Monetary Policy in Pacific Basin Countries

Monetary Policy in Pacific Basin Countries

Papers Presented at a Conference Sponsored by the Federal Reserve Bank of San Francisco

Edited by

Hang-Sheng Cheng

Federal Reserve Bank of San Francisco

Kluwer Academic Publishers

Boston Dordrecht London

Distributors for North America:
Kluwer Academic Publishers
101 Philip Drive
Assinippi Park
Norwell, Massachusetts 02061 USA

Distributors for the UK and Ireland:
Kluwer Academic Publishers
Falcon House, Queen Square
Lancaster LA1 1RN, UNITED KINGDOM

Distributors for all other countries:
Kluwer Academic Publishers Group
Distribution Centre
Post Office Box 322
3300 AH Dordrecht, THE NETHERLANDS

Library of Congress Cataloging-in-Publication Data

Monetary policy in Pacific Basin countries / sponsored by the Federal Reserve Bank of San Francisco; edited by Hang-sheng Cheng.
p. cm.
Based on papers prepared for a conference organized by the Federal Reserve Bank of San Francisco, held Sept. 23-25, 1987.
Includes index.
ISBN-13:978-94-010-7711-8 e-ISBN-13: 978-94-009-2685-1
DOI: 10.1007/978-94-009-2685-1
1. Monetary policy—Pacific Area—Congresses. I. Cheng, Hang-sheng, 1920- II. Federal Reserve Bank of San Francisco.
Hg1480.7.M66 1988
332.4'91823—dc19 88-23459
CIP

Softcover reprint of the hardcover 1st edition 1988

Contents

Preface vii

Overview

1. **Monetary Policy Changes in Pacific Basin Countries** 3
   Hang-Sheng Cheng and Reuven Glick

Issues

2. **Financial Market Changes and Monetary Policy in Pacific Basin Countries** 17
   Reuven Glick

3. **Exchange Rate Arrangements and Monetary Policy** 43
   Donald J. Mathieson

4. **Capital Mobility and Monetary Policy: Australia, Japan and New Zealand** 81
   Warren L. Coats, Jr.

5. **Monetary Policy and Foreign Debt: The Experiences of the Far East Countries** 95
   Homi J. Kharas and Miguel A. Kiguel

6. **Monetary Regimes and Fiscal Deficits: A Comparative Analysis** 125
   Donato Masciandaro and Guido Tabellini

7. **Monetary Policy in Pacific Basin Developing Countries** 153
   Maxwell J. Fry, David M. Lilien, and Wilima Wadhwa

Countries

8. **Exchange Rates and Monetary Policy in Singapore and Hong Kong** 173
Ramon Moreno

9. **U.S. Monetary Policy** 201
Thomas Mayer

10. **The Response of the Bank of Japan to Macroeconomic and Financial Change** 227
Thomas F. Cargill and Michael M. Hutchison

11. **The New Australian Monetary Policy** 247
Kevin Davis and Mervyn Lewis

12. **Financial Deregulation and Monetary Policy in New Zealand** 279
Carl E. Walsh

13. **Monetary Policy in Thailand** 303
John G. Greenwood

14. **Financial Reform and Monetary Control in Indonesia** 321
V. Sundararajan and Lazaros Molho

15. **Monetary Policy and Financial Reform in Korea** 353
Thomas A. Layman

16. **Monetary Policy in Taiwan, China** 381
Robert F. Emery

17. **Monetary Policy and Inflation in China** 401
Hang-Sheng Cheng

About the Authors 431

Conference Agenda 435

Conference Participants 439

Index 445

Preface

The chapters in this book are based on papers prepared for a conference organized by the Federal Reserve Bank of San Francisco, held at the bank September 23-25, 1987, to review and compare monetary policy experiences of Pacific Basin countries during the past 15 years.

The theme of the conference was conceived with two purposes in mind. First, there was (and still is) a great need to enhance knowledge on the workings of economies in the Pacific Basin, which has been the fastest growing region in the world economy during the past 30 years. While much has been written on Pacific Basin trade and economic growth, relatively few studies have been published on the conduct of monetary policy in these economies.

Second, as we in the United States and others elsewhere have learned, rapid financial market changes over the last 15 years have led to considerable adjustment in the conduct of monetary policy. A comparative study of various national experiences can yield insights into the interactions between monetary policy and financial market changes more than is obtainable by examining individual national experiences separately.

Twenty-three economists with an interest in Pacific Basin economies have contributed to the chapters in this book. They were selected not only on the basis of their expertise but also on the criterion that none was associated with the central bank of the economies on which they conducted study. The prepared papers, however, were distributed to the respective central banks as well as to all conference participants prior to the conference. On the basis of the discussion at the conference, all papers were subsequently revised prior to inclusion in this volume.

This book is a joint product of many people. Besides the authors of the chapters, special thanks are due to Reuven Glick and Ramon Moreno, who helped in organizing the conference and provided comments on early drafts of the conference papers; Sylvia Papa and Donna Payne, who assisted with conference and book production; Marilyn Wallace, who assisted in style editing; and Elizabeth Redil and Thomas Wood, who helped in typing.

Finally, the authors of all the chapters in this book wish to state that the views expressed in their contributions are their own, not necessarily reflecting the views of the organizations with which they are associated.

Overview

1
Monetary Policy Changes in Pacific Basin Countries

Hang-Sheng Cheng and Reuven Glick

Over the last 25 years, the Pacific Basin region -- defined to encompass all of the countries and territories in Asia, Oceania, and North America that border on the Pacific Ocean -- has become widely recognized as the most dynamic region in the world economy. Over this period the average output growth rate and the degree of economic transformation in the Pacific Basin have significantly surpassed that of any other region in the world.

Since the mid-1970s, almost all countries in the region have undertaken steps to liberalize their domestic financial systems and remove restrictions on international capital flows. At the same time, the conduct of monetary policy in these countries has undergone unprecedented changes, as monetary authorities have shifted away from heavy regulation of financial institutions and markets as a means of influencing private savings-investment flows and financing fiscal deficits toward more market-oriented policies.

The forces that prompted these changes have included rapid advances in communications technology that helped break down both domestic and international financial market barriers, inflationary pressures in the 1970s that rendered regulated interest rates increasingly ineffectual, and the development of new financial instruments and markets to circumvent traditional monetary controls. These forces have been world-wide. Because of the diversity of historical backgrounds, stages of economic development, and financial market environments, the Pacific Basin region offers a wide spectrum of examples of the conduct of monetary policy in response to these forces. The Pacific Basin region thus provides an almost ideal laboratory for a comparative study of the interactions between the formulation of monetary policy and economic market forces.

To provide such a study, the Federal Reserve Bank of San Francisco invited economists specializing in the area to prepare 16 papers covering the monetary policy experiences of a number of countries and territories in the Pacific Basin region. The papers were presented in a conference held at the Bank on September 23-25, 1987. Central bank officials from the region -- including several central bank governors and Federal Reserve presidents -- and scholars from various international organizations, U.S. government agencies, commercial and investment banks, universities, and research institutes also participated. The conference provided an opportunity for the participants to exchange views on the monetary policy experiences of Pacific Basin countries over the past 15 years. This book is the result.

Together, the papers that follow have attempted to assess the varied experiences within the Pacific Basin region from two directions. Ten of the papers focus on the specific monetary policy experiences of individual Pacific Basin countries and territories. Six other papers take a cross-sectional approach to compare and synthesize Pacific Basin monetary experiences in the last 15 years, focusing on the relation of monetary policy to factors such as financial market change, fiscal policy, exchange rate policy, capital mobility, foreign borrowing, and external shocks.

As an introduction to the papers in this book, we describe the general changes in financial markets that have taken place in the region, and provide an overview of the monetary policy regime shifts that have occurred in a number of Pacific Basin countries by contrasting where they are today with what they were like during the mid-1970s. Our purpose is to give an overview of the changes in monetary policies of Pacific Basin nations, focusing on common elements and trends, while leaving the details and unique experiences to the individual chapters presented in the book.

TRADITIONAL FINANCIAL MARKET ENVIRONMENTS

During the mid-1970s, the degree of financial market development and sophistication varied widely among countries in the Pacific Basin. Correspondingly, the degree of financial market restrictiveness and the conduct of monetary policy varied as well. Some nations, notably the United States, Hong Kong, and Singapore, possessed relatively free financial environments and well-developed financial markets. At the other end of the spectrum were countries with heavily regulated financial systems, such as Indonesia, Korea, Taiwan, and China.

Notwithstanding this diversity, in the early 1970s the financial systems of almost all countries in the Pacific Basin were characterized by one or more of a range of restrictive financial measures, including interest rate regulations, credit allocation controls, explicit and implicit taxes on financial institutions, and international capital controls. Such measures were employed by authorities to affect private savings-investment flows through their influence on the flow of credit and to finance government expenditures by extracting seigniorage through money creation and regulation of the financial sector.

Control over the flow of loanable funds from savers and investors was considered of critical importance in the development process in many countries because of the apparent presumption that the normal financial intermediation process did not ensure socially optimal use of resources. From this view, interest rate regulations and credit controls were seen as appropriate instruments of monetary policy. Interest rate regulations generally involved ceilings on deposit and loan rates. Credit controls included quantitative restrictions on lending by financial institutions, as well as measures that encouraged loans and central bank rediscounting of credits at subsidized rates to priority sectors. Controls on both inflows and outflows of international capital prevented financial institutions from evading domestic financial controls by undertaking transactions in external markets.

In many cases, constraints on the ability to raise revenue from conventional sources -- such as income, sales, and property taxes, and the underdevelopment of capital markets -- implied that fiscal authorities were unable to market government bonds outside the banking system. In this environment the domestic financial system was treated as an important revenue source to finance fiscal deficits.

Central bank purchases of government securities through money creation served as a major means of financing government expenditures. Taxes on financial transactions and on the income of financial institutions also provided a source of government revenue. Application of various reserve requirements and liquidity ratios to financial institutions ensured demand for government securities or high-powered money at low cost to the public sector and yielded implicit revenues. Required purchases of government debt by the banking system through liquidity ratios and reserve requirements enabled access to bank credit at low cost to the public sector.

FINANCIAL MARKET ENVIRONMENT CHANGES

Since the mid-1970s, a variety of forces have been at work to change the financial market environments of countries in the Pacific Basin region. These forces have prompted almost all countries to undertake steps to liberalize their domestic financial systems and remove restrictions on international capital flows. Of course, those countries with the least restrictive financial environments to begin with have undergone relatively less change.

In part, financial reforms were prompted by the market forces generated by the efforts of monetary authorities to control both the rate of credit creation and interest rate levels. Because bank deposit rates were often arbitrarily set by the monetary authorities in most Pacific Basin countries in the mid-1970s, inflationary monetary creation drove private savings from the regulated banks to financial institutions and markets that lay outside these controls. In time, the acceleration of financial disintermediation led to the growth of unregulated financial markets and nonbank institutions, thereby reducing the effectiveness of monetary policy.

To forestall financial disintermediation, monetary authorities in a number of countries sought to prohibit unregulated financial institutions and markets from arising. However, this impeded the development of financial markets and institutions in those countries. Ultimately, as the international integration of financial markets progressed, in many instances despite the efforts of national authorities to maintain domestic market insulation, these actions were seen to be futile and injurious to national interest and were abandoned. Similarly, when bank loan rates were set by national authorities in order to insure low cost financing, inflationary money creation resulted in excess demand for bank credit and impetus for the development of alternative channels of financing.

Financial reforms were also motivated by a desire to improve domestic economic efficiency and by external macroeconomic developments which made it increasingly difficult to maintain a tightly regulated financial system.

With experience, authorities in most countries came to recognize that financial restrictions hindered economic growth. Ceilings on interest rate, by depressing real interest yields, especially in high inflation environments, worked to reduce incentives to accumulate domestic financial assets. Domestic investment was consequently dampened. Credit controls often resulted in inefficient credit allocation by emphasizing credit flows to finance government deficits or capital-intensive projects by large firms at the expense of small firms, which were forced to seek credit in unorganized financial markets.

The desire to lessen the government's role in directing resource allocation and to permit market forces to reduce domestic distortions and inefficiencies was thus an important factor in the liberalization process for many countries. As a result, almost all countries have relaxed interest rate controls on bank deposits, lowered reserve requirements and liquidity ratios, and eliminated rules over the allocation of credit or provision of special credit at preferential rates. In many instances the authorities have also sought to encourage the development of new financial instruments, with open-market determined interest rates.

Because liberalization of financial markets also eroded the tax and seigniorage revenue extracted from the financial sector, those countries faced with the need to market growing amounts of government debt found it desirable to reform their domestic financial systems in order to raise the capacity of commercial banks and private securities markets to absorb the debt. The growing independence of monetary authorities implied that fiscal authorities were compelled to place less reliance on money creation as a means to finance budget imbalances. To increase the incentives of private financial institutions and investors to acquire this debt, financial reform was deemed desirable.

External macroeconomic developments and competitive pressures from abroad made it more difficult to maintain tightly regulated financial systems and created another motivation for reform in many countries. In particular, rising foreign interest rates stimulated the demands of domestic investors for higher returns on financial assets and intensified pressures for reductions in exchange and capital controls. Inflation in the presence of interest rate ceilings lowered real returns and increased incentives of domestic savers and investors to seek higher return investment vehicles abroad. In addition, other disturbances, such as large changes in oil and commodity prices, caused many economies in the region to allow greater exchange rate flexibility.

TRADITIONAL MONETARY POLICY REGIMES

It is within the changing financial environment described above that most countries in the Pacific Basin have altered the conduct of their monetary policy. To provide an overview of the monetary policy regime shifts that have taken place in the Pacific Basin countries considered in this study it is useful to categorize regimes by two principal characteristics: (1) the degree to which monetary authorities have relied on the market mechanism, instead of administrative directives, to carry out monetary policy; and (2) the extent to which the effects of monetary policy on national economic activity have been transmitted through the banking sector rather than through alternative financial market channels.

During the mid-1970s, the monetary policy regimes of Hong Kong and Singapore were undoubtedly among the most market-oriented in the Pacific Basin region in the sense that authorities intervened very little in the operation of financial markets and in determination of the money supply. Hong Kong, in particular, was (and still is) unique in that it did not even have a central bank, even though it had its own currency. The volume of base-money (currency) issue was regulated by requiring the two currency-issue banks to acquire full backing of currency issue in the form of Certificates of Indebtedness of the Government Exchange Fund. Since the Certificates of Indebtedness were issued freely on demand, the regime relied entirely on the market to determine the volume of currency issue. Without a central bank, there was no active monetary policy for influencing the level of domestic economic activity.

In 1975, Singapore ceased using administrative directives for conducting monetary policy. Instead the Monetary Authority of Singapore relied on market forces in conducting monetary policy. Currency issue of the Currency Board was fully backed by its holdings of foreign exchange. By pegging the Singapore dollar to a basket of currencies, the monetary authorities relinquished some control over the domestic money supply as well as domestic interest rates. However, in contrast to Hong Kong, where there was no active monetary policy to influence domestic economic activity, the currency peg in Singapore was adjusted to offset inflation.

U.S. monetary policy in the mid-1970s was also relatively market oriented. Monetary policy was pursued by adjusting the supply of bank reserves through open market operations rather than administratively setting interest rates or controlling credit. In contrast to Hong Kong and Singapore, however, the monetary authority in the United States, the Federal Reserve, possessed greater scope in conducting an independent monetary policy in part because of the international position of the United States as a reserve currency country and in part because the dollar was allowed to float. Hence, monetary policy was used more actively to influence economic activity.

Australia, New Zealand, and Thailand were characterized by somewhat less free-market-oriented monetary regimes than in the countries above. During the mid-1970s, the monetary authorities in all three countries conducted activist monetary policies by frequently adjusting bank reserve ratios, varying the discount rate, and administratively setting domestic interest rates. In all three, these measures were directed against commercial banks. This created considerable incentives for the growth of financial institutions and markets outside the regulated channels. In Australia and New Zealand this led to the growth of domestic nonbank financial institutions. By contrast, in Thailand, which allowed unrestricted international capital flows and maintained pegged exchange rates, free access to world money markets served as the financial outlet for domestic residents.

Japan, Indonesia, Taiwan, and Korea were characterized by an absence of alternative channels of domestic finance outside their respective banking sectors. In these countries, the monetary authorities relied heavily on administrative directives to banks in conducting monetary policy. Korea, Taiwan, and Indonesia, however, differed from Japan in that their banking systems were dominated by state-owned banks, which, though operating as separate profit centers, carried out the central banks' policy edicts. Thus, although all three had essentially private-enterprise, market economies, though with varying degrees of government industrial intervention, their conduct of monetary policy was the least market-oriented among Pacific Basin countries, except China. In contrast, Japan's banking system was predominantly privately owned. However, because commercial banks in Japan were perennially encouraged to overlend and hence were dependent on the Bank of Japan for accommodation, the Bank of Japan was able to regulate bank lending closely through "window guidance."

Monetary policy in China during the mid-1970s was the least market oriented in the region. Prior to 1980, its monetary policy consisted of accommodating the decisions of economic planning authorities concerning the budget deficit, enterprise capital formation, and the nation's exports and imports. As prices and output were both set by the planning authorities, there was no room for active monetary policy for affecting the nation's aggregate economic activity.

MONETARY POLICY REGIME CHANGES

In the last 15 years, the conduct of monetary policy in all these countries and territories has undergone significant changes. While the extent and manner of these changes has varied across countries, their direction has all been toward the more market-oriented use of monetary policy.

Not surprisingly, the least changes have taken place in Hong Kong, where the market pressures for changes were least. The only significant policy shift occurred in Hong Kong, when in 1983 it changed from floating to fixed exchange rates, thus securing an anchor for its currency issue. This shift reflected Hong Kong's recognition that in a regime without a central bank the market could not be relied on to determine both domestic interest rates and the exchange rate without risking monetary instability. By pegging its currency to the U.S. dollar, Hong Kong reverted to a regime that had prevailed prior to 1972, when its currency was on a sterling standard.

In Singapore, the shift from direct controls to a market-oriented monetary policy occurred early, and was largely accomplished by 1975. In the United States, despite rapid liberalization of financial markets, the mode of the conduct of monetary policy has altered relatively little since the mid-1970s. The Federal Reserve has continued to rely on the market mechanism in conducting monetary policy, specifically, on open-market operations for affecting the level of bank reserves.

The greatest shifts in monetary policy regime have occurred among the other countries in the Pacific Basin. Australia and New Zealand both completely discarded the use of administrative directives for the conduct of monetary policy. Both have abolished interest rate controls and exchange controls. However, unlike Hong Kong and Singapore, both have floated their exchange rates, thereby retaining some degree of monetary independence from external influences on domestic interest rates. Both central banks have shifted to extensive use of open-market operations for adjusting the level of bank reserves. The development of money markets operating outside the regulated banking sector has facilitated the central banks' open-market operations Monetary policy in both countries has thus moved closer to the U.S. model.

Indonesia, in a dramatic leap, has cast off all its direct controls in both the domestic financial markets and the foreign exchange market as instruments of monetary policy. It, too, has floated its exchange rate. In addition, it has assiduously nurtured the growth of domestic money markets by issuing large volumes of central bank certificates and establishing institutions to ensure the liquidity of the new instruments in secondary markets. As a result, domestic money markets have developed sufficiently for the central bank to engage in open-market operations in domestic securities in order to supplement operations in the foreign exchange market.

Japan has shifted far less than Indonesia in altering its monetary policy regime. With drastic changes in the direction of domestic funds flows from corporate debt financing to government deficit financing, the overlending condition of the banking system has dissipated. The pressing need for financing large government deficits from outside the banking system has forced Japan to dismantle interest rates controls and to permit new financial instruments and markets to arise, although the pace has been gradual. It, too, has removed capital controls. Floating exchange rates have enabled the Bank of Japan to retain some indirect control of domestic interest rates.

Korea and Taiwan have also tried to develop their financial systems by creating money markets outside the banking sector. Taiwan especially has issued large volumes of central bank certificates in order to help absorb the huge increases in bank reserves arising from its trade surpluses in the

1980s. However, to the extent that the certificates have been sold primarily to the state-owned banks, it is not clear how much such sales can be regarded as genuine open-market operations. Both Korea and Taiwan have partially liberalized their exchange controls, but both have tried to peg their exchange rates, with different degrees of success. Monetary policy in both has continued to be conducted primarily through direct controls of the state-owned banks, although nominally, interest rates have been set free to reflect market conditions. Thus, both Korea and Taiwan can be characterized as having moved a considerable way toward greater liberalization, but to date not as much as other countries.

Thailand has thus far made relatively little change in the mode of the conduct of its monetary policy. Monetary growth in Thailand over the last 15 years has alternated between periods of acceleration and deceleration, as the domestic financial market has been buffeted by alternating capital inflows and outflows that resulted from the central bank's attempt to stabilize both the exchange rate and domestic interest rates in the face of widely fluctuating world interest rates. Recent policy changes appear to suggest a move toward greater exchange rate stability and more domestic interest rate flexibility.

Lastly, monetary policy in China is undergoing substantial changes, as the nation undertakes drastic economic reform to move away from a rigid planned economy to one that is more market oriented. In the process, a central bank has emerged, and state-owned banks have been allowed to engage in deposit taking and business financing under the central bank's close administrative controls. A rudimentary interbank money market has emerged, but there is as yet no significant open money market. The country is still in an early stage of development of a market-oriented banking system. Correspondingly, the conduct of its monetary policy is still far short of being as market oriented as other countries in the region. Nevertheless, given the direction of economic reform in the last ten years, monetary policy in China is already assuming an important role in macroeconomic stabilization that it did not have under the old regime.

CONCLUSIONS

The changes in the conduct of monetary policy by Pacific nations over the last 15 years have been partly a response to the rapidly changing economic and market environment of the 1970s and 1980s and partly a reflection of fundamental revisions in the regulatory thinking of national authorities. Changes in domestic and international financial markets have altered the environment in which monetary policy operates. At the same time monetary authorities have increasingly perceived that restrictive financial policies have lost much of their effectiveness and have caused economic distortions and inefficiencies.

Of course, those countries with the least restrictive financial environments to begin with (e.g., Hong Kong and Singapore), have had the least reason to change. On the other hand, those countries which possessed the most restrictive financial markets in the mid-1970s have not necessarily since undergone the most change. In those countries in which monetary authorities have only slowly revised their attitudes toward the appropriate conduct of monetary policy relatively limited changes in monetary regimes have been undertaken (e.g., Korea and Taiwan). The most dramatic changes in the conduct of monetary policy have occurred in those countries which were initially characterized by relatively restrictive financial systems and in which monetary authorities have most sharply revised their regulatory thinking (e.g., Australia, New Zealand, and Indonesia).

While the degree of actual change has varied from country to country, the general nature of monetary policy for all countries in the region is fundamentally different from that which prevailed in the mid-1970s. Several general conclusions concerning the conduct of monetary policy emerge from examination of the experiences of all countries in the Pacific Basin region.

First, monetary authorities have gained greater independence from fiscal authorities as a result of the liberalization of financial markets Financial reform reduced the revenues collected by the government through explicit and implicit forms of money seigniorage. By thus compelling fiscal authorities to place less reliance on seigniorage and money creation as means to finance budget imbalances, monetary policy has become more independent. With this independence monetary authorities have become able to operate more actively in financial markets.

Second, the development of money and capital markets has enhanced the use of particular monetary policy instruments. Open market operations are no longer limited by the thinness of private markets in government debt. As a result, less emphasis has been placed on discount policy, the use of reserve requirements, and direct central bank control of credit as a source of bank liquidity and reserve growth. As the proportion of financial instruments carrying market-determined interest rates has grown, there has been a greater emphasis by most central banks on more market-oriented instruments and the control of monetary aggregates through the active use of open-market operations.

Lastly, the greater links between domestic financial systems with international financial markets have opened up new dimensions to monetary policy. Increased international capital mobility has tied domestic interest rates more closely to world interest rates. Fixed exchange rates and relatively free capital flows were found to be incompatible with effective ceilings on credit or reserve money. The greater opportunities for domestic residents to acquire credit from abroad as a result of financial deregulation weakened the effectiveness of domestic credit ceilings. In this new environment individual countries have pursued different approaches. Some, particularly the small, open economies, with high international capital mobility and exchange rate targets, have let domestic interest rates be determined by foreign markets (e.g., Hong Kong and Singapore). Others (e.g., United States, Japan, Australia, and New Zealand) have let their currencies float and retain at least some influence in the short run over nominal interest rates. In contrast, Korea, China, and Taiwan, although the latter undertook important steps to liberalize controls in 1987, still have relatively restrictive capital controls with pegged exchange rates.

STRUCTURE OF THE BOOK

The chapters in the book are divided into two parts. The first part consists of "issue" papers, while the second contains the "country" papers. The issue papers take a cross-sectional approach and are presented first in order to present the reader with a broader understanding of the general issues and problems concerning the conduct of monetary policy before examining the individual country experiences.

The chapter by Glick describes how financial reform in the Pacific Basin has affected the channels through which monetary policy operates, created new concerns for monetary authorities, and led monetary authorities to reconsider the mix and types of money and credit market instruments to be employed. Mathieson's chapter focuses particularly on what developments have led many developing countries in the Pacific Basin to undertake changes in their exchange rate arrangements, as well as in the use of money and credit market instruments. The chapter by Coates discusses the particular implications of international capital mobility for the conduct of monetary policy.

Kharas and Kiguel explore the dynamic relationships between domestic credit policy, the exchange rate, and foreign borrowing and the mix of fiscal and monetary policies. Masciandaro and Tabellini analyze the dynamic interrelationship between monetary and fiscal policies and how institutional features of the monetary regime are linked to the magnitude of fiscal deficits.

The chapter by Fry, Lilien, and Wadhwa examines the extent to which developing countries can and do pursue independent monetary policies. They find evidence that Pacific Basin countries generally followed more "prudent" policies than other developing countries in the sense that they did not allow their currencies to depreciate as much in response to net capital outflows, responded more strongly to fight inflation, and accommodated government credit creation to a lesser degree.

The individual country chapters presented in the second part of the book are ordered roughly by the extent of the market orientation of their monetary regimes. Because the individual country experiences have varied widely, these papers are best left to speak for themselves.

Issues

2

Financial Market Changes and Monetary Policy in Pacific Basin Countries

Reuven Glick

In recent years, almost all countries in the Pacific Basin have undertaken steps to liberalize their domestic financial systems and remove restrictions on international capital flows. Hong Kong and Singapore were the first to do so by removing or relaxing interest rate regulations and abolishing exchange controls in the early 1970s. Significant financial reforms have been undertaken in Japan and Malaysia since the late 1970s, in the Philippines, Australia, and Indonesia in the early 1980s, and in New Zealand in 1984.[1] More limited movements toward liberalization have occurred in Thailand. Although Korea and Taiwan (China) have also taken some steps toward financial liberalization in recent years, they still maintain relatively restrictive controls on most financial transactions, particularly international financial flows.[2] Thus, although the timing and extent of liberalization steps have varied across countries, virtually all countries in the region have allowed domestic and, in most cases, foreign market forces to play a greater role in their financial markets.

As the structure of financial markets has changed, both the conduct and effectiveness of monetary policy in Pacific Basin countries have been affected. The relaxation of interest rate regulations and the expanding range of sources of credit have allowed changes in interest rates to be transmitted more rapidly and pervasively to all sectors of the economy. The increased mobility of international capital has made the balance of payments and the exchange rate increasingly important channels for the transmission of monetary policy.

As a result, the authorities in these countries have had to reconsider the mix and types of money and credit market instruments employed to achieve internal and external objectives. The earlier emphasis on influencing the quantity of bank credit generally has been replaced by a greater emphasis on the control of monetary aggregates and on influencing interest-sensitive expenditures. Many countries in the region have moved from pegged to more flexible exchange rate regimes.

The purpose of this study is to review the financial market changes that have taken place among Pacific Basin countries and to discuss how these changes have affected their conduct of monetary policy. The general nature of many of the problems encountered are similar among all countries in the region.[3] Should central banks focus on control of prices, such as interest rates, or on quantities, such as money or credit aggregates, in financial markets? If the latter, should the targeted quantities be narrow or broad? How can the control of monetary aggregates be maintained and the exchange rate managed in the face of increasingly more mobile international capital flows? How can the stability of financial institutions be maintained as liberalization proceeds?

Although the general nature of the problems faced by all countries in the Pacific Basin are similar, the specific problems faced by individual countries often vary because of differences in market structure and financial institutions and in the extent to which the countries have allowed financial liberalization to advance. The economic and financial systems of these countries display a wide diversity, ranging from a high degree of government control, as in Korea, to more market-oriented systems, as in Hong Kong. Some, such as Japan, Australia, and New Zealand, and to a lesser extent the Philippines and Malaysia, had well developed nonbank financial institutions prior to the beginning of the reform process; others, such as Indonesia, Korea, and Taiwan, did not. In some countries, such as Korea and Taiwan, the presence of unorganized money markets outside of central bank control has played a role in the operation of monetary policy. In most countries the pace of liberalization has been gradual; in some, such as Australia and New Zealand, it has been unusually rapid It is this diversity of experience among countries in the region that provides a wealth of insight concerning the nature of the problems that financial liberalization creates for the conduct of monetary policy.[4]

The plan of the chapter is as follows. First, it discusses the channels through which monetary policy works under varying degrees of domestic and international financial controls. It then examines the nature of the various financial market and monetary policy changes that have occurred in countries of the Pacific Basin region as financial liberalization has proceeded. Next, it focuses on several specific issues that have arisen concerning the conduct of monetary policy as the result of financial liberalization, including: the identification of an appropriate money aggregate to utilize as an intermediate target of policy; the effective use of monetary policy instruments; policy responses to international capital flows; and the implementation of measures for assuring domestic financial stability. Conclusions are summarized at the end.

CHANGING CHANNELS OF MONETARY POLICY

Monetary policy is a major tool for achievement of medium-term goals of price stability and output growth and of short term stabilization in response to economic disturbances. The channels through which monetary policy operates depend on the financial structure of the economy. Financial liberalization, by removing various restrictions on financial institutions and changing the structure of financial markets, influences the relative importance of these different channels. Financial market changes in turn influence the relative effectiveness of different monetary instruments. As a background to understanding recent developments in Pacific Basin countries, it is useful to discuss in general terms the operation of these channels as the financial structure of an economy is liberalized.[5]

Economies with underdeveloped and/or repressed financial systems are characterized by interest rate regulations, restrictions on portfolio holdings of particular domestic and foreign assets, domestic credit controls, entry restrictions on new financial institutions, and international capital controls. Interest rate ceilings depress nominal and real interests rates, especially in high inflation environments, and lower the levels of savings and investment. Portfolio restrictions and credit allocation controls hinder the development of open markets in primary securities and claims. Restrictions on entry to the financial system lead to high concentration and segmentation of financial markets. Controls on international capital flows limit access to external sources of credit.

In such an environment, the effects of monetary policy work primarily through changes in credit availability rather than through adjustments of interest rates and exchange rates. When bank credit is the major source of finance, a tightening of monetary policy through central bank guidance of commercial banks to restrict credit levels results in the credit rationing of bank customers. The resulting financial crowding-out squeezes aggregate demand and dampens inflation. Expansionary monetary policy effected through an easing of credit rationing works conversely.[6] As long as financial flows are channeled primarily through the banking system, almost all instruments of control of bank credit, such as reserve requirements, interest rate ceilings, and direct constraints on the growth and composition of banks' credit, work effectively as tools of monetary policy.

However, both contractionary and expansionary monetary policies in an underdeveloped financial system encourage private agents to transfer funds through unregulated channels. When credit from regulated commercial banks is tightened, agents have an incentive to seek alternative sources of funds in unregulated markets. Monetary expansion leading to inflationary pressures may also channel funds outside the regulated banking market. In the absence of alternatives to holding currency and deposits as financial assets, inflation pressures, by lowering real deposit rates, can make commodities and other tangible assets increasingly attractive substitutes for bank assets. Inflation pressures may also tend to stimulate the growth of nonbank financial substitutes as agents seek to escape deposit rate limits in the banking sector.

The development of close substitutes for bank credit and the decline in the share of banks in intermediation alter the channels of monetary policy as well as the relative effectiveness of monetary instruments. In particular, the creation of financial assets not subject to reserve and liquid asset requirements and interest rate ceilings not only increases competition by other financial institutions but also weakens the effectiveness of credit rationing as an instrument of monetary control. Rationing of bank credit tends to be offset either by recourse to new types of banking operations, such as off-balance-sheet transactions, or by an expansion of credit from unconstrained financial institutions and money markets.

The growth of unregulated financial institutions and markets and the elimination of interest ceilings on bank deposits increase the range of financial instruments affected by variations in interest rates. These changes create a greater role for interest rates in transmitting monetary policy effects. To the extent that interest rates rise in response to contractionary monetary policy, for example, the private sector is induced to hold more financial assets, and real aggregate demand, especially for inventory accumulation and fixed investment, is depressed. Monetary policy also has adverse supply-side effects to the extent that rising interest rates create an increase in the cost of working capital. As the range of sources and types of domestic credit with market-related interest rates expand, changes in market interest rates are transmitted more rapidly and pervasively to all sectors of the economy, and the effectiveness of the interest rate as a transmission channel for monetary policy is increased.

In a completely closed economy, changes in monetary policy are transmitted through the economy entirely by changes in the availability of credit and, when permitted, by interest rates. In an open economy, other channels operate as well. With unrestricted international goods flows, limited capital mobility, and a pegged exchange rate regime, monetary restraint tends to improve the current account as falling domestic demand reduces imports. The resulting foreign exchange inflows create an offset to the initial decline in domestic credit. Thus, under a pegged exchange rate, control of credit and money aggregates is difficult since any balance of payments imbalances tend to generate offsetting movements in the foreign exchange sources of the money supply, despite control by monetary authorities of the domestic credit component. Under such a regime there is limited scope for aggregate demand management by the monetary authorities, since the authorities must adjust the money supply so as not to gain or lose reserves. Targets for money growth require the central bank to sterilize the impact of balance of payments imbalances by reducing domestic credit. The sustainability of such a policy is not clear, however, particularly in the case of continuing foreign reserve losses.

Relaxation of restrictions on international capital transactions increases capital mobility and sensitivity to fluctuations in foreign interest rates and to changes in exchange rate expectations. The problem of maintaining a pegged rate and controlling the money supply is exacerbated the greater the degree of international capital mobility. A contractionary monetary policy that raises domestic rates above foreign rates induces capital inflows that dampen the change in domestic interest rates and offset the initial credit reduction. Thus when exchange rates are pegged and capital mobility is high, the effective control of credit and money is even more severely limited.

With flexible exchange rates, control of the money supply and the ability to influence domestic interest rates are improved, and the exchange rate operates as another channel through which monetary policy affects the economy. Monetary restraint, for example, creates pressure for the nominal value of domestic currency to appreciate. The appreciation dampens the offsetting effect of tight money on domestic credit through incipient balance of payments surpluses.[7] The adjustment of the exchange rate enhances the effectiveness of the monetary contraction by further curbing demand for domestic output and reducing inflationary pressures. With high capital mobility the exchange rate becomes an increasingly important channel for the transmission of monetary policy effects, since actual or perceived shifts in relative domestic and foreign monetary conditions rapidly affect exchange rates.

The relative adjustment of interest and exchange rates in response to a change in monetary policy also depends on expectations about the future exchange rate. Because changes in expectations in the exchange market induce adjustment in the spot exchange rate more rapidly than the real economy can adjust, changes in monetary policy can cause the exchange rate to initially overshoot its new long-run level.

While more flexible exchange rates lessen concern about the effects of balance of payments imbalances, the closer tying of national capital markets creates other limitations on monetary policy. In particular, foreign monetary shocks become a more important concern to domestic monetary authorities. For example, changes in foreign monetary policy leading to higher foreign interest rates may compell the domestic central bank to make matching changes in policy in order to limit the necessary adjustment of the exchange rate. Thus while international capital mobility in some respects enhances the effectiveness of monetary policy, it may also place other limitations on the independence of domestic policymakers, particularly if the country is small.

PACIFIC BASIN FINANCIAL MARKET CHANGES

Recent reforms undertaken by Pacific Basin countries to liberalize their financial systems have included the relaxation of interest rate restrictions, reduction in the use of direct credit allocation or provision of special credit at preferential rates, development of open markets in primary securities, and liberalization of economic links with the rest of world through freer international capital transactions. To various extents, the relative importance of different channels of monetary policy have been affected within each individual country.

Motivations for Reform

The motivations for these reforms have arisen from a number of sources. As in many developed countries, a primary factor has been the desire to lessen the government's role in directing resource allocation and to permit market forces to reduce domestic distortions and inefficiencies.[8] Ceilings on interest rates, often justified on the grounds that high rates discourage investment, resulted in depressed real yields, which reduced incentives to save and invest. Selective and general credit controls by central banks, while often justified by the presumption that the normal channeling of funds did not ensure socially optimum use of resources, often led to inefficient, low-return investments. Subsidized loan rates for priority sectors often resulted in inefficient credit allocation by channeling funds to large capital-intensive projects, at the expense of small firms forced to seek credit in unorganized financial markets.

The desire for financial reform has also been stimulated by the concern of monetary authorities about the development of alternative channels for domestic financial flows that arose in response to existing restrictions on financial activities. In Australia, for example, interest rate controls on commercial bank deposits led to the growth of unregulated, nonbank financial institutions, thereby reducing the effectiveness of monetary policy. In Korea and Taiwan, restrictions on financial institutions led to the development of unofficial, unregulated, "curb" markets involving small borrowers and lenders. In the mid-1970s the aggregate size of the curb market in Taiwan was as large as all other financial institutions put together. In 1980 it accounted for roughly 30 percent of total domestic assets.[9]

External macroeconomic developments and competitive pressures from abroad created another motivation for reform in many countries.[10] In the face of high foreign interest rates, particularly in the United States in the early 1980s, it became more difficult to maintain tightly regulated financial systems. Faced with the demands of domestic investors for higher return investment assets, many countries introduced new money market instruments with freely determined interest rates, such as certificates of deposit, bankers acceptances, and commercial paper. In addition, as domestic markets became more liberalized, pressures for reductions in exchange and capital controls intensified as well.

The role of external considerations in the motivation to reform may be seen in the example of Thailand. Given its fixed exchange rate regime and the absence of controls on capital movements, Thailand found that credit controls and interest rate ceilings were unsustainable in the face of large international capital flows. As a result, Thai authorities introduced some measure of flexibility in the setting of interest rates and the exchange rate, in order to restore control of money aggregates. Indonesia had similar motivations for liberalizing measures that began in 1983.

Some countries found it desirable to reform their domestic financial systems in order to increase the capacity of commercial banks and private securities markets to absorb growing amounts of government debt. The governments in these countries traditionally had financed their deficits by borrowing from the central bank or commercial banks, often compelling them to hold government securities at below-market interest rates. To avoid the inflationary consequences of monetization of growing volumes of debt by the central bank and to increase the incentives of private financial institutions and investors to acquire this debt, financial reform was deemed desirable

In Japan, for example, the total amount of government debt outstanding increased from less than 10 percent of gross domestic product in the mid-1970s to more than 30 percent in the early 1980s. The difficulties banks in Japan experienced with absorbing these government debt issues prompted reforms that enabled greater distribution of bonds among the Japanese public. Indonesia and Malaysia were also motivated to develop money markets in order to finance government sector deficits, although for the former, a desire to reduce the need for foreign borrowing was also a significant factor.[11]

Interest Rate Liberalization

Almost all countries have relaxed interest rate controls on bank deposits. In many instances the authorities have also sought to encourage the development of new financial instruments with open market determined interest rates.

Some countries have proceeded rapidly. Singapore, for example, removed restrictions on bank rates in July 1975 and also allowed the establishment of a variety of money market instruments.[12] In Australia, beginning in 1980, interest rate ceilings on deposits and loans were relaxed rapidly; currently there are no controls on deposit rates, and a ceiling exists only on small bank loan rates. Indonesia liberalized many interest rates in 1983 and announced the formation of several short-term money markets in 1985. In New Zealand, as part of a general reform, all interest ceilings were removed in 1984.

Other countries have moved more slowly in lifting controls on deposit rates and encouraging the development of money markets. For example, prior to the start of financial reform in the mid-1970s, the interbank and gensaki (repurchase) markets were the only financial markets in Japan not subject to explicit interest rate controls, though even these markets were still subject to administrative guidance. In the late 1970s the Japanese authorities allowed the development of markets for several new financial instruments with market determined interest rates, including negotiable certificates of deposit and money market certificates. They have proceeded more cautiously, however, with reforms that would affect bank deposit rates. As of the end of 1986, roughly 70 percent of bank deposits still remained subject to interest rate controls.

Even in countries that have lifted controls on most financial transactions, provisions are still made to ensure favorable interest rates on loans to priority sectors of the economy. In October 1978, Malaysia announced measures which reduced administrative guidance, made bank interest rates more flexible, and established markets for bankers' acceptances and CDs. However, despite the fostering of price competition, sectoral allocations of bank loans are still regularly imposed, and priority sectors are favored with low interest rates. In the Philippines, interest rate ceilings were removed on deposits of more than two years' maturity in August 1980, and on bank savings and time deposits by the end of 1981. At the same time, a large proportion of domestic credit is still allocated by public sector financial institutions on nonmarket terms.

In other countries, even though formal interest rate controls no longer exist, rates are still determined oligopolistically. For example, since 1964 Hong Kong banks have restricted the interest rates they pay on deposits with maturities less than twelve months to a level determined by the Hong Kong Association of Banks or its predecessor, the Exchange Banks' Association.[13] However, there are indications that, as the 1970s progressed, competition from the Euro-market and from the deposit-taking companies, which are not subject to the interest-fixing agreement, have compelled the Association to adjust the deposit rates more frequently in order to keep the rates in line with market conditions.[14]

Some countries, such as Korea and Taiwan, have been much more reluctant to reduce interest rate controls, particularly on bank deposits. In these cases, concern about the effects of a rapid, widespread rise in interest rates on the economy, and particularly on the industrial sector, have limited the extent of decontrol of bank deposit rates. Although Korea continues to set all deposit rates in the commercial banking sector, it has allowed short-term finance companies greater freedom to set interest rates within a range between the banks' rates and those of the unofficial curb loan market, where interest rates are market determined. Taiwan did relax official restrictions on bank lending rates in 1980, but allows rates to be set by a bankers cartel, the Taipei Bankers' Association. It has sought to meet the demands of investors for higher return investment assets by establishing some open-money markets in recent years, including certificates of deposit and bankers acceptances. However, as the volumes in these officially sanctioned money markets and in the illegal curb market have grown, pressures on the regulated institutional markets have intensified.[15]

Thailand has also been reluctant to fully relax regulation of bank interest rates. Interest rate ceilings on both bank deposit and loan rates are still employed, although more flexible adjustment of these ceilings has been exercised in the 1980s. Nonbank financial institutions, however, have been permitted to develop relatively freely.

Reduction in Credit Controls

In addition to lifting interest rate controls, most countries have reduced the use of credit allocation rules and window guidance as instruments of monetary policy. Quantitative bank lending guidance was terminated in Australia in June 1982, selective credit ceilings were abandoned in Indonesia in June 1983, and guidelines on credit to the private sector were abolished in New Zealand in 1984. Window guidance of commercial banks in Japan has gradually diminished. Singapore and Hong Kong impose no credit allocation requirements on their banking systems.

However, many countries, including Korea, Malaysia, Philippines, Taiwan, and Thailand, still continue to make use of credit allocation rules to some extent as instruments of monetary policy. Korea, for example, terminated direct credit controls on lending by individual banks in 1982, and ended preferential rates for specified borrowers in November 1984, yet continues preferential rediscounting facilities to banks which lend to exporters and other designated industries, and maintains credit allocation requirements for banks as well.

Reductions in Exchange and Capital Controls

The authorities in most Pacific Basin countries have relaxed their exchange and international capital controls following the liberalization of domestic financial markets. Accompanying the relaxation of controls has been movement toward greater flexibility in exchange rates.

In Hong Kong the last official exchange controls were abolished in December 1972, and there are no controls on international capital flows by residents or nonresidents. The Hong Kong dollar was allowed to float freely in November 1974; however, since October 1983 it has been pegged to the U.S. dollar.

Singapore completely liberalized foreign exchange transactions in June 1978. In principle, near-perfect international capital mobility exists: residents are free to make transactions in any currency as well as to invest in any currency. While nonresidents are similarly free to transact in Singapore dollars, the authorities have sought to limit linkages between domestic money markets and the Asia dollar market, an offshore currency market, where rates are freely determined. This has been done by prohibiting the use of the Singapore dollar in the Asia dollar market, by levying a high interest tax on investment transactions by foreigners conducted in the domestic markets of Singapore, and by limiting local borrowing by nonresidents. Since 1975, the Singapore dollar has been pegged to a trade-weighted basket of currencies.

In Malaysia there are virtually no restrictions on capital inflows, nor on capital outflows as long as they are not financed by local borrowing. The Malay dollar has been allowed to float since 1973.

Thailand allows relatively free capital movements, although certain private capital outflows are restricted. It has tied its currency to the U.S. dollar, with devaluations in July 1981 and November 1984. Since the latter devaluation, the currency has been pegged to a currency basket.

As in the case of domestic financial transactions, Japan has followed a gradual process of deregulation of international financial transactions. In May 1979, foreigners were allowed for the first time to acquire gensaki (repurchase) securities. A new foreign exchange law was initiated in December 1980 which liberalized most capital controls. In 1984, in an agreement with the United States, actions were announced enabling further liberalization steps affecting international capital transactions. Throughout this process the yen has been allowed to float freely.

Other countries have eliminated capital controls more rapidly. Australia moved to a floating rate regime in December 1983, while at the same time abolishing almost all foreign exchange controls. New Zealand removed many restrictions on international capital movements in 1984, simultaneous with its domestic financial liberalization, and allowed its currency to float in 1985. Indonesia also liberalized its foreign capital transactions rapidly in 1983 and 1984.

International capital movements remain greatly restricted in Korea and, until only recently, in Taiwan as well. In December 1978 residents of Taiwan were permitted to hold foreign exchange deposits in designated banks and to buy and sell foreign exchange through these banks. In February 1979, the exchange rate was allowed to float within limits set by a small group of commercial banks together with the central bank. In July, 1987 new measures relaxing restrictions on some international capital flows were adopted.

Instruments of Monetary Policy

As the proportion of financial instruments carrying market-determined interest rates has grown, there has been a greater emphasis by most central banks on the control of monetary aggregates rather than bank credit. To an increasing extent, the control of monetary aggregates is accomplished through the active use of open market operations, accompanied by a tightening of access to the discount window. The use of other instruments, such as reserve and asset requirements, has diminished significantly.

The Philippines began open market operations in the late 1970s, and increasingly has relied on them as its primary instrument for controlling money growth; access to the rediscount system has been restricted considerably. A repurchase market for government securities was set up in Thailand in 1979 to facilitate open-market operations. Since 1985 open-market operations in the government bond market have been the main instrument in controlling the supply of reserve money. As part of a financial reform in June 1983 in Indonesia, domestic credit ceilings were abandoned, access to preferential rediscount facilities was tightened, and greater emphasis was placed on controlling money aggregates. In February 1984 the central bank of Indonesia began active open-market operations in terms of its own debt certificates, although it still relies greatly on rediscounting. Open-market operations became more important in Malaysia during the 1980s as well, but reserve and liquidity ratios and credit allocation rules continue to be used as instruments. Since 1979, Korea has used the growth rate of its M2 money stock as an intermediate target of monetary policy.

Monetary control in Japan has been based upon control over the interbank call and bills markets. This control is exercised through open-market operations, in addition to discount policy and reserve ratios, and to a lessening extent, window guidance of the large city banks.[16] The Bank of Japan has also used M2 plus CDs as a major monetary policy indicator since 1976.

Until the mid-1970s, the principal instruments of monetary policy in Australia were changes in reserve requirements and informal controls on bank lending. Commercial (trading) banks had to hold a proportion of their deposits as required reserves with the Reserve Bank and government securities as liquid assets, while savings banks were restricted to holding housing loans and government securities. Open-market operations were relatively limited, partly because of the narrowness of the market, which was in turn a result of extensive regulation. Since the late 1970s, the orientation of monetary policy has turned increasingly toward the use of open-market operations to control the growth of money aggregates.

New Zealand formerly relied on the varying of reserve requirements and of asset ratios by banks, as well as credit controls as instruments of monetary policy. With the reforms initiated in 1984, it switched to targeting a monetary base measure (primary liquidity) through open-market operations; asset ratio requirements were dropped totally in February 1985.

Singapore and Hong Kong conduct monetary policy somewhat differently than the countries above. Singapore maintains an unannounced exchange rate target by intervention in the foreign exchange market. Open-market operations in domestic assets are limited, since the government securities market is still thin.[17] This policy effectively subordinates control of the money supply to external considerations. While Singapore still maintains reserve and liquid asset requirements, they are not currently important instruments for monetary control; asset ratios are not binding.

Hong Kong, which does not have a formal central bank, generally allows market forces to determine the volume and allocation of credit, with base money creation effected by two private note-issuing banks. The government does not engage in open-market operations, nor is there any mechanism for government lending to banks. Since 1983 the note-issuing banks have been required to back their issues by foreign assets; the Hong Kong dollar was pegged in October 1983. Even though Hong Kong does not have a central bank that itself intervenes in the foreign exchange market to sustain the peg, under the present institutional arrangement market arbitrage effectively gives the same result.[18]

PROBLEMS IN THE CONDUCT OF MONETARY POLICY

The process of financial liberalization has created a number of general problems for countries in the Pacific Basin concerning the conduct of monetary policy. Most of the problems are similar to those faced by developed countries in other regions that have recently experienced financial innovations.[19] Should central banks focus on control of prices, such as interest rates, or quantities, such as money or credit aggregates, in financial markets? If the latter, should the targeted quantities be narrow or broad? Narrowly defined quantities are more easily controlled, but the links to the real sector have become more tenuous as the interest elasticity of demand for money has risen as a result of liberalization. Broader aggregates, while more closely related to the real sector, are less susceptible to control. Moreover, shifts in the relations between monetary aggregates on the one hand, and GNP and prices on the other, have called into question reliance on any single money target. Maintaining control of monetary aggregates if exchange rates are fixed in the face of increasingly more mobile international capital flows is another area of concern. The problem of financial stability, while also of concern to developed countries, is of even greater concern to the developing countries in the region because of the potentially greater fragility of their financial institutions and their relative inexperience in financial supervision.

What To Target?

Financial liberalization has created new concerns for monetary authorities formerly accustomed to relying on interest rate and direct credit controls in conducting monetary policy. As they have permitted greater flexibility of interest rates and freedom in financial market transactions, they have had to decide whether to conduct monetary policy primarily in terms of targeting prices, such as interest rates, or quantities, such as money or other credit aggregates.

In most cases, as liberalization has proceeded, emphasis has been placed on influencing monetary quantities. This emphasis is in large part a result of the increasing desire by most national monetary authorities to use monetary policy to achieve greater price stability rather than to allocate credit within the economy.

The greater opportunities for domestic residents to acquire credit from unregulated financial intermediaries or from open markets resulting from financial liberalization have weakened the effectiveness of credit controls by providing a source of credit outside the regulated channels. Thus, direct controls on lending have become less effective in limiting credit expansion, as regulated intermediaries have ceased to be the sole sources of large amounts of funds.

The central banks that have focused on greater control of monetary aggregates face the same problems as countries in other regions in the choice of appropriate money aggregate indicators and in determining the relation between the chosen indicator and the ultimate objectives of monetary policy. Authorities typically find it easier to achieve a narrow target for items in the central bank's own balance sheet. New Zealand, for instance, has used a monetary base measure, growth in "primary liquidity," defined currently as the deposits of trading banks with the central bank plus government securities with less than one month maturity. Two issues, in particular, have arisen with respect to the use of this target in New Zealand.

The first issue relates to the appropriate circumstances under which the level of the target should be adjusted.[20] A recent increase in the national sales tax was perceived by some as being inflationary and therefore requiring a lowering of the monetary base target level. An increase in the interest rate paid on bank reserves (settlement cash), perceived as leading to an increased demand for primary liquidity, has caused some to call for a rise in the base target level.[21] As yet, New Zealand's central bank has not adjusted its target.

The second issue concerns the appropriate definition of the monetary base. When base targeting was begun, the definition included government securities with up to six months' maturity, but over the period December 1985 to April 1986 this was changed to include only securities with up to one month's maturity, under the presumption that the latter was more controllable. This issue is symptomatic of the general problem of defining how broad a target on which to focus.

The growth of available financial instruments has made it more difficult to determine which money aggregate to use as an indicator of monetary policy. The distinction between narrow and broad money is less meaningful since many financial instruments can have both transaction and investment features. Furthermore, the decline in transaction costs has widened the spectrum of liquid assets. The increase in closer substitutes for narrow money aggregates as a medium of exchange has reduced the predictable effects of changes in the supply of money on the interest yields of other financial instruments.

This has led many countries to target broader aggregates in order to retain a stable statistical relation between aggregates and key nominal spending variables such as GNP or inflation.[22] However, financial reform has made the assessment of even broad movements in money and credit aggregates more difficult. As in the United States and elsewhere, the changing role of nonbank intermediaries for monetary policy has become a source of concern.

The experience of Australia is illustrative. Prior to financial liberalization monetary policy impacted predominantly on banks and bank lending. Because of deposit rate ceilings, banks lost funds to nonbank financial intermediaries. Liberalization, by removing interest ceilings, portfolio restraints, and other direct controls on banks, improved the competitive position of banking institutions. As a result of the reintermediation of funds by the banking sector, any previously stable relationships between monetary aggregates and key economic variables have tended to break down.[23] In January 1985, Australia abandoned its M3 (defined to include currency plus demand and time deposits with trading and savings banks) target range for monetary growth. It has since adopted an eclectic approach, by monitoring an assortment of indicators, including interest rates, the exchange rate, and the underlying economic trends, as well as the main monetary aggregates. In addition, the government has sought to increase public information about the future pattern of government finance.

The monetary authorities in Japan, like Australia, profess to use an eclectic approach in the determination of monetary policy. Some have attributed the relative stability of the Japanese economy over the last decade to a monetarist policy on the part of the Bank of Japan, based on the observation that the fairly steady decline in Japanese broad money growth since the mid-1970s has coincided with a decline in the inflation rate.[24] However, others contend that there is little institutional or empirical evidence that the Bank of Japan adheres to money aggregate targeting.[25] Announced money targets for the main aggregate indicator -- M2 plus CDs -- are more forecasts of actual money change than guidelines for policy.[26] In actuality, the evidence appears to be that Japan continues to use the interbank rate as an operating target but also looks at other indicators such as the aggregates and the exchange rate.

In some countries, such as Korea and Taiwan, the presence of unorganized, curb money markets outside of central bank control has created similar problems concerning the targeting of broad money aggregates. In Korea, for example, although some adjustment of interest rates on bank deposits and some growth in nonbank financial institutions have been allowed, the development of open money markets has been discouraged,[27] and many borrowers and lenders operate in unauthorized markets. Recent financial changes, such as the raising of interest rates on some demand deposits accounts relative to other callable deposits, have weakened the relation between the narrow aggregate, M1, and economic activity. But because the flow of funds from nonbank financial institutions to private curb money markets is also very volatile, M3 and broader credit aggregates have become much less easily controllable in the view of Korean authorities. Consequently, since 1979 Korea has used M2 as a planning target.[28] Taiwan has been similarly concerned about the effects of arbitrage flows between the highly regulated deposit banks, the curb market, and also the gradually growing open money markets.

In contrast to most countries in the region, Hong Kong and Singapore have both chosen to target financial market prices -- their exchange rates. Singapore has generally tightened its money supply in order to raise the exchange value of its currency and reduce foreign pressures on its interest rate and price level.[29] In Hong Kong, which, as noted above, has no central bank, current institutional arrangements effectively allow market forces to maintain a pegged exchange rate. In particular, because Hong Kong's government Exchange Fund stands ready to buy or sell local currency at a fixed dollar rate from private note-issuing banks, market arbitrage sustains the peg.[30] Thus, as in the case of Singapore, the monetary base and the money supply change primarily in response to balance of payments imbalances, as under a gold standard.

Thus, in general, the increased difficulties of identifying and measuring money aggregates and changes in the channels of monetary policy have created problems for monetary control and targeting in almost all Pacific Basin countries. The problem of targeting aggregates is particularly acute for those countries where, as liberalization proceeds, new and changing channels of intermediation between financial sectors are arising.

Policy Instruments

Changes in the financial environment have also required monetary authorities in Pacific Basin countries to reconsider the mix of their policy instruments. While the ultimate goals of monetary policy -- price stability and noninflationary growth -- may have remained constant, changes in the relative use of various instruments of monetary policy have occurred.

Prior to recent developments, reserve requirements were a commonly used instrument among Pacific Basin countries. In the late 1970s legal reserve requirements on deposits were as high as 30 percent in Indonesia and 20 percent in Malaysia, well above levels that prevail in most developed countries. Relatively few countries currently use reserve requirements as major monetary instruments. Most countries have either dropped use of liquid asset ratios or these ratios are not presently binding. For example, Singapore dropped asset ratios following the reform of its banking system in 1975. New Zealand dropped the use of asset ratios in February 1985. In Hong Kong the legal minimum liquidity ratio is 25 percent, but the ratio typically held is 50 percent.[31]

These developments reflect a wide recognition that changes in reserve requirements and asset ratios are too blunt as instruments and can have adverse effects on the long-term development of the financial system. Small changes in the required reserve ratio necessitate relatively large shifts among commercial bank assets which take time to accomplish if they are not to be disruptive. In addition, overreliance on reserve requirements, by increasing the costs of financial intermediation, results in higher costs to bank customers.[32] Another consideration is that the discriminatory effects of changes of reserve requirements on banking institutions compared to nonbanking institutions may encourage disintermediation from the banking system.

The use of the discount mechanism as a monetary instrument has also declined in many countries. With greater emphasis being placed on restraining money growth in order to contain inflation pressures, many central banks have found it impractical to use the discount mechanism as a tool to reduce commercial bank credit. For reduction in central bank lending to be effective in decreasing the growth of commercial bank credit, it is necessary for banks to be substantially indebted to the central bank. However, in those countries where this is so, discount policies typically involve subsidy elements or credit allocation requirements.[33] Consequently, reductions in discount financing may impose unsustainable losses upon commercial banks and continued credit flows to priority sectors may still be required.

Open-market operations possess the advantage of flexibility in comparison to the instruments discussed above. However, the use of open-market operations is not without problems. In many Pacific Basin countries, open-market operations were limited in the past by the thinness of private money markets. To enhance their ability to conduct open-market operations, authorities have sought to encourage the development of private secondary markets in government securities, as well as of callable loan markets in which banks can lend excess funds. This has compelled the elimination of the common practice of keeping the yields on government securities artificially low and/or forcing commercial banks and the central bank to absorb them. In addition, it has necessitated more restrictive access to discount facilities, with the discount rate raised high enough above market rates to preclude financial institutions from evading the effects of contractionary open market operations by borrowing at the discount window.

In fact, in many countries government bond issues are now sold increasingly through market auctions or syndicates to the private sector. However, in many cases where government issues are primarily long term, the short-term markets remain thin. This limits the use of open-market operations and has prompted monetary authorities in some countries to advocate a shortening of the term structure of government debt.

In Japan, substantial issues of medium- and long-term debt have been marketed to the private sector since the late 1970s. Only recently have short-term issues become more common. At present, however, the Bank of Japan is required to purchase short-term government securities directly from the Ministry of Finance at below market rates. These securities cannot be sold in private markets.[34] In fact, the Bank of Japan has become a strong advocate for a more open market in short-term government securities in order to provide more flexibility in using open-market operations as a monetary tool. Japan's Ministry of Finance, concerned about the implications for its financing costs, has been hesitant to allow this to happen. The continued lack of development of short-term markets is one reason why other tools, such as the discount rate, are still used actively as a monetary instrument in Japan.

In some countries where short-term government securities markets remain limited, central banks have sought to remedy the situation by issuing their own liabilities in which to conduct open-market operations. The Philippine National Bank, for example, did so in the mid-1970s. The central bank of Indonesia also has issued its own instruments recently.

International Capital Flows

High international capital mobility also presents problems for the conduct of monetary policy. As discussed earlier, maintaining effective domestic monetary control is difficult when the authorities simultaneously peg the domestic currency and permit relatively free international capital flows. Under such circumstances, changes in the domestic credit component of the money supply generate offsetting movements in foreign exchange assets through balance of payments imbalances, rendering monetary policy ineffective. In order to maintain the effectiveness of monetary policy and also to offset the effects of foreign real shocks -- such as divergent fiscal trends abroad and large changes in oil and commodity prices -- many of the countries in the Pacific Basin have moved to greater exchange rate flexibility. Some of the smaller countries in the Pacific Basin region that allow relatively free international capital movement (Hong Kong and Singapore, for example) have chosen to maintain pegged exchange rates and give up control of their money supplies altogether. Other countries, such as Korea and Taiwan, also peg their exchange rates but have preferred to limit the impact of international capital flows on monetary policy by maintaining capital restrictions.

For countries that have only partially liberalized their domestic and/or foreign financial markets, international capital flows potentially can create another concern for monetary authorities. As the experience of Thailand indicates, countries that liberalized their international capital transactions prior to liberalizing domestic financial markets expose their domestic interest rates to foreign arbitrage forces. In Thailand's case, the resulting capital outflows were a major factor in allowing greater adjustment of domestic interest rates and the beginning of domestic financial reform.[35] Thus, monetary authorities must be prepared to deal with the competitive pressures that international capital flows can create on domestic financial markets.[36]

The simultaneous removal of international capital controls and domestic interest rate restrictions can also adversely affect an economy. In particular, large-scale capital inflows in response to higher domestic interest rates can appreciate the domestic currency and hurt the tradables sector. This has been the experience of many Latin American countries. For this reason, it has been argued that international liberalization, particularly of the capital account, should be delayed until liberalization of the domestic financial sector is complete.[37]

Most countries in the Pacific Basin, in fact, have adopted a gradual approach to liberalization, beginning with domestic markets. Two notable exceptions, Australia and New Zealand, deregulated both domestic and external financial transactions within a relatively short period of time. In fact, their initial experiences following these steps involved both high interest rates and appreciating currencies, which in turn dampened domestic growth.

Assuring the Stability of Financial Institutions

For countries undergoing financial liberalization, supervisory and regulatory concerns also may play an important role in the conduct of monetary policy.[38] The stability of individual financial institutions is at relatively little risk when financial institutions' investment and pricing decisions are extensively regulated. The relaxation of interest rate controls and portfolio restrictions, however, can expose financial institutions to greater risks. For example, greater price competition among private financial institutions reduces profit margins, and greater fluctuations in interest rates can stimulate more speculative activity. In cases in which banks are government owned, the greater freedom allowed such banks in their operations may also result in riskier activity. Thus, concerns about existing methods of supervision of financial institutions may increase with liberalization.

There are two reasons why the extent of these concerns is potentially greater for the developing countries in the Pacific Basin than for the more developed countries. First, banks in developing countries in the past have been generally more restricted in portfolio diversification. Their acquisition of foreign assets has been limited or distorted by exchange and capital controls. They were often required to acquire certain domestic assets, such as government securities, at below-market value. Moreover, because the real economies of developing countries are typically highly specialized, portfolio holdings of domestic loan assets are not likely to be very diversified. The limited extent of portfolio diversification implies that banks in developing countries are likely to be more seriously affected by various shocks, such as fluctuating commodity prices, than are those in developed countries. In the transition from this environment to liberalized financial markets, greater concern about the solvency of private financial institutions is likely to arise. In the case of government-owned banks, concerns about solvency take the form of the potentially greater costs of subsidizing bank activity in a liberalized environment.

Second, developing countries typically lack standard accounting practices and credit rating systems. In addition, prior to liberalization, supervision and regulation in many developing countries have been directed primarily to ensuring satisfaction of government guidelines regarding credit pricing and allocation, rather than to whether institutions were making prudent credit decisions. The limited experience of both private markets and monetary authorities with the evaluation of credit risk thus also prompts concern about supervision and regulation in liberalized financial markets.

Hence, in implementing financial reforms, monetary authorities in developing countries need to consider what measures to undertake in order to promote financial stability. In particular, it may be desirable to give banks and other institutions greater freedom to diversify their portfolios by holding more foreign assets. It may also be desirable to allow financial institutions greater flexibility to hedge their interest rate risks. The elimination of various restrictions on private portfolio choice may need to be accompanied by an increase in prudential supervision by measures such as tighter auditing and strengthening of bank capital positions. Monetary authorities must also consider the need for increased deposit insurance and short-term bank borrowing from the central bank in order to maintain the solvency of individual institutions.

SUMMARY

In recent years, almost all countries in the Pacific Basin have undertaken steps to liberalize their domestic financial systems and remove restrictions on international capital flows. The resulting structural changes in financial markets have affected the relative importance of the channels through which monetary policy operates. The greater opportunities for domestic residents to acquire credit from unregulated financial intermediaries or from open markets resulting from financial liberalization have weakened the effectiveness of credit controls. Moreover, the developments have allowed the effects of changes in interest rates to be transmitted more rapidly and broadly through the economy. The increased mobility of international capital has enhanced the role of the balance of payments and the exchange rate as major channels for the transmission of monetary policy.

As the structure of financial markets has changed, almost all countries have replaced their earlier emphasis on influencing the quantity of bank credit by a greater emphasis on the control of monetary aggregates. This emphasis is in large part a result of the increasing desire by most countries to use monetary policy to achieve greater price stability rather than to allocate credit within the economy. Many countries in the region have also moved from pegged to more flexible exchange rate regimes.

At the same time, financial liberalization has in many cases increased the difficulties of choosing appropriate monetary aggregates to target. The increase in close substitutes for narrow money aggregates as a medium of exchange has reduced the predictability of the relation between narrow monetary aggregates on the one hand and inflation on the other hand. In countries where unorganized money markets outside of central bank control continue to play a major role in domestic finance, complicating the targeting of monetary targets, the authorities have adopted an eclectic approach in the determination of monetary policy, on the basis of a number of monetary aggregates and economic variables.

Financial market changes in Pacific Basin countries have required the use of more flexible monetary instruments in order to adjust to changing demand and supply conditions in financial markets. Changes in reserve requirements and asset ratios have become widely recognized as instruments that are too blunt and that have adverse effects on the long-term development of the financial system. With greater emphasis being placed on restraining money growth, many central banks have found it impractical to use the discount mechanism for controlling commercial bank credit.

Consequently, open-market operations have become the main instrument of monetary policy in most countries. To facilitate the greater use of open-market operations as a monetary policy instrument, however, monetary authorities must continue to encourage the development of private money markets, particularly in short-term government securities.

The issuance of central bank liabilities as debt instruments may serve as an effective alternative.

As liberalization proceeds, central banks in the region must also balance the objective of promoting the effectiveness of monetary policy with that of maintaining a sound financial system. The limited extent of portfolio diversification by financial institutions in many developing countries implies they may be very sensitive to the effects of various economic shocks. In many countries the experience of both private markets and monetary authorities with the evaluation of credit risk is inadequate. Thus, during the transition to liberalized financial markets, monetary authorities must consider effective measures for monitoring the soundness of private financial institutions and the costs of subsidizing government-owned banks. Such measures may include stricter auditing, strengthening of bank capital requirements, and more deposit insurance.

The process of financial liberalization in most Pacific Basin countries is still ongoing. While significant changes have occurred, relatively few countries thus far have fully liberalized all of their financial markets. As the process continues, the monetary authorities in each country will need to continue to adapt to the new changes in their financial systems.

NOTES

1. New Zealand experienced a brief period of interest liberalization between 1976 and 1981 that was abruptly reversed and not resumed until 1983.

2. Greenwood (1986) provides a survey of the financial deregulation process in seven East Asian countries, including Taiwan, South Korea, Hong Kong, Malaysia, Singapore, Thailand, and Indonesia.

3. These problems are similar to those encountered by the United States and European countries that have recently experienced bursts of financial innovation. The experience of developed countries with financial innovation has been well summarized by Ahktar (1983) and the Bank for International Settlements (1986).

4. Aghevli and others (1979) provide an earlier discussion of monetary policy in several Asian countries.

5. A useful analysis of the workings of monetary policy in a repressed economy can be found in Buiter (1986).

6. The presumption that money has nonneutral effects on real activity, at least in the short to medium run, may be explained by rigidities in the adjustment of wage and other contracts. As nominal wages and prices adjust over time, the real effects of monetary policy tend to disappear, with only changes in nominal magnitudes persisting in the long run.

7. These adjustments presume satisfaction of the appropriate elasticity conditions and the availability of resources.

8. Growing empirical evidence (for example, McKinnon, 1973; Lanyi and Saracoglu, 1983; and Townsend, 1983) indicates that such financial restrictions have retarded economic growth by most developing countries. There is generally a positive relationship between the degree of development of the financial sector, including in particular freer interest rates, and economic performance in developing countries.

9. See Cheng (1986, p. 151).

10. Greenwood (1986), in fact, has argued that a main impetus for liberalization in some countries came from local foreign banks, who sought access to lower cost local funds in order to finance trade credit.

11. A desire to limit the growth of foreign indebtedness was also a factor behind interest liberalization in the Philippines.

12. Competition in Singapore's banking industry has been intensified by the presence of a government institution, the Post Office Savings Bank, which has aggressively competed for funds.

13. These regulations were implemented obstensibly to prevent the destabilizing interest rate competition experienced during banking crises in the early 1960s. They were formalized in legislation in 1981 that established the Association and empowered it to require banks to observe the interest rates it set.

14. See Moreno (1986).

15. In 1984 Taiwanese authorities allowed local and foreign banks to establish offshore banking units. These units were permitted to accept deposits and make loans in foreign currency at free market rates. However, domestic borrowers and lenders are restricted from operating in this offshore market.

16. See Cargill and Hutchison (1987).

17. This in part is a result of the requirement placed upon Singapore's monetary authority to sell government bonds in order to finance government budget surpluses.

18. While the Hong Kong dollar was allowed to float from 1974 to 1983, some have characterized this system as unstable (Greenwood, 1983). Also see Moreno (1986, 1987).

19. The experience of developed countries with financial innovation has been summarized by Ahktar (1983). The major changes he describes include: the greater reliance by banks and other financial institutions on interest-sensitive funds to finance their activities as interest controls have been relaxed; increasingly widespread use of variable or floating rate financial techniques; and the growth of marketable financial instruments, including the development of specialized financial techniques which unbundle and facilitate the transfer of market and credit risks. These changes have resulted in greater competition among financial institutions and the systematic breakdown of segmentation between financial markets. Also see a study by the Bank for International Settlements (1986).

20. This issue is the same as the "base drift" argument in the United States. See Walsh (1986).

21. See Walsh (1987).

22. Judd and Trehan (1987) argue that a broad-based money aggregate like M3 appears to provide more useful information for conducting U.S. monetary policy than M1.

While the Federal Reserve has used M1 as its leading indicator of real GNP and inflation since the mid-1970s, this policy presumes that M1 is a stable function of the macro variables of interest to U.S. policymakers -- GNP, prices, and interest rates. However, the increase in closer substitutes for M1 as a medium of exchange as a result of financial liberalization in the 1980s reduced the predictable effects of changes in the supply of money on the interest yields of other financial instruments. They conclude that gradual, piecemeal deregulation may present bigger problems for the implementation of monetary policy when targeting monetary aggregates than once and for all or, at least rapid, deregulation.

23. See Dougherty (1986).

24. See, for example, Friedman (1983).

25. See Hutchison (1986) and Dotsey (1986).

26. Publically announcing targets for monetary expansion may directly affect private expectations of inflation. However, the potential benefit of, say, lowering inflation expectations by announcing a lower money growth rate must be balanced against the undesirable effects of subsequently exceeding the targets.

27. In fact, Korean authorities outlawed an unofficial repurchase market in 1984.

28. See Shin (1986). Current plans are to add CDs to M2 as a monetary target because of the high substitutability of the former with bank deposits.

29. See Fry (1985).

30. The debt of the Exchange Fund (certificates of indebtedness, or CIs) backs the note issues of private banks. The Fund passively sells or redeems this debt when approached by the private banks. Since the banks are also required to back all holdings of CIs by foreign assets, the volume of note issues effectively is linked to the foreign exchange reserves of the banking system. See Moreno (1986, 1987).

31. See Scott (1986). While Hong Kong also has reserve requirements, they are irrelevant given the absence of any limits on the ability of private banks to obtain currency (CIs) from the Exchange Fund. See note 30.

32. These costs can be especially high since central banks rarely pay interest on required reserves.

33. See Aghevli and others (1979, pp. 796-800).

34. See Royama (1986).

35. Concern about the tendency of domestic credit to be strongly affected by external developments has at times also prompted authorities in Thailand to reimpose some restrictions on domestic financial markets. See Greenwood (1986).

36. Glick (1987) provides an empirical analysis of real interest linkages between several Pacific Basin countries and the United States. He finds evidence that the extent of these linkages is generally comparable to that between most European countries and the United States.

37. The appropriate order of liberalization of domestic and foreign financial markets is an important topic in the development economics literature. See, for example, Edwards (1984), Frenkel (1982), and Mathieson (1986).

38. These issues are well discussed in Dooley and Mathieson (1986).

REFERENCES

Aghevli, Bijan, Mohsin Khan, P.R. Narvekar, and Brock Short (1979). "Monetary Policy in Selected Asian Countries." IMF *Staff Papers* (December).

Ahktar, M.A. (1983). *Financial Innovation and Their Implications for Monetary Policy: An International Perspective.* Basel, Switzerland: Bank for International Settlements (December).

Buiter, Wilem (1986). "Macroeconomic Responses by Developing Countries to Changes in External Economic Conditions." NBER Working Paper No. 1836 (February).

Bank for International Settlements (1986). "Recent Innovations in International Banking." Paper prepared by G-10 study group (April).

Cargill, Thomas and Michael Hutchison (1987). "The Bank of Japan's Response to Macroeconomic and Financial Change." Paper prepared for the Federal Reserve Bank of San Francisco Conference on "Challenges to Monetary Policy in Pacific Basin Countries" (September 23-25).

Cheng, Hang-Sheng (1986). "Financial Policy and Reform in Taiwan, China." In *Financial Policy and Reform in Pacific Basin Countries*, edited by Hang-Sheng Cheng. Lexington, Mass: Lexington Books.

Dooley, Michael and Donald Mathieson (1987). "Financial Liberalization and Stability in Developing Countries." IMF Working Paper 87/19 (March).

Dotsey, Michael (1986). "Japanese Monetary Policy: A Comparative Analysis." *Monetary and Economic Studies*, Institute for Monetary and Economic Studies, The Bank of Japan (October).

Dougherty, H.R. (1986). "The Evolution of the Australian Financial System." Paper prepared for the Seventh Pacific Basin Conference on Economic Modeling, Sydney, Australia (December 1-4).

Edwards, Sebastian (1984). "The Order of Liberalization of the External Sector in Developing Countries." *Princeton Essays in International Finance*, No. 156 (December).

Frenkel, Jacob (1982). "The Order of Economic Liberalization: Discussion." In *Economic Policy in a World of Change*, edited by Karl Brunner and Allan Meltzer. Amsterdam: North-Holland.

Friedman, Milton (1983). "Monetary Variability: United States and Japan." *Journal of Money, Credit, and Banking* (August).

Fry, Maxwell (1985). "Financial Structure, Monetary Policy and Economic Growth in Hong Kong, Singapore, Taiwan and South Korea, 1960-83." In *Export Oriented Development Strategies*, edited by Anne Krueger, Vittorio Corbo, and Fernando Osso. Colorado: Westview Press.

Glick, Reuven (1987). "Interest Rate Linkages in the Pacific Basin." Federal Reserve Bank of San Francisco *Economic Review*, No. 3 (Summer).

Greenwood, Jeremy (1983). *Asian Monthly Monitor* (December).

Greenwood, Jeremy (1986). "Financial Liberalization and Innovation in Seven East Asian Economies." In *Financial Innovation and Monetary Policy: Asia and the West*, edited by Yoshio Suzuki and H. Yomo. Tokyo: University of Tokyo Press.

Hutchison, Michael (1986). "Japan's 'Money Focused' Monetary Policy." Federal Reserve Bank of San Francisco *Economic Review*, No. 3 (Summer).

Judd, John and Bharat Trehan (1987). "Portfolio Substitution and the Reliability of M1, M2, and M3 as Monetary Indicators." Federal Reserve Bank of San Francisco *Economic Review*, No. 3 (Summer).

Lanyi, Anthony and Rusdu Saracoglu (1983). "The Importance of Interest Rates in Developing Countries." *Finance and Development* (June).

Mathieson, Donald (1986). "International Capital Flows, Capital Controls, and Financial Reform." In *Financial Policy and Reform in Pacific Basin Countries*, edited by Hang-Sheng Cheng. Lexington, Mass: Lexington Books.

McKinnon, Ronald (1973). *Money and Capital in Economic Development.* Washington, D.C.: The Brookings Institution.

Moreno, Ramon (1986). "Monetary Policy Without a Central Bank: The Case of Hong Kong." Federal Reserve Bank of San Francisco *Economic Review*, No. 2 (Spring).

Moreno, Ramon (1987). "Monetary Policy in Singapore and Hong Kong." Paper prepared for the Federal Reserve Bank of San Francisco Conference on "Challenges to Monetary Policy in Pacific Basin Countries" (September 23-25).

Royama, S. (1986). "An Open Market for Treasury Bills." *Economic Eye* 7, Keizai Koho Center, Tokyo, Japan (June).

Scott, Robert Haney (1986). "Monetary Policy in Hong Kong." In *Hong Kong's Financial Institutions and Markets*, edited by Robert Haney Scott, K.A. Wong, and Yan K. Ho. Oxford: Oxford University Press.

Shin, Hyunchul (1986). "The Money-GNP Relationship in Korea." Paper presented at the Seventh Pacific Basin Conference on Economic Modeling, Sydney, Australia (December 1-4).

Townsend, Robert (1983). "Financial Structure and Economic Activity." *American Economic Review* (December).

Walsh, Carl (1986). "In Defense of Base Drift," *American Economic Review* (September).

Walsh, Carl (1987). "Financial Deregulation and Monetary Policy in New Zealand." Paper prepared for the Federal Reserve Bank of San Francisco Conference on "Challenges to Monetary Policy in Pacific Basin Countries" (September 23-25).

3

Exchange Rate Arrangements and Monetary Policy

Donald J. Mathieson

In recent years, many countries have relied on monetary policy as the principal means not only for offsetting external and domestic cyclical shocks but also for containing secular inflation, especially when fiscal policies have been constrained by large structural deficits. However, it has been long recognized that the ability of monetary policy to achieve such objectives in an open economy is influenced by such factors as country size, the degree of integration between domestic and international goods and financial markets, and the country's exchange rate arrangements. Since the current international monetary system encompasses countries of divergent economic sizes, with varying degrees of integration with international markets, and with sharply different degrees of exchange rate flexibility, it is difficult to make general statements about the effectiveness of monetary policy without specifying the particular economic and financial structures being considered.

Traditionally there have been two alternative approaches to examining the issue of the effectiveness of monetary policy under alternative exchange rate arrangements: an examination of the effect on the economy of a change in a given monetary policy instrument, or consideration of the factors that lead a country to select monetary policy instruments and exchange rate arrangements. The second of these approaches, the analysis of optimal monetary and exchange rate policies, is broader in the sense that it explicitly takes into account the authorities' objectives. This chapter adopts the latter approach and examines the relationship between monetary and exchange rate policies by considering the factors that have led the authorities in developed and developing countries in the Pacific Basin to alter their use of monetary policy instruments and exchange rate arrangements during the past decade.

The chapter has three sections. The first section examines the monetary policy instruments and exchange rate arrangements that have been used in selected Asian countries during 1975-1985. This was a period of substantial structural change for almost all of these countries, including changes in exchange rate arrangements, substitution of monetary for credit policy instruments, major reforms of the domestic financial systems, a growing integration of domestic and external financial markets (often accompanied by a relaxation of restrictions on capital flows), and the need to adapt to large external and internal macroeconomic shocks.

Next, the question of which changes in economic conditions would lead countries to substitute monetary for credit policy instruments and introduce greater flexibility into exchange rate arrangements is examined. Although the recent literature on the choice of optimal exchange rate regimes and monetary policy instruments offers some important answers to this question, the analysis has been hampered by the typical assumption of perfect substitutability between domestic and foreign securities. Only by relaxing that assumption can one examine the conditions that would influence the authorities' choice between credit ceilings and limits on the expansion of monetary aggregates as their principal monetary policy instrument under alternative exchange rate arrangements. The types of monetary and exchange rate policies that have been adopted by countries undertaking extensive trade and financial liberalizations are considered in the discussion of the influence of ongoing structural changes on the selection of policy instruments.

The final section summarizes the main conclusions concerning the relationship between monetary and exchange rate policies.

ACTUAL EXPERIENCES

The changes in exchange rate arrangements and financial market policies of 13 Asian countries since 1975 are summarized in Table 1. (Details on individual countries are presented in the Appendix.) Since the specific experiences of a number of these countries are addressed in other chapters included in this book, this information on changes in exchange rate arrangements, capital controls, and monetary policy instruments is intended to provide only an overview of general developments.

Four key trends are evident. First, countries have increased the flexibility associated with their exchange rate arrangements.[1] This is especially true with the industrial countries in the region; for instance, Australia and New Zealand moved from initially being classified as "pegged" to "independent floaters." However, although the number of developing countries in the region that are classified as employing some form of exchange rate flexibility rose from three in 1975 to five in 1985, five other developing countries pegged their exchange rates in one form or another throughout the period. This pattern of some developing countries continuing to peg their exchange rates while many other countries

Table 1
Exchange Rate Arrangements, Capital Controls, and Monetary Policy Instruments in 11 Selected Asian Countries[a]

Exchange Arrangements[b]

	Pegged to U.S. Dollar	Pegged to Other Currencies or Composites	Other Flexible Arrangements	Managed Flexibility	Independent Floaters
1975	2	7	1	2	1
1976	2	6	1	3	1
1977	2	5	1	3	2
1978	1	5	2	3	2
1979	1	5	2	3	2
1980	0	5	2	4	2
1981	0	4	2	6	1
1982	0	4	3	5	1
1983	0	4	1	7	1
1984	0	4	1	6	2
1985	0	5	0	4	4

Capital Controls[c]

	Required Surrender of Export Proceeds	Advanced Import Deposits	Limitations or Advanced Approval on Payments for Invisibles	Limitations on Foreign Currency Deposits by Residents	Prior Approval Required for Foreign lending or Borrowing by Financial Institutions	Tax or Special Reserve Requirement on Foreign Borrowing
1975	11	4	9	11	10	2
1976	11	5	9	11	10	1
1977	11	4	9	11	11	2
1978	10	3	8	10	11	2
1979	10	3	8	10	11	1
1980	10	3	8	10	11	1
1981	10	2	8	10	11	1
1982	9	1	8	10	10	1
1983	7	1	8	9	8	1
1984	7	1	6	8	8	1
1985	7	2	6	8	8	1

(a) *The countries are: Australia, Burma, Fiji, Indonesia, Japan, Korea, Malaysia, New Zealand, the Philippines, Singapore, Sri Lanka, Thailand, and Western Samoa.*

(b) *Number of countries with given exchange arrangement.*

(c) *Number of countries utilizing a given capital control.*

Table 1 (continued)

Monetary and Credit Policy Instruments[(d)]

	Required Reserve Ratio	Liquidity Ratio	General Discount Facility and Discount Rate	Open-Market Operations[(e)]	Announced Monetary Aggregates Targets or Projections
1975	12 (4)	6 (2)	13 (2)	3 (1)	0
1976	12 (4)	6 (2)	13 (2)	3 (1)	1 (0)
1977	12 (4)	6 (2)	13 (2)	3 (1)	1 (0)
1978	12 (3)	6 (2)	13 (2)	3 (2)	2 (0)
1979	12 (3)	6 (2)	13 (2)	4 (2)	2 (0)
1980	12 (2)	6 (2)	13 (3)	4 (2)	2 (0)
1981	12 (0)	6 (0)	13 (2)	5 (3)	2 (0)
1982	11 (0)	6 (0)	13 (3)	6 (4)	3 (0)
1983	11 (0)	5 (0)	13 (3)	6 (4)	4 (0)
1984	10 (0)	5 (0)	13 (3)	9 (4)	2 (0)
1985	9 (1)	5 (1)	13 (2)	9 (5)	1 (0)

Monetary and Credit Policy Instruments (continued)

	Ceiling on Overall Credit Expansion	Credit Allocation Rules	Sectoral Rediscount Facilities	Ceiling Interest Rate
1975	10 (4)	10 (2)	3 (0)	12 (1)
1976	10 (4)	11 (2)	3 (0)	12 (1)
1977	10 (4)	11 (2)	3 (0)	12 (1) 1R[(f)]
1978	10 (4)	10 (2)	3 (0)	12 (0) 2R[(f)]
1979	10 (4)	10 (2)	3 (0)	12 (0) 2R[(f)]
1980	9 (4)	10 (2)	3 (0)	12 (0) 4R[(f)]
1981	9 (4)	10 (3)	3 (0)	12 (0) 4R[(f)] IT[(g)]
1982	6 (2)	9 (2)	3 (0)	12 (0) 4R[(f)]
1983	5 (1)	8 (1)	3 (0)	10 (0) 5R[(f)]
1984	5 (1)	7 (1)	3 (0)	9 (0) 4R[(f)]
1985	5 (1)	7 (1)	3 (0)	9 (0) 4R[(f)]

(d) *The first number represents the countries reported employing a given instrument, whereas the number in parentheses represents those countries for which this is a principal instrument.*

(e) *Including foreign exchange swap operations and repurchase agreements.*

(f) *The number before the letter R denotes the number of countries with interest rate ceilings that had freed some deposit or lending rates (typically on longer term deposits).*

(g) *The number before the letter T denotes the number of countries reimposing interest rate ceilings on previously freed rates.*

(especially industrial countries) introduced greater flexibility into their exchange rate arrangements is consistent with the changes that have occurred in other regions of the world. (See Goldstein, 1984; Crockett and Goldstein, 1987.)

A second major change has been the movement away from implementing monetary policy through credit market instruments toward the employment of monetary instruments (Table 1). In this chapter, monetary instruments are defined as those which principally affect the price and nominal quantity of base money, and credit policy instruments are those which primarily affect the price and nominal quantity of credit to the private sector. By this criteria, ceilings on the expansion of commercial bank credit to the private sector, credit allocation rules, and ceiling interest rates are classified as credit instruments, whereas open-market operations and discount window policies are treated as monetary instruments. Reserve and liquidity ratios fall between these two polar cases in that they can affect both the demand for base money and the availability of credit to the private and public sectors. In the mid-1970s, most of the countries represented in Table 1 implemented their monetary policies through the use of credit instruments, including limitations on the expansion of total bank credit, rules for the allocation of credit to particular sectors or borrowers, and ceiling interest rates on loans and deposits. By the mid-1980s, in contrast, monetary policy was most often implemented through open-market operations, changes in the terms and conditions under which discount windows could be accessed, and the employment of intermediate targets or projections for monetary aggregates. This change has been most evident in the industrial countries and those developing countries in which the most extensive financial reforms have been undertaken. Nonetheless, credit instruments have remained the principal monetary policy tools in a number of developing countries, especially those with pegged exchange rates.

Third, the greater flexibility of exchange rate arrangements and the increased use of monetary instruments has also been accompanied by some relaxation of restrictions on capital flows. While many of the developing countries represented in Table 1 still retain extensive controls on external financial transactions, the industrial countries and a number of the developing countries have either eliminated many of these controls or, where the controls have remained "on the books," have limited the types of portfolio and financial flows subject to controls. Where these controls have been relaxed, domestic residents have rapidly diversified their portfolios; domestic financial conditions have been increasingly influenced, too, by developments in international markets. The countries retaining the most extensive controls over capital flows have also tended to peg their exchange rates and rely on credit instruments in the conduct of monetary policy. Nonetheless, even where capital controls do not inhibit the arbitrage of financial market conditions, the linkages between domestic and international markets still appear to be far from perfect, with large borrowers or lenders from the industrial countries having much greater access to international markets than small and medium-sized entities from developing countries, and with short-term markets being much more closely linked than medium- or long-term markets.

A final characteristic of many of these Asian countries has been their willingness to undertake extensive liberalization of their domestic financial systems. The extent of these reforms has naturally differed considerably across countries, but they have often involved removing or relaxing ceilings on loan and deposit interest rates, increasing the degree of competition through the entry of new domestic and foreign financial institutions, reducing required reserve and liquidity ratios, paying interest on bank reserves, and eliminating the rules governing the allocation of credit or the provision of special credits at preferential rates.[2] In some cases (e.g., Australia, Japan, and New Zealand), these reforms have been accompanied by significant relaxations of capital controls.

These structural changes in the Asian economies, represented in Table 1 and the Appendix, raise a number of questions about the effectiveness of monetary policy under alternative exchange rate arrangements. First, which domestic and international developments have led some countries to undertake extensive changes in their exchange rate arrangements, their mix of money and credit market instruments, their use of capital controls, and the structure of their domestic financial markets, while other countries have shown much more limited structural change? Second, how have these changes altered the effectiveness of monetary policy in terms of its ability to help the authorities achieve their internal and external objectives? Finally, since real and financial structural changes seem likely to continue, how can monetary and exchange rate arrangements be designed not only to obtain the best performance from a given economic structure but also to cope with the problems encountered during periods of ongoing structural changes? In this chapter, these issues will be considered from two traditional points of view. The first focuses on a single country linked, to varying degrees, with exogenously determined conditions on international markets for goods, factors, and financial assets, while the second focuses on the interdependent effects of countries' policies.

THE CHOICE OF POLICY INSTRUMENTS

Since countries select the policy instruments which best allow them to achieve their internal and external objectives, it is usually argued in the literature on the optimal design of monetary and exchange rate policies that the set of most effective instruments depends on each instrument's time pattern of effects on domestic and external variables (which will reflect the economy's real and financial structure and degree of openness), the disturbances or other factors which need to be offset by policy measures, and the relative importance the authorities attach to their objectives. Thus, the changes in the use of monetary policy instruments and exchange rate arrangements evident in Table 1 and Appendix I should be explained as responses to such shifts. However, it has also been emphasized that the relative importance of each of these factors depends significantly on the degree of integration between domestic and international goods and financial markets. It is, therefore, useful to divide the discussion of the most effective monetary and exchange rate policies into those policies that should be adopted under perfect market integration and those that should be selected under less than perfect integration.

The Case of Highly Integrated Markets

It has been argued that, when domestic and international financial markets are highly integrated (i.e., domestic and foreign securities are perfect substitutes), monetary and exchange rate policies are not independent. However, this conclusion reflects a particular view of the potential monetary and exchange rate instruments available to the authorities.[3] The authorities' exchange rate arrangements are typically described in terms of a foreign exchange market intervention rule which specifies the scale of the authorities' purchases or sales of foreign exchange for domestic base money in reaction to the departures of the exchange rate from a target level or to the movements in the exchange rate ("leaning against the wind").[4] Monetary policy is conducted through open-market operations which alter the domestic component of base money. Thus, monetary and exchange rate policies are linked through their effects on domestic base money. Moreover, since it is often assumed that domestic and foreign assets are perfect substitutes and that interest rate parity conditions are satisfied, these two policies are collapsed into one policy and " monetary policy is exchange rate policy."[5] With perfect asset substitution across countries, open-market purchases of domestic securities or foreign exchange each set in motion portfolio and spending adjustments of a comparable nature.

In this situation, the exchange rate intervention rule (or equivalently, the money supply rule) that best allows the authorities to achieve their objectives depends on the nature of the internal and external shocks affecting the economy, the economy's structural rigidities, the asymmetries in the information sets available to the authorities and the private sector, the country's size, and the degree of integration of its goods and financial markets with those in the rest of the world. The importance of these factors was indirectly illustrated by Helpman (1981) who showed that, in a frictionless world of perfect certainty with purchasing power parity and interest rate parity, the consumption patterns associated with alternative exchange rate arrangements would be identical unless the arrangements involved a permanent transfer of resources from one country to another.[6] While such a world is unlikely ever to exist, the analysis implies that the appropriateness of a particular mix of exchange rate arrangements and monetary policy will depend on the exact nature of the market failures and frictions that exist.

Real and Monetary Shocks. The nature of the real and monetary shocks affecting the economy have been viewed as especially important determinants of optimal exchange rate arrangements. The policy recommendations for dealing with these shocks, however, differ somewhat depending on the extent of the feedback between the domestic and external economies. One possibility is that the domestic economy is "small" and that domestic developments, therefore, have no impact on external prices or incomes. Alternatively, a two-country framework has been used in which the levels of income, prices, and interest rates are affected by the policies adopted in both countries. In the case of a small country, for example, Frenkel and Aizenman (1982) showed that the higher the variance of shocks to real output, the more desirable is a fixed exchange rate. With a fixed exchange rate, changes in the current account balance can cushion the effects of real shocks on domestic consumption. Countries faced with relatively large real shocks should hold large stocks of international reserves to allow for large variability in the balance of payments. However, the importance of this consideration diminishes as the economy's degree of integration with world capital markets increases, since the same cushioning can be achieved through international borrowing or lending. In contrast, a greater variability of monetary shocks[7] increases the desirability of exchange rate flexibility since exchange rate adjustments can offset these monetary shocks and prevent them from altering real output and consumption. When both types of shocks are present, the optimal exchange rate regime involves a system of managed floating with a degree of intervention that allows the external economy to serve as the most efficient buffer for the domestic economy.

If there are two economies of comparable size, the policy recommendations change somewhat since neither country will find it optimal to act as the sole buffer in the system. Moreover, a distinction must be made between high and low degrees of financial and goods market integration between the two countries. In a two-country context, the notion that a floating exchange rate insulates a country from foreign shocks is more likely to be true when capital mobility is low than when it is high. For example, with low capital mobility, an exogenous increase in foreign demand for money might raise the foreign interest rate sharply but still generate few capital flows. Flexible exchange rates would then only have to respond to offset the changes in trade flows induced by the adjustments in aggregate demand in the foreign country. With a high degree of capital mobility, the increased capital flows would necessitate a sharper exchange rate adjustment that would, at least in the short run, affect prices and output to a greater degree than would low capital mobility.[8] In particular, Obstfeld (1985, p.405) has argued that under conditions of high capital mobility,[9]

> The risk-sharing argument suggests that the two regions will prefer a fixed exchange rate, together with appropriate international settlement arrangements, when monetary shocks are dominant, and especially when they are negatively correlated across regions, but will prefer a floating rate when aggregate demand shocks are the main concern.

In terms of explaining the evolution of the exchange rate arrangements for the countries represented in Table 1 and the Appendix, these analyses suggest that one first needs to identify the nature of the shocks that have dominated during the period 1975-1985 and the relative size and degrees of openness of the economies involved. With regard to the nature of the shocks that have occurred, Obstfeld (1985) has argued that the divergent fiscal trends across the major industrial countries, the extensive changes in oil and commodity prices, and the fact that exchange rates and stock market prices have not moved together in the way one would expect if the shocks were monetary in origin[10] all point to the fact that the past decade has been one in which real shocks have dominated monetary shocks.[13] If real shocks have dominated in the period since the mid-1970s, then the changes in exchange rate arrangements evident in Table 1 and the Appendix are consistent with the predictions of the theoretical analysis. The dominance of real shocks would imply that a small country confronted with low capital mobility (possibly a result of the presence of capital controls) would choose a pegged exchange rate, and the smaller developing countries with relatively restrictive capital controls represented in Table 1 and the Appendix have tended to adopt pegged rates. In contrast, larger economies or developing economies more closely integrated with international capital markets have moved, as expected, toward greater exchange rate flexibility. However, since there is no information about the relative sizes of the real and monetary shocks affecting each country, one cannot specify the most appropriate degree of exchange rate flexibility. Moreover, the optimal degree of exchange rate flexibility would be expected to vary over time with changes in the authorities' perceptions regarding the nature and severity of these shocks.

Other Considerations. In addition to real and monetary shocks, a number of other determinants of the most appropriate degree of exchange rate flexibility have been identified in the literature on optimum currency areas. Optimum currency area analyses have focused on the cost and benefits associated with expanding the area linked by fixed exchange rates. For example, Mundell (1961) first argued that a country should peg its exchange rate with another country if the two countries shared a high degree of factor mobility which would ensure real adjustment even without exchange rate adjustments. In contrast, McKinnon (1963) stated that the key factor determining whether a country should fix its exchange rate was the openness of the economy. In the short run, a relatively closed economy could use an exchange rate depreciation to switch expenditures from traded to nontraded goods, but a highly open economy would most likely just increase its price level. Subsequent analyses suggested that a country should be included in an optimum currency area if, relative to the existing members, it has a similar fiscal system, comparable size, limited geographic or commodity diversification of exports, a willingness to share a common rate of inflation, and close trade and financial relationship with the existing currency bloc.[12] While it is generally recognized that an optimum currency area would in most cases not correspond to the political boundaries of modern nation-states, these discussions do suggest that countries will tend to adopt greater exchange rate flexibility, the lower the degree of factor mobility between countries, the greater the divergence of fiscal systems, the more dispersed are inflation objectives, the less open are the individual economies, and the less they are associated with existing currency blocs.

The Case of Imperfect But Increasing Market Integration

While the analysis of monetary and exchange rate policy under conditions of perfect asset substitution helps to identify factors influencing the optimal combination of monetary and exchange rate policies, it provides little insight into the questions of why countries use different mixes of monetary and credit policy instruments and of the considerations that would lead the authorities to alter this mix over time. With perfect asset substitution, for example, a ceiling on the expansion of domestic commercial bank credit would have no effects on domestic activity if borrowers could immediately substitute foreign for domestic credit. As already noted, the set of monetary and exchange rate instruments included in most analyses of exchange rate policy is much narrower than is typically used by the authorities (Table 1 and Appendix).

The changes in the mix of monetary policy instruments and exchange rate arrangements in the past decade in part reflect a response to increasing but less than perfect degrees of integration of goods and assets markets. While international trade and financial transactions have become increasingly important for all countries, empirical studies -- e.g., Isard (1977) -- have found that purchasing power parity conditions can be violated for extended periods even among industrial countries. Moreover, Yuan (1986) recently argued that the overall degree of financial market integration across Asian countries is still low for most countries, especially for medium- or long-term credits.[13] Nonetheless, the gradual relaxation of capital controls has resulted in increasingly close-linked short-term financial markets, especially across the major countries.[14]

With less than perfect integration of domestic and international markets, monetary and exchange rate policies no longer can be represented by a single combined policy since many monetary and exchange rate policy instruments may have differential effects on the domestic economy and external transactions.[15] This naturally makes the choice of the most effective instruments more complex, but some of relevant factors influencing that choice can be illustrated by considering the conditions under which a country would use as its principal monetary policy instrument either a ceiling on the expansion of commercial bank credit or controls over the growth of domestic monetary aggregates. While many other policy choices could be examined, this choice is most closely related to the switch from credit to monetary instruments evident in Table 1 and the Appendix.

The Choice of Money and Credit Instruments. Whether the authorities' ability to achieve their domestic and external objectives will be enhanced by establishing and maintaining a ceiling on a given monetary or credit aggregate will depend on a number of characteristics of the domestic economy including the strength of linkages between domestic and external goods and financial markets, the structure of the domestic financial system, the state of the fiscal accounts, and the the nature of the country's exchange rate arrangements.[16]

Integration of Domestic and External Goods Markets. The strength of the linkages between domestic and international markets for goods is a key factor influencing the use of ceilings for monetary or credit aggregates. If domestic and international traded goods markets are closely integrated, for example, movements in the domestic prices of tradable goods would be tied to changes in the exchange rate and international prices. If international traded goods prices are stable, domestic traded goods prices would then change only in response to an exchange rate movement. Stable domestic prices of tradable goods would also help stabilize the prices of nontraded goods. In this situation, inflation would generally be associated only with the changes in prices produced by an exchange rate depreciation, regardless of the type of credit or monetary ceiling used.[17]

For most countries, however, the linkages between domestic and international goods markets are far less direct as a result of the existence of trade barriers, transactions costs, and shipping charges. These weaker linkages provide scope for extended periods of domestic inflation and create the possibility of a conflict between the attainment of the authorities' external balance and inflation objectives. Domestic prices would respond not only to exchange rate adjustments but also to such factors as increases in reserve money generated by the conversion of foreign exchange or issuance of domestic credit by the central bank. In this situation, a ceiling on domestic monetary growth could be an important element in limiting inflation.

Integration with External Financial Markets. The strength of the linkages between domestic and international markets for financial instruments is also a key factor influencing the use of ceilings for monetary and credit aggregates. Access to international financial markets affects the economy's structure in at least two important ways: (1) it gives residents an opportunity to acquire *net* credit (and goods and services) from abroad; and (2) reserve money can expand as a result of the conversion of foreign exchange acquired through current account imbalances or external borrowing. Depending on their size and sustainability, capital flows can weaken the effectiveness of credit ceilings both by providing a source of credit from outside the banking system and also by creating an incentive for the development of unregulated domestic sources of credit.

It has been suggested that the problems created by capital flows could be mitigated by placing a ceiling on the expansion of reserve money. Such a ceiling on reserve money would require the central bank to sterilize the impact of the capital inflows on reserve money by reducing the domestic credit of the central bank. While sterilization is always possible in a technical sense, the sustainability of such a policy depends on the cost of reducing central bank domestic credit and on the scope and persistence of the inflows. The domestic cost of sterilization is, in part, related to the fact that the firms obtaining credits from the external sector may be quite different from those economic units that obtain the central bank credits. In an economy where credit is rationed and interest rates are constrained, it may be quite difficult for firms or enterprises that obtain credits from the central bank to obtain credits from any other foreign or domestic source. Thus, the sterilization of capital inflows may involve a sharp redistribution of credit within the private sector; this could create serious financing difficulties for certain sectors of the economy.[18]

The feasibility of sterilizing capital inflows is also determined by the nature of the capital flows. In some situations, the capital inflow may represent a once-and-for-all movement of capital between domestic and international markets. For example, there could be a reflow of funds to the domestic market following a currency realignment. In cases where it was judged necessary to offset any price level effect of this inflow, either the credit ceilings could be adjusted in advance by the anticipated size of this inflow or a ceiling on reserve money could ensure that automatic sterilization takes place.

There is a far more serious problem when the capital flows represent the continuing arbitrage of financial market conditions between domestic and international markets. In economies with severe credit rationing, there are large incentives to obtain credit from international sources. In this case, sterilization of the capital inflow may not only involve a sharp redistribution of credit within the private sector (from those obtaining credits from the central bank to those with access to international financial markets) but also would not eliminate the original incentives for further capital flows. Thus, in the presence of distortions or other conditions that give rise to continuing capital inflow, a ceiling on reserve money could lead to continuing increases in the central bank's foreign exchange reserves and an ongoing redistribution of credit within the private sector. Alternatively, the absence of such a ceiling on reserve money could result in a rapid increase in reserve money and thereby in inflationary pressure.[19]

Fiscal Imbalances and the Structure of Domestic Financial Markets. A country's fiscal position and the structure of its domestic financial markets often interact to influence strongly whether a given monetary or credit aggregate will be effective and controllable. In particular, the absence of control over the fiscal accounts may mean that neither a monetary nor a credit ceiling would be effective. With regard to the former type of ceiling, a large fiscal deficit financed by the provision of central bank credit to the government would clearly make it difficult to maintain a reasonable rate of expansion for any monetary aggregate. Moreover, the maintenance of a banking system credit ceiling could involve an extensive redistribution of credit within the economy, since any increase in central bank credit to the government (which would also increase reserve money) would have to be matched by a reduction of credit to private borrowers by either the central bank or the commercial banks. While an increase in central bank credit to the government matched by a reduction in commercial bank credit to the private sector is neutral in terms of satisfying the overall credit ceiling on the financial system, such a shift may still strongly affect the level and distribution of economic activity. In countries where credit is rationed more by administrative procedure than by market interest rates, firms that are excluded from their traditional sources of credit (e.g., central bank's special lending programs) may have considerable difficulty in finding new sources of funds. This would be especially true for firms already in serious financial difficulties. Thus, if an overall credit ceiling is maintained when there is a large government budget deficit, there could be a major redistribution of credit between the private and public sectors which could lead to a sharp crowding out of private spending and thereby a fall in real output and investment.

Another threat to the effectiveness of a ceiling on domestic credit of the banking system arises when an extensive system of unregulated financial intermediaries exists or develops. In this case, any increase in reserve money (from whatever source) would allow increased lending by the unregulated nonbank financial institutions even if credit from the banking system remained at a ceiling level. The existence of such an alternative source of credit naturally weakens the relationship between a ceiling on credit of the banking system and the levels of spending and real output.

Exchange Rate Policy. In general, a country's exchange rate arrangements will more strongly influence the use of a ceiling on a monetary aggregate rather than a credit aggregate. With a commitment to hold the exchange rate fixed, or to adjust it only gradually (e.g., to reflect inflation differentials), the authorities may find it difficult to control the growth of domestic monetary aggregates over any extended period. Even when the authorities limit the issuance of reserve money from domestic sources, portfolio and spending adjustments in the private sector would lead to external payments imbalances that could expand reserve money as the authorities intervene in the foreign exchange markets to maintain their exchange rate policy. In contrast, a flexible exchange rate would allow the authorities to control the growth of reserve money, making a monetary aggregate ceiling a potentially effective instrument.

To an important degree, the effectiveness of ceilings on domestic credit depends more on the extent to which unregulated domestic and foreign sources of credit are available than on the nature of the country's exchange rate arrangements. If sources of credit other than through the domestic banking system are limited, then a ceiling on domestic credit of the banking system can be quite effective in affecting domestic spending and activity regardless of the exchange rate structure. As noted earlier, however, capital flows can create difficulties under a domestic credit ceiling, which may, therefore, require some degree of exchange rate flexibility. For example, if the exchange rate has been substantially depreciated in an effort to secure favorable trade balance, then substantial capital inflows could be generated by yield differentials which reflect, in part, the expectation that further large exchange rate depreciations are unlikely. If such flows occur, there could be substantial inflationary pressure in the economy. To limit this inflation, a greater degree of exchange rate flexibility may be required since a fixed exchange rate, relatively unrestricted capital flows, and the establishment of effective ceilings on credit or reserve money may at times be incompatible.

The combined influence of such characteristics of an economy on the selection of a particular monetary or credit aggregate can be illustrated by comparing the conditions under which a ceiling on domestic credit would generally be preferred with the situation under which a ceiling on a monetary aggregate would be most appropriate. A ceiling on the domestic credit of the banking system would allow the authorities to have the greatest influence on domestic spending and activity and on the country's external balance in cases where most domestic financial institutions are part of the banking system, domestic tradable goods prices are closely tied to world prices, and linkages between domestic and international financial markets are relatively weak. With no alternative sources of domestic or foreign credit, control over the nominal level of domestic credit could be maintained with most types of exchange rate arrangements. Moreover, with a fixed exchange rate, a ceiling on domestic credit generally would be more readily attained than a ceiling on a monetary aggregate. The effectiveness of a credit ceiling would also be enhanced by the existence of relatively close ties between domestic and international markets for goods. With such ties, there would be little possibility of extended periods of domestic inflation in the absence of continuing exchange rate or external price movements.

In contrast, a ceiling on a monetary aggregate would be most useful when the economy has a flexible exchange rate, domestic goods prices are not closely tied to world prices, strong linkages exist between the domestic and international financial markets, and a variety of unregulated domestic financial intermediaries provide credit that is not subject to the banking system ceiling. Since credit ceilings are typically defined with regard to the lending of the banking system, the existence of significant credits either from abroad or from nonbank financial intermediaries could seriously undermine any relationship between the ceiling on banking system credit and economic activity or the current account balance. In addition, with a flexible exchange rate, control over the growth of domestic monetary aggregates would be feasible since the authorities would not be required to undertake exchange market intervention. Such monetary control would be especially important for limiting inflation if domestic goods prices were not very strongly linked to international tradable goods prices.

These considerations provide some explanation for the changing pattern of the use of monetary and credit policy instruments evident in Table 1 and the Appendix. For example, those countries continuing to use credit instruments typically have had the most extensive controls on both their domestic financial systems and foreign financial transactions and have some form of pegged exchange rate. Since residents of these countries have limited access to external financial markets, credit instruments retain their effectiveness unless unorganized financial markets of significant size emerge. However, when domestic financial regulations have been liberalized and capital controls relaxed, countries have shifted toward greater exchange rate flexibility and the increased use of monetary instruments. In such a situation, ceilings on credit from the organized financial sector can be readily evaded, whereas monetary instruments impose more effective constraints, especially under flexible exchange rates.

Structural Changes. Although the importance of real and monetary shocks in the determination of optimal monetary and exchange rate policies has been recognized, it has often been implicitly assumed that the underlying real and financial structure of the economy is unchanged when the choice of policy instruments is made.[20] However, the period since 1975 has witnessed extensive and ongoing structural changes.

The need to formulate monetary and exchange rate policies in the face of often unanticipated and rapid structural changes has created a variety of problems. In particular, the effectiveness of traditional instruments has often been eroded, thereby creating the need to develop and employ new policy instruments. Moreover, even when a given instrument remains effective, the nature of its impact can vary over time as structural changes alter the channels through which the instrument affects spending and portfolio decisions. The authorities, therefore, have faced not only the traditional problem of identifying how to use their existing set of instruments to achieve the best performance of a given economic structure but also how to use or modify the types of instruments that they employ over time.

While the optimal intertemporal pattern of monetary and exchange rate policies has recently been examined in a number of studies -- see Eaton (1985), Frenkel and Razin (1986), and Helpman and Razin (1987) -- the desire to arrive at closed-form solutions for the complex theoretical models needed to analyze the issues involved has necessarily limited the types of policies examined. Moreover, the problem of uncertainty regarding likely structural changes has not been addressed. However, many of the issues have been considered in a somewhat less formal framework dealing with the design of monetary and exchange rate policies during periods of extensive trade, fiscal, and financial reforms -- see Khan (1987), McKinnon (1986), Mussa (1987), and Lal (1987). These analyses have often dealt with an inflationary and partially indexed economy with an uncontrolled fiscal deficit and extensive distortions in goods, factor, and financial markets. It is generally argued that the optimal mix of exchange rate arrangements and monetary (or credit) policies that should accompany the structural reforms will vary over time depending on the initial conditions facing the economy, the pace of the structural reforms, and the speed with which domestic and external markets integrate.[21]

While the long-run objective of the reform program is to remove policy-induced distortions in order to achieve greater efficiency, discussions of the sequencing of reform measures and stabilization policies have been most concerned with ensuring that smooth adjustment to long-run equilibrium could be achieved. The policy recommendations have often reflected the view that complete and instantaneous liberalization of goods, financial, and factor markets in an environment of high inflation and general uncertainty about likely macroeconomic developments does not work well. If prices in all markets were fully flexible and expectations certain, then there would be no sequencing problem -- the policy distortions could be removed immediately and prices would quickly adjust to establish a new equilibrium.[22] However, since asset markets adjust more rapidly than goods or factor markets, it has been argued that the immediate removal of capital controls and interest rate ceilings could lead to capital inflows, resulting in a real appreciation of the exchange rate; this would work against the reallocation of resources from the nontraded to traded goods sectors that is the objective of the trade reforms. As a result, a more careful sequence of reforms is needed.

While there is far from a consensus about the most appropriate sequencing of policies, it is frequently recommended that the *fiscal accounts* should be brought under control at the beginning of the reform period. The rationale for first undertaking fiscal reform is that the other reforms are unlikely to be successful if a large fiscal imbalance is generating rapid monetary growth and high inflation. It is also argued that *trade reforms* (the removal of quotas and lowering of tariffs) should be announced early in the reform period and should be phased in a preannounced manner. The objective in adopting this gradualist program is to provide factors of production with time to move between sectors and also to indicate to investors the types of relative prices (at least for traded goods) that are likely to prevail in the future.[23]

Monetary and exchange rate policies have been viewed as pursuing three often contradictory objectives: (1) removing financial system distortions; (2) implementing a "forward-looking" monetary policy designed to stabilize prices; and (3) establishing external payments balance and thereafter avoiding an excessive real appreciation of the exchange rate. While it is generally agreed that positive real interest rates should be established at an early stage, there has not been a consensus about how best to achieve this objective. Some have argued that this can best be accomplished by immediately removing interest rate ceilings, reducing required reserve ratios, eliminating portfolio selection restrictions, and allowing for more entry into the financial system; others have favored a more gradual elimination of these distortions, especially in a highly inflationary environment where past entry into the banking system was severely restricted.[24] Moreover, while some have favored establishing a floating exchange rate -- e.g., Lal (1987) -- McKinnon (1986) has argued for a more managed exchange rate policy encompassing a "passive" crawling peg policy (adjusting the exchange rate to reflect inflation differences) to be used during the initial stages of the reform program when inflation is still high, and an "active" crawling peg to be used when the budget deficit has been brought under control and inflation has slowed. The active crawl would be designed to provide an unambiguous signal around which private expectations about inflation could coalesce. However, to be successful, this active crawling peg policy would have to be supported by appropriate labor and financial market policies to prevent a real appreciation of the exchange rate.[25]

To support this managed exchange rate policy, it has been argued that the removal of *capital controls* should be delayed until the end of the reform period. Without such controls, high domestic real interest rates, coupled with an improved prospect for the economy's future performance, could induce a large capital inflow which would tend to appreciate the real exchange rate. The resulting changes in relative goods prices would induce inappropriate investments and distort the reallocation of resources across sectors, thereby helping to destabilize the reform process. However, Lal (1987) has argued that capital controls should be removed (and the exchange rate floated) relatively early in the reform period because it is unlikely that such immiserizing investment would take place when expectations are rational and announcements are credible.[26]

Three conclusions seem warranted regarding the roles of monetary and exchange rate policies during a period of structural reforms. First, there are a number of reasons why some differentiation exists between the effectiveness of exchange market intervention, provision of credit to the government, changes in interest rate ceilings, and modification of credit controls. These reasons include the fact that assets are not perfect substitutes; markets adjust at different speeds; wages, prices, and interest rates do not immediately adjust to their long-run equilibrium values (and may actually overshoot); and expectations are uncertain (as opposed to irrational). Second, the optimal mix of stabilization policies adopted will vary over the reform program. For example, the exchange rate arrangements best suited for the turbulent period at the beginning of the reform would be expected to be quite different from those at the end of the reform period. Third, the optimal set of policy instruments would change over the course of the reform period as such instruments as credit controls and interest rate ceiling would be replaced by more market-oriented instruments (e.g., open-market operation in government securities). This change would be a response to the fact that adjustment in the economy would increasingly rely on changes in the relative prices of goods, factors, and assets rather than on credit rationing or quantitative restrictions.

CONCLUSIONS

One common element in the experiences of almost all countries during the past decade has been the need to adjust their exchange rate arrangements and monetary policy instruments in order to respond more effectively to extensive external and domestic disturbances. In the Pacific Basin, these changes have encompassed the employment of greater exchange rate flexibility and a switch from credit to monetary instruments; they have been accompanied by a growing but still incomplete integration of domestic and external financial markets and often substantial liberalizations of domestic financial systems. However, the formulation of monetary and exchange rate policies has been complicated by the need to undertake extensive structural changes in the real and financial sectors in order to improve economic efficiency and adapt to a changing international environment. Many of the adjustments in monetary and exchange rate policies have been consistent with the policies recommended in recent theoretical analyses for countries confronted with a period in which real shocks have dominated monetary shocks.

NOTES

The author would like to thank Joseph Bisignano, Jeffrey Frankel, Peter Isard, Jürg Niehans, Liliana Rojas-Suarez, and Nicholas Sargen for comments on an earlier draft. The views presented in this paper are those of the author and should not be taken as representing those of the International Monetary Fund.

1. Exchange rate arrangements have been classified according to the categories employed in the IMF's *Annual Report on Exchange Arrangements and Exchange Restrictions*. These categories represent a spectrum of exchange rate arrangements ranging from those with little flexibility (e.g., the exchange rate peggers) to those allowing for considerable flexibility (the independent floaters). The divisions between these two extremes are necessarily somewhat arbitrary. Examination of changes in the spectrum of arrangements may either understate or overstate the degree of exchange flexibility employed by countries. For example, although a country could formally peg its exchange rate to a particular currency, this would not rule out the possibility that it would undertake frequent adjustments of that rate. In contrast, a country that was independently floating could still undertake extensive exchange market intervention designed to limit exchange rate movements.

2. In some countries, these financial reforms were accompanied by changes in commercial policy and trade reforms designed to open domestic goods markets to external competition.

3. Much of the recent work has focused on extending the earlier analyses by Fleming (1962) and Mundell (1962) to allow for a more complete portfolio specification, stochastic monetary and real disturbances, traded and nontraded goods, rational expectations, the possibility of asymmetric information and wage-price rigidities, and the implications of intertemporal budget constraints. See Marston (1985a) and Branson and Henderson (1985) for comprehensive surveys of the development of this literature. The most recent models typically have four basic components. There is first a set of relationships describing the portfolio behavior and budget constraints facing the public and private sectors. For the private sector, this often consists of the specification of the demand for money, the degree of substitution between domestic and foreign securities, and any wealth and income constraints. In much of this literature, domestic and foreign securities are taken as perfect substitutes and uncovered interest rate parity is assumed to hold (i.e., the domestic interest rate equals the sum of the foreign interest rate plus the expected rate of depreciation of the exchange rate). The public sector is typically entered either very simply via a money supply rule (or alternatively via an exchange market intervention rule) or in a more complex manner via both a money supply rule and an intertemporal budget constraint representing the limitations imposed by international markets on the ability of the authorities to finance their deficits through borrowing. A second set of relationships describes the linkages between external and domestic goods prices, and the determinants of domestic output. Some form of purchasing power parity relationship usually links (apart from stochastic shocks) domestic and foreign prices. Output is either specified as an exogenous (stochastic) variable or is determined via a stochastic production function that depends on the amount of labor employed. As the third basic component of these models, the supply of labor is then taken as a function of the real wage, and wages are set to equate the expected demand and supply of labor. Finally, there is a specification of how expectations regarding prices and wages are formed. While earlier analyses used static wage-price expectations, more recent discussions have focused on rational expectations although certain types of contract rigidities have been incorporated into even this framework. Examples of the use of these models for analyzing either the choice of optimal exchange rate arrangements or

exchange rate dynamics are provided by the articles by Aizenman (1985), Aoki (1985), Bhandari (1985a), Carlozzi and Taylor (1985), Driskill and McCafferty (1985), Flood and Hodrick (1985), Flood and Marion (1982), Frenkel and Mussa (1985), Gray (1976), Harkness (1985), Helpman (1984), Hodrick (1982), Marsten (1985b), Mussa (1985), Obstfeld (1983), Obstfeld and Rogoff (1984), Obstfeld and Stockman (1985), Turnovsky (1985a and 1985b), and Weber (1981).

4. In addition to this "unsterilized" intervention, there have also been discussions of "sterilized" intervention where the effects on the domestic monetary aggregates are offset by open-market operations. Such sterilized intervention has generally been regarded as ineffective.

5. Daniel (1985), p. 253.

6. Mussa (1983) has argued that such exchange rate system neutrality requires that: (1) Ricardian equivalence must hold with regard to the evaluation of government securities as wealth; (2) a pegged rate must not be maintained through foreign exchange operations involving assets that are not part of the efficient portfolio that would be maintained by the private sector under a flexible exchange rate regime; (3) the redistribution of wealth that occurs because of unanticipated changes in nominal prices and the exchange rate in the presence of bonds must be absent or have no effect on world demands; (4) money must play no role in the real economy; and (5) problems with imperfect information must be absent. These issues are also discussed in Aschauer and Greenwood (1983), Helpman (1979), and Stockman (1983). Aschauer and Greenwood argue, in particular, that Helpman's neutrality conclusions do not hold when output is taken as endogenous rather than exogenous.

7. In the Frenkel and Aizenman (1982) analysis, monetary shocks encompass not only shocks to the money demand or supply but also shocks to foreign prices or purchasing power parity conditions.

8. Saidi (1980) has argued, however, that these conclusions have arisen out of models that assume the existence of price rigidities and/or agents that neglect available information in forming expectations crucial to current decisions. In the context of a general equilibrium model with rational expectations, he argued that a flexible exchange rate does not insulate domestic employment and output from foreign disturbances. The importance of the information sets of the authorities and private sectors have also been discussed in Bhandari (1985a), Eaton (1985), Flood and Hodrick (1985 and 1986), Frenkel (1981), and Glick and Wihlborg (1986).

9. Hsieh (1984) also examines this risk-sharing argument.

10. Obstfeld (1985) examined the relative importance of real and monetary shocks by considering the correlation between changes in nominal exchange rates and in nominal stock prices. He argued that if domestic monetary shocks are the dominant source of disturbance, the nominal prices of stocks and foreign exchange should be highly positively correlated, whereas if the shocks are real, the correlation should be much lower or even negative. In considering these correlations for the Federal Republic of Germany, Japan and the United States for various subperiods between 1976 and 1985, he generally found low negative correlations.

11. This does not rule out the possibility that unanticipated monetary policy changes were also important.

12. For a summary of these arguments see Tower and Willett (1976).

13. Dooley, Frankel, and Mathieson (1986) found that the analysis of savings and investment patterns across both industrial and developing counties suggests that, while some financial markets are closely integrated, this integration does not extend to the markets for physical capital.

14. The nature of these linkages, even in the presence of capital controls, are discussed in Canto (1985) and De Macedo (1986).

15. The choice of policy instruments has been considered by Ahn and Jung (1985), Bryant (1980), Cottarelli, Galli, Reedtz and Pittaluga (1986), Gardner (1983), Mantel and Martirena-Mantel (1982), Rojas-Suarez (1987a), and Wickham (1985).

16. A general discussion of the role of money and credit, especially in developing countries, is presented in Rojas-Suarez (1987a, 1987b).

17. There is still the issue of whether a fixed exchange rate could remain fixed if there were excessive domestic credit expansion by the central bank. This possibility implies that the choice among monetary and credit instruments may have to be based on the authorities' other objectives.

18. It is also important to note that in economies where credit is rationed primarily by interest rates, such sterilization would be much less likely to have these sectoral effects since credit could flow from one sector to another in response to changes in relative interest rates.

19. The potential inflationary effect of a continuing capital inflow would also depend on how the borrowed funds are used. For example, foreign borrowing used to purchase foreign capital goods employed in the domestic economy could yield a flow of resources more than sufficient to service any external obligations. Moreover, to the extent that this greater investment led to higher growth, it could be deflationary (with a flexible exchange rate and given money supply).

20. An exception to this has been the discussion of the optimal degree of wage indexation under alternative exchange rate regimes. See Gray (1976) and Frenkel and Aizenman (1982).

21. In a sense, however, even these analyses do not deal fully with the problems created by unanticipated structural changes; since they focus on policy-induced structural changes that are typically preannounced.

22. Even with flexible prices, there could be a once-and-for-all capital inflow and a new equilibrium real exchange rate.

23. There is also the question of whether the trade reforms are perceived to be permanent or temporary. A temporary trade reform may be worse than no reform at all.

24. There is also the question of whether the full institutional structure needed for the operation of competitive markets is likely to exist at the beginning of the reform and, if not, how they can be developed. The implications of this issue for the reform process have been discussed by Dooley and Mathieson (1987).

25. The use of real exchange rate policies is also subject to a potential inflationary bias. See Adams and Gros (1986) for a discussion of this possibility.

26. The issue in all reforms is how to make policies credible in a situation where past reforms may have been reversed and the "staying power" of the current reform is unclear. Even if private sector participants have a complete understanding of the effects of the reforms (e.g., in the rational expectations sense, they "know" the model), they may still be uncertain about whether the reforms will be sustained. In these circumstances, investors may significantly shorten the maturity of their investments, attempt to make investments or loans that they feel they can get out of quickly if things go wrong, and delay long-term investments that would be appropriate if the reform should be successful.

REFERENCES

Adams, Charles and Daniel Gros (1986). "The Consequences of Real Exchange Rate Rules for Inflation: Some Illustrative Examples." *Staff Papers* 33. Washington, D.C.: International Monetary Fund, pp. 439- 476.

Ahn, Chul Won and W. Jung (1985). "The Choice of a Monetary Instrument in a Small Open Economy: The Case of Korea." *Journal of International Money and Finance* 4, pp. 469-484.

Aizenman, Joshua (1985). "Openness, Relative Prices, and Macro-Policies." *Journal of International Money and Finance* 4, pp. 5-18

Aoki, Masanao (1985). "Misadjustment to Anticipated Shocks: An Example of Exchange Rate Responses." *Journal of International Money and Finance* 4, pp. 415-420.

Aschauer, David and Jeremy Greenwood (1983). "A Further Exploration in the Theory of Exchange Rate Regimes." *Journal of Political Economy* 91, pp. 868-875.

Benavie, Arthur (1983). "Achieving External and Internal Targets with Exchange Rate and Interest Rate Intervention." *Journal of International Money and Finance* 2, pp. 75-85."

Bhandari, Jagdeep S. (1985a). "Informational Regimes, Economic Disturbances, and Exchange Rate Management." In *Exchange Rate Management Under Uncertainty*. Cambridge, Mass.: The MIT Press, pp. 126-153.

Bhandari, Jagdeep S. (1985b). "World Trade Patterns, Economic Disturbances, and Exchange Rate Management." *Journal of International Money and Finance* 4, pp. 331-360.

Bhandari, Jagdeep S., ed. (1985). *Exchange Rate Management Under Uncertainty*. Cambridge, Mass.: The MIT Press.

Branson, William H. and Dale W. Henderson ((1985). "The Specification and Influence of Asset Markets." Ch. 15 in *Handbook of Interenational Economics* Vol. II edited by Ronald W. Jones and Peter B. Kenen. New York: North-Holland, pp. 749-805.

Bryant, Ralph C. (1980). *Money and Monetary Policy in Interdependent Nations*. Washington, D.C.: The Brookings Institution.

Calvo, Guillermo A. (1985). "Reserves and the Managed Float: A Search for the Essentials." *Journal of International Money and Finance* 4, pp. 43-60

Canto, Victor A. (1985). "Monetary Policy, 'Dollarization,' and Parallel Market Exchange Rates: The Case of the Dominican Republic." *Journal of International Money and Finance 4*, pp. 507-522.

Carlozzi, Nicholas, and John B. Taylor (1985). "International Capital Mobility and the Coordination of Monetary Rules." In *Exchange Rate Management Under Uncertainty*, edited by Jagdeep S. Bhandari. Cambridge, Mass.: The MIT Press, pp. 186-211.

Corden, W.M. (1985). *Inflation, Exchange Rates and the World Economy*. 3rd edition. Oxford: Clarendon Press.

Cottarelli, Carlo, Giampaolo Galli, Paolo Marullo Reedtz, and Giovanni Pittaluga (1986). "Credit Ceilings." *Economic Policy* 3, pp. 673-695.

Crockett, Andrew and Morris Goldstein (1987). *Strengthening the International Monetary System: Exchange Rates, Surveillance, and Objective Indicators*. Occasional Paper No. 50. Washington, D.C.: International Monetary Fund.

Daniel, Betty (1985). "Optimal Foreign Exchange Policy for a Small Open Economy." *Journal of International Money and Finance* 4, pp. 523-536.

De Macedo, Jorge Braga (1986). "Trade and Financial Interdependence Under Flexible Exchange Rates: The Pacific Area." In *Pacific Growth and Financial Interdependence*, edited by Augustine H. H. Tan and Basant Kapur. London: Allen Unwin, pp. 237-291.

Dooley, Michael and Donald J. Mathieson (1987). "Financial Liberalization and Stability in Developing Countries." Working Paper WP/87/19. Washington, D.C.: International Monetary Fund.

Dooley, Michael, Jeffrey Frankel, and Donald J. Mathieson (1987). "International Capital Mobility: What do Saving-Investment Correlations Tell Us?" Staff Papers 34, Washington, D.C.: International Monetary Fund, pp. 503-530.

Dornbusch, Rudiger (1983). "Flexible Exchange Rates and Interdependence." *Staff Papers* 30. Washington: International Monetary Fund, pp. 3-38.

Driskill, Robert and Stephen A. McCafferty (1985). "Exchange Market Intervention under Rational Expectations with Imperfect Capital Substitutability." In *Exchange Rate Management Under Uncertainty*, edited by Jagdeep S. Bhandari. Cambridge, Mass.: MIT Press, pp. 83-95.

Eaton, Jonathan (1985). "Optimal and Time Consistent Exchange Rate Management in an Overlapping-Generations Model." *Journal of International Money and Finance* 4, pp. 83-100.

Fleming, Marcus (1962). "Domestic Financial Policies Under Fixed and Under Floating Exchange Rates." *Staff Papers* 9. Washington, D.C.: International Monetary Fund, pp. 309-380.

Flood, Robert J. and Robert J. Hodrick (1985). "Central Bank Intervention in a Rational Open Economy: A Model with Asymmetric Information." In *Exchange Rate Management Under Uncertainty*, edited by Jagdeep S. Bhandari. Cambridge, Massachusetts: MIT Press, pp. 154-185.

Flood, Robert J. and Robert J. Hodrick (1986). "Real Aspects of Exchange Rate Regime Choice with Collapsing Fixed Rates." *Journal of International Economics* 21, pp. 215-232.

Flood, Robert J. and Nancy Peregrim Marion (1982). "The Transmission of Disturbances Under Alternative Exchange Rate Regimes with Optimal Indexing." *Quarterly Journal of Economics* 96, pp. 43-66.

Frenkel, Jacob A. (1981). "Flexible Exchange Rates, Prices, and the Role of 'News': Lessons from the 1970s." *Journal of Political Economy* 89, pp. 665-705.

Frenkel, Jacob A. and Assaf Razin (1986). "Fiscal Policies in the World Economy," *Journal of Political Economy* 94, pp. 564-594.

Frenkel, Jacob A. and Joshua Aizenman (1982). "Aspects of the Optimal Management of Exchange Rates." *Journal of International Economics* 13, pp. 231-256.

Frenkel, Jacob A. and Michael L. Mussa (1985). "Asset Markets, Exchange Rates, and the Balance of Payments." Ch.14, in *Handbook of International Economics* II, edited by Ronald W. Jones and Peter B. Kenen. New York: North-Holland, pp. 679-747.

Gardner, Grant W. (1983). "The Choice of Monetary Policy Instruments in an Open Economy." *Journal of International Money and Finance* 2, pp. 347-354.

Glick, Reuven and Clas Wihlborg (1986). "The Role of Information Acquisition and Financial Markets in International Macroeconomic Adjustment." *Journal of International Money and Finance* 5, pp. 257-284.

Goldstein, Morris (1984). "The Exchange Rate System: Lessons of the Past and Options for the Future." Occasional Paper No. 30. Washington, D.C.: International Monetary Fund.

Gray, J. (1976). "Wage Indexation: A Macroeconomic Approach." *Journal of Monetary Economics* 2, pp. 221-236.

Harkness, Jon (1985). "Optimal Exchange Intervention for a Small Open Economy." *Journal of International Money and Finance* 4, pp. 101-112.

Helpman, Elhanan (1981). "An Exploration in the Theory of Exchange Rate Regimes." *Journal of Political Economy* 89, pp. 865-901.

Helpman, Elhanan (1979). "Toward a Consistent Comparison of Alternative Exchange Rate Regimes." *Canadian Journal of Economics* 12, pp. 394- 409.

Helpman, Elhanan (1984). "The Role of Saving and Investment in Exchange Rate Determination Under Alternative Monetary Mechanisms." *Journal of Monetary Economics* 13, pp. 307-325.

Helpman, Elhanan and Assaf Razin (1987). "Exchange Rate Management: Intertemporal Tradeoffs. *American Economic Review* 77, pp. 107-123.

Hodrick, Robert J. (1982). "On the Effects of Macroeconomic Policy in a Maximizing Model of a Small Open Economy." *Journal of Macroeconomics* 2, pp. 195-213.

Hsieh, David A. (1984). "International Risk Sharing and the Choice of Exchange Rate Regime." *Journal of International Money and Finance* 3, pp. 141-152.

Isard, Peter (1977). "How Far Can We Push the Law of One Price?" *American Economic Review* 67, pp. 942-948.

Khan, Mohsin S. (1987). "Macroeconomic Adjustment in Developing Countries: A Policy Perspective." *The World Bank, Research Observer* 2, pp. 23-42.

Lal, Deepak (1987). "The Political Economy of Economic Liberalization." *The World Bank Economic Review* 1, pp. 273-300.

McKinnon, Ronald I. (1986). "Interest Rate and Foreign Exchange Management During Monetary Stabilization: Further Lessons from Chile and Korea." Unpublished.

McKinnon, Ronald I. (1963). "Optimum Currency Areas." *American Economic Review* 53, pp. 717-725.

Mantel, Rolf and Ana M. Martirena-Mantel (1982). "Exchange Rate Policies in a Small Economy: The Active Crawling Peg." *Journal of International Economics* 13, pp. 301-320.

Marsten, Richard C. (1985a). "Stabilization Policies in Open Economies." Ch. 17 in *Handbook of International Economics II* edited by Ronald W. Jones and Peter B. Kenen. New York: North-Holland, pp. 859-916.

Marsten, Richard C. (1985b). "Financial Disturbances and the Effects of an Exchange Rate Union." In *Exchange Rate Management Under Uncertainty*, edited by Jagdeep S. Bhandari. Cambridge, Mass.: The MIT Press, pp. 272-291.

Mundell, Robert A. (1961). "A Theory of Optimum Currency Areas." *American Economic Review* 60, pp. 657-665.

Mundell, Robert A. (1962). "The Appropriate Use of Monetary and Fiscal Policy Under Fixed Exchange Rates." *Staff Papers* 9. Washington, D.C.: International Monetary Fund, pp. 70-77.

Mussa, Michael L. (1987). "Macroeconomic Policy and Trade Liberalization: Some Guidelines." *The World Bank Research Observer* 2, pp. 61-78.

Mussa, Michael L. (1985). "Official Intervention and Exchange Rate Dynamics." In *Exchange Rate Management Under Uncertainty*, edited by Jagdeep S. Bhandari. Cambridge, Mass.: MIT Press:, pp. 1-30.

Mussa, Michael L. (1983). "Empirical Regularities in the Behavior of Exchange Rates and Theories of the Foreign Exchange Market." In *Theory, Policy, Institutions; Papers from the Carnegie-Rochester Conferences on Public Policy*, edited by Karl Brunner and Allan H. Meltzer. New York: North-Holland, pp. 165-312.

Obstfeld, Maurice (1983). "Intertemporal Price Speculation and the Optimal Current Account Deficit." *Journal of International Money and Finance* 2, pp. 135-146.

Obstfeld, Maurice (1985). "Floating Exchange Rates: Experience and Prospects." *Brookings Papers on Economic Activity* 2, pp. 369-450.

Obstfeld, Maurice, and Kenneth Rogoff (1984). "Exchange Rate Dynamics with Sluggish Prices Under Alternative Price-Adjustment Rules." *International Economic Review* 25, pp. 159-174.

Obstfeld, Maurice and Alan C. Stockman (1985). "Exchange Rate Dynamics." In *Handbook of International Economics* II, edited by Ronald W. Jones and Peter B. Kenen. New York: North-Holland, pp. 917-977.

Rojas-Suarez, E. Liliana (1987a). "The Role of Financial Constraints on the Short-Run Behavior of Prices and Output Under Alternative Exchange Rate Regimes." Unpublished.

Rojas-Suarez, E. Liliana (1987b). "Devaluation and Monetary Policy in Developing Countries: A General Equilibrium Model for Economies Facing Financial Constraints." *Staff Papers* 34, Washington, D.C.: International Monetary Fund, pp. 439-470.

Saidi, Nassar H. (1980). "Fluctuating Exchange Rates and International Transmission of Economic Disturbances." *Journal of Money, Credit and Banking* 12, pp. 575-591.

Stockman, Alan C. (1983). "Real Exchange Rates Under Alternative Nominal Exchange Rate Systems." *Journal of International Money and Finance* 2, pp. 147-166.

Tan, Augustine H. H. and Basant Kapur, eds. (1986). *Pacific Growth and Financial Interdependence*. London: Allen and Unwin.

Tower, Edward and Thomas D. Willett (1976). "The Theory of Optimum Currency Areas and Exchange Rate Flexibility." *Special Paper in International Economics* 11.

Turnovsky, Stephen J. (1985). "Optimal Exchange Market Intervention: Two Alternative Classes of Rules." In *Exchange Rate Management Under Uncertainty*, edited by Jagdeep S. Bhandari. Cambridge, Mass.: The MIT Press, pp. 55-72.

Turnovsky, Stephen J. (1985). "Domestic and Foreign Disturbances in an Optimizing Model of Exchange Rate Determination." *Journal of International Money and Finance* 4, pp. 151-171.

Weber, Warren E. (1981). "Output Variability Under Monetary Policy and Exchange Rate Rules." *Journal of Political Economy* 89, pp. 733-751.

Wickham, Peter (1985). "The Choice of Exchange Rate Regime in Developing Countries." *Staff Papers* 32. Washington, D.C.: International Monetary Fund, pp. 248-288.

Yuan, Tsao (1986). "Capital Flows Among Pacific Basin Economies." In *Pacific Growth and Financial Interdependence*, edited by Augustine H.H. Tan and Basant Kapur. Sydney: Allen and Unwin, pp. 68-94.

Appendix

(1) Australia

A. Exchange Rate Arrangements

1975	Pegged to composite indicator
1976-1983	Managed floating
1984-1985	Independently floating

B. Monetary and Credit Policy Instruments

During 1975-1980, authorities initially focused on use of a required reserve ratio (Statutory Reserve Deposits), a liquidity ratio, controls on lending of financial institutions, and ceilings on interest rates. First public reference to possible outcomes for growth of broadly defined money (M3) was in 3/76. Open market operations and direct sales of government securities to nonbanks increasingly used to limit monetary expansion.

Major reforms in the period 1980-1985. In December 1980, most ceilings on deposit rates removed and those relating to loan rates relaxed. Quantitative bank lending guidance terminated at end-June 1982. Exchange controls liberalized, and portfolio restrictions on banks (e.g., minimum maturity of deposits) and other nonbank financial institutions removed - December 1983. Reserve requirement little changed after 1981. Main instrument was open-market operations.

C. Capital Controls

			Restrictions on			Tax or Special Reserve Require-ments on Foreign Borrowing
	Required Surrender of Export Proceeds	Advanced Import Deposits	Payments for Invisibles	Foreign Currency Deposits by Residents	Foreign Lending or Borrowing by Financial Insitution	
1975	*	--	*	*	*	--
1976	*	--	*	*	*	--
1977	*	--	*	*	*	--
1978	*	--	*	*	*	--
1979	*	--	*	*	*	--
1980	*	--	*	*	*	--
1981	*	--	*	*	*	--
1982	*	--	*	*	*	--
1983	--	--	--	--	--	--
1984	--	--	--	--	--	--
1985	--	--	--	--	--	--

* *Denotes presence of the measure.*

-- *Indicates absence of the measure.*

(2) Burma

A. Exchange Rate Arrangements

1975-1985 Pegged to SDR

B. Monetary and Credit Policy Instruments

The banking system has been principally concerned with supplying the financial resources needed to fulfill the authorities' overall national economic plan. The volume and allocation of credit, interest rates, and foreign borrowing are determined so as to be consistent with the plan's objectives. The banking system has been the primary -- often the sole -- source of credit, and the banks are state owned.

C. Capital Controls

			Restrictions on			
	Required Surrender of Export Proceeds	Advanced Import Deposits	Payments for Invisibles	Foreign Currency Deposits by Residents	Foreign Lending or Borrowing by Financial Insitution	Tax or Special Reserve Require-ments on Foreign Borrowing
1975	*	--	*	*	*	--
1976	*	--	*	*	*	--
1977	*	--	*	*	*	--
1978	*	--	*	*	*	--
1979	*	--	*	*	*	--
1980	*	--	*	*	*	--
1981	*	--	*	*	*	--
1982	*	--	*	*	*	--
1983	*	--	*	*	*	--
1984	*	--	*	*	*	--
1985	*	--	*	*	*	--

* *Denotes presence of the measure.*

-- *Indicates absence of the measure.*

(3) Fiji

A. Exchange Rate Arrangements

1975-1985 Pegged to composite

B. Monetary and Credit Policy Instruments

Throughout this period, there have been both cash reserve and government security ratios. The allocation of credit has been affected by portfolio allocation rules for banks. In June 1981, the ceiling on large deposit rates was removed, and other steps taken during 1982-1985 for gradual deregulation of interest rates. Open-market operations have not been used actively.

C. Capital Controls

			Restrictions on			
	Required Surrender of Export Proceeds	Advanced Import Deposits	Payments for Invisibles[a]	Foreign Currency Deposits by Residents	Foreign Lending or Borrowing by Financial Insitution	Tax or Special Reserve Require-ments on Foreign Borrowing
1975	*	--	*	*	*	(b)
1976	*	--	*	*	*	--
1977	*	--	*	*	*	--
1978	*	--	*	*	*	--
1979	*	--	*	*	*	--
1980	*	--	*	*	*	--
1981	*	--	*	*	*	--
1982	*	--	*	*	*	--
1983	*	--	*	*	*	--
1984	*	--	*	*	*	--
1985	*	--	*	*	*	--

* *Denotes presence of the measure.*

-- *Indicates absence of the measure.*

(a) *Generally free but large amounts subject to approval.*

(b) *Net foreign liabilities of banks subject to a 5 percent reserve requirement.*

(4) Japan

A. Exchange Rate Arrangements

1975-1985 Independently floating

B. Monetary and Credit Policy Instruments

Throughout most of this period, broad money (M2) has been used as a monetary policy indicator. To influence M2, the central bank has relied on a complex mechanism of short-term money market operations to meet short-run changes in demand for reserve money and bond market operations to provide for trend growth in the demand. These operations were supported through discount policy, reserve ratios, and (during the period until 1980) window guidance policy. While most interest rates were controlled in 1975, there has been a gradual removal of such ceiling rates. As the proportion of financial instruments carrying market-determined interest rate has increased, there has been increasing emphasis on control of monetary aggregates as opposed to bank credit.

C. Capital Controls

			Restrictions on			Tax or Special Reserve Require-ments on Foreign Borrowing
	Required Surrender of Export Proceeds	Advanced Import Deposits	Payments for Invisibles	Foreign Currency Deposits by Residents[d]	Foreign Lending or Borrowing by Financial Insitution	
1975	--	--	(a)	*	*(e)	--
1976	--	--	(a)	*	*(e)	--
1977	--	--	(b)	*	*(e)	--
1978	--	--	--	*	*(e)	*
1979	--	--	--	*	(f)	*
1980[c]	--	--	--	*	(f)	--
1981	--	--	--	*	(f)	--
1982	--	--	--	*	(f)	--
1983	--	--	--	*	(f)	--
1984	--	--	--	*	(f)	--
1985	--	--	--	*	(f)	--

* *Denotes presence of the measure.*

-- *Indicates absence of the measure.*

(a) *Certain limitations on large payments.*

(b) *Payments subject to verification but without limitation.*

(c) *Since the Foreign Exchange and Foreign Trade Control Law became effective in December 1980, capital transactions are in general permitted unless specifically prohibited.*

(d) *Foreign currency deposit overseas subject to prior approval if not carried out by authorized bank.*

(e) *Foreign exchange banks subject to controls over their overall net position in foreign currencies.*

(f) *Generally free but certain transactions require prior notice and waiting period.*

(5) Korea

A. Exchange Rate Arrangements

1975-1979	Pegged to U.S. dollar
1980-1985	Managed floating

B. Monetary and Credit Policy Instruments

From 1975 to 1982, authorities relied on reserve ratios, ceilings on interest rates, limits on volume of bank credits, and rules governing allocation of credit. Interest rate ceilings were nonetheless used flexibly. As part of a financial reform in 1982, direct credit controls on lending by individual banks were replaced by indirect control through use of reserve requirements, open-market operations, and the rediscount mechanism. Preferential interest rates were eliminated, but credit allocation rules were retained. Regular reserve requirements have been supplemented by monetary stabilization accounts (effectively a marginal reserve requirement).

C. Capital Controls

			Restrictions on			
	Required Surrender of Export Proceeds[a]	Advanced Import Deposits	Payments for Invisibles	Foreign Currency Deposits by Residents	Foreign Lending or Borrowing by Financial Insitution	Tax or Special Reserve Requirements on Foreign Borrowing
1975	*	*	*	(b)	*	--
1976	*	*	*	(b)	*	--
1977	*	--	*	(b)	*	--
1978	*	--	*	(b)	*	--
1979	*	--	*	(c)	*	--
1980	*	--	*	(c)	*	--
1981	*	--	*	(c)	*	--
1982	*	--	*	(c)	*	--
1983	*	--	*	(c)	*	--
1984	*	--	*	(c)	(d)	--
1985	*	--	*	(c)	(e)	--

* *Denotes presence of the measure.*

-- *Indicates absence of the measure.*

(a) Or *deposited in foreign exchange accounts in domestic banks.*

(b) *Certain residents may hold foreign currency deposits at foreign exchange banks.*

(c) *All residents may hold foreign currency deposits at foreign exchange banks.*

(d) *Borrowing above certain minimum amounts require approval.*

(e) *Subject to ceilings on conversion of foreign borrowing. All outward bound capital requires approval.*

(6) Malaysia

A. Exchange Rate Arrangements

1975-1985 Pegged to composite

B. Monetary and Credit Policy Instruments

During 1975 and 1976, the authorities' instruments included reserve and liquidity ratios, controls on interest rates, and credit allocation rules. Since October 1978, interest rates have been gradually liberalized. During the 1980s, open-market operations, foreign exchange swap operations,[a] and the recycling of government deposits became important instruments, but the authorities continue to use reserve and liquidity requirements and credit allocation rules as instruments.

C. Capital Controls

			Restrictions on			Tax or Special Reserve Require-ments on Foreign Borrowing
	Required Surrender of Export Proceeds[b]	Advanced Import Deposits	Payments for Invisibles[c]	Foreign Currency Deposits by Residents	Foreign Lending or Borrowing by Financial Insitution	
1975	--	--	--	*n*	*n*	--
1976	--	--	--	*n*	*n*	--
1977	--	--	--	*n*	(d)	--
1978	--	--	--	*n*	(d)	--
1979	--	--	--	--	(d)	--
1980	--	--	--	--	(d)	--
1981	--	--	--	--	(d)	--
1982	--	--	--	--	(e)	--
1983	--	--	--	--	(e)	--
1984	--	--	--	--	(e)	--
1985	--	--	--	--	(e)	--

* *Denotes presence of the measure.*

-- *Indicates absence of the measure.*

n *Indicates no information.*

(a) *Swap of foreign exchange between central bank and financial institution at current exchange rate accompanied by agreement to unwind the transaction at a more favorable exchange rate for the financial institution at the end of one to three months.*

(b) *Limited exchange control governing reporting and payments structure.*

(c) *Few restrictions.*

(d) *If above certain limits.*

(e) *Banks could borrow freely, but there was a limit on their net foreign currency position. Nonbanks could borrow freely from abroad sums which were less than M$100,000, but they also faced a limit on their net foreign currency position.*

(7) New Zealand

A. Exchange Rate Arrangements

1975-1980	Pegged to composite
1981-1984	Managed floating
1985	Independently floating

B. Monetary and Credit Policy Instruments

Until 1984, the authorities' instruments included reserve ratios, government security ratios, rules governing the allocation of expansion of credit and (at times) controls on the expansion of credit. While interest rate controls were relaxed during 1977-1980, they were reinstituted during 1981-1982. Monetary growth was also limited through market financing of the government deficit. In 1984, all ratio requirements were abolished, open market operations were used more actively, discount policy was tightened, guidelines on credit to private sector were abolished, interest rate ceilings were removed, and capital controls were liberalized.

C. Capital Controls

			Restrictions on			
	Required Surrender of Export Proceeds	Advanced Import Deposits	Payments for Invisibles[(a)]	Foreign Currency Deposits by Residents	Foreign Lending or Borrowing by Financial Insitution	Tax or Special Reserve Requirements on Foreign Borrowing
1975	*	--	*	*	*	--
1976	*	*	*	*	*	--
1977	*	*	*	*	*	--
1978	*	--	*	*	*	--
1979	*	--	*	*	*	--
1980	*	--	*	*	*	--
1981	*	--	*	*	*	--
1982	*	--	*	*	*	--
1983	--	--	*	*	*	--
1984	--	--	--	--	(b)	--
1985	--	--	--	--	--	--

* *Denotes presence of the measure.*

-- *Indicates absence of the measure.*

(a) *Prior to 1984, certain payments required reserve bank approval.*

(b) *Limitations on borrowing by corporate entities.*

(8) Singapore

A. Exchange Rate Arrangements

1975-1985 Pegged to composite

B. Monetary and Credit Policy Instruments

Since a government budget surplus (especially for the retirement fund) has acted to reduce base money growth, rediscount operations have been the main domestic source of monetary growth. Balance of payments flows have also been a major source of monetary growth. While there were reserve and liquidity ratios, they tended to be changed infrequently.

C. Capital Controls

			Restrictions on			Tax or Special Reserve Require-ments on Foreign Borrowing
	Required Surrender of Export Proceeds	Advanced Import Deposits	Payments for Invisibles	Foreign Currency Deposits by Residents	Foreign Lending or Borrowing by Financial Insitution	
1975	(a)	--	(b)	*	*n*	--
1976	(a)	--	(b)	*	*n*	--
1977	(a)	--	(b)	(a)	*n*	--
1978	--	--	--	--	--	--
1979	--	--	--	--	--	--
1980	--	--	--	--	--	--
1981	--	--	--	--	--	--
1982	--	--	--	--	--	--
1983	--	--	--	--	--	--
1984	--	--	--	--	--	--
1985	--	--	--	--	--	--

* *Denotes presence of the measure.*

-- *Indicates absence of the measure.*

n *Indicates no information.*

(a) *Above certain minimum amounts.*

(b) *Above certain maximum amounts.*

(9) Sri Lanka

A. Exchange Rate Arrangements

1975	Pegged to sterling
1976	Pegged to composite
1977-1980	Independently floating
1981-1985	Managed floating

B. Monetary and Credit Policy Instruments

Instruments have included interest rate ceilings, limits on access of individual banks to Central Bank credit, and credit allocation rules. By 1978, principal instruments were the Bank rate, the amount the Central Bank would finance at that rate, and the penalty rate for further discounts. In June 1984, the Central Bank began auctions of Central Bank securities.

C. Capital Controls

	Required Surrender of Export Proceeds	Advanced Import Deposits	Restrictions on Payments for Invisibles	Restrictions on Foreign Currency Deposits by Residents	Restrictions on Foreign Lending or Borrowing by Financial Insitution	Tax or Special Reserve Require-ments on Foreign Borrowing
1975	*	--	*	*	*	--
1976	*	--	*	*	*	--
1977	*	--	(a)	*	*	--
1978	*	--	(a)	*	*	--
1979	*	--	(a)	*	*	--
1980	*	--	(a)	*	*	--
1981	*	--	(a)	*	*	--
1982	*	--	(a)	*	*	--
1983	*	--	(a)	*	*	--
1984	*	--	(a)	*	*	--
1985	*	--	(a)	*	*	--

* *Denotes presence of the measure.*

-- *Indicates absence of the measure.*

(a) *Certain payments require exchange control permission.*

(10) Thailand

A. Exchange Rate Arrangements

1975-1984	Other flexible arrangements
1985	Pegged to composite

B. Monetary and Credit Policy Instruments

Instruments have included ceiling interest rates, reserve and liquidity ratios, rediscount facilities, credit allocation rules, and occasional ceilings on credit expansion by banks. In 1979, a repurchase market for government securities was created. By 1985, unwanted fluctuations in reserve money were principally offset by operations in the government bond market.

C. Capital Controls

	Required Surrender of Export Proceeds	Advanced Import Deposits	Restrictions on: Payments for Invisibles	Restrictions on: Foreign Currency Deposits by Residents	Restrictions on: Foreign Lending or Borrowing by Financial Insitution	Tax or Special Reserve Require-ments on Foreign Borrowing
1975	*	--	(a)	*	*	--
1976	*	--	(a)	*	*	--
1977	*	--	(a)	*	*	--
1978	*	--	(a)	*	*	--
1979	*	--	(a)	*	*	--
1980	*	--	(a)	*	*	--
1981	*	--	(a)	*	*	--
1982	*	--	(a)	*	*	--
1983	*	--	(a)	*	*	--
1984	*	--	(a)	*	(b)	--
1985	*	--	(a)	*	(b)	--

* *Denotes presence of the measure.*

-- *Indicates absence of the measure.*

(a) *Some limitation (e.g., on travel).*

(b) *A limit existed on financial institutions net foreign currency position.*

(11) Western Samoa

A. Exchange Rate Arrangements

1975-1985 Managed floating

B. Monetary and Credit Policy Instruments

Instruments have included interest rate ceilings, required reserve ratios, credit allocation rules, and controls over volume of bank lending.

C. Capital Controls

	Required Surrender of Export Proceeds	Advanced Import Deposits	Restrictions on: Payments for Invisibles	Restrictions on: Foreign Currency Deposits by Residents	Restrictions on: Foreign Lending or Borrowing by Financial Insitution	Tax or Special Reserve Require-ments on Foreign Borrowing
1975	*	(a)	*	*	*	--
1976	*	(a)	*	*	*	--
1977	*	(a)	*	*	*	--
1978	*	(a)	*	*	*	--
1979	*	(a)	*	*	*	--
1980	*	(a)	*	*	*	--
1981	*	(a)	*	*	*	--
1982	*	--	*	*	*	--
1983	*	--	*	*	*	--
1984	*	*n*	*	*	*	--
1985	*	(a)	*	*	*	--

* *Denotes presence of the measure.*

-- *Indicates absence of the measure.*

n *Indicates no information.*

(a) *For motor vehicles.*

4

Capital Mobility and Monetary Policy: Australia, Japan, and New Zealand

Warren L. Coats, Jr.

The past two decades, but particularly the 1980s, have seen dramatic changes in financial markets characterized by the dissolution of traditional institutional structures and the proliferation of financial instruments and the ease with which they can be obtained and used. These developments have greatly enhanced capital mobility around the world, in part by better mediating the preferences of savers and investors, in part by increasing information about investment opportunities, and in part by greatly limiting the ability of authorities to effectively restrict capital movements with direct controls.

Freely mobile capital worldwide contributes to the ability of savings to finance the most profitable investments and, hence, to the efficient utilization of resources and maximization of wealth. It should, therefore, be welcomed and encouraged along with other policies that contribute to the efficient use of resources. For a variety of reasons, however, the free flow of capital across national boundaries has not always been welcomed by authorities.

The significant increase in international capital mobility has reduced the ability of national monetary authorities to conduct domestic monetary and fiscal policies independent of external considerations, even with flexible exchange rates. The increased ease with which capital flows internationally means that it is now more difficult and costly than it once was to attempt direct control, even in the short run. This suggests that domestic interest rates now need to conform more closely than before to international levels. This necessitates more careful coordination of the mix of monetary and fiscal policies so as to pursue domestic policy objectives while maintaining interest rates consistent with external balance.

Whether increased capital mobility facilitates or impedes an economy's adjustment to disturbances depends on the nature of the shocks it experiences. In light of the increased sensitivity of exchange rates to relative interest rate changes resulting from increased capital mobility, the case has been strengthened for closer coordination of macro policies among countries in order to minimize the risk of precipitating inappropriate, temporary, but costly reallocations of resources as a consequence of unnecessary, temporary fluctuations in exchange rates. The well-known impediments to fine-tuning stabilization policies (information and reaction lags, and the political difficulties of adjusting macro policies as desired) suggest the desirability of avoiding policy inconsistencies that will require more dramatic adjustment in the future.

This chapter briefly reviews the implications of increasing capital mobility for the conduct of domestic monetary policies and examines the experiences of Australia, Japan, and New Zealand with capital controls relaxation and financial sector liberalization in relation to their effects on the conduct of monetary policy.

CAPITAL MOBILITY AND MONETARY CONTROL

Perfectly mobile capital renders the domestic money supply endogenous in nominal as well as real terms for (relatively small) countries that fix the exchange rates of their currencies in terms of some other currency. The fixed exchange rate makes the domestic price level exogenous, while freely mobile capital makes the domestic interest rate exogenous. This makes it impossible for the monetary authorities to change permanently the domestic money supply from the nominal quantity the public wishes to hold at the exogenously determined price level and interest rate.[1]

Given output growth, an increase in the quantity of money would depress domestic interest rates, leading to a capital outflow. If capital is perfectly mobile, no interest rate differential can persist across national boundaries, and the capital outflow would continue until the initial interest differential is eliminated, i.e., until the domestic increase in the money supply is exactly reversed.

Allowing exchange rates to float restores to the central bank the ability to control the domestic nominal money supply, because the domestic price level is allowed to behave independently of the world price level. With highly mobile capital, however, floating exchange rates cannot restore domestic policy independence from the foreign sector because domestic policies that create a demand by foreigners for domestic assets (or vice versa) affect exchange rates, which affect the allocation of domestic resources.

Perfect capital mobility ties the level of domestic real interest rates to that of the world. Temporary differences in the level of domestic and international interest rates, such as might result from an unexpected change in the domestic money supply, cause exchange rate changes that lead to real resource transfers, which in turn will eventually eliminate any real interest rate differential. The exchange rate changes imply changes in the relative prices of tradables and nontradables, which help establish (or preserve) external and overall balance but can also cause a reallocation of resources between these sectors. These resource reallocations are costly, often involving a temporary increase in unemployment, idling of capital equipment, and heightened political strains that are associated with any redistribution of costs and benefits in a society. Moreover, frequent changes in exchange rates can cloud resource allocation decisions and lead to reallocations that prove to be mistaken; exchange rate movements that are expected to be temporary can lead to political support for protection in the form of trade and capital controls. These costs of resource reallocation in response to exchange rate changes are the basis of the often expressed desire for exchange rate stability.

The mechanism by which capital mobility links interest rates and exchange rates may be summarized as follows. Capital flows internationally to the extent that savings are invested across national boundaries as a result of current account deficits or surpluses, i.e., to the extent there are net transfers of real resources across national borders. With freely floating exchange rates, the inducement for capital to flow internationally as a result of a change in relative interest rates is offset by exchange rate movements; capital flows would arise only after the exchange rate changes had brought about current account adjustments.[2]

An increase in the domestic money supply that reduced domestic interest rates relative to foreign rates, for example, would raise the premia in the forward exchange market of the domestic currency in terms of other currencies sufficiently to eliminate any financial gain from investing in foreign assets with higher interest rates. As a result of this increase in forward premia, the spot purchase and investment of foreign exchange, and the forward repurchase of the domestic currency would result in the same yield as would investing in domestic assets at the lower interest rate. However, investors prepared to take the risk could buy the foreign exchange spot and hold foreign assets uncovered by future commitments to reacquire the domestic currency, if they believed that the forward premia overstated the likely appreciation in the future spot exchange rates of the domestic currency. If this were the market's general view, speculation would lower the spot exchange rate until it was expected to appreciate to the same extent as implied by the forward premia.[3]

Through these channels, market forces would tend to eliminate any net advantage from shifting financial assets across national borders, so that the public would be satisfied holding the existing stock of assets at the new interest rates. The depreciation of the spot exchange rate in the low interest rate country, however, would result over time in the current account surplus needed to realize the desired net capital outflow.

It can be seen in this simplified account that while floating exchange rates with capital mobility allow divergent inflation rates and nominal interest rates and therefore domestic control of the nominal money stock by the central bank, they do not isolate the domestic economy from the world economy, nor allow domestic monetary policy to operate without regard for the foreign sector. The freer capital is to respond to interest rate differences, the more efficient long-run resource allocation will tend to be, but the larger will be the exchange rate effects (and hence real economy effects) of such differentials. If these interest differentials and exchange rate effects are in fact temporary, but are not correctly perceived as such by market participants, they could impede the efficient allocation of resources by causing unnecessary and costly short-term reallocations between tradable and nontradable goods sectors. This is simply a specific example of the general case against macro instability and results, for a given degree of variability, from information and transactions (adjustment) costs.

This raises two policy issues that are of interest in this paper: Are there circumstances in which the cross-border mobility of capital should be resisted by the use of capital controls? What are the implications of capital mobility, and the very limited prospects for controlling it, for the stance and conduct of domestic monetary policy? Five circumstances are considered: low interest rate growth strategy; domestic financial liberalization and stabilization policy; external financial shocks originating from changes in the interest rate; external real shocks; and countercyclical stablization.

Low Interest Rate Growth Strategy

Artificially low real interest rates are sometimes adopted as part of a country's growth strategy in order to encourage investment or to minimize the cost of government borrowing. In fact, low interest rates tend generally to reduce investment (because of reduced domestic savings, and/or misallocation of domestic savings, e.g., into commodity hoards, and induced capital flight), and to reduce the productivity of investment (because of the need to rely more heavily on nonprice allocation of savings).[4] Moreover, such policies require capital controls to restrain the capital flight (in search of higher yielding and/or less risky investments) that normally accompany them.

The authorities' ability to control capital movements is increasingly limited by the proliferation of financial instruments internationally and the ease with which they can be obtained or traded. This, and an increased understanding of the shortcomings of "low interest rate" policies and of the repressed financial sectors that result from the more extreme versions of such policies, have diminished the interest of authorities in adhering to them.

Fortunately, the policies needed to avoid capital flight, e.g., realistic exchange rates, acceptable fiscal deficits, attractive domestic financial assets, a healthy, competitive financial sector, and economic and political stability,[5] are the same policies that are needed for efficient resource allocation in general. Authorities wishing to liberalize their domestic economy's financial sector and the international movement of capital should liberalize their domestic financial sector first in order to minimize the prospects of capital flight.[6]

Domestic Policy Reforms -- "High" Interest Rate Policy

The ability of authorities to effectively tax traditional financial institutions and instruments through interest rate regulations, reserve and similar requirements, inflation, etc., has led to the development of alternative, unregulated, or less regulated forms of financial intermediation. For this and other reasons (e.g., a shift by many authorities to the view that market forces generally allocate resources more efficiently than regulation[7]) a growing number of countries have moved to liberalize their financial sectors.

While financial sector liberalization should improve the efficiency of financial intermediation in the long run, the short-run effect is generally to raise interest rates, especially where interest rates were repressed. When this is coupled with monetary restraint to lower the rate of inflation, as has often been the case, the short-run interest rate effect is even more pronounced. Especially when combined with other policies that collectively improve an economy's growth prospects, these reforms may induce large capital inflows that temporarily appreciate the exchange value of the domestic currency and frustrate the economy's adjustment to the new policies. McKinnon explained this potential market failure as the result of individual lenders and borrowers assessing profitability myopically and "... not taking into account what will happen if they all transfer foreign capital simultaneously." While this behavior seems irrational, it may be difficult for individuals to "... see through what will happen to the general equilibirium of the economy in the future."[8]

The implication is that the relaxation of capital controls should be the last step of a liberalization-stabilization reform. While, as already noted, these controls are not likely to be effective in the long run, they may contribute in the short run to the success of the reform by reducing or avoiding the exchange rate overshooting that tends to occur during the adjustment period. It may also be that controls to reduce the inflow of capital, as required to avoid currency appreciation, can be made somewhat more effective than controls on the outflow of capital.

External Financial Shocks

Capital controls are sometimes linked to efforts to shelter domestic interest rates from temporary swings in foreign real interest rates,[9] such as the sharply rising interest rates in the United States and other industrial countries in the late 1970s and early 1980s. There is no doubt that the inflationary policies of many industrial countries during the 1970s in reaction to dramatic oil price increases and other developments imposed a cost on the developing countries, which were not responsible for the inflation and its accompanying high nominal interest rates. It does not necessarily follow, however, that the maintenance of domestic interest rates at historic levels and the imposition of capital controls for maintaining existing exchange rates would be the best policy response to that unfortunate situation. The desirability of avoiding temporary swings in interest rates and investment should be weighed against the higher yields abroad, and the enforcement costs and other costs of capital controls. In addition, the viability of maintaining the existing exchange rate rests on the judgment that the change in international interest rates is all real, when, in fact, large swings in interest rates are generally mainly nominal. It also depends on the confidence the authorities can attach to their assessment of the duration of the "temporary" interest rate swings.

External Real Shocks

Greater international capital mobility can reduce the extent to which domestic interest rate and exchange rate adjustments are needed in order to induce the real capital flows to finance changes in the current account balance. Take the case of the 1973 oil price increase. For oil-importing countries with short-run inelastic demand for oil, the externally induced current account deficit and consequent capital inflow required an increase in domestic interest rates or a depreciation of the domestic currency. With perfect capital mobility, a negligible increase in domestic interest rates would bring about the required balance of payments financing with no change in the exchange rate. Ultimately, external balance would require a depreciation of the exchange rate in order to restore the original current account balance.

The initial increase in expenditures on oil imports before any interest rate adjustments will reduce domestic savings and consumption, which may disturb internal balance. The fall in domestic savings in relation to domestic investment creates the financing gap that is covered by the capital inflow (current account deficit). The fall in domestic savings could occur with unchanged income -- by increasing expenditures for imports without reducing expenditures on domestic output -- but will more generally result in a fall in income as a result of a shift of expenditures from domestic to foreign goods. In short, the externally imposed current account deficit will generally result in a decline of domestic aggregate demand. This might be moderated by increased fiscal stimulus (increased government borrowing).[10]

The obvious contribution of capital mobility to the process of adjusting to an external shock is that the longer run correction of the current account balance can take place more gradually with less disturbance to domestic interest rates and exchange rates than otherwise. Thus, an overshooting of the exchange rate that would be likely without capital mobility can be avoided.

Countercyclical Stabilization

The effect of international capital mobility on the automatic stabilizing tendencies of an economy will depend on such factors as the source of a disturbance (real or monetary, internal or external); the degree of openness of the economy (share of imports and exports in the total economy); the degree of development of domestic financial and other markets; the elasticities of export supply and import demand; and the degree of price and wage flexibility.[11] Capital mobility with floating exchange rates transmits domestic interest rates changes into exchange rate movements. Whether the induced exchange rates changes contribute to economic stability or instability depends on whether their impact on aggregate demand is in the "right" direction or not.

For example, consider a monetary disturbance in the form of an autonomous increase in the demand for money in an open economy with moderately flexible wages and prices and an unchanged money supply. The increased demand for money (a leftward shift of the LM curve) creates a deficiency in aggregate demand at prevailing prices and increases interest rates. Employment and price levels tend to fall, and a current account surplus (capital outflow) is likely to arise at the prevailing exchange rate. Prices will fall until real money balances reach the level compatible with the increased demand for money, and interest rates, employment, and the current account have returned to their initial levels. With capital mobility, the initial increase in interest rates appreciates the exchange rate of the domestic currency. Depending on the size and elasticities of current account flows, the resulting exchange rate appreciation, by increasing imports, tends to aggravate the contraction of aggregate demand, and thus retards the adjustment process. Capital mobility, in this case, would slow the adjustment process.[12] On the other hand, countercyclical monetary policy would be more powerful in the presence of capital mobility, as the contribution it would make to domestic aggregate demand would be augmented by the external sector's response to induced changes in exchange rates.

Freer capital mobility reinforces international equalization of real interest rates; hence, the interest rate and exchange rate effects of domestic monetary policies need to be taken into account more than otherwise. When combined with domestic financial sector liberalization, it has increased market pressure for international harmonization of regulations in such areas as banking (e.g., reserve and capital requirements) and fiscal policy.

If the world economy is stable, the closer adherence of domestic policies to international conditions will contribute to domestic stability as well. If the world economy behaves erratically, there is no longer any opportunity to escape its adverse consequences domestically. This closer link underlies the world community's mutual interest in the economic health and well-being of each of its members, but especially of its trend-setting major members.

REVIEW OF NATIONAL EXPERIENCES

Three developed Pacific Basin countries, Australia, Japan and New Zealand, have recently liberalized their financial sectors, floated the exchange rates of their currencies, and relaxed capital controls. These developments are reviewed in other chapters in this book. It is interesting to look at these nations' monetary policy experiences in an environment of greater international capital mobility.

Australia. Australia's financial sector liberalization started in earnest in 1980 and is still underway. However, a great deal had been accomplished by the end of 1983, when virtually all exchange controls were lifted and the Australian dollar was allowed to float. Since then, Australia's real effective exchange rate has depreciated at a rate of about 8 percent per year. The rate of inflation as measured by the consumer price index fell from an average of 11.4 percent a year during the decade 1974-1983 to 6.6 percent a year from 1984 to March 1987, and the rate of real GDP growth rose from about 2 percent a year to more than 5 percent a year over the same periods. Australia's current account deficit, however, rose to 5.25 percent of GDP on average over the most recent period compared with a 3.3 rise on average over the ten years ending in 1983.

Money, both narrow and broad, grew at roughly the same rate during each of these two periods, but was less volatile in the more recent period, which also saw a 1.5 percent per year growth in the ratio of broad money to GDP. Government expenditures and borrowing requirements remain relatively large.

The new monetary exchange rate regime has facilitated the increased focusing of monetary policy on external stability. The earlier objective of keeping interest rates down in order to support the expansion of investment was replaced by the twin objectives of containing domestic demand in order to dampen imports, and of increasing the attractiveness of domestic investment by containing inflation, raising interest rates, and bringing greater stability to the exchange rate of the Australian dollar. Increased capital mobility does not seem to have interfered with the attainment of these objectives.

Japan. Japan's approach to financial deregulation has been gradual and is not yet complete. Deregulation and development of Japan's domestic financial markets have not fully kept pace with liberalization of international capital flows. This led to a recent sharp rise in gross capital inflows and outflows as a result of the increased use of free markets outside Japan for intermediating financial flows between Japanese residents. Responding to these strains, the government undertook a number of measures which facilitated the development of a market for public sector securities. The emergence of a secondary market for government bonds stimulated trading of other instruments as well. In addition, foreign investor interest in the Japanese market was stimulated by the ability to acquire liquid and risk-free government bonds. Notwithstanding this significant progress, the government bond market remained under-developed relative to that of many countries. Particularly noteworthy was the lack of a full-fledged Treasury bill market.

The shift to slower growth in the 1970s was accompanied by the birth of a structural current account surplus of the Japanese economy. The need to keep an essentially protected financial system in order to stem capital outflows gradually disappeared. However, during the 1970s, the authorities only selectively dismantled the exchange control system, depending on Japan's current account position. In fact, at times of external deficit, the authorities restored some restrictions on capital outflows, although definite progress toward liberalization was achieved during those years.

The second oil shock (1979) caused the external position to deteriorate again. This was met by additional exchange control measures by the authorities. Rather than restricting outflows, however, they were practically all in the direction of liberalizing capital inflows to achieve external objectives. Existing restrictions on the purchase of short to medium-term yen bonds, bank CDs, and Gensaki bonds by nonresidents were lifted, as were restrictions on yen deposits remunerated at free interest rates.

Resident companies were allowed to issue bonds abroad with fewer restrictions, while foreign currency-denominated loans to residents by both resident and nonresident banks were liberalized. Prudential guidelines to resident banks' foreign lending and temporary measures to limit capital outflows through restrictions on private placement of foreign bonds in Japan were issued.

These measures significantly altered the conduct of monetary policy in Japan. The system of window guidance in which each commercial bank was allocated loan quotas had become ineffective by the late 1970s. Quantitative credit controls were replaced by more market-oriented mechanisms. The Bank of Japan placed increasing emphasis on targeting the money supply, and ensured that the prevailing interest rates were consistent with this target.

A fundamental change occurred in 1980 with the passage of the New Foreign Exchange Law. It established the principle that all external capital transactions are free from restrictions unless specifically prohibited. Prior to this law, all transactions were prohibited unless specifically authorized. The law did not, however, abolish all exchange controls. In practice, authorities retained the right to issue prior approval for some transactions, and to invoke emergency measures should the external position of Japan require them. A new banking act was also introduced in 1981 allowing greater freedom of activities to banks and security companies, thus erasing some of the long-standing differences between the two types of institutions.

With the rapid strengthening of the current account situation, and in response to foreign pressures, authorities undertook yet another series of liberalization measures in 1984. The regulation limiting foreign exchange transactions to those related to trade was abolished; a rapid increase in the volume of such transactions resulted. Further liberalization of transactions in the Euroyen market was enacted.

The authorities' approach to financial liberalization can be summarized as being careful, gradual, and perhaps hesitant. In undertaking the step-by-step liberalization, the authorities have sought to curtail major disruptions in the financial markets and in the conduct of monetary policy, as well as to continue to protect Japanese financial institutions and companies.

New Zealand. New Zealand's very recent, very rapid, and very extensive economic policy reforms, including deregulation of its financial and trading sectors, have not yet had time to show many positive results. As part of this economic strategy, a number of measures were taken with a view to promoting efficiency and competition in the economy, and the tradable goods sector in particular, and to restoring over time a sustainable external position. Macroeconomic policy was given a medium-term, rather than a short-term, focus. These measures included the devaluation of the New Zealand dollar by 20 percent in July 1984; the phasing out of the main export subsidies; the acceleration of the process of import liberalization; the abolition of exchange controls in December 1984; and the floating of the New Zealand dollar in early March 1985.

New Zealand's trading sector and its domestic and international financial sectors and exchange rates were deregulated simultaneously rather than being phased in in any particular order. In the two years following (i.e., in 1985-1986), money growth rates and short-term interest rates rose considerably and became more volatile, and the rate of inflation first increased and then declined. While the Reserve Bank has attempted to produce more consistently tight monetary conditions from a medium-term perspective, the dramatically changed regulatory and policy environment has made it difficult to establish operating procedures consistent with this objective. Swings in monetary conditions resulted in fairly sizable swings in New Zealand's real effective exchange rate, which rose above its 1984 pre-devaluation level toward the end of 1985, dropped back to the neighborhood of its post-devaluation low in mid-1986, and then appreciated to within 5 percentage points of its pre-devalution level. These exchange rate movements have closely reflected interest rate differentials between New Zealand interest rates and Eurodollar rates.

The persistence of interest rates higher than those abroad since 1984, together with the improved confidence of foreign investors in the medium-term outlook of the economy as a result of the policy measures taken by the authorities, contributed to sizable private capital inflows, mostly in the form of foreign borrowings by New Zealand residents. Since the floating of the New Zealand dollar, official borrowing abroad has been undertaken only to finance scheduled amortization payments in order to improve the maturity structure of outstanding debt and to bolster external official reserves. As the authorities have also refrained from intervening in the foreign exchange market, net private capital inflows have generally matched the deficit on currency account.

Though New Zealand's foreign sector performance has improved, stabilization efforts have been hampered by the erratic behavior of money, interest rates, and exchange rates, and by the disproportionate burden of anti-inflation policy falling on monetary policy as a result of the relatively slow progress in reducing fiscal deficits. This policy mix has put additional upward pressure on real interest rates and exchange rates. The appreciation in the real exchange value of the New Zealand dollar is likely to slow the process of reducing the current account deficit to a more sustainable level. The negative impact of the appreciation on the demand for domestic output has contributed to sluggish output and employment. The resulting relative price signals, if they prove temporary, could slow the restructuring of the allocation of New Zealand's production resources needed for long-term competitiveness.

The freedom with which capital may flow in and out of New Zealand means that the need to establish a mix of monetary and fiscal policies to lower real interest rates while reducing inflation is even stronger than it otherwise would be. New Zealand authorities have stressed the need to reduce fiscal deficits in order to help lower domestic interest rates and exchange rates, rather than attempting to influence exchange rates by reintroducing capital controls.

NOTES

1. The real quantity of money is basically demand determined in any event. This is not meant to deny that the rate of growth of the nominal money supply, by determining the rate of inflation, influences the cost of holding money, and hence is an important determinant of the demand for real money balances.

2. Borrowing abroad for the purpose of financing the purchase of foreign goods, of course, results in an immediate current account adjustment (and therefore capital flow) with no effect on exchange rates (except as might result from changing foreign perceptions of credit-worthiness, etc.).

3. This is the overshooting phenomenon in the Dornbusch sense. See Dornbusch (1976).

4. For a general critique of such policies see Coats and Khatkhate (1984), and the literature cited there.

5. Khan and Ul-Haque, (1987).

6. Edward (1985).

7. Dooley and Mathieson (1987).

8. McKinnon (1984) pp. 477-478.

9. Swings in nominal interest rates matched by exchange rate movements--as would result, for example, from a fully anticipated inflation--do not provide any unusual profit opportunities.

10. An expansionary monetary policy and its tendency to lower interest rates would result in a more dramatic fall in the exchange rate.

11. Otani and Tiwari (1984).

12. An autonomous reduction in aggregate demand emanating from the real sector, on the other hand, would be accompanied by a reduction in interest rates, hence a depreciation of the exchange rate, which would augment aggregate demand. Capital mobility in this case would have a stabilizing effect.

REFERENCES

Boughton, James M., Richard D. Hass, and Paul R. Masson (1986). "The Role of Exchange Rate Movements in Transmitting International Disturbances." Washington, D.C.: International Monetary Fund, IMF Working Paper, WP/86/4.

Buiter, Willem (1986). "Macroeconomic Responses by Developing Countries to Changes in External Economic Conditions." NBER Working Paper Series, Cambridge, Mass. (February).

Cargill, Thomas F. (1985). "A U.S. Perspective on Japanese Financial Liberalization." *Bank of Japan Monetary and Economic Studies* 3, No. 1 (May), pp.115-161.

Coats, Warren L. and Deena Khatkhate (1980). *Money and Monetary Policy in Less Developed Countries: Survey of Issues and Evidence.* Oxford, England: Pergamon Press.

Coats, Warren L. and Deena Khatkhate (1984). "Monetary Policy in Less Developed Countries: Main Issues." *The Developing Economies,* Tokyo: Institute of Developing Economies XXII, No. 4 (December), pp. 329-348.

Corden, W. Max (1986). "The Japanese Current Account Surplus: Some Reflections." Washington, D.C.: International Monetary Fund (December).

Corden, W. Max (1987). "How Valid is International Keynesianism?" Washington, D.C.: International Monetary Fund, IMF Working Paper, WP/87/56.

Crockett, Andrew and Morris Goldstein (1987). "Strengthening the International Monetary System: Exchange Rates, Surveillance, and Objectives Indicators." *Occasional Paper No. 50,* Washington, D.C.: The International Monetary Fund (February).

Dodsworth, J., M.A. El-Erian, and D. Hammann (1987). "Foreign Currency Deposits in Developing Countries -- Origins and Economic Implications." Washington, D.C.: International Monetary Fund, IMF Working Papers, WP/87/12.

Dooley, Michael P. and Donald J. Mathieson (1987). "Financial Liberalization and Stability in Developing Countries." Washington, D.C.: International Monetary Fund, IMF Working Paper, WP/87/19.

Dornbusch, Rudiger (1976). "Expectations and Exchange Rate Dynamics." *Journal of Political Economy* 84, pp. 1161-1176.

Edward, Sebastian (1985). "The Sequency of Economic Liberalization in Developing Countries." *Ecomonic Policy Notes,* The World Bank (November).

Gros, Daniel (1987). "The Effectiveness of Capital Controls and Their Implications for Monetary Autonomy in the Presence of Incomplete Market Separation." Washington, D.C.: International Monetary Fund, IMF Working Paper, WP/87/4.

Kahkonen, Juha S. (1987). "Liberalization Policies and Welfare in a Financially Repressed Economy." Washington, D.C.: International Monetary Fund, IMF Working Paper, WP/87/23.

Kahn, Moshin S. and Nadeem Ul-Haque (1987). "Capital Flight from Developing Countries." *Finance and Development,* Washington, D.C., 23, No. 1 (March).

Kowada, Takamasa (1986). "Financial Deepening and Liberalization in Japan." Daiwa Investment Trust, Tokyo, Japan (September).

Mathieson, Donald (1986). "International Capital Flows, Capital Controls and Financial Reform." In *Financial Policy and Reform in Pacific Basin Countries*, edited by Hang-Sheng Cheng. Lexington, Mass: D.C. Heath & Co..

McKinnon, Ronald I. and Wallace E. Oates (1966). "The Implications of International Economic Integration for Monetary, Fiscal and Exchange Rate Policy." *Princeton Studies in International Finance 16* (Princeton).

McKinnon, Ronald I. (1984). "The International Capital Market and Economic Liberalization in LDCs." *The Developing Economies* XXII, No. 4 (December), pp. 476-481.

Mundell, Robert A. (1986). *International Economics*. New York: The MacMillan Company.

Otani, Ichiro and Siddharth Tiwari (1984). "Capital Controls, Interest Rate Parity and Exchange Rates: A Theoretical Approach." Washington, D.C.: International Monetary Fund, Mimeographed (May 23).

Takagi, Shinji (1986). "Recent Developments in Japan's Bond and Money Markets." Washington, D.C.: International Monetary Fund, Mimeographed (August 29).

5

Monetary Policy and Foreign Debt: The Experiences of the Far East Countries

Homi J. Kharas and Miguel A. Kiguel

In its heyday, foreign borrowing from private international capital markets was seen by the governments of many less developed countries (LDC) as a double blessing. First, it helped balance their external accounts, which had been weakened by the first oil shock and the consequent requirements of domestic investment for adjustment to the relative price changes. Second, it provided a mechanism for financing large government budget deficits without recourse to inflationary domestic credit expansion. Over time, however, perceptions have changed. Foreign debt is now more widely viewed as a double curse: high interest payments have worsened both the current account balance and the fiscal deficit, triggering higher inflation through exchange rate depreciation and more rapid growth in domestic credit. This dynamic relationship between foreign indebtedness, domestic credit policy, inflation, and the real exchange rate is explored in this chapter. The analysis is illustrated with the historical experiences of a small group of East Asian countries: Indonesia, Korea, Malaysia, the Philippines, and Thailand.

In this chapter, a highly stylized model of government policy rules and objectives is developed to trace the evolution over time of public foreign debt, domestic credit, and international reserves. A full employment economy producing traded and nontraded goods is considered along the lines of the models presented in Kouri (1976), Bruno (1976), and Khan and Lizondo (1986). Government budget deficits in this model are financed through foreign borrowing and domestic credit from the central bank, clearly linking the choice of monetary[1] and fiscal policies with foreign borrowing decisions. In particular, in countries where the budget deficit remains relatively stable over time, domestic credit policies play a key role in determining the level and growth of foreign debt. Monetary policy is also relevant to the balance of payments, because different combinations of domestic and foreign financing will have a dissimilar impact on changes in international reserves.

There is extensive literature on the relationship between domestic credit policies and the balance of payments. Most work on this issue is based on the monetary approach to the balance of payments, as presented in Frenkel and Johnson (1976), which links balance of payments problems to imbalances in the domestic money market. The importance of domestic policies for external balance is also highlighted in recent work on balance of payments crises, for instance in Obstfeld (1986), van Wijnbergen (1986), and Ize and Ortiz (1986). In these models, the choice of inconsistent monetary, fiscal, and exchange rate policies potentially leads to the depletion of central bank foreign exchange reserves. In countries where the central bank or other government agencies have access to international funds, however, a run on reserves can be postponed by increasing foreign borrowing.

This is the case considered in this chapter: the adoption of inconsistent domestic policies are prone to lead to excessive borrowing and result in a debt crisis. The stability of the system and the evolution of foreign debt, domestic credit, and international reserves under alternative policy rules is investigated. The model is used for examining the "sustainability" of government economic policies.[2]

One important feature of this model is the joint consideration of gross external debt and international reserves. The possibility for a two-way financial flow, whereby utilization of international credit is accompanied by a buildup of international reserves, sometimes even above normal desired levels, is a key characteristic of the monetary aspects of foreign borrowing. By contrast, most of the existing analysis of LDC indebtedness has been dominated by real economy paradigms which emphasize the gaps between saving and investment or exports and imports. This latter approach, therefore, focuses exclusively on net debt, defined as gross debt less foreign exchange reserves of the banking system, or equivalently, the net transfer of real resources to the country from abroad. See, for example, Cohen (1988), Cooper and Sachs (1985), and Cline (1982).

The first section of this chapter gives descriptive background on selected East Asian countries, and documents the importance of the financial, as well as real-resource, aspects of foreign borrowing. Next, an analytical model is presented which relates the results to specific historical episodes in the borrowing countries, focusing on the impact of monetary policy on foreign debt and international reserves. From this, inferences are drawn on certain current policy concerns of the countries in the region, including debt-equity swaps, substitution of domestic for foreign debt, and sterilization of money creation resulting from current account surpluses. The conclusions are summarized in the final section.

FINANCIAL ASPECTS OF FOREIGN DEBT FLOWS

Almost all foreign borrowing by East Asian countries has been in the form of public or publicly guaranteed debt contracted at market interest rates.[3] The growth of such debt has been rapid, in line with the experience of other developing countries (Table 1). Net debt, defined as total foreign debt minus foreign reserves, has followed a similar pattern. Private debt has been growing steadily but remains a small proportion of total foreign debt. Absolute volumes have also been large. Korea, for example, is now the fourth largest LDC debtor in the world. East Asian countries, with the exception of the Philippines, are among the few developing countries that still have access to voluntary lending from commerical banks. Their debt-GNP ratios have remained within reasonable bounds, while their debt-export ratios have remained much lower than the major Latin American debtor countries. This has been helped by the continuous reduction in current account deficits in the last years. Furthermore, both Korea and the Philippines had sizeable current account surpluses in 1986, the first in two decades.

The rapid growth of public foreign debt is closely linked with the expansionary fiscal-conservative monetary policy stances of these countries for most of this period. As East Asian countries have had relatively thin domestic financial markets, there has been a constraint on the feasibility of financing fiscal deficits through domestic bonds. The only alternatives are borrowing from abroad and obtaining domestic credit from the central bank. As discussed in the Appendix, adjustment of domestic credit has been the main instrument used by the authorities to maintain external balance. Through the late 1970s, Korea and Indonesia financed their budget deficit primarily through foreign borrowing, which has helped to support a conservative monetary policy. A similar pattern seems to hold for Thailand, although the data are not readily available. The benefit of this policy is that these countries, with the exception of the Philippines, have been able to contain monetary growth and have enjoyed reasonable price stability (Table 2). The major inflationary episodes were short-lived, resulting from the oil shocks of the early 1980s.

A second benefit of this monetary-fiscal policy mix was the resultant reasonable degree of stability of the real exchange rates in these countries (Table 2). In Korea, for example, the range of fluctuation in the real exchange rate between 1980 and 1985 was 10.6 percent. The stability is particularly surprising in view of the wide fluctuations of the real exchange rates of the OECD countries during this period. Moreover, it appears that changes in the budget deficit also have an impact on the real exchange rate (Table 2). This is particularly clear in the Philippines, which had large

Table 1
External Debt Indicators

(Billions of U.S. Dollars)

		Indonesia	Korea	Malaysia	Philippines	Thailand
Public Debt[a]	1975	8.0	5.8	1.3	1.4	0.6
	1980	15.0	16.2	3.9	6.6	4.1
	1985	26.6	29.1	13.8	13.6	9.9
Private Debt[a]	1975	2.4	0.6	0.5	1.4	0.7
	1980	3.1	2.3	1.3	2.5	1.7
	1985	3.8	6.6	4.1	3.0	3.4
Short-Term Debt	1975	NA	NA	NA	NA	NA
	1980	2.8	10.6	NA	7.6	2.3
	1985	5.3	10.7	NA	8.6	3.2
Total Debt	1975	NA	NA	NA	NA	NA
	1980	20.9	29.8	NA	17.5	8.3
	1985	35.8	48.0	NA	26.2	17.5
			(Percent of GNP)			
Public Debt	1975	26	28	14	9	4
	1980	20	27	16	19	13
	1985	33	35	48	42	26
Total Debt	1975	NA	NA	NA	NA	NA
	1980	28	49	NA	50	25
	1985	45	58	NA	81	47
			(Percent of Exports)			
Public Debt	1975	114	97	31	44	21
	1980	67	72	26	83	48
	1985	133	88	78	171	97
Total Debt	1975	NA	NA	NA	NA	NA
	1980	94	132	NA	218	97
	1985	179	145	NA	330	171

(a) *Medium- and long-term debt only, outstanding and disbursed.*

Source: World Bank, World Debt Tables.

Table 2
Financial Indicators

	Consumer Price Index (percent)	Real Exchange Rate[a] (1980 = 100)	Current Account Balance (US$,billions)	Foreign Reserves: Ratio to Imports (percent)	Foreign Reserves: Amount (US$,billions)	Net Foreign Debt (US$, billions)
Indonesia						
Avg: 1975-80	19.4	87.8	0.0	45.8	2.8	11.8
1981	12.2	93.8	-0.5	35.6	5.0	14.1
1982	9.5	87.1	-4.8	17.6	3.1	20.2
1983	11.8	106.4	-6.3	21.0	3.7	22.6
1984	10.5	110.5	-1.9	31.3	4.8	23.5
1985	4.7	113.5	-1.8	29.5	5.0	22.9
Korea						
Avg: 1975-80	22.4	101.1	-2.1	22.3	2.4	9.0
1981	21.3	98.1	-4.6	11.0	2.7	25.9
1982	7.3	97.2	-2.7	11.9	2.8	29.7
1983	3.4	101.5	-1.6	9.4	2.3	31.9
1984	2.3	103.6	-1.3	10.1	2.8	33.3
1985	2.5	122.3	-0.9	10.8	2.9	37.0
Malaysia						
Avg: 1975-80	5.4	94.4	0.2	63.0	3.0	-0.7
1981	9.7	94.6	-2.5	34.8	4.1	1.5
1982	5.8	91.3	-3.6	29.6	3.8	4.3
1983	3.7	88.4	-3.5	28.6	3.8	7.0
1984	3.9	92.5	-1.7	27.7	3.7	8.5
1985	0.4	109.0	-0.7	42.5	4.9	8.9
Philippines						
Avg: 1975-80	13.1	107.0	-0.9	56.6	1.9	9.4
1981	13.1	98.2	-1.8	30.6	2.1	15.0
1982	10.2	96.0	-2.9	12.8	0.9	19.4
1983	10.0	112.3	-2.6	10.7	0.7	19.2
1984	50.3	112.4	-1.2	10.2	0.6	20.5
1985	23.1	103.8	0.0	12.0	0.6	21.5
Thailand						
Avg: 1975-80	10.9	102.9	-1.2	49.1	1.8	2.4
1981	12.7	97.8	-2.6	19.4	1.7	6.3
1982	5.3	97.4	-1.0	20.3	1.5	7.6
1983	3.7	94.6	-2.9	17.5	1.6	8.7
1984	0.9	95.0	-2.1	20.8	1.9	9.2
1985	2.4	106.0	-1.5	26.1	2.2	10.9

(a) *Trade-weighted exchange rates deflated by the corresponding consumer price indices. A rise in the real exchange rate means a real devaluation of the national currency.*

Table 2 (continued)
Financial Indicators

	Money (M1)		Growth in Central Bank		Public Sector Deficit	
	Ratio to GDP (percent)	Growth (percent)	Domestic Credit (percent)	Foreign Assets (percent)	Ratio to GDP (percent)	Foreign Financing (percent)
Indonesia						
Avg: 1975-80	10.6	38.9	59.3	66.7	1.4[(b)]	88.0
1981	12.0	29.2	27.8	-4.3	0.2	100.0
1982	12.0	10.0	49.0	-8.7	4.1	83.0
1983	10.7	6.4	4.5	44.1	3.0	100.0
1984	10.4	13.2	28.4	51.4	0.8	100.0
1985	10.5	18.0	1.9	5.8	1.4	100.0
Korea						
Avg: 1975-80	11.1	31.6	31.8	101.2	1.6	79.1
1981	8.5	4.6	31.0	-2.1	3.4	34.0
1982	11.0	45.6	15.3	13.9	3.1	41.1
1983	11.1	17.0	22.1	-15.5	1.1	60.8
1984	10.0	0.6	22.6	25.3	1.2	37.3
1985	10.0	10.8	20.6	6.7	1.3	46.9
Malaysia						
Avg: 1975-80	18.8	19.0	57.8	23.5	NA	43.3
1981	19.1	12.9	57.9	-5.0	16.4	38.7
1982	20.0	13.3	182.8	-4.8	15.4	50.9
1983	19.3	7.7	76.1	1.3	9.5	69.1
1984	16.8	-0.6	36.4	2.1	6.4	61.0
1985	18.2	5.8	-48.7	29.2	5.7	21.6
Philippines						
Avg: 1975-80	9.1	19.9	32.0	19.4	1.2	50.1
1981	7.7	4.4	36.7	-19.0	4.0	49.6
1982	6.9	-0.1	25.7	-21.6	4.1	82.0
1983	8.5	38.3	37.6	-22.9	1.9	73.0
1984	6.1	3.5	20.2	46.1	1.8	19.4
1985	5.7	6.4	0.4	16.8	1.8	NA
Thailand						
Avg: 1975-80	11.5	16.8	33.8	10.7	4.1	22.6
1981	9.3	2.6	17.2	0.5	3.2	22.2
1982	9.3	6.9	18.5	-2.7	5.8	19.6
1983	8.9	4.5	13.1	-3.6	4.1	21.6
1984	9.4	14.1	-0.3	24.1	3.7	12.8
1985	8.6	-3.5	13.4	9.7	5.1	33.8

(b) *1978-1980 only.*

Source: International Monetary Fund, International Financial Statistics; and World Bank, World Debt Tables.

budget deficits (compared with previous years) and an appreciation in 1981 and 1982, and in Malaysia where large budget deficits from 1981 to 1983 are also correlated with exchange appreciation. Notice that after those episodes, there was a subsequent depreciation when fiscal policy was tightened.

A third benefit has been the retention of comfortable levels of foreign exchange reserves. Prior to 1981, Indonesia, Thailand, Malaysia, and the Philippines had reserves equivalent to six months of imports. In the immediate aftermath of the second round of oil price increases, fiscal deficits widened while domestic credit tightened. The Philippines is the exception; domestic credit continued to grow rapidly, causing a drastic erosion of reserves. More recently, it appears that monetary and fiscal policy stances have again shifted in response to changing international conditions. Domestic credit remains tight, but fiscal deficits have begun to shrink, accelerating the restoration of reserves to prior levels. This is most apparent in the Philippines, where between 1983 and 1985 a drastic reduction in the budget deficit (from 4 to 1.8 percent of GDP) and low rates of growth in the money supply have turned a $2 9 billion current account deficit into a surplus.

In summary, in the five East Asian countries over the last ten years, the public sector has played a major role in determining the volume of foreign borrowing through public debt financing Private foreign borrowing has been relatively minor. Inflation has been close to international levels, except in the Philippines, where it accelerated substantially during the early stages of the debt crisis. Domestic credit policy has been used to maintain control over foreign exchange reserves.

THE ANALYTICAL FRAMEWORK

The Basic Model

The following section develops an analytical framework within which the appropriateness of alternative policy stances can be assessed. Consider a small open economy that produces one tradable and one nontradable (home) good. At a constant real exchange rate, output of both goods has a constant natural rate of growth (n), which is equal to productivity change plus labor force growth. This constant, therefore, represents overall real GDP growth. The share of each sector in real GDP, however, depends on the real exchange rate (r), defined as the price of the tradable good in terms of the nontradable good.

$$y_i = y_i(r) \qquad i=t,h \qquad y_{tr} > 0;\ y_{hr} < 0 \tag{1}$$

where y_i is the share of the ith sector in real GDP; the subscripts t and h denote the tradable good sector and the home good sector, respectively; and y_{tr} the effects of a change in the real exchange rate on the shares of the tradable good sector and the home good sector, respectively, in real GDP. There is perfect arbitrage in the market for the tradable good, which means $P_t = EP_t^*$ (i.e., the price of the tradable good in terms of the domestic currency (P_t) is equal to the exchange rate (E) times its price in terms of the foreign currency (P_t^*)).

Demand is divided into two components, public and private. Public sector expenditure falls entirely on the home good.[4] Private sector demand for each good depends on wealth -- proxied here by the holding of real money balances in terms of the tradable goods (m) -- and on the real exchange rate (r). As the demand functions are homogenous of degree one with respect to wealth and government expenditure, the demand for the two goods can be simply expressed as ratios to GDP:

$$D_h = C_h(m,r) + rg \qquad C_{hm} > 0 \, ; C_{hr} > 0 \tag{2}$$

$$D_t = C_t(m,r) \qquad C_{tm} > 0 \, ; C_{tr} < 0 \tag{3}$$

where g, C_h, C_t, and m are expressed as ratios to GDP; g is government spending in terms of the tradable good; C_h, C_t are private spending on the home and the tradable goods, respectively. In the home good market, supply and demand are equated through instantaneous adjustment of the price of the home good. Combining (1) and (2) gives a reduced form equation for r.

$$r = r(m,g) \qquad r_m < 0 \, ; r_g < 0 \tag{4}$$

As real money balances (m) increase, private spending on the home good increases; equilibrium in the home good market is restored through an increase in the price of the home good relative to that of the tradable good, which means a real exchange rate appreciation, i.e., a decline in r. A similar equilibration holds for an expansion in government spending (g).[5] It is assumed that the central bank has a target for the nominal exchange rate, which it devalues at a constant rate. A fixed nominal exchange rate would be a special case in which the rate of devaluation is zero.

Money balances are given as the sum of two stock variables: domestic credit (d) and reserves (R), both expressed in terms of the tradable good as ratios to GDP.

$$m = d + R \tag{5}$$

At any point in time, d and R are predetermined. Thus, once the level of government spending is known, the real output, the demand in each sector, and the real exchange rate are determined. To investigate the dynamics of the system one need only to specify the behavior over time of the stock variables and of government spending.

Because developing countries typically have limited open-market operations, changes in the net domestic credit of the central bank are determined by the need to finance the government deficit. It is supposed that the government has only two sources of funds: domestic credit, which is free of interest, and foreign indebtedness (f), which is incurred at a fixed and exogenous real interest rate (i). Changes in the stock of credit from these two sources represent the resource flows available to fund government expenditure. Again, expressing all lower case variables as fractions of GDP, the government budget constraint can be written as:

$$\dot{d} = g + (i - n) f - (\pi + n) d - \dot{f} \tag{6}$$

where π is the domestic inflation rate, and where a dot over a variable denotes the rate of change of that variable over time. Equation (6) states that changes in government debt ($\dot{d} + \dot{f}$) are equal to the budget deficit ($g + if$) minus the inflation tax (πd) and minus the reduction in the asset ratios resulting from economic growth $(f + d)n$.

The dynamic path of reserves can be deduced from the balance of payments. The change in reserves is simply the sum of the trade balance, less interest payments on foreign debt, plus net capital inflows from abroad. Neglecting any private capital flows, reserve changes can be expressed as:

$$\dot{R} = s(m,g) + \dot{f} + (n - i) f - nR \qquad s_m < 0;\ s_g < 0 \tag{7}$$

where s, the ratio of the trade balance to GDP, is simply the excess of the tradable good output over its demand, $s = y_t - C_t(m,r)$.

Equation (7) represents the condition for external balance. As money balances expand, the trade deficit widens because of the direct impact of increased money balances on the demand for the tradable good and because of the indirect impact of larger money balances causing a real exchange rate appreciation. Government spending also enters, even though no spending is directly on imports, because of the exchange rate effect.

Dynamic Behavior

The differential equations (6) and (7) illustrate the interdependence of changes in domestic credit, foreign debt, and reserves. The government can only set one of these in an arbitrary fashion. It can also adjust its real spending and inflation targets. The stability of the system and the properties of the long-run, steady-state solution depend on how these policy choices are made.

Initially, assume the following policy mix: The government holds real spending at a constant fraction of GDP, $g = \bar{g}$. It also has a desired long-run inflation rate, $\pi = \bar{\pi}$, (which could be zero), which is accommodated by a steady depreciation of the nominal exchange rate at the target inflation rate, $\bar{\pi}$. Finally, it fixes some level of foreign exchange reserves as a target, $\bar{R}$ (for instance, three months of imports), to which the steady-state level of reserves, R^*, should converge.

Equations (6) and (7) give two dynamic equations describing the government budget constraint and the condition for external balance for determining three unknowns: $\dot{f}$, $\dot{d}$, and $\dot{R}$. A third equation is needed to complete the system; this can be obtained by assuming that the central bank uses one of the two policy variables: foreign borrowing ($\dot{f}$), or domestic credit ($\dot{d}$) to achieve its reserve target ($\bar{R}$). For the stability properties of the system, it does not matter which of the two policy variables is used. However, on the basis of the data for the 1970-1985 period, it appears that in fact the East Asian countries relied primarily on domestic credit policy to achieve reserve targets (Appendix). Hence, it is assumed

$$\dot{d} = a\,(R - \bar{R}) \tag{8}$$

Equation (8) is a simple policy rule which sets the change in domestic credit as a linear function of excess reserves, such that when reserves are below their target, domestic credit is tightened, and vice versa.

Now, denote the steady-state levels of the state variables by an asterisk and linearizing around the steady-state to obtain

$$\begin{bmatrix} \dot{f} \\ \dot{d} \\ \dot{R} \end{bmatrix} = \begin{bmatrix} i-n & -a & -(\pi+n) \\ 0 & 0 & a \\ 0 & s_m-\pi-n & -a \end{bmatrix} \begin{bmatrix} f - f^* \\ d - d^* \\ R - R^* \end{bmatrix} \tag{9}$$

As each of the state variables, f, d, and R, is predetermined, stability requires that the real parts of the three roots of (9) be negative. Thus, the determinant of the matrix on the right hand side of equation (9) must be negative. The expression for the determinant $|A|$ is $a(i-n)(-s_m+\pi+n) < 0$ if $n > i$.[6] The first result, therefore, is that the system is stable and the chosen policy rules are sustainable if and only if the growth rate of the economy is greater than the real interest rate on external debt. If the interest rate is greater than growth, foreign debt as a proportion of GDP will continuously expand. Domestic credit and reserves, however, will reach and remain at their steady-state levels.

The expression $n > i$ as a condition for debt stability is not novel. It has been derived in a famous paper by Domar (1944) and is incorporated in more recent works such as Solomon (1977) and Cohen (1988), among others, and is closely related to the conditions for stability in the economic growth literature. In a sightly different guise, it is also referred to as the Simonsen rule.[7] What is new here is that the instability derives not from the real economy side but from the demand of government deficit financing. With the inflation rate exogenous and domestic credit targeted to reserves, the amount of seigniorage (from the inflation tax plus growth) is predetermined. If this is insufficient to fill government spending and debt service requirements, then foreign debt must grow and in fact, accelerate as the government financing gap widens with ever-increasing interest obligations.

In the long run,[8] there is substitution between domestic credit and foreign debt. The external constraint in equation (7) implies that an increase in the long run stock of domestic credit would tend to deteriorate the balance of payments. To restore external balance, there should be a reduction in the budget deficit to offset higher private expenditure on goods; otherwise, reserves will fall. Higher d^*, in turn, provides more government revenue through seigniorage and reduces the requirement for foreign financing to fill the budget deficit.

The budget constraint and the external balance condition impose a somewhat different outcome for government spending and inflation. As government spending rises, more foreign borrowing is required to finance the budget deficit. This more than compensates for the incipient deterioration in the balance of payments, and permits an expansion in domestic credit as well. Similarly, a decline in inflation reduces government seigniorage; the financing gap is met by more foreign borrowing and higher domestic credit.

Surprisingly, the impact of a change in the natural growth rate on foreign debt is ambiguous. It does not appear that faster growing countries will always be characterized by higher debt/GDP ratios. On the one hand, faster growth necessitates a more rapid accumulation of reserves and hence a more restrictive domestic credit stance. This tends to increase the demand for more foreign debt. On the other hand, there is an offsetting tendency as seigniorage and net foreign transfers from a given foreign debt stock both rise. Finally, one can ascribe a rise in long-run debt to an increase in the real interest rate.

One feature of the system of equations (9) is that it can be partitioned. There is a subsystem giving the dynamics of domestic credit and reserves that is independent of the stock of foreign debt or of new capital inflows from abroad. This is a direct result of the assumption that all foreign borrowing is undertaken by the public sector. Thus, information on government spending and/or domestic credit fully determines the current and capital accounts of the balance of payments.

The dynamics of the domestic credit reserves subsystem are illustrated in Figure 1. Equations (7) and (8) show the combination of points for which $\dot{d} = 0$ and $\dot{R} = 0$, respectively. From inspection of equation (8), $\dot{d} = 0$ coincides with the horizontal axis. At any point below (above) the $\dot{d} = 0$ schedule, the stock of reserves is less (more) than the desired level and hence the authorities contract (expand) domestic credit. The $\dot{R} = 0$ schedule shows the combinations of reserves and domestic credit at which the balance of payments is in equilibrium. It is downward sloping because an increase in reserves results in a higher money supply and hence in a larger trade deficit; domestic credit must fall to restore external balance. At points to the right (left) of this schedule, the country experiences a balance of payments deficit (surplus). The stationary equilibrium is the point at which both schedules intersect, which in this case coincides with the origin.

Suppose that the economy is initially at point A in Figure 1(a), with reserves below the desired level. Contractionary domestic credit policies lead to a continuous balance of payments surplus. At point B the target level of reserves is achieved, but domestic credit is below its equilibrium level and the economy continues to experience a balance of payments surplus. As the level of reserves rises above $\bar{R}$, the central bank loosens its domestic credit policy, thereby accommodating larger trade deficits. In our example, the economy will go through cycles in which international reserves first rise and then fall until the stationary equilibrium is finally reached.

As the economy cycles, money supply and the real exchange rate will also be affected. From equation (4), it can be seen that for a given flow of real government expenditure, the dynamics of the real exchange rate are uniquely determined by real money balances. Taking into account equation (5), the identity between real money balances and the sum of central bank domestic and foreign assets, the long-run equilibrium real exchange rate can be expressed as a function of steady-state domestic credit and reserve levels:

$$r^* = r(d^* + R^*, g). \qquad (4')$$

Equation (4′) implies that relative to the long-run level, the current real exchange rate will appreciate when real money balances exceed the long run equilibrium level (m^*), and vice versa. Figure 1(b) shows the areas of real appreciation and real depreciation of the exchange rate. The rr line (which has a slope = −1) shows the combinations of R and d for which $R + d = m^*$. To the right of that schedule, $m > m^*$ and hence the exchange

Figure 1
Domestic Credit and Foreign Reserves Adjustment Mechanism

(a) Balance of Payments Dynamics

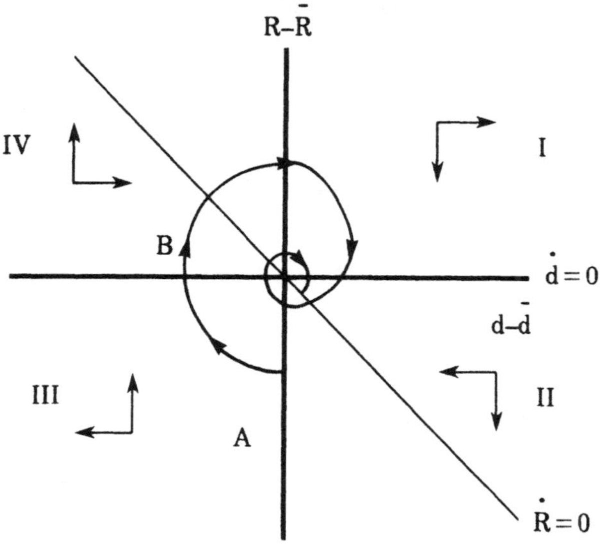

(b) Real Exchange Rate Dynamics

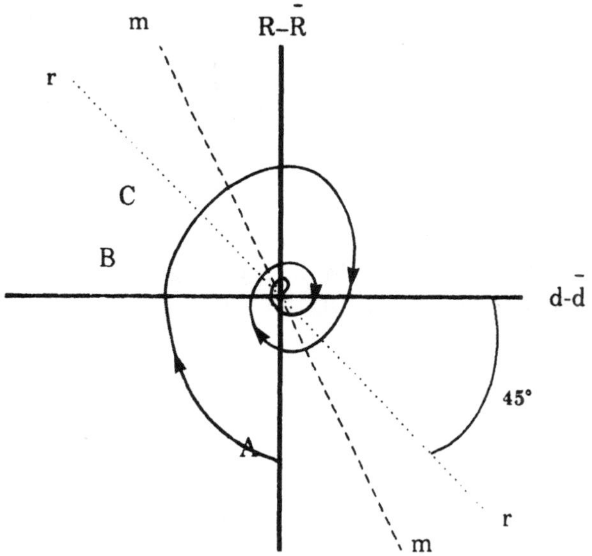

rate will appreciate; to the left, m < m*, hence the real exchange rate will depreciate.

A full description of the behavior of the real exchange rate is based on the dynamics of the real money supply. Differentiating (5) and substituting equation (7) and (8) yields

$$\dot{m} = \dot{R} + \dot{d} = s(d + r;\ g) + g - (\pi + n)\,d \qquad (5')$$

Notice that although both $\dot{R}$ and $\dot{d}$ are affected by the composition of financing between domestic credit and foreign borrowing, their sum is independent of the composition and depends only on the total level of the real budget deficit, g. Linearizing this equation in the neighborhood of the long run equilibrium and making it equal to zero yields

$$\left.\frac{(R-R^*)}{(d-d^*)}\right|_{\dot{m}=0} = -\frac{s_m - \pi - n}{s_m} < -1 \ \text{for}\ n+\pi > 0.$$

This line is shown as mm in Figure 1(b) which, in this example, is assumed to be steeper than the schedule for external balance.[9] To the right (left) of the mm schedule, real money balances are falling (rising) and the exchange rate is depreciating (appreciating).

The cyclical adjustment to equilibrium implies that there can be sizeable leads and lags in the behavior of key variables. For example, even when reserves are above their long-run level -- for instance, at a point above B in Figure 1(b) -- the exchange rate may continue to depreciate, causing still greater accumulation of reserves. The model also depicts "overshooting," in which the exchange rate depreciates even if it is already undervalued relative to its long-run equilibrium -- after point C, for example.

It is interesting to note that the system described by equation (9) can generate overborrowing (increases in foreign debt concommitant with reserve growth above desired levels).[10] Overborrowing can result from the decentralized decision process in the economy. While the treasury decides on a target for the budget deficit, the monetary authorities independently set the deficit that they are willing to finance through expansion in domestic credit. In terms of Figure 1, this is likely to occur when the economy is in the fourth quadrant (IV), where $d - d^* < 0$ and $R - R^* > 0$. The first differential equation in (9) is

$$\dot{f} = (i-n)(f-f^*) - a(R-R^*) - (\pi+n)(d-d^*)$$

If the economy initially has low debt ($f<f^*$ and $d < d^*$), and the growth rate is higher than the international interest rate, then the first and third terms on the right-hand side are positive, and $\dot{f}$ may well be positive even if $R > R^*$.

In this model, overborrowing results as part of the equilibrium adjustment process rather than as the choice of "suboptimal" policies. In fact, a stronger type of overborrowing could also occur. That is, countries could still be borrowing from abroad when $R > R^*$ and $f > f^*$. This could happen when the stock of domestic credit (d) as well as its change ($\dot{d}$) -- that is, $a(R - \bar{R})$ -- are at very low levels. In that case, the government does not generate enough income from the inflation tax or domestic credit expansion to finance its deficit, and is forced to borrow abroad in spite of the high stock of foreign debt.

Indonesia is a good example of overborrowing. Between 1982 and 1985, the country continuously increased its stock of international reserves, while its foreign debt also grew from 20 percent of GDP in 1982 to 33.4 percent in 1985. Foreign borrowing is particularly difficult to justify between 1984 and 1985, since at that time international reserves were already above 25 percent of annual imports.[11] Thailand in the 1971-1972 and 1983-1985 periods and Malaysia in 1973-1974 and 1984-1985 are other examples of overborrowing.

Debt Crisis and Adjustment

There is mounting agreement that the current debt crisis[12] was caused by unfavorable international events beyond the control of developing countries, combined with their adoption of inconsistent domestic policies. More specifically, higher world interest rates and reduced LDC growth rates in conjunction with large budget deficits appear to have been central to the crisis.

The sharp increase in the world interest rates during the early 1980s was a critical factor in determining the appropriateness of countries' domestic credit and foreign debt policies. The worldwide recession and the adjustment to the 1979-1980 oil shock compounded the situation by reducing the growth potential of nonoil economies. As mentioned in the previous section, a reversal in the stability condition $n > i$ would put the economy onto an unstable path, given fixed real government deficits, inflation, and reserve targets.

The data presented in Table 3 indicate that for most of the East Asian developing countries there was indeed a reversal in the stability condition. As a result of these changes, an adjustment in policies was required to restore stability. Without such adjustment in real spending, this model shows that the budget deficit grows as debt service on public debt grows. One common way of adjusting is to link the inflation target to the government deficit. A higher inflation would generate real resources

Table 3
Comparison Between Growth and Interest Rates
(Percent)

	Average: 1975-80	1981	1982	1983	1984	1985
World Interest Rate						
Nominal[a]	10.3	17.7	14.6	10.9	12.3	9.6
Real[b]	1.2	8.6	12.6	9.7	9.9	10.1
Indonesia						
Output Growth	7.5	7.9	2.2	4.2	NA	NA
Export Growth	12.0	8.7	-2.4	-6.5	8.5	-10.6
Korea						
Output Growth	7.6	6.9	5.5	9.5	7.9	5.2
Export Growth	18.9	-10.2	-1.2	9.9	10.8	0.7
Malaysia						
Output Growth	7.3	6.7	5.8	6.1	7.9	-1.0
Export Growth	14.5	16.9	0.5	12.9	17.1	-7.3
Philippines						
Output Growth	6.3	3.9	2.9	0.9	-5.7	-4.0
Export Grwoth	4.8	-0.2	-8.0	1.8	9.8	-11.6
Thailand						
Output Growth	7.5	6.3	4.1	3.8	6.2	4.0
Export Growth	10.9	-1.9	-2.9	-8.9	13.6	-3.3

(a) *This corresponds to six months LIBOR plus 1 point spread.*

(b) *This is the nominal interest rates minus the wholesale price inflation in the United States.*

Source: International Monetary Fund, International Financial Statistics.

through the inflation tax.[13] Assume that the government is prepared to accommodate higher inflation in response to changes in external debt as follows:

$$\pi = \pi(g + if) = \pi(f); \quad \pi' > 0 \tag{10}$$

where $g = \bar{g}$. Control over the inflation level is achieved through managing the rate of depreciation of the nominal exchange rate. When equation (10) is substituted for the exogenous inflation assumed earlier, the system (9) is transformed to give:

$$\begin{bmatrix} \dot{f} \\ d \\ R \end{bmatrix} = \begin{bmatrix} i-n-\pi'd & -(\pi+n) & -a \\ 0 & 0 & a \\ 0 & s_m-\pi-n & s_m-n-a \end{bmatrix} \begin{bmatrix} f & - & f^* \\ d & - & d^* \\ R & - & R^* \end{bmatrix} \quad (11)$$

The condition for the determinant to be negative is

$$\pi' > \frac{(i-n)\,(-s_m + \pi + n)}{-ds_m} > 0 \quad (12)$$

when i > n.[14] Inequality (12) can be interpreted as the necessary tradeoff between inflation and the fiscal deficit that would make inflation, spending, and reserve targets mutually consistent. Clearly, the higher the interest rate or the lower the growth rate, the greater the required inflation increase per unit increase in the deficit. Also, as the level of inflation rises, the tradeoff becomes increasingly costly.

This type of analysis is particularly relevant for the Philippines experience of 1984-1985. The Philippines was the hardest hit of the East Asian countries. It entered the 1980s with the largest external debt relative to exports, and with the least robust economy. During the 1970s, output growth had been artificially inflated through production behind a highly protective trade and tax regime. At world prices, output growth would have been considerably smaller. Export growth rates are perhaps more indicative of economic performances over this period. The collapse of exports during the 1980s reflects two factors: a downturn in world markets for traditional commodity exports (sugar, coconut, copper) and poor performance in the nontraditional manufactures (semiconductors and garments) because of an appreciating real exchange rate. Government fiscal and monetary policy, however, did not adjust to these changing circumstances. The fiscal deficit actually expanded to bolster faltering growth. Although a contractionary monetary policy was installed, stability was not achieved. As argued above, the counterpart to the domestic credit contraction was a surge in external borrowing, culminating in a foreign-exchange crisis in October 1983. As shown in Table 1, medium- and long-term debt doubled as a percent of GNP between 1980 and 1985.

This analysis suggests that an important factor in the development of the Philippine debt crisis was a fundamental dynamic inconsistency between government spending, inflation, external financing, and foreign exchange reserve targets. Reliance on tight monetary policy to achieve balance of payments equilibrium only made matters worse. In the absence of a fiscal adjustment, the demand for foreign borrowing accelerated. The situation was complicated by the increase in world interest rates, which increased the size of the budget deficit and fostered instability. The crisis was caused by the inability of the government to reduce the fiscal deficit either through higher taxes or lower spending, and their unwillingness to raise revenue initially through an inflation tax. Such measures were especially needed under the new circumstances in the international financial markets.

With $i > n$, in the new steady state, foreign indebtedness and inflation must be higher. If creditors prevent the system from reaching the steady-state debt level, the economy will be unable to obtain the necessary external resources, and it may fall into an external financial crisis. At this point, any viable solution requires that the authorities correct the budgetary situation in order to reduce the steady state debt level below the creditors' ceiling. Indeed, the Philippine government embarked on a radical stabilization program in October 1985, featuring a substantial reduction in the fiscal deficit.

Other East Asian countries were also faced with a reversal of the $n > i$ condition, but have managed to avoid debt crises. In some cases, this was because of more favorable initial conditions. Thailand, for example, pursued similar policies to the Philippines during 1981 and 1982: that is, tight money combined with fiscal expansion. As predicted, this led to a rapid growth in external debt, from 25 to 47 percent of GDP between 1980 and 1985. To a large extent, this occurred despite official attempts to reduce public foreign borrowing by financing the fiscal deficit through sales of domestic bonds. In the thin financial markets of Bangkok, this simply pushed the private sector offshore into greater foreign borrowing. Thailand essentially postponed adjustment until the end of 1984.

Two other strategies are visible. In Korea, the government has allowed foreign exchange reserves to fluctuate and has focused instead on explicitly controlling the level of foreign debt. In Malaysia and Indonesia, adjustment has come about through a reduction in fiscal deficits.

The stability properties of these two strategies of adjustments are discussed next.

Lower Government Spending. One option for resolving instability is to reduce real government spending. In most stabilization programs, a cutback in government spending is effected in response to the decline in new foreign borrowing. Indeed, many governments are heavily reliant on external capital inflows to maintain their investment programs. Thus, rather than assuming a fixed level of spending, $g = \bar{g}$, it is assumed instead:

$$g = g(\dot{f}), \quad g' > 0 \tag{13}$$

Substituting (13) into the original system yields

$$\begin{bmatrix} \dot{f} \\ d \\ R \end{bmatrix} = \begin{bmatrix} \frac{i-n}{1-g'} & \frac{-(\pi+n)}{1-g'} & \frac{-a}{1-g'} \\ 0 & 0 & a \\ \frac{(1+s_g)(i-n)g'}{1-g'} & \frac{s_m-(\pi+n)}{1-g'} & \frac{s_m-n-a}{1-g'} \end{bmatrix} \begin{bmatrix} f - f^* \\ d - d^* \\ R - R^* \end{bmatrix} \tag{14}$$

The key stability condition can be derived as:

$$\frac{-s_m-(\pi+n)}{(\pi+n)(1+s_m)-s_g} > g' > 1 \tag{15}$$

Inequality (15) gives the required change in government spending in response to changes in foreign borrowing.

Two properties are worth noting. First, stability requires that government spending be reduced by more than the reduction of net foreign inflows. As the latter can drop very sharply as in a debt crisis, stability requires a more than proportionate cut in government expenditures. In the Philippines, for example, the government deficit by 1985 was reduced to 1.8 percent of GNP from 4.0 percent in 1981, while public net foreign inflows fell from 2.0 to -0.2 percent in these years, respectively. This is approximately a one-for-one reduction, perhaps not quite sufficient to restore stability.

In Indonesia, control over the public deficit has been a centerpiece of the adjustment strategy. The deficit in Indonesia has been steadily reduced in the 1980s despite falling oil revenues. In 1985, the national government deficit stood at 1.4 percent of GDP. In Malaysia, the budget deficit has also been cut, although it remains high by the standards of East Asian countries. However, deficits have recently begun to rise again, primarily as a result of falling oil prices and a rising domestic and foreign debt service burden. Malaysia does not appear to have successfully adjusted yet. Unless the fiscal deficit is brought under control, or growth picks up to a level above the world interest rate, the future could bring either inflation or an external debt crisis.

The second notable feature of inequality (15) is that government spending should not be cut too far. That is, there is also an upper bound on g′. This stems from the basic fiscal balance. If g is reduced below $\dot{f}$ by too large an amount, then net domestic credit will be excessively tightened and reserves will tend to increase without bound. Thus, while the debt problem will be resolved, macroeconomic balance will not be attained as the country builds up foreign assets too rapidly. Indeed, although they started at an extremely low level, reserves in the Philippines have grown by some 3 percent of GDP during both 1985 and 1986. As a result, g in 1987 has expanded again, seeking a proper balance. Note that the growth rate of GDP has been treated as exogenous in (15). If n were also to depend positively on g, then the potential decreases for using a cutback in g to stabilize foreign debt and the rest of the macroeconomy, because as the deficit declines, growth would decline and seigniorage would fall.

A Foreign Debt Target. An obvious solution to accelerating foreign indebtedness is to stipulate a foreign debt target and to adjust new foreign borrowing to achieve this target. Let $f^* = \bar{f}$ replace $R^* = \bar{R}$ in the system given by (9). Accordingly, one must replace (8) by

$$\dot{f} = a(\bar{f} - f) \qquad (16)$$

Equation (16) says that if the external debt/GNP ratio is below its long-run target, then net borrowing is positive, and vice versa. Adoption of equation (16) clearly ensures that debt will always tend to its equilibrium level. What is of interest here is whether this ensures stability of the rest of the system. Using (16), (6), and (7) we obtain

$$\begin{bmatrix} \dot{f} \\ d \\ R \end{bmatrix} = \begin{bmatrix} -a & 0 & 0 \\ i-n+a & -(\pi+n) & 0 \\ -a-(i-n) & s_m & s_m-n \end{bmatrix} \begin{bmatrix} f - f^* \\ d - d^* \\ R - R^* \end{bmatrix} \qquad (17)$$

This system is unambiguously stable, since $a(\pi + n)(s_m - n) < 0$. It permits the authorities to hit any foreign debt target, but in so doing, the composition of money between net domestic credit and net foreign assets of the central bank must be endogenously determined.

If foreign borrowing is predetermined as in equation (16), the change in net domestic credit will be driven exclusively by the need for budget deficit financing, and the change in reserves will respond to the current account and capital account positions. That is to say, choice of a foreign debt target requires relaxation of the choice of a foreign reserve target. Indeed, as Table 2 shows, Korea, which seems to have adopted an explicit foreign debt target, operates with an extremely low reserves/imports ratio.

Of all the East Asian countries, Korea apparently gives least weight to maintaining high reserves.

There are several advantages to choosing a foreign debt target over a reserves target. First, as shown in equation (17), it ensures stability, even with an arbitrary choice of government spending and inflation. Second, a suitable choice of foreign debt target can be made to fall within the limits set by external creditors. It is now recognized that credit rationing is an appropriate mechanism to deal with the risk of debt repudiation (Eaton and Gersovitz, 1981), in international lending as well as in domestic banking. Both lenders and borrowers would, therefore, gain from a mutual agreement on a long-run debt target.

On the other hand, the disadvantage of a foreign debt target is that it precludes control over foreign reserves if spending and inflation are fixed. The magnitude of domestic credit must be such that seigniorage covers the budget deficit. Real money balances will be set to ensure balance of payments equilibrium. The level of reserves, $R = m-d$, is therefore a residual, and in fact may not necessarily be positive.[15] Furthermore, the higher the debt target, the lower will be the steady-state reserve level. Thus, care must be taken in setting the debt target within a feasible range.

POLICY INFERENCES

The analytical framework developed above can be used to illustrate the impact of policy issues currently of concern in the region. Three issues are discussed: the swapping of debt for equity; the substitution of domestic debt for foreign debt; and the sterilization of rising foreign exchange reserves.

Debt/Equity Swaps

Debt/equity swap mechanisms have become popular among high debt countries. The Philippines has a formal arrangement through which investors can obtain domestic equity by purchasing foreign debt at a discount on the face value of the debt (less transaction fees), which is equivalent to obtaining the equity at a preferential exchange rate. Other countries (Korea and Malaysia, for example) have also actively pursued a substitution of debt for equity through the initiation of equity funds.

In the framework developed in this chapter, equity is not included and the only domestic asset is domestic money. Debt for cash swaps have similar financial properties.

Consider a situation, such as in the Philippines right now, in which a country loses its access to the international capital markets and has a large stock of public debt. One way to reestablish its ability to borrow abroad is to reduce the stock of foreign debt by offering to pay back part of it with domestic currency. For simplicity, assume that the debt is purchased at a discount with dollars held abroad by domestic residents. The debt is then presented to the central bank, which issues domestic currency to the investor and retires the external obligation. As a result of this transaction the stock of government foreign debt falls while domestic credit and the money supply increase. In this scenario, however, there is initially no net effect on the balance of payments, as claims on foreigners and liabilities to foreigners are reduced by the same amount. The future impact on the balance of payments depends on the relative strength of two effects which work in opposite directions. On the one hand, there will be smaller interest payments because of the lower debt stock, which helps to improve the balance of payments; on the other hand, larger real money balances will increase aggregate expenditure, leading to higher prices of domestic goods and to an appreciation of the real exchange rate, contributing to a deterioration in the current account. What is important to note, however, is that to the extent that the swap is not accompanied by a correction in the domestic policies, it only changes the *initial conditions* of the system. The long run steady-state values of d, f, and R remain the same. So do the conditions for stability. Thus, in this case a debt/equity swap can only be considered a short-term solution for a debt crisis. It neither removes instability, nor does it lower steady-state debt below a ceiling imposed by lenders. At best, it postpones the inevitable for a brief period. For a swap to provide more lasting relief, it must be accompanied by an improvement in the underlying policies.

One problem with debt/cash swaps is that they produce an initial increase in the domestic money supply and hence in prices of nontraded goods. When there is a market for government bonds, the monetary authorities can reduce the monetization effect of this transaction through open-market sales of these bonds. However, in countries such as the Philippines, with less than fully developed capital markets, this transaction is likely to produce significant upward pressure on the domestic real interest rate. In addition, when the cost of borrowing in the domestic market is higher than the cost of borrowing abroad, the swap of domestic for foreign debt increases total government interest payments thus increasing future budget deficits. These side effects would further exacerbate instability problems.

Substitution of Domestic Debt for Foreign Debt

Many governments have sought to avoid the dangers of inflation or of excess foreign indebtedness by financing public deficits through the issuance of domestic bonds. Although this model does not explicitly incorporate domestic debt, the outcome of such a system can be conjectured. First consider a situation where the domestic interest rate is controlled by the monetary authorities and is set equal to the foreign interest rate, both expressed in terms of tradables. If domestic debt is issued at the prevailing interest rate, then the dynamics of the government budget equation are unaffected; f must simply be reinterpreted as total debt. At the same time, because interest rates are fixed, domestic saving and investment stay the same. Hence, the balance of payments equation is also unchanged, with f now representing public and private foreign borrowing. In this case, public domestic borrowing simply crowds out private sector domestic borrowing and forces the private sector to borrow offshore. National foreign indebtedness remains the same, and the conditions under which a debt crisis could occur are unaltered.

In practice, the government does not offer bonds at market-equivalent interest rates. In most cases, the government bond market is very thin. To all intents and purposes, these bonds are like private placements at predetermined interest rates with captive institutions. In these schemes, commercial banks, social security agencies, pension plans, and insurance companies are requested to hold a certain negotiated amount of public debt.

Malaysia offers an example of such a scheme, where the Employee Provident Fund (EPF) finances the public deficit in amounts approximately equal to 8 percent of GNP. The interest rate charged the government by the EPF is much below the foreign interest rate. Furthermore, it should be noted that the private sector in Malaysia runs a very sizeable surplus of savings over investment. Government borrowing from the EPF then does not force additional private foreign borrowing, but substitutes for private foreign asset accumulation. Typically, one would expect the return on foreign assets to be below the government cost of borrowing from abroad. In this case, government domestic borrowing improves national welfare. Moreover, insofar as public foreign borrowing is still the marginal source of funds for the public sector, the stability criterion remains unaffected. The process of inframarginal borrowing at low domestic interest rates slows down the process of explosive fiscal deficits, but does not alter the long-run trend. Malaysia must still adjust in the future, either through inflation, lower government expenditure, or higher fiscal revenues. The last represents the least costly form of adjustment for which the country can hope. It may occur automatically if oil prices improve.

The case of Thailand is somewhat different. Since 1980, government has attempted to stabilize foreign debt accumulation by financing public deficits through domestic bond sales. In Thailand, however, there are no cheap, captive sources of domestic funds. The government offered financial institutions high real interest rates on domestic debt (about 10 percent in terms of tradables) in part to encourage the development of a secondary market in domestic debt. This was higher than the equivalent interest rate on foreign debt of about 6 percent in real terms. Furthermore, as financial institutions increased their portfolio share of government debt, they reduced lending to the private sector. The latter turned to offshore sources to finance investments. The terms that were available to private borrowers, however, were typically worse than those offered to the government. Thus, both the balance of payments and the budget deficit deteriorated. Rather than stabilizing debt accumulation, government debt management exacerbated the problem.

Thailand has nevertheless been able to avoid a crisis situation in part because of an initially low stock of debt and in part because of successful economic growth. Recent real growth in exports at the double-digit level may have permitted Thailand to regain stability by once more restoring $n > i$. This is in sharp contrast to Malaysia, where growth is flat. However, stability cannot be ascribed in either case to the official policy of substituting domestic for foreign debt.

Dealing with Current Account Surpluses

Some countries of the Pacific Basin are now facing a problem somewhat unusual for developing countries: they have large current account surpluses. Taiwan, certainly the most extreme example, had surpluses of US$9.8 billion in 1985 and US$12 billion in 1986. As a result, Taiwan now holds above 50 billions of international reserves, the equivalent of one and a half years of imports. During 1986, Korea also experienced a large current account surplus, estimated at US$4 billion, but it avoided the accumulation of reserves through repayment of part of its foreign debt.

Current account surpluses could create problems for policymaking on two grounds. First, when they are not sterilized, there is an increase in the money supply that increases aggregate expenditure and creates inflationary pressures in the market for nontradable goods. This also leads to a real appreciation of the exchange rate and could damage growth prospects in the critical tradable sectors of these economies. Second, if the surpluses are sterilized through open-market sales of government bonds, there will be upward pressure on the domestic interest rate. In the presence of higher domestic interest rates firms will start to borrow abroad. There will be capital inflows, leading to further increases in the money supply.

One possible way to overcome the undesirable monetary effects of a current account surplus is to induce capital outflows of a similar magnitude. In this model, this corresponds to the case considered in which the government has a foreign debt target. If the government lowers the target, the immediate impact, as is clear from equation (17), is that reserves fall as capital flows out and debt is run down to its new equilibrium level. However, when foreign debt has been brought down, government interest obligations also decline. There is a lower demand for domestic credit to finance the budget deficit. This, in turn, has repercussions on the trade balance. The trade surplus grows in response to tight domestic credit; meanwhile, foreign interest payments also decline, adding further to the current account surplus. Reserves, therefore, start to accumulate again. To restore equilibrium in the balance of payments, an appreciation of the real exchange rate is necessary. In the new steady state, with a lower external debt, reserves are actually *higher* than before. Thus, a policy of using reserves to repay external debt will result in lower reserve levels in the short run but higher reserves in the long run.

Two further points need clarification. First, for those countries such as Taiwan that have a very small foreign debt, repayment of foreign obligations should be interpreted as an ongoing process which may conclude with the country becoming a net creditor. Second, current account surpluses and reserve accumulation may be transitory phenomena which will disappear once the economy reaches stationary equilibrium. In the long run, the problems of inflation, exchange rate appreciation, and excess reserve accumulation may never actually come to pass. For example, governments could, through changing their policy stance, alter the adjustment of the economy and the future long-run steady state. One possibility would be the adoption of expansionary fiscal policy, which would increase aggregate demand and lead to a further expansion in domestic credit (through the budget constraint). The resulting outcome would be a deterioration in the current account and lower reserves in the stationary equilibrium. The only drawback of this policy is that it still puts pressure on domestic prices and leads to an appreciation of the real exchange rate. The monetary authorities, however, can avoid the inflationary scenario through an appreciation of the nominal exchange rate. Thus, expansionary fiscal policy and an appreciation of the nominal exchange rate seems to be a reasonable response to excess reserves. This is hardly surprising, after all, as it is simply the reverse of the standard recommendation that countries experiencing balance of payments problems tighten fiscal policy and depreciate the exchange rate.

SUMMARY

This chapter has analyzed the effects of alternative monetary rules on foreign debt and the balance of payments. A simple analytical macroeconomic framework has been used to capture the most relevant factors affecting the developing countries of the Pacific Basin. Foreign borrowing is undertaken by the government, the exchange rate is pegged, and there are no domestic bonds. Budget deficits are financed through foreign debt and central bank credit.

The basic model highlights the relationship between monetary policy and foreign debt. For a given budget deficit, tighter monetary policy leads to an increase in foreign borrowing and to an improvement in the balance of payments.

The model is particularly useful to discuss the existence of overborrowing and to provide alternative explanations of the debt crisis. It is argued that when countries target monetary policy toward external balance, as suggested by Mundell (1962), there will be a period during which the economies will borrow in the international markets despite holding international reserves above their desired level. Regarding the debt crisis, the framework here provides two main reasons for its development: high world interest rates, and an inconsistency between fiscal, monetary, and exchange rate policies. Reducing the budget deficits and increasing the revenue from the inflation tax are considered as possible solutions for countries with very high foreign debt.

Also discussed are policy issues that arise regarding debt to equity swaps, the substitution of domestic for foreign debt, and large current account surpluses. In recent years, an increasing number of countries have developed institutional mechanisms to encourage debt/equity swaps. This model suggets that in the absence of other policy changes, debt/equity swaps do not provide a feasible long-run solution to the debt crisis. When the swap is entirely monetized, it leads to increases in the rate of inflation and to a deterioration in the trade balance and most likely also in the balance of payments. If the government attempts to sterilize the money supply growth through open-market operations, it is likely to face an increase in interest rates and hence in the budget deficit. Finally, in the absence of any substantive corrections in fundamental domestic policies, the swap will only have a transitory effect on foreign indebtedness.

The large current account surpluses recently experienced in some of these countries has become a matter of concern. In the absence of sterilization or offsetting capital outflows, the countries have experienced a significant increase in the money supply and, with it, inflationary pressures. Central bank sterilization is a dangerous game because it would

lead to high real interest rates, and imperil growth. While capital outflows, either through loans to foreigners or repayment of outstanding debt, provide a short-term solution to reserve accumulation, in the long run they will lead to increasing current account surpluses and to growing pressure on reserves and the exchange rate. Instead, these countries should expand fiscal policy and appreciate the nominal exchange rate.

NOTES

We are grateful to Willem Buiter, Bill Easterly, Ruben Lamdani, Johannes Linn, Ramon Moreno, Nicholas Sargen, and Hang-Sheng Cheng for useful comments on an earlier draft.

1. When the central bank pegs the exchange rate, money supply is endogenous. The central bank, though, still keeps control over the expansion of domestic credit. What we term monetary policy in this chapter is in fact the central bank's target on domestic credit. See Guitian (1973).

2. In common parlance, "sustainability" often seems to refer to the ability of governments to maintain current account or budget deficits at existing levels into the distant future. This is, of course, a rather problematic definition because there is no reason to assume that it is *planned* to keep the deficits at such targets. A correspondence between stability of a system under given rules and "sustainability" is somewhat more precise. In this sense our discussion is analogous to Sargent and Wallace (1981).

3. However, a significant volume of funds has been obtained from official multilateral and bilateral sources. These have not carried concessional terms.

4. This assumption can easily be relaxed. The key is the assumption of a fixed proportion of public spending on each sector.

5. Implicitly we are assuming a Cambridge-type demand-for-money function of the form $m^d = dE$ where E represents private spending. This equation implies a positive relationship between the stock of money and expenditure.

6. For stability the following conditions must also be satisfied:

$$tr(A) = (i-n) - a < 0$$

$$\sum_i A_{ii} = -(i-n)a - a(s_m - \pi - n) > 0$$

where A is the matrix of partial derivatives in equation (9). Thus $i - n < 0$ is a necessary and sufficient condition for stability.

7. Simonsen looks at the balance payments and argues that the growth of exports must exceed the interest rate. See Simonsen (1985).

8. The long-run equilibrium values of the state variables can be computed as functions of the exogenous parameters by solving (6) – (8) with the left-hand-side variables equal to zero in each case. By construction, equilibrium reserves equal their target level $\bar{R}$. Domestic credit and foreign borrowing can be expressed as

$$d^* = d^*(\overset{(+)}{y_t},\ \overset{(+)}{\bar{g}},\ \overset{(-)}{\bar{R}},\ \overset{(-)}{n},\ \overset{(-)}{\pi})$$

$$f^* = f^*(\overset{(-)}{y_t},\ \overset{(+)}{\bar{g}},\ \overset{(+)}{\bar{R}},\ \overset{?}{n},\ \overset{(-)}{\pi},\ \overset{(+)}{i}) \qquad \text{if } n > i/$$

where the signs above each argument refer to the partial derivative of the function.

9. When $s_m = -a$ this schedule will coincide with the one for external balance. In our example we consider the case in which $-s_m < a$.

10. Accumulating foreign debt to add to reserves is termed overborrowing because there is typically an interest differential between the cost of borrowing and the return on reserves. At the margin, therefore, the country pays this spread without any benefits in the form of an increased inflow of real resources from abroad. In our model the cost of borrowing is i^*, while the return on reserves, for simplicity, was made equal to zero.

11. A good rule of thumb is that international reserves should cover three months of imports. This is consistent with the results obtained in Lizondo and Mathieson (1987).

12. In general terms, we refer to a debt crisis as a sharp contraction in the availability of external financing to a debtor country.

13. Most estimates of money demand indicate that for economies experiencing low to moderate inflation, the value of real inflation tax revenues rises as the level of inflation grows.

14. The necessary and sufficient conditions for stability are:

1) $$i < 2n + \pi' d - s'_m + e$$

2) $$\left(i - n - n'd\right)\left(s_m - n - a\right) - a\left(s_m - \pi - n - \pi' d\right) > 0$$

where the second condition is always satisfied.

15. In what follows, in order to simplify the analysis, we will assume that reserves are always positive.

REFERENCES

Bruno, Michael (1976). "The Two Sector Open Economy and the Real Exchange Rate." *American Economic Review* 66: pp. 566-577.

Cline, William (1983). *International Debt and the Stability of the World Economy.* Washington, D.C.: Institute for International Economics.

Cohen, Daniel (1988). "The Management of the Developing Countries' Debt: Guidelines and Application to Brazil." *The World Bank Economic Review*, Vol. 2, No. 1.

Cooper, Richard and Jeffrey Sachs (1985). "Borrowing Abroad: The Debtors Perspective." In *International Debt and the Developing Countries*, edited by G. Smith and J. Cuddington. Washington, D.C.: The World Bank.

Domar, Eusey (1944). "The Burden of the Debt and the National Income." *American Economic Review* 34 No. 5, pp. 798-827.

Eaton, Jonathan and M. Gersovitz (1981). "Debt with Potential Repudiation: Theoretical and Empirical Analysis." *Review of Economic Studies* 48, pp. 289-309.

Frenkel Jacob and Harry Johnson (1976). *The Monetary Approach to the Balance of Payments.* London: Allen and Unwin.

Guitian, Manuel (1973). "Credit vs. Money as an Instrument of Control." *IMF Staff Papers* 20 No. 3, pp. 785-800.

Ize, Alan and Guillermo Ortiz (1987). "Fiscal Rigidities, Public Debt and Capital Flight." *IMF Staff Papers* 32 No. 2, pp. 311-32.

Khan, Mohsin and Saul Lizondo (1987). "Devaluation, Fiscal Deficits and the Real Exchange Rate." *The World Bank Economic Review* 1, pp. 357-74.

Kouri, Penti (1976). "The Exchange Rate and the Balance of Payments in the Short Run and in the Long Run." *Scandinavia Journal of Economics* 78, pp. 280-304.

Lizondo, Saul and Donald Mathieson (1987). *The Stability of the Demand for International Reserves*, IMF, Mimeo.

Mundell, Robert (1962). "The Appropriate Use of Monetary and Fiscal Policy Under Fixed Exchange Rates." *IMF Staff Papers* 9, pp. 70-79.

Obstfeld, Maurice (1986). "Rational and Self-Fulfilling Balance of Payments Crisis." *American Economic Review* 76, pp. 72-81.

Sargent, Thomas and Neil Wallace (1981). "Some Unpleasant Monetarist Arithmetic." *Federal Reserve Bank of Minneapolis, Quarterly Review* (Fall), pp. 1-17.

Simonsen, Mario H. (1985). "The Developing Country Debt Problems." In *International Debt and the Developing Countries*, edited by G. Smith and J. Cuddington. Washington, D.C.: The World Bank.

Solomon, Robert (1977). "A Perspective on the Debt of Developing Countries." *Brookings Paper on Economic Activity* 2, pp. 479-510.

van Wijnbergen, Sweder (1986). "Fiscal Deficits, Exchange Rate Crisis and Inflation." The World Bank, Mimeo.

APPENDIX

The data presented in Table 3 suggest that the authorities have used domestic credit as a mechanism to achieve their external balance, or foreign exchange reserve, targets. Tight domestic credit limits public and private expenditures and reduces the trade deficit. Thus, the mechanism works primarily through the current account of the balance of payments. Tight domestic credit limits public and private expenditures and reduces the trade deficit. An alternative mechanism would be to adjust public foreign borrowing to ensure that the capital account of the balance of payments is always sufficiently positive to maintain adequate reserves. To test which of these two mechanisms prevailed in actual experience, we regress reserves on domestic credit and foreign debt for each of the five countries included in this study. In these regressions, international reserve and foreign public debt are measured as a ratio to total imports; domestic credit is the ratio of the domestic assets of the central bank to nominal GDP. All the variables are measured in terms of deviations from their trend. We use annual data from 1970 to 1985. The sources are IMF *International Financial Statistics* and the *World Bank Debt Tables*.

We find a negative and statistically significant coefficient on the domestic credit variable in all the five cases. It seems that domestic credit has been an important instrument affecting reserve accumulation. On the other hand, foreign borrowing does not appear to be significant in three of the five cases. Holding domestic credit constant, higher foreign borrowing implies higher government expenditure, but significant changes in reserve.

Appendix Table

$$Res = Q_1\, DC + Q_2\, FD + \varepsilon_t$$

	Q_1	Q_2	R^2	$\bar{R}^2$	DW
Indonesia	-3.49 (-4.15)	0.84 (2.25)	0.66	0.60	1.42
Korea	-2.03 (-4.15)	0.0006 (0.605)	0.33	0.23	1.71
Malaysia	-5.19 (-2.41)	0.17 (1.27)	0.33	0.22	1.33
Philippines	-4.92 (-3.68)	-0.17 (-1.88)	0.58	0.51	1.75
Thailand	-4.88 (-4.37)	0.53 (4.61)	0.64	0.59	1.37

Note: All equations were estimated using OLS except for Indonesia where we corrected for autocorrelation of errors. The t-statistics are in parentheses.

6

Monetary Regimes and Fiscal Deficits: A Comparative Analysis

Donato Masciandaro and Guido Tabellini

In the 1980s, most industrialized countries have experienced large fiscal deficits and rapidly growing public debt. These events are likely to leave a legacy of tight government budget constraints to future fiscal administrations for many years to come.

At the same time, for many countries the 1980s have been years of financial liberalization and reform. A by-product of these reforms is to shift a larger share of the burden of satisfying the intertemporal budget constraint on fiscal policy, away from monetary and regulatory policies. The reforms have the general effect of abrogating hidden and implicit forms of taxation on financial markets, of raising the real cost of deficit financing, and of shrinking the revenue collected through explicit and implicit forms of money seignorage.

Therefore, a tension might develop in the future between the goal of satisfying the government budget constraint and the survival or completion of the financial reforms. This chapter investigates the nature of this potential tension. In particular, it asks whether in the long run financial deregulation and tight monetary policy make the task of correcting the present fiscal imbalances more difficult. This question is addressed in the chapter from two points of view.

From a theoretical point of view, it is argued that the reforms, if credible and long lived, might facilitate the task of reducing fiscal deficits. The thrust of the argument here is that financial deregulation and tight monetary policy enhance the fiscal authorities' incentive for reducing fiscal deficits. This argument is elaborated in the next section with the aid of a game-theoretic model of monetary and fiscal policy coordination. The central result is that the equilibrium size of fiscal deficits depends on the institutional features of the monetary regime. The less accommodative the monetary regime, the smaller is the equilibrium fiscal deficit.

The remainder of the chapter considers, in the light of these theoretical results, some cross-sectional empirical evidence relating fiscal deficits and monetary institutions of different Pacific Basin countries: Australia, Canada, Japan, New Zealand, and the United States. The focus is on the relative degree of independence of the central banks from the fiscal authorities, and the extent to which the monetary and financial systems are geared toward facilitating the financing of fiscal deficits. Moreover, the extent of debt monetization and the size of fiscal deficits in these five countries are quantified and compared. The comparison tends to support the results derived in our model: the countries with more accommodating and captive monetary institutions and with largely monetized public debt also tend to have larger fiscal deficits and a larger stock of public debt outstanding.

THEORY

This section considers a model with the following property: In equilibrium, the intertemporal choices of the fiscal authority (and hence the size of fiscal deficits) depend on the institutional features defining the monetary regime. In particular, the size of fiscal deficits is determined by the "degree of fiscal dominance" of the monetary regime; that is, by the extent to which the burden of satisfying the intertemporal budget constraint falls on monetary rather than on fiscal policy. (See Sargent and Wallace, 1981.)

The key idea is as follows. Money seignorage and regulatory constraints on captive financial institutions are hidden sources of fiscal revenue for the government. Deficit financing is the way in which these implicit taxes are imposed on the economy. A monetary regime that cuts the link between fiscal deficits and (direct or indirect) debt monetization deprives the Treasury of these hidden taxes. But because of that, such a monetary regime also reduces the incentive for the government to run a deficit. In such a non-accommodative regime, a deficit today has to be met with higher explicit taxes or smaller expenditures tomorrow. In other words, a monetary regime that does not automatically provide debt monetization forces the government to fully internalize the political and economic costs of running a budget deficit. To the extent that these costs are taken into account in the fiscal policy decision process, a non-accommodative monetary regime tends to limit the size of budget deficits.

This simple idea (that the method of deficit financing influences the size of budget deficits) is elaborated in the remainder of this section by means of a game theoretic model. The model presumes that monetary and fiscal policies are chosen by two partially decentralized agencies with conflicting objectives. This assumption is strictly appropriate for countries like the United States or West Germany, where the central bank and other regulatory agencies are largely politically and administratively independent of the Treasury. However, the same general concepts and results should be applicable, though less literally, to countries with a much smaller degree of decentralization between monetary and fiscal policies. The model is analyzed and discussed in more detail in Tabellini (1987).

The Model

The model is the simplest possible to analyze the ideas summarized above. In particular, only direct money seignorage (i.e., creation of fiat money) is considered as a source of fiscal revenue associated with monetary policy. No attempt is made to model regulatory constraints on captive financial institutions, or to analyze other fiscal repercussions of monetary policy through its impact on the cost of issuing public debt. However, the nature of the results should extend to much more general settings, even though the analysis would be more complex.

The economy is open to the rest of the world and is a price taker in international capital markets. The only tool of monetary policy is the domestic component of the monetary base. Thus, exchange rates are perfectly flexible. Moreover, purchasing power parity is assumed, so that there is no need to distinguish between the price level and the nominal exchange rate. The time horizon lasts two periods. At the end of the second period, all debt (private or public) has to be repaid.

The private sector consists of a representative consumer who lives two periods and maximizes utility, V:

$$V = Max\left\{ln\, C_1 + \beta\, ln\, C_2 + ln\, m_1 + \beta\, ln\, m_2\right\}, \quad 1 > \beta > 0 \qquad (1)$$

where: $C_i \equiv$ consumption in period i; $m_i \equiv M_i/P_i \equiv$ real money balances held at the end of period i, M_i and P_i being, respectively, nominal money balances and the price level in period i. Real money balances enter the utility function because of the liquidity services that they provide. β is a rate of time discount.

The consumer is endowed with a positive quantity E of real income in each period; this endowment is taxed at the rate τ_i in period i. Moreover, at the beginning of the first period, he also owns a positive quantity of nominal money balances, M_0, and of real government debt, B_0.[1] Finally, the consumer faces a given real interest rate in international capital markets, r, that coincides with his subjective rate of intertemporal preference: $1/(1+r) = \beta$. Under all these assumptions, and denoting the inverse of the gross expected inflation rate in period 2 by $\pi_2^e \equiv P_1/P_2^e$, the consumer's intertemporal budget constraint can be written as:

$$W \equiv E(1-\tau_1) + \beta E(1-\tau_2) + B_0 + \frac{M_0}{P_1}$$

$$\geq C_1 + m_1\left(1-\beta \pi_2^e\right) + \beta C_2 + \beta m_2 \tag{2}$$

where W denotes his lifetime real wealth.

The first order conditions of this simple optimization problem yield the consumer's demand for private consumption and for real money balances in the two periods:

$$C_1 = C_2 = m_2 = \frac{W}{2(1+\beta)},$$

$$m_1 = \frac{W}{2(1+\beta)(1-\beta \pi_2^e)} \tag{3}$$

There are two policymakers: the central bank, which controls the money supply, and the fiscal authority, which sets taxes and public expenditures. These two policymakers are partially decentralized. In some of the countries considered in the following sections, the central bank is really an agency of the Treasury, with little independence to pursue its own goals. This lack of independence is modeled here as an explicit constraint on monetary policy choices in the second period of the game, rather than as affecting the central bank preferences directly. Thus, the two policymakers are assumed to pursue different goals. This diversity is not meant to reflect the independence of the monetary from the fiscal authorities, but rather the fact that the individuals representing these two bodies face different political incentives. For simplicity, this diversity in the final goals of the two policymakers is assumed to be extreme. Specifically, the fiscal authority only cares about public expenditure, G, and maximizes:

$$U = Max\left\{ln\,G_1 + \beta\, ln\,G_2\right\} \tag{4}$$

The central bank, by contrast, only cares about the private sector and totally disregards public consumption. Making a less extreme hypothesis about the divergence of preferences between the two policymakers would complicate the notation and the algebra but would not alter the nature of the results in any respect.

The action of the two policymakers is constrained by the intertemporal government budget constraint:

$$G_1 + B_0 \le \tau_1 E + \beta B + \frac{M_1}{P_1} - \frac{M_0}{P_1}$$

$$G_2 + B \le \tau_2 E + \frac{M_2}{P_2} - \frac{M_1}{P_2} \tag{5}$$

where B is the (real) public debt issued by the government in period 1 that has to be repaid in full at the end of period 2. Both τ_1 and τ_2 are given and equal to each other.[2]

To simplify the notation, the excess of public expenditure over tax revenue is denoted by $g_i = G_i - \tau_i E$. Thus, g_i is the fiscal deficit net of interest payments in period i. The fiscal authority chooses g_i and the central bank chooses M_i, $i = 1,2$.

The imposition of the government budget constraint implies the loss of one degree of freedom in setting monetary and fiscal policies. Who is going to bear the residual burden of satisfying this constraint? Obviously, there is no general answer; it depends on the institutional setup.[3] In this model, it is assumed that a fraction $(1-\theta)$ of the burden of satisfying the budget constraint falls on the fiscal authority, and that the remaining fraction θ falls on the central bank. Thus, in the second period of the game, g_2 and M_2 are constrained by:

$$g_2 \le -(1-\theta)B$$

$$\frac{M_2}{P_2} - \frac{M_1}{P_2} \le \theta B \tag{6}$$

If $\theta = 1$, a regime exists where fiscal policy is dominant and the burden of repaying the debt falls entirely on monetary policy. This regime resembles the one analyzed by Bryant and Wallace (1979); it corresponds to a situation in which the fiscal authority acts as the Stackelberg leader and has the first move in each period of the game. If $\theta = 0$, the opposite extreme exists -- a regime where monetary policy is dominant and the burden of repaying the debt falls exclusively on fiscal policy. This regime would arise if the central bank could act as the Stackelberg leader and could precommit to a course of action for the current period before fiscal policy has been chosen. Intermediate regimes correspond to values of θ between 0 and 1. Throughout the paper, θ is referred to as the "degree of fiscal dominance." Equivalently, θ could be interpreted as an indicator of central bank independence from the fiscal authority. If $\theta = 1$, the central bank is completely subordinated to the fiscal needs of the government. Conversely, if $\theta = 0$, the central bank is free to pursue its own monetary goals. However, the term "central bank independence" is somewhat ambiguous and often means different things to different people. For this reason, throughout this chapter only the more neutral and precise concept of "degree of fiscal dominance" of the monetary regime is used.

In the real world, θ is determined by factors beyond the control of policymakers, or at least by factors that the policymakers can change only indirectly and in the very long run, such as institutions, intellectual climate, and political variables. The next section seeks to assess the relative degree of fiscal dominance in five Pacific Basin industrialized countries by comparing their monetary institutions. First, an investigation of how the equilibrium rate of inflation and the size of fiscal deficits depend on θ in this model is in order.

The Macroeconomic Equilibrium

The demand for real money balances in period 1, and hence the price level in that same period, depend on expected future inflation. Under rational expectations, expected future inflation is determined by the equilibrium condition of the money market in period 2. In equilibrium, (6) will hold as equality. Hence, from (6) and (3):

$$m_2 = \theta B + m_1 \pi_2 = \theta B + \frac{m_2 \pi_2}{\left[1 - \beta \pi_2^e\right]} \tag{7}$$

Equating π_2 and π_2^e, and using (3) again, equation (7) can be solved for the actual and expected inverse of the inflation rate:

$$\pi_2 = \pi_2^e = \frac{W - 2\theta(1+\beta)B}{[W - 2\theta\beta B](1+\beta)} \tag{8}$$

By taking partial derivatives of (8), it can be shown that π_2 is increasing in W and decreasing in θ and (if $\theta > 0$) in B. Thus a higher debt to be repaid, B, or a higher proportion of debt to be monetized in the second period, θ, tend to raise the inflation rate in that period. However, higher private real wealth, W, by increasing the demand for real balances in period 2, has the opposite effect of reducing the inflation rate in period 2.

The price level in period 1, P_1, is also determined by the equilibrium condition in the money market:

$$\frac{1}{P_1} = \frac{m_1}{M_1} = \frac{W}{2(1+\beta)(1-\beta\pi_2^e)M_1} \tag{9}$$

Defining $\mu = M_1/M_0$ as the gross rate of growth of money supply in period 1, recalling from (2) that $W = B_0 + M_0/P_1$, and using (8) to form π_2^e, we can solve (9) for the inverse of the price level:

$$\frac{1}{P_1} = \frac{2B_0 - \theta\beta B}{2(2\mu-1)M_0} \tag{10}$$

Equation (10) implies:

Proposition 1 P_1 *is increasing in* μ *and* B. *The effect of* B *on* P_1 *is proportional to* θ.

That is, an expansionary monetary policy (a larger μ) increases prices in the current period. Also, issuing more public debt, B, is inflationary in the current period, since the private sector realizes that issuing debt leads to future inflation and hence reduces real money demand today. Moreover, the larger the degree of fiscal dominance (the larger is θ), the more inflationary are the consequences of issuing public debt. In the limit, if monetary policy is dominant (that is, if $\theta = 0$), issuing debt has no effect on prices, since the debt will not be monetized at all in the future. This result suggests an empirical conjecture, namely, that the association between fiscal deficits and inflation should be more marked in those countries with a higher degree of fiscal dominance. Protopapadakis and Siegel (1986), among others, provide empirical evidence supporting this result.

Fiscal Deficit and Financial Reforms

It is now possible to evaluate the effects of changing θ on the behavior of the fiscal authorities and on the players' welfare in a feedback-Nash equilibrium. In such an equilibrium, the two policymakers move simultaneously in each period and take into account the effect of the state variable on the outcome of the game in the second period (i.e., they take into account equations (6) and (8)). This is the appropriate solution concept, given that neither player can precommit to a course of action forever.[4]

Using equation (10), the government budget constraint in period 1 -- equation (5) -- can be written as:

$$B = g_1 \phi(\mu, \theta) + \Omega(\mu, \theta) \tag{11}$$

where

$$\phi(\mu, \theta) = \frac{4\mu - 2}{\beta[(4-\theta)\mu + \theta - 2]}$$

$$\Omega(\mu, \theta) = \frac{2B_0}{\beta[(4-\theta)\mu + \theta - 2]} \tag{12}$$

The fiscal authority maximizes (4) with respect to g_1 and B, subject to (6), (11), and (12), and taking current monetary policy, μ, as given. Its first order conditions imply:

$$\frac{1}{G_1} \geq \frac{\beta(1-\theta)\,\phi(\mu, \theta)}{G_2} \tag{13}$$

with an equal sign in an interior optimum. The left hand side of (13) is the marginal utility of public expenditures in the current period. The right hand side is the marginal cost of financing it by issuing public debt. This cost is given by the marginal disutility of the future reduction in expenditures necessary to repay the debt, under the existing monetary regime, as defined by θ.

Monetary policy is chosen by the central bank in order to maximize the private sector welfare, subject to the private sector first order conditions (equation (3)), the equilibrium condition in the money market (equations (8) and (10)), the government budget constraints (equations (5) and (6)), and for a given value of the fiscal policy variable, g_1. Tabellini (1987) characterizes more precisely the central bank optimization problem and applies the envelope theorem to prove that, under plausible conditions, the central bank welfare (and hence the private sector welfare under the hypothesis of this model) is a monotonically decreasing function of θ. That is, the more dominant monetary policy is, the better off the central bank is. Not surprisingly, given the assumptions of the model, the optimal monetary arrangement for the private sector's welfare has the central bank completely shielded from fiscal pressures (that is, the optimal value of θ is 0).

This result would survive several generalizations of the underlying model, as long as one retains the assumptions that the rate of inflation desired by the central bank is closer to the social optimum than the inflation rate the Treasury would choose.

Finally, applying the implicit function theorem to (13) and to the central bank first order conditions, it is possible to prove that, for large values of B_0 and for θ not too close to 1:

Proposition 2 The fiscal deficit net of interest payments in period 1, g_1, is an increasing function of θ.

That is, a monetary regime with a low degree of fiscal dominance, θ, forces the fiscal authority to limit the size of the budget deficit in period 1. The intuition is straightforward. The cost of issuing public debt is mitigated by its future monetization. A monetary regime that cuts the link between public debt and subsequent monetization tends to raise the marginal cost of running a fiscal deficit. In the limit, if monetary policy is dominant and money creation is absolutely independent of the stock of public debt in circulation (that is, if $\theta = 0$), equation (13) reduces to $G_1 = G_2$, in which case the fiscal authority finds it optimal to balance the budget in both periods.

Further Remarks

These results seem in strident contrast with two related common sense considerations that recur in many public policy discussions of how to finance fiscal deficits: first, that fiscal deficits are *de facto* determined independently of the stance of monetary policy; and second, that their size is purely the macroscopic consequence of several myopic political decisions, rather than being the deliberate and strategic choice of a rational agency.

The first consideration, however, reflects a confusion between monetary policy actions and monetary regimes. In this model, it is true that fiscal policy is not affected by current monetary policy. The crucial determinant of fiscal policy is the monetary regime, that is, the link between current deficits and future monetization. This link does not depend on the good will (or bad will) of the central bank. It is determined exclusively by factors that the monetary authority controls only indirectly and in the very long run, such as institutions, political constraints, and intellectual climate. The analytical results of this section therefore should not be interpreted as an argument in favor of more restrictive monetary policies within the current institutional setup. Such a policy choice would merely substitute less monetization today for even more monetization in the future, as in the model of Sargent and Wallace (1981). The results may, however, argue in favor of monetary regimes with a low degree of fiscal dominance. Such monetary regimes credibly constrain future debt monetization, and it is this fact that decreases the incentives of the fiscal authority to run a deficit.

The second objection to the approach taken in this section is more damaging and more difficult to handle. But even if fiscal policy decisions are not taken by a rational player, the fact that monetary regimes with a low degree of fiscal dominance may tend to increase the cost of running a fiscal deficit remains valid. All that is necessary for the validity of the argument then is that, at some stage of the political decision process, these costs be taken into account.

MONETARY REGIMES AND FISCAL DOMINANCE

Having identified the degree of fiscal dominance of the monetary regime as one of the crucial determinants of budget deficits and of the equilibrium rate of inflation, we now seek to assess the actual relative degree of fiscal dominance in five industrialized countries in the Pacific Basin region: Australia, Canada, Japan, New Zealand, and the United States.

We focus on two aspects of the regime that determine the institutional position of the central bank: the "political" aspect, determined by the legislative and administrative rules concerning the appointment and the composition of the members of the central bank governing bodies, and their relationship with the legislature and the government; and the "economic" aspect, determined by the involvement of the monetary authorities in the process of deficit financing, by the tools of monetary policy that are regularly used, and by the nature and fiscal repercussions of the regulatory controls on the financial system. These two aspects jointly determine the degree of fiscal dominance.

Obviously, the degree of fiscal dominance of any regime also depends on much more intangible features of the environment, such as the evolution of the institutions over time, the actual performance record of the policymakers themselves, the expectations of the private sector and the public opinion created by the policymakers' past performances, the intellectual and political climate, and so on. Even though these intangible factors change only very slowly over time, they are very difficult to capture in any cross-sectional study.

Political Rules

The political aspect of the monetary regime in the five Pacific Basin countries is presented and compared in Table 1 in terms of the appointment of the Governor and the Members of the Board of the central bank, as well as the reporting relationship of the central bank to the legislature and the government. (See Appendix for details.) These rules define the formal responsibilities of the central bank, and shape the incentives and the constraints of the individuals in charge of the major monetary policy decisions.

Table 1
The Central Bank in the Government Structure

	Australia	Canada	Japan	New Zealand	United States
The Governor					
Appointed by	Gov't	Board	Gov't	Gov't	President
Term (years)	7	7	5	5	4
Reappointability	Yes	Yes	Yes	Yes	Yes
Members of the Board					
Number	9	15	7	9	7
Appointed by	Gov't	Minister of Finance(13)	Gov't	Gov't	President
Term (years)	5	3	4	5	14
Reappointability	Yes	Yes	Yes	Yes	No
Gov't Member	Secretary of Treasury	Deputy Minister of Finance	From two Ministries[a]	Secretary of Treasury	No
Report to Parliament	Annual	On call	On call	Annual	Semi-annual
Relation with Government					
Responsibility	Informing	Consultation	Approval	Approval	Informal Contacts
In Case of Conflict	Gov't directives[b]	Gov't directives[b]	Not possible	Not possible	No provision

(a) *Representatives from the Ministry of Finance and the Ministry of Economic Planning.*

(b) *Informing the legislature.*

In general, one can conjecture that the degree of fiscal dominance tends to be low if the central bank is isolated from the political pressures originating from the Treasury. This is most likely to happen if:

- The Governor and the Board are appointed by self-representatives of the Bank, with the approval of the legislature.
- The Governor is directly responsible to the legislature (rather than to the government) for the conduct of monetary policy.
- The Governor and the Board can be reappointed, with the approval of the legislature.

Conversely, the political pressures originating from the fiscal authorities tend to be reinforced if:

- The government is represented in central bank bodies.
- Legal directives exist that automatically subordinate the central bank's will to that of the government in cases of explicit conflict between them.

Comparing these rules in the five countries suggests that the U.S. Federal Reserve System enjoys more political autonomy from the government than any of the other central banks. Next in line is probably Canada. New Zealand seems to have the least autonomous central bank. Australia and Japan are presumably situated in between Canada and New Zealand.

Financial Relationships

The central question in this regard is the influence of the Treasury in determining how much it can borrow from the central bank. In the limit, if the Treasury has full discretion in determining the monetary financing of the deficit, then the central bank can control the monetary base only through open-market operations in the foreign exchange market and/or the secondary market for public debt. For technical reasons (imperfections in the secondary market for public debt, exchange rate or balance of payments targets), such a situation weakens the capacity of the central bank to control the monetary aggregates. Moreover, under these circumstances, the central bank would find it difficult to resist political pressures to maintain low levels of interest rates or to impose regulatory controls on captive financial institutions, since the level of interest rates is perceived by the public opinion to be determined by monetary actions rather than by the size of fiscal deficits. Hence, a high degree of fiscal dominance exists in a regime in which the Treasury has easy access to direct monetary financing, for at least two reasons: the Treasury directly controls a major determinant of the revenue collected through money seignorage; and the

Treasury's political influence in directing the general thrust of monetary policy is large.

The central bank can extend credit to the government in two ways: through its direct credit facilities; and by buying public debt in the primary market. The first source of credit, where it is available, is designed to help the government to bridge temporary cash shortfalls. The second source enables the central bank to facilitate the issue of government debt. Table 2 compares the legal rules that constrain Treasury access to these two sources of credit in the five countries under examination. (See Appendix for more details.)

Table 2
Treasury Financing through Monetary and Regulatory Measures

	Australia	Canada	Japan	New Zealand	United States
Central Bank					
Direct Credit	Direct placement[a]	Advances[b]	Advances	Overdraft[c]	No
Participation in Primary Issue of Securities	Yes	Yes	Yes	Yes	No
Commercial Banks					
Required Holding of Government Securities	Yes	Yes	Prior to 1980	Prior to 1985	No
Interest Rate Ceilings					
Deposit Rate	Prior to 1984	1972-74	Prior to 1987	Prior to 1984	Prior to 1986
Loan Rate	Prior to 1982	Prior to 1967	No	Prior to 1984	No

(a) *Treasury bills.*

(b) *Not used since the 1960s.*

(c) *Limit of NZ$1 billion.*

The U.S. Federal Reserve System is the only central bank among the five Pacific Basin countries not involved in direct financing of the Treasury in any respect. In the other countries, monetary policy is not always clearly separated from debt management policies. In Canada and Japan, the central bank seems to be less involved in direct deficit financing than in Australia and New Zealand.

The Regulation of Financial Markets

The degree of fiscal dominance of a monetary regime is also determined by the central bank's relationship with the banking system and by the nature of the tools of monetary policy. In particular, several financial regulations have the by-product of facilitating the financing of budget deficits. Thus, other things being equal, the degree of fiscal dominance of the regime tends to be higher the easier it is for the monetary and fiscal authorities to discretionally impose such regulations, and the more frequently they have been imposed. In general, regulatory restrictions on financial institutions, such as credit controls, portfolio constraints, and interest rate ceilings, tend to increase artificially the private sector's demand for government liabilities, and thereby reduce the cost of government borrowing.

Among the five Pacific Basin countries, the United States stands out as the one in which financial market regulation has been both the lightest and the least geared toward the goal of facilitating deficit financing. Among the remaining countries, Canada is the most similar to the United States. Up to 1984, New Zealand had the most heavily regulated markets, but has since undergone drastic deregulation, as has Australia. The same has happened in Japan, though to a much smaller extent.

A Tentative Ranking

It is difficult to quantify the various factors determining the degree of fiscal dominance in a country. Nevertheless, on the basis of the preceding analysis, one can arrive at some tentative ranking of the conditions prevailing in the five Pacific Basin countries during the 1970-1985 period.

Two extremes can be readily identified. The degree of fiscal dominance was clearly the lowest in the United States; the Fed has greater political autonomy than any other country in the group. Its monetary rules prevent any direct financing of the fiscal deficit by the central bank, and its main instruments of monetary control have very limited fiscal repercussions. Even though U.S. financial markets are strictly regulated, the main purpose of this regulation is financial stability, not money seignorage.

At the other extreme, New Zealand was clearly the country with the highest degree of fiscal dominance, at least up to 1984. Its Reserve Bank was the most subordinated to the political will of the government. Moreover, monetary financing of the fiscal deficit was facilitated by both the Treasury's direct access to central bank funds, and, until very recently, by financial regulations.

Between these two extremes lay the remaining monetary regimes. Canada was presumably closer to the low fiscal dominance end, whereas Australia and Japan seem to have leaned more toward the high fiscal dominance end.

According to the theory presented above, therefore, we should expect to find that debt monetization and fiscal deficits tend, on average, to be highest in New Zealand and lowest in the United States.

COMPARISON OF MONETARY AND FISCAL POLICIES

As indicated in Table 3, the fiscal deficits of all countries are larger in the second half of the 1970s than in the first half. For all countries except Australia, the growth of deficits is further accentuated in the 1980s. Table 3 suggests that, at least for some countries, the higher deficits of the 1980s are the result of higher public expenditures. In all countries, public expenditures as a fraction of GDP are larger in the 1980s than in the second half of the 1970s. For the same period, total revenues remain approximately constant as a fraction of GDP, or rise only marginally for some countries.

These common trends however, are associated with some differences across the five countries. Specifically, New Zealand stands out as the country with the largest fiscal deficit and the largest level of public expenditures throughout the time period considered. The total public debt outstanding is also larger in New Zealand than in any country in the sample (Table 3).

These facts are consistent with the results of the monetary regime comparisons presented above: New Zealand also has the monetary regime with the highest degree of fiscal dominance (at least up to 1984). According to these theoretical results, therefore, New Zealand would be expected to have a tendency toward larger deficits and larger public debt outstanding than the other countries in the sample.

Table 3 provides further evidence of this point. The annual average real interest rate on public debt was negative in New Zealand in the three periods 1970-1974, 1975-1979, and 1980-1985. It was also much lower than in all the other countries. This fact presumably reflects the heavy portfolio requirements on New Zealand's financial institutions. New Zealand also had the highest inflation rate. This is consistent with the predictions of the theoretical section. Moreover, the stock of public debt held by New Zealand's monetary sector as a fraction of GDP in 1984 tends to be higher than in most other countries. All these numbers reinforce the result of the preceding institutional comparisons: the degree of fiscal dominance, as

Table 3
Fiscal and Monetary Indicators

	Australia	Canada	Japan	New Zealand	United States
Fiscal Deficit[a]					
Average: 1970-74	0.6	1.4	1.2[b]	2.6	1.3
1975-79	3.8	3.8	4.9[b]	6.7	3.0
1980-85	2.2	5.0	4.9[b]	7.7	4.4
Public Expenditure[c]					
Average: 1975-79	27.0	19.9	15.8	33.8	21.7
1980-85	28.3	22.7	18.2	39.2	24.3
Central Government Debt in 1984[d]					
Total	22.6	38.7	53.8	70.0	36.5
Monetized[e]	--	7.2	24.4	17.2	9.0
Real Interest on Public Debt[f]					
Average: 1970-74	-3.1	-1.4	-4.0	-3.5[g]	-0.4
1975-79	-3.2	-0.1	0.5	-5.1[g]	-1.4
1980-85	3.9	4.4	4.2	-1.2	3.5
Consumer Price Inflation[h]					
Average: 1970-74	8.1	5.9	10.9	8.7	6.1
1975-79	11.6	8.9	7.3	14.3	8.1
1980-85	8.6	7.9	3.6	12.9	8.3

(a) *Percent of GDP, except otherwise noted.*

(b) *Percent of GNP.*

(c) *Percent of GDP.*

(d) *Percent of GDP.*

(e) *Debt held by the central bank and commercial banks.*

(f) *Percent; Treasury bill rate, except otherwise noted.*

(g) *Government bond yield.*

(h) *Percent.*

Sources: International Monetary Fund, Government Financial Statistics; International Monetary Fund, International Financial Statistics; OECD, Japan: Economic Survey.

reflected in the actual behavior of the monetary authorities, was higher in New Zealand than in the remaining countries.

The financial reforms implemented in New Zealand are likely to cause a sharp increase in the marginal cost of government borrowing, precisely because government borrowing was facilitated by the financial regulations that have been removed. This fact will tend to inflate the government budget in the short run. However, the reforms, if credible and long lasting, are also going to reduce the degree of fiscal dominance of New Zealand's monetary regime. Theoretical results and empirical comparisons suggest that this fact is likely to change the incentives of New Zealand's fiscal authorities, and thus will likely bring about smaller budget deficits (not including interest payments). The next few years will tell whether this conjecture will prove to be correct.

The rest of the information contained in Table 3 is more ambiguous and harder to interpret. For instance, Japan monetized public debt to a relatively large extent. At the same time, Japan is also the country with the lowest inflation rate and one of the highest real interest rates, at least in the 1980s. Perhaps this ambiguity of its monetary regime explains why Japan has relatively large fiscal deficit and public debt outstanding.

Finally, the tables reported above indicate that the U.S. monetary and fiscal policies (and particularly its budget deficit) do not differ significantly from those of the other countries in the sample. This is somewhat surprising, given the important differences between the U.S. monetary regime and those of the remaining countries. Alesina and Tabellini (1987) and Persson and Svensson (1987) offer some tentative explanations of why the United States may have chosen a policy of larger fiscal deficits in the 1980s than in previous periods. These explanations stress political institutions (as opposed to monetary institutions) as determinants of budget deficits.

CONCLUDING REMARKS

It has been argued here that the intertemporal choices of the fiscal authorities are influenced by the institutional features of the monetary regime. In particular, they are influenced by the degree of fiscal dominance of the regime; that is, by the extent to which the burden of satisfying the intertemporal government budget constraint falls on monetary rather than on fiscal policy. The higher the degree of fiscal dominance of the regime, the larger the tendency for the government to run a fiscal deficit.

This argument was developed here both from a theoretical point of view and by comparing the fiscal policies pursued in five industrialized countries with different monetary institutions. The empirical evidence lends support to the theoretical results. The country with the highest degree of fiscal dominance in its monetary institutions, New Zealand, is also the country that on average had the largest deficits and largest debts.[5] The obvious future next step in this line of research is to extend the analysis to a larger number of countries. Parkin (1986) examines 12 industrial countries from the same point of view taken in this chapter. His institutional comparisons, however, focus exclusively on what here has been called the "political" aspect of the regime, neglecting the "economic" aspect. His conclusions support the results of our chapter.

NOTES

We wish to thank, without implicating, Hang-Sheng Cheng, Alberto Alesina, Thomas Cargill, and several conference participants for helpful comments on a previous version.

1. The assumption that public debt is indexed to the price level simplifies the analysis but does not affect the results in any respect.

2. Given the government's objective function as in equation (4), if the tax rates were endogenous, then they would be set at 100 percent.

3. Note that this issue is not an artifact of having a finite horizon. It would also arise in an infinite horizon model, as long as the time path of public debt is bounded from above. Specifically, the question that would arise in an infinite horizon version of this same model is: Who will bear the burden of satisfying the budget constraint when the upper bound of public debt is reached? The answer to this question will determine the strategic interaction among the monetary and fiscal authorities throughout the rest of the game, just as in the two-period model analyzed in the text.

4. Because of the feedback nature of the strategies chosen by both players, the equilibrium is subgame perfect and hence *a fortiori* time consistent.

5. It could be argued that New Zealand had more accommodating monetary institutions, and hence a regime with higher fiscal dominance, because it had a larger deficit to be financed, rather than the other way around. However, the accommodating feature of its regime dates back to the 1960s, when fiscal deficits were not such a big problem. Moreover, the financial reforms of 1985 and 1986 which reduced the degree of fiscal dominance have been taken at a time when the problem of deficit financing seemed most pressing.

REFERENCES

Alesina, A. and G. Tabellini (1987). "A Positive Theory of Budget Deficits and Government Debt in a Democracy." NBER Working Paper.

Banker Research Unit (1980). *Banking Structures and Sources of Finance in the Far East.* Financial Times Business Publishing.

Bryant, J. and N. Wallace (1979). "The Inefficiency of Interest Bearing National Debt." *Journal of Political Economy* (April).

Cargill, T.F. (1986). "Financial Reform in the United States and Japan: A Comparative Overview." In *Financial Policy and Reform in Pacific Basin Countries*, edited by Hang-Sheng Cheng. Lexington, Mass.: Lexington Books.

Cargill, T.F., H.S. Cheng, and M.M. Hutchison (1986). "Financial Market Changes and Regulatory Reforms in Pacific Basin Countries: An Overview." In *Financial Policy and Reform in Pacific Basin Countries*, edited by Hang-Sheng Cheng. Lexington, Mass.: Lexington Books.

Cargill, T.F. and S. Royama (forthcoming). *The Transition of Finance in Japan and the United States: A Comparative Perspective.* Hoover Insitution Press.

Carron, A.S. (1986). "Financial Reform in Australia and New Zealand." In *Financial Policy and Reform in Pacific Basin Countries*, edited by Hang-Sheng Cheng. Lexington, Mass.: Lexington Books.

Cheng, H.S.(1986). *Financial Policy and Reform in Pacific Basin Countries*, ed. Lexington, Mass.: Lexington Books.

Cheng, H.S. (1983). "Financial Reform in Australia and New Zealand." *Federal Reserve Bank of San Francisco Economic Review* 1(Winter).

Dean, R.S. (1972). "Papers on Monetary Policy, Credit Creation, Economic Objectives and the Reserve Bank." Research Paper, Reserve Bank of New Zealand.

Dean, R.S. (1986). "Financial Sector Policy Reform: The Case of New Zealand." In *Financial Policy and Reform in Pacific Basin Countries*, edited by Hang-Sheng Cheng. Lexington, Mass.: Lexington Books.

Fair, D. (1980). "Relationships Between Central Banks and Government in the Determination of Monetary Policy." SUERF Working Paper.

Hutchison, M.M. (1986). "Financial Effects of Budget Deficits in the Pacific Basin." In *Financial Policy and Reform in Pacific Basin Countries*, edited by Hang-Sheng Cheng. Lexington, Mass.: Lexington Books.

Mittra, S. (1978). *Central Bank versus Treasury: An International Study.* University Press of Austria.

Nicholl, P.W.E. (1977). "New Zealand Monetary Policy in the 1970s: Analysis and Perspective." Research Paper, Reserve Bank of New Zealand.

OECD (1982). *Budget Financing and Monetary Control.* Monetary Studies Series, Paris.

OECD (1983). *Government Debt Management: Debt Instruments and Selling Techniques*, Committee on Financial Markets.

OECD (1981-1986). *Financial Market Trends*, Paris.

OECD (1986). *Canada*, Economic Surveys Series (March), Paris.

OECD (1986). *Japan*, Economic Surveys Series (November).

OECD (1986). *United States*, Economic Surveys Series (November).

OECD (1987). *Australia*, Economic Surveys Series (March), Paris.

OECD (1987). *New Zealand*, Economic Surveys Series (May).

Parkin, M. (1986). "Domestic Monetary Institutions and Deficits." In *Deficits*, edited by J. Buchanan, C. Rowley and R. Tollison. Oxford, England: Basil Blackwell.

Persson, T. and L. Svensson (1987). "Checks and Balances on the Government Budget." Mimeo, University of Rochester.

Pigott, C. (1983). "Financial Reform in Japan." *Federal Reserve Bank of San Francisco Economic Review* 1 (Winter).

Phillips, M.J. (1986). "Financial Reform: The Australian Experience." In *Financial Policy and Reform in Pacific Basin Countries*, edited by Hang-Sheng Cheng. Lexington, Mass.: Lexington Books.

Protopapadakis, A. and J. Siegel (1986). "Is Money Growth and Inflation Related to Government Deficits? Evidence from Ten Industrialized Economies." Working Paper No. 86-11, University of Pennsylvania, The Wharton School.

Sargent, T. and N. Wallace (1981). "Some Unpleasant Monetarist Arithmetics." *Federal Reserve Bank of Minneapolis Quarterly Review*.

Skanland, H. (1984). *The Central Banks and Political Authorities in Some Industrial Countries*. Oslo: Norges Banks.

Skully, M. T. (1985). *Financial Institutions and Markets in the Southwest Pacific*. London, England: The McMillan Press.

Tabellini, G. (forthcoming). "Monetary and Fiscal Policy Coordination with a High Public Debt." In *Surviving with a High Public Debt: Lessons from the Italian Experience*, edited by F-Giavazzi and L. Spaventa. Cambridge, England: Cambridge University Press.

APPENDIX: MONETARY REGIMES IN FIVE PACIFIC BASIN COUNTRIES

Political[a]

Australia. The presence of the government in the central bank's organizational structure is notable. The governor and the deputy governor are appointed by the government for seven years. The remaining seven board members are similarly appointed, for five years. No more than two of the seven members may be officers of the Reserve Bank or public service employees. All members are eligible for reappointment. Board members are usually selected for their eminence in academic, agricultural, or general business activity. The Secretary of the Treasury is an ex-officio member of the Board. Six members, including the governor or deputy governor, are required for a quorum.

In the conduct of monetary policy, the Reserve Bank is under a legal obligation to keep the government informed of monetary and banking policies. If differences of opinion exist, the government has statutory power, after due process of consultation, to direct the Reserve Bank to carry out a given policy; the Parliament must be informed within 15 days. By law, if a matter cannot be resolved by negotiation between the two authorities, the board would furnish to the Treasury a statement in relation to the matter. The statements of the government and the board are required to be tabled in Parliament. The minister would make a recommendation to the governor-general, who on this basis would decide the matter. In this way, the government assumes responsibility for the decision. Finally, an annual report and a financial statement are presented to both Houses of Parliament. Overall, the monetary action of the Reserve Bank seems to be strongly influenced by the government, directly and indirectly. The relationship of the Bank with Parliament is limited to an informational role.

Canada. The governor of the Bank of Canada is appointed by the directors, with the approval of the government. The term of office is seven years, but is subject to a "good behavior" condition; the governor is eligible for reappointment. The Board of Directors has 15 members: the governor, a senior deputy governor, 12 directors, and the deputy minister of finance (the latter without voting rights). The 12 directors are appointed by the minister of finance with the government's approval, for terms of three years; they may be reappointed. There is a general requirement that the directors be selected from "diversified occupations." The Executive Committee consists of five members of the Board of Directors: the governor, his deputy governor, two directors, and the deputy minister of finance without voting rights.

In its relationships with the government, the board is under a legal obligation to consult regularly with the Department of Finance, and vice versa. Following the forced resignation of the governor of the Bank of Canada in 1961, the result of his pursuing a tight monetary policy in opposition to the government's wishes, the power to issue directives to the Bank in case of conflict was conferred on the minister of finance by the addition of a clause (S14) to the Bank of Canada Act in 1967. Specifically, the minister of finance, with the agreement of the government, may issue directives in matters of monetary policy valid for a limited period of time. Such directives must be published in the Canada Gazette and laid before Parliament within 15 days. This procedure has never been invoked, probably because it would be too costly for the government (from a political point of view) to enter into an explicit conflict with the central bank. Finally, the governor is frequently directly asked to appear before committees of both the House of Commons and the Senate to explain and defend his policies. Other witnesses may be summoned to verify his evidence. This procedure can clarify the respective positions of the government and the central bank in case of conflict, and eventually reinforce the monetary priorities.

Japan. The governing bodies of the Bank of Japan are the Executive Board and the Policy Board. Even though the latter is the formal policymaking entity of the Bank, in practice it is the Executive Board that has the major responsibility for the formulation of monetary policy. The Executive Board consists of the governor, the vice governor, and several executive directors. The governor is appointed by the cabinet for a term of five years and may be reappointed. The vice governor and the executive directors are selected by the governor, but are subject to the approval of the minister of finance. The Policy Board consists of seven members; two are representatives of the Ministries of Economic Planning and Finance. The remaining members must consist of two with financial experience, one with industrial experience, and one with agricultural experience. They are appointed by the cabinet with the consent of both houses of the Diet for four-year terms. They may be reappointed. The two government representatives on the Board have no voting rights, and Board decisions are taken by a simple majority.

The Bank of Japan is subject to the general directions of the government. Any change in banks' reserve ratios requires approval of the minister of finance. The discount rate policy and the open market operations are independently determined. In practice, the minister of finance is likely to exercise a strong influence on all policy aspects. No conflict between the two authorities is likely to arise, because the government has complete authority over the central bank. The central bank law has no explicit provisions to prevent or solve such conflicts. This tends to increase the degree of fiscal dominance.

The government can be called directly to explain the conduct of monetary policy to the Diet. The Board must also submit an annual report on the state of financial markets and on the policies implemented by the Bank.

New Zealand. The governor of the Reserve Bank of New Zealand is appointed by the governor general upon recommendation of the minister of finance, for a term of five years. He is eligible for reappointment. The deputy governor and seven directors are similarly appointed. Appointments are intended to reflect a diversity of interests, including industrial or commercial experience. The Secretary of the Treasury is a member of the Board with voting right. Since decisions are taken by consensus, the Treasury has a vote. Moreover, the monetary actions may be subject to directions of the minister of finance; the Bank has no independence in the policy area and is required by its statute to support the monetary policy of the government. The conflict between the two authorities is unlikely to arise because the government has complete authority over the central bank. There are no provisions in case of conflict. An annual report is submitted to Parliament, but the governor is not examined by Parliament. He is, however, subject to questioning by Treasury officials in private sessions of government committees.

United States. The seven members of the Federal Reserve Board in the United States are appointed by the president, with the approval of the Senate, for staggered fixed terms of 14 years, nonrenewable. The president designates two members of the Board to be chairman and vice chairman for four-year terms, renewable. By tradition, the members of the Board are selected in order to maintain a geographical balance, and both bankers and nonbankers are included. Major monetary policy decisions are made by the Federal Reserve Open Market Committee (FOMC), which consists of the members of the Board, plus the presidents of five regional Reserve Banks who serve one year terms on a rotating basis, except the president of the Federal Reserve Bank of New York who is always present and by tradition is the vice chairman of the FOMC. The chairman of the Board is also the chairman of the FOMC. The decisions of the Board are reached by a simple majority vote.

The government has no formal authority over the Fed. This reinforces the Fed's capacity to pursue its monetary goals in case of conflict with the government. The Congress can issue directives to the Fed Board, and the Fed chairman is required to report twice a year to both houses of Congress on the goals and conduct of monetary policy. This exclusive power of Congress to direct the Fed represents a guarantee for the chairman, and presumably contributes to limiting the overall degree of fiscal dominance.

Economic Aspects: The Central Bank and the Treasury[(b)]

Australia. In Australia government borrowing from the central bank is guaranteed by the issue of "public" Treasury bills, not available for public subscription. No formal ceiling on such borrowing is imposed; however, periodic approval in advance by the executive council is required The central bank may also hold substantial amounts of Treasury notes and bonds.

The Treasury, subject to the approval of the Australian Loan Council (consisting of the prime minister and the six state premieres), is responsible for financing the Commonwealth government's budget. The terms of borrowing by the Commonwealth government are fixed by the Council in the light of market conditions, with advice received from both the Treasury and the Reserve Bank.

Canada. In Canada, government borrowing from the central bank is guaranteed by advances from the Bank of Canada at the bank rate. However, this has not been done since the early 1960s.

The Department of Finance, in collaboration with the Bank of Canada, has responsibility for the Canadian government debt management. The Bank advises the government and administers marketable bond issues, which are allocated to a network of commissioned dealers about seven times a year. The Bank is also prepared to purchase government securities from authorized dealers who agree to repurchase them at a later date.

Japan. The Bank of Japan may acquire substantial amounts of Treasury bills, which are only issued by the minister of finance for cash management purposes. The minister of finance has responsibility for funding the deficit of the central government. The term of issue of public debt instruments, mainly long-term bonds, are negotiated with an underwriting syndicate which normally consists of the commercial banks and securities companies. Short-term Treasury bills provide a residual source of finance for temporary shortfalls of cash within a given fiscal year.

It is specifically mentioned in the central bank law that the monetary authorities may make advances to the government without collateral and may participate in government bond issues. However, the fiscal law prevents the Bank from participating in such issues; in practice the bank's financing of the Treasury is carried out through purchases in the secondary market.

New Zealand. In New Zealand, government borrowing from the central bank is guaranteed by overdraft facilities with current limit of NZ$1 billion. The balance in the overdraft account must be reduced to zero at the end of each financial year. Moreover, the Reserve Bank takes up Treasury bills and government bonds.

United States. In the United States, there is no institutional mechanism for the government to borrow from the Fed. Until June 1981, with a vote of five out of seven governors and under "unusual and exigent" circumstances, the Fed could buy newly issued government securities (up to a ceiling of US$5 billion) for a renewable 30-day period.

The United States Treasury has responsibility for meeting the Federal Government's borrowing needs. Except to the extent that the Fed makes purchases of Treasury debt in the open market, it does not play a direct role in financing the budget deficit. Since 1951, there has been no presumption that the Fed conducts open-market operations with the aim of supporting Treasury debt issues.

Economic Aspects: The Central Bank and Financial Markets[c]

Australia. Banks used to be controlled in their lending, deposit collection, asset holding activities, and in their charges. Many of these controls have been recently abolished. Specifically:

- All deposit banks were subject to lending restrictions, aimed at affecting domestic activity without inducing large swings in interest rates. The restrictions were withdrawn in 1982.
- The major trading banks were subject to the "Liquidity Assets and Government Securities Convention" (LGS). This agreement states that, in return for the trading banks' investing a percentage in specific liquid assets (cash, Treasury bills and notes, and other Commonwealth securities), the Reserve Bank will make a less stringent use of the statutory reserve-deposit system (SRD). This agreement limits the extent to which banks can sell LGS assets to offset tensions on their liquidity. The constraints implicit in this agreement have been substantially relaxed in most recent years.
- The banking law gives the central bank authority, with the approval of the Treasury, to fix the maximum interest rates. In recent times, the central bank has not formally promulgated regulations, but has informed the banks of its goals concerning the rates of interest, following discussions between the central bank and the banks concerned. Prior to 1984, there was a limit on the size and term of wholesale deposits accepted by trading and savings banks. Prior to 1980, retail deposit rates were subject to ceilings set by the authorities. The government still retains controls of interest rates on specific loans.

The SRD system traditionally was the most important instrument of monetary policy implementation. It remains important today, given that the secondary market for public debt is still relatively shallow.

Canada. The central bank has no direct powers through selective credit controls; administrative ceilings or discriminatory controls on certain types of lending have rarely been used in Canada. The portfolio requirements amount to a secondary reserve requirement (excess cash reserves, Treasury bills, and other liquid assets), varying between 0 and 12 percent. In the period 1972-1974, wholesale deposit rates were subject to ceilings set by the authorities. Lending rates were subject to restrictions by the authorities until 1967.

The open-market policy is the most important instrument of the Bank of Canada, in addition to manipulation of the location of government deposits. The Bank is authorized to adjust the proportion of government funds held with the 11 chartered banks rather than with itself. By transferring government deposits to or from the Bank, cash may be withdrawn from or injected into the system in the same way as with open-market operations, but without the same direct impact on securities prices.

In Canada, the central bank determines reserve requirements; they are stable and the law limits how quickly they can be changed. In practice, cash requirements are fixed by law, rather than administratively, and are very rarely changed. Cash reserves and secondary reserves are statutory requirements laid down by the central bank. In monetary policy, the discount policy is of little significance because banks have a traditional inclination not to borrow from the central bank.

Japan. In Japan, there are no explicit or formal investment requirements on financial institutions. There used to be an informal obligation to hold government debt, but this was phased out in the late 1970s and early 1980s.

All institutions used to be subject to interest rates controls, either formally or *de facto*. Now, maximum deposit rates and lending rates of banks and other financial institutions are set by the Temporary Interest Rates Adjustment Law. Within the range stipulated by the law, each bank freely determines the lending rates actually applied. As for deposit rates, guidelines were provided by the central bank. Up to 1978, the wholesale deposit rates were subject to direct nonmarket influence by the authorities. Since 1979, rates on three- to six-month certificates have not been regulated, but controls are imposed on minimum CD size. Rates on large denomination deposits and restrictions on size and maturity of CDs have been liberalized in 1985-1987. The existence of a high degree of regulation of bank interest rates is not conducive to applications of a cash base system of monetary control. Furthermore, the absence of a developed secondary market for public debt has reduced the effectiveness of open-market operations. Under these conditions, the Bank of Japan has continued to resort to the extensive use of direct quantitative ceilings on commercial bank lending. At the same time, steps are being taken toward a more efficient system of monetary control. This is intended to counter disintermediation through financial institutions not covered by the ceilings and other market distortions caused by such controls.

Finally, the Bank of Japan has traditionally set a relatively low cash reserve requirement. Formal approval from the Minister of Finance is required whenever the reserve ratio is changed.

New Zealand. Direct administrative intervention in the operation of financial institutions has traditionally been a feature of monetary policy in New Zealand. Since 1973, trading banks were required to hold a minimum percentage of their deposits in specified public sector assets. The ratios were varied by the bank, with the approval of the minister of finance. Government security investment ratios, under which financial institutions have a statutory obligation to invest specified proportions of their total assets or deposits in public sector securities, were also applied by law to all saving banks, building societies, finance companies, official market dealers, stock and station agents, private pension funds, and life insurance offices. Most of these constraints were removed in 1985.

Credit restrictions on nonpriority overdrafts were imposed on trading banks to influence domestic activity and, prior to 1963, credit allocation. Sectoral guidelines were also applied to bank lending. These guidelines have not been subject to formal enforcements. The Bank exercised influence over nonbank credit, too.

Up to 1969, wholesale deposit rates were set by the authorities, as were retail deposit rates in the periods 1972-1976. Some of these controls were reintroduced in 1981-1984. Since 1984, active and passive interest rates have been completely liberalized.

In the most recent years, an important shift has occurred toward indirect forms of monetary control. Together with the dismantling of compulsory ratio requirements and credit guidelines, there has been a move toward more active use of open-market operations and discount policy. If this change is lasting, it implies a significant reduction in the degree of fiscal dominance of the monetary regime.

United States. The primary instrument for implementing monetary policy is open-market operations, predominantly in Treasury bills. Given the characteristics of the U.S. financial system, this instrument is highly flexible as to both timing and size of operations. As a consequence, supplementary instruments of control have played a secondary role. The Fed has generally avoided using direct administrative measures to ration credit.

The Federal Reserve Board used to fix reserve requirements only for the banks that were members of the Federal Reserve System. Since 1980, all banks are required to hold minimum cash reserves. If the reserves are not provided by the federal funds market, they must be borrowed at the Fed discount window.

Up to 1986, retail deposit rates were subject to ceilings set by the authorities. Credit restrictions were used briefly in 1980 to reduce inflation.

NOTES TO APPENDIX

(a) The bibliographical sources for this subsection are: Fair (1980), Skanland (1984), Cargill (1987).

(b) The bibliographical sources here are: Deane (1972), Mitra (1978), OECD (1982-1983).

(c) The main references for this subsection are: Banker Research Unit (1980), Cargill et al. (1986), Cargill (1986), Carron (1986), Cheng (1983), Dean (1986), Hutchison (1986), Nicholl (1977), OECD (1985), Phillips (1986), Pigott (1983), Skully (1985), and various OECD economic surveys.

7
Monetary Policy in Pacific Basin Developing Countries

Maxwell J. Fry, David M. Lilien, Wilima Wadhwa

In its most extreme form, the monetary approach to the balance of payments assumes that central banks in open economies with fixed exchange rates have no ability to affect the nominal money stock. Among others, Aghevli and others (1979, p. 776) and Smaghi (1982) have used this proposition in more moderate form to assert that Pacific Basin developing countries have only limited monetary policy independence. Even if these developing countries were able to pursue independent monetary policies, Connolly and Taylor (1979) find that developing countries generally do not appear to pursue any systematic monetary policy.

This chapter, therefore, will attempt to answer three questions: Can developing countries pursue independent monetary policies? If so, do developing countries pursue systematic discretionary monetary policies? Are the Pacific Basin developing countries different from other developing countries with respect to the first two questions?

The developing countries in the Pacific Basin have posted significantly higher rates of economic growth than developing countries in other parts of the world. For the sample of 19 developing countries analyzed here, the continuously compounded rate of growth in real GNP averaged 5.0 percent annually over the period 1968-1985 for the 14 countries in the control group and 6.3 percent for the five Pacific Basin countries (Indonesia, Korea, Malaysia, the Philippines, and Thailand). The question arises as to whether behavior or policies in the Pacific Basin countries are substantially different. This examination will include one behavioral equation determining net capital inflows and two policy equations explaining the behavior of the monetary authorities with respect to domestic credit expansion and exchange rate depreciation.

The conclusion is that the implementation of monetary policy in the Pacific Basin developing countries has been significantly different from monetary policy implementation in the other sample countries. This conclusion supports Harberger's (1985, p. 15) finding that economic policy was indeed quite different in the Latin American countries from what it was in East Asia. On the other hand, it is also shown that despite the difference in policy regimes, private behavior with respect to capital flows in the Pacific Basin developing countries has not differed significantly from behavior in a sample of other developing countries. This does not suggest that behavior in other respects is unaffected by the policy regime. Indeed, previous work on the rate of economic growth (Fry and Lilien, 1986) supports Lucas's (1973 and 1976) theoretical and empirical work on the effects of policy regimes on private sector behavior. The conclusion here, however, is that monetary policy regimes need not affect, and have not affected, private behavior with respect to the balance of payments on capital account.

THE MODEL

The three equations examined here are embedded in a macroeconomic model designed for a small semi-open developing economy. In this economy, the government sets or manipulates the foreign exchange rate and uses domestic credit as its target for monetary policy purposes. The assets available to residents of this country are money (M), capital and other inflation hedges (K), and foreign bonds (F).

Net holdings of foreign bonds are negative when foreign borrowing exceeds foreign lending. Developing countries borrow abroad by selling dollar-denominated bonds in world financial markets. In practice, developing country bonds are not perfect substitutes for industrial country bonds. Hence, developing countries face a downward sloping demand curve for their bonds on world markets. Both the supply and the demand for foreign bonds are, therefore, specified here.

In most developing countries, neither corporate nor government bonds are traded in open markets. Indeed, corporate bonds simply do not exist in many developing countries. Typically the commercial banks are captive buyers of domestic government bonds at low fixed rates of interest by virtue of liquidity ratio requirements. Government deficits are financed almost entirely by loans from the central and commercial banks. As a rough approximation, therefore, the budget deficit equals the change in net domestic credit to the government sector (ΔDCg) plus loans from abroad. Since the nonbank private sector provides virtually no direct lending to the government, we exclude domestic bonds from this model.

The capital flow equation derived here is based on the quasi reduced-form equation derived by Kouri and Porter (1974, pp. 447-454) which has been used recently by Kamas (1986, pp. 471-472) and Laskar (1983, pp. 317-321). These authors all treat the current account as exogenous. The model proposed here endogenizes the current account and recognizes that developing countries face country-specific risk premia when they borrow abroad.

Table 1 presents the parts of the underlying model that are of immediate relevance. There are three assets: domestic money (M), foreign bonds (F), and domestic capital and other inflation hedges (K) -- e.g., land, grain. The nominal returns on these three assets are zero on money, i on foreign bonds (as measured by the rate of return in terms of the domestic currency), and expected inflation π^e on capital and other inflation hedges. The market for capital and other inflation hedges is not specified since it can be derived by using Walras's Law.

The remaining endogenous variables in the ten equations specified in Table 1 are real GNP (y), the domestic price level (P), nominal GNP (Y), the domestic-currency return on foreign bonds (i, the domestic-currency cost of borrowing abroad), inflation (π), expected inflation (π^e), exchange rate depreciation (ε), expected exchange rate depreciation (ε^e), the country-specific risk premium (ρ), net foreign assets (NFA), domestic credit (DC), domestic credit to the private sector (DCp), net domestic credit to the government sector (DCg), capital flows (CF), and the current account balance (CA).[1]

The exogenous variables in equations (1) to (10) are government and government-guaranteed foreign debt in current prices (D), wealth (W), foreign inflation (π^*, U.S. wholesale price inflation), foreign wealth (W^*), and the rate of change in the world dollar price of oil (π^0).

Equation (1) is a money demand function. It includes expected inflation (π^e) as the return on K and the domestic-currency return on foreign assets (i). This return consists of the dollar rate on foreign bonds (i^*) plus the country-specific risk premium on foreign borrowing (ρ) -- since net foreign bond holdings of all the sample developing countries examined here are negative, i.e., they are net borrowers -- plus the expected exchange rate depreciation (ε^e).

One characteristic of this model is that money demand is also determined by government and government-guaranteed foreign debt (D). As households see foreign debt rise, they may anticipate increased future tax burdens, including inflation, for its servicing. They will, therefore, have an increasing incentive to transfer assets abroad. Furthermore, households may perceive that a high and rising foreign debt ratio could goad the government into stimulating exports. This would involve a devaluation in the real exchange rate. In such case the real returns on assets held abroad would be higher than the real returns on domestic assets. For both these reasons, therefore, a higher value of D may be expected to reduce money demand.

Table 1
Key Elements of the Model

Money demand:

$$M = \xi(\overset{+}{y}, \overset{+}{P}, \overset{-}{\pi^e}, \overset{-}{i}, \overset{-}{D}, \overset{+}{W}); \tag{1}$$

Money supply:

$$M \equiv NFA + DC; \tag{2}$$

Domestic credit:

$$DC \equiv DCg + DCp; \tag{3}$$

Net demand for foreign bonds:

$$F = \theta(\overset{-}{y}, \overset{-}{P}, \overset{-}{\pi^e}, \overset{+}{i}, \overset{+}{D}, \overset{+}{W}); \tag{4}$$

Net supply of foreign bonds:

$$F = \omega(\overset{-}{i-\varepsilon^e}, \overset{-}{D}, \overset{-}{\Sigma CA}, \overset{+}{W^*}); \tag{5}$$

Wealth:

$$W \equiv M + K + F; \tag{6}$$

Capital flow:

$$CF \equiv -\Delta F; \tag{7}$$

Change in net foreign assets:

$$\Delta NFA \equiv CA + CF; \tag{8}$$

Central bank domestic credit reaction function:

$$\Delta DC = \mu\left(\Delta NFA, \pi_{t-1} - \pi^*_{t-1}, \Delta DCg, \pi^o, D_{t-1}\right) \tag{9}$$

Central bank exchange rate reaction function:

$$\varepsilon = \eta\left(\Delta NFA, \pi_{t-1} - \pi^*_{t-1}, \Delta DCg, \pi^o, D_{t-1}\right) \tag{10}$$

Equation (2) is the money supply function that takes the form of a simplified balance sheet of the consolidated banking system. The liability -- money (M) -- is created by banking system holdings of net foreign assets (NFA) and domestic credit (DC). Equation (3) decomposes domestic credit into net domestic credit to the government sector (DCg) and domestic credit to the private sector (DCp); both components are endogenous.

Equation (4) is the net demand for foreign bonds (F). It takes exactly the same form as equation (1). Since foreign bond holdings are negative, this equation determines the level of net foreign indebtedness that the country wishes to incur, given the interest rate on the debt in domestic currency. Part of F consists of government and government-guaranteed foreign debt (D).

Equation (5) is derived from work by Hanson (1974), Eaton and Gersovitz (1981), Edwards (1986), and Sachs (1984) on the determinants of the country-specific risk premium. Here, the net supply of foreign bonds (or, equivalently, the net demand for dollar-denominated developing country bonds) is determined by the world nominal interest rate plus the country-specific risk premium ($i^* + \rho$), but not by the expected exchange rate depreciation (ε^e), since foreign lenders are unaffected by domestic currency depreciation. Since $i = i^* + \rho + \varepsilon^e$, it follows that $i^* + \rho$ equals $i - \varepsilon^e$.

The net supply of foreign loans is also affected by the level of government and government-guaranteed foreign debt (D). As debt rises, the expected probability of repayment falls. Hence, the net supply of foreign loans declines as foreign debt increases. The net supply of foreign credit is also affected by the size of a country's cumulative current account position (ΣCA).[2] In flow terms this implies that a large current account deficit makes the rest of the world less inclined to lend more to this developing country. Finally, the net supply of foreign bonds is determined by foreign wealth (W^*). Clearly this supply function is appropriate only for negative supplies of foreign bonds, i.e., for net lending by the rest of the world to the developing country.

Government and government-guaranteed foreign debt is treated as exogenous to this model. This would be inappropriate if all net capital inflows produced a corresponding change in government and government-guaranteed foreign debt. There is, however, virtually no correlation between total net capital flows and the change in government and government-guaranteed foreign debt. Although analysis of government debt-guaranteeing decisions would be of considerable interest, it is beyond the scope of this chapter. The assumption is that they are not based on current values of any endogenous variables in this model.

Equation (6) indicates that the exogenous wealth (W) at the beginning of each period can be allocated among money (M), domestic capital and other inflation hedges (K), and foreign bonds (F). Equation (7) defines the capital account or capital inflows (CF) as the change in the holdings of foreign bonds (ΔF), which can, of course, be negative. Using the balance-of-payments identity, equation (8) expresses the change in net foreign assets (ΔNFA) as the sum of current account (CA) and the capital account (CF).

Equation (9) is the central bank's reaction function determining the change in domestic credit, while equation (10) is its reaction function toward the rate of change in the nominal exchange rate. Following the early work on monetary policy reaction functions by Reuber (1964) and Froyen (1974), central bank objectives have typically been taken to include a balance-of-payments target (ΔNFA), an inflation target expressed here as the lagged gap between domestic and foreign inflation ($\pi_{t-1}-\pi^*_{t-1}$), and possibly some response to exogenous shocks such as oil price inflation (π^o). The extent to which central banks accommodate the credit requirements of the government sector (ΔDCg) without squeezing private sector credit availability is also determined. In both reaction functions, the hypothesis that developing country governments do worry about foreign debt (D_{t-1}) is tested.

Combining equations (1), (2), and (8) gives

$$CA + CF + \Delta DC = \Delta[\xi(y, P, \pi^e, i, D, W)]. \tag{11}$$

Equations (4) and (7) produce

$$CF = -\Delta[\theta(y, P, \pi^e, i, D, W)]. \tag{12}$$

Equations (5) and (7) yield

$$CF = -\Delta[\omega(i-\varepsilon^e, D, \Sigma \mathrm{CA}, W^*)]. \tag{13}$$

Equations (11), (12), and (13) can be solved simultaneously to eliminate the two price variables, expected inflation (π^e) and the domestic return on foreign bonds (i). For expositional simplicity, a simple linear system in which all coefficients take positive values is considered with W and W* omitted. For this illustration, equations (11), (12), and (13) take the specific forms:

$$CA + CF + \Delta DC = a_1\Delta y + a_2\Delta P - a_3\Delta\pi^e - a_4\Delta i - a_5\Delta D; \tag{14}$$

$$CF = b_1\Delta y + b_2\Delta P + b_3\Delta\pi^e - b_4\Delta i - b_5\Delta D; \tag{15}$$

$$CF = c_1(\Delta i - \Delta\varepsilon^e) + c_2\Delta D + c_3 CA. \tag{16}$$

Equations (15) and (16) can be rearranged in terms of $\Delta\pi^e$ and Δi:

$$\Delta \pi^e = \frac{CF}{b_3} - \frac{b_1}{b_3}\Delta y - \frac{b_2}{b_3}\Delta P + \frac{b_4}{b_3}\Delta i + \frac{b_5}{b_3}\Delta D; \tag{17}$$

$$\Delta i = \frac{CF}{c_1} + \Delta \varepsilon^e - \frac{c_2}{c_1}\Delta D - \frac{c_3}{c_1} CA. \tag{18}$$

Inserting (17) and (18) into equation (14) gives the capital flow equation:

$$CF = \left[-\Delta DC - \left(1 + \frac{a_4 c_3}{c_1}\right) CA + \left(a_1 + \frac{a_3 b_1}{b_3}\right)\Delta y + \left(a_2 + \frac{a_3 b_2}{b_3}\right)\Delta P \right.$$
$$\left. - \left(a_4 + \frac{a_3 b_4}{b_3}\right)\Delta\varepsilon^e - \left(a_5 + \frac{a_3 b_5}{b_3} - \frac{a_3 b_4 c_2}{b_3 c_1} - \frac{a_4 c_2}{c_1}\right)\Delta D \right] /$$
$$\left[1 + \frac{a_3}{b_3} + \frac{a_3 b_4}{b_3 c_1} + \frac{a_4}{c_1}\right]. \tag{19}$$

Clearly, signs of all coefficients except that of D are unambiguous. The log-linear version of equation (19) scaled by nominal GNP (not wealth) actually estimated here takes the form

$$CFR = \overset{-}{b_{11}} DDCR + \overset{-}{b_{12}} CAR + \overset{+}{b_{13}} GG + \overset{+}{b_{14}} INF$$
$$+ \overset{-}{b_{15}} EDEXG + \overset{?}{b_{16}} DDETY + \overset{?}{b_{17}} DDEYS, \tag{20}$$

where CFR is the ratio of capital inflows to GNP, DDCR is the change in domestic credit divided by GNP, CAR is the ratio of the current account balance to GNP, GG is the rate of growth in real GNP, INF is the inflation rate, EDEXG is the expected change in the rate of depreciation in the foreign exchange rate, DDETY is the change in the ratio of foreign debt to GNP, and DDEYS is the change in the squared debt ratio. The initial specification search indicated that the effect of government and government-guaranteed foreign debt on capital flows was nonlinear. Hence, the squared debt/GNP ratio is included in addition to the debt/GNP ratio.

It is assumed that expectations are formed rationally, and hence the change in the rate of exchange depreciation estimated by variables known at time t-1 is used as the expected change in the rate of exchange depreciation. Specifically, the expected change in the rate of exchange depreciation is estimated separately for each country by ordinary least squares (OLS), using lagged values of the change in, and level of, exchange rate depreciation, world real interest rate, world economic growth, domestic economic growth, money (M2) growth, inflation, the ratio of domestic credit to GNP, and the ratio of capital flows to GNP.

The offset coefficient is b_{11}. Its value can lie between 0 and -1. A value of -1 implies monetary policy impotency because the private sector is reducing its holdings of net foreign assets to offset exactly any increase in domestic credit. In this case, changes in domestic credit, the only monetary aggregate controllable by central banks in open economies, have no effect on the money supply.

The change in income and price in equations (11) and (12) are converted into the growth and inflation variables in equation (20), since first differences of logarithms are taken. These variables exert positive effects on capital inflows through their positive effects on money demand and negative effects on the demand for foreign bonds.

The coefficient of the current account ratio (b_{12}) in equation (20) is negative. If a large current account deficit makes the rest of the world less inclined to lend to this developing country as implied by equation (5), a larger current account deficit could reduce capital inflows. In such case, a higher current account deficit would cause a more than one-for-one reduction in net foreign assets. While b_{11} has a lower bound of -1, the value of b_{12} has no lower bound.

The expected change in exchange rate depreciation reduces capital inflows because of the asymmetry between foreign bond demand and supply functions with respect to this variable. A rise in ε^e encourages capital outflows but has no effect on capital inflows. Hence, a rise in ε^e reduces *net* capital inflows. Only the debt coefficients (b_{16} and b_{17}) in equation (20) are ambiguous in theory, since debt exerts opposite effects on demand and supply.

The reaction functions are specified to discover whether or not the developing countries examined here sterilize inflows of net foreign assets to achieve some money supply target. There is also an analysis of whether or not the monetary authorities reacted to any other economic events. In particular, developing country central banks might squeeze credit when domestic inflation exceeded U.S. inflation or when oil prices rise. Central banks might squeeze domestic credit to the private sector when the credit requirements of the government increase. In such case the coefficient of the change in government credit would be significantly less than 1. The reaction function estimated here is also scaled by GNP:

$$DDCR = b_{21}DNFAR + b_{22}INFGAP_{t-1} + b_{23}DDCGR + b_{24}DOILP + b_{25}LDETY + b_{26}LDEYS, \qquad (21)$$

where DNFAR is the change in net foreign assets divided by GNP, INFGAP is the difference between domestic and U.S. inflation, DDCGR is the change in net domestic credit to the government sector divided by GNP, DOILP is the rate of change in the world market dollar price of oil, LDETY is the lagged ratio of foreign debt to GNP, and LDEYS is the square of the lagged debt/GNP ratio. Complete sterilization implies a value of -1 for b_{21}.

Finally, we specify an identical reaction function for the rate of exchange rate depreciation:

$$EXG = b_{31}DNFAR + b_{32}INFGAP_{t-1} + b_{33}DDCGR + b_{34}DOILP + b_{35}LDETY + b_{36}LDEYS, \qquad (22)$$

where EXG is the rate of change in the nominal exchange rate.

THE ESTIMATES

The regression estimates presented here use 338 observations from 19 developing countries heavily indebted to the World Bank. National income and foreign debt data came from the World Bank's *Bank Economic and Social Database*, and financial statistics from the *International Financial Statistics* tape. The 19 countries are Algeria, Brazil, Cameroon, Colombia, Egypt, India, Indonesia, Ivory Coast, Jamaica, Korea, Malaysia, Mexico, Morocco, Pakistan, Philippines, Sudan, Thailand, Tunisia, and Turkey. For most of the sample countries, the regression period is 1968-1985; for Cameroon, Mexico, Morocco, and Sudan, the period ends in 1984.

Initially, separate equations for each of the 19 countries in the sample were estimated. With a maximum of 18 observations, however, the coefficients often exhibited large standard errors and implausible values.

Pooling the data constrains the coefficients of the equation to be identical across countries, a hypothesis that was tested with an F test. The appropriateness of pooling without country dummy intercepts is always rejected at the 99 percent confidence level. With country dummies, however, coefficient equality for the remaining coefficients cannot be rejected, except in the exchange rate reaction functions. Even for the exchange rate equations for which pooling is rejected formally, the pooled estimates appear to be more useful than the individual country estimates, given the data limitations. In the results that follow, separate F tests of the pooling assumption are reported for each estimated equation.

The estimation method employed for all the equations reported here is two-stage least squares on pooled time series data with individual country intercepts included (but not reported). Pooling raises the issue of the choice of instruments for the two-stage least squares model. If all the exogenous variables together with the lagged endogenous variables of the full model are used as instruments, there are more instruments than the 18 observations per country. This large number of instruments can be used only if coefficient equality is imposed in the first stage of the two-stage estimation procedure. Alternatively, a smaller number of instruments can be chosen so that their coefficients can differ between countries. The pooled model was estimated in both ways. The second stage equations fit the data somewhat better when fewer instruments were used, and their coefficients were not restricted to be the same across countries. In fact, the results were very similar and the basic conclusions are the same whichever method is used.

For all the estimates reported in this section, coefficient equality was imposed over countries within a group in the equation being estimated, but not on the unestimated equations of the model. In other words, the instruments are allowed to have different coefficients for each country in the first stage of the two-stage estimation procedure. The instruments used for the capital flow equations reported here are the world real interest rate; world economic growth; the expected change in exchange rate depreciation; changes in the debt/GNP ratio and the squared debt ratio; and lagged values of domestic economic growth, money (M2) growth, inflation, the change in the ratio of domestic credit to GNP, the change in the ratio of government sector credit to GNP, and the current and capital account ratios.

The estimates of three versions of the capital flow equation are given in Table 2. In equation (23), the Pacific Basin countries have the same coefficients as the rest of our sample. The estimated offset coefficient in equation (23) is -0.32. The size of this offset coefficient is inconsistent with the assertion that active monetary policy cannot be pursued in a

Table 2
Estimated Capital Flow (CFR) Equations

Equation	(23)	(24)	(25)
	Dependent Variable: CFR		
$\widehat{\text{DDCR}}$	-0.320 (-5.925)	-0.297 (-5.042)	-0.290 (-5.120)
$\widehat{\text{CAR}}$	-0.763 (-14.418)	-0.745 (-12.437)	-0.745 (-12.730)
$\widehat{\text{GG}}$	0.076 (1.506)	0.055 (0.966)	0.083 (1.635)
$\widehat{\text{INF}}$	0.065 (3.498)	0.065 (2.988)	0.063 (3.379)
EDEXG	-0.019 (-1.280)	-0.019 (-1.168)	-0.018 (-1.230)
DDETY	0.162 (1.999)	0.153 (1.741)	0.144 (1.745)
DDEYS	-0.144 (-2.277)	-0.137 (-2.033)	-0.126 (-1.937)
Shift Parameters for Pacific Basin Countries			
$\widehat{\text{DDCR}}$		-0.361 (-2.024)	-0.297 (-1.786)
$\widehat{\text{CAR}}$		-0.273 (-1.698)	-0.173 (-1.310)
$\widehat{\text{GG}}$		0.266 (1.733)	
$\widehat{\text{INF}}$		-0.040 (-0.834)	
EDEXG		0.021 (0.540)	
DDETY		-0.236 (-0.571)	
DDEYS		0.353 (0.515)	
R^2	0.585	0.588	0.587
S.E.E.	0.0311	0.0314	0.0311
F against unpooled	1.048	1.090	1.051
F against equation (23)		0.323	0.856

Note: Variables with a "hat" are endogenous variables.

representative developing country. Indeed, this coefficient is considerably smaller than offset coefficients estimated for most industrial countries. Not surprisingly, capital accounts seem to be more open in the industrial countries than they are in our sample of developing countries. For example, Kouri and Porter (1974, pp. 455-456) estimate offset coefficients averaging -0.57 for Australia, Germany, Holland, and Italy, while Laskar (1983, p. 329) reports his preferred offset coefficients averaging -0.64 for Britain, Canada, France, Germany, Holland, Italy, and Japan.

Obstfeld (1982, pp. 47-48) points out that the Kouri-Porter estimate of -0.77 for Germany is severely biased toward -1 as a result of the ordinary least squares estimation procedure. Laskar's estimates are corrected for simultaneous equation bias, as are the estimates reported here, by the use of two-stage least squares. Hausman's (1978) test for simultaneous equation bias rejects exogeneity of both the change in domestic credit and the current account ratios at the 99 percent confidence level. Although these test results indicate that simultaneous equation bias would occur if these two variables had been treated as exogenous, their coefficients change by only minuscule amounts when these two variables are in fact treated as exogenous in these estimates. The paradox is explained by the fact that these estimates use a relatively large number of observations.

Whether or not the Pacific Basin developing countries in this sample (Indonesia, Korea, Malaysia, Philippines, and Thailand) exhibit significantly different offset coefficients is examined next. Equations (24) and (25) include interaction terms between a Pacific Basin dummy variable (taking the value 1 for Pacific Basin countries and 0 for all the other sample countries) and the other variables in the capital flow equation. Equation (24) is equivalent to estimating a separate equation for the Pacific Basin. To calculate the effect of a variable on a Pacific Basin country, the coefficient for the total sample must be added to the Pacific Basin shift parameter or slope dummy.

The only significant difference (just significant at the 95 percent confidence level) for the Pacific Basin countries is the offset coefficient of -0.66 (equal to -0.30 plus -0.36). The offset coefficient for the other countries in this sample is only -0.30. The offset coefficient for the Pacific Basin countries is comparable to offset coefficients estimated for most industrial countries. That the Pacific Basin developing countries seem to be more open than the other sample countries is not surprising. Nevertheless, the F test indicates that one cannot reject the hypothesis that no difference exists at all between the Pacific Basin and the other developing countries with respect to the determinants of capital flows. While the data clearly reject an offset of -1 for all of the countries in our sample, the results do suggest somewhat less monetary independence among the Pacific Basin countries.

The next topic is government policy equations. The first three columns of Table 3 comprise variants of the monetary reaction function DDCR while the next three columns contain exchange rate adjustment reaction functions EXG. Again, coefficient equality is imposed over country groups in the equation being estimated, but not on the unestimated equations of the model. For both reaction function equations, the instruments chosen are the world real interest rate; world economic growth; the rate of change in world oil prices; and lagged values of the debt/GNP ratio and the squared debt ratio, domestic economic growth, money (M2) growth, the gap between domestic and U.S. inflation, the change in the ratio of domestic credit to GNP, the rate of exchange rate depreciation, and the current account ratio.

Equation (26) in Table 3 forces the same reaction coefficients on all the sample countries. It displays little use of sterilization by this sample of developing countries. The coefficient of DNFAR indicates that these developing countries sterilize less than 15 percent of the change in net foreign assets. However, the F statistic rejects at well over the 99 percent confidence level the hypothesis that monetary policy in the Pacific Basin developing countries is explained by the same equation as monetary policy in the rest of the sample. Indeed, equations (27) and (28) indicate that the Pacific Basin developing countries sterilized 54 percent of the increase in net foreign assets (-0.10 plus -0.44), compared with only 10 percent in the other developing countries.

The small sterilization coefficient for the non-Pacific Basin countries may well result from the fact that some countries in this group actually increased domestic credit when net foreign assets rose. Porzecanski (1979, pp. 434-435) finds that in Mexico and Venezuela higher net foreign assets led to more rapid domestic credit expansion. Fry (1978, pp. 50-52) finds the same phenomenon in Turkey. Indeed, Turkey's bouts of double digit inflation in the 1950s and 1970s originated in rapid increases in foreign exchange receipts. Rather than sterilizing the effect of higher net foreign assets on the money supply, the Turkish central bank responded by expanding domestic credit to finance a greater volume of imports of capital equipment and raw material. Although this reduced rapidly the level of net foreign assets, it sustained the expansionary monetary impulse. The Turkish central bank then followed its own version of the real bills doctrine toward domestic credit expansion, accommodating demand pressures generated by the accelerating rise in nominal GNP with a lag.

The developing countries outside the Pacific Basin accommodated domestically generated inflationary pressures, the government's credit requirements, and increases in oil prices. They did, however, reduce domestic credit expansion when foreign debt rose. Porzecanski (1979, pp. 434-435) finds that two countries in the sample -- Argentina and Chile --

Table 3
Government Policy Equations

Equation	Dependent Variable: DDCR			Dependent Variable: EXG		
	(26)	(27)	(28)	(29)	(30)	(31)
DN$\hat{F}$AR	-0.145 (-2.987)	-0.099 (-1.921)	-0.105 (-2.026)	-0.303 (-1.171)	-0.467 (-1.656)	-0.472 (-1.682)
INFGAP	0.029 (2.158)	0.057 (3.515)	0.062 (3.927)	0.653 (9.160)	0.862 (9.668)	0.865 (10.015)
DD$\hat{C}$GR	0.922 (16.904)	0.929 (16.731)	0.936 (17.036)	0.698 (2.398)	0.445 (1.468)	0.463 (1.550)
DOILP	0.022 (2.755)	0.018 (1.925)	0.025 (3.129)	-0.062 (-1.424)	-0.039 (-0.764)	-0.048 (-1.125)
LDETY	0.173 (4.943)	0.166 (4.050)	0.145 (4.209)	0.466 (2.489)	0.486 (2.175)	0.438 (2.344)
LDEYS	-0.211 (-5.324)	-0.206 (-4.670)	-0.187 (-4.836)	-0.404 (-1.914)	-0.463 (-1.922)	-0.417 (-1.987)
Shift Parameters for Pacific Basin Countries						
DN$\hat{F}$AR		-0.439 (-3.226)	-0.433 (-3.317)		0.475 0.639	0.588 (0.828)
INFGAP		-0.065 (-2.341)	-0.080 (-3.108)		-0.573 (-3.791)	-0.588 (-4.207)
DD$\hat{C}$GR		-0.686 (-2.716)	-0.670 (-2.700)		0.810 (0.588)	0.976 (0.724)
DOILP		0.018 (0.979)			-0.045 (-0.463)	
LDETY		0.068 (0.512)			-0.263 (-0.363)	
LDEYS		-0.266 (-0.893)			0.330 (0.203)	
R^2	0.780	0.800	0.798	0.547	0.570	0.569
S.E.E.	0.0244	0.0235	0.0235	0.1304	0.1283	0.1279
F against unpooled	1.701	1.458	1.451	2.268	2.180	2.128
F against equation (26) or (29)		5.057	9.071		2.705	5.165

Note: Variables with a "hat" are endogenous variables.

accommodated domestically generated inflation either to supplement government revenue through monetary expansion or to maintain a certain level of real liquidity in the economy.

In contrast, the Pacific Basin developing countries reduced rather than increased credit when domestic inflation exceeded U.S. inflation. They also accommodated government credit requirements to a much smaller degree (by squeezing private sector credit) than the rest of the sample. Harberger (1985, p. 15) finds that when East Asian countries deviate from the average developing country behavior, they deviate on the side of prudence.

Results in this study contrast with those of Connolly and Taylor (1979, p. 287), who find no evidence that developing countries pursue any systematic monetary policies. Results also contrast with estimates of substantial or complete sterilization in industrialized countries (except for Switzerland) reported by Artus (1976, p. 326), Darby (1983, pp. 307-308), Laney and Willett (1982, pp. 144-147), and Obstfeld (1983).

The exchange rate equations (29) - (31) in Table 3 present roughly the same picture as the domestic credit equations (26) - (28). Non-Pacific Basin developing countries devalued their currencies in response to a decline in net foreign assets and an acceleration in domestic inflation. The Pacific Basin developing countries, however, were much more reluctant to take that course. Equations (30) and (31) indicate that a decline in net foreign assets actually led to a small but statistically insignificant revaluation of their currencies. In the Pacific Basin countries, domestic inflation induces devaluations of roughly one-third the magnitude of inflation-induced devaluations in the other sample countries. In fact, the hypothesis that the Pacific Basin countries maintain currency stability in the face of changes in either net foreign assets or domestic inflation cannot be rejected.

CONCLUSION

In this chapter, one quasi reduced-form behavioral equation determining capital flows and two reaction functions embedded in a macroeconomic model have been used to compare the monetary and exchange rate policies of Pacific Basin developing countries with those of other developing countries. It has been found that the monetary and exchange rate policies pursued by the Pacific Basin developing countries have been significantly less accommodative, and hence less inflationary, than policies followed by the others in the sample.

Despite the different policy regimes, the capital flow equations exhibit only one significant behavioral difference -- a considerably greater offset in the Pacific Basin than in the other sample countries. The F test fails to reject the hypothesis that capital flows in the Pacific Basin countries are determined in exactly the same way as capital flows in the other sample countries. Even in the Pacific Basin, however, the offset is certainly not great enough to make monetary policy impotent. Hence, it may be concluded that the more conservative monetary and exchange rate policies pursued by the Pacific Basin countries in the sample were effective in containing inflation, in spite of international capital flows.

Empirical analysis of the rate of economic growth reported elsewhere (Fry and Lilien, 1986) indicates that accommodative, discretionary monetary and fiscal policies have negative effects on economic growth in the long run. Monetary accommodation of exogenous shocks adds noise to the economic environment by increasing the variance of money growth shocks. Harberger (1985) suggests that erratic exchange rate policies in Latin America have reduced export supply elasticities in that part of the world. However, the analysis reported in this chapter hardly allows the inference that policy rather than behavioral differences explains the superior economic performance of the Pacific Basin developing countries. It is plausible that the different monetary and exchange rate policy regimes in the Pacific Basin developing countries detected in this study may have contributed to the distinctly superior economic performance in these countries. Nevertheless, a positive identification of such contributions goes beyond the scope of this chapter.

NOTES

Our thanks go to Reuven Glick, Giovanna Mossetti, Edward Shaw, and Joseph Whitt for comments on an earlier version of this paper and to the University of California's Pacific Rim Research Program for financial support.

1. The full model would also treat national saving, domestic investment, the rate of economic growth, terms of trade, income growth attributable to terms-of-trade improvements, the real exchange rate, imports, and exports as endogenous. Hence, none of these variables is used as an instrument in the two-stage least squares estimates reported below.

2. A cumulative current account deficit equals cumulative capital inflows minus net foreign assets. It does, therefore, provide a rough measure of the relative exposure of the rest of the world to the vagaries of this country's economic performance.

REFERENCES

Aghevli, Bijan B., Mohsin S. Khan, P.R. Narvekar, and Brock K. Short (1979). "Monetary Policy in Selected Asian Countries." *International Monetary Fund Staff Papers* 26, No. 4 (December), pp.775-824.

Artus, Jacques R. (1976). "Exchange Rate Stability and Managed Floating: The Experience of the Federal Republic of Germany." *International Monetary Fund Staff Papers* 23, No. 2 (July), pp. 312-333.

Connolly, Michael B. and Dean Taylor (1979). "Exchange Rate Changes and Neutralization: A Test of the Monetary Approach Applied to Developed and Developing Countries." *Economica* 46, No. 183 (August), pp. 281-294.

Darby, Michael R. (1983). "Sterilization and Monetary Control: Concepts, Issues, and a Reduced-Form Test." In *The International Transmission of Inflation*, edited by Michael R. Darby, James R. Lothian and others. Chicago: University of Chicago Press for the National Bureau of Economic Research, pp. 291-313.

Eaton, Jonathan and Mark Gersovitz (1981). "Debt with Potential Repudiation: Theoretical and Empirical Analysis." *Review of Economic Studies* 48, No. 2 (April), pp. 289-309.

Edwards, Sebastian (1986). "The Pricing of Bonds and Bank Loans in International Markets: An Empirical Analysis of Developing Countries' Foreign Borrowing." *European Economic Review* 30, No. 3 (June), pp. 565-589.

Froyen, Richard T. (1974). "A Test of the Endogeneity of Monetary Policy." *Journal of Econometrics* 2, No. 2 (July), pp. 175-188.

Fry, Maxwell J. (1978). "The Money Supply Mechanism in Turkey." *METU Studies in Development* 21 (Autumn), pp. 49-60.

Fry, Maxwell J. and David M. Lilien (1986). "Monetary Policy Responses to Exogenous Shocks." *American Economic Review* 76, No. 2 (May), pp. 79-83.

Hanson, James A. (1974). "Optimal International Borrowing and Lending." *American Economic Review* 64, No. 4 (September), pp. 616-630.

Harberger, Arnold C. (1985). "Growth, Industrialization and Economic Structure: Latin America and East Asia Compared." Canberra: Australian National University, Conference on Explaining the Success of Industrialization in East Asia (September).

Hausman, Jerry A. (1978). "Specification Tests in Econometrics." *Econometrica* 46, No. 6 (November), pp. 1251-1271.

Kamas, Linda (1986). "The Balance of Payments Offset to Monetary Policy: Monetarist, Portfolio Balance, and Keynesian Estimates for Mexico and Venezuela." *Journal of Money, Credit and Banking* 18, No. 4 (November), pp. 467-481.

Kouri, Pentti J.K. and Michael G. Porter (1974). "International Capital Flows and Portfolio Equilibrium." *Journal of Political Economy* 82, No. 3 (May/June), pp. 443-467.

Laney, Leroy O. and Thomas D. Willett (1982). "The International Liquidity Explosion and Worldwide Inflation: The Evidence from Sterilization Coefficient Estimates." *Journal of International Money and Finance* 1, No. 2 (August), pp. 141-152.

Laskar, Daniel M. (1983). "Short-Run Independence of Monetary Policy under a Pegged Exchange-Rate System: An Econometric Approach." In *The International Transmission of Inflation*, edited by Michael R. Darby, James R. Lothian and others. Chicago: University of Chicago Press for the National Bureau of Economic Research, pp. 314-348.

Lucas, Robert E., Jr. (1973). "Some International Evidence on Output-Inflation Tradeoffs." *American Economic Review* 63, No. 3 (June), pp. 326-334.

Lucas, Robert E., Jr. (1976). "Econometric Policy Evaluation: A Critique." *Carnegie-Rochester Conference Series on Public Policy* 1, pp. 19-46.

Obstfeld, Maurice (1982). "Can We Sterilize? Theory and Evidence." *American Economic Review* 72, No. 2 (May), pp. 45-49.

Obstfeld, Maurice (1983). "Exchange Rates, Inflation, and the Sterilization Problem: Germany, 1975-1981." *European Economic Review* 21, No. 1 and 2 (March/April), pp. 161-189.

Porzecanski, Arturo (1979). "Patterns of Monetary Policy in Latin America." *Journal of Money, Credit and Banking* 11, No. 4 (November), pp.427-437.

Reuber, Grant L. (1964). "The Objectives of Canadian Monetary Policy, 1949-61: Empirical 'Trade-Offs' and the Reaction Function of the Authorities." *Journal of Political Economy* 72, No. 2 (April), pp. 109-132.

Sachs, Jeffrey D. (1984). "Theoretical Issues in International Borrowing." *Princeton Studies in International Finance* 54 (July).

Smaghi, Lorenzo Bini (1982). "Independent Monetary Policy and Capital Mobility in LDCs: The Case of Malaysia, 1978-1981." Washington, D.C.: International Monetary Fund, DM/82/72 (November).

Countries

8

Exchange Rates and Monetary Policy in Singapore and Hong Kong

Ramon Moreno

Two lessons of general interest may be derived from the monetary policy experiences of Singapore and Hong Kong since the early 1970s. The first concerns the role of exchange rate policy in the conduct of monetary policy in open economies. The second has to do with the interactions between monetary policy on the one hand and other economic policies (fiscal, incomes, etc.) and economic structures (e.g., the government role in the economy) on the other hand.

Exchange rate policy has been the centerpiece of monetary policy in both these economies. In the case of Singapore, exchange rate policy was a key element in maintaining effective monetary control and achieving policy objectives as financial and exchange markets were liberalized. In Hong Kong, a fixed exchange rate regime was necessary to effectively regulate the money supply and to ensure stability in its system of private money creation.

Differences in exchange rate policy also help explain differences in the macroeconomic performance of the two economies. In the late 1970s and early 1980s, a strengthening currency contained inflation in Singapore by contributing to an increase in the demand for money, while a weakening currency produced the opposite result in Hong Kong. On the other hand, a contractionary fiscal policy, and policy-induced rigidity in labor markets exacerbated the deflationary impact of Singapore's strong currency policy over the 1980s and produced a recession in 1985. Yet, a parallel strengthening of the Hong Kong dollar after 1983 had a smaller contractionary effect because of flexibility in labor markets and in the approach to fiscal policy.

With respect to economic structure, Singapore has clearly defined economic and social objectives that underlie monetary, fiscal, and wage policies. Its experience of carefully managed transition from direct controls to market-based instruments of monetary policy as financial markets were liberalized, and of the effective and deliberate use of an exchange rate target, provides useful examples for other developing economies.

Hong Kong's economic policy, in contrast, has aimed at achieving the least amount of government regulation or intervention consistent with economic stability. Thus, Hong Kong has no central bank, and the money supply is largely determined at the initiative of the market, rather than by the government. How the government has solved the problems of monetary control under such conditions may be highly instructive for countries that hesitate to deregulate financial markets for fear of losing monetary control and destabilizing the economy.

This chapter starts with a sketch of the institutional background of the money creation process in Singapore and Hong Kong. It reviews the macroeconomic performance of both economies, as well as the behavior of monetary aggregates, exchange rates, and interest rates. It assesses the role of monetary policy in relation to economic performance in the two economies, and concludes by reviewing the main lessons offered by their experiences.

MONEY CREATION IN SINGAPORE

The Financial Sector

The Monetary Authority of Singapore was established in 1971 as a wholly owned government corporation. It performs all the functions of a central bank (except currency issue) such as regulating and supervising banks; holding reserve deposits of banks, issuing and managing public debt; discounting treasury bills; underwriting approved loans; and financing economic development in Singapore.

The Currency Board issues currency when presented with acceptable foreign assets for conversion. It is required to maintain a fund with at least 100 percent external asset cover (valued at current exchange rates) for currency issued. Unlike the Monetary Authority of Singapore, the Currency Board has no discretionary powers.

Banks doing business in Singapore may, subject to varying restrictions, engage in domestic or offshore banking. Over most of the period under discussion, domestic banking activities were subject to a minimum cash ratio of 6 percent and a liquid asset ratio of 20 percent (now 18 percent) of deposit liabilities,[1] and to a 40 percent (now 33 percent) tax on profits. Offshore banking is undertaken in Singapore's Asian dollar market by creating segregated accounting entries known as Asian currency units. Since 1972, offshore banking activities conducted in the Asian dollar market have been exempt from liquidity-asset ratio or cash ratio requirements, and profits on offshore operations with foreign residents are taxed at only 10 percent. This preferential treatment is designed to encourage foreign banks to concentrate their activities in the offshore, rather than in the domestic financial sector, and to make the Asian dollar market more attractive to foreign residents. However, transactions in Singapore dollars in the Asian dollar market are forbidden in order to discourage the internationalization of the currency and minimize speculative transactions by foreign residents which could increase exchange rate volatility.

There are three categories of commercial banks. *Fully licensed banks* do most of their business with Singapore residents, and may engage in all domestic banking activities permitted by the 1967 Banking Act. *Restricted license banks* can operate only in one location, and may not accept checking accounts, savings accounts, or time deposits of less than S$250,000. In addition to these restrictions, *offshore license banks* may not accept deposits in Singapore dollars from foreign residents, and lending to nonbank Singapore residents may not exceed S$30 million at any one time without the approval of the Monetary Authority of Singapore.

The closest deposit-taking competitors to banks in Singapore are finance companies, which may accept time and savings deposits but may not provide checking facilities. Unlike those in many other countries (such as Hong Kong before 1981), Singapore finance companies have been subject to cash reserve and liquid asset requirements similar to those for banks. The finance companies, therefore, had no competitive advantage over the banks. Moreover, Singapore's moderate inflation rate in the second half of the 1970s, as well as the absence of restrictions on bank deposit rates, reduced the incentive to shift funds from banks to finance companies. As a result, finance companies in Singapore in the 1970s did not grow as rapidly as in other countries.[2] Although their situation improved greatly in the early 1980s, their share of M3, at 10 percent in 1986, has remained small.

At the beginning of 1986, 135 commercial banks were operating in Singapore. Thirty-seven of them were fully licensed. Of these, 13 were incorporated in Singapore and controlled locally, and four have historically accounted for roughly 75 percent of the total assets of local banks. There were 14 banks with restricted licenses and 84 banks with offshore licenses. The commercial banks and other financial institutions accounted for 180 offshore Asian currency units operations, up from one in 1968 and 66 in 1975. In 1985, domestic banks accounted for approximately 25 percent of total deposits (including Asian currency units), foreign banks with full or restricted licenses for 48 percent, and offshore banks for 27 percent.

Money Creation and Monetary Control

Up to the first half of the 1970s, the Singapore government relied on extensive regulation of the banking sector to control money creation in order to contain high money growth rates and inflation. Singapore's strategy for controlling money growth over this period had two components. First, the government attempted to reduce growth in bank deposits. The minimum cash ratio was raised from the 3.5 percent rate prevailing until June 1972 to 9 percent by January 1973. In March 1974, quantitative and selective credit guidelines were issued to banks. To dampen loan demand, bank lending rates were raised by the bank-interest-setting cartel (in consultation with the Monetary Authority of Singapore) in April and December 1973 and in March of 1974, for a total of up to 2 percentage points.

Second, the government sought to limit the availability of foreign assets to domestic banks. Foreign assets could be readily converted into domestic liquid assets as well as currency, particularly under the fixed exchange rates prevailing up to June 1973. Banks could offset rising cash ratios by borrowing and selling foreign assets for domestic currency. The problem was exacerbated by speculative capital inflows caused by the perception that the Singapore dollar was undervalued as a result of its peg to a weakening U.S. dollar. In January 1973, the Monetary Authority imposed a special reserve requirement of 5 percent on banks' net foreign interbank liabilities, and raised this requirement to 9 percent in March of that year. Finally, the Singapore dollar was floated in June 1973.

While these measures did reverse rapid money growth and inflation in Singapore in the first half of the 1970s, the use of such blunt instruments as credit controls and reserve requirements to regulate money creation was inconsistent with Singapore's objective of developing and deepening its financial sector. As inflationary pressures eased, the government sought to replace these instruments with more sophisticated market instruments for monetary control.

Step by step, the panoply of regulations and controls was liberalized or dismantled. The special reserve requirement on banks' net foreign interbank liabilities was reduced from 9 percent to 5 percent in December 1973 and was eliminated altogether in May 1974.[3] Minimum cash ratios were reduced in steps to 6 percent by July 1975, and have not been changed since. Credit guidelines were lifted in January 1975, and the interest-setting cartel was discontinued in July 1975. Foreign exchange controls on domestic residents were eased in 1975 and lifted completely in June 1978, as were restrictions on transactions of domestic residents with the Asian dollar market.

To replace these controls, the government needed to develop effective market instruments for monetary control. Starting in 1975, it shifted to intervention in foreign exchange markets, as well as to rediscounting of commercial bills (specifically for the export sector), to control the supply of base money. At the same time, an exchange rate target was adopted to determine the extent of its intervention.

The importance of exchange market intervention in regulating Singapore's money supply is illustrated in Chart 1, which decomposes the determinants of reserve money. Government deposits and other liabilities of the Monetary Authority of Singapore have consistently tended to contract the money supply, partly reflecting the impact of persistent fiscal surpluses since the early 1970s. Exchange market intervention has offset this liquidity drain. Starting in 1975, the role of exchange market intervention was to adjust the money supply sufficiently to satisfy the government's exchange rate target.

Chart 1
Sources of Reserve Money: Singapore

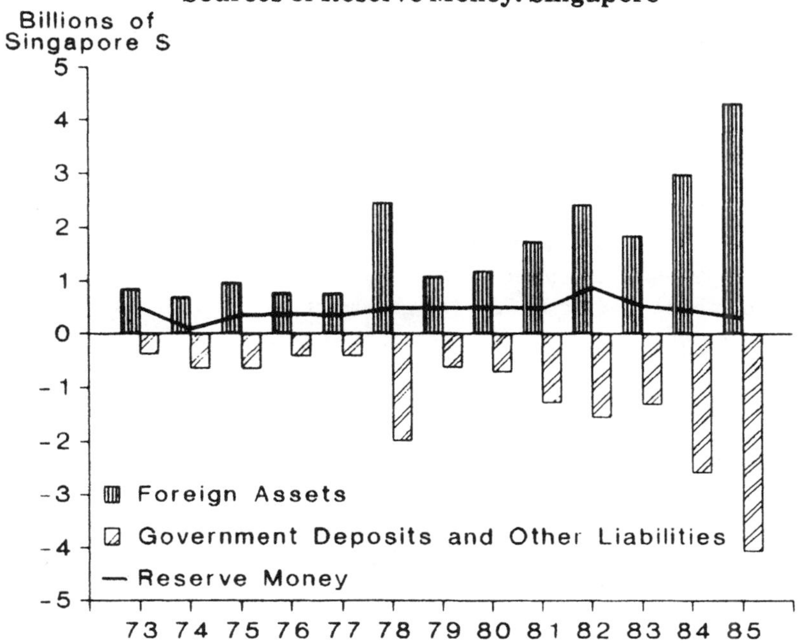

The shift to a market based instrument for monetary control is particularly remarkable because Singapore's domestic financial sector remains relatively undeveloped in contrast to its international banking and exchange markets. In particular, the scope for open-market operations in government securities has been limited by the small volume of issue resulting from perennial budget surpluses, the fact that most government securities are held to maturity, and that few government securities are held outside banks and a small number of institutional investors.

The development of active trading in government securities and of the financial market in general probably also has been slowed by government efforts to discourage foreign resident holdings of domestic financial assets through preferential treatment of the Asian dollar market, and also by the very heavy tax burden imposed on the private sector, which in effect limits the choice of savings vehicles for households.[4] A large proportion of private sector savings are placed in the Central Provident Fund, a government-administered pension scheme for all workers, rather than in domestic financial markets.

In 1987, the government took a number of steps to stimulate the development of the bond market and the marketability of government securities. While differential tax treatment between domestic markets and the Asian dollar market is maintained, the government has attempted to increase the volume of government securities held by the private sector by reducing the tax burden, issuing more government securities, allowing individuals to hold government securities via the Central Provident Fund, and increasing the minimum proportions of government securities that banks are required to hold.

A number of factors may explain recent efforts to develop a market for government securities in Singapore, even if the government appears to have no intention of becoming a net debtor in the near future. First, to regulate domestic credit creation, the government may wish to replace the rediscounting of commercial paper by open-market operations in government securities. Second, channeling savings away from Central Provident Fund contributions toward more marketable government securities, or making the Central Provident Fund itself a more flexible savings vehicle, is consistent with Singapore's efforts to develop deeper and more sophisticated financial markets, and should result in welfare gains for savers. Third, the availability of a market in government securities may improve monetary control by facilitating sterilized intervention in exchange markets, and the independent targeting of interest rates as well as exchange rates, at least in the short run.[5]

Since 1975, the Singapore dollar has been pegged to an undisclosed basket of currencies,[6] with emphasis on maintaining a strong Singapore dollar to contain inflation and instill confidence in Singapore's financial markets. The precise intervention rule has not been disclosed, but the government appears to have responded to increases in the domestic price level by appreciating the Singapore dollar. At the same time, the exchange rate target had to be calibrated to offset the liquidity drain created by persistent fiscal surpluses, thus "ensuring sufficient liquidity to accommodate real economic growth."[7]

While the overall thrust of Singapore's monetary policy is clear, it is hard to reconcile its various elements. A strong exchange rate policy geared to curtail inflation implies a relatively tight monetary policy, and it is not obvious how this is consistent with ensuring sufficient liquidity.[8] That the answer was not completely clear to the Singapore authorities either is apparent in the policy-induced recession of 1985 to be discussed later in this chapter.

Nevertheless, the adoption of an exchange rate target in Singapore was a prerequisite for the successful transition from direct controls to the use of market intervention to regulate money supply, and also enhanced domestic monetary control as exchange controls were lifted. It also proved highly effective in containing inflation.

MONEY CREATION IN HONG KONG

Financial Institutions

Hong Kong has no officially designated central bank, but a number of institutions perform some central banking functions under the overall direction of the Financial Secretary. A Banking Advisory Committee provides policy advice on banking and banking legislation, while a Commissioner of Banking regulates banking activity and on rare occasions intervenes in the operations of individual banks when their financial integrity is threatened.[9] A government Exchange Fund authorizes the issue of domestic currency by two private note-issuing banks, by providing these banks with certificates of indebtedness in exchange for acceptable asset backing for the note issue.[10] Currency issue is the only source of base money creation in Hong Kong, and it largely occurs at the initiative of the private sector. This poses interesting questions for monetary control.

Hong Kong banking legislation requires that banks maintain a ratio of liquid assets to deposits of at least 25 percent.[11] A 100 percent liquid asset cover is required on interbank liabilities. Since 1979, the short-term Hong Kong dollar deposits of the Exchange Fund with licensed banks are considered interbank liabilities and also require a 100 percent liquid asset cover.

Since 1964, banks in Hong Kong have restricted the interest they pay on deposits with maturities of less than 12 months to a level determined by the Hong Kong Association of Banks or by its predecessor, the Exchange Banks' Association. This restriction was designed to prevent the destabilizing interest rate competition experienced during banking crises in the early 1960s.

In contrast to Singapore, no particular effort has been made to insulate domestic from Eurocurrency banking operations in Hong Kong.[12] No preferential tax or regulatory treatment was given to Eurocurrency transactions, except for the elimination of the 15 percent withholding tax on foreign currency deposits in 1982, which applied to domestic as well as foreign residents. Restrictions on capital movements were eliminated in 1972 when Hong Kong abandoned the sterling standard; there is no effort to discourage Eurocurrency transactions denominated in Hong Kong dollars.

Since 1981, a three-tier banking structure segments the deposit-taking market into licensed banks, licensed deposit-taking companies (mostly banks with an international background), and registered deposit-taking companies (smaller finance companies). Licensed banks were authorized to engage in the full range of commercial banking operations. Registered deposit-taking companies were restricted to time deposits of HK$50,000 or more with a term of at least three months, while licensed deposit-taking companies could accept time deposits of less than three months' duration, for deposits of at least HK$500,000.

In contrast to the finance companies in Singapore,[13] Hong Kong deposit-taking companies grew very rapidly in the 1970s because they could offer better deposit rates than banks and were not subject to capital or liquid asset ratio requirements (they did not have to comply with the rates set by the bank interest-setting cartel). However, concern over deposit-taking companies' contribution to inflation and their impact on the profitability of banks, prompted the imposition of liquid asset ratio requirements on deposit-taking companies starting in 1980 and the far more severe restriction of their activities in 1981. The share of deposit-taking companies in total deposits fell from 36 percent in 1981 to 12.7 percent in 1986.

In the first half of 1985, there were 141 licensed banks, 33 licensed deposit-taking companies, 307 registered deposit-taking companies, and 117 bank representative offices of foreign banks operating in Hong Kong.

Money Creation and Monetary Control

Hong Kong has a freewheeling banking tradition, and policy toward the financial sector developed less deliberately than it did in Singapore. In implementing its mandate to "regulate the exchange value of the Hong Kong dollar," the government Exchange Fund has for the most part not resorted to direct manipulation of the monetary base, through such familiar instruments as open-market operations, or changes in reserve requirements or the discount rate. Instead, it has allowed the market to determine the money supply, while regulating the terms on which two private note-issuing banks issue currency.

Since 1972, Hong Kong has experimented with two approaches for regulating base money creation: floating exchange rates from 1974 to 1983, and fixed exchange rates since 1983.

Floating Exchange Rates, 1974-1983. Between July 1972 and October 1983, the two note-issuing banks could obtain certificates of indebtedness by crediting the Exchange Fund with the equivalent in Hong Kong dollar deposits. The Exchange Fund would then seek to achieve full foreign currency backing of the resulting domestic note issue by purchasing foreign assets with these deposits; it did not require banks to provide the backing themselves. For reasons that will become apparent, this led to floating exchange rates in 1974. In contrast, under the sterling standard that had prevailed up to 1972, and the fixed exchange rate regime in place since 1983, banks were required to surrender foreign currency to the Exchange Fund to purchase the right -- at a fixed exchange rate -- to issue domestic currency.

The major difficulty with Hong Kong's monetary regime during this period was the lack of constraint on domestic money creation by banks. Instead, the banking sector could create base money at will, by creating deposit liabilities in domestic currency against the government Exchange Fund. Unless some market mechanism existed to limit money creation, continuous increases in lending, money growth, and inflation could result.[14] Rapid money growth and rising inflation did occur in the late 1970s and early 1980s, leading to attempts to curtail money creation. In 1980 the government imposed liquid asset ratio requirements on deposit-taking companies, to limit their rapid deposit creation and mandated a 100 percent liquid assets requirement on deposits of the Exchange Fund, which had the effect of requiring note-issuing banks to hold either currency or foreign exchange assets against their currency issue.

In the late 1970s, it appears that the Hong Kong government also attempted to use the private bank interest-setting cartel as an instrument for monetary control. Thus, deposit rates were raised with greater frequency in the second half of the 1970s, and the interest-setting agreement that had been in place since 1964 was strengthened in 1981 by legislation that required banks to observe the interest rates established by the Hong Kong Association of Banks .

These measures were probably ineffective in containing money growth and inflation. Banks and deposit-taking companies could readily obtain foreign assets to satisfy liquidity requirements in the course of engaging in Eurocurrency transactions or by borrowing abroad. Furthermore, as the Hong Kong dollar depreciated in the late 1970s, a fixed amount of foreign assets used to serve the liquidity requirement could support an increasing amount of domestic currency creation. The fact that the Hong Kong dollar was floating thus diluted the effectiveness of liquid asset ratio requirements. The ease with which liquid asset ratios could be satisfied is illustrated by the end-of-year liquid asset holdings of banks from the early 1970s up to 1985. These holdings were typically in excess of 40 percent of deposit liabilities, well above the statutory 25 percent.

As for the interest-setting mechanism, it is likely that international competition and, up to 1981, the growth of nonbank deposit-taking companies eroded the ability of the Hong Kong Association of Banks to influence interest rates. Although the rise in bank deposit rates in the late 1970s was apparently in line with government desires to curtail money creation,[15] market conditions would probably have prompted such revisions anyway. The frequency with which deposit rates were revised is indicative. In 1981, just before major additional restrictions were imposed on deposit-taking companies, the Hong Kong Association of Banks revised its deposit rates 13 times, up from a single revision in 1976. The rate of revisions subsequently declined as competition from deposit-taking companies was effectively curtailed. However, revisions were once more stepped up to a peak of 16 in 1984.

In addition, the private Hong Kong Association of Banks could not always be expected to base its decisions on macroeconomic policy concerns. For example, during the attack on the Hong Kong dollar in 1982-1983, a rise in domestic deposit rates might have helped stabilize the Hong Kong dollar. However, the Hong Kong Association of Banks reportedly was reluctant to raise interest rates, because of concern about the financial condition of its members, and the government was not inclined to insist.[16]

Another difficulty with Hong Kong's monetary regime between 1972 and 1983 was that independent money creation by banks could neutralize any efforts by the government to stabilize exchange rates. This became apparent shortly after the sterling standard was abandoned in 1972, and prompted the government to discontinue fixed exchange rates in November 1974. In effect, Hong Kong went into a floating rate regime by default because it had adopted an institutional arrangement inconsistent with a fixed exchange rate.

In addition, efforts by the Exchange Fund to purchase foreign asset backing for note issue may have contributed to the persistent tendency for the Hong Kong dollar to depreciate after 1977. To see this, suppose that at prevailing exchange rates and interest rates, there were an excess demand for domestic currency. If the banks accommodated this demand by increasing currency issue, there would be no change in interest rates and exchange rates. However, if the Exchange Fund then purchased foreign assets to back the increased domestic currency issue, the Hong Kong dollar would tend to depreciate.

The lack of effective instruments to stabilize the currency is most dramatically illustrated by the 1982-1983 attack on the Hong Kong dollar. During this period, uncertainty about the future of Hong Kong provoked a general shift out of Hong Kong dollar assets into foreign currency assets, and resulted in a drop in the trade-weighted value of the Hong Kong dollar of 27 percent over 15 months. Furthermore, the crisis may have put the exchange market on a speculative path, where expectations about further declines in the Hong Kong dollar created further pressure on the currency and thus tended to be self-fulfilling. In July 1982, when the Hong Kong dollar began its sharp decline, the annualized rate of depreciation was 7.7 percent. By September 1983, the last month of the crisis, the Hong Kong dollar was depreciating at a 65 percent annual rate.

The data suggest that the Exchange Fund may have intervened to stabilize the Hong Kong dollar between March and July 1983, as the stock of currency outstanding declined at an average annual rate of about 18 percent.[17] However, in August and September 1983, before the monetary regime was changed, the stock of currency grew very rapidly, at a 57 percent average annual rate. It is possible that banks at this point had stepped up currency creation to acquire foreign currency assets, overwhelming any attempts at intervention by the Exchange Fund.

Fixed Exchange Rates, 1983 to Present. In what proved to be a successful measure to end the attack on the Hong Kong dollar, the government changed the arrangements for note issue in October 1983. Since then, banks have been required to exchange foreign assets for certificates of indebtedness of the Exchange Fund, at the exchange rate set by the government.[18] The note-issuing banks may then issue paper currency for the value of the certificates of indebtedness. In turn, the Exchange Fund stands ready to redeem domestic currency at the fixed exchange rate. The pre-1972 sterling standard had functioned essentially in the same way.

Three characteristics of this regime guarantee stability. First, the level of base money creation and currency issue in Hong Kong under the present regime depends on the volume of foreign assets which banks wish to convert into Hong Kong currency at the exchange rate set by the government. This in turn depends on their vault cash requirements, the public's demand for currency, and ultimately, on the extent to which banks wish to accommodate money demand at prevailing interest rates. Because banks have alternative uses for the foreign assets, they try to limit currency issue. No such constraint limited note issue between 1972 and 1983.

Second, the readiness of the Exchange Fund to buy or sell Hong Kong dollars at a fixed exchange rate ensures that arbitrage would regulate money creation in such a manner as to maintain the exchange rate set by the government. For example, if the Hong Kong dollar depreciated below the officially set exchange rate, banks would find it profitable to convert domestic currency for foreign assets with the Exchange Fund, and then sell the foreign currency at a profit in the open-market. This arbitrage process would continue until the reduced supply of domestic currency eliminated the incipient depreciation.[19] The role of the Exchange Fund is in this respect similar to that of a central bank which engages in unsterilized currency market intervention to peg the exchange rate.

Third, asset holders can be confident that the government holds a sufficient amount of foreign exchange reserves to redeem all the base money created. This accounts for the remarkable success of the present monetary regime in ending the speculative attack on the Hong Kong dollar in 1983. Under the monetary regime in place between 1972 and 1983, banks could create money in excess of the value of the foreign asset cover at the prevailing exchange rate. This contributed to the expectation that a currency peg would be unenforceable and made it impossible to contain the attack on the Hong Kong dollar. The fact that money is not created at the initiative of the government and that Hong Kong has historically adopted a conservative fiscal policy is also of importance. In other economies, it is money creation by the government, often to finance budget deficits, that creates doubts about the enforceability of the currency peg and prompts speculative attacks that ultimately result in currency depreciation.

MACROECONOMIC PERFORMANCE AND THE POLICY STANCE

From the first quarter of 1971 to the fourth quarter of 1985, the average real GDP growth of both Singapore and Hong Kong was a little over 8 percent (Table 1). Both economies exhibited resiliency in the face of external shocks, as they rebounded strongly after the first oil shock and were relatively unaffected by the second oil shock. There is a close correspondence in the cyclical patterns of growth, indicating the strong dependence of both economies to similar external markets. However, GDP growth in Singapore has lagged behind Hong Kong's in recent years. As discussed more fully below, the decline in Singapore's growth, which has since been reversed, reflects the impact of fiscal contraction, a high wage policy, and a strong currency in Singapore over the 1980s.

Unemployment has not been a significant problem in either economy, except for certain episodes. Between 1975 and 1985, Singapore's unemployment rate averaged 3.6 percent, although in 1985 it was at a 10-year high of 4.1 percent.[20] Over the same period, Hong Kong's unemployment rate averaged 4.2 percent, notwithstanding periodic surges in the labor force caused by immigration, such as the half million immigrants from the Chinese mainland between 1978 and 1981.[21]

Table 1
Macroeconomic Performance
(percent)

	Real GDP Growth		**Inflation**[a]	
Year	**Singapore**	**Hong Kong**	**Singapore**	**Hong Kong**
1971	12.5	7.3	1.8	3.2
1972	13.4	11.0	2.1	6.4
1973	11.5	12.7	19.3	17.9
1974	6.3	2.2	23.0	15.2
1975	4.1	0.2	2.7	2.7
1976	7.5	17.1	-1.9	3.8
1977	7.9	12.5	3.3	5.6
1978	8.6	9.5	4.7	5.8
1979	9.4	11.7	4.0	11.7
1980	10.3	10.9	8.5	14.8
1981	9.9	9.4	8.2	13.8
1982	6.4	3.0	4.0	10.7
1983	7.9	6.5	1.2	9.9
1984	8.1	9.5	2.6	8.5
1985	-1.9	0.6	0.5	3.5
1986	2.0	8.7	-1.4	2.6
1971–1985	8.1	8.3	5.2	8.9
1975–1983	8.0	9.0	3.9	8.8

(a) *Average of changes in quarterly indices over corresponding quarters of the preceding year.*

Source: International Monetary Fund International Financial Statistics and the Hong Kong Monthly Digest of Statistics.

In contrast, inflation over the period 1971-1985 was significantly lower in Singapore than in Hong Kong. In particular, between 1975 and 1983, when Singapore had a "strong currency" policy and the Hong Kong dollar was floating, Singapore's inflation rate averaged 3.9 percent, less than half Hong Kong's average inflation of 8.8 percent. Both economies experienced transitory increases in inflation following the 1973 and the 1979 oil shocks, and subsequent disinflation in the 1980s. However, Hong Kong's inflation rate rose much more than Singapore's in the late 1970s, and did not fall as much in the 1980s.

The money growth in both economies is shown in Table 2. Both economies experienced very fast narrow money growth in the early 1970s. Between 1975 and 1983, average M1 growth in Singapore of 13.4 percent a

Table 2
Money Growth[a]
(Percent)

Year	Singapore M1	Singapore M2	Hong Kong[b] M1	Hong Kong[b] M2
1971	9.4	10.7	20.3	23.7
1972	24.1	19.3	35.9	26.2
1973	22.4	20.1	24.5	13.0
1974	8.5	13.9	-4.0	14.4
1975	18.8	17.6	8.9	17.4
1976	17.7	14.5	15.3	18.0
1977	10.2	7.3	10.6	20.2
1978	11.3	10.3	25.2	26.2
1979	13.7	11.2	22.8[c]	24.3[c]
1980	13.9	27.8	20.1	27.9
1981	11.5	22.0	2.9[c]	13.8[c]
1982	13.8	14.5	6.3	20.9
1983	10.0	16.5	11.0	14.3
1984	1.5	8.2	14.5	23.1
1985	2.1	3.6	26.1	19.0
1971-1985				
average	12.6	14.5	16.0	20.2
maximum	24.1	27.8	35.9	27.9
minimum	1.5	3.6	-4.0	13.0
standard deviation	6.2	6.1	10.0	4.8
coefficient of variation	0.5	0.4	0.6	0.2
1975-1983				
average	13.4	15.7	13.7	20.3
maximum	18.8	27.8	25.2	27.9
minimum	10.0	7.3	2.9	13.8
standard deviation	3.0	5.9	7.2	4.7
coefficient of variation	0.2	0.4	0.5	0.2

(a) *Average of changes in quarterly aggregates over corresponding quarters of the preceding year.*

(b) *All currencies to 1980; Hong Kong dollars, 1981-1985.*

(c) *Adjusted for change in definition. Only December-to-December change available for 1981.*

Source: International Monetary Fund International Financial Statistics and the Hong Kong Monthly Digest of Statistics.

year was about the same as M1 growth of 13.7 percent in Hong Kong.[22] Since then, however, Singapore's M1 growth dropped off sharply, while M1 growth in Hong Kong has accelerated. Narrow money growth in Hong Kong has been very erratic, with periods of very rapid growth alternating with periods of contraction. In fact, the coefficient of variation for narrow money between 1975 and 1983 is two and a half times higher in Hong Kong than in Singapore. It would appear that sharp fluctuations in narrow money growth are a characteristic of Hong Kong's system of private money creation, even under the fixed exchange rates adopted since 1983.

Between 1975 and 1983, M2 growth averaged 15.7 percent in Singapore. Of particular interest is the acceleration in growth starting in the second half of 1979, which, it will be argued, reflected strong demand for Singapore dollar assets and helped contain inflation. M2 growth was even faster in Hong Kong over the period, but the data are more difficult to interpret, particularly since they include foreign currency deposits up to 1980.

The behavior of exchange rates on a trade-weighted basis[23] is illustrated in Chart 2. Between 1975-1983, after Singapore adopted an exchange rate target and the Hong Kong dollar floated, the trade-weighted Singapore dollar appreciated 10.3 percent while the trade-weighted Hong Kong dollar depreciated 37 percent.

Chart 2
Trade Weighted Exchange Rates
Singapore and Hong Kong

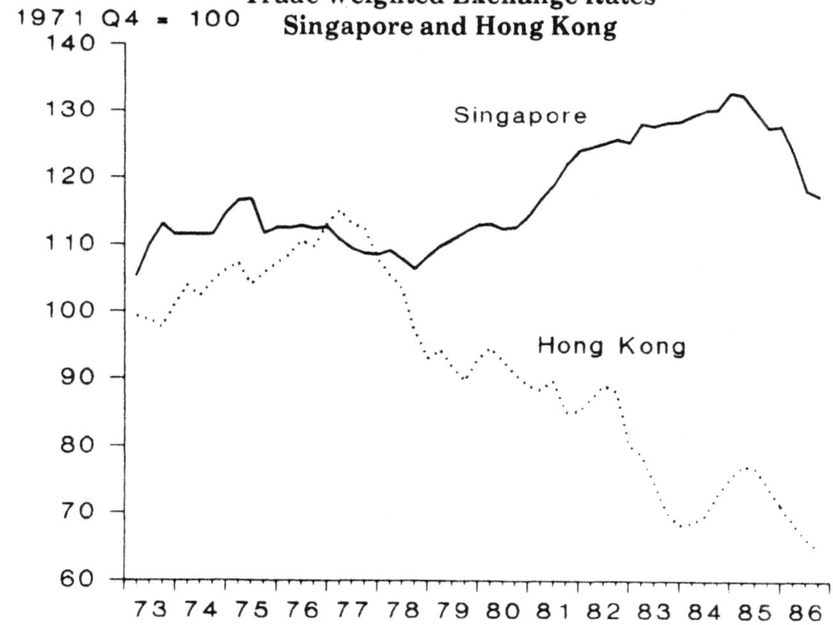

Chart 3
Interest Rate Differentials
Singapore and Hong Kong

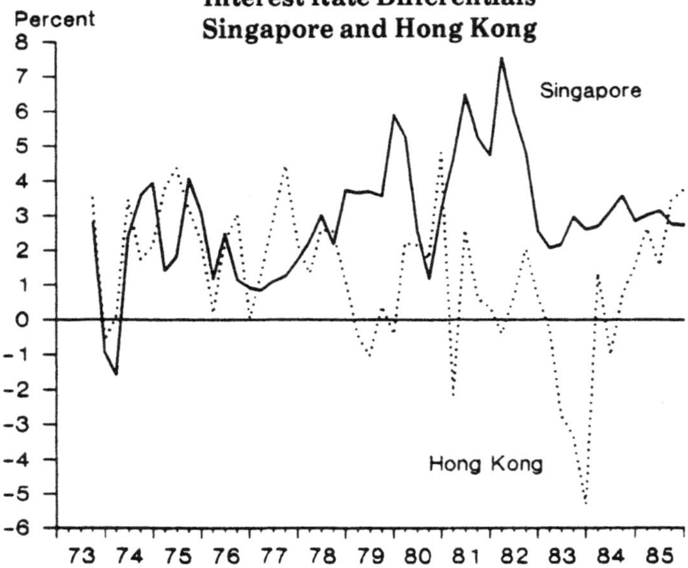

Between 1975 and 1978, Singapore apparently pegged its currency to the U.S. dollar, resulting in a slight depreciation on a trade-weighted basis over the period. This was still consistent with a strong currency policy, as the value of the Singapore dollar with respect to the U.S. dollar was approximately 25 percent above its levels at the beginning of the 1970s. The Singapore dollar began to appreciate against the U.S. dollar and on a trade-weighted basis in 1978, the year in which exchange controls were lifted.

Like the Singapore dollar, the Hong Kong dollar appreciated significantly on a trade-weighted basis from the early 1970s to about 1977. In contrast to the Singapore dollar, however, the Hong Kong dollar then began an extended period of decline which accelerated in 1982 and 1983 because of a speculative attack on the currency. The stability of the Hong Kong dollar after 1983, therefore, is particularly striking.

As shown in Chart 3, the differential between the three-month London interbank offer rate (LIBOR) and a comparable Singapore rate widened from 1977 to 1982 (except in 1980, when monetary policy in Singapore tightened in response to rising inflation). As world interest rates rose to unprecedented levels, the increase in Singapore interest rates was comparatively moderate. The pattern of interest rates implied expectations of continued appreciation of the Singapore dollar in the late 1970s and early 1980s.

In contrast, the differential between the LIBOR and the comparable Hong Kong rate[24] does not suggest any consistent premium in favor of the Hong Kong dollar in the late 1970s; it even turned negative in the late 1970s and in 1983. However, since 1983 it has been steadily rising. The pattern reflects a weak Hong Kong dollar in the late 1970s and early 1980s, as well as credibility of Hong Kong's monetary and exchange rate regime after 1983.

POLICY IMPACT

Exchange Rate Policy and Inflation

Surprisingly, the rates of money growth do not fully explain the difference in Hong Kong and Singapore's inflationary performances. Between 1975 and 1983, when Hong Kong's inflation rate was on average more than double that of Singapore's, the average M1 growth was about the same in the two economies.[25] Furthermore, M1 growth in Hong Kong in 1985 reached 26 percent, above the most rapid growth rates achieved in the late 1970s. Nevertheless, Hong Hong's average inflation in 1985 and 1986 was far below the peak inflation rates of the late 1970s and early 1980s.

The impact on money demand of the different exchange rate policies in the two economies up to 1983 may explain differing inflation performances. In particular, Singapore's strong currency policy after 1975 may have dampened inflation by increasing money demand, while Hong Kong's depreciating currency had the opposite effect. A simple indicator of money demand is the velocity of money, or the ratio of nominal GDP to money, which measures the money stock that supports a given level of nominal spending on goods and services. A decline in velocity indicates a rise in money demand, which tends to be disinflationary; a rise in velocity indicates a fall in money demand, which is typically associated with higher inflationary pressures.

Table 3 reports the variations in money velocity in Singapore and Hong Kong since the early 1970s.[26] In Singapore, M1 velocity declined an average of 0.4 percent between 1975 and 1983, while M2 velocity declined an average of 2.4 percent. In contrast, the growth of M1 velocity in Hong Kong from 1975 to 1983 averaged 4.7 percent, while M2 velocity on the average declined 1.2 percent. The data for Singapore suggest stable and even increasing demand for M1 and a strong increase in the demand for M2, while the data for Hong Kong indicate falling demand for M1.

Two reasons may be offered for this contrasting velocity performance. First, differing perceptions about the effectiveness of monetary control may have increased money demand in Singapore, while lowering it

Table 3
Changes in Money Velocity[a]
(Percent)

Year	Singapore M1	Singapore M2	Hong Kong M1	Hong Kong M2
1971	7.6	6.4	-4.3	-6.9
1972	-3.7	0.0	-10.9	-4.5
1973	2.9	4.5	7.6	14.3
1974	13.8	8.3	20.6	0.3
1975	-10.3	-9.4	-4.1	-11.3
1976	-7.2	-4.6	10.7	8.2
1977	-0.6	2.1	5.4	-3.1
1978	-0.3	0.6	-6.0	-6.7
1979	1.3	3.7	7.3	6.0
1980	6.4	-5.7	7.7	0.9
1981	7.0	-2.3	14.0	3.2
1982	-2.0	-2.5	6.6	-6.0
1983	1.8	-3.9	0.6	-2.2
1984	8.4	1.5	4.8	-2.5
1985	-8.1	-9.5	-15.1	-10.3
1971-1985				
average	1.1	-0.7	3.0	-1.4
maximum	13.8	8.3	20.6	14.3
minimum	-10.3	-9.5	-15.1	-11.3
standard deviation	6.6	5.2	9.3	6.8
coefficient of variation	5.8	-7.2	3.1	-4.9
1975-1983				
average	-0.4	-2.4	4.7	-1.2
maximum	7.0	3.7	14.0	8.2
minimum	-10.3	-9.4	-6.0	-11.3
standard deviation	5.3	3.9	6.3	6.0
coefficient of variation	12.3	1.6	1.3	-4.9

(a) *Average of changes in quarterly velocities over corresponding quarters of the preceding year.*

Source: Federal Reserve Bank of San Francisco staff estimates based on data in International Monetary Fund International Financial Statistics and the Hong Kong Monthly Digest of Statistics. See also note 26.

in Hong Kong, reflecting different perceptions of the risk of holding money in the two economies. Second, it appears that the moderate rise in nominal interest rates in Singapore relative to Eurorates in the second half of the 1970s (Chart 3) strengthened the demand for M1 and produced the slight decline in M1 velocity.

The increased demand for Singapore dollar assets is reflected in a sharp increase in capital inflows that started in 1978, when capital controls for domestic residents were ended. These inflows, which far exceeded the current account deficit, rose from US$607 million in 1977 to a peak of US$2,709 million in 1983.[27] Of particular interest are the positive net errors and omissions in the capital account of Singapore after 1978, which may indicate capital repatriation by domestic residents in response to the lifting of exchange controls. This component rose from US$1.1 million in 1977 to US$103.9 million in 1978, and to an average of close to US$400 million in 1979 and 1980. Capital inflows would also help explain the sharp drop in M2 velocity starting in 1979, as domestic residents may have placed funds previously held abroad in domestic interest-bearing bank deposits.[28]

On the other hand, the combination of rising M1 velocity and comparatively stable M2 velocity in Hong Kong suggests a decline in narrow money demand in response to inflationary pressures and rising domestic interest rates, resulting in a shift from transactions balances toward interest-bearing deposits. The absence of an effective peg on the Hong Kong dollar over the period contributed to the rise in nominal interest rates by reinforcing inflationary expectations and leading investors to demand a premium on assets denominated in Hong Kong dollars.

The pattern of velocity in Hong Kong after 1983 more closely resembles that of Singapore for the period 1975-1983, suggesting that the peg to an appreciating U.S. dollar enhanced the demand for money in Hong Kong. M1 velocity in Hong Kong grew much more moderately, while there appears to have been a strong increase in demand for M2, reflected in continuous declines in velocity.

Aside from affecting money demand, exchange rate policy also had an impact on imported inflation, which may also partly explain the differences in inflationary performance. Between 1975 and 1981, a period of high world inflation, the Singapore dollar appreciated 12 percent against the U.S. dollar, while depreciating 17 percent against the Japanese yen and 6 percent against the German mark. In contrast, even before the 1982-1983 attack on the Hong Kong dollar, the Hong Kong dollar had depreciated 12 percent against the U.S. dollar, implying even stronger depreciation against the yen and the mark. Among the three, the United States experienced the highest rate of inflation, averaging 9.1 percent over the period, compared to 6.2 percent for Japan and 4.4 percent for Germany. The United States was also the second largest source of imports for Singapore, with a share of 14 percent in Singapore's imports in 1980. Thus, Singapore's exchange rate policy tended to attenuate imported inflation in the second half of the 1970s, while the absence of a mechanism to stabilize exchange rates may have amplified imported inflation in Hong Kong.[29]

Exchange Rate Policy and the Policy Mix

In 1979 Singapore adopted a policy favoring high wages, apparently aimed at shifting the composition of output away from labor-intensive (and presumably low technology) manufacturing sectors.[30] At the same time, it also maintained a continually appreciating currency and a contractionary fiscal policy. Notwithstanding relatively low inflation, between 1978 and 1985 unit labor costs (nominal wage rates adjusted for productivity increases) in Singapore doubled. Over the same period, the nominal trade-weighted Singapore dollar appreciated 22 percent, while fiscal surpluses in Singapore increased from a low of 0.25 percent of nominal GDP in 1978 to a high of 5.2 percent in 1984.

Tight money and the cheaper import costs of intermediate goods associated with a strong currency were not sufficient to offset the effect of higher real wages on external competitiveness. As a result, Singapore's terms of trade (the ratio of export to import prices) rose 14 percent from the first quarter of 1979 to its peak in the first quarter of 1983. While Singapore's terms of trade declined subsequently, it was too late to avert a recession in 1985 which resulted in a 1.9 percent decline in real GDP.

The recession prompted a major reassessment of the approach to policy in Singapore, and accounts for recent efforts at fiscal stimulus and a reduction in intervention in the labor market.[31] For example, the levy on employers for the Central Provident Fund was reduced from 25 to 10 percent of gross wages, and corporate tax rates were reduced from 40 to 33 percent. Other taxes and user charges have also been reduced. At the same time, the Singapore dollar has depreciated along with the U.S. dollar since the first quarter of 1985 (about 9 percent on a trade-weighted basis to 1986), providing a boost to competitiveness and economic growth in 1987.

The recent modifications to policy in Singapore are more in line with the policy mix adopted by Hong Kong in the 1980s. Hong Kong appreciated its currency after 1983, but it did not experience a loss of competitiveness or economic contraction to the degree experienced by Singapore in recent years. This was partly because of wage flexibility in its labor markets,[32] which meant that unit labor costs in Hong Kong rose much less than they did in Singapore between 1978 and 1985, and declined on a U.S. dollar basis. Hong Kong's terms of trade over the same period also declined.[33] At the same time, a relative relaxation of fiscal policy helped offset the contractionary effect of currency appreciation, as the overall budget balance moved from a peak surplus of about 7.3 percent of GDP in 1980, to deficits averaging 1 percent of GDP in 1982-1984.

Exchange Rate Policy and Offshore Markets in Singapore

Hewson (1981) has argued that the lifting of exchange controls in Singapore in 1978 was premature. In particular, the differential treatment of the Asian dollar market and domestic deposits could adversely affect monetary control by encouraging a "round trip" between domestic banking markets and the Asian dollar market. Under such a round trip, domestic residents would shift deposits to the Asian dollar market to avoid reserve requirements, and convert these funds for use in domestic markets at some future date. Currency risk would be hedged in the forward market.[34]

However, Singapore's monetary policy may actually have discouraged round tripping for purposes of reserve avoidance. If the government's policy of maintaining a strong currency, in effect since 1975, created an expectation of an appreciating Singapore dollar, banks acquiring U.S. dollars in the Asian dollar market for the purpose of reserve avoidance would find it costly to hedge their positions, as market participants would demand a forward premium on the Singapore dollar. If the forward premium were sufficiently large, it could offset any savings on reserve requirements.

Two indicators cited earlier suggest that a strong currency may have curtailed round tripping. First, the data on interest differentials in Chart 3 indicates a significant and rising premium on Singapore dollar assets after exchange controls were lifted, which must have raised the cost of round tripping significantly. Second, the strong rise in M2 in Singapore after 1979 and the data on capital inflows reflect a rising demand by domestic residents for assets denominated in Singapore dollars, which presumably limited their desire to shift deposits out of these assets into the Asian dollar market.[35]

CONCLUSIONS

Taken together, the experience of Singapore and Hong Kong highlights the effectiveness of an exchange rate target in controlling inflation in small open economies. In the case of Hong Kong, an enforceable exchange rate target is actually a necessary condition for effectively regulating its system of private money creation.

Nevertheless, rapid money growth in Hong Kong during the period when its currency was floating does not fully explain its higher inflation in comparison to Singapore; the impact of exchange rate policy on money demand appears to have been of importance as well. By dampening the rise in domestic interest rates, the strong currency policy adopted by Singapore appears to have increased money demand and slowed inflation.

Conversely, the weak Hong Kong dollar in the late 1970s and early 1980s appears to have reduced money demand and accelerated inflation.

The experience of both economies also highlights the importance of allowing sufficient flexibility in domestic economic policy to offset the disinflationary impact of a strong currency policy. Hong Kong's performance has been better than Singapore's in recent years precisely because it adopted a more appropriate policy mix. While Hong Kong, like Singapore, has allowed its currency to appreciate since 1983, Hong Kong has maintained competitiveness by allowing real wage flexibility and some fiscal stimulus at the same time as its currency appreciated. Singapore introduced a policy of rising wages that adversely affected competitiveness and also exacerbated the contractionary pressures by adopting tight fiscal and monetary policies.

Nevertheless, the largely conservative approach to fiscal policy in both economies reduced the policymakers' need to exploit the seigniorage from money creation and is therefore a key ingredient in the successful conduct of monetary policy in both economies. In the case of Singapore, it gave the government the freedom to pursue a disinflationary strong currency policy; in the case of Hong Kong, it probably accounts for the government's willingness to maintain a monetary regime where the private sector determines money creation.

Other lessons may also be drawn from the experiences of these two economies. By actively intervening in exchange markets and adopting an exchange rate target, Singapore was able to abandon direct control measures as instruments of monetary policy, even if its domestic financial markets were relatively undeveloped. A strong currency target was important in encouraging capital inflows and providing an ample foreign asset base for intervention in exchange markets.

Furthermore, a currency target had several advantages over its alternatives. A monetary aggregate target might not have provided the flexibility required to offset imported inflation or stimulate the demand for Singapore dollar assets. An interest rate target would become unattainable by the growing integration with international financial markets. A strong currency target may also have reduced the impact of the lifting of exchange controls on the effectiveness of monetary policy by discouraging round tripping into the Asian dollar market.

Hong Kong's experience dramatically illustrates the feasibility of a regime where the money supply is determined by the private sector, so long as currency issue is linked to foreign assets at a fixed exchange rate. A policy of market creation of money enhances the credibility of the fixed exchange rate. It accounts for the remarkable success in ending a speculative attack on the Hong Kong dollar in 1983. The experience may be instructive for economies that fear to deregulate financial markets, but nevertheless have experienced far more instability than has Hong Kong.

NOTES

Thanks to Hang-Sheng Cheng for helpful comments and to John Duffy and Laura Shoe for expert research assistance.

1. The first 10 percent tier of the liquid asset ratio consisted of primary liquid assets: cash; balances with the Monetary Authority of Singapore in excess of minimum cash balances; net money at call with discount houses; Singapore treasury bills and government securities; and trade bills of less than one year's maturity. The second 10 percent tier of liquid assets consisted of primary assets in excess of the first 10 percent tier; government securities of over one-year maturity; and up to 5 percent of liabilities (of the 10 percent provided in the second tier) in bills of exchange payable within three months. On May 21, 1987, the liquid asset ratio requirement was lowered to 18 percent, but the portfolio must now consist of at least 10 percent in Singapore government securities.

2. See Lee and Jao (1982).

3. The floating of the Singapore dollar in 1973 facilitated the eventual abolition of the special reserve requirement on net foreign interbank liabilities.

4. This is a point made by Hewson (1982). However, it may be argued that using the tax mechanism to satisfy certain social investment objectives is to be preferred to the use of selective credit guidelines or preferential interest rates, which has been common in other countries. The latter approach creates severe distortions in the financial system and may restrict the availability of credit even to the sector being favored. An example is New Zealand. See Harper (1986).

5. A very interesting discussion of the issues involved in developing a government securities market and of the experience of Indonesia is provided by Sundararajan and Molho (1988) in their chapter in this book.

6. A basket was deliberately chosen to dampen the effects of fluctuations of any individual currency. Casual inspection and empirical analysis reported by Branson (1981) indicate that a heavy weight is assigned to the U.S. dollar, which is also the currency of intervention.

7. In its 1981-1982 annual report, the Monetary Authority of Singapore explains its monetary target as follows: ". . . the (monetary) policy . . . was aimed . . . at maintaining a strong exchange rate for the Singapore dollar, while ensuring sufficient liquidity to accommodate real economic growth. Underlying this shift in emphasis away from targets for interest rates and money supply growth . . . is the view that the exchange rate is a relatively more important anti-inflation instrument in the context of the small and open Singapore economy. Price stability then, continued to be the prime objective. The emphasis given to a strong exchange rate policy also facilitates the policy of upgrading and restructuring the domestic economy."

8. A similar point is made by Hewson (1981, 1982).

9. The private Hongkong and Shanghai Bank has in the past served as a lender of last resort on a voluntary basis, for example during the banking crises in the early 1960s. In the 1980s, however, the government has departed from previous practice and intervened directly to save failing banks.

10. Since 1976, the Secretary for Monetary Affairs heads a Monetary Affairs Branch responsible for managing the accounts of the government, for relations with international monetary institutions and for administering the Coinage Security Fund and the Exchange Fund.

11. In Hong Kong, liquid assets may include freely remittable bills of exchange and net balances with other banks -- both foreign and domestic -- approved certificates of deposit and money market instruments, treasury bills and government issued or guaranteed securities, as well as noninterest-bearing legal tender notes and coins, and gold coins or bars. Given the limited amount of marketable government securities, foreign assets have typically accounted for the bulk of interest-bearing liquid assets, although certificates of deposits have grown in importance since 1983.

12. Government statistics did not even distinguish between domestic and foreign currency deposits until 1981.

13. For purposes of monetary control, Hong Kong's deposit-taking companies may be compared with Singapore's finance companies because they may accept deposits from the public. Hong Kong's deposit-taking companies also perform merchant banking activities. Merchant banks in Singapore operate mainly in the offshore Asian dollar market and may accept deposits only from banks and other financial institutions.

14. Observers of the Hong Kong scene have argued that the monetary system during this period was inherently unstable. This view was buttressed by traditional critiques of (real bills) regimes where money is created at the initiative of the private sector. Instability in such regimes occurs in a closed economy and under certain conditions in an open economy which is fully insulated by floating exchange rates. For a succinct recent discussion of the "real bills" doctrine, see Humphreys (1982). Laidler (1981) discusses Adam Smith's demonstration of the stability of private money creation under fixed exchange rates. A fuller discussion of all these issues in the context of Hong Kong is given in Moreno (1986).

15. See Standard Chartered Bank (1986).

16. *Asian Monetary Monitor*, Vol. 7, No. 6 (November-December 1983). Market rates did rise in Hong Kong in response to the downward pressure on the Hong Kong dollar, although they did not contain the currency depreciation. The differential between the overnight London interbank offer rate and an estimate of the Hong Kong overnight interbank rate, which has on the average been positive since 1973, dropped precipitously starting in the second half of 1982 and bottomed at a negative 5 percentage points in the last quarter of 1983, when the monetary regime was changed (see Chart 3). The rise in interest rates may have been caused by the decline in currency cited earlier and the competition by banks for funds to be converted into foreign currency.

17. Such intervention has never been officially confirmed. However, banks had no incentive to retire domestic currency during the attack on the Hong Kong dollar in 1983. On the contrary, they may have had the incentive to create currency to acquire foreign assets.

18. At HK$7.80 per U.S. dollar.

19. The arbitrage process is discussed by John Greenwood in *Asian Monetary Monitor*, Vol. 7, No. 6 (November-December 1983). Hsu (1985) has analyzed this arbitrage process in more detail. He notes that the demand for currency may be such that banks do not fully exploit the arbitrage opportunities when exchange rates deviate from the official rate of HK$ 7.80 to the U.S. dollar. However, the deviations are small. Hsu estimates that the coefficient of variation for the exchange rate vis-á-vis the U.S. dollar between November 1983 and December 1984 is 0.0022, with a maximum range (the difference between the maximum and the minimum exchange rate as a percentage of the minimum exchange rate) of 0.69 percent.

20. Singapore lost 96,000 jobs in 1985, two-thirds of which were held by guest workers.

21. The unemployment figures for Hong Kong and Singapore are not necessarily comparable.

22. In both economies M1 consists of currency and demand deposits, while M2 consists of M1 plus interest-bearing savings, time deposits, and negotiable CDs of banks.

23. The effective exchange rate for Hong Kong is a trade-weighted (imports and exports) index, using 1981 trade weights with Hong Kong's 15 principal trading partners. The source is Table 7.17, Hong Kong *Monthly Digest of Statistics*. Countries included (percentage weights in parentheses) are Australia (2.74), Belgium (1.23), Canada (1.65), China (17.99), France (1.69), Germany (5.19), Italy (1.34), Japan (16.81), Netherlands (1.21), Singapore (7.26), South Korea (3.58), Switzerland (2.21), Taiwan (6.83), U.K. (7.15), and U.S.A. (23.14). The effective exchange rate index for Singapore was calculated using 1980 trade weights with Singapore's 10 principal trading partners, based on the IMF direction of trade data. The countries in the index are U.S. (20), Japan (13), U.K. (4.16), Germany (4.87), Australia (6.5), Hong Kong (12.47), Malaysia (24.24), Thailand (7.04), India (3.98), and France (3.53).

24. The Hong Kong rate is the average of the maximum and minimum Hong Kong overnight interbank offer rate.

25. The reasons why money growth in Hong Kong did not approach the rates reached by some Latin American countries are not immediately obvious, given the potential instability of Hong Kong's monetary regime. Moreno (1986) suggests that Hong Kong's monetary regime under flexible exchange rates could be consistent with limited money growth if two conditions held: (a) domestic output were not fully insulated from the external sector; and (b) the real loan supply -- and therefore the real quantity of money supplied by profit-maximizing banks -- were positively related to interest rates. The first condition implies that the domestic prices could be stabilized by the external sector, even under floating rates. The second condition implies that banks would not passively accommodate loan demand, which could lead to the cycle of accelerating inflation and money growth described by Wicksell. A conservative fiscal policy may also play a role, by limiting the demand for credit and the incentive for banks to create money.

26. The growth in velocity is calculated on a quarter to previous year's quarter basis. Only annual GDP data are available for both economies. To estimate quarterly velocity, a quarterly GDP series was generated using quarterly industrial production in Singapore and quarterly industrial employment in Hong Kong as instruments.

27. These data are taken from the IMF *Balance of Payments Statistics Yearbook* (1985). The SDR figures are converted into U.S. dollars at the rate indicated in the yearbook.

28. The Monetary Authority of Singapore has suggested that the strong increase in M2 after 1979 was due to substitution from noninterest-bearing into interest-bearing assets, in response to rising interest rates and inflation. However, this does not seem to be the complete story. Since M1 is part of M2, a substitution into interest-bearing components of M2 would not necessarily have increased the total size of M2 to the extent observed in Singapore.

29. However, the relationship between the wholesale price index and the consumer price index raises some questions about the significance of imported inflation in explaining domestic inflation, particularly in Singapore. In the late 1970s, Singapore's wholesale price index, which is very highly correlated with the import price index, rose as much as three times faster than the consumer price index, which suggests deflationary pressures in Singapore's nontraded goods sector. As argued earlier, such deflationary pressures appear to have resulted from a significant increase in money demand in Singapore. Exchange rate policy may thus have affected domestic inflation in the two economies largely through its impact on money demand rather than through its effect on imported inflation.

30. This approach is remarkable because wage policy in other countries is usually employed to contain labor costs, particularly if the exchange rate policy will tend to erode competitiveness.

31. In September 1985, the National Wages Council was instructed to stop recommending broad band annual wage rises for the work force in general and leave employers and unions to do their own negotiating. A report of the National Wages Council (1986) argues for a more flexible bargaining system which ties salary increases to corporate performance.

32. The organization of the labor market is very different in the two economies. The Hong Kong government does not get involved in wage setting, while the National Wages Council of Singapore has set guidelines for wage increases every year between 1972 and 1985.

33. Although Hong Kong's inflation has been much higher than Singapore's, the unit labor cost index for Hong Kong rose 58 percent between 1978 and 1985 compared to over 100 percent for Singapore. (See Balassa and Williamson, 1987, p. 92.) Hong Kong also enjoyed a competitive edge over Singapore because the trade weighted appreciation of the Hong Kong dollar since 1983 did not fully reverse its earlier weakness. The trade weighted Hong Kong dollar was 17 percent lower at its most recent peak in 1985 in comparison to its 1978 level, whereas the Singapore dollar appreciated 13 percent over the period. As a result, the unit labor cost index in Hong Kong was about 5 percent lower in 1985 than in 1978 on a U.S. dollar basis.

34. Hong Kong residents had no similar incentive for round tripping because no reserve requirements are imposed on either domestic or foreign currency deposits, and in general, no preference is given to offshore markets. Even the elimination of the 15 percent

withholding tax on foreign currency deposits in Hong Kong in 1982 (a tax was maintained on domestic currency deposits) would not necessarily produce round tripping by domestic residents unless they could successfully avoid the scrutiny of tax authorities.

35. Between 1977 and 1983, the Asian dollar market deposit holdings by Singapore residents as a percent of total assets of domestically oriented financial institutions in Singapore rose from under 3 percent to around 7 percent (Bryant, 1985). While this would seem to support Hewson's hypothesis, an alternative explanation is that domestic residents were simply diversifying their portfolios, without necessarily covering their positions or round tripping in a manner that could affect monetary policy systematically. Domestic residents may also have taken funds held abroad and placed them in Singapore's Asian dollar market once they were permitted to do so.

REFERENCES

Aghevli, Bijan B. and others (1979). "Monetary Policy in Selected Asian Countries." *IMF Staff Papers* (December).

Argy, Victor (1984). "The Optimal Mix of Monetary and Exchange Rate Management in Conditions of Perfect Asset Substitution – A Formal Analysis." MacQuarie University, Centre for Studies in Money, Banking and Finance, Working Paper No. 8450-B (April).

Asian Monetary Monitor. Various issues. Hong Kong.

Balasa, Bela and John Williamson (1987). *Adjusting to Success: Balance of Payments in The East Asian NICs*. Washington, D.C.: Institute for International Economics.

Benavie, Arthur (1983). "Achieving External and Internal Targets with Exchange-Rate and Interest Rate Intervention." *Journal of International Money and Finance*, 2, pp. 75-85.

Blejer, Mario I. and Mohsin S. Khan (1983). "The Foreign Exchange Market in a Highly-open Developing Economy: The Case of Singapore." *Journal of Development Economics* 12, Nos. 1/2 (Feb/April), pp. 237-249.

Boyer, Russell (1978). "Optimal Foreign Exchange Market Intervention." *Journal of Political Economy* 86, No. 6, pp. 1045-1055.

Branson, William (1981). "Monetary Stability and Exchange Rate Objectives in Singapore." In *Papers on Monetary Economics*, Monetary Authority of Singapore.

Bryant, Ralph (1985). "Financial Structure and International Banking in Singapore." Brookings Discussion Papers in International Economics 29 (May).

Bryant, Ralph C. (1986). "The Evolution of Singapore as a Financial Center." Brookings Discussion Papers in International Economics 45 (April).

Effros, Robert C. (1982). *Emerging Financial Centers: Legal and Institutional Framework*. Washington, D.C.: International Monetary Fund.

Fry, Maxwell J. (1985). "Financial Structure, Monetary Policy and Economic Growth in Hong Kong, Singapore, Taiwan and South Korea. 1960-1983." In *Export Oriented Development Strategies*, edited by A. Krueger et al. Colorado: Westview Press.

Goodhart, C.A.E. (1985). "The Development of Asset Ratios as a Monetary Policy Instrument." In *Papers on Monetary Economics*, Monetary Authority of Singapore.

Haddon-Cave, Sir Phillip (1984). "Introduction." In *The Business Environment of Hong Kong*; 2nd ed., edited by D. Lethbridge. Hong Kong: Oxford University Press.

Harper, David A. (1986). "The Financial Services Industry: Effects of Regulatory Reform." Wellington: New Zealand Institute of Economic Research, Research Paper No. 35.

Hendrie, Anne (1986). *Banking in the Far East. Structures and Sources of Finance*. London: Financial Times Business Information.

Hewson, John R. (1982). "Offshore Banking in Australia." In *Australian Financial System Inquiry: Commission Studies and Selected Papers*. Canberra: Australian Government Publishing Service, p. 501.

Hewson, John R. (1981). "The Asian Dollar Market and Monetary Policy." In *Papers on Monetary Economics*, Monetary Authority of Singapore.

Hong Kong Monthly Digest of Statistics. Various issues. Hong Kong: Census and Statistics Department.

Hsu, John C. (1985). "Exchange Rate Management without a Central Bank: The Hong Kong Experience." *Hong Kong Economic Papers* 16.

Humphreys, Thomas M. (1982). "The Real Bills Doctrine." *Economic Review*, Federal Reserve Bank of Richmond (September/October).

International Monetary Fund. Various issues. *International Financial Statistics*, Washington, D.C.

International Monetary Fund (1985). *Balance of Payments Statistics Yearbook*, Washington, D.C.

Jao, Y.C. (1984). "The Financial Structure." In *The Business Environment of Hong Kong*; 2nd ed., edited by D. Lethbridge. Hong Kong: Oxford University Press.

Laidler, David (1981). "Adam Smith as a Monetary Economist." *The Canadian Journal of Economics* XIV, No. 2 (May).

Lee, S.Y. and Y.C. Jao (1982). *Financial Structures and Monetary Policies in Southeast Asia*. New York: St. Martin's Press.

Monetary Authority of Singapore. Various issues. *Annual Report*.

Moreno, Ramon (1986). "Monetary Control Without a Central Bank: The Case of Hong Kong." Federal Reserve Bank of San Francisco, *Economic Review* (Spring).

National Wages Council Secretariat (1986). "Report of the National Wages Council Subcommittee on Wage Reform." Singapore (November).

Short, Brock K. (1977). "Velocity of Money in Malaysia and Singapore: Reply." *Journal of Development Studies* 13, No. 3 (April).

Simkin, Colin (1984). "Does Money Matter in Singapore?" *Singapore Economic Review* (April).

Standard Chartered Bank (1986). "Hong Kong." In *Banking in the Far East*, edited by Anne Hendrie, Financial Times Business Information.

Sundararajan, V. and Lazaros Molho (1988). "Financial Reform and Monetary Control in Indonesia." This volume.

9

United States Monetary Policy

Thomas Mayer

The policy of the Federal Reserve since 1973 can conveniently be divided into four episodes: the inflationary policy until October 1979; the quasi-monetarist experiment from October 1979 to October 1982, the current episode, for which it is hard to find a label; and the response to the two oil shocks and large changes in the exchange rate. Discussion of these topics will focus on the following questions: Why did the Fed pursue an inflationary policy prior to October 1979? To what extent was its policy monetarist after October 1979? Why and to what extent did the Fed change its policy in 1982? How did it respond to business cycles and to shocks? An appendix describes some features of the U.S. economy and policy-making that are relevant for understanding U.S. monetary policy.

SECULAR INFLATION UNTIL OCTOBER 1979

The Fed turned to a secular inflationary policy in the 1960s. From 1953 to 1965 the United States had been a low-inflation country for reasons difficult to ascertain. One would expect that in a country in which such a large proportion of the population had contracted fixed-rate mortgages there would be great political pressure for inflation. Perhaps the explanation is that in an economy with such an elaborate financial system, and with so many nominal claims, inflation is particularly damaging. Or perhaps it reflected the political weakness of labor unions and of left-wing parties.

But in the mid-1960s, the United States joined the ranks of nations with growing inflation. From 1966 to 1980 the GNP deflator rose by 145 percent. The culprit for such a secular inflation is not hard to find. It is by now generally agreed that the high growth rate of money can be blamed.[1] But to say that the high growth rate of money was the culprit is not a sufficient answer. Why was monetary policy so expansionary? Four potential answers are worth examining. One is that, while the growth rate of money was high, it was not too high; the secular inflation resulted from an appropriate policy. The second answer is that monetary growth was excessive, and that this was due to unrealistic goals the Fed had set. The third answer also points to the goals used by the Fed, but argues that these goals were not the Fed's own choice, but were imposed by its political masters. The fourth is that the fault lay not with the Fed's goals, but with the intermediate targets and instruments that it used. Let us consider each of these explanations.

Inflation as an Appropriate Policy

The advocacy of secular inflation has a long history in economics, though modern economists are more likely to consider it a second-best solution.[2] Those who argue that the Fed followed mainly correct policies claim that not only would a feasible restrictive policy have imposed major costs, it would also have failed to prevent inflation because much of the inflation was the result of supply shocks. If one omits the years most directly impacted by supply shocks, 1973-1974 and 1979-1980, then in the remaining years since 1973 the inflation rate reached 7.0 percent or more in only two years: 1975 and 1981, both years in which the effects of the oil shocks were still working their way through the economy. Hence, in this view, despite vociferous complaints about inflation, monetary policy in the 1970s was essentially correct.

This interpretation has a certain attraction, since it points to the often ignored fact that even correct policy cannot eliminate all macroeconomic problems. (It has been said that an optimist is someone who believes we live in the best of all possible worlds, and a pessimist is someone who agrees with him.) All the same, this interpretation is not wholly convincing. While it is true that the years of double-digit inflation were years of supply shocks, Chart 1 shows a more troublesome picture. Since 1953 the inflation rate, not just the price level, has been rising. In a world of naive expectations that does not matter so much. But while the public's expectations may not meet all the tests of rationality, the public is not stupid; it does learn from experience. And with the public expecting more inflation, eventually any favorable effects of inflation on output disappear, while the unfavorable effects remain. Undoubtedly, it was the years of supply-shock inflation that provided the political support for Volcker's disinflationary policy. But even if there had been no supply shocks, eventually such a policy would have had to be adopted.

Can one argue that the short-run benefits of the expansionary policy exceeded its long-run costs? This is doubtful. If the choice really were to have greater unemployment now or to have a permanently higher -- but stable -- inflation rate, then one might well choose the latter. But the notion of a high but steady inflation rate is implausible. If the central bank settles for a higher inflation rate now, what will prevent it from choosing a still higher inflation rate in the future? He who fights and runs away, lives to *run* another day. And the public knows this.

Chart 1
Consumer Price Inflation, 1953-1986
(Quarterly change at annual rates)

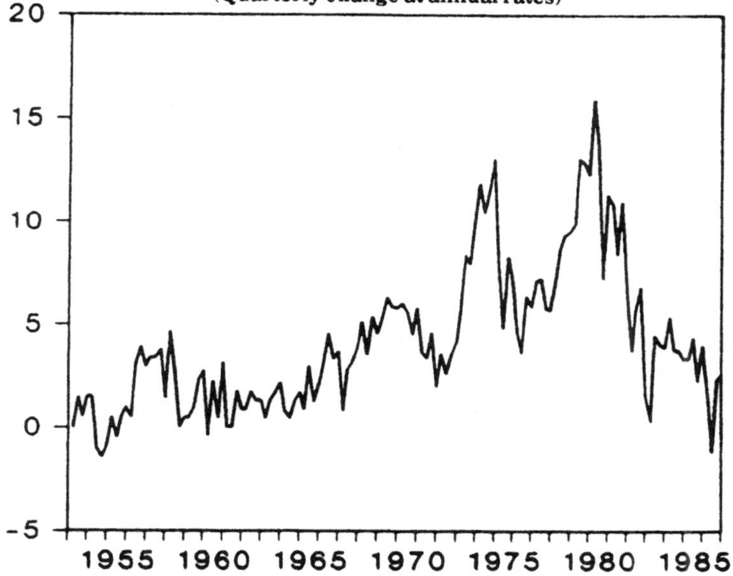

Errors in Choosing Goals

One way to generate accelerating inflation is to set as the goal of monetary policy too low a rate of unemployment. While there are no data on the Fed's estimate of the natural rate of unemployment, several reasons suggest that the Fed underestimated it.

First, the actual unemployment rate was below the natural rate for a long time in the 1960s (see Weiner, 1986), probably for long enough to generate inflationary expectations. One can make a plausible (though not compelling) argument that had the Fed known this, it would have adopted a more restrictive policy.

Second, as Raymond Lombra (1986) pointed out, a perusal of Federal Open Market Committee (FOMC) documents suggests that the Fed tends to underestimate the future inflation rate. The Fed was not alone in this. Stephen McNees (1985, p. 37) provided the forecast errors for the GNP deflator of a sample of private forecasters. For the period 1973.I -1979.III, the mean error (not the mean *absolute* error) of these forecasts was -1.3 percent.

Third, one can make some sort of a case, though not a persuasive one, that a central bank should operate with a low estimate of the natural unemployment rate. Suppose that it overestimates the natural rate and is therefore too restrictive. More people than necessary then suffer the misery of unemployment, and assuming that there is little downward price flexibility, there is not much benefit on the inflation front. By contrast, if the central bank underestimates the natural rate, it can then offset the resulting inflation by a more restrictive policy later on. Hence, it should experiment by first using a low estimate of the natural rate.[3]

Moreover, Lombra (1986) suggested that the Fed's policy procedures impart an inflationary bias to its selection of a short-run unemployment-inflation trade-off. The Fed makes policy on a short-run basis in part because it does not trust its longer-run forecasts, and in part because political pressures focus on the immediate effects of a policy. And when one looks at the short run, the negative effects of a restrictive policy seem much more salient than its positive effects.

Another reason why the Fed may well have set too high a monetary growth target is that it may have underestimated the costs of inflation. Economists in general had difficulty explaining the public's great concern about inflation. In the economist's model of anticipated inflation, shoe-leather costs that result from a lower real stock of money do not justify much concern about inflation. Only gradually did the more serious cost of inflation, arising from increased uncertainty, become apparent to economists. A related explanation is the replacement of traditional central bankers by economists, both on the Board of Governors and at the Federal Reserve Banks. Traditionally, central bankers have had two dominating aims: to preserve the stability of the currency and to prevent financial panics. Economists have a different outlook.[4]

Political Pressures

As described briefly in the Appendix, the Fed's independence is severely circumscribed; the main thrust of its policy must be one that the President can accept. Was the inflation between 1973 and 1979, therefore, the fault of the White House?

One piece of evidence is the voting records of the governors who were nominated during this period. If a President believes that the Fed is too restrictive, he is likely to nominate governors who will press for a more expansionary policy. Did this happen? The twelve governors appointed between January 1973 and October 1979 registered as many dissents on the expansionary side as on the restrictive side in this period. This hardly suggests that the White House was pressing the Fed to be more restrictive. Moreover, in 1972, just prior to the period on which I focused, President

Nixon put extraordinarily strong pressure on the Fed to adopt more expansionary policies (see Pierce, 1979). One component of this pressure continued into 1973. As part of the incomes policy imposed in August 1971, President Nixon appointed Chairman Burns to head a Committee on Interests and Dividends that was supposed to keep interest rates and dividends from rising excessively. Burns's appointment to head that Committee was the worst infringement of Fed independence since the Accord of 1951, because the only way Burns could prevent interest rates from rising was by having a monetary policy that was sufficiently accommodative.

President Ford, who took over in August 1974, was a strong opponent of inflation. Unfortunately, he allowed his correct intuition, which called for a restrictive policy in the midst of a recession, to be overruled by the derision of economists. It may be conjectured that he did not pressure the Fed to become expansionary. President Carter's impact on the Fed is harder to gauge. By his nomination of Chairman Volcker in 1979, and by refraining from speaking out against Volcker's policy, he deserves much credit for this policy. But, it is less clear what his position was before the crises of 1978 and 1979 showed the failures of the old, too expansionary policy. President Carter, it would appear, was quite conservative, but would reverse himself under pressure from the left wing of his party. It seems likely that after August 1974 the Fed was not under much pressure to be more expansionary.

But this does not necessarily mean that such pressure would not have materialized had the Fed, in 1975, adopted as strong a disinflationary policy as it did in 1979. It seems highly plausible that the Fed would not have been permitted to adopt such a policy until, at the earliest, the 1978 crisis. Even then the restrictive policy was strongly criticized in Congress.

Should one therefore attribute the too-expansionary monetary policy to the Fed, or should one blame the potential pressures from the White House, Congress, and the public that would not have permitted a much more restrictive policy had the Fed tried to adopt one? Given the ever-present threat to the Fed's independence, the political opposition to restrictive policies was probably a sufficient condition for the expansionary policy (see Hetzel, forthcoming). It was also a necessary condition in the sense that had the White House and Congress demanded a severely disinflationary policy, the Fed would have adopted such a policy, judging by its past record. By contrast, given the limits to the Fed's independence, the Fed's preference for a too-expansionary policy was neither a necessary nor a sufficient condition.

It might therefore be tempting to say that, since the preferences of the public and of its political leaders were both a necessary and a sufficient condition for the too expansionary policy, these preferences were the "cause" of this policy. But that is too facile. Most of the time the Fed was not limited in the sense that it wanted to be more restrictive, but was constrained by political realities. The Fed did not use the autonomy that it does have to press against the political limits of a restrictive policy. It was not merely going along with a policy that it disagreed with. Because it was not as restrictive as it could have been, the Fed must take some of the responsibility for the inflationary policy that it pursued.

Technical Errors

Another possible explanation of the Fed's inflationary policy attributes it not to the Fed's goals but to the specific targets, instruments, and institutions through which policy was carried out, to what Lombra (1986) calls the "plumbing" of monetary policy.

In the 1970s the Fed was generally seen by economists, and perhaps by itself, as choosing between two targets: the monetary growth rate and the interest rate. The choice was usually discussed in terms of the relative stability of the IS and LM curves. There is still little agreement about the relative stability of these curves, but the Fed probably has an institutional bias toward thinking that the demand for money, and hence the LM curve, is less stable, and was therefore biased in favor of using the interest rate as its target. An unstable money-demand function explains away undesirable events that would otherwise be attributed to the money-supply function, and hence to the Fed. Moreover, someone who watches the money market on a day-to-day basis is more likely to be impressed by its instability than is someone who, like most academic economists, works with quarterly or annual data.

But if it is actually the IS curve that is shifting upwards, then a central bank that has an interest rate target accommodates inflation. Moreover, the inflationary effects of a nominal interest rate target are cumulative. Any inflation that occurs lowers the real rate represented by a given nominal interest rate target, so that the nominal interest rate target falls more and more below its appropriate level.[6]

However, the extensive debate about using the interest rate or the money stock as a target missed a central point: The Fed used its interest rate target in a way that differs radically from what most economists mean when they refer to an interest rate target. In the economist's interpretation of an interest rate target, the numerical setting of this target is changed whenever the IS curve shifts. Ever since Wicksell explained the relation of the natural rate and the market rate, it has been clear that to keep income stable, when the natural rate varies, the market rate must vary along with it. But in the 1970s the Fed was reluctant to let the nominal market rate vary. It confounded two quite different concepts, an appropriate interest rate, and a stable interest rate.[7]

There are two reasons for the Fed's reluctance to let interest rates vary. One is that a rise in interest rates often generates congressional criticism of the Fed.[8] Second, rising interest rates impose costs on financial institutions, particularly on the heavily leveraged government-security dealers.

If confronted with a clear-cut choice between following an accommodative policy that stabilizes interest rates but destabilizes GNP, or a policy that destabilizes interest rates but stabilizes GNP, the Fed would almost surely make the correct choice and let interest rates vary. But such clear-cut choices are rare. Given the short-run focus of Fed policy, the choice that appears on the agenda of each FOMC meeting is not whether to change interest rates, or instead to have the monetary growth rate miss its target. Rather, the choice is whether to change the interest rate right now, or whether to wait and see if the change is really necessary. Estimates of the monetary growth rate are continually being revised, and by large amounts. Moreover, they contain a great deal of noise; David Pierce (1981) found that the standard error in the underlying trend of the monthly M1 growth rate was 4.5 percent! In such a situation, procrastination seems almost a virtue, and highly capable and dedicated policymakers are likely to make what by hindsight seem obviously bad decisions.

Hence, while the Fed had both monetary targets and interest rate targets in the 1970s, it is hardly surprising that in the frequent conflicts between the two, the interest rate targets almost always won out, and the money targets seemed to be little more than decoration.[9] As Chart 2 shows, monetary growth was rarely constrained by its target ranges. Since the Fed sets its targets for the monetary growth rate as a percentage measured from wherever the money stock happens to be at the time, the actual growth of money may have had more influence on the targets than the targets had on the actual growth rate. The Fed met congressional demand that it set monetary targets by doing so *pro forma*, but with only a limited impact on actual policy.[10]

Moreover, even if the Fed had tried to stay within its monetary target ranges, there was an institutional "detail" that would have complicated this task. The reserve requirement was lagged, so that the reserves that banks needed in one period depended on their deposits in the previous period. Hence, there was nothing that banks could do within a period to reduce the reserves they needed.[11] As a result, the Fed had to supply banks with the necessary reserves, so that the demand for reserves determined the supply of reserves. Admittedly, the Fed could do so through the discount window rather than through open-market operations, and the

Chart 2
M1 Target Rates, 1975-1985

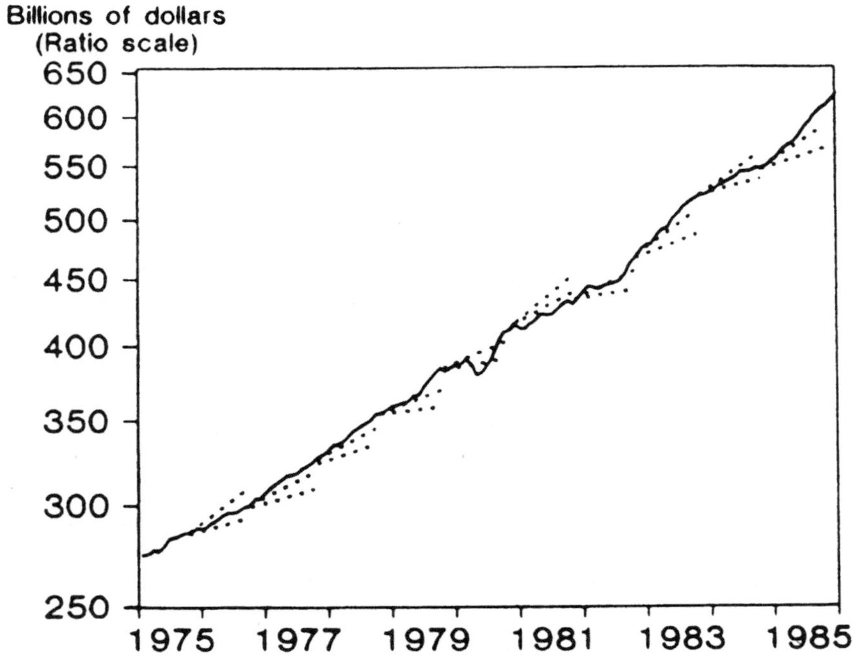

Source: William T. Gavin, "The M-1 Target and Disinflationary Policy," Federal Reserve Bank of Cleveland, Economic Commentary, October 1985, p.3.

Fed has claimed that banks are reluctant to expand deposits on the basis of borrowed reserves. But are they reluctant enough?

Thus, the Fed's choice of target variables, as well as the lagged reserve-requirements system, operated to limit the Fed's control over the money supply and hence its ability to control inflation. Can these "technical" factors, therefore, be held responsible for the inflation? No, they cannot, for three reasons. First, the timing is wrong. The Fed stayed with lagged reserve requirements until 1983, when it switched to almost contemporaneous reserves, but by that time the disinflation was already well under way. Moreover, in 1982 the Fed abandoned its quasi-monetarist experiment and switched to a system of targets and instruments that is more or less similar to the system in effect prior to October 1979. Yet, the inflation rate continued to decline through 1986. The lags of monetary policy may be long, but they are not that long.

Second, the Fed's targets and the lagged reserve requirements made it harder to control inflation, but they did not make it impossible. Suppose that the public, Congress, and the President had, in 1976, all shown a great fear of inflation and had been willing to tolerate high interest rates and a deep recession to end inflation. Had the Fed responded by setting its interest rate targets high enough, it would have brought the inflation rate down. Monetarists were right when they argued in the 1970s that the Fed's targets and instruments were clumsy and likely to destabilize the economy. But clumsy and destabilizing tools can be used to generate recessions as well as inflations. In the 1930s the Fed's operating procedures that focused on short-term interest rates and on free reserves worsened a depression, not an inflation.

Third, despite all this, assume that the lagged reserve requirements and the Fed's use of interest rates as targets would somehow have prevented a disinflationary policy that the Fed wanted. It could then have changed to contemporaneous reserve requirements and used a different target.

As far as the inflation of the 1970s was concerned, the October 1979 shift in the Fed's operating procedures was an epiphenomenon. What is more significant is that in March 1980, when asked whether current monetary and fiscal policies would lead to a recession, Chairman Volcker could reply: "Yes and the sooner the better" (Farnworth, 1980). As Michael Keran (1985) has suggested, traditionally the Fed would wait for an inflation to occur before it tightened. Now the Fed tightens whenever the growth rate of nominal GNP reaches a level that, if continued, would be too inflationary.

The conclusion, therefore, is that while the inflationary monetary policy of the 1970s had many "causes," the salient cause was that the public and its political leaders were not willing to pay the necessary costs of terminating or moderating the inflation.[12]

THE QUASI-MONETARIST EXPERIMENT

On October 6, 1979, the Fed dramatically announced a change in its policy.[13] From now on it would focus on reducing the inflation rate. To do so, it would allow the funds rate to fluctuate much more than before, it would place much greater emphasis on its monetary targets, and it would use unborrowed reserves rather than the funds rate as its instrument for controlling the monetary growth rate.

This policy is frequently referred to as "the monetarist experiment," but not by monetarists. They reject this label because the monetary growth rate, far from becoming more stable, became even more volatile. From January 1971 to September 1979 the standard deviation of monthly changes in M1 was 0.35 percent. From November 1979 to August 1982 it was 0.86 percent. All the same, the policy was more monetarist than the prior policy in two ways: it put more focus on reducing inflation, and it allowed the funds rate to vary much more. Quasi-monetarist might be the appropriate name for it.

Its most important and most enduring component was disinflation. The Fed's announcement that its dominant target would be the monetary growth rate, and not an interest rate, was probably a necessary condition for a disinflationary policy. Given the public's inability to distinguish between nominal and real interest rates, as well as the political and ideological power of debtor interests, the Fed could allow interest rates to rise very substantially only if it denied responsibility for them.

Accordingly, the FOMC removed its previous tight constraints on the funds rate, allowing it to fluctuate freely in a range of 5 percent or more, compared to 1 1/4 percent previously. And fluctuate it did, as Chart 3 illustrates. But these fluctuations should be put into their proper perspective. As Rosenblum and Stronin (1983, p. 13) have pointed out, the volatility of the funds rate was neither new nor excessive *if* one considers the whole period since 1953. In part, it was the contrast with the unusually stable funds rate of the 1970s that made the funds rate of the early 1980s look so unstable.

That the funds rate became more volatile once the Fed lifted its tight constraints is hardly surprising. What is surprising is that the monetary growth rate became more volatile, too. Previously the Fed had been limited in its attempt to control the monetary growth rate by its commitment to interest rate stability. It was the old story, familiar to every economist: you can control either the price (the interest rate) or the quantity, but you cannot control both at the same time. So now that the Fed had essentially relinquished its control over the price, why did it not succeed in controlling the quantity?

The anti-monetarist's gleeful answer is that in a modern economy a central bank cannot control the growth rate of money, at least in the short run. The monetarist's answer is that the Fed had not made the necessary institutional changes. It had not switched from lagged reserve requirements to contemporaneous reserve requirements, and it was trying to control the monetary growth rate not through total reserves, as monetarists recommended, but through unborrowed reserves.

The latter seems like a trivial technical detail but it is not, and hence needs discussion. The Fed set a target for unborrowed reserves, and used open-market operations to attain this target. If banks wanted more

Chart 3
Monetary Target Ranges, 1975-1985

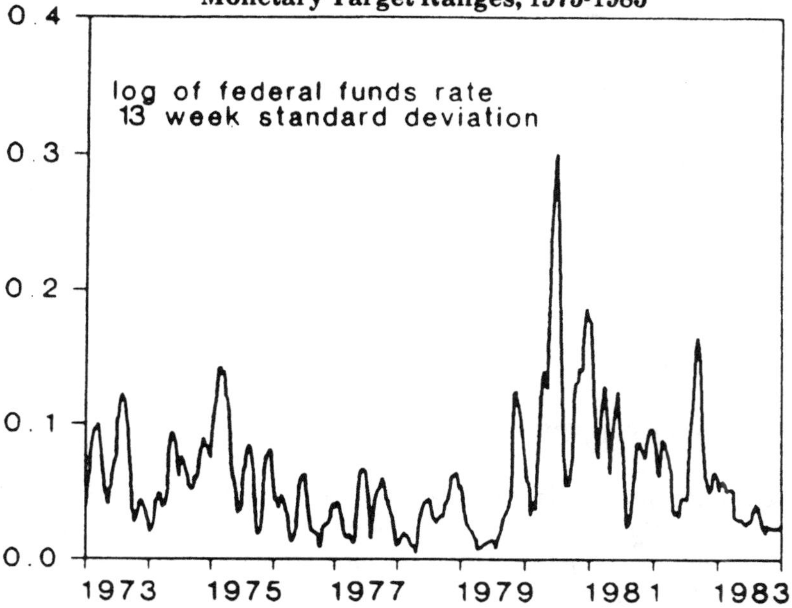

Source: Harvey Rosenblum and Steven Strongin, "Interest Rate Volatility in Historical Perspective," Federal Reserve Bank of Chicago, Economic Perspectives, January-February, 1983, p.11.

reserves, they could obtain them only by borrowing at the discount window. But since individual banks are reluctant to borrow from the Fed and prefer to borrow on the federal funds market, an increase in borrowings from the Fed is accompanied by a rise in the funds rate. And when the funds rate is higher, the public wants to hold less money. Hence it sells securities to banks and repays bank loans, so that the supply of money falls. This is a subtle and sophisticated mechanism, but whether it is effective is another question. A rise in borrowings from the Fed might not raise the funds rate by enough to have a sufficient effect on the demand for money. The Fed seems to have a tendency to overestimate the reluctance of banks to borrow from it.[14]

In principle, the Fed could, of course, offset a change in borrowed reserves by an opposite change in unborrowed reserves, but the Fed had been unable to estimate borrowings with any degree of accuracy. In fact, it frequently assumed that borrowings during the current period would more or less equal borrowings in the previous period. As a result, changes in the demand for reserves were accommodated to a considerable extent by changes in borrowed reserves. The Fed was still following an accommodative policy.[15]

This accommodative policy is only a partial explanation of the increased volatility of the monetary growth rate during the quasi-monetarist experiment. The variance of the money multiplier rose sharply, presumably in response to the greater fluctuations of the funds rate. The answer to the question of why the variability of the monetary growth rate rose rather than fell, therefore, consists of two parts. First, although in principle abandonment of the accommodative policy of funds rate targeting allowed the Fed to keep the base and reserves growing at a much more stable rate than before, the Fed permitted the variance of the base and of reserves to increase.[16] Second, the variance of the money multiplier rose substantially (see Mayer, 1987).

THE CURRENT POLICY[17]

The quasi-monetarist experiment did not last long. The Fed abandoned it around the summer or early fall of 1982 for several reasons. An obvious reason, though probably not the most important one, was that the Fed was under great political pressure to reduce and stabilize interest rates. Both Democratic and Republican leaders in Congress supported legislation that would have severely curbed the Fed's independence. To be sure, there was a good chance that President Reagan would veto such legislation, but given the anger of supply-siders directed at the Fed, the Fed could not be certain, and besides a veto might be overridden.

Probably a more important reason was the severity of the 1982 recession, the worst since the 1930s. Domestically there were fears of major bankruptcies that might cause a financial panic. Internationally, high interest rates threatened default on LDC debts. By hindsight it is obvious that the Fed had been too tough for too long.

The reason the Fed's policy had been too tough is that in setting its monetary targets it was making the wrong assumption about velocity. Velocity had been growing steadily at an an annual rate of approximately 3 percent for a long time and the Fed, as well as many economists, assumed that it would continue to grow at this rate.[18] Instead, as Chart 4 shows, in early 1981 velocity began to fall. In the period 1981-1986, M1 velocity fell by 16 percent. The Fed therefore had to raise the monetary growth rate to avoid disaster. But given the public's focus on the growth rate of money, a rise in the monetary growth rate might generate expectations of higher inflation. It was therefore sensible for the Fed to complement its more expansionary policy with a deemphasis of monetary targeting.

Chart 4
M1 Velocity, 1959-1986
(Quarterly)

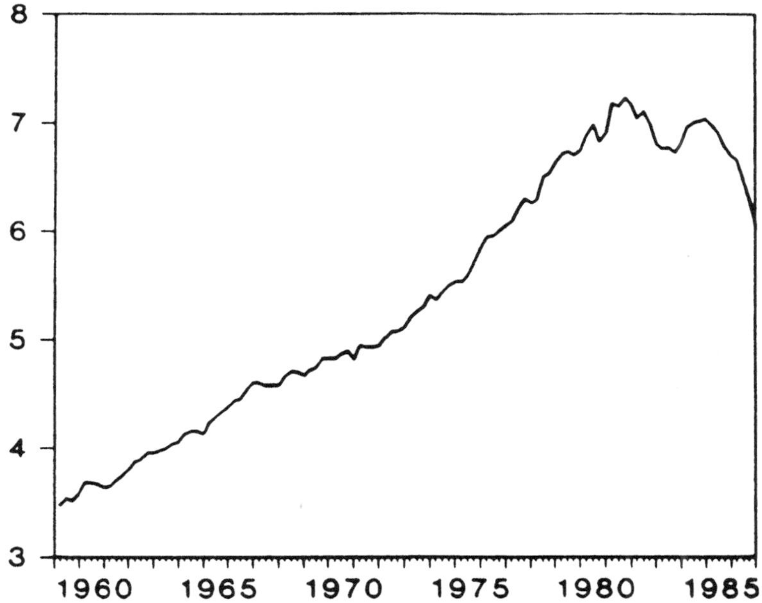

Moreover, rightly or wrongly, the deemphasis of monetary targeting seems justified by the erratic behavior of velocity shown in Chart 4. Money demand functions also became less stable. It was widely believed that financial innovations had destroyed the old relation between M1 and nominal GNP. With interest-paying NOW accounts becoming available everywhere, M1 balances currently include to a much greater extent than before genuine savings, that is, funds not held for immediate expenditures. One would expect such funds to be sensitive to changes in interest rates. While sufficient data for a firm conclusion are not yet available, preliminary evidence suggests that the demand for money has become more interest-elastic. In addition, with varying differentials between deposit rates and open-market rates, the incentive to shift between money market instruments and bank deposits changes over time. Under these circumstances, can one expect velocity to be stable?

More generally, can money be defined in a measurable way in such a deregulated financial system? A number of economists doubt it. However, the same question was raised in the 1960s when savings and loan associations were growing rapidly. We were told that the old quantity theory of money no longer applied, and yet velocity grew at a remarkably stable rate. So, *perhaps* the instability of velocity and of money-demand functions is only a transitional phenomenon.

It is not clear to what extent financial innovations were a major motivation in the Fed's abandonment of the quasi-monetarist experiment, and to what extent they merely provided a convenient rationalization. Since shifts among the various components of M2 and M3 internalize most of the relevant financial innovations, the velocities of M2 and M3 have not become as volatile as the velocity of M1, so that M2 and M3 targets might be used in place of an M1 target.

The Fed's current procedure is to set what it calls "targets" for M2 and M3, but as of this time, not for M1. However, in announcing targets for M2 and M3 the Fed is using the word targets in a peculiar way. Webster's Dictionary defines a target as follows: "a goal set or proposed for achievement." This definition of a target seems implied when the FOMC states, as it frequently does, that a certain growth rate of money is "acceptable."

But recently Gary Stern, the president of the Minneapolis Fed, described the Fed's target ranges for money in a very different way, writing:

> What the money ranges are meant to be are indicators to the public of the general course of monetary policy *if the economy performs as expected*.... Any specific ranges tell the public just what the Fed's actions will imply for the growth of money during that period if the usual economic patterns persist.... *In this strategy the Fed's money measures are not targeted.* They are, instead, among the many variables the Fed uses to determine how next to aim at its goals by adjusting its instruments. They are thus known as *information variables*.... Unlike targeting, the information variable strategy uses all available information.... If an information variable were targeted, the Fed's efforts to keep it on target might make the Fed ignore information that other variables were offering about its real goals.... This best way to conduct monetary policy is quite different from the view that many people seem to have of the Fed's strategy....The Fed does not in a strict sense target these measures (Stern, 1986, pp. 3-5, first two italics added).

This is confusing. An information variable is quite different from a target variable. One uses information variables to lead one to the target. If one has only a single information variable, that variable then serves as a manifestation of the target, and could loosely be called a target. But if one has several information variables, one blends the information they provide, and will typically not use any of them as a "goal set for achievement." Suppose, for example, that a central bank uses three information variables, the interest rate, credit growth, and the growth rate of money, and thinks all three are equally reliable guides to its ultimate goal, a certain growth rate of GNP. Suppose further that money is growing 3 percent too fast, while the other two variables are growing 3 percent too slowly. Despite the fact that money is growing too rapidly, this central bank should adopt a more expansionary policy. Hence, if the Fed is using money as one of several information variables, it is confusing to call it a target. It is much less than a target.

Is the Fed using the monetary growth rate as an information variable, as Stern explained, or as a target variable as is implied by FOMC statements about "acceptable" growth rates of money? The evidence from Chart 2 supports Stern's interpretation. If the Fed would treat the monetary growth rate as a genuine target, it would frequently miss its target ranges because the monetary growth rate is hard to control. But its errors would be random, and not as systematic as Chart 2 shows them to be.

However, it would be wrong to go to the other extreme and claim that the Fed's monetary targets have no meaning. First, the Fed is using the monetary targets to communicate with the public. Its monetary targets are, so to speak, a hostage given to the public, to assure it that the Fed will prevent a sharp acceleration of the inflation rate. Thus, Stephen Axilrod (1985, p. 22) when he was the FOMC's senior economist wrote:

> . . . it is virtually undeniable that an expression of the central bank's objectives is needed to establish public accountability and responsibility. That accountability on an ongoing basis is best indicated by a financial variable that is reasonably subject to control, with some measure, or measures, of the money supply being on balance the most advantageous.

Moreover, if the inflation rate does accelerate the Fed is likely to put more emphasis on the monetary growth rate because of the familiar relation between excessive monetary growth and inflation. In addition, having monetary targets helps the Fed to resist those who call for more expansionary policies to lower interest rates.

All the same, it seems that the Fed now does not use monetary targets in the proper sense of the term "targets." It operates eclectically with its most important target probably being nominal GNP, even though a nominal GNP target is not made public, and is, in all likelihood, not even made explicit in FOMC discussions.

The borrowed-reserves operating procedure that the Fed now uses is highly accommodative. Suppose that banks need $100 million more reserves because deposits are expanding. They borrow $100 million from the Fed. The Fed then brings borrowings back to target by providing the needed $100 million of reserves through open-market operations. During the quasi-monetarist experiment, when the Fed targeted *un*borrowed reserves, an increase in borrowings raised the funds rate, and this reduced, at least somewhat, the demand for, and hence the supply of money. But now this stabilizing mechanism is no longer here; when banks borrow more, the Fed simply provides them with additional unborrowed reserves to substitute for the borrowed reserves.

The new procedure is quite similar to the pre-1979 procedure when the FOMC explicitly targeted the funds rate. Now it does so indirectly. In setting its target for borrowed reserves the Fed selects that level of borrowed reserves that it thinks will generate an appropriate funds rate. Hence, only to the extent that the Fed makes errors in estimating the relation between borrowings and the funds rate does the funds rate differ from what the Fed wants. It is therefore not surprising that the current operating procedure has kept the bill rate as stable as it was prior to the quasi-monetarist experiment. From October 1982 to December 1986 the mean absolute variation in the monthly average of the 90-day Treasury bill rate was 0.26 percent, compared to 0.28 percent from October 1975 to September 1979. With respect to operating procedures the quasi-monetarist experiment has been almost entirely abandoned, with one exception. Previously, when the Fed controlled the funds rate directly, it admitted doing so. Now it controls the funds rate in a less obvious way. This reduces the political pressures on the Fed to hold the funds rate down, and hence gives it more autonomy.

COUNTERCYCLICAL POLICY

The phrase "the Fed's countercyclical policy" is a questionable one; the Fed may well have acted procyclically rather than countercyclically. Here are the growth rates of M1 and M2 in the cycle phases since 1973:

In every expansion the growth rate of money was higher than in either the prior or the subsequent contraction. The sample is small, in fact, tiny, but (at least for M1) the results are consistent with those from earlier cycles. Since July 1953, the M1 growth rate was always higher in expansions than in the following recession.[19]

Average Monthly Growth Rate
(Percent)

Upper Turning Point	M1		M2	
	Contraction	Expansion	Contraction	Expansion
11/73	.39	.58	.55	.84
01/80	.24	.71	.66	.79
07/81	.68	NA	.77	NA

This does not necessarily mean that monetary policy has been destabilizing. By a lucky coincidence, the lag of monetary policy *could* be just long enough to transform a procyclical growth rate of money into a countercyclical impact of monetary policy. More important, though it is often claimed, it is *not* true that to be countercyclical, monetary policy should raise income in the recession phase and lower it in the expansion phase. In a smooth and symmetrical cycle, income is above its mean during half the contraction phase, as well as during half the expansion. It is therefore more meaningful to compare changes in the growth rates of M1 and M2 to cyclical changes in unemployment. In such a comparison, the monetary growth rate emerges as countercyclical. However, this does not mean that monetary policy has actually been countercyclical, because this comparison ignores the lag in the impact of monetary policy. Given the great uncertainties in measuring this lag, one cannot say whether postwar U.S. monetary policy has been procyclical or countercyclical.

This does not deny, of course, that business fluctuations have played an important role in Fed policy. For example, as just mentioned, the Fed appears to respond to changes in the level of unemployment.[20] A history of U.S. monetary policy that ignores such responses would be utter nonsense. If monetary policy has been procyclical, it is because of the lag in the impact of monetary policy, and because the Fed's efforts to stabilize interest rates have frequently caused it to behave procyclically.

THE FED'S RESPONSE TO SHOCKS

In addition to recessions, the Fed also had to deal with two types of shocks: oil shocks and exchange-rate shocks. The first oil shock, in 1973, at the beginning of the period discussed here, came at a time when two other supply shocks -- bad harvests and a falling dollar -- were working their way through the economy. There is disagreement about whether a price rise that results from a major supply shock should be accommodated by monetary expansion. But there can be little disagreement that the Fed's response was inappropriate. Its initial response was to generate, or at least to allow, a sharp decline in the monetary growth rate, accompanied by rising interest rates. As a result, there was a threat of a financial crisis. Then, the Fed reversed course sharply and adopted a too-expansionary policy. One might say in the Fed's defense, that it faced a new problem and was groping for a solution. But given the size of its staff, it should have had contingency plans ready.[21]

Its response to the second oil shock in 1979 was different. In part because of the sharp rise in the inflation rate and in inflationary expectations, and in part because of the exchange rate crisis, the Fed adopted on October 6, 1979, the disinflationary policy already described.

There have been several exchange rate shocks since 1973. The first consisted of a sharp deterioration in the U.S. current account balance in 1977-1978 accompanied by a decline of the dollar. The response was a program to borrow foreign currencies to prop up the dollar, as well as the adoption of "voluntary" wage and price controls, and the inauguration of a restrictive monetary policy. But eventually even the smallest flow will swallow the largest stock, so that borrowing foreign currencies is no long-run solution. And neither the "voluntary" wage and price controls nor the restrictive monetary policy turned out to be serious policy measures; although the monetary growth rate fell initially, it soon rose again and stayed high.

The second exchange rate shock occurred in the fall of 1979 when the dollar fell dramatically. This time the response was serious and sustained -- the disinflationary policy inaugurated on October 6, 1979.

A subsequent exchange rate shock was the rise of the dollar: in the first quarter of 1985 the nominal multilateral trade-weighted value of the dollar was 25 percent higher than it had been in 1983. This appreciation probably had little direct effect on U.S. monetary policy. While a falling exchange rate often generates a feeling of crisis, a rising exchange rate is traditionally accepted with more equanimity. Moreover, the Fed was focusing on disinflation, where the rising dollar certainly helped. All the same, it *may* have had substantial indirect effects. Had it not been for the plight of the import-competing industries and the export industries, perhaps the Fed *might* have adopted a more restrictive policy. This is hard to determine.

The final exchange rate shock is the recent decline of the dollar. Again, there is no definitive way of determining what role this has played in Fed decision-making, but it seems likely that it has contributed, probably significantly so, to a firming of monetary policy. Chairman Volcker, as befits a central banker, was worried about the apparently small but potentially scary probability that the dollar would go into a free-fall.

CONCLUSION

Rather than summarize this historical survey, I will suggest some implications of the recent history of monetary policy for current and near-term monetary policy. First, having disinflated at great cost to the economy, the Fed is not likely to let inflation accelerate substantially. Barring major supply shocks, a sustained inflation rate of 6 percent or more seems unlikely. Rightly or wrongly, the quasi-monetarist experiment probably left the Fed with an even greater distaste for monetarism than it had before. It is unlikely to let monetary targets dominate its policy at most times. This does not mean that monetary targeting has been completely abandoned. The FOMC will pay *some* attention to its monetary targets, because the experience of the 1970s taught it that monetary targets are useful for determining longer run policy, and thus provide a desirable complement to its short-run focus in making policy. Moreover, talking in terms of monetary growth rates rather than interest rates is politically beneficial for the Fed, and what one says has *some* effect on what one thinks. Large fluctuations in interest rates, such as occurred during the quasi-monetarist experiment, will probably not be permitted and hence the FOMC is likely to stay with some highly accommodative operating procedures. To prevent these operating procedures from letting the monetary growth rate get too far from its target, the Fed will probably continue with its stop-go policy.

NOTES

1. In principle, a rise in velocity could also generate inflation, but except in hyperinflations, the potential increase in velocity is limited. Moreover, even if velocity is rising, the central bank could offset this by reducing the monetary growth rate.

2. See Tobin (1980), pp. 43-44.

3. What underlies this asymmetry is an asymmetry in price behavior; prices are less flexible downward than upward. Hence, if the Fed is too restrictive in the first period, it reaps little benefit on the price side, while losing on the unemployment side. But this argument is vulnerable to the response that if, as is normal now, there is inflation in any case, then a too-restrictive policy can reduce the inflation rate even if nominal prices and wages are inflexible downward. This response is, however, not entirely correct. Even with ongoing inflation there are some industries in which nominal prices are not rising.

4. In the early 1950s I heard a Fed governor argue before a congressional committee against more expansionary policy. As I listened to him I thought, Good Lord, he sounds as though he is opposed to greater expansion, not because it would be inflationary but because it would make moderate-income families too well off. I may well have done him an injustice, but I cannot imagine getting the same impression from the testimony of a recent governor.

5. See Poole (1970).

6. The same cumulative effect works, in principle, in a deflationary direction if one starts with a nominal market rate that is too high. But it is less likely that the Fed would stick with a too-high nominal interest rate than that it would stick with too low a rate.

7. Since I am criticizing the Fed at many points it is only fair to admit that academic economists also made a serious mistake in being slow to realize that the issue was more the Fed's preference for a stable interest rate rather than its choice of an interest rate target.

8. Political pressures *directly* inhibit only rises in interest rates. But if the Fed lowers interest rates now, sooner or later it will have to raise them again. Hence, it prefers to keep them stable.

9. The *Review* of the St. Louis Federal Reserve Bank carries an article each year describing the FOMC's actions. The charts in these articles show dramatically how the FOMC usually kept the federal funds rate within its targets, while missing the associated monetary targets.

10. Congress, by and large, did not object. Since Congress reflects the immediate concerns of constituents, it is more upset by rising interest rates than by a rising growth rate of money.

11. With a contemporaneous reserve requirement banks can reduce their required reserves in the same week. When, to replenish its reserves, a bank sells securities to the public, deposits and hence required reserves fall.

12. This is also the conclusion of Raymond Lombra (1986).

13. For the details of new policy see William Melton (1985).

14. It is likely that much of the Fed's belief that banks are reluctant to borrow from it comes from its experience in administering the discount window. But, due to an aggregation problem, this experience can be misleading. The basic issue is whether banks borrow only for "need," or also for profit. Suppose that each bank borrows only for need, and not to expand its deposits. The banking system, as a whole, may still be borrowing to expand deposits. This comes about because as some banks expand their deposits they borrow from nonbanks, e.g., government security dealers. As a result, some other banks now lose reserves, and borrow from the Fed for "need." For a more detailed discussion of operating procedures during the quasi-monetarist experiment, see Hetzel (1986).

15. William Poole (1982) argued that this was because the Fed implicitly targeted borrowed reserves, so that if the demand for reserves increased, the Fed provided additional unborrowed reserves to keep borrowed reserves at their target level. This interpretation of Fed policy has been challenged by Spindt and Tarhan (1987) who use Granger tests to reject Poole's hypothesis. But Granger tests have been criticized extensively.

16. This is not *necessarily* inconsistent with the Fed attempting to stabilize the monetary growth rate. The Fed might have introduced greater variance into the base to offset expected fluctuations in the money multiplier.

17. This section draws heavily on Mayer (forthcoming). Alton Gilbert (1985) provides a detailed and clear comparison of the various operating procedures used since the 1970s.

18. It should have been obvious that the growth rate of velocity would fall as inflation, and hence nominal interest rates, declined. Academic economists are also guilty of not taking this effect of disinflation sufficiently into account.

19. If one compares the monetary growth rate in recessions with the growth rate in the subsequent expansion, then there is one case in which the growth rate was higher in the recession than in the expansion.

20. Thus, a number of studies of the Fed's reaction functions have found that the level of unemployment has a positive effect on the monetary growth rate. But other studies of the Fed's reaction functions do not confirm this conclusion. I have not made use of the reaction-function literature because its findings lack robustness (see Khouri, 1986).

21. For a discussion of Fed thinking during this episode, see Mayer (1982).

REFERENCES

Axilrod, Stephen (1985). "The Formulation and Reporting of Monetary Policy Objectives." In *Monetarism, Inflation and the Federal Reserve*, U.S. Cong., Joint Economic Committee, 99th Cong., 1st sess., pp. 16-23.

Farnworth, Clyde (1980). "Washington Watch." *New York Times* (March 17), p. D2.

Gilbert, Alton (1985). "Operating Procedures for Conducting Monetary Policy." Federal Reserve Bank of St. Louis, *Review* 67, No. 2, pp. 13-21.

Keran, Michael (1985). "The New Business Cycle and the Fed." *Economic Review*, The Prudential (March).

Khoury, Salwa (1986). "The Federal Reserve Reaction Function: A Specification Search." Unpublished dissertation. University of California, Davis.

Hetzel, Robert (1986). "Monetary Policy in the Early 1980s." Federal Reserve Bank of Richmond, *Economic Review* 72, No. 2 (March-April), pp. 20-32.

Hetzel, Robert (forthcoming). "The Making of Monetary Policy in a Democracy." In *The Political Economy of American Monetary Policy*, edited by Thomas Mayer. Cambridge University Press.

Lombra, Raymond (1986). "Monetary Policy: The Rhetoric vs. the Record." Unpublished paper.

Mayer, Thomas (1982). "Federal Reserve Policy in the 1973-75 Recession: A Case Study of Fed Behavior in a Quandary." In *Crises in the Economic and Financial Structure*, edited by Paul Wachtel. Lexington, Mass.: Lexington Books, pp. 41-84.

Mayer, Thomas (1987). "An Explanation of the Variability of Monetary Growth Rate in the Early 1980s." In preparation.

Mayer, Thomas (forthcoming). "Federal Reserve Policy since October 1979: A Justified Response to Financial Innovations?" In *Monetary Policy and Financial Innovations in Five Leading Industrial Countries*, edited by Stephen Frowen. London: Macmillan.

McNees, Stephen (1985). "Which Forecast Should You Use?" Federal Reserve Bank of Boston, *New England Economic Review* (July-August), pp. 45-42.

Melton, William (1985). *Inside the Fed.* Homewood, Ill.: Dow Jones-Irwin.

Pierce, David (1981). "Trends and Noise in Monetary Aggregates." In *New Monetary Control Procedures* 1, Board of Governors, Federal Reserve System. Washington, D.C. (duplicated).

Pierce, James (1979). "The Political Economy of Arthur Burns." *Journal of Finance* 24 (May), pp. 485-96.

Poole, William (1970). "Optimum Choice of Monetary Policy Instruments in a Simple Stochastic Macro Model." *Quarterly Journal of Economics* 84 (May), pp. 197-216.

Poole, William (1982). "The Federal Reserve Operating Procedures." *Journal of Money, Credit and Banking* 14, No. 4, Part 2 (November), pp. 575-596.

Rosenblum, Harvey and Steven Strongin (1983). "Interest Rate Volatility in Historical Perspective." Federal Reserve Bank of Chicago *Economic Perspectives* 7, No. 1 (January), pp. 10-19.

Spindt, Paul and Vefa Tarhan (1987). "The Federal Reserve's New Operating Procedures: A Post Mortem." *Journal of Monetary Economics* 19, No. 1 (January), pp. 107-124.

Stern, Gary (1986). "The Fed's Money Supply Ranges: Still Useful after All these Years." In Federal Reserve Bank of Minneapolis, *Annual Report.* Minneapolis, Minn., pp. 1-15.

Tobin, James (1980). "Stabilization Policy Ten Years After." *Brookings Papers on Economic Activity* 1, pp. 19-72.

Weiner, Stuart (1986). "The Natural Rate of Unemployment: Concepts and Issues." Federal Reserve Bank of Kansas City, *Review* (January).

Woolley, John (1984). *Monetary Politics.* New York: Cambridge University Press.

APPENDIX

Economic Developments

A cyclical peak occurred in November 1973, with the recession lasting until March 1975. At the time, this was the worst recession since the Great Depression. Part of its severity was, of course, a result of the first oil shock and other supply shocks. The subsequent expansion continued until January 1980 and was followed by a short recession until July 1980. The expansion that followed was cut short in July 1981, and resulted in only an incomplete recovery with the economy operating well below capacity. Since it started from such a low level, the subsequent recession was extraordinarily severe, the worst since the Great Depression. A long, as yet unfinished, expansion then started in November 1982. Table 1

Table 1
Some Major U.S. Macroeconomic Variables, 1961-1986

Year	Real GNP Growth Rate (percent)	Unemployment Rate[a]	Federal Surplus (+) or Deficit (-) (percent of GNP)	Inflation: GNP Deflator	Inflation: CPI[b]
1961	2.6	6.5	-0.7	1.0	.7
1962	5.3	5.4	-0.7	2.2	1.2
1963	4.1	5.5	0.0	1.6	1.6
1964	5.3	5.0	-0.5	1.5	1.2
1965	5.8	4.4	+0.1	2,7	1.9
1966	5.8	3.7	-0.2	3.6	3.4
1967	2.9	3.7	-1.6	5.0	4.7
1968	4.1	3.5	-0.7	5.0	4.7
1969	2.4	3.4	+0.9	5.6	6.1
1970	-0.3	4.8	-1.2	5.5	5.5
1971	2.8	5.8	-2.0	5.7	3.4
1972	5.0	5.5	-1.4	4.7	3.4
1973	5.2	4.8	-0.4	6.5	8.8
1974	-0.5	5.5	-0.8	9.1	12.2
1975	-1.3	8.3	-4.3	9.8	7.0
1976	4.9	7.6	-3.0	6.4	4.8
1977	4.7	6.9	-2.3	6.7	6.8
1978	5.3	6.0	-1.3	7.3	9.0
1979	2.5	5.8	-0.6	8.9	13.3
1980	-0.2	7.0	-2.2	9.0	12.4
1981	1.9	7.5	-2.1	9.7	8.9
1982	-2.5	9.5	-4.6	6.4	3.9
1983	3.6	9.5	-5.2	3.9	3.8
1984	6.4	7.4	-4.5	3.8	4.0
1985	2.7	7.1	-5.0	3.3	3.8
1986	2.5	6.9	-4.8	2.7	1.1

(a) *Unemployment rate, all workers.*

(b) *December to December.*

Source: *Economic Report of the President, 1987, pp. 247, 249, 331, 285, 311.*

shows the salient data. In interpreting the unemployment rate shown in this table, one must remember that because of demographic developments and such factors as changes in the unemployment-compensation system, the natural unemployment rate rose in this period.

Table 2 shows some financial variables. The high growth rate of M1 in recent years should, of course, be interpreted in light of the decline in its velocity. The high nominal interest rates are explained by the high inflation rate. In the second half of the 1970s, the real rate was usually negative. What is surprising is not that nominal bill rates were so high but that they were so low.

Table 2
Some Financial Variables, 1973-1986

	Growth Rates of[a]		Interest Rates		Exchange Rates[b]	
Year	M1	M2	Treasury Bills[c]	Treasury Bonds[d]	Nominal	Real
1973	5.5	6.9	7.0	6.8	99.1	98.8
1974	4.4	5.5	7.9	7.6	101.4	99 .2
1975	4.9	12.6	5.8	8.0	98.5	93.9
1976	6.6	13.7	5.0	7.6	105.6	97.3
1977	8.0	10.6	5.3	7.4	103.3	93.1
1978	8.3	8.0	7.2	8.4	92.4	84.2
1979	7.1	7.8	10.0	9.4	88.1	83.2
1980	6.6	8.9	11.5	11.5	87.4	84.8
1981	6.5	10.0	14.0	13.9	102.9	100.8
1982	8.8	8.9	10.7	13.0	116.6	111.7
1983	9.8	12.0	8.6	11.1	125.3	117.3
1984	6.0	8.6	9.6	12.4	138.3	128.5
1985	12.2	8.1	7.5	10.6	143.2	132.0
1986[b]	16.6	9.3	6.0	7.7	112.0	103.4

(a) *Percent change from year earlier.*

(b) *Multilateral trade-weighted value of the dollar, 1973 = 100.*

(c) *Three months new issues.*

(d) *Ten-year maturities.*

Source: *Economic Report of the President, 1987, pp. 319, 325. 365.*

The Making of Fiscal Policy

Fiscal policy is made in a decentralized way. The President proposes a budget, but Congress often departs widely from the President's recommendations. The President can then veto specific tax and spending legislation. It is tempting to relate the large deficits of recent years to this decentralization. However, it is only part of the explanation. From the end of World War II until 1965 the federal budget was virtually in balance. Though there were many more years of deficits than of surpluses, in those years in which surpluses did occur they were large enough to offset the deficits of other years.

The Making of Monetary Policy

Monetary policy is made in a complex way. The Federal Open Market Committee (FOMC) that decides on open-market operations consists of the seven governors and five presidents of Federal Reserve Banks. The New York Bank has a permanent seat, the others serve in rotation. Actually, all the Reserve Bank presidents normally attend, and since the FOMC's discussion seeks a consensus, the nonvoting presidents also exert some influence. Reserve requirement changes and discount rate changes are controlled by the Board of Governors. Although formally the Fed is independent, in actuality it is subject to Presidential influence. It would be rare for monetary policy to be one that the President is seriously unhappy with (see Woolley, 1984). The main sources of the President's influence are the moral suasion that he exercises as a result of his having been elected, his power to appoint governors, and the Fed's need for his support in its congressional struggles. To a lesser extent the Fed is also sensitive to congressional pressures, since Congress could, subject to a Presidential veto, reduce the Fed's independence. Moreover, as a bank-regulating agency the Fed frequently asks Congress for legislation, which gives Congress a way of influencing the Fed.

10

The Response of the Bank of Japan to Macroeconomic and Financial Change

Thomas F. Cargill and Michael M. Hutchison

The Japanese economy has undergone significant structural changes over the past two decades and has been exposed to numerous domestic and external macroeconomic shocks. These changes have posed a strong challenge to the traditional approach to monetary policy in Japan.

On the domestic side, important developments have included a significant decline in economic growth after the early 1970s, major shifts after 1975 in established flow-of-fund patterns, steady innovation and liberalization in financial markets throughout the past decade, and episodes of money-demand instability. On the external side, major changes in the economic environment have included large fluctuations in exchange rates after 1973 when the floating exchange rate framework was introduced, oil price shocks in 1973 and 1979, internationalization of the Japanese financial market, and political pressures by the United States to restructure Japan's economy in an effort to address the external trade imbalances.

This chapter reviews and analyzes the evolution of Japanese monetary policy over the past two decades, and focuses on the way the Bank of Japan has responded to the changing economic and financial environment of the 1970s and the first half of the 1980s. This will involve a review of the details of the Bank of Japan's monetary control procedures, shifts in the strategy and stance of monetary policy, and important changes in the transmission mechanism of monetary policy to economic activity and inflation. In addition, the chapter will analyze the extent to which these changes have contributed to the stability of the Japanese economy.

This chapter considers the three major stages in the evolution of Japanese monetary policy. The first section focuses on the macroeconomic environment, Bank of Japan's operating procedures, and the transmission mechanism of monetary policy prior to the initiation of financial liberalization in the mid-1970s. This phase is termed the "high growth period" (Suzuki, 1980 and 1986). The next section analyzes the macroeconomic shocks and the response of monetary policy during the turbulent years between 1971-1975, the "transition period," and the following section considers the macroeconomic environment and monetary policy in the post-1975 period, the "stable period." Several unresolved issues concerning Japanese monetary policy are considered in the next section, in particular the debate surrounding the role of the Bank of Japan in contributing to general macroeconomic stability in Japan since 1975. The chapter concludes with several policy implications of the analysis and suggests avenues of potentially fruitful future research.

THE PRE-LIBERALIZATION PERIOD

Macroeconomic Background

Japan began a period of sustained high economic growth after the end of occupation in 1952 which continued until the early 1970s. Real gross national product grew at an average rate of about 10 percent annually, cyclical swings were relatively mild, and inflation ranged from 3 to 7 percent. Rapid economic growth over this two-decade period was largely sustained internally by a very high level of corporate investment in plant and equipment, as Japan moved to rebuild the productive capacity of its war-torn economy, and to a much lesser extent was sustained by expansion of the export sector. This developmental period was characterized by rapid employment gains, high productivity growth, and a substantial movement of labor from traditional low productivity sectors of the economy -- particularly agriculture -- to the high productivity manufacturing sector.

The financial system in Japan during the high growth period was highly concentrated and extensively regulated. Open-money and capital markets did not exist, and interest rates for the most part were administratively controlled. The yen exchange rate was fixed to the U.S. dollar, and extensive controls of foreign exchange transactions were maintained. The Japanese financial system during the high growth period has been termed "undeveloped" (Suzuki, 1985), but served certain functions quite well. In particular, the official desire to funnel low cost credit to the rapidly expanding manufacturing sector was made possible by the highly centralized banking system, the administratively regulated interest rate structure, and the lack of alternative financial instruments through which low-priority borrowers could raise funds.

The stance of monetary policy during the period was generally expansionary, with the fundamental purpose of supporting the rapid real growth potential of the Japanese economy. Short periods of monetary restraint were exercised to maintain current account balance. As a consequence, the average growth of the narrow and broad money aggregates ranged between 16 and 18 percent annually from 1967-1971 and experienced relatively little variation around this trend (Table 1). The policy stance at the beginning of the 1970s was particularly expansionary, partly in response to the accumulation of foreign exchange reserves associated with the beginning of large Japanese external surpluses, and partly attributable to Bank of Japan's support of the Tanaka Plan aimed at maintaining continued rapid economic growth in the 1970s.

Table 1
Money and Economic Activity in Japan

	Money[a]			Economic Variables[b]		
Time Period	**M1**	**M2**	**M2+CDs**	**Y**	**Q**	**P**
Early Period:						
1967.Q2 - 1971.Q2						
Average Growth	17.98	16.28	16.28	15.45	9.54	5.77
Standard Deviation	3.15	2.06	2.06	6.73	6.38	2.46
Coefficient of Variation	.17	.12	.12	.43	.67	.43
Interim Period:						
1971.Q3 - 1974.Q4						
Average Growth	19.20	18.36	18.36	16.84	4.63	12.12
Standard Deviation	9.85	6.82	6.79	6.45	6.80	6.99
Coefficient of Variaton	.51	.37	.37	.38	1.47	.58
Later Period:						
1975.Q1 - 1986.Q1						
Average Growth	6.49	9.59	9.86	7.46	4.18	3.24
Standard Deviation	5.84	2.77	2.54	3.56	2.69	2.59
Coefficient of Variation	.90	.28	.26	.48	.64	.80

(a) *All money aggregates are defined as the daily average outstanding, quarterly percent changes at seasonally adjusted annual rates. Source: Bank of Japan.*

(b) *Y, Q, P are nominal GNP, real GNP (1980 prices) and the GNP price deflator, respectively; quarterly percent changes at seasonally adjusted rates.*

Financial Environment

The transmission of monetary policy prior to 1975 was based on four unique aspects of Japan's financial environment which provided a close link between the Bank of Japan's policy instruments and the final policy targets: (1) the well-established flow-of-fund patterns between nonfinancial and financial entities; (2) the dependence of the corporate sector on intermediation credit in general, and bank credit in particular; (3) the extensive regulatory constraints on the portfolio activities of financial, and to a lesser extent, nonfinancial market participants in combination with binding constraints on virtually all interest rates; and (4) the absence of open-money and capital markets in general, and the absence of a government securities market in particular.

The pre-liberalization transmission process of monetary policy was based on three flow-of-fund patterns. First, the flow of funds among the nonfinancial sectors was characterized by large personal sector surpluses, large corporate sector deficits, and relatively small public sector deficits which were mainly concentrated in the local authorities and public corporations sector. In fact, the central government operated with small surpluses for much of the period prior to the initiation of liberalization. Net financial flows between Japan and the rest of the world were small, reflecting Japan's tendency toward current account balance and extensive restrictions on capital flows. The average financial surpluses relative to gross national product over the 1954-1974 period for the personal, corporate, and public sectors were 8.6, -7.1, and -2.4 percent, respectively.

The second flow-of-fund pattern involved flows between the city banks and other financial institutions. The city banks stood at the center of corporate finance, since they were the largest of the private financial intermediaries, had direct access to credit at the Bank of Japan discount window at below market rates, and played the key role in the main bank system (Cargill and Royama, forthcoming; Elston, 1981; and Nakatani, 1984). As a result, and also because strict limitations were placed on their deposit base, city banks were net demanders of funds from the interbank market. On the other hand, because they primarily served the less expansionary sectors of the economy, regional banks and other private financial institutions were net suppliers of funds to the interbank market (Suzuki, 1980; Cargill, 1986b).

The third flow-of-fund pattern involved the flow of direct Bank of Japan credit to private financial institutions. The city banks were the most dependent on such direct credit, receiving 87 percent of such credit during the 1969-1975 period, with the remainder allocated to the long-term credit banks and several large regional banks. This high dependence existed because regulation limited alternative sources of funds (e.g., a broader deposit base or access to a CD market), and because the Bank of Japan generally set the discount rate well below the interbank rate.

The corporate sector's heavy dependence on intermediation credit, particularly bank credit, was another characteristic of the Japanese financial system prior to the early 1970s which was relied upon to provide an important linkage in the transmission of monetary policy. In 1974, the last year of large corporate deficits, the corporate sector obtained 73 percent and 9 percent of external funding from private and public financial intermediaries, respectively. The 13 city banks, the larger regional banks, and the three long-term credit banks played a particularly important role in providing intermediation credit to the corporate sector.

Extensive portfolio and interest rate constraints, combined with the absence of open-money markets and capital markets, were also structural aspects of the Japanese financial system prior to reform which had important implications for the transmission of monetary policy. With the exception of the gensaki rate on repurchase agreements based primarily on government bonds but also on corporate and other bonds, all interest rates prior to liberalization were regulated to some extent. Even the interbank market was subject to administrative guidance by the Bank of Japan and thus functioned as something less than a competitive market. Portfolio restrictions limited the sources of funds for both financial and nonfinancial entities, and foreign sources of funding were virtually nonexistent.

Moreover, with the exception of the gensaki market, open-money and capital markets were undeveloped before 1975. Private financial institutions, especially the large city banks, stood at the center of Japan's industrial structure and provided the primary conduit for transferring the surpluses of the personal sector to finance the deficits of the corporate sector. This arrangement effectively satisfied the external funding requirements of the corporate sector, thus limiting internal pressures for the development of open-money and capital markets. The absence of a government securities market further limited the potential development of private direct markets (Hutchison,1986a).

Monetary Policy Instruments and Transmission Mechanism

Figure 1 illustrates the general framework of monetary policy prior to 1975. The policy instruments included: credit rationing at the discount window; changes in the discount rate; purchases and sales of bills in the bill component of the interbank market; sales of self-addressed bills of exchange; administrative guidance over transactions in the interbank market; and "window guidance" loan limits on individual financial institutions. These policy instruments were used to control the availability of credit to the corporate sector both directly by influencing the ability of financial institutions to make loans, and indirectly by influencing the price of credit. Because the corporate sector had few alternative sources of funding beyond financial intermediaries, the effect of the controls had a major influence on corporate spending and hence on the overall level of economic activity.

Figure 1: Monetary Tactics and Strategy

1. *Policy Instruments*
   a. *Discount window credit to the city banks and other larger banks*
   b. *Discount rate*
   c. *Purchases and sales of bills in the interbank market*
   d. *Sales of self-addressed bills*
   e. *Lending limits imposed on financial institutions or "window guidance"*
2. *Operating Target and Policy Indicator*
   a. *Interbank loan rate*
3. *Private Financial Institutions*
   a. *Portfolio decisions of city banks, regional banks, long-term credit banks, trust banks, and other financial institutions*
4. *Intermediate Financial Target*
   a. *Loans to the corporate sector*
5. *Intermediate Real Target*
   a. *Corporate investment spending*
6. *Final Policy Target*
   a. *Prices, real GNP, exchange rate, etc.*

Both direct controls on bank lending (window guidance) and changes in the interbank rate played key roles in the transmission of monetary policy (Figure 2). The Bank of Japan focused on both the interbank rate and the quantity of intermediation credit as policy targets and indicators of monetary policy.

The Bank of Japan influenced the interbank rate in three ways. Its purchases and sales of bills in the interbank market and administrative guidance of interbank transactions directly influenced interbank interest rates. Credit rationing at the discount window indirectly influenced the interbank rate by influencing the availability of borrowed reserves and hence the excess demand for short-term funds of the city banks.

Figure 2: Transmission of Monetary Policy

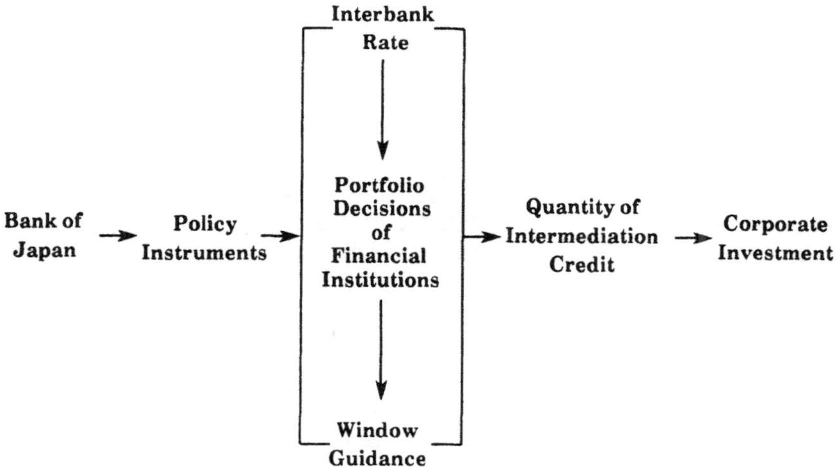

Interbank interest rate movements initiated by the Bank of Japan influenced the quantity and price of lending to the corporate sector, and hence the state of aggregate demand in the economy. City banks were the only net borrowers in the interbank market. Although posted loan rates were adjusted only periodically in response to discount rate changes, city banks effectively passed on changes in cost of funds (interbank rate) to corporate customers by varying the deposit/loan ratio (the so-called "compensating balances") which borrowers were required to maintain as a condition for new loans. City banks also frequently adjusted the effective loan rate by varying the amount of loans qualifying for the prime loan rate, and requiring a higher interest rate for loan amounts in excess of the new limits. Thus, not only the price (i.e., effective loan rates) but also the quantity of bank loans was directly affected by the Bank of Japan's operations in the interbank market.

While the main focus of the policy instruments was directed toward the city banks, other private financial institutions were also influenced by Bank of Japan's operations in the interbank market. For example, when the Bank of Japan pursued monetary restraint and rationed credit to city banks at the discount window, an excess demand for reserves would result. The resultant rise in interbank rates would induce other private financial institutions, which were net lenders on the interbank market, to reduce their businesses loans so as to increase their lending of reserves to city banks. In addition, although smaller financial institutions were not dependent on the Bank of Japan's direct credit, they respected the window guidance limits because the limits were set in such a fashion as to maintain market share (Yasuda, 1981).

In sum, part of the transmission process relied on an interest rate-expenditure effect; i.e., the indirect effect of interest rate changes on the demand for total credit and thereby aggregate expenditure in the economy. However, given the highly regulated and rigid nature of the interest rate structure in Japan, this transmission channel was secondary to the direct credit availability effect on aggregate expenditures associated with credit rationing. This in turn was achieved by changing the reserve base of the financial institutions, by administrative guidance imposed on city banks at the discount window, and by the window guidance loan limits established by the Bank of Japan.

The relative importance of these two channels for the transmission process of monetary policy is an important identifying characteristic of the pre-reform period. In the face of a fairly rigid and administratively controlled interest rate structure, the direct and indirect control of the total quantity of credit (and control over the allocation of credit through the banking system) -- as opposed to the price of credit -- was the primary linkage between Bank of Japan operations and its ultimate policy objectives.

THE TRANSITION PERIOD

The Japanese economic system began to undergo fundamental changes in the early 1970s. The rapid output growth of the high growth period was simply not sustainable. A significant part of the potential productivity gains associated with the restructuring of the Japanese economy from traditional employment areas to manufacturing had been realized by the early 1970s. Moreover, Japan's growth potential was also presumably limited by its dependence on imported energy supplies, which became a major constraint following the first oil price shock in 1973. Japan depended on imported oil for almost 75 percent of its energy requirements at the time. Finally, the move to floating exchange rates in the early 1970s also greatly affected the economic environment.

The transition period of the early 1970s was marked by significant macroeconomic instability and uncertainty in the economy. Real GNP growth shifted from the 10 percent range during the high growth period to a range of 3 to 5 percent. The combination of a drop in the underlying growth potential of the economy, an expansionary monetary policy at the beginning of the 1970s, and the oil price shock in 1973 pushed the inflation rate to double-digit levels, averaging over 12 percent annually between

1971-1973. Moreover, the variability of both output growth and inflation rates increased significantly (Table 1).

A significant part of the rise of inflation in Japan in the early 1970s was associated with expansionary monetary policy (Pigott, 1980; Oritani, 1979; and Shimpo, 1979), rather than simply the pass-through effects of the oil price shock in 1973. The inflationary effects of expansionary monetary policy were at first not fully appreciated in Japan, however. But as inflation accelerated, reaching an annual rate of 20.6 percent in 1973, as measured by the GNP deflator, the Bank of Japan embarked on an extremely tight monetary policy, which was at least partly responsible for the rapid fall in the inflation rate to less than 8 percent by 1974 (Suzuki, 1986; Pigott, 1980).

The inflationary effects of the expansionary monetary policy and the need to institute a tight monetary policy at a time when the economy was being subjected to a severe oil price shock were to have a major impact on monetary policy in Japan after 1974. The Bank of Japan has adopted a strategy of gradually reducing the growth rate of the money supply and by some measures has achieved a more stable monetary growth than before 1975. There is some question as to how important the money supply has become as an intermediate target, or whether the Bank of Japan should continue to focus primarily on interest rates and intermediation credit. (This is discussed in Section 5.) However, there is no debate over the fact that since the inflationary experience of the early 1970s, the Bank of Japan has become quite conscious of the link between rapid money growth and inflation, and has focused on price stability as one of the primary policy objectives (Suzuki, 1985).

THE STABLE PERIOD

Macroeconomic Background

Since the mid-1970s, the Japanese economy has adapted remarkably well to a lower economic growth and other fundamental changes in the economic environment. Inflation has declined significantly, averaging since 1975 around 3 percent annually. As Figure 3 illustrates, the decline in inflation has coincided with a marked downward trend in money growth since 1975. Broad money growth (M2 + CDs) has averaged less than 10 percent annually, and narrow money growth (M1) has averaged less than 7 percent annually over the 1975-1986 period. The average annual growth rates of M2 + CD and M1 over the 1967-1974 period were 18 and 17 percent, respectively.

Figure 3: Quarterly Growth Rates of Money Supply in Japan, 1968-1986

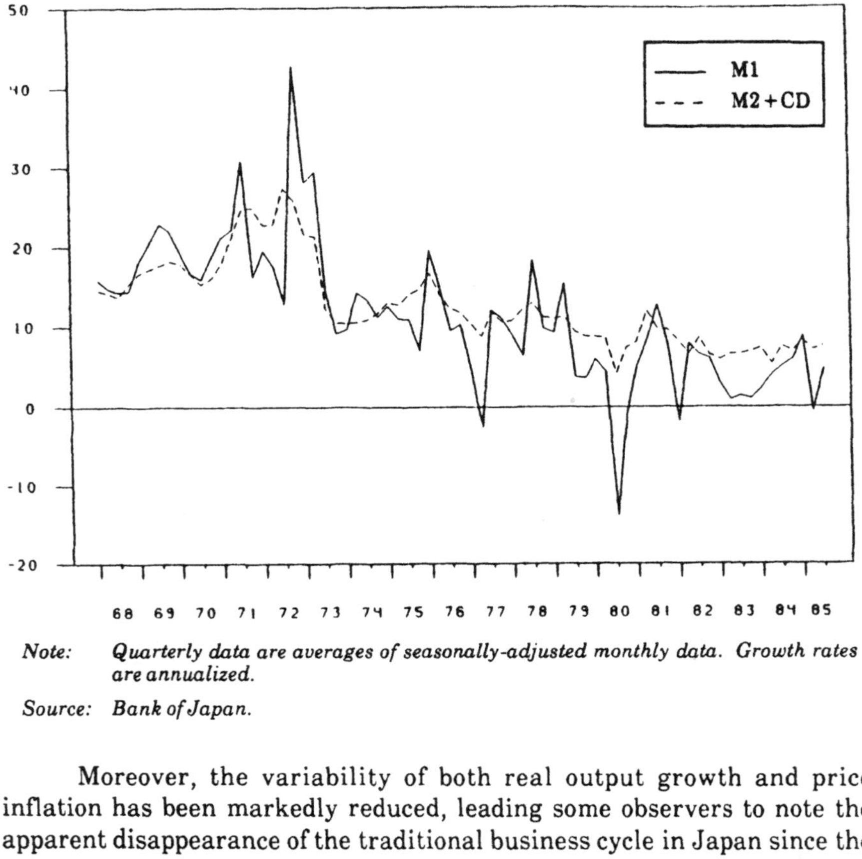

Note: *Quarterly data are averages of seasonally-adjusted monthly data. Growth rates are annualized.*

Source: *Bank of Japan.*

Moreover, the variability of both real output growth and price inflation has been markedly reduced, leading some observers to note the apparent disappearance of the traditional business cycle in Japan since the mid-1970s (Hutchison, 1987). Particularly noteworthy is that Japan alone among the major industrial countries quickly contained inflation after the second oil price shock in 1979 while at the same time avoiding a recession (Hamada and Hayashi, 1985).

Financial Environment

The financial liberalization that emerged after 1975 and fundamentally changed the environment for Japan's money policy, has continued to the present. The seeds of financial liberalization were sowed by the lower growth potential of the Japanese economy of the 1970s, which had a profound impact on established flow-of-fund patterns (Cargill, 1986a; Cargill and Royama, forthcoming; Suzuki, 1985 and 1986; Feldman, 1986;

Pigott, 1983). In the mid-1970s, the corporate sector's deficit position was reduced by almost 50 percent, and the overall government budget deficit increased by almost 100 percent. The latter increased largely because the central government budget, which had previously exhibited small surpluses, shifted to a deficit after 1973. The personal sector surplus remained essentially unchanged during this period.

The corporate sector deficit declined because of a reduced need for external financing as output growth and business investment declined. The central government deficit increased as a consequence of an expansionary fiscal policy to offset the contractionary effects of the oil price shock, and of reduced revenue growth associated with a lower economic growth. The new flow-of-fund patterns and the increasing need to internationalize domestic finance initiated the liberalization process in Japan. The need to fund increasing amounts of government debt and the growing market resistance to absorbing the large amounts of debt at subsidized prices forced the regulatory authorities to make the government debt offerings more sensitive to market forces. The declining market share of the banking system resulting from reduced corporate demand for external funding generated pressure on the regulatory authorities to permit new portfolio opportunities in order for the banks to regain and enhance their market share. Finally, the reduced profit opportunities in the real sector for corporations brought pressure on the regulatory authorities to provide new portfolio opportunities to restore profit levels.

The shift to a floating exchange rate added momentum to the liberalization process. Japan's internationally isolated financial system was incompatible with floating exchange rates. The myriad of restrictions on international capital movements required to maintain fixed exchange was no longer necessary.

The catalysts for financial reform were well in place by the end of the 1970s (Cargill, 1985, Cargill and Royama, 1987). Although the pace of liberalization has not been rapid, the financial environment of the 1980s differs significantly from that which existed prior to 1975. Market participants have been granted greater portfolio flexibility, interest rates on key financial assets are now unregulated, regulated interest rates are adjusted more frequently, differentials between regulated and unregulated interest rates have been narrowed, and the inflow and outflow of capital have expanded significantly.

The financial structure has also undergone fundamental changes. The government has become the major deficit sector in Japan. City banks have experienced a decline in the share of intermediation finance, and are less dependent on the interbank market or the discount window for funds. Direct finance through money and capital markets has gained relative to indirect finance through financial institutions. In addition, corporate spending has become more sensitive to interest rate changes (Akhtar, 1983).

Monetary Policy Instruments and Transmission Mechanism

In many ways, the Bank of Japan's monetary policy operating procedure is very similar to that which was used before 1975. According to a prominent Bank of Japan official, the Bank continues to focus primarily on the interbank rate as both the operating target and the indicator of monetary policy (Fukui, 1986). Academic research supports this view (Cargill, 1986b; Dotsey, 1986; Hutchison, 1986b and 1986c). In fact, the outline of Japan's monetary policy presented in Figure 1 remains essentially accurate. Nevertheless, changes in both the policy tactics and the transmission mechanism are discernable.

Liberalization has permitted regulated interest rates to be more responsive to market forces. New unregulated financial assets have been authorized: CDs in 1979; money market certificates and yen-denominated banker's acceptances in 1985; and, most recently, unregulated large time-deposit certificates. As a result, there has been a gradual deemphasis on the availability of credit as the intermediate monetary policy target and an increasing emphasis on interest rates as a major channel of monetary policy (Cargill, 1986b, Fukui, 1986).

The Bank of Japan has placed increasing emphasis on open-market operations in the interbank market, relative to window guidance limits and administrative intervention in the interbank market. In addition, it has become a vocal advocate for the development of a short-term government securities market that would enable it to use open-market operations as a monetary policy instrument. At present, the Bank of Japan is required to absorb short-term government securities issued by the Ministry of Finance, since they are priced above market levels (Royama, 1986).

Figure 4 indicates the new transmission process of monetary policy. It differs from Figure 2 by the deletion of window guidance as a significant policy instrument and constraint on the portfolio decisions of financial institutions, and by the addition of a new channel of monetary policy transmission via the increased flexibility of interest rates. At the same time, the "quantity of intermediation credit" channel still remains a part of the transmission process, although its importance has been reduced during the past decade.

At the same time, an increasing emphasis has been placed on price stability as an objective of monetary policy. Not only has this new emphasis been expressed in numerous Bank of Japan policy statements (e.g., Shimamoto, 1982) but it has also been reflected by the gradual reductionof

Figure 4: Monetary Policy Transmissions -- After Liberalization

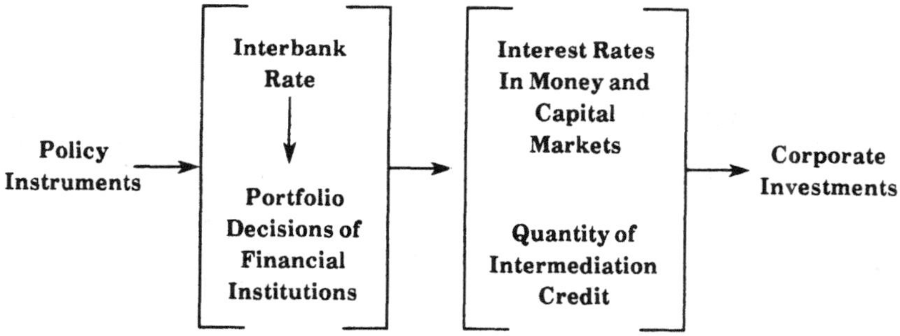

the growth rate of the broad money aggregate (M2+CDs) since 1975. The Bank of Japan's rapid response to the second oil price shock in 1979 -- increase of the interbank interest rates by more than 800 basis points over a 12-month period -- was designed to quickly avert continued inflationary pressures and curb a rise in inflation expectations. The action must be judged a success, as Japan has been able to avoid both significant inflation and recession, a degree of macroeconomic stability not achieved by the majority of industrial economies.

UNRESOLVED ISSUES

A number of interesting, and as yet unresolved, issues remain regarding the workings of Japanese monetary policy and its linkages to the economy. A short list includes the extent to which monetary policy, as opposed to other factors, is responsible for the remarkable stability of the Japanese economy; the extent to which the Bank of Japan is following a "monetarist" policy in its desire to maintain price stability; the effectiveness of the Bank of Japan's response to the major appreciation of the yen exchange rate over the past two years; the effects on the transmission mechanism of monetary policy of the increasing internationalization of the Japanese financial system; the role of open-market operations and window guidance in Japan's monetary policy; and the relationship between monetary policy and financial liberalization in Japan. Not all these issues can be explored in the remainder of this chapter.

Monetarism

Several economists have attributed the stability of the Japanese economy, as well as the low rate of Japanese inflation since the mid-1970s, to the adoption by the Bank of Japan of a monetarist policy of stable long-run monetary growth (Cargill and Royama, forthcoming; Friedman, 1985; Greenwood, 1985). Friedman, for example, has argued that "... the Bank of Japan has been the least monetarist central bank in its rhetoric, the most monetarist in its policy." Friedman bases his observation on the fact that Japan's broad-money growth has followed a fairly steady decline since the mid-1970s, and this trend has coincided with a decline in the rate of Japanese price inflation.

Allan Meltzer (1985, 1987) also attributes stability in the Japanese economy to Bank of Japan's monetary policy, but characterizes the shift in monetary regimes in terms of the adoption of a more credible monetary policy, as opposed to the adoption of monetary targeting. The evidence marshalled by Meltzer in support of his credibility thesis is that the forecast error variance (generated from time series forecasting equations) of nominal GNP, real GNP, and prices in Japan decreased markedly after the country's switch to fluctuating exchange rates in 1971. He associates reduced forecast errors to a more stable and credible monetary policy.

Hutchison (1986b, 1987) takes issue with the view that the Bank of Japan has adopted a traditional monetarist policy, and also questions the empirical support for the credibility hypothesis. He argues that there is little institutional or empirical evidence suggesting that the Bank of Japan has adhered to money aggregates targeting, and that the public announcement of money projections starting in July 1978 are, in fact, forecasts and not policy targets. Moreover, Hutchison points out that Japan's money growth has not become significantly more predictable (in terms of a reduction in forecast error variance) since the mid-1970s. Dotsey (1986) also argues against the monetarist interpretation of Bank of Japan's policy since 1975, and has noted that "... Japan achieves results that are monetarist in nature without using the procedures frequently advocated by monetarists." Cargill (1986b) concludes that one can discern only gradual changes in the framework of monetary policy since the initiation of financial liberalization in the mid-1970s.

The issue is debatable as to whether the Bank of Japan has consciously adopted a monetarist strategy or whether it has achieved what appear to be monetarist results via an operating strategy that is nonmonetarist in nature. It is also debatable whether or not its policy has become more predictable, in some sense of the term. Most importantly, nonmonetary factors (e.g., labor market adjustment) must also take credit for the undeniable stability of the Japanese economy during the past decade.

There are, however, less debatable aspects of the evolution of monetary policy in Japan during the last decade. As discussed above, the operating tactics of the Bank of Japan have not changed significantly during the past decade in terms of the role of the interbank rate and the role of the cost and availability of credit in the transmission of monetary policy. There has also been a subtle and gradual shift toward policy instruments designed to exploit the enhanced role of interest rates in the financial system. In this respect, the transmission mechanism of monetary policy has been modified. Finally, there has been a significant shift in the strategy of monetary policy designed to maintain greater price stability than in the pre-1975 period. While the evidence suggests that the Bank of Japan does not target monetary growth according to monetarism, the effect of its policies has been to achieve a well-defined long-run monetary growth path. Given the close long-run relationship between inflation and money and the undeniable importance of price stability in Japan, the Bank of Japan has de facto achieved a monetarist outcome. Perhaps it would be better to characterize the policy as a form of eclectic monetarism in which the Bank of Japan does not adhere to specific monetary growth targets and controls the money supply via a policy focused on interest rates. However, the commitment to stable and low inflation is necessarily reflected by a long-run stable monetary growth rate.

It is noteworthy that the Bank of Japan's commitment to a noninflationary policy also has made a major contribution to the financial reform process in Japan. Financial reform in Japan has progressed at a slow and gradual pace compared to the discrete and frequently disruptive pace of reform in the United States. A slow, predictable, and gradual financial reform process has a number of advantages; however, it requires a noninflationary environment to minimize the differential between unregulated and regulated interest rates. In Japan, the differential has been considerably smaller than in the United States (Cargill and Royama, forthcoming), and this has resulted in smaller disruptions to the flow of funds than in the United States. Thus, the Bank of Japan's commitment to price stability provides a lesson to other central banks. Not only will price stability contribute to a more favorable macroeconomic performance but it will additionally allow a more gradual and consistent approach to financial reform.

Policy Instruments

Another important unresolved issue concerns whether the Bank of Japan has in fact substantively modified its operating instruments. We have documented several notable changes in its policy instruments during the past decade, specifically, an increasing emphasis on open-market operations and a decreasing emphasis on credit allocation instruments, particularly window guidance loan limits. Two caveats regarding this shift in policy instruments are necessary, however.

First, open-market operations in Japan, frequently emphasized during the 1970s, have only until recently been employed as a general instrument of policy, and are limited by the absence of an open and broad short-term government securities market. Prior to February 1986, the only short-term security issued by the Ministry of Finance was routinely purchased by the Bank of Japan, since it was priced above market levels and not marketable to syndicate members. The Bank of Japan objected to this procedure because the amount of short-term debt was becoming a large part of the supply of high-powered money (Fukio, 1986); the Bank was forced to use other instruments to offset the expansionary effect on the money supply. In response to this and to external pressure to increase the pace of financial liberalization, the Ministry of Finance recently began to issue a six-month Treasury bill at competitive rates. This is a limited, but important, first step toward establishing a short-term government securities market. Should further efforts be directed toward an open and broad Treasury bill market, the Bank of Japan will eventually have access to a policy instrument more consistent with a financially liberated system than at any time in the past decade.

There is no doubt that less emphasis is being placed on window guidance. At the same time, however, the Bank of Japan has had little opportunity to use window guidance since 1979-1980 when monetary policy was very tight. During that period, window guidance limits were effective and were respected, at least by the city banks. Until the Bank of Japan is again faced with a need to adopt tight monetary policy, it is difficult to judge the importance or lack of importance of window guidance as a policy instrument, though it is not unreasonable to suggest that window guidance has declined in importance (Figures 2 and 4).

CONCLUSION

The environment in which monetary policy in Japan is conducted has changed significantly since the mid-1970s. Along with the relaxation of a formal exchange rate objective, the conduct of monetary policy has been affected by a gradual liberalization of the Japanese financial system: interest rate decontrol; the development of new financial instruments and financial markets; and fewer constraints on the asset and liability choices of investors, borrowers, and financial institutions.

These changes, in turn, have induced the Bank of Japan to modify its traditional approach to monetary policy. In particular, the transmission of interest rate changes to economic activity is now more significant in the emerging deregulated Japanese financial environment. Partly in response to these changes, the Bank has emphasized interbank interest rates as the primary operating instrument of policy to a greater extent than before, and has virtually discontinued direct controls over bank lending.

It is also apparent that the high inflation of the early 1970s and its association, at least in part, with high money growth has induced the Bank of Japan to rethink its traditional strategy of monetary policy. In particular, there has been a new emphasis on price stability as a final policy objective. As a consequence, it has sought and achieved lower average money growth in the last decade compared with the pre-1975 period. Moreover, its rapid move to increase interbank interest rates in response to the second oil price shock in 1979 demonstrated its resolve to maintain a low-inflation environment.

The economic and financial conditions of the late 1980s will undoubtedly pose new challenges to the Bank of Japan in its attempts to support economic growth and maintain low inflation. Examples are not difficult to find. Most recently, the sharp rise in the value of the yen exchange rate and the associated slowdown in the Japanese economy has put the Bank in a delicate position. This position is made even more difficult because of Japan's unsurpassed string of trade account surpluses. Japan's major trading partners, particularly the United States, have demanded that Japan introduce measures designed to stimulate domestic aggregate demand and thereby help to redress the trade imbalance. In response, the Bank of Japan lowered the discount rate four times in 1986 to a level below the historical low of 3.29 percent set in April 1936 (Bank of Japan, 1987). While money supply growth has increased somewhat (8.4 and 8.6 percent in 1985 and 1986, respectively), it is too early to determine whether the Bank has embarked on an expansionary policy path that may ultimately deviate from the stable policy of the past decade.

Another challenge to Japan's monetary policy could be presented by the increasingly international nature of the Japanese financial system. It is probable that the transmission mechanism of monetary policy may be modified, or that the Bank of Japan's control over domestic interest rates may be weakened as a consequence of the internationalization. But if the past is any indication, it is likely that the Bank will respond to these new challenges in a pragmatic and flexible manner.

The authors thank Hang-Sheng Cheng, Reuven Glick, Tomohiko Sakamoto, and Koichi Takata for valuable comments on an earlier draft of this chapter, and Donna Payne for production support. Cargill's research on this project has been partly funded by the U.S.-Japan Friendship Commission, and Hutchison's work supported by a Pacific Rim Grant from the President's Office of the University of California.

REFERENCES

Akhtar, M. A. (1983). *Financial Innovation and Their Implications For Monetary Policy: An International Perspective.* Basel, Switzerland: Bank for International Settlements (December).

Bank of Japan (1987). "Quarterly Economic Outlook." Research and Statistics Department, Special Paper No. 148 (Winter).

Cargill, Thomas F. (1985). "A U.S. Perspective on Japanese Financial Liberalization." *Monetary and Economic Studies.* Institute for Monetary and Economic Studies. Bank of Japan. 3 (May), pp. 115-161.

Cargill, Thomas F. (1986a). "Financial Reform in the United States and Japan: A Comparative Overview." In *Financial Policy and Reform in Pacific Basin Countries*, edited by Hang-Sheng Cheng. Lexington, Mass.: D.C. Heath and Company, pp. 39-57.

Cargill, Thomas F. (1986b). "Japanese Monetary Policy, Flow of Funds, and Domestic Financial Liberalization." *Economic Review.* Federal Reserve Bank of San Francisco (Summer), pp. 21-32.

Cargill, Thomas F. (1988). "A Perspective on United States Trade Policies Toward Japan." *Columbia Journal of World Business* (forthcoming).

Cargill, Thomas F. and Ramon Moreno (1986). "A New Direction for Japan." *Weekly Letter.* Federal Reserve Bank of San Francisco (June).

Cargill, Thomas F. and Shoichi Royama (1985). "Japanese Banking and Corporate Finance in Transition." *Bank Structure and Competition.* Federal Reserve Bank of Chicago , pp. 19-33.

Cargill, Thomas F. and Shoichi Royama (1988). *The Transition of Finance in Japan and the United States: A Comparative Perspective.* Hoover Institution Press, Stanford University, forthcoming.

Dotsey, Michael (1986). "Japanese Monetary Policy, A Comparative Analysis." *Monetary and Economic Studies.* Institute for Monetary and Economic Studies, The Bank of Japan 4 (October), pp. 105-127.

Elston, C.D. (1981). "The Financing of Japanese Industry." *Quarterly Review.* Bank of England (December), pp. 510-518.

Feldman, Robert A. (1986). *Japanese Financial Markets: Deficits, Dilemmas, and Deregulation.* Cambridge, Mass.: The MIT Press.

Friedman, Milton (1983). "Monetary Variability: United States and Japan." *Journal of Money, Credit and Banking* 15 (August), pp. 339-343.

Friedman, Milton (1985). "The Fed's Monetarism Was Never Anything but Rhetoric." *Wall Street Journal* (December).

Fukui, Toshihiko (1986). "Recent Developments of the Short-term Money Market in Japan and Changes in Monetary Control Techniques and Procedures by the Bank of Japan." Research and Statistics Department, The Bank of Japan, Special Paper No. 130 (January).

Greenwood, John (1984). "The Japanese Experiment in Monetarism 1974-1984." *Manhattan Report on Economic Policy* 4.

Hamada, Koichi and Fumio Hayashi (1985). "Monetary Policy in Postwar Japan." In *Monetary Policy in Our Times*, edited by Ando et al. Cambridge, Mass.: MIT Press.

Hutchison, Michael (1986a). "Financial Effects of Budget Deficits in the Pacific Basin." In *Financial Policy and Reform in Pacific Basin Countries*, edited by Hang-Sheng Cheng. Lexington, Mass.: D.C. Heath and Company.

Hutchison, Michael (1986b). "Japan's 'Money Focused' Monetary Policy." Federal Reserve Bank of San Francisco *Economic Review* 3 (Summer), pp. 33-47.

Hutchison, Michael (1988). "Monetary Control with an Exchange Rate Objective: The Case of Japan, 1973-1986." *Journal of International Money and Finance* (forthcoming September).

Hutchison, Michael (1988). "The Bank of Japan's Response to Exchange Rate Shocks: Evidence from VAR Models." *Geld, Banken und Versicherungen*, 1987/Bandl, VVW Karlsruhe (forthcoming).

Hutchison, Michael (1987). "A Model Central Bank?" *Weekly Letter*. Federal Reserve Bank of San Francisco (April 3, 1987). This publication was incorrectly dated April 3, 1982, when first released by the Federal Reserve Bank of San Francisco.

Meltzer, Allan H. (1985). "Japanese Monetary Policy." *The Foxhall Review* Volume 3, No. 18 (May 23).

Meltzer, Allan H. (1985). "Variability of Prices, Output and Money Under Fixed and Fluctuating Exchange Rates: An Empirical Study of Monetary Regimes in Japan and the United States." Bank of Japan *Monetary and Economic Studies* 3 (December), pp. 1-46.

Nakatani, Iwao (1984). "The Economic Role of Financial Corporate Grouping." In *The Economic Analysis of the Japanese Firm*, edited by Aoki Masahiko, Amsterdam: Elsevir Science Publishers, pp. 227-258.

Okina, Kunio (1986). "Relationship Between Money Stock and Real Output in the Japanese Economy." Bank of Japan *Monetary and Economic Studies* 4 (April), pp. 41-77.

Okubo, Takashi (1983). "Money, Interest, Income and Prices." Bank of Japan *Monetary and Economic Studies* 1 (October), pp. 111-146.

Pigott, Charles (1980). "Wringing Out Inflation: Japan's Experience." Federal Reserve Bank of San Francisco *Economic Review* (Summer), pp. 21-42.

Pigott, Charles (1983). "Financial Reform in Japan." *Economic Review*. Federal Reserve Bank of San Francisco. (Winter), pp. 25-46.

Royama, Shoichi (1986). "An Open Market for Treasury Bills." *Economic Eye*. Keizai Koho Center, Tokyo, Japan. 7 (June), pp. 13-15.

Simamoto, Reiichi (1982). "Monetary Control in Japan." In *Central Bank Views on Monetary Targeting*, edited by Paul Meek. Federal Reserve Bank of New York (May).

Suzuki, Yoshio (1980). *Money and Banking in Contemporary Japan*. New Haven: Yale University Press.

Suzuki, Yoshio (1984). "Monetary Policy in Japan: Transmission Mechanism and Effectiveness." Bank of Japan *Monetary and Economic Studies*, 3 (December).

Suzuki, Yoshio (1985). "Japan's Monetary Policy Over the Past 10 Years." Bank of Japan *Monetary and Economic Studies*. 3 (September), pp. 1-18.

Suzuki, Yoshio (1986). *Money, Finance, and Macroeconomic Performance in Japan*. New Haven: Yale University Press.

Yasuda, Tadashi (1981). "A Theoretical Interpretation of the Window Guidance: A Game-Theoretic Interpretation." Bank of Japan, Special Economic Studies Department (February).

11
The New Australian Monetary Policy

Kevin Davis and Mervyn Lewis

Throughout most of the postwar years, monetary policy in Australia has been carried out in the context of rigid controls over the banking system, government securities markets, and foreign exchange markets. In the early 1980s, these controls were swept away. Beginning late in 1980 with the removal of interest rate ceilings on bank deposits, a rapid succession of moves followed, including a reorganization of the government securities markets and a liberalization of the foreign exchange market that culminated in December 1983 with the lifting of exchange controls and the floating of the Australian dollar. (The Appendix provides a chronology of major financial deregulatory changes.)

The shift of monetary policy from direct control to more market-oriented methods accompanied and encouraged changes in banking, securities markets, and the foreign exchange market. With the entry of 16 new banks in 1985, the number of banks more than doubled. The turnover in the secondary markets for government bonds increased from \$12.6 billion in fiscal 1980/81 to \$167 billion in fiscal 1986/87.[1] Trading in the foreign exchange market increased fivefold from 1985 to 1987. With a daily turnover of \$25 billion, the Australian foreign exchange market now ranks sixth or seventh in the world, above Paris and not much below Singapore.[2] These developments in turn have prompted a further evolution in monetary policy in Australia.

The first section of this chapter provides a brief description of the institutional framework in which monetary policy operates in Australia. The next section reviews Australia's macroeconomic performance in recent years. The third section discusses the rise of the new Australian monetary policy. The fourth section analyzes the instruments of transmission of the new monetary policy. The final section focuses on certain current issues arising from the conduct of the new monetary policy.

INSTITUTIONAL FRAMEWORK

When the Commonwealth of Australia was formed in 1901, the trading banks (i.e., commercial banks) held 60 percent of the assets of all financial institutions in Australia.[3] They still are the financial group with the largest assets (see Table 1), and are the key financial institutions in the Australian financial system.[4] This pivotal position owes much to their dominance of the domestic and international payments system; to public perception that as "banks" they are government guaranteed; and to their central role in monetary policy.

Prior to 1980, interest rate controls and other restrictions upon banking liabilities and assets induced banks to follow the holding company approach by establishing finance company subsidiaries, taking equity interests in merchant banks, and seeking nondeposit-based financing through issuing bank acceptances and other off-balance-sheet activities. Nevertheless, their dominant role diminished. In the retail market, building societies and credit unions, which were subject to less restrictive state government legislation than the federally regulated banks, were able to offer more attractive deposit facilities and greater availability of housing and personal loans. In the wholesale market, banks were handicapped by being barred from accepting interest-bearing time deposits of less than 30 days' maturity. These restrictions provided openings for merchant banks, many of which were subsidiaries of foreign banks excluded from operating as banks in Australia.

Table 1 shows a resurgence of domestic commercial banks in the 1980s. However, the previous distinctions between banks and nonbank financial institutions have become blurred as a result of liberalization of bank regulations, the provision of payments services by building societies and credit unions, and the opening of foreign exchange dealership to merchant banks. In addition, the data in Table 1 are distorted by the increase in the number of banks in 1985, when 16 foreign banks were permitted to operate as banks and the foreign banks transferred some of their nonbank businesses to their new banking arms.

Significant changes occurred in the foreign exchange market as well. Australia clung to fixed exchange rates longer than most other major countries. From 1976 to 1983, the exchange rate was administered daily by government officials, much along the lines of a crawling peg.[5] As is often true in adjustable peg arrangements, the system was bedevilled by speculation. Exchange controls, introduced in World War II, became primarily concerned with regulating short-term capital movements. Official forward cover was limited. Although a thriving private hedge market developed, based on the mutual indemnity principle, international financial integration was not complete, and covered interest parity did not always hold.

Eventually, speculation forced the end of exchange controls. The authorities began in December 1983 to issue new licenses to deal in foreign exchange, an activity previously permitted (with one or two minor

Table 1
The Australian Financial System Pre- and Post-Deregulation

	June 1979		June 1986		Compound Annual Growth Rate of Assets			
	No. of Institutions	Share of Assets	No. of Institutions	Share of Assets	Five Years to June		Four Years to June	
					1973	1978	1982	1986
Reserve Bank	1	7.8	1	6.1	16	11	10	17
Trading Banks	13	22.5	29[(a)]	27.6	14	14	18	21
Savings Banks	13	16.0	16[(a)]	12.2	10	12	9	15
Life Insurance Funds	50	9.6	n.a.	8.4	11	9	11	17
Pension Funds	n.a.	8.2	n.a.	9.2	12	14	16	21
Nonlife Insurance Offices	200	5.3	n.a.	4.7	13	19	17	12
Finance Companies	166	12.1	146	7.5	26	16	15	4
Money Market Corporations	40	3.8	113	8.0	69	13	32	27
Permanent Building Societies	120	6.9	64	5.1	40	21	16	10
Authorized Money Market Dealers	9	1.2	9	0.5	11	11	-2	10
Credit Cooperatives	202	1.3	302[(b)]	1.7	39	30	22	22
Other	n.a.	5.3	n.a.	9.0	n.a.	n.a.	n.a.	n.a.
All Financial Institutions	n.a.	100.0	n.a.	100.0	15	14	16	18

(a) Includes State Banks.

(b) Change in coverage of statistics.

Source: Australia Financial System Inquiry Interim Report, Tables 3.1, 3.3, 6.1, 6.2. Reserve Bank of Australia Bulletin, various issues.

exceptions) only to trading banks. Trading in both spot and forward Australian dollar has grown strongly, and covered-interest parity now consistently holds. While the Reserve Bank retains the power to reintroduce exchange controls, the power remains unused. Nevertheless, there were still several impediments (interest withholding tax and oversight of direct investment by the Foreign Investment Review Board, for example) to various types of international capital flows. Changes in both areas have been in the general direction of liberalization, and they have affected the type, rather than the volume, of capital flows.

Controls over new issues of government securities have switched from price setting to quantity setting. Until 1979, an unlimited quantity of three- and six-month Treasury notes at an officially determined yield was issued under a tap system. Since 1979, a tender system has been in place. The Treasury announces the amount of issue virtually every week, with the yield determined by auction.

Longer term (one year and over) Treasury bonds were issued under an intermittent tap system. Three or four times a year, new securities would be made available at an officially determined yield. This was replaced in 1979 by a tap system, which prevailed until replaced by the current tender system in July 1982. Approximately eight tenders are held each fiscal year, which starts on July 1.[6]

These changes have insulated monetary flows from the effects of developments in the government securities and foreign exchange markets in a way which is unique in Australian postwar history.[7] The tender system has enabled the government to meet its own need for funding without recourse to borrowing from the Reserve Bank, as was necessary under the previous system when new issues were mispriced. Since fiscal 1984/85, the central government has fully funded its deficits by primary issues, thereby creating a separation of monetary and debt management. In addition, the floating of the Australian dollar has similarly neutralized the impact of foreign exchange flows upon domestic monetary flows.

These changes have brought home the point that the government budget deficit and private foreign exchange transactions do not of themselves create money. Increases in money arise from these sources only when the Reserve Bank buys government debt or foreign exchange. Of course, this was equally true under the previous arrangements, but conventions and institutional realities focused attention upon the deficit and the exchange rate rather than on the Bank's open-market operations.

The nine authorized money market dealers, created in 1959, hold a central position in Australia's money market. Their function is to facilitate open-market operations. Like the banks, they also have exchange settlement accounts with the Reserve Bank, but, in contrast to the banks, the money market dealers alone have recourse to loans from the Reserve Bank. In this respect, they are like the discount houses in the United Kingdom, serving as the designated intermediaries between the central bank and the trading banks. However, open-market transactions in Australia, unlike those in the U.K., do not involve "bank bills," i.e., bank acceptances.[8] Instead, they are confined to Treasury notes and bonds either on an outright basis or by means of repurchase agreements. Market operations in securities of less than one year[9] are conducted through the dealers, who hold short-term government debt and bank bills financed by call loans and other types of short-term funds from banks and other customers.[10]

Bank loans to money market dealers play a key role in the functioning of the Australian financial system. Because of settlement practices adopted by the Reserve Bank, from the banks' viewpoint loans to dealers are as good as funds held in exchange settlement accounts at the Reserve Bank; moreover, because they bear interest, the loans are preferred to the latter. Dealers also avoid holding exchange settlement funds, because lags in the official settlements process enable them to "play the float" by increasing or decreasing deposits from nonbank customers. Float comes about because dealers' exchange settlement accounts at the Reserve Bank are instantaneously debited or credited when they withdraw or deposit funds, but the offsetting credits or debits to banks' exchange settlement accounts resulting from the dealers' customers' use or deposit of funds are lagged one day. Fluctuations in the float affect market liquidity and hence impinge upon short-term interest rates.

In all its activities, the Reserve Bank is ultimately answerable to the Federal Government, as the Treasurer has an effective veto over the Reserve Bank Board's decisions. The Reserve Bank Act provides that in the event of a disagreement between the Treasurer and the Reserve Bank, the difference must be presented to Parliament. However, in fact, the veto power has never been invoked. Much as in the U.K., the Reserve Bank is the central banking arm of a centralized macroeconomic executive, and the authority of the Bank rests on the personality and style of the Reserve Bank Governor and his officials. The Bank's authority has also been strengthened by financial deregulation and by the swing to market-based monetary policy, which have removed interest rate and exchange rate determination from the political process. Many of the direct controls that made up the Bank's old armory required the Treasurer's explicit permission before use. Unlike the Treasury, the Bank is a participant in both the government securities market and the foreign exchange market. As such, it requires considerable operational latitude. In practice, over the years there has been little disagreement between Treasury and the Reserve Bank on major policy issues.

MACROECONOMIC PERFORMANCE

During the 1950s and 1960s, Australia seemingly enjoyed an economic nirvana. Over the years 1950-1970, unemployment averaged 1.3 percent of the work force. From 1952-1970, the inflation rate averaged 2.7 percent per year. However, these indicators masked a moderate growth rate and a structure of manufacturing protected by high tariff walls.

Macroeconomic performance since then has been less positive. Unemployment rose sharply from 1974 to around 6 percent in the late 1970s, until a major economic downturn took it above 10 percent in late 1983. A reduction to around 8 percent was relatively rapid during the boom of 1983-1985, but no further reductions have ensued. Inflation peaked at nearly 17 percent per year in 1975 and was brought down to around 10 percent per year from 1978 to 1983. The subsequent two years saw a temporary fall in inflation to below 5 percent -- reflecting in part a pause in wage increases -- but has since stayed at just under 10 percent a year (Table 2).

Domestic policy goals have been overshadowed in recent years by external concerns. A large increase in the current-account deficit occurred early in the 1980s, and was accompanied by a sharp rise in the net external debt position and a major depreciation of the exchange rate (Table 3). The exchange depreciation far exceeded the prevailing domestic-international inflation differential, resulting in an improvement in the nation's international competitiveness. However, relatively little improvement in the current account has yet taken place.[11]

A massive decline in the terms of trade of nearly 20 percent in 1985 and 1986 and the associated national income loss has underscored a continued emphasis on the need for real-wage restraint. Since the economic downturn of 1974, a fundamental premise of policy has been that economic recovery requires a return of labor costs to levels more in line with those prevailing before the wages explosion of the early 1970s. Most indicators of labor costs suggest that such parity now prevails. However, in view of the need to absorb the terms of trade loss and rectify the current-account imbalance, further real-wage restraint may be in order.

The persistent current-account deficit has also directed attention to the size of the public sector deficit. In 1974-1975, the public sector deficit increased markedly from below 2 percent to almost 5 percent of the gross domestic product (GDP). Budgetary policy over the next seven years was directed at reducing the deficit, to avoid crowding out of domestic private expenditures. Some minor success in that objective was achieved, but the economic downturn of 1982-1983 and the policy responses to it saw a rise in the public sector deficit to 6.8 percent of GDP in 1983-1984. Since then,

Table 2
Macroeconomic Indicators

Year Ending June	Unemployment Rate[a]	Output Growth Rate[b]	Inflation Rate[c]	Exchange Rate[d]	Interest Rate[e]
1972	2.3	4.4	6.8	98.5	5.9
1973	2.7	3.5	5.9	107.9	6.7
1974	2.2	3.8	13.1	117.3	9.5
1975	4.1	1.3	16.7	105.3	9.5
1976	4.9	2.1	12.8	105.3	10.0
1977	5.2	2.3	14.0	92.5	10.4
1978	6.3	0.9	9.5	86.2	9.1
1979	6.3	5.2	8.2	83.1	10.0
1980	6.2	1.6	10.1	85.0	11.8
1981	5.9	3.1	9.4	92.9	13.2
1982	6.2	2.3	10.4	88.2	16.4
1983	9.0	-1.1	11.5	77.7	14.9
1984	9.6	5.4	6.8	79.2	13.8
1985	8.6	4.4	4.3	65.0	13.5
1986	7.9	4.3	8.4	56.3	13.0
1987	8.3	2.0	9.3	56.6	12.8

(a) *Average for year.*

(b) *Real Gross Domestic Product, percentage change from previous year.*

(c) *Consumer Price Index (average for year) percentage change from previous year.*

(d) *Trade weighted Index, at end of year (May 1970 = 100).*

(e) *10-year bond rate, end of year.*

Source: Reserve Bank of Australia Bulletin (various issues).

Table 3
Indicators of Potential Imbalance

Year Ending June	Public Sector Deficit /GDP[a]	Real Unit Labor Costs[b]	Current Account /GDP[c]	Terms of Trade[d]	International Competitiveness[e]	International Indebtedness[f]
1972	1.2	101.2	-0.9	0.99	105.8	n.a.
1973	2.0	100.1	-1.7	1.16	113.0	n.a.
1974	1.4	104.5	-1.8	1.23	127.0	n.a.
1975	4.9	108.5	-2.0	1.14	122.7	3.4
1976	4.9	106.9	-1.9	1.09	120.4	3.5
1977	4.1	105.9	-2.9	1.05	113.8	4.7
1978	5.1	108.0	-3.3	0.96	105.9	6.9
1979	4.7	104.4	-3.5	0.97	98.3	7.9
1980	3.7	102.9	-1.7	1.00	100.0	6.1
1981	3.1	104.0	-4.1	1.00	101.6	6.2
1982	3.6	109.0	-5.9	0.98	107.6	10.6
1983	6.2	110.1	-4.1	0.96	102.3	13.6
1984	6.8	102.5	-3.8	0.99	102.5	15.4
1985	5.2	101.3	-5.2	0.97	92.9	23.8
1986	4.9	100.7	-5.9	0.87	78.8	30.4
1987	n.a.	100.7	-5.1	0.83	72.1	31.4

(a) *Net Public Sector Borrowing Requirement/Gross Domestic Product (as percentage).*

(b) *Private nonfarm corporate sector. (Average 1966-1967 to 1972-1973 = 100. Break in series at 1977-1978.)*

(c) *As percentage (Average 1969-1970 to 1972-1973 = -1.0).*

(d) *Ratio of deflators for exports to imports of goods and services (1979-1980 = 100).*

(e) *Australian CPI divided by the weighted average of exchange rate-adjusted CPIs of four major trading partners. (1987 figure is for March.)*

(f) *Net external debt as percentage of GDP.*

Source: *The Roundup. Australian Treasury; National Economic Summit Conference, Information Paper on the Economy April 1983 (AGPS).*

policy has again been concerned with reducing the deficit, as an aid to the reduction of the current-account deficit and of the nation's external indebtedness.[12]

THE CHANGING ROLE OF MONETARY POLICY

As stated, monetary policy in Australia is carried out by a unified executive branch in conjunction with other government agencies. It has not been the focal point of economic policy-making in the same way that it appears to be in some other countries. Thus, it can be misleading to talk of an "assignment" of monetary policy. Nevertheless, the Fraser government's "inflation first strategy" from 1976 to 1983 did give greater prominence to monetary policy especially vis-á-vis fiscal policy, and budgetary outcomes were formulated much more with monetary consequences in mind.

The relationship between monetary policy and the other arms of policy is difficult to disentangle. The setting of money-supply targets by the Reserve Bank was initially meant to signal a greater reliance upon market forces in wage and price setting mechanisms. By declaring that future monetary policy would not accommodate inflationary wage claims even in the face of increased unemployment, it was expected that such wage claims would be seen as futile and hence would not arise. It was on this unproven assumption of rational expectation behavior that the M3 growth rate was lowered successively from 1976 to 1979 (Table 4).

Inflation did recede, but the contribution of this monetary-deceleration strategy can be questioned on a number of grounds. First, periodic issues of money supply statistics did not begin until August 1974, and the M3 aggregate was not widely known at the start of the targeting experience. Second, the targets were announced as conditional projections, and after the first two years were not adhered to nor adjusted in order to prevent base drift. Third, most of the rationale for monetary-aggregate targeting came from evidence, mainly overseas, that excess money balances created inflationary pressures. But the effectiveness of a policy of monetary deflation was largely untested. Moreover, there is no firm evidence demonstrating a link between inflation and M3 growth in Australia stronger than the links between inflation and tradeable goods prices and the wage settlements of the Arbitration Commission.[13]

In practice, an old-style wages policy in the form of government submissions to the Arbitration Commission continued in conjunction with the monetary projections strategy. Wages policy then, as now, involved two aspects of wages: real wages, as the price of labor for employment decisions,

Table 4
Monetary Indicators: Percentage Change

Year Ending June	Base Money[a]	M1[b]	M3[c]	Target[d]	Broad Money[e]	LP[f]	LPF[g]
1972	n.a.	9.1	10.5	-	n.a.	13.0	19.7
1973	n.a.	26.3	25.7	-	n.a.	17.2	34.6
1974	n.a.	2.3	14.5	-	n.a.	14.8	24.6
1975	n.a.	12.6	15.4	-	n.a.	11.1	10.5
1976	n.a.	14.1	14.4	11-13	n.a.	13.1	17.5
1977	25.0	8.4	11.0	10-12	13.3	13.1	17.8
1978	-7.6	8.6	8.0	8-10	11.7	12.2	15.3
1979	9.6	16.7	11.8	6-8	14.8	12.9	15.7
1980	7.0	12.9	12.3	10	13.4	13.8	16.2
1981	10.6	12.0	12.7	9-11	15.7	19.5	17.4
1982	14.0	1.6	11.3	10-11	13.9	19.9	15.9
1983	5.4	5.9	12.5	9-11	11.4	14.4	10.9
1984	11.9	9.9	10.9	9-11	11.5	11.2	12.1
1985	15.0	17.1	17.5	8-10	16.0	17.3	20.8
1986	10.7	1.5	13.0	-	13.4	18.0	20.1
1987	8.1	11.4	12.9	-	10.0	15.1[h]	14.1

(a) *Notes, coin and other monetary liabilites of the Reserve Bank.*

(b) *Currency plus checking accounts at trading banks.*

(c) *M1 plus other deposits at trading banks plus deposits at savings banks.*

(d) *For 1975-1976 for second half of year; for 1982-1983 expressed on an annual average basis; for 1983-1984 based on June quarter averages and increased to 10-12 during the year; 1984-1985 target abandoned in January 1985.*

(e) *M3 plus borrowings from private sector by nonbank financial institutions.*

(f) *Liabilities of the private nonfinance sector.*

(g) *Liabilities of the private nonfinance sector to financial intermediaries.*

(h) *Year to December 1986.*

Source: Reserve Bank of Australia: Bulletin (various issues).

and money wages, as part of the inflationary policy. It was often difficult to sort out which aspect was being pursued. Money supply targets could be interpreted as one way of defining the path for nominal magnitudes, but the exchange rate policy was also fashioned with wage and price outcomes in mind. Indeed, government spokesmen often mentioned the exchange rate as the single most important price they could set. Until the very end of the administered system, a certain fixity of exchange rates was justified as needed to counteract the rigidity of Australia's system of centralized wage determination.

While the Fraser government's performance in pursuing market-based policies fell short of its declarations, the Labor government's policy approach, after 1983, threatened a severe curtailment to the role of monetary policy. The old approach -- facing a choice between constraining wage growth and accepting increased unemployment -- smacked of a combative style ill-attuned to the Australian "mateship" psyche. In contrast, the new approach played on the public's collectivist mentality by attempting to lock players into a cooperative approach. Thus, the approach was an attempt to enable pursuit of multiple (i.e., unemployment-inflation) objectives by obtaining agreement from the unions not to thwart expansionary macroeconomic policy by demanding inflationary wage increases -- known as the "Accord." It was predicated on the assumption that by adopting a "corporatist" style, the major economic players would be locked into an institutional framework in which they would look for points of cooperation by which all would gain -- in effect, a positive-sum game.[14] Empirical support for the strategy came from the apparent economic successes of European countries that pursued this type of policy in the labor market.[15]

This approach fitted in naturally with the view of the inflation process that gives greater emphasis to competing income claims than to the role of market forces. In the Australian case, the available evidence indicated that centrally determined wage decisions had an important influence on prices. That same evidence also indicated that monetary restraint had a relatively quick and predictable influence upon unemployment, but a lagged and less certain bearing on inflation (Davis and Lewis, 1978).

These considerations all seemed to set the stage for an economic policy in which inflation was to be attacked from the wages arena, with fiscal policy directed to relieving the unemployment position through public spending. With the balance of payments taken care of by the floating dollar, this seemingly left monetary policy adrift, with no role to play other than passively accommodating wage increases. In essence, under the Accord a Hicksian labor standard had been put in place of a monetary standard.

Such a passive role for monetary policy was not new. After the government's aggressive anti-inflationary stance of 1976 to 1979, monetary policy appeared to have slipped into a neutral gear. Inflation had settled down at around 10 percent per year, and monetary growth targets of the same order of magnitude suggested that policy seemed to aim first at consolidating the inflationary gains which had been won, and then living with that rate.

These were also the years that saw major reviews of the financial system. Both the Campbell Inquiry into the Financial System (Campbell et al., 1981) and the group appointed by the Labor government to review its findings (Martin et al., 1983) paid minimal attention to the conduct of monetary policy and focused instead upon the efficiency of the monetary system and its "micro" aspects.

However, despite the passive role of monetary policy, a clear change was occurring in its implementation. Variable statutory reserve deposits (SRDs) were the traditional workhorse of Australian monetary policy and were used intensively until the 1980s. The ratio was adjusted six times in each year 1976 and 1977, and three times in each year 1978 and 1979. The average of each change was one percentage point; the ratio ranged between 3.5 and 10.0 percent. The trading bank LGS (liquid and government securities) ratio was increased from 18 to 23 percent between February 1976 and March 1977, a break with tradition in response to the high budget deficit prevailing at the time. Embargoes on certain types of overseas borrowings existed until 1978, and lending guidelines to the banks were used from time to time.

Since 1979, the SRD ratio has been changed only once (in January 1981), quantitative lending guidelines for the banks were ended (in mid-1982), and the asset portfolio restrictions on savings banks significantly reduced. Greater flexibility in official interest rates also became evident, although even as late as the last half of 1981, the ten-year bond yield remained unchanged for five months. Adoption of the bond tender system in mid-1982 marks this period as the start of the new monetary policy in Australia. No longer were open-market operations in the secondary market constrained to operate in the context of a pegged yield set in the primary issue market, and the stage was set for separation between debt management policy and monetary policy. Completion of the transition to the new policy regime, however, came later with the floating of the exchange rate.

This change in the relative importance of policy instruments is only one aspect of the new monetary policy. Also significant has been a change in official views about the links between primary assets issued by the authorities (base money, government debt) and financial market behavior.

Consequently, operating strategies have changed in the light of a different vision of the money supply process (considered in Section 4 below).

One other set of changes is also relevant in assessing the development of the new monetary policy. Prior to August 1981, trading banks could not offer interest-bearing accounts of less than 30 days maturity, nor certificates of deposit (CDs) of less than three months' maturity. The scope for liability management was thus extemely limited. In August 1981, the minimum maturity for CDs was reduced to 30 days and in March and April 1982 the minimum maturity for CDs and time deposits was reduced to 14 days. In August 1984, these minimum maturities were abolished.

This last change presaged the abolition of the M3 target, but the previous changes were relevant in explaining a major change in bank portfolio management. Prior to those changes, the scope for banks to practice liability managment existed but was circumscribed, resulting in significant holdings of LGS assets in excess of the requirement. Changes in the SRD ratio reduced excess reserves and forced asset portfolio adjustment. Over the 1980s this practice declined, reflecting an increased scope of banks to manage their liabilities and a reduced use of the SRD mechanism.[16] With the abolition of the LGS convention in 1985, excess LGS holdings are now an historical curiosum.

These dynamic evolutions in banking, government securities and foreign exchange markets have rescued monetary policy from its essentially accommodative role implicit in the Accord. A number of developments have been important in this process.

Monetary targets, previously set in a "neutral" gear in line with wage increases as determined under the Accord and changes in the velocity of money, were abolished in January 1985.[17] The abandonment of targeting reflected a perception that velocity was distorted to an unknown degree by re-intermediation from nonbanking intermediaries to the banking system. In the absence of a monetary target, the Reserve Bank outlined its actions as being guided by a checklist of indicators. The list included all of the major monetary aggregates; interest rates; the exchange rate and the external accounts; the current performance; and the outlook for the economy, including movements in asset prices, inflation, and inflationary expectations. This switch gives the Reserve Bank and the government considerable discretion in the short run; accountability is far less direct. Under money supply targeting, market participants had an indicator, however imperfect, by which to judge policy. Until the 1980s, monetary policy actions were highly visible, as alterations to the SRD ratio and interest rates were announced publicly; their impact was clearly understood, through familiarity with long-standing practices. With the new techniques, however, few outside the inner sanctums of the Reserve

Bank's market division understood how markets were supposed to respond to policy initiatives in the new environment.

It is this new market environment that has contributed most to the increasingly significant role of monetary policy. As noted earlier, the aftermath of deregulation has seen an explosion of new market trading and innovative financing methods in line with developments overseas. Following the move to the bond tendering system, both savings banks and life insurance companies, which accounted for some 40 percent of non-official holdings, were released in August 1982 and September 1984 from their role as captive holders of government debt.[18] Increased prospects for trading profits in the secondary market led to a much deeper market. Table 5 illustrates how the turnover of government debt has grown. In addition, a rapid growth in new financial markets has occurred. Secondary mortgage markets have been established. Forward markets in foreign exchange have developed significantly since the float, and banks now provide loan and deposit facilities in foreign currencies to Australian residents. Forward markets in various financial instruments have grown in significance, and second board markets have been established on the nation's stock exchanges.

Table 5
Bond Market Activity

Year to June	Total Turnover ($ billions)	Nonofficial Transaction (b) ($ billions)	Turnover Rate (c) (percent)
1975-1978 (average)	11.5	7.0	0.8
1979-1982 (average)	14.0	10.4	0.8
1983	24.5	22.3	1.1
1984	57.8	54.0	2.0
1985	85.1	80.2	2.4
1986	119.9	113.1	3.1
1987(a)	167.0	161.0	4.2

(a) *Annual figures based on half year to December 1986.*

(b) *Excludes transactions involving the Reserve Bank.*

(c) *Nonofficial transactions as a ratio of the stock of bonds outstanding at the end of the period.*

Source: Reserve Bank of Australia Bulletin, January 1987.

Volatility in the financial markets has emerged as a major concern, especially in the foreign exchange market where variability translates into currency risk for either the foreign holders or domestic issuers of Australia's now extensive external debt. Monetary policy has been directed at the balance-of-payments position in recent years. Initially, the proximate objective was the capital account, with high interest rates designed to induce capital inflow and support the dollar. From November 1985, the disinflationary policy also meant the seeking of a dampening effect on income growth and thus on the growth of imports.

The Reserve Bank's operations in the foreign exchange market have also assumed greater importance. The Bank's policy, enunciated at the time of the float, envisaged that "intervention could be required from time to time in order to test market trends, or smooth large transactions."[19] In the initial stages of floating, market testing and smoothing transactions were minimal, and the float was a "clean" one. After August 1986, the Bank moved away from testing and smoothing to "dealing in the market on its own account to enhance market efficiency and promote stability."[20] During 1986-1987, the Bank's purchases and sales of foreign exchange totalled U.S. $13 billion, averaging U.S. $50 million per day. Many market participants interpreted the Reserve Bank's aim as one of putting a collar -- i.e., ceiling and floor -- upon movements of the Australian dollar. To some degree, greater intervention is in line with that of other central banks over the past year, but reflects also the changed status of the Australian dollar internationally as an important currency in the Euro-currency markets, especially for swap-related transactions.

Intervention has also been in response to the large within-day and day-to-day variability that had become a feature of the exchange rate. As a result of the Reserve Bank's prudential regulation, the Australian banks apparently have low limits relative to their capital base on the net open overnight positions that they are permitted to hold on their Australian books. However, the banks do not appear to be large position-takers, so that there is a large element of "pass the parcel" in the daily turnover. Since the Reserve Bank began its policy of steadying the market, short-term variability of the exchange rate has declined sharply (Marsden and Jones, 1977).

These operations by the Bank have involved some trading by the Bank in markets outside Australia. They have enhanced the Bank's status in policy-making, and monetary policy has gained importance in the policy arena through interventions and actions designed to moderate exchange market disturbances.

The government has increasingly sought to employ monetary policy for economic stabilization while other slow-acting policy instruments are brought into play. This brings the Reserve Bank's operating techniques in the money market and channels of transmission of monetary policy to the center stage in the discussion that ensues.

THE NEW MONETARY POLICY

Under the Reserve Bank Act of 1959, the Bank has a clear mandate to undertake discretionary measures which will best contribute to "(a) the stability of the currency of Australia, (b) the maintenance of full employment in Australia, and (c) the economic prosperity and welfare of the people of Australia."[21] It is endowed under the Act with sweeping powers, among which the main provisions are:

Regulation of Bank Liquidity. Each trading bank that is subject to the Banking Act (excluding state government banks) is required to maintain in a statutory reserve deposit (SRD) account at the Reserve Bank an amount equal to a specified percentage of the average level of the bank's domestic deposits in the previous month. Changes in the SRD ratio have traditionally acted against the fulcrum of the liquid and government securities (LGS) ratio, which each bank maintains by convention, in order to adjust banking liquidity and influence banks' capacity and willingness to lend.

Credit Control. The Reserve Bank is empowered to issue guidelines to be followed by the trading banks with respect to the total volume of lending and to the distribution of loans among various industries and purposes.

Interest Rates. With the approval of the Treasurer, the Bank has authority to control the rates of interest paid or received by banks or others in the course of any banking business transacted by them.

Foreign Exchange. The Act gives the Reserve Bank exclusive custody of the banks' foreign reserves and forbids all foreign exchange dealings unless they have the express approval of the Reserve Bank or its agents.

Open-Market Transactions. The Reserve Bank is authorized by the Act to deal in any type of security in the open-market.

Under the new monetary policy, only the last of these provisions is actively used. Those relating to interest rates, advances policy, and foreign exchange lie dormant. The SRD ratio has become *de facto* a fixed required cash reserve ratio at an arbitrary level of 7 percent on which banks are paid an interest rate of 5 percent per year. The LGS ratio, which had no statutory basis but was based on a "firm understanding,"[22] has been replaced by the *prime assets ratio*. The latter comprises notes and coin, balances with the Reserve Bank, treasury notes and other Commonwealth government securities, and loans to authorized money market dealers. It is intended to engender public confidence in banks, rather than to be an instrument of monetary policy.[23]

In examining the Reserve Bank's open-market operations, it is useful to distinguish between two components of the official cash market, which is an equivalent of the Federal funds market in the United States. The first is that of banks' exchange settlement accounts at the Reserve Bank which, together with deposit accounts of the authorized dealers at the Reserve Bank, constitute a small part of base money. In June 1986, currency accounted for 67 percent of base money, SRDs 25 percent, and notes held by banks as till money for almost 7 percent.

The second part of the official cash market is the indirect link between the Reserve Bank and the banks through the official money market dealers. Banks in Australia must meet their required SRD reserves at all times; no shortfall is permitted and excess holdings do not occur. Banks cannot borrow reserves in order to meet the SRD requirements, although they can obtain lender-of-last-resort support if they are in difficulty. Like any other holder of Treasury notes, the banks could rediscount the notes to obtain reserves, but they try to avoid doing so because the rediscount rate involves a penalty. Thus, the banks must themselves hold excess reserves in order to meet day-to-day needs for funds.

Banks' balances with the official money market dealers (called loans to the market) are as good as cash, because withdrawals of the loans would yield exchange settlement funds to the banks. Since loans to dealers bear interest, but exchange settlement funds do not, banks hold virtually no free cash reserves at the Reserve Bank, relying upon money market loans for free cash holdings. Dealers, in turn, are able to work with virtually zero exchange settlement accounts as a result of the arrangements that exist between them and the Reserve Bank.

The arrangements between dealers and the Bank place the dealers at the center of open-market operations.[24] Short-term trading in securities by the Bank is generally with the dealers; the dealers finance their holdings, predominantly short-term government securities, by loans from banks and from the nonbank sector. They avoid a need for cash holdings because of access to a number of safety valves: (1) overnight settlements float extended by the Reserve Bank; (2) the Treasury note rediscount facility at the Reserve Bank; and (3) the Bank's loans to dealers.

Reserve bank loans are usually for a minimum of seven days, and the interest rate is determined at the discretion of the Bank. Like the rediscount rate, the loan rate is usually pitched at a level above the rate at which dealers can obtain funds from nonbank entities. Consequently the latter two of the safety valves are not frequently used, and variations in float smooth the transition from easy to tight monetary conditions or the reverse.

When the Bank sells government securities to the dealers, for instance, the dealers fund those purchases by taking loans from nonbank customers who provide funds by checks drawn upon their bank accounts. (We assume that banks have no surplus exchange settlement funds to lend to dealers as a result of the previous nights clearings at the Reserve Bank.) Transactions between the dealers and the Reserve Bank are in what is known as "same-day funds" so that the security purchase and dealers' borrowings are credited and debited to the dealers' accounts on the same day. Transactions between banks and the nonbank customers by contrast, are in next-day funds; that is, all transactions are aggregated at the end of each day and debited to banks' exchange settlement accounts in the Reserve Bank on the following morning. Because the dealers' exchange settlement accounts are credited immediately but those of the banks are not debited until the next day, an overnight settlements float is thus created.[25]

The float is extinguished the next morning when the bank checks are cleared through the Reserve Bank, resulting in a decline in the banks' reserves. Since banks do not keep excess reserves, they must call in loans from dealers, who in turn are forced to obtain further loans from the nonbank sector, or to rediscount Treasury notes, or to seek loans from the Reserve Bank. But, with the Reserve Bank being the only source of cash to the system, dealers and banks bidding for funds in the money market would push interest rates up without any change in the aggregate amount of cash. Dealers might borrow from the Reserve Bank, and for a time mitigate the cash losses but at a higher than market cost. Eventually, increased interest rates charged on loans would reduce the demand for loans and, together with security sales made by banks to the nonbank sector, would reduce bank deposits. As deposits and advances fall and interest rates increase, the public's desired currency holdings will fall as will required reserves, thus providing an inflow of free cash to the financial system and restoring market equilibrium.

In this scenario, the overnight settlements float enables the system to replace temporarily the reduced supply of Reserve Bank reserves. Over time, the interest rate consequences of the shift in the supply will affect banks' balance sheets and reduce their demand for reserves.[26]

If this depiction of the mechanisms is correct, then in broad terms the overall process of adjustment to a reserve contraction is similar to that often envisaged as occurring in the United States (see Melton, 1985), with various safety valves that can be triggered. In both systems, it is possible for a central bank to choose to focus upon the initial interest rate changes rather than the later consequences for monetary aggregates, and to keep adjusting the supply of reserves accordingly. But, as is well known in the theory of stabilization policies, the lagged effects seem likely to create a complication for policy in later periods in terms of instrument instability. (See, for example, Goodfriend, 1987.)

In the Australian system, instrument instability might arise from the need for the Reserve Bank to initially withdraw or inject larger amounts of cash than are ultimately needed to achieve a desired change in monetary conditions. The safety valve arrangements moderate such effects, but complicate any assessment of how policy is operating by making base money a demand-determined variable in the short run. A more general complication arises from the perfect substitutability of cash and bank loans to dealers from the banks' viewpoint. In these circumstances, the relevance of the base money as a policy indicator is further called into question, although this is not a novel situation in the Australian environment.

MONETARY POLICY - CURRENT ISSUES

The Role of the Monetary Base and Required Reserves

Official views about the relationships between the primary liabilities of the authorities and other monetary aggregates have passed through a number of stages. Until 1984, the authorities held the view that bank credit creation did not rest upon base (or high powered) money but upon the LGS base, which also encompassed bank holdings of government debt. Under the policy of fixed interest rates, a close substitutability between bonds and base money may in fact have existed.[27] In such circumstances, it is easy to see the perceived need for reliance on direct controls.

Equation 1 presents an identity describing changes in the stock of LGS assets -- the change in base money (B) plus the change in government securities holdings of banks (GS_B) -- and the change in government securities holdings of nonbanks (GS_{NB}) as the sum of private sector foreign-exchange transactions (PSFET) and the budget domestic deficit (BDD):

$$\Delta B + \Delta GS_B + \Delta GS_{NB} = PSFET + BDD \qquad (1)$$

Prior to the exchange-rate float, the total of LGS assets could not be *controlled* by the authorities because of variations in private sector foreign-exchange transactions (PSFET). In addition, since there was no mechanism on the supply side for determining the distribution of government securities holdings between the banks (GS_B) and nonbanks (GS_{NB}), control of the LGS base ($B + GS_B$) did not exist. Rather, the LGS base reflected banks' demands for such assets arising from changes in bank deposits and bank lending brought about by private sector foreign-exchange transactions, which were outside the Reserve Bank's direct control.

Under the new monetary policy, flexible interest rates and floating exchange rates have enabled the Reserve Bank to control the monetary base and hence the banks' balance sheets. However, the relationship between banks' balance sheets and the monetary base does not appear to match the descriptions in standard textbooks. There is no mechanical link between the total reserves and the monetary aggregates as envisaged in the money multiplier analysis. The causation runs, rather, from reserves adjusting to monetary aggregates, rather than the reverse.[28] Underpinning this analysis, which is espoused by the Reserve Bank, is the view that safety valves such as the float make base money demand-determined in the short run. Like many other central banks, the Reserve Bank argues that under lagged reserve accounting it has no alternative but to supply banks with the reserves that are needed to validate deposit growth, if stability of the banking system is to be ensured. All that the central bank can do is to influence the cost at which cash is made available to the system.

Current arrangements further reduce the value of base money as an indicator of monetary changes. As our description of the money market mechanism indicated, the principal form of reserves held by banks is loans to dealers. It suggests that movements in this latter aggregate may be a better indicator of the changes in system liquidity than is base money. Control of bank loans to dealers is achieved through the lagged settlement arrangements and restrictions on banks swapping government securities for loans to dealers.

Reserve Bank officials also see little role for the SRD ratio in Australia, asserting that it would make no difference to the Reserve Bank's ability to influence market conditions if SRDs were removed from the Bank's balance sheet.[29] The validity of this assertion hinges on the question of whether interest rates or monetary aggregates are the appropriate fulcrum of monetary actions. As stated earlier, in our opinion, changes in required reserves play an equilibrating part in the lagged market responses to interest rate changes. Moreover, under the new monetary policy, by operating continuously in the market to adjust the availability of funds, the Reserve Bank has made banks almost passive spectators in the process of monetary control. In response to cash shortages, it falls to the banks to raise interest rates in line with money market rates. If borrowers are not daunted by higher interest rates, the banks bid for deposits and are supplied with cash to prevent them running out of reserves. If this supply comes at penalty rates, then the official dealers would bear the main brunt of the higher cost. Banks would be thereby penalized to the extent that higher interest rates increase the tax burden of the reserve requirement; they would no longer find it profitable to bid for liabilities. This again points to the possible role that the ratio plays in the current policy.

It is important not to confuse what is with what could be. If banks can get cash at little additional cost, they are unlikely to worry about potential cash shortages. However, if forced to make up reserve shortages at penalty rates, banks would likely exercise greater care when granting overdraft facilities and open credit lines. There would be an incentive for banks individually to refrain from lending and to build up reserves when cash shortages are anticipated. Surges in monetary growth may be less likely to occur.

In the absence of an SRD requirement, this type of scenario could still hold, since banks and dealers would need to hold a positive inventory of cash to cope with system-wide movements in liquidity. However, existing money market arrangements enable banks to economize on their holdings of cash reserves -- in fact, to hold zero cash reserve balances. To remove the SRD requirement while maintaining arrangements that result in a zero demand for free cash could have quite different implications for monetary control.[30]

One question raised by this analysis of the money market is the continued usefulness of the official money market dealers. They have outlived their original purpose of broadening and deepening the market for government securities. Their present role as the chosen conduit between the Reserve Bank and the banking system seems merely to separate banks from the consequences of excessive monetary growth without adding much to the working of the system. Overnight settlements float could, conceivably, be replicated in a number of ways, including a more flexible use of the rediscount facility and a revival of direct lending to the banks at discretionary rates as allowed for under the old LGS arrangements. Replacement of the LGS ratio by the prime assets ratio seems to have had little consequence for monetary control, as banks have been operating with prime assets sufficiently in excess of the requirement not to find the ratio binding. Ultimately, though, such gearing constraints, while being prudent in their intent, do place a ceiling upon balance sheet expansion.

Targeting Versus the Checklist Approach

The decision to abandon targeting, at least temporarily during the deregulatory transition phase, appeared to have sound basis. If portfolio disturbances, a key characteristic of a transition period, dominate real-sector disturbances, interest rate targets would lead to smaller fluctuations in economic activity and prices than would money stock targets. In addition, if these disturbances also affect the money multiplier, short-term interest rates rather than base money would be a superior operating target.[31] Because of the layering of financial claims, brought about by nonbank financial intermediaries using bank deposits as reserves, the process of reintermediation causes a shift in the base money/broad money relationship.[32] Since deregulation has focused upon banks, the demand for broad money could be expected to be less distorted than the demand for M3. Hence, shifts in the relationship between base money and broad money are more pertinent to policy choice than any relative stability of the base money/M3 relationship.

While portfolio disturbances have undoubtedly occurred, limiting the value of monetary targets, the strategy that replaced it has some weaknesses, in the light of hindsight. As a matter of practical policy, the decision to abandon monetary targets undoubtedly unsettled the foreign exchange market.

On economic grounds, deregulation was said to produce re-intermediation, resulting in both a move from direct to intermediated finance and a shift in financing patterns from nonbank intermediaries to banks. There is mixed evidence on the extent to which these have occurred. It is true that borrowings of the nonbank private sector from financial intermediaries increased faster than the former's total financial liabilities, but that was in line with the trend over the entire 1972-1987 period, as shown in Table 4. Increased intermediation at the expense of direct financing is inconsistent with the enormous expansion of banks' off-balance sheet business, much of which facilitates nonintermediated financing. At the time, it was argued that deregulation would slow the growth of borrowings by nonbank financial intermediaries.[33] The fact is, when the lending figures are adjusted for asset conversion by newly established banks, lending by nonbanks has grown just as rapidly as that of banks since 1984 -- at a rate much in line with earlier years (Mohl, 1987).

In any event, the case for dropping the target rested not on any argument about credit, but on whether deregulation increased the demand for money. To suppose that increases in desired liquidity necessarily equal increases in bank lending appears to confuse the demand for money with the demand for credit.

With the switch in strategy, the Reserve Bank has been at great pains to point out to the financial community that it has not swung to the opposite extreme of targeting interest rates. Rather, it monitors a range of economic information (the checklist) and does not precommit itself publicly to specified outcomes for any financial variables. In its internal delegation of operating responsibilities, very short-run operating targets are presumably specified, but the notion of a commitment to any target over any macroeconomically relevant time period is disavowed.

Since a return to targeting has not been ruled out, the question remains whether arguments previously advanced in favor of or against targeting still carry the same weight. Targeting was said to fulfill an information role as an anchor for expectations and as a yardstick for interpreting current developments.

Information is now in more plentiful supply. Daily estimates of the market's cash position, the outlook for the forthcoming week, annual projections of the pattern of government transactions, regular reviews of bank operations over the previous quarter, and periodic assessments by bank officials are all relatively recent developments -- certainly not in existence when targeting was introduced in 1976. But it is not at all certain that this adds up to a set of clear signals to the market. Operating procedures in the money market are still not widely understood. Discretion is the order of the day, and combining the Bank's activities in the bond, foreign exchange and money markets creates an index number problem that the checklist approach fails to solve.

When targeting first began, most central banks perceived that they had to settle for one target if they were to establish credibility and thereby gain a handle upon expectations. A single, simple, monetary target lends itself to that prescription in a way that a more complicated rule could not, since flexibility can be mistaken for permissiveness, undoing the whole intent. Once credibility is established, a more complex strategy seems possible, and that has been the story of the mid-1980s as, one by one, central banks have moved on from single targets. In the Australian case, the rapid deregulation brought new uncertainties; the abandonment of targeting without a credible alternative in place in that environment was perhaps premature. To the extent that it works, the cooperative approach to wage fixing since 1983 removes the need for a monetary policy directed toward establishing the credibility of anti-inflationary policy. While the Accord has been remarkably successful when measured against the history of incomes policies, it is not clear that it was as helpful in 1985 as it is now in making up for the absence of a monetary policy rule.

Monetary targeting was also designed to discipline government budgetary decisions. That argument has always lacked substance, since it ignores the prior question of what constitutes the optimal form of discipline. Reactions of overseas investors and speculators to government budgetary decisions can play a similar disciplining role. As noted, the informal practice of fully funding the budget domestic deficit through bond tenders has been followed in recent years. For those concerned about fiscal discipline, formalizing such arrangements may have greater appeal than the reinstatement of monetary targets.

A necessary condition for monetary targeting is that there exists an intermediate variable which is controllable and has a reliable link to ultimate policy goals. With open-market operations as the instrument and the official cash rate apparently as the operational target (Dotsey, 1987), we turn to the question of the relative usefulness of alternative financial aggregates for indicating monetary conditions.

Credit and Monetary Aggregates

Transactions balances, liquid assets, and credit are all aggregates involved in the transmission mechanism of monetary policy. In Australia, the market for transactions balances has been accorded relatively little attention in policy discussion, and a credit market perspective has implicitly supported official thinking. Bank credit was the preoccupation of monetary policy in early postwar years, and the instruments of monetary policy were fashioned with control of credit in mind. An M3 target had the advantage of encompassing both savings bank and trading bank credit, and was amenable to control by traditional methods.

Now, according to the Reserve Bank, a squeeze in the cash market would mean that "the higher cost of cash . . . gradually . . . would feed also into rates paid and charged by banks and other financial intermediaries; and thus into the demand for money and credit. Over time the effects would show up in money and credit aggregates."[34] Again, bank credit features in the story. In the current environment of deregulated interest rates, credit expansion or contraction requires loan interest rates to adjust, resulting in adjustments in bank deposits arising from bank sales of securities to and from the nonbank sector. As part of the same adjustment, banks also vary deposit interest rates. The relative movement of bank deposit and loan rates is an important component of the adjustment process.

It is difficult to reach any firm conclusions without making specific assumptions about how banks adjust deposit rates. Our own analyses (Davis and Lewis, 1982 and 1983) concluded that deregulation would make monetary policy more effective. Based on likely responses in asset markets, we argued that interest rates would be more variable, and that interest rates would need to rise more in order to produce a given degree of monetary tightness. This was a closed economy analysis that ignored interest rate volatitility induced by exchange rate changes. But the prediction about interest rates seems to be borne out (Johnston, 1986), and we suggest that the revival of monetary policy owes something to its greater effectiveness in the new environment.

The Australian practice of paying a market-related rate of interest on banks' free reserves and a positive below-market rate of interest on required reserves provides an interesting case for study. Where banks receive a full market-related rate of interest on reserves, they are constrained in adjusting deposit rates to market rates primarily by the extent of their maturity transformation. An overlap thus exists between prudential regulation of the degree of maturity transformation and the transmission process of monetary policy.

When comparing credit and monetary aggregates, it is apparent that those private sector credit aggregates recently constructed by the Reserve Bank demonstrated significant variations in short-run behavior that were different from those of the monetary aggregates (see Table 4). Also noticeable in Table 4 is the dramatic variability in the M1 aggregate. Although deregulation has undoubtedly distorted the meaning of the figures somewhat, M1 appears to be the most responsive of the aggregates to changing economic conditions. Whether the demand function for this or other aggregates has remained stable throughout deregulation is, as yet, not fully answered. [35]

In Australia, as in Britain, an M1 target has always been held to be somewhat cosmetic. Higher interest rates would lead depositors to shift funds out of demand deposits into time and savings deposits, without altering the total. This would enable the target to be achieved, but nothing essentially would be altered. Interest rates would then feed through to expenditures, but if so it seems better to focus upon the interest rates and not on the transactions balances. The situation is also affected by uncertainty about the stability of the demand function for transactions balances when institutional arrangements -- such as those making "own rates" sticky -- are changing. The official publication of the M1 aggregate ceased in 1985 partly because transactions accounts outside the trading banks were thought to be reducing the significance of M1.

Whether monetary control separate from interference with intermediation is an appropriate approach for policy is looming as an important question in Australia; the authorities appear to be preparing the ground for a removal of the required SRD ratio. As the introduction of the SRD ratio was recommended in 1936, and its origins can be traced to 1940, it is remarkable that it has lasted so long, though the Reserve Bank has never been in a hurry to give up controls (Harper, 1986). Less clear is whether in its absence there will be as stable a fulcrum for reserves policy. As noted above, monetary control in Australia appears to work through credit markets, and then deposit and transactions markets. It might be argued that some of the greatest instabilities arise in credit markets, as changes in market psychology lead to leveraged attempts to purchase existing financial and physical assets.[36]

This adds up to support for the current checklist approach to Australian monetary policy, in that it does not stand nor fall on a particular theory of the transmission mechanism. But the combination of the unanswered questions above and a rapidly changing institutional structure leaves an examination of the alternative means of conducting Australian monetary policy firmly on the research agenda. It is ironic that Australia's two wide-ranging enquiries into the financial system paid so little attention to the operation of monetary policy in the deregulated environment that they helped to bring about.

NOTES

1. Reserve Bank of Australia Bulletin, January 1987, p. 13. Australia's fiscal year runs from July 1 to June 30.

2. Phillips (1986, 1987).

3. Lewis and Wallace (1985, p. 2).

4. At the end of 1983, there were four major banking groups (two mergers having occurred in 1982) incorporating both trading (commercial) and savings bank arms Seven other (small) trading banks existed, and there were also six (more significant) savings banks. More detail on these and other institutional characteristics can be found in Lewis and Wallace (1985).

5. The exchange rate officially set was for the Trade Weighted Index, although the $A–$US rate was generally believed to be a major consideration for policy. (See Polasek and Lewis, 1985, for an outline of the transition to floating.)

6. In addition to these changes in new issue arrangements several other changes warrant mention. First, various "captive market" arrangements (requiring banks and life offices to hold certain proportions of assets as government debt) were reduced in significance. Second, new forms of debt were created. In 1976, a retail bond (the Australian savings bond) had been introduced and in 1985 indexed bonds were tentatively introduced. At the state government level the creation of Central Borrowing Authorities has led to an increased homogenization of semi-government debt. (State governments obtain loan funds from two sources. The federal government borrows on their behalf and advances the funds via its budget, and the states also borrow directly, these borrowings being referred to as semi-government debts. The federal government controls, to varying degrees in the past, these borrowings by its dominance of the Loan Council. For further details see Davis and Lewis, 1988.

7. In the 1930s, the central bank adopted a highly independent stance toward governmental requests for loan funds, but had little control over the banking system.

8. Under the Reserve Bank Act, the Bank is empowered to deal in any type of security. During the liquidity shortage in 1974 and 1976, the Reserve Bank purchased private securities in the form of bank bills.

9. The Reserve Bank now also has a moderately large list of bond dealers, including some banks, with whom it undertakes transactions in bonds of at least one year to maturity.

10. The assets which dealers can hold are restricted by regulation and the size of the dealers is potentially constrained by gearing ratios.

11. See Pitchford (1986).

12. For a discussion of Australia's economic performance in 1975-1986, see Davis (1988), Perkins (1987), and various editions of *State of Play*, the latest of which is Indecs (1988).

13. Davis and Lewis (1978) survey and present evidence on the extent of any link. More recent studies are Horne and Monamedji (1985) and Valentine (1982).

14. See Gruen (1984).

15. Bruno and Sachs (1985) in their survey of macroeconomic policy among OECD countries find that those countries adopting a degree of cooperation in the labor market were able to achieve a greater decline in inflation, relative to unemployment outcomes, than could the other countries.

16. Davis (1985) provides evidence on the decline of excess LGS holdings in the first half of the 1980s.

17. Valentine (1984) argued the case for such a neutral monetary policy.

18. The tax arrangements which had made life offices captive holders of public sector debt had lost most of their effectiveness by the early 1980s.

19. "Foreign Exchange Arrangements," Reserve Bank Bulletin, January 1984, p.473.

20. Proctor (1987).

21. Reserve Bank Act, 1959.

22. Reserve Bank of Australia (1969), p. 9.

23. Reserve Bank of Australia (1987), p.2. Interestingly, the LGS ratio was also designed in part "as a protection to depositors" (Coombs, 1971, p.70).

24. These arrangements are outlined in, for example, Reserve Bank (1985). We have benefitted considerably in our understanding of the system by reading Battelino and Macfarlane (1987).

25. Each morning since mid-1985 the bank has published estimates of the opening cash position of the market which reflects the outcome of overnight settlements and known cash transactions for that day. The bank also announces its dealing intentions for the day regarding transactions in Treasury notes, short-term bonds and repurchase agreements which are conducted with the official short-term money market dealers and change same day cash in the market. Dealings in longer-term bonds through other reporting bond dealers do not affect the cash position until two days later. Payment is made on the day following the transaction but with settlement by check, cash is not affected until the second day. The daylight overdrafts on exchange settlement accounts resulting from the opening cash position on same-day cash transactions must be rectified by the day's end, when the system is said to be "square."

26. Davis and Lewis (1983) provided an early analysis of how monetary policy would work in the deregulated environment proposed by the Campbell Inquiry. Jonson and Rankin (1986) survey recent literature.

27. Davis and Lewis (1980) survey the pre-1980s debate over the appropriate base concept. Sharpe (1980) provides empirical evidence.

28. Battelino and Macfarlane (1987), pp. 7-8.

29. Battelino and Macfarlane (1987), p. 5.

30. There are a number of studies which address the question of how the level of banks' required reserve ratios affect the volatility of monetary aggregates in a financial system subject to random disturbances (see, for example, Froyen and Kopecky, 1983). Unfortunately, they do not provide definitive results -- but neither do they point to the optimality of a zero cash reserve requirement, however desirable on "efficiency" grounds.

31. See Poole (1970) for the initial idea and Sellon and Teigen (1982) for a survey of subsequent developments and extension.

32. See Valentine (1985) and Davis (1985) for discussions of this point.

33. "Meeting on Monetary Issues," p.2. *Reserve Bank Bulletin* (insert) December 1985.

34. Reserve Bank of Australia (1985), p. 815.

35. See Reserve Bank of Australia, 1987.

36. Despite historically high real interest rates, the Australian stock market reached record levels in 1987, and a large upsurge in takeover activity has occurred.

REFERENCES

Battelino, R. and I. Macfarlane (1987). "Research Report: Open Market Operations - Some International Comparisons." *Reserve Bank of Australia Bulletin* (December) pp. B2-B11.

Brady, N.J. (1986). "Supervision of Banks in a Changing Financial Environment." *Programme in Monetary and Financial Economics, Occasional Paper No. 1*, University of Melbourne (June).

Bruno, M. and J.D. Sachs (1985). *Economics of Worldwide Stagflation.* Cambridge: Harvard University Press.

Campbell, J.K. et al. (1981). *Australian Financial System Inquiry Final Report.* AGPS Canberra.

Coombs, H.C. (1971). *Other People's Money: Economic Essays.* Canberra: ANU Press.

Davis, K.T. (1985). "Australian Monetary Policy: Recent Experience and Some Current Issues." *Australian Economic Review*, No. 72, Summer, 4th Quarter, pp.37-50.

Davis, K.T. (1988). "Economic Policy." In *From Fraser to Hawke,* edited by B. Head and A. Patience. Oxford: Oxford University Press, forthcoming.

Davis, K.T. and M.K. Lewis (1978). "Money and Income: Evidence from Simple Models." In *The Australian Monetary System in the 1970s*, edited by M. Porter. Melbourne: Monash University, pp. 127-140.

Davis, K.T. and M.K. Lewis (1980). *Monetary Policy in Australia*. Melbourne: Longman Cheshire.

Davis, K.T. and M.K. Lewis (1982). "Can Monetary Policy Work in a Deregulated Capital Market?" *Australian Economic Review* No. 57, First Quarter, pp. 9-21.

Davis, K.T. and M.K. Lewis (1983). "Monetary Tactics and Monetary Targets: A Guide to Post Campbell Monetary Policy." *Economic Papers*, Special Edition (April), pp. 82-100.

Davis, K.T. and M.K. Lewis (1988). "The Bond Markets in Australia." In *International Bond Markets*, edited by D. Gowland. London: Croom Helm, forthcoming.

Dotsey, M. (1987). "Open Market Operations in Australia: A US Perspective." *Research Discussion Paper 8702*, Reserve Bank of Australia (May).

Friedman, B. (1983). "The Roles of Money and Credit in Macroeconomic Analysis." In *Macroeconomics Prices and Quantities*, edited by J. Tobin. Washington, D.C.: Brookings, pp. 161-200.

Froyen, R. and K. Kopecky (1983). "A Note on Reserve Requirements and Monetary Control with a Flexible Deposit Rate." *Journal of Banking and Finance* 7, No. 1 (March), pp. 101-109.

Goodfriend, M. (1987). "Interest Rate Smoothing and Price Level Trend Stationarity." *Journal of Monetary Economics*, Vol. 19, No. 3 (May), pp. 335-348.

Gruen, F.H. (1984). "Australia's Long Term Economic Strategy." *C.E.P.R. Discussion Paper No. 96*, ANU (May).

Harper, I. (1986). "Why Financial Deregulation?" *Australian Economic Review*, No. 73, First Quarter, pp.37-49.

Horne, J. and M. Monameji (1985). "Debt Credit and Monetary Targeting in Australia." *Economic Record, 61*, No. 173 (June), pp. 522-534.

Indecs (1988). *State of Play 5: The Australian Economy Up to Date*. Sydney: Allen and Unwin.

Johnston, R.A. (1985). "Monetary Policy - The Changing Environment." *Reserve Bank of Australia Bulletin* (June), pp. 807-813.

Johnston, R.A. (1986). "The Role of a Central Bank." *Reserve Bank of Australia Bulletin* (February), pp. 1-7.

Jonson, P.D. and R.W. Rankin (1986). "On Some Recent Developments in Monetary Economics." *Economic Record 62*, No. 178 (September), pp. 257-267.

Laidler, D.E.W. (1984). "The 'Buffer Stock' Notion in Monetary Economics." *Economic Journal* supplement, pp. 17-34.

Lewis, M.K. and R.H. Wallace, eds. (1985). *Australia's Financial Institutions and Markets*. Melbourne: Longman Cheshire.

Macfarlane, I.J. (1986). "Open Market Operations Since the Float." *Reserve Bank Bulletin* (December), pp. 6-10.

Marsden, J. and P. Jones (1987). "Monetary and Exchange Rate Policy: A Volatility Based Perspective." Paper presented at *Australian Monetary Policy Post Campbell Conference*, Baxter, Victoria (August), mimeo.

Martin, V. et al. (1983). *Report of the Review Group*. AGPS Canberra.

Melton, W.C. (1985). *Inside the Fed: Making Monetary Policy*. Homewood, Il: Dow-Jones Irwin.

Mohl, A. (1987). "Patterns of Financing Post Deregulation." Paper presented at *Australian Monetary Policy Post Campbell Conference*, Baxter, Victoria (August), mimeo.

Perkins, J.O.N. (1987). *Australian Macroeconomic Policy 1974-1985*. Melbourne: Melbourne University Press.

Phillips, M. (1986). "The Foreign Exchange Market -- A Central Banker's View." *Reserve Bank of Australia Bulletin* (December), pp. 1-5.

Phillips, M. (1987). "The Role of the Australian Foreign Exchange Market." *Reserve Bank of Australia Bulletin* (March), pp. 1-6.

Pitchford, J. (1986). "The Australian Economy: 1985 and Prospects for 1986." *The Economic Record* 62, No. 176 (March), pp. 1-21.

Polesek, M. and M. Lewis (1985). "Australia's Transition from Crawling Peg to Floating Exchange Rate." *Banca Nazionale del Lavoro Quarterly Review*, No. 153 (June), pp. 187-210.

Poole, W. (1970). "Optimal Choice of Monetary Policy Instruments in a Simple Stochastic Macro Model." *Quarterly Journal of Economics* LDXXXIV No. 2 (May), pp. 197-216.

Poole, W. (1981). "Australian Monetary Policy: An Outsider's View." Paper presented at *ANZAAS Congress*, Brisbane (May).

Proctor, C. (1987). "The Australian Foreign Exchange Market." *Reserve Bank of Australia Bulletin* (August), pp. 14-18.

Radcliffe, Lord et al. (1959). *Committee on the Working of the Monetary System, Report.* HMSO London.

Reserve Bank of Australia (1979). *Conference in Applied Economic Research*, Sydney.

Reserve Bank of Australia (1985). "The Reserve Bank's Domestic Market Operations." *Reserve Bank of Australia Bulletin* (June), pp. 814-819.

Reserve Bank of Australia (1987). "Research Report: Notes on February 1987 Meeting on Monetary Issues." *Reserve Bank of Australia Bulletin* (July), B2-B7.

Roosa, R.V. (1956). *Federal Reserve Operations in the Money and Government Securities Markets*. Federal Reserve Bank of New York.

Sellon, G.H. and R.L. Teigen (1982). "The Choice of Short-Run Targets for Monetary Policy." *Issues in Monetary Policy II*. Federal Reserve Bank of Kansas City, pp. 27-50.

Sharpe, I.G. (1980). "Australian Money Supply Analysis: The Relationship Between the Monetary Base, Secondary Reserve and the Money Supply." *Journal of Banking and Finance* 4, No. 32 (September), pp.283-300.

Tobin, J. (1985). "Financial Innovation and Deregulation in Perspective." *Bank of Japan Monetary and Economic Studies* 3, No. 2 (September), pp. 19-29.

Valentine, T.J. (1982). "Monetary Targeting Revisited." *Bulletin of Money, Banking and Finance*, 1982-83, No. 2, pp. 1-41.

Valentine, T.J. (1984). "The Financial System." *EPAC Discussion Paper*, 84-01.

Valentine, T.J. (1985). "The Effect of Deregulation on M3 Growth: A Note." *Bulletin of Money Banking and Finance*, 1984-85, No. 3, pp. 42-48.

APPENDIX

Financial Deregulation in Australia: Major Events

December 1980	Interest rate ceilings on most bank deposits removed.
March 1982	Maturity controls on bank deposits relaxed, permitting increased competition in short-term markets.
May 1982	Interest rate on trading bank SRD accounts increased from 2.5 percent to 5 percent.
June 1982	Lending restrictions on trading banks abolished.
July 1982	Treasury bond tender introduced.
August 1982	Savings bank LGS-type requirement reduced from 40 to 15 percent; they are permitted to accept corporate deposits, and are given greater asset flexibility.
December 1983	Australian dollar floated and exchange control regulations largely abolished.
June 1984	Forty new foreign exchange dealers authorized.
August 1984	Interest rate prohibition on check accounts removed. Maturity restrictions on bank deposits removed.
September 1984	(1) Applications for bank licences from foreign banking interests invited. (2) Foreign investment guidelines regarding merchant banking temporarily suspended. (3) 30/20 rule for life offices and pension funds abolished.
January 1985	M3 projection suspended.
February 1985	Sixteen new banks invited to commence operation.
April 1985	Interest rate ceiling on "small" bank loans (under $100,000) removed, leaving the housing interest rate the only one subject to control.
May 1985	LGS convention of 18 percent abolished and gradual phasing in of prime assets ratio of 12 percent announced.
April 1986	Removal of interest rate ceiling on bank home mortgage lending announced.
April 1987	Prescribed assets ratio for savings banks reduced from 15 to 13 percent.

12

Financial Deregulation and Monetary Policy in New Zealand

Carl E. Walsh

Since 1984, the New Zealand government has undertaken a series of policy actions designed to increase the economy's reliance on private markets and promote greater economic competition. As a result of these policy actions, the financial sector has moved rapidly from being one of the most heavily regulated among industrialized economies to being one of the most unregulated. Interest rate controls have been removed, reserve requirements on depository institutions have been abolished, and barriers to entry in banking have been significantly reduced. At the same time, a new framework for monetary policy has been adopted. The impact of these major institutional changes on the structure of the financial sector and on the performance of the New Zealand economy are likely to be profound.

In the early 1980s, New Zealand's institutions and instruments of macroeconomic policy experienced increasing difficulty in achieving conflicting goals of government policy. The need to finance large fiscal deficits, reduce inflation, maintain a low level of interest rates, and defend a pegged exchange rate placed severe strains on the existing tools of monetary policy. These tools, consisting of direct controls on interest rates and on the balance sheets of financial institutions, generated microeconomic inefficiencies while failing to achieve macroeconomic control of the money supply. The reforms instituted in 1984 were designed to address both these shortcomings. Deregulation of the financial sector was intended to yield a more efficient allocation of credit, and the associated development of open market operations was designed to aid the Reserve Bank of New Zealand in achieving monetary control.

This chapter has two purposes. First, it discusses the changes in New Zealand's financial regulation since 1984, with particular emphasis on the impact these changes have had on the tools available for the conduct of monetary policy. Second, the policy procedures adopted by the Reserve Bank of New Zealand for implementing monetary policy in the new environment are evaluated.

The sections that follow outline the macroeconomic developments that led to deregulation, describe the regulatory framework and the tools of monetary policy prior to 1984, note the reforms carried out since 1984, review the role of monetary policy and its implementation, and summarize conclusions.

MACROECONOMIC DEVELOPMENTS, 1975-1984

During the decade leading up to the economic reforms that began in 1984, New Zealand's economic performance was characterized by low average rates of real income growth and high rates of inflation. Data on real gross domestic product (GDP) growth, inflation, and other macroeconomic variables are presented in Table 1. A major motivation for economic reform in New Zealand, both financial and nonfinancial, was the belief that the poor economic performance could be traced, at least partially, to institutional and regulatory rigidities that reduced the economy's ability to adjust to structural changes in the economic environment.

The major external shocks faced by New Zealand since 1972 included the oil price increases and the entry of Britain into the European Economic Community (EEC). The oil price increases presented New Zealand with problems similar to those faced by other energy-importing countries. The decision by Britain to join the EEC restricted New Zealand's access to its major agricultural export market. These shocks required domestic economic adjustments that the New Zealand economy was slow to achieve.

From 1970 to 1976, the annual growth rate of real GDP averaged 5.2 percent; between 1976 and 1984, average real GDP growth dropped to only 1.5 percent. Over this same 1976-1984 period, growth among the Organization for Economic Cooperation and Development (OECD) countries averaged 2.8 percent. Performance was equally poor on the inflation front in New Zealand. As measured by the annual percentage change in the GDP price deflator, inflation averaged over 14 percent from 1976 to 1982. While inflation decelerated during 1983 and 1984 to the 6-7 percent range, this reflected the impact of a comprehensive wage and price freeze, and was not the result of a policy shift aimed at addressing the causes of the high inflation. In a reflection of the slow expansion in real GDP, unemployment had been rising steadily since the mid-1970s.

An important domestic development during the 1970s and early 1980s was the continued growth of the government's budget deficit. As a fraction of GDP, the deficit rose from just under 3 percent in 1970 to over 9 percent by 1984. Strong fiscal expansion helped to stimulate the economic upturn that began in 1983 and continued into 1984. Normally in a small open economy, price increases and a worsening of the current account both act as automatic stabilizers in the face of an expansion in

Table 1
Macroeconomic Variables

	Real GDP Growth	Inflation: GDP Deflator	Inflation: CPI	Unemployment Rate[a]	Gov't Deficit[b]
1976	1.68	13.6	18.9	0.4	5.1
1977	0.14	20.8	17.2	0.6	8.6
1978	-2.72	8.6	12.8	0.8	5.3
1979	2.66	10.1	10.9	1.9	6.3
1980	2.70	13.9	15.6	2.0	7.2
1981	1.03	15.5	16.4	3.1	7.4
1982	4.66	15.7	15.5	3.7	6.9
1983	0.59	11.2	15.3	4.2	6.3
1984	2.57	6.3	5.2	5.7	9.1
1985	6.62	6.9	8.6	4.4	7.2
1986	1.54	12.6	15.3	3.8	4.2

	M1 Growth Rate	Current Account[c]	Terms of Trade[d]	Exchange Rate[e]
1976	19.8	-7.0	72	106.1
1977	5.9	-4.2	79	105.3
1978	1.8	-3.4	78	105.3
1979	18.3	-2.8	82	105.3
1980	5.5	-4.2	86	96.2
1981	14.2	-3.6	76	90.1
1982	17.4	-5.8	77	84.5
1983	4.3	-6.4	74	78.4
1984	8.3	-4.2	75	78.4
1985	2.7	-8.4	73	62.1
1986	21.6	-7.5	71	64.7

(a) *Registered unemployed as a fraction of estimated labor force.*

(b) *Deficit before borrowing as fraction of nominal GDP.*

(c) *Current account as a fraction of nominal GDP.*

(d) *December year, 1957 = 100.*

(e) *Index, June 1979 = 100.*

Source: Reserve Bank of New Zealand Bulletin (various issues) and Monthly Abstract of Statistics (various issues). Data are for March years unless otherwise noted.

domestic demand. However, the fiscal stimulus took place while comprehensive wage and price controls were in effect. As a result, price increases were limited by the controls, forcing more of the adjustment onto the current account. The strong increase in demand in 1983 led to an economic expansion and a sharp deterioration in the trade balance.

The major failure of monetary policy during this period was its inability to provide a restrictive policy stance to offset the fiscal expansion. As indicated in Table 1, money supply growth (as measured by M1) was both high and variable. The annual growth rate of M1 from 1976 to 1984 averaged 10.6 percent. To understand why monetary policy failed to control the growth in the monetary and credit aggregates, it is necessary to describe the financial system and the instruments of monetary policy in the pre-1984 period.

FINANCIAL REGULATION AND MONETARY POLICY PRIOR TO 1984[1]

Prior to 1984, the financial sector in New Zealand was shaped by a highly regulated environment designed to affect both the total volume of credit flow in the economy and its sectoral allocation. The regulations acted to segment domestic financial markets, impose direct controls on financial institutions, and limit entry into the financial industry. Regulations affected the microeconomic structure of the financial sector and provided the tools for macroeconomic control over aggregate credit.

Financial regulation in New Zealand typically consisted of a set of limitations on the lending activities of financial institutions, together with the conferring of specific cost advantages in the regulated lines of business. For example, lending by building societies was limited to long-term, fixed rate mortgages. But building societies were allowed to issue deposit liabilities that paid higher nominal yields than deposits at trading banks. In turn, trading banks had a monopoly on the issuance of transaction accounts and on access to the Reserve Bank's lender-of-last-resort facility.

A major justification for this segmentation of the financial sector was the perceived leverage this gave the authorities to influence the flow of credit to particular sectors of the economy. For example, agriculture, manufacturing exports, and housing were viewed as priority sectors. Using regulations to generate specialized financial institutions was viewed as a means to insure the provision of credit to these priority sectors.

Direct Control

Direct controls on both interest rates and lending activity played a major role as part of the regulatory regime. Four categories of these direct controls are discussed by Harper (1986): interest rate controls; restrictions on the composition of assets and liabilities; restrictions on total lending; and foreign exchange controls. For example, trading banks, the most heavily regulated of the financial institutions, were prohibited from paying interest on deposits of less than 30 days, and ordinary savings accounts had an interest rate ceiling of 3 percent. Interest rates restrictions were also applied to time deposit liabilities of the trading banks, although these limits were removed during the period of temporary financial decontrol between 1976 and 1981.

The composition of trading bank assets was restricted by reserve asset ratios -- minimum required holdings of certain assets as a fraction of total deposits -- introduced in 1973. Only cash, deposits at the Reserve Bank, and government securities qualified as reserve assets. This ratio requirement constituted an active tool of monetary policy and was varied frequently.[2] Much of the variation was designed to offset seasonal factors, but the reserve asset ratio was also used as a major instrument of monetary policy to affect total credit flows.

In addition, all major financial institutions were required to hold government or local authority debt to meet required public sector security ratios. These ratios, usually expressed as minimum fractions of the institution's deposits (private savings banks, trustee savings banks) or total assets (life insurance offices, private superannuation funds, finance companies, building societies) generated a captive demand for government debt.[3] The ratios in effect in April 1984 ranged from 30 percent for finance companies to 60 percent for official money market dealers.[4]

Reserve asset ratios and public sector security ratios were used as tools to affect total credit, as were explicit credit growth guidelines. For instance, to restrain the growth of credit, the government established a set of guidelines in early 1983 that required financial institutions to limit credit growth to 1 percent per month.[5]

Prior to the change of government in 1984, low interest rates also constituted an objective of government economic policy. Ceilings existed on many deposit and lending rates, and rates on government securities were kept artifically low.[6] Demand for these securities was then generated by including government securities among the assets trading banks could hold to satisfy their reserve asset ratios and through the use of public sector security ratios applied to nonbank financial institutions.

Because assets satisfying the reserve asset and public sector security ratios paid below market rates of interest, the system imposed a discriminatory tax on the activities of regulated financial institutions. Given free exit from the financial sector, the tax should be completely shifted by these institutions to their borrowers and depositors. However, this tax adversely affected their competitive position relative to those not so subject and to those with lower ratios.

Pressures for Decontrol

As in other countries,[7] the rising inflation rates of the 1970s greatly increased the incentives to avoid activities subject to reserve asset ratios or direct nominal interest rate controls. The growth of relatively unregulated institutions, such as finance companies, was stimulated at the expense of the more heavily regulated institutions. For example, from 1976 to 1984, the share of M3 deposits[8] accounted for by deposits at savings banks declined from 47 percent to 32 percent, while the share accounted for by finance company deposits rose from 6 to 18 percent. The process by which credit flows were channeled toward those institutions that were the least regulated, a process common in many other countries as well, tended to reduce the effectiveness of credit policies operating through direct controls.

New Zealand's long history of strict governmental control over interest rates was broken most recently during the period from 1976-1981. In March 1976, many existing interest rate regulations were abolished, and rates on government securities were raised. In the following year, controls were removed to allow savings banks freedom to set interest rates on their term liabilities. These tentative moves toward market determined interest rates had a significant effect in increasing the competitiveness of the financial sector. With inflation averaging more than 15 percent annually during this period,[9] market rates rose to high levels, reflecting the prevailing expectations of inflation.

An important effect of the rise in interest rates on government securities was the reduction in revenues generated by the inflation tax on the government's nominal debt. As long as interest rate ceilings are in place and binding compulsory ratio requirements insure the debt is held, increases in inflation will generate seigniorage on both the noninterest-bearing debt of the government and its interest-bearing debt denominated in New Zealand dollars. The actual seigniorage earned will be reduced to the extent that the government issues debt denominated in foreign currencies or issues inflation-indexed domestic debt.[10]

The effect of the 1976-1981 period of decontrol on government security yields is illustrated in Table 2. Despite the partial decontrol of interest rates, rates on government securities were not increased sufficiently to prevent ex post real rates from remaining very low throughout the 1976–1981 period. In late 1981, the government moved to reestablish control over interest rates. The reinstituted system of controls was then extended in June 1982 as part of a comprehensive wage and price control package put forward as an anti-inflation program.

Table 2
Interest Rates on Government Securities and Inflation[a]

Fourth Quarter	Nominal Rate	Inflation	Real Rate[b]
1973	6.05	9.78	-5.73
1974	6.11	11.78	-8.46
1975	6.64	14.57	-7.85
1976	8.71	14.52	-5.53
1977	10.08	14.24	0.40
1978	10.02	9.68	-5.18
1979	12.98	15.20	-2.03
1980	12.97	15.01	-1.56
1981	12.68	14.53	-1.58
1982	12.87	14.26	9.31
1983	10.56	3.56	1.58
1984	16.72	8.98	2.54
1985	17.37	14.18	-0.83

(a) *Data source: International Financial Statistics, 1986 Yearbook.*

(b) *The real rate is calculated as the nominal rate minus actual inflation over the next four quarters.*

Monetary Policy Constraints

Under a policy of pegging interest rates on government debt at below market clearing levels,[11] the Reserve Bank stood ready to buy or sell government debt at administratively set prices. From a monetary control perspective, this discount window policy precluded any independent monetary policy, as the Reserve Bank had no control over the composition of its own portfolio. Such a policy of interest rate pegging raises serious questions of price level determinancy,[12] and may not provide a sufficient description of monetary policy to allow economic agents to form rational forecasts of future inflation.[13]

The Reserve Bank also stood ready during this period to buy and sell foreign exchange at a pegged exchange rate. Such a commitment further reduced New Zealand's ability to achieve monetary control. Thus, two major reforms necessary for the development of an independent monetary policy were a move to flexible exchange rates and the market determination of yields on government debt.[14]

The impact on the monetary base of fiscal injections shows up clearly in an empirical analysis of the sources of movements in the base. Using data constructed by Dick (1984), a vector autoregression (VAR) estimated over the 1955 to 1983 period was used to derive the implied effect of various shocks on the base.[15] The estimated effect of a positive fiscal injection on the monetary base was initially close to zero, as the private sector provides an offset. Eventually, however, the fiscal injection led to a steady increase in the total monetary base. In contrast, an injection by the Reserve Bank had a more immediate impact on the base, but Reserve Bank shocks appeared to be transitory and did not produce sustained increases in the base. Similarly, private sector injections initially caused a rise in the base, but this effect then was reversed, leaving little long-run impact. This evidence seems consistent with the view that fiscal injections provided the strongest impact on the growth of the monetary base during this period.

Summary

Three factors prior to 1984 contributed to the need to move away from the previous reliance on direct controls. First, high rates of inflation increased the opportunity cost of holding assets subject to interest rate ceilings and required ratios. As a result, funds flowed from the heavily regulated financial institutions such as the trading banks toward institutions less heavily controlled. This reduced the share of the broad monetary aggregates that represented liabilities of those institutions over which the Reserve Bank had the most control, and reduced the effectiveness of direct controls as monetary policy instruments.

Second, economic distortions were generated by interest rate restrictions and direct controls on the allocation of credit. The artificial segmentation produced by the regulatory structure, with the resulting lack of competition between financial institutions, was a hindrance to the development of an efficient financial sector. Government actions to direct the flow of credit to sectors with high political priority lowered real income growth, as government's evaluation of a project's prospective return replaced market expectations. The heavy financial regulation was, therefore, a contributing factor in the slowness with which New Zealand was perceived to have adjusted to economic shocks.

Third, because of the government's low interest rate policy, the Reserve Bank was forced to monetize the large fiscal deficits. Debt not successfully sold to the nonbank public increased the reserves of the banking sector. Thus, the low interest rate objective clashed directly with any attempt to restrict the growth of monetary aggregates as an offset to the expansionary fiscal policy.

The inability of direct interest rate and credit controls to simultaneously limit money growth and maintain low interest rates, without producing unacceptable inefficiencies and distortions in the financial sector, provided strong arguments for financial deregulation and for movement toward indirect methods of maintaining monetary control.

FINANCIAL REFORM SINCE 1984

Since the election of the Labour party in July 1984, major changes in the conduct of monetary policy and in the scope of financial regulation have occurred. The objectives of the changes were to improve efficiency in the financial sector and enhance the ability of the Reserve Bank to conduct monetary policy. These micro and macro objectives were to be met by deregulating the financial sector. Table 3 highlights the major policy actions that have taken place since July 1984, including: the removal of interest rate controls; the elimination of all compulsory reserve asset ratios; the institution of interest payments on bank settlement balances; the acceptance of market-determined rates on government debt; and the floating of the New Zealand dollar.

The removal of interest rate controls in 1984 went much further than the 1976 decontrol. Controls were initially removed in July 1984 from all institutional deposits except for deposits of less than 30 days at trading banks and passbook savings banks. However, even these were decontrolled one month later.

The effects of interest rate decontrol on the efficiency of the financial services industry in New Zealand constituted the chief argument in support of their removal. Attempts to circumvent the pattern of financial regulation would be likely to waste resources and reduce the overall level of intermediation services provided by the financial sector. To the extent that financial intermediaries reduce informational cost in financing economic activity,[16] limitations on the degree of intermediation due to interest rate controls lowers real income.

Even with the removal of all interest rate controls, a zero interest rate on required reserves imposes a tax on those institutions subject to the compulsory reserve ratios. This interferes with the goal of policy neutrality with respect to private asset choice by imposing a differential tax rate on institutions engaged in similar activities. Accordingly, in early 1985 all compulsory ratio requirements were abolished.

A third distortion to private market incentives was removed by the introduction of interest payments on settlement balances. In the absence of reserve requirements, cash and short-term government securities discountable at the Reserve Bank will be held as liquid asset reserves by financial institutions engaged in the payments system. If short-term government debt bears interest and settlement balances do not, inefficiencies arise from the existence of two assets with similar risk characteristics that pay different rates of return.[17] During January 1985, the Reserve Bank began paying interest on cash settlement balances held at the Reserve Bank. Initially, the interest rate on settlement balances was set at 5 percent.

Table 3
Major Monetary Policy Measures: July 1984 - January 1987

July 18, 1984:	Interest rate controls removed. All lending and deposit rates decontrolled except those on trading bank deposits of less than 30 days and ordinary 3 percent savings accounts.
August 15, 1984:	Open-market operations by the Reserve Bank commenced on a regular basis. The Reserve Bank's discount window for government securities opened to all persons.
August 30, 1984:	Interest rate controls on trading bank deposits of less than 30 days and ordinary savings accounts abolished.
October 31, 1984:	Controls on private overseas borrowing relaxed.
December 21, 1984:	Automatic access to the Reserve Bank's discount window for government securities with more than six months to maturity removed.
January 1, 1985:	Reserve Bank payment of interest (5 percent) on settlement balances begun.
January 29, 1985:	Government debt marketed by a tender system.
February 11, 1985:	All compulsory ratios on financial institutions abolished.
March 4, 1985:	New Zealand dollar floated.
December 3, 1985:	Reserve Bank discount window access limited to government securities with less than one month to maturity. (Previously, securities with up to six months' maturity were discountable.) This change phased in gradually and completed by April 1, 1986. Interest rate paid on settlement balances to be adjusted daily in line with market yields.

Source: Adapted from Financial Policy Reform (1986, Chapter 13).

However, at this rate, institutions still had a large incentive to minimize cash balances and hold Treasury bills in their place. In 1986, the Reserve Bank raised the rate on cash balances to a level equal to 65 percent of the seven-day market rate.

A traditional argument against the payment of interest on reserves focuses on the implications for monetary control. Any reduction in the opportunity cost of holding reserve assets will increase average excess reserve holdings. It is then argued that with higher levels of excess reserves, open-market operations to reduce total reserves will have a less restrictive impact on bank lending and the money supply. However, a reduction in the supply of reserves will still raise interest rates and reduce the demand for monetary assets.

By May 1986, the administration of the discount window by the Reserve Bank was changed to allow automatic discounting, at a penalty rate, only of government securities with less than one month to maturity. Initially, maturities of up to six months had been discountable. Thus, an institution wishing to liquidate longer term government securities must now sell them in the open market. As a result, attempts by financial institutions to liquidate medium and long-term government securities have no effect on the stock of reserve assets.

Of major importance was the government's willingness to accept market-determined yields on debt issued through auction. This shift made possible the active use of open-market operations as a tool of monetary policy. Under the auction system, interest rates on government securities are market determined by the requirement that the public be willing to hold the outstanding stock of debt.

MONETARY POLICY SINCE 1984

The wholesale deregulation of the New Zealand financial sector has eliminated the former tools of monetary policy -- interest rate controls, asset ratios, and credit guidelines. New, less direct instruments of policy have been created by the reforms, and the use of these new instruments has been guided by the objective of achieving moderate growth in the monetary aggregates.[18] However, the broader monetary aggregates have not been directly used as either targets or indicators of monetary policy. Instead, actual policy has been guided by the requirement that fiscal deficits be financed through the sale of medium-term government securities to the private sector. This policy is described by the Reserve Bank of New Zealand as one of "fully funding" fiscal deficits via debt sales.

Operationally, the funding objective has been implemented through a focus on "primary liquidity," defined as cash plus discountable government securities, i.e., the assets held by the private sector that can be used for the settlement of transactions with the Reserve Bank. By financing fiscal deficits with medium-term, nondiscountable securities, the funding policy is designed to insulate primary liquidity from fiscal influences.

Several issues are raised by a policy that maintains control over a very narrow monetary aggregate like primary liquidity. Should the instrument of monetary policy be a quantity variable, like primary liquidity, or should it be a short-term interest rate? If a quantity variable is the appropriate instrument, is primary liquidity the right quantity to use? What problems are likely to arise in using the quantity variable as a policy instrument? Finally, what is the role of the broader monetary aggregates, interest rates, and the exchange rate as indicators of monetary policy?

Interest Rates Versus Monetary Aggregates

The pre-1984 policy of maintaining below-market-clearing nominal interest rates was clearly incompatible with the achievement of price stability. So, policy reform did require some shift toward the use of monetary aggregates. The relevant issue confronting the Reserve Bank centered around formulation of policy. Should policy smooth short-run movements of an aggregate around some targeted value? Should policy smooth movements of a short-term interest rate around a target where the target would be adjusted over time in response to economic developments?

The theory of optimal instrument selection[19] shows that the choice between an interest rate and an aggregates policy depends on the principal source of disturbances to the economy. Thus, the major disruptions to the New Zealand economy resulting from the removal of import controls and deregulation of the real side of the economy would suggest the desirability of choosing a monetary aggregate as the instrument of monetary policy. However, in an environment of wholesale deregulation of the financial sector, the relationship between monetary aggregates and such goals of policy as price stability will be uncertain. An unstable financial sector favors the use of an interest rate as the instrument of monetary policy. In fact, a major problem facing the Reserve Bank is the uncertain relationship between monetary aggregates, interest rates, inflation, and real income in the new economic environment. As the financial sector and the rest of the economy adjusts, the linkages between policy instruments and policy goals are likely to be unstable. An unstable link between monetary aggregates and nominal income argues against the use of any rigid quantity control.

Indicative of the changes resulting from financial reform is the behavior of monetary aggregate velocities. From 1980 to 1983, the velocity of M1 declined at a 4 percent annual rate. Then, in 1985, it fell 12 percent, followed by a rise of 9 percent during 1986. M3 velocity fell at an annual rate of 2 percent from 1980 to 1983. It then rose 9 percent in 1985 and 8 percent in 1986. Until the relationship between the monetary aggregates and nominal income becomes stabilized, a policy to focus on a narrow aggregate is likely to be inadequate as a means of achieving price stability goals.

The Level of Primary Liquidity

Clearly, 1985 and 1986 were a transition period for the New Zealand Reserve Bank as it attempted to insulate primary liquidity from fiscal influences. However, the Reserve Bank's stated policy of offsetting the impact of fiscal injections on primary liquidity is an incomplete prescription for policy. Equally important is the choice of a base level. Indeed, determining the appropriate adjustments to the level of primary liquidity as financial markets evolve in response to deregulation will constitute a major challenge to policymakers.

Structural shifts in the financial sector require adjustments in the level of the base under any policy that targets a nominal aggregate.[20] The need for such adjustments has been recognized by the Reserve Bank,[21] and modifications to the level of primary liquidity and even to its definition have occurred over the last three years.

Early in 1986, for example, the Reserve Bank gradually phased out access to the discount window for securities with more than one month to maturity. This change in discount policy was accompanied by a corresponding change in the definition of primary liquidity. Under the old definition, seasonal fluctuations had to be reflected in debt with maturity exceeding six months if primary liquidity was to be unaffected.[22] Since government securities with maturities of between one and six months could no longer be used for the settlement of transactions with the Reserve Bank, they were excluded from the definition of primary liquidity. This change was instituted to allow the outstanding stock of debt with one to six months' maturity to reflect seasonal fluctuations in government expenditures and revenues.

Factors that influence the demand for primary liquidity also require adjustments in the base level if price level effects are to be neutralized. For example, economic developments in late 1986 were strongly influenced by the introduction of a general sales tax in October. In nominal terms, retail sales rose 20.5 percent in September in anticipation of the tax. The price level effects of the tax produced a temporary bulge in the rate of inflation -- the CPI rose at an annual rate of over 35 percent during the fourth quarter. The ultimate price level effects of the sales tax will depend on the extent to which the base level of primary liquidity is adjusted by the Reserve Bank.

Similar monetary adjustment problems were posed by the 20 percent devaluation of the New Zealand dollar, engineered by the Labour government when it took office, and by increases in government user charges in early 1985. Both are price level effects whose impact on inflation should be temporary unless they induce the Reserve Bank to raise the level of primary liquidity. By early 1986, the inflation rate had begun to come down, although wage increases in 1985 averaged 17-18 percent.

Recent changes in financial regulation promise to have major impacts on both the demand for primary liquidity and for the linkages between this narrow aggregate and the broader monetary and credit aggregates. The abolition of reserve asset ratios and the payment of interest on cash balances at the Reserve Bank are particularly relevant in this regard.

The requirement of holding noninterest-bearing reserve assets acts as a tax on the provision of financial intermediation services.[23] The reserve tax can be removed either by the elimination of compulsory reserve ratios or by the payment of market interest rates on reserve assets. The recent financial reforms in New Zealand have moved in both these directions. In determining the desired level of primary liquidity, the Reserve Bank must determine how the elimination of this tax affects the demand for primary liquidity.[24]

In 1986, the Reserve Bank began to intervene more frequently to smooth short-run fluctuations in liquidity. By reducing the risk of a liquidity shortage, this change reduced the precautionary demand by financial institutions for cash settlement balances. The lower demand for primary liquidity led the Reserve Bank to lower its base level in September 1986 in order to avoid easing policy. However, the reduction appears to have been an overadjustment, producing a monetary tightening. Short-term interest rates rose relative to long-term rates, peaking at almost 25 percent in the first quarter of 1987. The downward trend of the exchange rate through the second and third quarters of 1986 was also reversed, and by December the real exchange rate was only about 3 percent below its level just prior to the 20 percent devaluation of July 1984.

Private Sector Actions and Primary Liquidity

The choice of a particular definition for primary liquidity determines the set of private sector actions, if any, that will be allowed to automatically influence the monetary base. For example, currency in the hands of the nonbank public -- an item roughly of the same order of magnitude as primary liquidity -- is excluded from the Reserve Bank's definition of the monetary base. Thus, shifts in the relative demands for currency and bank deposits by the nonbank public can affect the level of Reserve Bank liabilities.

The exclusion of nonbank currency holdings from the definition of primary liquidity amounts to a policy of accommodating shifts in currency demand. For example, an increase in the demand for currency on the part of the nonbank public would, in the absence of Reserve Bank actions, drain reserves from the banking sector and lead to a fall in primary liquidity. Under the Reserve Bank's primary liquidity management policy, this effect is offset in order to prevent primary liquidity from declining.

When primary liquidity was initially adopted as the main instrument of monetary policy, New Zealand was still maintaining a pegged exchange rate. As long as the Reserve Bank was constrained to defend the exchange rate, private sector transactions between foreign and domestic currencies would automatically influence primary liquidity. The impact of exchange flows could be quite large. For example, when markets reopened on July 18, 1984, after the 20 percent devaluation of the New Zealand dollar, an exchange inflow doubled the reserve assets of the trading banks in less than 14 hours. In early 1985, a shift from a position of net capital inflows to one of net outflows produced a liquidity shortage as the contribution of the fiscal deficit to domestic liquidity was more than offset by Reserve Bank open-market operations and a capital outflow. This liquidity shortage drove 30-day interest rates to as high as 45 percent.

On March 4, 1985, the New Zealand dollar was floated. This step broke the automatic link between the foreign capital flows and the level of domestic liquidity. Under a floating exchange rate system, the Reserve Bank is able to exercise control over primary liquidity in the face of swings in New Zealand's net capital account.

Finally, the definition of primary liquidity affects the type of open-market operations necessary to exert base control. As long as short-term government securities are included in the definition, open market operations in such securities will leave primary liquidity unaffected. Thus, effective control over the monetary base requires that the Reserve Bank engage in open-market operations in government securities with maturities exceeding one month.

Indicators of Monetary Policy

The removal of interest rate controls in August 1984 and the February 1985 abolition of all compulsory asset ratios have reduced the usefulness of traditional monetary aggregates as indicators of monetary policy. Financial deregulation reversed the earlier process of disintermediation and produced rapid growth in the deposit liabilities of those institutions that had been heavily regulated under the previous regime. Since the liabilities of these same institutions constituted the major monetary aggregates, these aggregates exhibited large increases. Table 4 presents growth rates for three monetary aggregates: M1, M3, and Private Sector Credit (PSC). All have grown very rapidly in recent years, but the high growth rates of M3 and Private Sector Credit relative to M1 during 1985 and 1986 presumably reflect effects of financial deregulation.[25] M3, for example, grew in excess of 20 percent in 1985 (December over December). These adjustments distorted the informational content for monetary policy of the aggregates and have reduced the value of the broader monetary aggregates as indicators of monetary policy.

Table 4
Annual Growth Rates: December over December

	M1	M3	PSC
1979	7.99	17.45	20.90
1980	4.58	12.01	16.91
1981	14.28	15.27	24.30
1982	5.67	10.23	10.02
1983	13.85	11.18	13.15
1984	10.52	16.98	15.55
1985	11.61	18.57	20.50
1986	14.75	16.39	26.72

Source: RBNZ Bulletin, various issues.

The deterioration of the indicator value of the broad aggregates contrasts with the recent experience in the United States. Recent breakdowns in the relationship between M1 and nominal income due to financial innovation and deregulation have shifted the focus of monetary policy toward the broader aggregates such as M3.[26] Financial deregulation has increased the degree of substitutability among the components of the broader aggregates, leaving aggregates like M3 more stable than their component parts like M1. In New Zealand, deregulation has affected the competitiveness of financial institutions whose liabilities are part of the broad aggregates relative to those institutions whose liabilities are not counted in the aggregates. Thus, interest rate decontrol and the removal of reserve asset ratios has led to a rapid growth in the components of New Zealand's M3 at the expense of non-M3 items.

The Reserve Bank has stated that moderate growth in the broader monetary aggregates is an ultimate policy objective. Such an objective presupposes that price stability is consistent with an environment in which each aggregate grows at a rate determined by the growth rate of potential income minus the trend growth rate of velocity. The object of policy is then to smooth the deviations of each aggregate from its trend growth path. However, there is considerable evidence that most macroeconomic time series do not exhibit a tendency to return to a trend path after a deviation.[27] Deviations tend to be permanent so that a period of faster-than-trend growth is not followed by slower-than-trend growth.

If the velocities of the various aggregates are subject to such permanent shifts in their levels, then the paths of the aggregates will tend to diverge permanently. They will present conflicting indications of the stance of monetary policy unless the permanent velocity shocks have a common source. If the same source is responsible for the random-walk behavior of all the monetary aggregates, then, in the terminology of Engle and Granger (1987), the various aggregates would be "cointegrated."[28] If the aggregates are not cointegrated, then they can drift apart and follow very divergent paths.

Tests for cointegration among the broader aggregates M3 and Private Sector Credit using monthly data for the period since July 1984 found no strong evidence that the two were cointegrated. A lack of cointegration between these two variables would suggest that difficulties will arise if the Reserve Bank attempts to use both aggregates in the formulation of monetary policy.

The Reserve Bank has focused on the term structure of interest rates and the exchange rate as indicators of the stance of monetary policy, while maintaining primary liquidity as the operational target of policy. A strong New Zealand dollar and short-term interest rates that exceed long-term rates are interpreted as indications of a tight monetary policy stance. For example, the New Zealand dollar strengthed during the autumn of 1984 as short-term rates in New Zealand exceeded overseas rates. Short-term rates were also above rates on long-term securities. These developments were interpreted as evidence of a tight monetary policy. The lower long-term rates in particular were taken to reflect market expectations of lower future inflation in the belief that the Reserve Bank's "fully funding" policy would prevent the monetization of the fiscal deficits.

Problems may arise in using the domestic term structure of interest rates as an indicator of domestic monetary conditions as New Zealand financial markets become increasingly internationalized. The deregulation of external financial transactions will make the level of domestic interest rates increasingly subject to foreign arbitrage forces. Changes in domestic monetary conditions will be reflected in exchange rate movements, not in interest rate movements. Thus, the Reserve Bank may need to reduce its current reliance on the term structure as an indicator of monetary policy.

Summary

The objective of monetary policy since the change of government in 1984 has been to insulate a narrow monetary aggregate from the influences of fiscal deficits. In the aftermath of financial deregulation and major changes in the financial sector, exclusive reliance on an aggregate as the instrument of monetary policy is probably unwarranted. As the removal of reserve ratios, the payment of interest on settlement balances, and the freeing of interest rates all affect the demand for primary liquidity, the Reserve Bank will have to determine the appropriate adjustment in its targeted level of primary liquidity. During this period of financial restructuring, the broader monetary aggregates are unlikely to provide a reliable indication of the stance of monetary policy, while the increasing integration of domestic and foreign capital markets will reduce the usefulness of domestic interest rates as indicators of monetary policy.

CONCLUSIONS

New Zealand clearly fits the pattern, identified in other countries by Germany and Morton (1985), in which the need to finance large fiscal deficits in an inflationary environment produced pressures leading to financial deregulation. The system of regulations created incentives that led to the expansion of those markets least subject to control, thereby reducing the credit flows that were subject to direct control. The regulations generated microeconomic distortions while failing to provide the macroeconomic tools necessary for an effective anti-inflation policy.

New Zealand is perhaps unique in the speed with which deregulation occurred,[29] but because the adjustments initiated by deregulation are probably not yet complete, any lessons drawn from the New Zealand experience must necessarily be preliminary. This is particularly true with respect to the efficiency gains to be realized from a more competitive financial sector.

Freed from the need to both defend the exchange rate and maintain artifically low interest rates on government debt, the Reserve Bank now has the tools to conduct an independent monetary policy. It has chosen to do so by employing a narrow monetary aggregate, primary liquidity, as the main instrument of policy. The broader monetary aggregates are likely to be unreliable indicators of monetary policy while the economy continues to adjust to deregulation. However, it will also be some time before a reliable relationship between primary liquidity and nominal income can be established to serve as a guide to policy. Hence, a strict adherence to primary liquidity as an instrument of monetary policy would be inadvisable.

An examination of the Reserve Bank's operating procedures does indicate a recognition that a policy of maintaining a constant level of primary liquidity should not be adhered to rigorously. A primary liquidity policy is appropriate from a price stabilization perspective only if the demand for primary liquidity is stable. This is unlikely to be the case, particularly during a period of major change in the financial sector. The removal of required reserve ratios and the introduction of interest payments on settlement balances are examples of recent changes that will affect the demand for primary liquidity. Demand will also be affected by nonfinancial developments such as the general sales tax introduced last year. The ultimate price level effects of each of these changes will depend on the manner in which the Reserve Bank adjusts primary liquidity.

Even after the immediate effects of deregulation have been completed, a successful anti-inflation policy is likely to produce a large increase in the demand for monetary assets. This will require that the Reserve Bank adjust upwards its target for primary liquidity.

The Reserve Bank has been employing the exchange rate and the term structure of domestic interest rates as indicators of the impact of monetary policy. The value of domestic interest rates as indicators may decline as New Zealand capital markets are increasingly integrated with international financial markets. As this occurs, the exchange rate may take on greater importance. However, if price stability is a goal of policy, control must ultimately be exercised over a nominal quantity, no matter what variable is used as the short-run indicator of policy.

Until enough time has passed to allow reasonable confidence to be gained in modeling the demand for primary liquidity, an eclectic approach to implementing monetary policy will continue to be in order.

NOTES

The author would like to thank Ramon Moreno, Fred Furlong, and Hang-Sheng Cheng for helpful comments.

1. The discussion of regulation in this section borrows heavily from David Harper's recent study of the New Zealand financial sector (Harper 1986). See also Cheng (1983) and Reserve Bank of New Zealand (1983).

2. Between January 1981 and December 1984, the reserve ratio ranged between 10 percent (October and November 1982) and 32 percent (March 1984).

3. For a discussion of the traditional justifications for the compulsory ratio requirement system, see Reserve Bank of New Zealand *Bulletin* (1985a).

4. These ratios applied to total deposits at trading and saving banks, to investments at finance companies, to selected assets at life insurance offices, and to the total portfolio of money market dealers.

5. These guidelines met with limited success. From late 1983 through the first half of 1984, however, "the lending growth of virtually every institutional group . . . has been either close to or in excess of the guideline rate of growth" (Reserve Bank *Bulletin*, June 1984, p. 242). Ratio requirements were tightened, but credit growth remained high.

6. A good example of the reliance on direct interest rates control is provided by the government's attempt to lower mortgage interest rates in November 1983. "In November, reductions in mortgage loan interest rates were considered insufficient and regulations were invoked to achieve satisfactory reductions" (Reserve Bank of New Zealand Bulletin, May 1984, p. 186).

7. See Germany and Morton (1985) for a discussion of the common factors leading to financial innovation and regulatory changes in industrial countries other than the United States.

8. M3 consists of notes and coin plus all deposits at trading banks, the Post Office Savings Bank, trustee and private savings banks, finance companies, official money market dealers (until August 1984), stock and station agents, and net of term deposits of the nonbank institutions with the trading banks.

9. As measured by the Consumer Price Index.

10. Estimates of the impact of inflation on the deficit can be found in "Interpreting the Fiscal Deficit," Reserve Bank of New Zealand *Bulletin*, 49, Dec. Quarter 1986, 497-502.

11. For example, government securities were marketed through auctions beginning in 1983, but of the first five auctions, the government only sold about 60 percent of the debt it tried to market; additional bids for the new securities were rejected because the government thought the implied yields were too high.

12. See Sargent and Wallace (1975).

13. See McCallum (1986).

14. The domestic and external influences on New Zealand's monetary base are discussed in Dick (1984).

15. Dick (1984) divides the total change in the monetary base into three component sources. The first arises from government's financial transactions with the private sector. The second arises from private sector's overseas transactions. The third source arises from Reserve Bank transactions with the private sector. Four lags of each variable, together with a constant, were included in each equation of the VAR system. In addition, all variables were scaled by the square root of the absolute change in the base to reduce heteroscedasticity.

16. A number of recent papers have emphasized the role of intermediaries in the presence of asymmetric information and economies of scale in monitering the outcome of investment projects. See Bernanke and Gertler (1986) and Williamson (1986a, 1986b).

17. See Friedman (1960). The issue of paying interest on reserves is discussed in Sargent (1987).

18. In the annual report of the Reserve Bank for the year ending March 31, 1986, the objectives for monetary policy seem to be stated in terms of real goals: "... a firm monetary policy is defined as one that will constrain the growth in aggregate domestic expenditure over time to a level which is broadly consistent with the potential growth in real economic activity."

19. See Poole (1975).

20. See Walsh (1986).

21. Reserve Bank *Bulletin* (December Quarter, 1986, p.510).

22. Reserve Bank of New Zealand *Bulletin*, 48, No. 12 (Dec. 1985, pp.683-684).

23. The traditional view seems to be that this tax is borne by depositors. However, Fama (1985) argues that it is borne by bank borrowers.

24. As pointed out by Grandmont and Younes (1973), the tax on base money cannot be eliminated by the explicit payment of interest if those interest payments are financed by increases in the supply of money. More recently, Sargent and Wallace (1985) have argued that tax-financed interest payments on bank reserves may result in price level indeterminacy.

25. The earlier period of limited interest rate decontrol ending in 1981 also experienced rapid growth in the broader aggregates.

26. See Trehan and Walsh (1987) and Judd, Motley, and Trehan (1986) for discussions of the impact of deregulation on the monetary aggregates in the United States.

27. See Nelson and Plosser (1982).

28. If two monetary aggregates are cointegrated, then there exists a linear combination of the two that is stationary. For example, a simple money multiplier model would imply that monetary aggregates should be cointegrated as long as multipliers are stationary.

29. Judd, Motley, and Trehan (1986) speculate that rapid deregulation in the United States might have reduced the continual problems for monetary policy that arose due to the gradual process of deregulation adopted in the United States.

REFERENCES

Cheng, Hang-Sheng (1983). "Financial Reform in Australia and New Zealand." Federal Reserve Bank of San Francisco, *Economic Review*, Winter, pp. 9-24.

Deane, R.S., P.W.E. Nicholl, and R.G. Smith, eds. (1983). *Monetary Policy and the New Zealand Financial System*, 2nd edition. Wellington: Reserve Bank of New Zealand.

Dick, R. Rodney (1984). "Influences on New Zealand's Monetary Base 1949-1983." Reserve Bank of New Zealand, Discussion Paper G84/7, July.

Friedman, Milton (1970). *A Program for Monetary Stability.* Bronx: Fordham University Press.

Germany, J. David and John E. Morton (1985). "Financial Innovation and Deregulation in Foreign Industrial Countries." *Federal Reserve Bulletin*, October, pp. 743-753.

Fama, Eugene F. (1985). "What's Different About Banks?" *Journal of Monetary Economics* 15, No.1, January, pp. 29-39.

Fuller, Wayne A. (1976). *Introduction to Statistical Time Series.* New York: John Wiley and Sons.

Harper, David A. (1986). *The Financial Services Industry: Effects of Regulatory Reform.* New Zealand Institute of Economic Research, Research Paper 35.

Judd, John P., Brian Motley, and Bharat Trehan (1986). "Financial Change and the Design of Monetary Policy: Lessons from the U.S. Experience." Federal Reserve Bank of San Francisco Working Paper 87-01, December.

Keeley, Michael C. (1986). "Monetary Policy in a Deregulated World." Federal Reserve Bank of San Francisco *Weekly Letter,* August 22.

Kimbrough, Kent P. (1986). "The Optimum Quantity of Money Rule in the Theory of Public Finance." *Journal of Monetary Economics* 18, November, pp. 277-284.

McCallum, Bennett T. (1986). "Some Issues Concerning Interest Rate Pegging, Price Level Determinacy, and the Real Bills Doctrine." *Journal of Monetary Economics* 17, No. 1. January, pp. 135-160.

Poole, William (1970). "Optimal Choice of Monetary Policy Instrument in a Simple Stochastic Macro Model." *Quarterly Journal of Economics* 84, May, pp. 197-216.

Reserve Bank of New Zealand (1983). *Monetary Policy and the New Zealand Financial System.*

Reserve Bank of New Zealand (1984a). "New Zealand Economy -- Six Monthly Review." *Bulletin* 47, No. 4, May, pp. 183-192.

Reserve Bank of New Zealand (1984b). "Quarterly Review of Monetary Conditions and Policy." *Bulletin* 47, No. 5, June, pp. 239-245.

Reserve Bank of New Zealand (1985a). "Abolition of Compulsory Ratio Requirements." *Bulletin* 48, No. 4, April, pp. 175-178.

Reserve Bank of New Zealand (1985b). "Monetary Policy in New Zealand." *Bulletin* 48, No. 6, June, pp. 293-300.

Reserve Bank of New Zealand (1985c). "Monetary Policy: Some Questions and Answers." *Bulletin* 48, No. 11, November, pp. 626-629.

Reserve Bank of New Zealand (1985d). "Modification to the Liquidity Management Policy." *Bulletin* 48, No. 12, December, pp. 683-684.

Reserve Bank of New Zealand (1986a). "The Fiscal Deficit, Monetary Policy and Interest Rates." *Bulletin* 49, No. 6, June, pp. 274-277.

Reserve Bank of New Zealand (1986b). "Interpreting the Fiscal Deficit." *Bulletin* 49, December Quarter, pp. 497-502.

Sargent, Thomas J. (1987). *Dynamic Macroeconomic Theory.* Cambridge: Harvard University Press.

Sargent, Thomas J. and Neil Wallace (1975). "'Rational' Expectations, the Optimal Monetary Instrument, and the Optimal Money Supply Rule." *Journal of Political Economy* 83, pp. 241-254.

Sargent, Thomas J. and Neil Wallace (1982). "The Real Bills Doctrine versus the Quantity Theory: A Reconsideration." *Journal of Political Economy* 90, No. 6, December, pp. 1212-1236.

Sargent, Thomas J. and Neil Wallace (1985). "Interest on Reserves." *Journal of Monetary Economics* 15, No. 3, May, pp. 279-290.

Sheppard, D.K. and J.L. Whitwell (1982). "The Post 1960 Management of the New Zealand Financial Sector: An Assessment." *New Zealand Economic Papers* 16, pp. 1-27.

Trehan, Bharat and Carl E. Walsh (1987). "Portfolio Substitution and Recent M1 Behavior." *Contemporary Policy Issues* 5, No. 1, January, pp. 54-63.

Walsh, Carl E. (1978). "Unemployment in New Zealand: An Errors in Variables Approach to Estimating the Number of Unemployed." *New Zealand Economic Papers*, pp. 12-48.

Walsh, Carl E. (1986). "In Defense of Base Drift." *American Economic Review* 76 (4), September, pp. 692-700.

Zanetti, G.N., et al. (1984). "Opening the Books." *New Zealand Economic Papers* 18, pp. 13-30.

13
Monetary Policy in Thailand

John G. Greenwood

The monetary history of Thailand over the past decade and a half offers an interesting study of progressive adaptation to a fixed or quasi-fixed exchange rate regime. Throughout the period since 1970, Thailand has experienced wide fluctuations in monetary growth in reaction to external and internal stimuli of both a monetary and non-monetary nature. While in the past the policy responses of the authorities were significantly constrained by domestic institutional rigidities, there is reason to believe that in the future the response of the authorities can be more flexible.

After a brief outline of the institutional framework of the monetary system in Thailand, this chapter provides an analysis of each episode of expansion or contraction in monetary growth since 1970 with a view to explaining how it came about and how the authorities reacted to the consequent effects. This treatment will highlight the progressive development of official policy responses to a rather unusual set of domestic constraints.

INSTITUTIONAL FRAMEWORK

Thailand has a wide variety of financial institutions (Table 1), all of which, except for the life insurance companies, are to a greater or lesser extent under the regulatory control of the Bank of Thailand.

Commercial Banks

There are presently 16 Thai commercial banks and 14 foreign banks licensed to operate in the country. Bangkok Bank is the dominant bank in terms of market size. Among the others, Thai Farmers Bank and Siam Commercial Bank offer a wide range of services, have branches overseas, and are also fairly sophisticated in banking terms. Krung Thai Bank is owned by the government, although the government now only accounts for 25 percent of its business. Thai Military Bank is controlled by the military, which owns in excess of 40 percent of the shares. It obtains a substantial amount of its business directly or indirectly from the military. Licensed foreign banks are generally limited to one branch, except for three that have two branches, and Standard Chartered, which has three branches.

Table 1
Financial Institutions in Thailand, December 31, 1985
(Billions of Baht)

Institutions	No.	Deposits Equiv-alent	Borrow-ing	Household Savings Mobilized	Credit Extended	Invest-ment	Total Assets
Commercial Banks	30	559.8	70.6	457.2	552.3	85.1	701.9
Finance Companies	100	84.0	23.0	58.1	98.1	11.0	131.0
BAAC	1	15.3	9.8	2.6	21.6	0.8	28.5
Industrial Finance Corp. of Thailand	1	--	9.4	--	7.8	0.3	15.0
Government Housing Bank	1	7.1	4.2	7.1	11.2	0.1	13.7
Small Industrial Finance Office[(a)]	1	--	--	--	--	--	0.1
Government Savings Bank	1	56.6	--	56.1	1.4	57.7	64.8
Agricultural Cooperatives	1,132	0.4	4.5	1.3	5.8	0.1	7.6
Savings Cooperatives	611	1.5	0.5	11.5	13.9	--	15.7
Pawnshops	333	--	3.2	--	4.6	--	5.1
Credit Foncier Companies	25	2.1	1.1	2.1	2.8	0.2	4.2
Life Insurance Companies	12	14.6	--	14.6	7.2	5.5	18.4
Total	2,248	741.5	126.3	610.6	696.8	160.9	1,005.8

(a) *Total Assets: 57 million baht, of which 41 million baht were in loans.*
Source: Bank of Thailand

Together, they account for a very small percentage of the total activity in the banking sector, although the foreign banks have a large share of the foreign exchange activity in Thailand.

Finance Companies

These operate in a similar way to commercial banks but are not empowered to take deposits from the public. Instead, they issue promissory notes of no less than 10,000 baht in Bangkok and two adjacent provinces, and 5,000 baht elsewhere in the country. At present, there are approximately 100 licensed finance companies, their activities ranging from short-term finance, hire purchase, underwriting, and security trade, to other investment and advisory services.

Bank for Agriculture and Agricultural Cooperatives (BAAC)

The bank's objective is to provide credit to farmers and agricultural cooperatives as part of the government's agricultural development strategy. In addition, all other banks are now forced to lend 20 percent of their deposits either directly to agricultural businesses (or small rural industry) at up to the ceiling rate of 13.5 percent per year, or to the BAAC at 7 percent. The BAAC obtains the majority of its funds from the commercial banks, but foreign sources and the Bank of Thailand account for 22 percent and 13 percent of its funding, respectively.

Industrial Finance Corporation of Thailand (IFCT)

Although established by government legislation, the IFCT is now principally owned by private interests, including Thai commercial banks. The IFCT functions along the lines of a development bank, through the extension of medium- and long-term loans. It also occasionally participates in the equity of a borrower. The IFCT's principal sources of funds in the past have been the Bank of Thailand, the Thai Government, the Asian Development Bank, and other international and quasi-governmental organizations. However, in recent years the bank has significantly increased its borrowing from private banking sources.

Government Housing Bank (GHB)

The basic function of the GHB is to help persons of moderate income obtain houses of their own. Its source of funds is principally deposits from the public. However, its activities account for only 1.5 percent of the lending of the financial sector as a whole.

Small Industries Finance Office (SIFO)

This is an arm of the Industry Ministry, lending to selected small industrial enterprises at low rates of interest to promote certain types of small-scale cottage industries.

Government Savings Bank (GSB)

The role of the GSB is to mobilize small savings through accepting deposits and issuing premium savings certificates, similar in manner to the Post Office Savings Bank in the United Kingdom. The bulk of GSB's funds are invested in government savings bonds.

Agricultural Cooperatives

At the end of December 1985, there were 1,059 agricultural cooperatives. The principal source of finance for agricultural cooperatives is the BAAC. Funds are then lent to members for agricultural purposes. The government has been encouraging the formation of these cooperatives in order to create a cheaper source of funds than the traders and middlemen who account for a significant percentage of rural lending and who offer loans at extremely high rates of interest.

Savings Cooperatives

At the end of December 1985, there were 611 savings cooperatives. The main source of finance is the members' own resources. These cooperatives lend to meet personal or occupational requirements. This form of cooperative is very popular among some professional groups, particularly teachers.

Pawnshops

There are three types of pawnshops: private, government, and municipal. These act as a source of finance for the poorest section of the community, usually to meet consumption requirements.

Credit Foncier Companies

These specifically finance the purchase of immovable property, their main source of funds being the public. Deposits must be a minimum of 1,000 baht per account.

EXCHANGE RATE REGIME

Throughout the period from 1970 to 1984, Thailand maintained a fixed exchange rate against the U.S. dollar, although there were two devaluations. The first devaluation occurred in July 1981, when the baht was devalued by 8.7 percent from Bt. 21 to Bt. 23 per U.S. dollar. This followed a period of three years of rapid monetary growth fueled mainly by domestic credit expansion, including the financing of growing central government budget deficits. The devaluation was necessitated by the resultant deterioration in the nation's balance of payments.

The second devaluation was in November 1984, when the baht was devalued by 14.8 percent from Bt. 23 to Bt. 27 per U.S. dollar. It came as a major shock both to the financial markets and to important political elements in Thailand. This adjustment in the exchange rate again followed a sustained three-year monetary expansion, but was only introduced after a series of measures had been implemented between December 1983 and March 1984 to control money growth. A principal contributor to the rapid money growth of this period was the rigidity and high level of domestic interest rates, which prompted Thai firms and financial institutions to borrow extensively abroad, resulting in a strong growth in the net foreign assets of the Bank of Thailand.

Following the November 1984 devaluation the authorities adopted a more flexible exchange rate policy, pegging the baht to a basket of currencies whose precise components were never disclosed but which private sector sources estimated to consist of roughly 50 percent U.S. dollars, the remainder being comprised of yen, deutsche mark, Singapore dollars, Malaysian dollars, Hong Kong dollars, and sterling. This strategy was maintained until it came under pressure in late 1985, on account of the large volume of private borrowing abroad and sensitive exchange rate speculations. Finally, after a 2 percent explicit depreciation in December 1985, a revised basket was adopted, in which the U.S. dollar or U.S. dollar-linked currencies are reckoned by private analysts to account for more than 90 percent of the total. This is the regime that persists today.

In effect, Thailand abandoned in November 1984 the rigid U.S. dollar peg which it had maintained throughout the postwar period, in an attempt to introduce more flexibility; after a brief period of experiment, it has returned to a quasi-U.S. dollar standard. The reasons for the failure of the basket experiment will be elaborated in the next section.

MONETARY CYCLES IN THAILAND, 1970-1986

In the analysis presented below, monetary cycles are measured by reference to year-on-year growth rates of M2, i.e., average rates of change over 12 months. Since most of the episodes of monetary acceleration or deceleration are quite clearly identifiable, the selection of year-on-year changes rather than changes over shorter periods does not appear to be a disadvantage. (See Table 2 for year-end monetary growth rate data.)

Monetary Acceleration, October 1970 - June 1973

As in many other East Asian economies, Thailand experienced an enormous monetary acceleration between 1970 and 1973. This episode of rapid monetary expansion began in the third quarter of 1970 with M2 growing at 10.1 percent a year, accelerating to 27.5 percent in June 1973. The source of this rapid money growth was the improving balance-of-payments position, which translated into the creation of new reserves of

Table 2
Main Economic Indicators

	Year-to-Year Changes (percent)				
	M1[(a)]	M2[(a)]	Nominal GDP	Real GDP	CPI[(a)]
1970	8.0	13.5	5.9	6.5	-1.2
1971	10.2	16.7	6.0	4.7	1.2
1972	16.4	23.8	13.6	4.8	8.9
1973	20.6	22.3	31.5	9.4	20.1
1974	9.3	20.5	25.9	5.4	17.8
1975	6.1	16.3	9.7	7.1	4.5
1976	16.8	21.1	12.6	8.7	3.4
1977	9.3	19.9	16.2	7.2	8.8
1978	19.4	19.2	18.8	10.1	-8.3
1979	15.9	13.9	17.6	6.1	15.0
1980	13.7	22.9	23.1	5.8	16.4
1981	3.3	16.3	13.7	6.3	12.3
1982	6.8	24.2	7.2	4.1	2.6
1983	6.1	24.0	9.7	5.8	3.8
1984	11.5	20.2	6.4	6.2	-0.4
1985	-3.5	10.2	4.5	4.0	3.3
1986	18.6	13.1	5.5	4.5	1.7

	Budget Balance/GDP (%) of GDP	Interest Rates (percent per year)		
		Discount Rate	1-Year Deposit Rate	Bank Lending Rate[(b)]
1970	-4.0	9.0	7.0	14.0
1971	-5.0	9.0	7.0	14.0
1972	-4.4	8.0	7.0	14.0
1973	-2.4	10.0	7.0	14.0
1974	-0.8	11.0	8.0	15.0
1975	-2.5	10.0	8.0	15.0
1976	-4.8	9.0	8.0	15.0
1977	-3.1	9.0	8.0	15.0
1978	-2.8	12.5	8.0	15.0
1979	-2.4	12.5	9.0	15.0
1980	-4.8	13.5	13.0	18.0
1981	-3.4	14.5	13.0	19.0
1982	-5.0	12.5	13.0	19.0
1983	-2.5	13.0	12.5	16.5
1984	-3.5	12.0	12.5	16.5
1985	-3.9	11.0	11.0	15.5
1986	-3.2	8.0	7.25	12.0

(a) *Data for M1, M2, the CPI and interest rates are as at year end.*

(b) *Until 1982 data for bank loan rates represent ceiling rates. After September 1982 bank lending rates were reduced below the ceiling rates.*

Source: Bank of Thailand, National Economic and Social Development Board.

baht for the commercial banks as the central bank intervened in the foreign exchange market to buy the excess foreign currency sold at the fixed exchange rate. The main source of strength in the balance of payments was the strengthening current account, which in turn reflected improving terms of trade (Table 3).

Also in common with other East Asian nations, no real attempt was made by the Bank of Thailand to sterilize the creation of money and credit through operations in the domestic money markets. Rather, the policy was one of passive acceptance of the monetary consequences of the external imbalance. As a result, nominal GDP saw a peak growth of 31.5 percent in 1973, and consumer prices rose at an annual rate of 28.8 percent in May 1974.

Thus, Thailand already exhibited most of the classic signs of overheating -- a deteriorating trade balance, accelerating price rises, and worsening terms of trade -- by the time the first oil price hikes began to take effect in early 1974. The oil price hikes, therefore, contributed mainly to a further acceleration of inflation in 1974 and a sharp slowdown in the economy, causing the real GDP growth rate to fall from 9.4 percent in 1973 to 5.4 percent in 1974.

Essentially, the Bank of Thailand played by the rules of the Bretton Woods system in this episode, with all of the adjustment occurring in the domestic economy rather than in the external exchange rate. Unlike a number of other countries, Thailand passively accepted the implications of maintaining a fixed exchange rate through this period. The consequences were predictable, even if uncomfortable.

Monetary Deceleration, July 1973 - December 1975

The deceleration that started in late 1973 saw monetary growth (M2) nearly halved, declining in annual rates from 27.5 percent at the peak to 16.3 percent at the trough in December 1975. In the initial stages of the monetary deceleration in 1973-1974, the overall balance of payments remained in surplus despite a deterioration in the current account. In 1974, there was a significant capital inflow more than offsetting the current account deficit, so that net foreign assets of the Bank of Thailand continued to rise strongly in 1974, and even climbed again in 1975.

The primary basis for the slowdown in monetary growth appears to have been the sale by the central bank of Treasury bills, which is reflected in the fall of the Bank of Thailand's net claims on government (Table 4), together with some build-up in government deposits at the central bank. In other words, instead of strictly playing by the Bretton Woods rules of the game as it had done in the 1970-1973 upswing, the Bank of Thailand switched to a more discretionary strategy to cope with the impact of the last

Table 3
International Balance of Payments

	Trade Balance	Net Services	Current Account
1970	-12.2	6.0	-5.2
1971	-9.9	5.4	-3.6
1972	-8.9	6.6	-1.1
1973	-10.8	6.8	-1.0
1974	-14.3	7.6	-1.8
1975	-20.2	6.2	-12.4
1976	-11.1	1.6	-9.0
1977	-25.6	2.4	-22.4
1978	-28.5	4.3	-23.4
1979	-47.1	3.2	-42.6
1980	-58.0	11.1	-42.4
1981	-65.8	6.0	-56.0
1982	-36.1	8.8	-23.1
1983	-89.2	16.6	-66.3
1984	-68.8	15.2	-49.5
1985	-61.7	14.6	-42.6
1986	-16.5	16.6	5.8

	Capital Movements				
	Direct Investment	Other Private Long-Term	Private Short-Term	Central and Local Govt.	Overall Balance
1970	0.9	1.3	0.2	0.1	-2.7
1971	0.8	0.6	0.2	0.2	-0.3
1972	1.4	2.0	0.3	-0.1	4.0
1973	1.6	-0.6	1.3	0.7	0.9
1974	3.8[(a)]	4.0	1.1	0.1	8.0
1975	1.7	3.6	2.6	-0.1	-2.9
1976	1.6	2.5	2.8	2.4	-0.1
1977	2.2	5.7	5.2	0.8	-7.5
1978	1.0	6.1	1.7	6.1	-13.3
1979	1.0	20.6	3.6	8.5	-7.9
1980	3.8	33.0	7.7	6.2	5.2
1981	6.4	38.3	2.5	8.0	2.5
1982	4.3	25.5	1.0	7.6	3.3
1983	8.2	17.5	2.9	6.1	-18.1
1984	9.6	37.2	5.8	5.7	10.6
1985	4.4	24.1	4.0	19.0	12.5
1986	6.7	4.4	6.3	-6.6	33.6

(a) *Includes oil concession fee of Baht 1070 millions, received in June 1974.*

Source: Bank of Thailand, Monthly and Quarterly Bulletins.

Table 4
Component Sources of the Monetary Base
(Billions of Baht)

End of Year	Monetary Base	Net Foreign Assets	Net Claims on Government	Claims on Financial Institutions	(less) Other Liabilities
1970	15.4	18.8	3.3	0.8	7.5
1971	17.0	17.7	6.7	1.3	8.6
1972	20.1	21.7	7.4	1.3	10.3
1973	23.7	25.9	6.9	2.9	12.0
1974	26.8	35.7	1.5	3.9	14.2
1975	29.8	36.5	3.9	7.2	17.9
1976	33.5	35.6	11.2	5.4	18.7
1976[a]	33.7	35.5	14.4	6.7	22.9
1977	36.9	35.5	21.7	6.9	27.3
1978	43.1	46.7	29.6	10.2	43.4
1979	50.3	56.4	38.2	19.5	63.9
1980	57.3	55.2	53.2	22.0	73.1
1981	61.1	43.0	65.4	24.6	71.9
1982	68.4	41.5	81.2	26.0	80.3
1983	75.6	34.8	94.8	28.0	82.0
1984	79.8	48.4	90.3	32.2	91.1
1985	86.5	50.1	98.9	38.3	100.8
1986	96.3	70.7	89.6	48.9	112.8

(a) *From 1970 to 1976, the base was derived as the sum of currency in circulation plus private sector, commercial bank and other deposits at the Bank of Thailand, from a table entitled 'Bank Liquidity' published in the Bank of Thailand's Monthly Bulletin. Since 1976, the Bank of Thailand has published a table entitled 'Monetary Base' giving "Uses and Sources of the Base," according to the standard IMF/IFS definitions and format.*

Source: Bank of Thailand.

stages of the 1973-1974 commodity price boom. The policy change explains why Thailand was able to go through the global recession of 1974-1975 without having to devalue the currency as well as accounting for its success in bringing inflation under control in 1974-1975 (Table 2).

Monetary Acceleration, January 1976 - November 1980

This second episode of monetary acceleration can be separated into three periods, starting with a modest acceleration from an annual 18.2 percent in January 1976 through a peak of 22 percent in mid-1977, declining somewhat afterwards but maintaining a rate above the previous trough until January 1979. There was then a distinct pause for 11 months from February 1979 until the end of 1979, with the M2 growth rate slowing to 13.9 percent year-on-year in December 1979. Thereafter, there was another short acceleration from January 1980 until November 1980, when M2 peaked at 23.2 percent.

During this episode, the nominal GDP accelerated fairly continuously from 9.7 percent in 1975 to 23.1 percent in 1980, and the consumer-price inflation rate rose from 4.1 percent in 1976 to the 7-8 percent range in 1977-1978 and to 24.5 percent in 1980.

The source of the rapid monetary growth during this episode was the domestic component of the monetary base, in the face of a continuing deterioration in the current account and a persistent deficit in the overall balance of payments. Most of the growth in the monetary base can be attributed to the rising government budget deficit and its financing by the Bank of Thailand's purchases of government bills, which more than offset the contractionary influence of the balance of payments.[1] In 1980, with improvements in the overall balance of payments and continued rapid growth of the budget deficit, monetary growth exploded, rising from 15 percent to 23 percent in 10 months, further fueling the inflation in 1979-1981.

Given the weakness of the current account, the economy ought to have been more severely affected by the second oil shock of 1979-1980 than by the first oil shock. Moreover, despite a temporary improvement in 1978-1979, the next two years saw an uninterrupted deterioration in the terms of trade. The reason that the economy was not so badly affected as might be supposed can be found in the substantial capital inflows from 1979 onward, the origins and consequences of which are examined in the next sections.

Monetary Deceleration, December 1980 - November 1981

In this episode, M2 growth fell from its peak of 22.9 percent in December 1980 to 14.0 percent by November 1981, while M1 growth fell even more steeply from 13.7 percent December 1980 to a negative 3.7 percent in November 1981. The sudden slowdown can be attributed partly to a reversal of the domestic conditions in 1980 and partly to external factors. First, the growth rate of national government expenditure was sharply curtailed from 31.1 percent in 1980 to 13.9 percent in 1981. Consequently, the budget deficit began to shrink, as did the need for Bank of Thailand financing of the deficit. Second, the overall balance-of-payments surplus halved in 1981, while net foreign assets at the Bank of Thailand fell from Bt. 55.2 billion to Bt. 43 billion. The primary factor in this development was a sharp decline in private capital inflow after the middle of 1980, particulary in an item designated "loans and credits to private enterprises" and included in "Other Private Long-Term Capital" in Table 3.

The drop in overseas borrowings in 1981 is attributable to the persistence of high interest rates overseas starting from the end of 1979, when the U.S. Federal Reserve changed its monetary policy to concentrate on monetary targets and allow increased interest rate flexibility. At the same time, interest rates in Thailand were fairly rigidly controlled. Thai borrowers switched to lower cost domestic borrowings and repaid their overseas debt.

The July 1981 devaluation was a significant break in the long-standing policy of fixed exchange rate, setting the value of the currency at Bt. 21 per U.S. dollar. Three factors contributed to the policy shift. First, there had been a persistently adverse trend in the terms of trade, which fell by 25 percent from the mid-1970s to 1981. Second, against the background of rapid money growth and accelerating domestic spending since 1976, the current account deficit increased from 2.8 percent of GDP in 1976 to 7 percent in 1981. Third, in the face of large destabilizing capital flows, the authorities attempted to inject an element of uncertainty into exchange rate expectations. In any event, the devaluation of July 1981 marked the first time the authorities tried to deal with the external imbalance by means other than passive domestic adjustment.

Monetary Acceleration, December 1981 - December 1983

The surge in M2 growth in this third episode of monetary acceleration was particularly strong in the period from March 1982 to December 1982, as M2 moved up from 15.9 percent growth in December 1981 to 26.0 percent by June 1983. There were two key elements in this resurgence of monetary growth. First, the consequences of the tight money policy of 1981 and the July devaluation were reflected very rapidly in an improved trade and current account. Imports fell 9.3 percent because of inventory run-downs and reduced consumer demand associated with the recession of 1981 and early 1982, and at the same time export values actually increased by 4.4 percent as a result of a bumper rice crop in 1981-1982. The current account was further aided by a marked increase in remittances from Thai contract workers in the Middle East. Second, the fall in U.S. interest rates below Thai interest rates during this period once more reversed capital flows, leading to another period of capital inflows and some improvement in the overall balance of payments in 1982.

Concerned at the sudden reversal in capital flows in 1982, the Bank of Thailand endeavored to reduce domestic interest rates and introduce some flexibility into the domestic interest rate structure. In September 1982, it succeeded in persuading the large commercial banks to reduce their maximum lending rate and the key one-year deposit rate below the official ceilings for the first time in Thai financial history. This was followed by further interest rate cuts in February 1983, when the Bank of Thailand reduced the ceiling on bank lending rates from 19 to 17.5 percent, and commercial banks lowered the rate on one-year deposits from 12.5 to 11.5 percent. In August and again in October of 1983, it reduced its discount rates for lending to banks. However, with a plentiful supply of reserves available to the commercial banks as a result of capital inflows, the effect on reserve borrowing from the Bank of Thailand was minimal.

The interest rate on government bonds was also cut, and rates in the bond repurchase market fell sharply.[2] Because of excess liquidity, commercial banks were the only buyers. The Bank of Thailand also attempted to create the expectation of falling interest rates by postponing financing of the Treasury's known borrowing requirements. It was hoped that postponing Treasury borrowing would create the expectation that such borrowing was to be undertaken later at lower interest rates.

These measures to reduce incentives for capital inflows were only partially successful. The continued large capital inflows in the second half of 1982 more than offset the deterioration in the trade account, resulting in an overall balance of payments surplus of Baht 3.3 billion for the year. The consequent increase in the Bank of Thailand's net foreign assets accounts for more than the total increase in the monetary base between March and December 1982.[3]

As overseas interest rates rose in 1983 and forward cover for U.S. dollar borrowings became more expensive in the wake of speculation against the baht, private enterprises repaid foreign borrowings and turned to domestic banks for credit. This led to a surge in domestic credit expansion. At prevailing interest rates, banks were not able to attract enough deposits to finance loan growth. They turned to overseas banks and the Bank of Thailand.[4] In the third quarter of 1983, domestic banks' borrowings from foreign banks increased by Baht 5.23 billion. In August and September 1983, direct loans from the Bank of Thailand increased by Baht 1.17 billion, or from 0.5 percent to 0.8 percent of total bank deposits.

At the same time, upward pressure on interest rates emerged. Following a rise in interbank rates in August, banks raised the minimum lending rate by 1 percent at the beginning of September. In early December 1983, banks raised deposit rates and loan rates again, putting the minimum lending rate at 17 percent, close to the maximum lending rate ceiling of 17.5 percent. By that time, interest rate differentials were more in favor of Thailand than at any time since 1978.

Monetary Deceleration, Direct Controls, and Devaluation, January 1984-December 1985

Faced with difficulties in curbing money growth and improving the balance of trade, the Bank of Thailand and the Ministry of Finance resorted to more drastic measures between December 1983 and March 1984, raising the discount rate by 1.5 percent to 13 percent, increasing the ratio of required government bond holdings to bank deposits from 10 to 14 percent, and introducing controls on bank credit for imports. More important, in January 1984 the Bank of Thailand instituted overall quantitative credit controls, restricting lending growth to 18 percent in 1984. In March, the Finance Ministry introduced a two-tier maximum lending rate ceiling: the maximum rate on loans for imports, luxury consumer durables, and buildings was set at 19 percent, while the ceiling rate on loans for agriculture, manufacturing, and exports remained unchanged at 17.5 percent. The interest rate ceiling on deposits of between three months' and one year's maturity was raised to 13 percent, the same as the ceiling on deposits of one to two years' maturity.

Basically, this set of responses was entirely retrograde. Instead of reducing the rigidities in the financial system, the authorities were reacting to problems that arose from the inflexibilities of the financial system by introducing more rigidities. Clearly, in an open economy with unrestricted capital flows, effective monetary control cannot be sustained while maintaining a fixed exchange rate against the background of rigid domestic interest rates. Either the Thai authorities would be compelled to introduce capital control or they would be obliged to float the exchange rate.[5]

In November 1984, the baht was devalued by 14.8 percent. At the same time, the authorities abandoned the rigid pegging of the currency to Bt. 23 per U.S. dollar of the preceding three years. Instead, the baht was pegged to a basket of currencies comprising the U.S. dollar, yen, deutsche mark, sterling, and the Malaysian, Singapore, and Hong Kong dollars, with the peg adjustable whenever warranted or made necessary by domestic or international considerations. In practice, the variations in the baht against the U.S. dollar turned out to be very small, as most of the currencies in the basket remained quite stable against the dollar. The Hong Kong dollar, for instance, was fixed to the U.S. dollar at a rigid rate from October 1983 on; the Singapore and Malaysian dollars were themselves managed in a very narrow range against the U.S. dollar; and the Japanese yen was relatively stable against the dollar from November 1984 until September 1985.

By the end of 1984, it was evident that the policies of increased controls adopted in late 1983 and early 1984 were on the way out. With the appointment of Bank of Thailand Governor Kamchorn Sathirakul in September 1984, the pendulum began to swing away from direct controls toward more market-oriented mechanisms. The 18 percent ceiling on bank credit expansion had been removed in August. Also, interest rates were becoming less "sticky," as Thai banking and financial management grew more flexible in to adapting to the volatile world environment. Banks actively began to discourage the bunching of deposits in maturities of one or two years, thus making it easier for them to lower interest rates without a squeeze on margins. This was helped by the Finance Ministry's announcement in March 1984 that the interest rate ceiling on all deposits of between three-month and two-year maturity would be equalized. In short, the links in the chain of causation running from the U.S.-Thai interest rate differential through private net foreign borrowing to money growth were being weakened at every stage. Not only were interest rates becoming less rigid but also there was an emerging trend for borrowers to use currencies other than the U.S. dollar. In addition, the Bank of Thailand's increased willingness to adjust the exchange value of the baht lessened the impact of capital flows on domestic monetary growth.

In any event, just one month after the November 1984 devaluation, capital inflows turned into capital outflows. As the U.S. dollar soared in January and February 1985, the baht declined in line with the yen, mark, and sterling components of the basket, and corporate borrowers made massive repayments of U.S. dollar borrowings in an attempt to avoid exchange rate losses. The baht reached a low of Bt. 28.33 per dollar in early March 1985, compared with the immediate post-devaluation fixing of Bt. 27.00 per dollar.

For the remainder of 1985, the authorities were constrained by the stickiness of domestic interest rates, being unwilling to lower rates for fear of the effects on private capital inflow. This fear was reflected in the official exchange rate policy. As the U.S. dollar depreciated after September, the Bank of Thailand did not let the baht appreciate against the dollar as far as would have been implied by the basket. Instead, it kept the baht at around the Bt. 26.5 level, as the dollar fell sharply against the yen and the mark. The immediate response was a capital outflow, as the market speculated against the baht. Finally, in December 1985 the Bank of Thailand announced a 2 percent depreciation of the baht against the dollar, adding that in the future it would further reduce the volatility of the baht/dollar rate, thus virtually abandoning the previous currency basket policy.

Although in 1984-1985 the Bank of Thailand attempted to create a financial environment more conducive to the operation of an independent monetary policy, monetary and exchange rate policies were increasingly constrained by the need to maintain sufficient private capital inflow to finance the nation's persistent current account deficits. This meant that the central government had to restrain its own external borrowings as well as those of state enterprises. In this respect, Thailand's external debt problem in 1984-1985 resembled Malaysia's in that for many years the current account deficits were to be financed by foreign borrowing -- except that Thailand's case was more acute, because roughly 25 percent of the current account deficit was financed by private foreign borrowings, which were highly volatile and very sensitive to international interest rate and exchange rate movements. After the experience of 1984-1985, the major policy alternative, devaluation, was virtually closed off because of a concern over the implications for capital movements of a loss of confidence in the baht.

Monetary Acceleration, Current Account Improvement, and Lower Interest Rates, January 1986 - Mid-1987

The monetary slowdown of 1984-1985 curtailed domestic demand in Thailand and restricted import growth well below export growth, so that the trade and current accounts started to improve markedly in late 1985 and 1986. At the same time, bank lending decelerated from growth rates exceeding 20 percent in mid-1984 to just 6 percent by March 1986. The scope for lowering interest rates finally emerged. Initially, the Bank of Thailand was reluctant to let rates drop, because there was a widespread view in official circles that the improvements in the external accounts were a windfall of a purely temporary nature because of the weaker U.S. dollar (and hence weaker baht) and falling oil prices. However, as it became clear that the improvements were likely to be more permanent, the case for lower interest rates became overwhelming.

From its trough of 10.2 percent in December 1985, M2 growth accelerated to just under 15 percent in April 1987. During the same period, M1 growth rose from 3.5 percent to almost 20 percent, partly reflecting the sharp declines in interest rates over the period and partly as a result of current account surpluses. As interbank rates fell from 15 percent in December 1985 to 6 percent by the end of 1986, the prime loan rate was reduced from 16.5 percent in January 1986 to 11.5 percent in early 1987, while one-year time deposit rates fell from 11.0 percent to 7.25 percent.

The rigidity of interest rates in Thailand came about partly because of banking practices in the country. On average since 1980, time deposits at fixed rates accounted for between 70 and 75 percent of banks' total liabilities to the private sector, and the turnover of these deposits averaged less than 1 percent, whereas most bank lending was predominantly short-term trade financing, one- to three-month loans, and overdraft lending. Because loan rates adjusted more quickly than deposit rates, bank profit margins tended to rise and fall with market interest rates. To the optimum extent, banks attempted to stabilize their profits by retarding adjustments in their loan and deposit rates. However, the long duration of declining interest rates in the present cycle has forced the banks to lower both deposit and lending rates -- even though the prime loan rate has not fallen as much as short-term interbank rates, basically reflecting the slow runoff of high-cost time deposits.

In the period ahead, the major challenge to the Thai authorities will be to ensure greater interest rate flexibility and thereby help promote greater stability in monetary growth. One step in this direction has been the introduction of greater flexibility in the pricing of government bonds, and another the development of a more active money market, where blue chip companies can raise short-term funds at rates substantially less than they pay for borrowing at the banks.

SUMMARY AND CONCLUSION

Over the past decade and a half, Thai monetary growth has been subject to wide swings mainly because of a policy of a fixed exchange rate for the baht combined with rigid domestic interest rates. In an attempt to break away from this straitjacket, the Bank of Thailand in November 1984 adopted a more flexible exchange rate policy. However, instead of solving the problem, the policy change aggravated instability because of interest-sensitive capital flows. As a result, Thailand has now reverted to an exchange rate regime more closely linked to the U.S. dollar, and has sought to introduce more flexibility into the interest rate structure. The fortuitous depreciation of the U.S. dollar since February 1985 combined with an improvement in Thailand's terms of trade -- thanks to the fall in oil prices -- has helped to create an environment of excess liquidity, and thereby put downward pressure on interest rates. The sustained gap between inter-bank rates and bank interest rates together with the emergence of a small domestic commercial paper market has provided some incentive for banks to free up their deposit and loan pricing structure. The future stability of Thai monetary policy will depend very much on the extent of interest rate flexibility introduced during this period of relatively low interest rates. There is no reason why Thailand should not maintain a fairly rigid exchange rate vis-à-vis the dollar, provided that interest rates are free to vary. However, institutional rigidities, which have proved a major source of monetary instability in the past, may not be easily removed.

NOTES

1. *Asian Monetary Monitor* 6, No. 4, July-August, 1982, pp. 26-28.

2. The bond repurchase market was at that time a relatively new market set up by the Bank of Thailand to encourage secondary trading in government bonds, with the central bank acting as an intermediary between banks to supply banks short of liquidity with funds, with government securities being used as collateral.

3. It should be noted that this increase in net foreign assets is obscured in the year-end data in Table 2 because the low point in the Bank of Thailand's net foreign assets was reached at the end of the first quarter of 1982. The balance of payments moved firmly into surplus during the final three quarters of that year.

4. *Asian Monetary Monitor* 8, No. 2, April 1984, pp. 17-19.

5. *Asian Monetary Monitor* 8, No. 2, April 1984, p. 10.

REFERENCES

Darrington, B. (1987). *Banking in Thailand: An Investment Appraisal.* Hong Kong: Crosby Research Ltd.

Lee, Tim J. (1982). "Thailand: Why Liquidity is Easing Sharply." *Asian Monetary Monitor* 6, No. 4, July-August.

Lee, Tim J. (1983). "Thailand: Causes and Consequences of Rapid Monetary Acceleration." *Asian Monetary Monitor* 7, No. 4, July-August.

Lee, Tim J. (1984a). "Thailand: A Third Year of High Money Growth?" *Asian Monetary Monitor* 8, No. 2, March-April.

Lee, Tim J. (1984b). "Thailand: Devaluation Paves the Way for More Rapid Money Growth." *Asian Monetary Monitor* 8, No. 6, November-December.

Lee, Tim J. (1984c). "Thailand: Rising External Indebtedness Constraints Monetary Policy." *Asian Monetary Monitor* 10, No. 1, January-February 1986.

Lee, S.Y. and Y.C. Jao (1982). *Financial Structure and Monetary Policies in Southeast Asia.* London: Macmillan Press.

14
Financial Reform and Monetary Control in Indonesia

V. Sundararajan and Lazaros Molho

The financial system in Indonesia has been strongly influenced by developments in the petroleum sector, which accounts for more than half of export receipts and of public sector revenues. In the 1970s, the expansion of oil revenues contributed to a rapid growth in real gross domestic product (GDP), averaging 8 percent annually, and to a sharp increase in domestic savings, from 12 percent of gross national product (GNP) in 1971 to 26 percent in 1980. The oil boom was also reflected in higher inflation, with the GDP deflator rising by an average rate of 16 percent a year between 1974 and 1982. The concomitant expansion of the financial sector was sizable, both in terms of volume of transactions and in the range of financial services. The situation changed drastically in 1982-1983, however. Declining oil exports contributed to a marked weakening of the external accounts and triggered a comprehensive adjustment effort that was initiated in 1983. Principal features of this effort included a 28 percent depreciation of the exchange rate, the streamlining of public sector subsidies and investment programs, and a reform of the tax system aimed chiefly at increasing nonoil tax revenue.

On June 1, 1983, as part of the adjustment policies, the Indonesian authorities also initiated a financial and monetary reform. The decision to initiate this reform was taken in response to the shortcomings of the previous system of direct restrictions on the policies of financial institutions; that system had distorted the pattern of financial intermediation, encouraged private capital outflows, and tended to become ineffective. The first stage of the reform entailed the removal of credit ceilings, the abolition of controls on state banks' interest rates, and the change in the funding role of the central bank, Bank Indonesia. The second stage included the introduction of new instruments of indirect monetary control and the adoption of measures to strengthen the money market.

This chapter analyzes the evolution and impact of the monetary control system from the early seventies to 1986, with a particular focus on the adaptations of the system in the context of the reforms initiated since 1983. It is argued that the financial reform measures have contributed significantly to the adjustment effort by restoring the competitiveness of the domestic financial institutions. In addition, these measures have enhanced the authorities' technical ability to control reserve money and have transformed the money markets. Nevertheless, the evolution of the monetary control system has been constrained by the continuing pressure on the exchange rate and interest rates -- reflecting, in part, the steady weakening of oil prices throughout the 1983-1986 period -- which encouraged the authorities to focus on targeting interest rates rather than monetary aggregates. Although interest rate targeting may have been more stabilizing in the presence of the large portfolio shifts during the early phases of the reform, greater flexibility of money market rates could help enhance both monetary control and money market development in the period ahead. In this regard, one of the lessons of the Indonesian experience may be that the progress of financial reform depends not only on institutional development but also on the overall macroeconomic environment. A more favorable external environment, in particular, would relax some of the constraints that may have slowed down the move toward market-determined money market rates, and would allow a fuller use of the arsenal of new instruments at the central bank's disposal.

BACKGROUND

As background to an understanding of monetary policy developments, it is useful to outline briefly the structure of the Indonesian financial system.

The financial system is dominated by Bank Indonesia (the central bank) and deposit money banks; the two together hold over 90 percent of total gross assets of the organized financial system. The deposit money banks -- hereafter, banks -- consist of 5 major state banks, 10 private Indonesian foreign exchange banks, 11 foreign banks, 59 purely domestic commercial banks, and 28 development banks. The state banks with their large branch systems dominate the banking scene, accounting for about 65 percent of total deposit liabilities and 70 percent of total credit of all banks.

Nonbank financial institutions, one of the fastest growing segments of the system, still account for only around 4 percent of gross assets of the organized financial system. Nonbank financial institutions fall into two categories -- development and investment. The development institutions, which are wholly or partly state owned, engage principally in medium- and long-term lending or equity participation. They derive their resources mainly from Bank Indonesia or international lending institutions and, to a lesser extent, from the issuance of short-term promissory notes. The investment institutions, which are privately owned, deal primarily in short-term commercial paper and promissory notes, thus constituting an important segment of the domestic money market. They hold commercial and financial paper issued by borrowers, which they fund by selling their own promissory notes. The sale of corporate promissory notes, with or without recourse, is negligible.

Before the financial reform, the Jakarta money market consisted of a fairly segmented interbank market and a small market for the liabilities of nonbank financial intermediaries. Maturities in the interbank market were generally quite short, from overnight to one week, and rates were set competitively. However, the market was dominated by the large state banks, which were normally the chief suppliers of funds to other participants. Following the financial reform, a significant transformation of the money market is underway.

Indonesia's exchange rate system is virtually free of restrictions, as is short-term external borrowing by residents. Bank Indonesia stands willing to trade unlimited amounts of foreign exchange for rupiah with authorized traders at rates that are established and adjusted by Bank Indonesia on the basis of a policy of managed float against a basket of currencies.

MONETARY POLICY: TARGETS AND INSTRUMENTS

Policy Objectives in Indonesia

One of the principal objectives of macroeconomic policy in Indonesia is the maintenance of external balance. Because the exchange rate system is virtually free of restrictions, any perceived misalignment between international and domestic interest rates -- corrected for exchange rate expectations -- could undermine financial stability by giving rise to massive capital movements. Macroeconomic policies can affect capital flows not only through their impact on the current account of the balance of payments but also through their effect on exchange rate expectations. The elusive relationships between these expectations on the one hand and policy actions and market developments on the other hand have made the coordination of exchange rate and financial policies one of the most challenging tasks for the Indonesian authorities.

In addition to external balance, other longer-run objectives of Indonesian policymakers include the promotion of saving and investment, satisfactory growth of output and employment, the maintenance of price stability, and the deepening of domestic financial intermediation. Although in the long run these objectives are attainable only in the context of a stable financial environment, in the short run there may be some conflicting considerations. For example, the rise in domestic interest rates that has been necessary to stabilize the external accounts in the wake of the terms of trade deterioration of recent years may have tended to weaken investment incentives. In the presence of such trade-offs, the Indonesian authorities have consistently adopted the longer view, making financial stability the foremost policy objective.

Choice of Monetary Targets

In an open economy such as that of Indonesia, the choice between interest rates and monetary or credit aggregates as policy targets will generally depend on the degree of substitutability between domestic and foreign currency assets, and on the exchange rate regime. If the exchange rate is fixed and expected to remain so, then the authorities will have little control over the money supply in the long run as increases (decreases) in domestic credit tend to be offset by losses (gains) in international reserves. Under perfect capital mobility the money supply cannot be controlled even in the short run, with incipient capital flows forcing the authorities to target the domestic interest rate in line with the international rate.

By contrast, when the exchange rate is flexible, as has been the case in Indonesia in recent years, the authorities may have much more autonomy in conducting monetary policy. In the short run, exchange rate flexibility may allow attaining external balance with alternative mixes of monetary, fiscal, and exchange rate policies, without any intervention in the foreign exchange market. These policies can be carried out by targeting either interest rates or the money supply.

Some monetary autonomy may be maintained even when the exchange rate remains temporarily pegged, through sterilized intervention in the foreign exchange market. In the long run, of course, a policy of pegging the exchange rate cannot be sustained if it is accompanied by an overly expansionary monetary policy; but, in the short run, the possibility of using sterilized intervention may substantially enhance the central bank's monetary autonomy. Indeed, thanks to the financial reform, Bank Indonesia has improved its ability to offset any undue changes in the money supply by developing the new money market instruments that are described in the next section.[1]

Given such autonomy, what criteria could guide the authorities' choice between interest rate and money supply targeting?

One set of criteria could be based on the ability of each kind of policy to minimize any deviations of output and prices from their targeted or expected levels. Such deviations could result from a variety of exogenous disturbances, including shifts in the public's spending, alterations in portfolio behavior, and changes in the terms of trade. For some types of disturbances, monetary policy may be more stabilizing with interest rate targeting, while for others money or reserve targeting may work better. In this regard, the generally accepted view is that interest rates are likely to be the preferred short-run and intermediate target when the dominant source of instability is in the financial sector, whereas the targeting of a monetary or credit aggregate could be preferable when real sector disturbances are more important.[2]

In practice, of course, no simple policy rule can ensure economic and financial stability. In an economy that may be simultaneously subject to multiple disturbances of varying intensities, on which there is imperfect information, policymakers may prefer to adopt a policy of discretionary adaptation by continuously reviewing the settings of policy targets in the face of the most recent information. Although it would still be necessary to choose between interest rate or money supply targets at any point in time, this choice would generally be subsidiary to the more important task of setting the target level.[3]

Following the financial reform, the Indonesian authorities seem to have shifted from targeting aggregate credit expansion to targeting interest rates, thereby allowing monetary and reserve aggregates to be demand-determined. Interest rates on the new money market instruments were occasionally adjusted in line with exchange rate considerations in the year following the money market crunch of September 1984, but they changed little thereafter. As a result, the net absorption or injection of bank reserves through these instruments was left largely to the discretion of the banking system.

The policy of targeting interest rates may have been appropriate in the wake of the financial reform initiated in 1983. Portfolio shifts were probably a dominant type of disturbance at least during the early part of the postreform period, warranting stabilization of interest rates according to the argument spelled out above. Rupiah time and savings deposits rose from the equivalent of less than 4 percent of gross domestic product in March 1982, to more than 12 percent of GDP in December 1986 (Table 1). Narrow money in relation to GDP also fluctuated during this period, albeit without any apparent trend, with its composition shifting in favor of currency. Targeting monetary and reserve aggregates in the wake of such significant financial sector changes could conceivably have resulted in undue increases or instability in the level of interest rates, with possible adverse effects on output.[4]

Notwithstanding these considerations, a more flexible interest rate policy could be more appropriate for Indonesia in the period ahead. Most of the portfolio shifts spurred by the reform may have already been completed,

Table 1
Monetary Aggregates, 1982-1986

(Trillions of rupiah)

	1982 Mar.	1983 Mar.	1984 Mar.	1985 Mar.	1986 Mar.	1985 Dec.	1986 Dec.
Rupiah broad money	8.9	10.1	13.3	16.0	20.3	19.7	23.3
Narrow money	6.8	7.4	8.1	9.0	10.5	10.1	11.5
Currency	2.5	3.0	3.6	3.8	5.0	4.4	5.3
Demand deposits	4.2	4.4	4.5	5.2	5.4	5.7	6.2
Time & savings deposits	2.2	1.8	5.2	7.0	9.8	9.6	11.7
Foreign currency deposits	1.2	2.1	2.5	3.3	3.9	3.4	4.8
Adjusted reserve money[(a)]	4.0	4.1	5.3	5.9	7.5	6.4	7.7

(Percent of GDP)[(b)]

	1982 Mar.	1983 Mar.	1984 Mar.	1985 Mar.	1986 Mar.	1985 Dec.	1986 Dec.
Rupiah broad money	15.4	16.2	18.0	18.3	21.1	20.5	24.4
Narrow money	11.7	11.8	10.9	10.3	10.9	10.5	12.1
Currency	4.4	4.8	4.8	4.3	5.3	4.6	5.6
Demand deposits	7.3	7.0	6.1	5.9	5.7	5.9	6.5
Time & savings deposits	3.8	4.4	7.1	8.0	10.2	10.0	12.3
Foreign currency deposits	2.1	3.4	3.4	3.8	4.1	3/6	5.0
Adjusted reserve money[(a)]	6.9	6.5	7.2	6.7	7.8	6.7	8.1

(a) *Adjusted for disparity between bank reserve figures according to Bank Indonesia and according to deposit money banks.*

(b) *In percent of GDP of previous calendar year for March balances, but current calendar year for December balances.*

Source: Bank Indonesia and IMF staff estimates.

and real sector disturbances may have become much more important following the recent oil price developments. After the exchange rate depreciation of September 1986, in particular, the authorities may be better able to contain inflation by using monetary and credit aggregates as intermediate targets of monetary policy. Focusing on these aggregates could also help prevent destabilizing speculation against the exchange rate by underscoring that domestic credit creation will not be accommodating.[5] Targeting the aggregates would require placing more emphasis on reserve money as an operational target while allowing interest rates to be more flexible. Irrespective of the chosen target, of course, the settings of target levels would need to be continuously reassessed in light of the most recent information on interest rates, exchange rates, reserve flows, and other relevant variables.

Choice of Monetary Instruments

Prereform Instruments. Before the financial reform of June 1, 1983, the major instruments of monetary policy were credit ceilings for individual banks, interest rate controls for state banks, and a selective rediscount mechanism designed to reallocate credit at subsidized interest rates. During each fiscal year, the authorities targeted aggregate credit expansion consistent with projected money demand and with their target for the balance of payments. The aggregate credit target was then allocated among groups of banks and individual banks on the basis of past performance, with additional subceilings for various credit types at each bank.

In addition, state banks were also subject to controls on deposit and loan rates, but private banks -- both domestic and foreign -- were free to set their own interest rates. As a result, state bank deposit rates were maintained significantly below those of private banks, with differentials ranging from 6 to12 percentage points depending upon maturity.

Finally, banks were induced to provide loans to selected priority sectors at below-market interest rates set by Bank Indonesia. These loans were eligible for rediscount (liquidity credits) from Bank Indonesia at highly subsidized rates and at varying rediscount proportions, depending upon the type of the loan. Between 1977 and 1982, liquidity credits rose by an average rate of 40 percent a year, becoming a major source of funds for deposit money banks, particularly state banks. By the end of 1982, loans supported by liquidity credits accounted for nearly 80 percent of total credit by all banks, while liquidity credits made up nearly one-third of the total liabilities of state banks.

The prereform system of monetary control proved effective in limiting the expansion of bank credit, but it also produced some undesirable side effects. The credit ceilings on banks were binding through most of the 1974-1982 period, with the realized amounts of credit generally falling short of the specified ceilings during 1974-1977 and slightly exceeding the ceilings during 1978-1982. However, with reserve money growing rapidly as a result of the fast expansion in Bank Indonesia's liquidity credits and net foreign assets, credit control was achieved at the expense of a large accumulation of surplus funds in the banking system, especially by state banks. Banks held these funds partly in the form of rupiah excess reserves and partly in foreign assets, thus raising their share in total net foreign assets at the expense of Bank Indonesia. In order to check this erosion in its share of international reserves, Bank Indonesia began paying interest on rupiah excess reserves in January 1978. In addition, between September 1982 and June 1983, it required state banks to hold special deposits with Bank Indonesia, using proceeds from repatriated assets and earning a return tied to the London interbank offer rate (LIBOR). Even so, deposit money banks raised their share of total net foreign assets from 8 percent at the end of 1977 to more than 50 percent by September 1983.

The combination of excess liquidity in the banking system and interest rate controls produced distortions in the pattern of domestic financial intermediation which could ultimately undermine both monetary control and external balance. The deposit rate ceilings that applied only to state banks reduced their ability to compete for private sector deposits, and made the state banks increasingly dependent on captive customers, such as public enterprises. As a result, between 1979 and 1982, the average annual rate of growth of time deposits was only 8 percent for state banks, compared with 75 percent for private banks. Concurrently, the assets of nonbank financial institutions, which were not subject to credit or interest rate ceilings, grew by an average annual rate of 42.5 percent. Thus, the monetary control system favored the growth of the less regulated types of institutions at the expense of the highly regulated state banks, possibly weakening the system's effectiveness.

Even if both interest rate and credit ceilings were to be extended throughout the financial system, the resulting lack of competitiveness of domestic financial institutions would discourage aggregate saving and could give rise to serious balance-of-payments difficulties. Indeed, increased competition from offshore financial markets, such as Singapore and Hong Kong, was already leading to a substantial buildup of Indonesian residents' offshore deposits.

Post-Reform Instruments. Against this background, and in view of the deteriorating macroeconomic environment, the Indonesian authorities initiated their financial reform on June 1, 1983. As part of this reform the authorities dismantled the old system of monetary control through direct restrictions on financial institutions, and replaced it by a more indirect system based on reserve-money management. Interest rate controls on state banks were eliminated, and a wide range of loan categories -- accounting for 50 percent of total loans outstanding prior to the reform -- were slated to become ineligible for liquidity credits. Credit ceilings on individual banks were also eliminated. The authorities introduced a new mechanism of monetary control that would rely principally on open-market operations complemented by a system of new rediscount facilities. The evolution of these new instruments since the reform is described below.

Open-market operations. The rationale for the adoption of open-market operations may be best understood in terms of the prereform monetary and institutional developments. The acquisition of an increasing share of the system's international reserves by banks was in itself undesirable, while the growing importance of the less-regulated nonbank financial institutions could also pose problems for monetary control in the long run. The introduction of open-market operations could minimize such possibilities by offering a rupiah asset as a substitute for foreign assets in the liquid asset portfolios of banks, and by allowing the authorities to absorb or inject reserves at their own initiative, so as to restore control over the system's lending capacity.

In this regard, the scope for using reserve requirements was limited. Competition from offshore markets constrained the interest spreads of Indonesian banks, while the segmentation of the domestic money market and the wide variation in excess reserve holdings across institutions also restricted the scope for changing reserve ratios.[6] Open-market sales of a rupiah asset, on the other hand, could readily be initiated in an environment of excess liquidity and could eventually help Bank Indonesia improve confidence in the domestic currency by reclaiming its share of net foreign assets. The new instrument could also serve to unify and strengthen the domestic money market and in the longer run could stimulate capital market development.

Taking into account these considerations, and given the lack of government debt instruments in Indonesia, Bank Indonesia decided to issue its own debt certificate, the Sertificat Bank Indonesia (SBI), beginning in February 1984. The SBIs were originally issued once a week with maturities of 30 and 90 days, in bearer form, and in denominations of Rp 50 million, Rp 250 million, and Rp 1,000 million. The frequency of SBI sales was subsequently increased to three times a week in October 1984, and to five times a week from July 1985 to August 1986. Since then, Bank Indonesia has reverted to weekly auctions. The issue of SBIs with 15-day maturities was also initiated in October 1984, but it was discontinued in May 1985. Only banks and nonbank financial institutions were authorized to buy SBIs directly from Bank Indonesia, but these institutions as well as the public were also allowed to trade in SBIs in the secondary market. In order to stimulate demand for SBIs, the interest rate on excess reserves held with Bank Indonesia was first reduced from 13 percent to 7 percent in February 1984, and eliminated three months later.

SBIs were initially sold at preannounced rates set by Bank Indonesia, but an auction system has been in use since March 1984. According to this system, each bidder indicates both the volume of SBIs he is willing to buy and the interest rate he is willing to accept, and Bank Indonesia sets the cutoff rate for each auction. Successful bidders -- those who offer to buy at rates lower than or equal to the cutoff rate -- generally receive an amount of SBIs equal to the quantity they demand at their bid rate. However, if the amount of successful bids exceeds the volume of SBIs that are for sale, the allocation of SBIs among the lowest bidders -- those who bid the cutoff rate -- is conducted pro rata, while all other bidders receive the requested amounts. Noncompetitive bidding is not accepted. In practice, the five state banks and the State Development Bank (BAPINDO) have been the main participants in the SBI auctions, together holding over 90 percent of outstanding SBIs in early 1986.

Data on cutoff rates in SBI auctions and on the amounts of SBIs outstanding over the last three years are presented in Table 2. The cutoff rate for 30-day SBIs peaked at 18 percent in September and October 1984, a period of extraordinary pressure on bank liquidity that resulted from speculation against the rupiah. With the subsequent easing in money market conditions, the cutoff rate on 30-day SBIs was reduced in steps to 14 percent in August 1985, and has since remained unchanged. The cutoff rate on 90-day SBIs, which has generally been kept at one percentage point above the 30-day rate, has also remained unchanged at 15 percent since October 1985.[7]

Sales of SBIs were initially modest, with the outstanding amount averaging only about Rp 34.4 billion during February-August 1984 (0.6 percent of reserve money). SBIs outstanding declined to Rp 7.3 billion in September 1984 owing to liquidity shortages faced by banks in the aftermath of speculative capital outflows. Subsequently, with the increase in the SBI cutoff rate, and the injection of liquidity through a special credit facility, SBI sales picked up. Since June 1985 there has been a significant growth in SBIs outstanding, despite the downward adjustment in the cutoff rates in July and August. The volume of outstanding SBIs reached a peak of Rp 2,393 billion in July 1986, and since then has declined to Rp 746 billion by the end of the year.

The sharp increase in banks' SBI holdings since June 1985 reflected, in part, policies to enhance the liquidity of the SBI. On August 1, 1985, banks and nonbank financial institutions were allowed to sell their SBIs before maturity to the First Indonesian Finance and Investment Corporation (FICORINVEST), an institution largely owned by Bank Indonesia, which has been the marketmaker in money market securities since February 1985. FICORINVEST stood ready to discount SBIs, at the interest rate of the original SBI issue without regard to its remaining maturity, and could automatically rediscount them with Bank Indonesia also at the original issue rate. Under these policies there was virtually no risk of capital loss on SBIs, in effect making them as liquid as excess

Table 2
Bank Indonesia's Operations in Money Market Instruments: Rates and Volume

	Interest Rates (Percent)				Volume (Billions of rupiah)		
	SBI Rate[a]	SBPU Rate[b]	Interbank Rate	Discount Rate[c]	SBI[d]	SBPU[e]	BI Credit[f]
Jan. 1984	--	--	19.3	--	--	--	--
Feb.	--	15.0	18.2	17.5	51	--	--
Mar.	15.0	--	16.4	17.5	46	--	--
April	14.5/14.8	--	13.7	16.5	56	--	--
May	14.5	--	17.4	16.5	31	--	--
June	14.5	--	16.5	16.5	17	--	--
July	14.5	--	16.8	16.5	19	--	--
Aug.	15.0	--	22.6	16.5	21	--	--
Sept.	18.0	--	46.8	26.0	7	--	--
Oct.	17.0	18.5	14.7	22.0	323	--	--
Nov.	17.0	--	11.0	21.0	358	--	--
Dec.	15.8	--	9.6	21.0	213	--	--
Jan. 1985	15.8	--	9.6	21.0	200	--	--
Feb.	16.0	20.5	12.2	21.0	185	--	--
Mar.	16.0	20.3	13.2	21.0	243	--	--
Apr.	16.0	20.3	12.2	21.0	187	192	105
May	16.0	18.3	10.7	21.0	5	164	65
June	16.0	16.3	9.2	21.0	3	182	48
July	16.0	17.2	6.9	19.5	222	113	5
Aug.	14.0/15.0	16.3	8.1	18.5	339	156	67
Sep.	14.0	15.3	10.2	18.5	407	131	19
Oct.	14.0	14.5	9.9	18.5	927	145	96
Nov.	14.0	14.5	10.2	18.5	984	233	196
Dec.	14.0	14.5	11.5	18.5	966	503	411
Jan. 1986	14.0	14.8	12.1	18.5	1064	441	293
Feb.	14.0	14.8	12.6	18.5	1,129	607	530
Mar.	14.0	14.8	15.2	18.5	1,394	659	614
Apr.	14.0	14.8	14.6	18.5	1,848	611	575
May	14.0	14.8	15.5	18.5	2,244	549	451
June	14.0	14.8	12.7	18.5	2,057	558	441
July	14.0	14.8	12.4	18.5	2,393	447	311
Aug.	14.0	14.8	12.2	18.5	1,551	598	446
Sep.	14.0	14.5	12.9	18.5	1,135	391	114
Oct.	14.0	14.5	12.6	18.5	1,473	455	225
Nov.	14.0	14.5	12.9	18.5	1,296	529	207
Dec.	14.0	14.5	14.8	18.5	746	1,086	967

(a) *Cutoff rate in 30-day SBI auctions.*

(b) *FICORINVEST buying rate of 30-day SBPUs for banks and nonbank financial institutions.*

(c) *Basic discount rate.*

(d) *Volume outstanding.*

(e) *Volume of outstanding SBPUs sold through FICORINVEST.*

(f) *Credit to FICORINVEST for the funding of its purchases of SBPUs (liquidity line).*

Sources: *Bank of Indonesia; FICORINVEST; and IMF, International Financial Statistics.*

reserves. This new feature of rediscountability was introduced in order to lessen the reluctance of banks to purchase SBIs in the absence of an organized secondary market for these instruments, and to strengthen Bank Indonesia's ability to inject liquidity into the banking system. However, since August 6, 1986, FICORINVEST began quoting secondary market discount rates for SBIs based on the remaining maturity, and Bank Indonesia limited its rediscounting to SBIs with remaining maturity of 21 days or less.

Discount facilities. In order to complement the new system of reserve money management through sales and redemptions of SBIs, Bank Indonesia established two new rediscount facilities in February 1984. The first was designed to facilitate day-to-day reserve management by financial institutions with short-term support. Each bank's access was limited to 5 percent of its third-party liabilities -- i.e., liabilities to the nonbank public -- with emphasis on intermittent and temporary use of the facility. The basic discount rate was generally determined in relation to the weighted average of time deposit interest rates in rupiah for one, three, and six months. This basic rate (currently 18.5 percent) applied to borrowings in the first basic period of 15 days, rising thereafter by a fixed margin (currently one percentage point) for each additional seven days, up to a maximum of 29 days. For intermittent usage of funds, a separate, graduated scale of discount rates was used, with the basic discount rate applying to the first 30 days of intermittent usage.

The second discount facility, which replaced the previous emergency credit facility, was designed to encourage long-term bank lending by giving temporary relief to banks facing maturity risks resulting from a shortening of deposit maturities following deregulation. Accordingly, access to the facility was based on variations in third-party funds of each bank in relation to its net disbursements of medium- and long-term credits. The discount credit was in effect for up to a maximum of four months; each bank's access was limited to 3 percent of its third-party liabilities. The basic discount rate was applied to the first 60 days, with the rate rising by a specified margin for each additional 30 days of access.

Only those banks categorized as "sound" and "sufficiently sound" were eligible for access to these windows. Access was based on the sale of banks' own promissory notes on a discount basis. Bank Indonesia circulars on the discount facilities emphasized the "lender of last resort" role of these facilities.

The two discount facilities remained largely unutilized except during the money market crunch of August-September 1984. Banks were generally reluctant to borrow from Bank Indonesia, lest such borrowing be interpreted by the market and Bank Indonesia as an indication that their solvency was compromised. Also, because the basic discount rate was kept at a penalty level, most of the time above both short-term deposit rates and interbank rates, the demand for borrowing from the discount window was relatively insensitive to variations in market rates (Table 2).

Special credit facility. The situation changed dramatically beginning in August 1984, when speculation against the rupiah resulted in a fall in local currency deposits, driving the weighted average interbank rates up to 47 percent (Table 2). In response, Bank Indonesia encouraged banks to borrow under its short-term discount facility. However, the access limit for individual banks to this facility proved inadequate. In addition, the situation highlighted the dangers of having some banks too heavily dependent on a segmented interbank market, where specific banks may face particularly acute limit problems vis-à-vis lending banks.

In order to stabilize money market conditions, effective October 1, 1984, the authorities imposed a limit on each bank's borrowing in the interbank market, equivalent to 7.5 percent of the bank's third-party liabilities.[8] At the same time, they introduced a special credit facility as a substitute for interbank borrowing by banks that had exceeded their limit, thereby relaxing the limitations of the regular discount facilities. One half of the borrowing under the special credit facility was to be repaid within six months, and the balance within a year.

The rate on the facility was originally set at 26 percent, but it was subsequently lowered, along with the basic discount rate, in four steps to 21 percent by November 1984. Borrowings under this facility peaked at Rp 297 billion in October 1984 and declined slowly thereafter with the first substantial decreases occurring in early 1985. Borrowings through the two discount windows remained insignificant throughout this period

Money market facility. In order to prevent any inadvertent monetary contraction as repayments on the special credit facility fell due, and in order to develop a way to inject bank liquidity in a more systematic fashion, a new money market facility was established in February 1985. This facility created new money market instruments and allowed banks and nonbank financial institutions to trade in these instruments among themselves or with Bank Indonesia. The First Indonesian Finance and Investment Corporation (FICORINVEST) was appointed marketmaker, standing ready to buy and sell money market paper and funding its holdings of this paper either in the market or through a "liquidity line" from Bank Indonesia.[9] The newly created money market instruments, which are known as SBPUs (Surat Berharga Pasar Uang), included promissory notes issued by customers in connection with borrowing from banks or nonbank financial institutions; promissory notes issued by banks and nonbank financial institutions (NBFIs) in connection with interbank borrowing;

trade bills drawn by one party and accepted by another in connection with a specific transaction, where either the drawer or the drawee is a customer of a bank or NBFI; and trade bills drawn by a bank or NBFI customer and accepted by the bank or NBFI in connection with a credit extension to finance a specific transaction. In order to be marketable, the securities have to be drawn up according to specified regulations and must be endorsed by the selling bank or NBFI. Originally, SBPU maturities were 30 to 90 days, and the minimum denomination was Rp 50 million, but since August 7, 1985, the maximum maturity has been raised to six months and the minimum denomination has been lowered to Rp 25 million.

The holdings by FICORINVEST of the SBPUs for which a particular bank acts as the first endorser are limited to 15 percent of the third-party liabilities of that bank. However, a bank which has already reached its SBPU limit with FICORINVEST can obtain additional funds from another bank (or NBFI) which is below its SBPU ceiling by issuing a promissory note which can be endorsed by the lending bank and sold to FICORINVEST. Thus banks and NBFIs can utilize each other's limit, and the sum of the specified limits applying to holdings of each bank's SBPUs at FICORINVEST becomes, in effect, the global limit on the total volume of SBPUs that can be created in the system, equivalent to 15 percent of the liabilities of eligible banks and NBFIs.[10] This has encouraged interbank trading, and thereby the development of the SBPU market.[11]

FICORINVEST, which is still the only marketmaker in SBPUs, is free to set its buying and selling rates within the limits established by Bank Indonesia. At the end of 1986, the maximum allowable rate, which is also the rate at which Bank Indonesia buys SBPUs directly from banks and NBFIs, was 17 percent.[12] FICORINVEST may set rates that are lower than Bank Indonesia's rate by up to four percentage points for all maturities, and by up to three percentage points for maturities of more than one month.[13] The rates at which FICORINVEST can rediscount SBPUs at Bank Indonesia were originally set at one half of a percentage point and one percentage point above FICORINVEST's buying rate for maturities of up to one month and more than one month, respectively. These intermediation margins, however, have effectively been reduced to 0.125 percentage point for all maturities since March 6, 1986.[14]

Effectiveness of New Monetary Instruments

Although the new instruments have enhanced the authorities' technical ability to control reserve money, the apparent targeting of the SBI cutoff rate and FICOR's SBPU rate has generated a high degree of monetary variability even after the reform. Taken together, the new monetary instruments have had the net effect of absorbing reserves through most of the period, with the magnitude of this effect varying substantially from month to month, by as much as the equivalent of 20 percent of reserve money. Nevertheless, owing to the targeting of interest rates, monetary policy has largely failed to offset the variations in reserve money caused by autonomous factors, i.e., factors not related to monetary policy (Table 3).[15] SBI sales offset a rather insignificant portion of the reserve money expansion caused by autonomous factors in 1983-1984, the first year after the reform. In 1984-1985, policy actions reinforced the expansionary impact of the autonomous factors, with net sales of SBIs more than offset by the supply of reserves through the special credit and SBPU facilities. In 1985-1986, net sales of SBIs were almost exactly equal to the net increase in total rediscounts, with a neutral net effect. Reflecting this policy stance, excess reserves have been quite variable, with quarterly changes amounting to as much as the equivalent of 7 percent of reserve money, suggesting that the authorities have not been overly concerned with controlling the system's excess liquidity.[16] Partly as a result, neither reserve money nor broad money seems to have become more stable following the reform.[17]

If the authorities were to refocus on targeting overall monetary or credit aggregates rather than interest rates, the present monetary control system could pose some constraints. The substitutability of SBIs and SBPUs in the portfolios of investors implies that arriving at an appropriate setting for the SBI-SBPU rate structure, consistent with the corresponding operating target for reserve money, could involve considerable trial and error, possibly causing slippages in monetary control. To attain their reserve targets, the authorities would then need to control both the volume of SBI sales in the primary market and the volume of SBI and SBPU rediscounts by Bank Indonesia.

However, in order to limit rediscounts effectively without choking off money market activity, complementary measures to develop a secondary market for SBIs and SBPUs would be necessary. The development of such a market would allow Bank Indonesia greater freedom to move the rediscount rate for SBPUs and SBIs, thereby enhancing its ability to attain its reserve money targets. In this regard, one important decision that would need to be made is whether to discourage variation in borrowed reserves -- by posting a penalty or market-related discount rate -- or whether to allow greater fluctuation in borrowed reserves, as seems to have been the case so far. A penalty or market-related discount rate would improve control over money -- albeit at the expense of greater volatility of interest rates -- if shifts in the money-demand function were the dominant source of financial system disturbance. By contrast, if instability in bank behavior or in non-borrowed reserves were the dominant type of disturbance, pegging the

Table 3
Factors Affecting Changes in Reserve Money
(Bilions of rupiah)

	Fiscal[a] 82/83	Fiscal 83/84	Fiscal 84/85	Fiscal 85/86	Q2 1986	Q3 1986
Reserve money	67	1,263	497	1,721	-463	168
Currency outside banks	459	554	231	1,259	-210	339
Bank reserves	-393	716	157	579	-305	-118
Required reserves	12.6	308.4	276.3	317.8	32.7	179.5
Excess reserves	-435.6	404.6	-54.3	116.2	-248.7	-249.5
Correction factor[b]	30	3	-65	145	52	-53
Other deposits	1	-7	109	-117	52	-53
Autonomous factors	67	1,308	318	1,717	-25	865
Net foreign assets	-88	2,238	1,625	290	-466	4,069
Net claims on government	320	-1,566	-2,704	1,051	128	-1,773
Claims on private sector	-244	-440	-159	142	106	21
Liquidity credits to banks	1,256	505	1,333	954	254	188
Net other items	-1,177	571	223	-720	-47	-1,640
Policy factors	0	-45	179	4	-438	-697
SBIs outstanding	0	-45	-198	-1,151	-663	922
SBIs rediscounted	0	0	0	904	412	-1,292
SBPUs rediscounted	0	0	205	409	-173	-327
Rediscount Facility I	0	0	7	7	-14	0
Rediscount Facility II	0	0	0	0	0	0
Special credit facility	0	0	165	-165	0	0

(a) *Fiscal year begins March 1.*

(b) *Reflects the difference between the figures on bank reserves in the accounts of Bank Indonesia and of deposit money banks.*

Source: *Bank Indonesia and International Monetary Fund staff estimates*

discount rate at a nonpenalty level would enhance monetary control, by allowing changes in borrowed reserves to neutralize the monetary effect of these disturbances.[18] The implications of the structure of SBI and SBPU rates for both monetary control and money market development are discussed further in the following section.

MONETARY POLICY AND THE DEVELOPMENT OF THE FINANCIAL SECTOR

The Development of the Money Market

Since 1985, with the introduction of new money market instruments, the role of the nonbank financial institutions in the money market has grown, a small market for acceptances has emerged, and the significance of the unsecured interbank market has been reduced. Nevertheless, the money market is still in its early phases of development with interest rates effectively set by Bank Indonesia.

The Role of SBPUs. The introduction of SBPUs in early 1985 altered significantly the structure of the interbank market. Reflecting their excellent liquidity and their exemption from reserve requirements, SBPUs have become the principal vehicle for interbank loans of one-week or longer maturities, while also serving as the primary means of obtaining rediscount credits. Partly as a result, the importance of the rupiah interbank market has diminished permanently. The weekly average volume of rupiah interbank transactions had risen steadily in 1983-1984, peaking in the third quarter of 1984 at the equivalent of more than 25 percent of commercial banks' required reserves (Table 4). In the last quarter of 1984, the volume of interbank transactions fell sharply -- to the equivalent of about 8 percent of commercial banks' required reserves -- in response to Bank Indonesia's restrictions on interbank borrowing. In August 1985, however, these restrictions were relaxed, with Bank Indonesia raising its ceiling on each bank's interbank borrowing from 7.5 percent to 15 percent of third-party liabilities. Even so, the weekly average volume of rupiah interbank transactions failed to recover, remaining at the equivalent of less than 10 percent of required reserves throughout 1986, well below 1983 levels.

The decreased utilization of the interbank market is attributable in large measure to the structure of SBPU rates quoted by FICORINVEST (Table 2). The posted margin between buying and selling rates for SBPUs -- which has ranged between 25 and 50 basis points -- has been lower than the margin that would be needed to offset the cost of reserve requirements on interbank borrowing, thus making borrowing through SBPUs more economical. As a result, non-SBPU interbank transactions

Table 4
Selected Indicators of Money Market Conditions
(Percent, except as otherwise indicated)

	Interest Rates				Exchange Rate Depre-ciation[b]	Interbank Transactions	
	30-day SBIs	30-day SBPUs	Inter-bank	3-month LIBOR[a]		Weekly Average[c]	Ratio to Required Reserves
1983							
Jan.-Mar.	--	--	17.9	9.4	9.6	122	12.9
Apr.-June	--	--	10.5	9.4	48.4	131	13.2
July-Sept.	--	--	10.6	10.2	4.8	213	19.4
Oct.-Dec.	--	--	13.7	9.9	2.7	251	21.6
1984							
Jan.-Mar.	14.5	--	18.0	10.3	2.7	290	23.2
Apr.-June	14.5	--	16.0	11.5	4.9	258	20.6
July-Sept.	15.8	--	28.7	11.9	12.7	347	25.8
Oct.-Dec.	16.8	--	11.8	10.0	10.0	115	8.1
1985							
Jan.-Mar.	15.9	20.4	11.7	9.0	9.1	148	9.7
Apr.-June	16.0	18.9	10.7	8.2	8.7	120	7.4
July-Sept.	14.8	16.3	8.5	8.1	2.4	228	13.2
Oct.-Dec.	14.0	14.5	10.5	8.2	1.5	175	9.4
1986							
Jan.-Mar.	14.0	14.8	13.3	7.9	1.5	175	9.5
Apr.-June	14.0	14.8	13.6	7.1	-0.1	153	8.1
July-Sept.	14.0	14.8	12.5	6.3	9.4	153	7.4
Oct.-Dec.	14.0	14.8	13.4	6.1	--	187	9.2

(a) *London interbank offer rate on three-month U.S. dollar deposits.*

(b) *Annualized rate of depreciation of the rupiah-U.S. dollar quarterly average exchange rate; except for 1983Q2, for which the depreciation from 1982Q2 is used.*

(c) *Billions of rupiahs.*

Source: Bank Indonesia; and IMF staff estimates.

have remained concentrated in the shorter maturities -- one to six days -- for which there is no obvious substitute, while SBPU transactions dominate in the longer maturities. This segmentation of the market by maturity partly explains the observed wide differentials between interbank rates on the one hand, and SBI and SBPU rates on the other (Table 4).

The Determination of Money Market Rates. Under current procedures, market forces seem to play a minor role in the determination of SBI and SBPU rates. Although SBI rates are technically determined by the market in the weekly SBI auctions, in practice Bank Indonesia has pegged the cutoff rate at 14 percent throughout 1986, leaving the quantity of SBI sales to be demand determined. SBPU rates, likewise, have moved very little during 1986, with FICORINVEST adjusting its buying rates by a mere 25 basis points in mid-1986 and leaving them unchanged thereafter, despite the large movements in the exchange rate. Thus, Bank Indonesia has continuously asserted its own view of money market rates, possibly discouraging the development of trading skills among market participants. In this regard, the continuous posting of a relatively inflexible term structure of interest rates by FICORINVEST may sometimes give rise to unwarranted arbitrage opportunities, or it may even discourage money market trading altogether. For example, in times of extraordinary pressure on the exchange rate, the market might dictate an inverted yield curve which would be inconsistent with the upward sloping curve that FICORINVEST has customarily posted. This inconsistency might generate an excess supply of short-term paper and an excess demand for long-term paper, with market funding of SBPUs virtually eliminated. The same principle would apply to the term structure of SBI rates.

To rationalize the structure of money market rates, it is necessary to increase the role of market forces in the determination of interest rates, so that the liquidity of money market instruments is provided primarily by the market rather than by Bank Indonesia's discount window. This transition is perhaps one of the most challenging tasks in any financial reform. In the early stages, the central bank may still need to assert its own views on interest rates, based on the signals provided by the market in the form of quantities of money market paper demanded and supplied. Eventually, the monetary authority could limit its intervention to the shortest maturities, allowing the market to determine the yield curve, with the intervention tailored to the objectives of monetary policy. Such a system would allow the authorities the discretion to intervene as necessary in order to reduce interest rate volatility, while also forging closer linkages between money market rates, deposit rates, and loan rates.[19] In particular, to the extent that SBPUs are viewed as a deposit substitute, their yields should be in line with those on deposits of like maturities adjusted for the cost of reserve requirements.[20] In the longer run, if participation in the SBPU market were to widen to include nonbank institutional investors, prime borrowers could sell their own promissory notes to investors either directly or through nonbank financial institutions, thus stimulating the development of a commercial paper market. Competition from this market could then be expected to keep SBPU rates at levels close to, but slightly below, the prime and commercial paper rates.[21]

Money Market Development and Monetary Control. Under a system of targeting monetary aggregates, both the further development of the money market and the effectiveness of monetary control would be critically influenced by the relative structure of SBI and SBPU rates. For example, the rate structure during 1985-1986, together with SBI rediscount-ability, made SBIs more attractive than short-term SBPUs as an outlet for banks' excess liquidity. At the same time, funding of loans through SBPUs has remained more attractive than funding through deposits because the SBPU rates have been generally lower than deposit rates adjusted for the cost of reserve requirements. Such a rate structure could weaken control over reserve aggregates by raising the demand for rediscount credit through SBPUs, while also hampering the development of the money market, by discouraging market funding of SBPUs. Bank Indonesia, in effect, may thus perform the interbank transfer of funds by supplying liquidity through SBPU and SBI rediscounts on the one hand, and absorbing a part of excess liquidity through SBI sales on the other. Such possibilities highlight the need to increase flexibility in SBI and SBPU rates in order to strengthen control over the volume of SBIs and SBPUs rediscounted with Bank Indonesia. The recent change in the rediscount policy for SBIs was an important step in this direction. Additional measures to strengthen money markets could include licensing new marketmakers to compete with FICORINVEST, and pursuing a more flexible SBPU rate policy designed to maximize market funding. As of December 1986, market funding of SBPUs had not shown much improvement, given the automatic rediscounting at one half the spread posted by FICORINVEST (Table 2).

The Pattern of Financial Intermediation

The reform measures proved highly effective in stimulating competition among banks and in spurring a rapid expansion in deposits with financial institutions. Reflecting the increased competition for deposits, time deposit rates offered by state banks were initially raised to levels that were close to, but somewhat below, the rates offered by private banks, and subsequently, the differential between the two rates has declined substantially (Table 5). Partly as a result, the historical decline in the state banks' share of deposits was arrested, the share of private domestic banks doubled from 14 percent in June 1983 to 30 percent by end-1985, and that of foreign banks was cut in half. The overall impact of deregulation thus seems to have strengthened the competitive position of both state and private domestic banks vis-à-vis foreign banks.

Perhaps the most conspicuous success of the reform was the rapid increase in the growth of total domestic currency deposits after June 1983.

Table 5
Bank Interest Rates
(Percent)

	Six-Month Deposit Rate			Average Loan Rate[a]			
	State Banks	Private Banks	Foreign Banks	State Banks	Private Banks[b]	Foreign Banks	Inflation Rate
1982							
Mar.	6.0	18.1	12.4	--	--	--	10.2
June	6.0	18.3	15.9	--	--	--	9.0
Sept.	6.0	18.5	18.7	--	--	--	9.0
Dec.	6.0	18.5	18.3	--	--	--	10.1
1983							
Mar.	6.0	18.6	18.5	17.7[c]	27.3[c]	22.2[c]	8.6
June	11.9	18.8	17.6	--	--	--	13.5
Sept.	11.6	18.3	16.9	--	--	--	13.5
Dec.	13.1	18.8	17.0	--	--	--	12.0
1984							
Mar.	14.6	18.7	18.5	18.2	24.9	21.3	13.3
June	16.9	19.2	18.9	--	--	--	10.4
Sept.	16.9	19.6	19.5	--	--	--	8.8
Dec.	17.2	20.7	21.4	--	--	--	9.1
1986							
Mar.	18.0	21.2	21.6	19.9	28.2	26.4	3.7
June	18.6	21.1	20.7	--	--	--	5.2
Sept.	17.7	20.0	18.5	--	--	--	4.8
Dec.	16.0	17.8	16.5	--	--	--	4.4
1986							
Mar.	14.5	16.7	15.4	19.0	25.5	22.2	5.8
June	14.8	16.5	15.1	18.8	25.2	22.1	3.6
Sept.	14.7	15.9	15.0	18.7	24.8	21.4	6.8

(a) *Nonpriority credit.*

(b) *Simple average of foreign-exchange and nonforeign-exchange private national banks.*

(c) *May 1983.*

Source: Information supplied by Indonesian authorities.

Rupiah time and savings deposits rose by the equivalent of about eight percentage points of GDP between March 1983 and December 1986, while foreign currency deposits with banks grew by only one and a half percentage points of GDP during the same period (Table 1). This pattern was a marked reversal of the prereform trend of faster growth in foreign currency deposits and was partly the result of the exchange rate adjustment in 1983. While data are not available on the effect of reform measures on deposits offshore, one can hypothesize that the total portfolio shifts from foreign to domestic currency deposits were even more pronounced, contributing substantially to the strengthening of Indonesia's external accounts.

The increased interbank trading in SBPUs has also permitted some easing of the regulation-induced segmentation in the loan market. Although state banks are prohibited from extending credits -- or acting as first endorser of such credits -- to joint ventures, they are permitted to buy SBPUs issued by joint ventures which are already endorsed by private banks or NBFIs. Similarly, even though there is a prohibition against foreign banks extending credit to enterprises outside Jakarta, these banks can buy securities issued by such enterprises if they are already endorsed by domestic banks or nonbank financial institutions.

STANCE OF MONETARY POLICY AND MACROECONOMIC PERFORMANCE

Following the 1983 reform, the new monetary control system, together with the appropriate fiscal and exchange rate adjustments, contributed to a substantial improvement in Indonesia's external accounts, consistent with the authorities' principal objective. Inflation was also brought under control -- after an upsurge that followed the 1983 depreciation of the rupiah -- and real output, which had stagnated in 1982, resumed growth. Nevertheless, partly owing to the steady weakening of oil prices, the exchange rate remained under pressure through much of the post-reform period. The resulting high level of domestic interest rates is perhaps one of the key policy issues still confronting the Indonesian authorities.

External Accounts

The financial reform of 1983 was part of a concerted effort to improve Indonesia's external accounts, which had registered an overall deficit of US$3.5 billion in 1982/83. In addition to the already discussed measures in the financial sector, this effort included large adjustments in both the exchange rate and fiscal policy. The maxi-devaluation of 1983 and the subsequent mini-adjustments in the exchange rate served to strengthen competitiveness; Indonesia's real effective exchange rate declined by 21.6 percent in 1983-1984 and, after appreciating slightly by 4.5 percent in 1984-1985 on account of the strength of the U.S. dollar, it declined again by 17.2 percent in 1985-1986 (Table 6). In the fiscal accounts, the adjustment was also substantial in both expenditures and revenues. The overall budget deficit narrowed from the equivalent of 4.8 percent of GDP in 1982-1983 to 2.6 percent of GDP in 1983-1984 and, after swinging into surplus in 1984-

Table 6
External Balance and Budget Balance

Balance of Payments

	(In billions of U.S. dollars)				
	1981/82	**1982/83**	**1983/84**	**1984/85**	**1985/86**
Current account	-2.8	-6.8	-4.4	-1.7	-2.0
Capital account	-2.9	3.3	6.9	4.0	1.3
Of which:					
Private short-term capital[(a)]	-0.6	-1.9	2.5	0.8	-0.5
Overall balance	0.1	-3.5	2.6	2.3	-0.5

Government Finance

	(In percent of GDP)				
	1981/82	**1982/83**	**1983/84**	**1984/85**	**1985/86**
Revenue and grants	21.3	19.1	20.9	20.9	20.1
Expenditure	23.7	23.9	23.5	20.0	23.0
Overall surplus or deficit	-2.3	-4.8	-2.6	0.9	-2.9
Borrowing from the banking system	-0.2	1.4	-2.4	-3.5	0.9
Foreign borrowing (net)	2.5	3.5	5.0	2.6	2.0

Memorandum Items

	(Percentage change)				
	1981/82	1982/83	1983/84	1984/85	1985/86
Terms of trade[(b)]	8.6	0.3	-5.3	3.1	-11.4
Real effective exchange rate[(c)]	3.6	1.2	-21.6	4.5	-17.2
Average crude oil price ($/barrel)	34.9	33.5	29.5	28.8	25.1
Real GDP[(d)]	6.8	-0.3	3.4	6.1	1.9
of which: Non-oil GDP	-8.7	-4.2	-4.0	-4.7	-3.5

(a) *Estimate based on net errors and omissions.*

(b) *Ratio of export prices to import prices.*

(c) *Trade-weighted exchange rates deflated by corresponding consumer price indices.*

(d) *Calendar year.*

Sources: Data provided by the Indonesia authorities and IMF staff estimates.

1985, it widened to 2.9 percent of GDP in 1985-1986, largely on account of higher development expenditures (Table 6).

Reflecting these measures, the overall deficit in the balance of payments moved into surplus -- averaging US$2.5 billion a year -- in 1983-1984 and 1984-1985 before registering a small deficit in 1985-1986. Private capital inflows played an important role in this improvement. In the three years following the implementation of the reform, these inflows are estimated to have amounted to a cumulative US$2.5 billion, thereby reversing the outflows that had occurred in the previous two years. This reversal in the pattern of private capital flows and the concurrent sharp expansion in rupiah time deposits (Table 1) suggest that the financial reform measures must have contributed significantly to the adjustment effort.

The Level of Interest Rates, Exchange Rate Expectations, and the Policy Mix

Despite the substantial adjustments in the real effective exchange rate, domestic interest rates have remained quite high in real terms over the last few years, posing a significant policy challenge. Assuming that inflation expectations can be approximated by actual inflation over the past 12 months, one notes that both real deposit and real loan rates peaked in 1985 at very high levels -- ranging from a low of 14 percent for real deposit rates up to 26 percent for real loan rates (Table 5). Thereafter, nominal interest rates declined by as much as five to six percentage points but, with the rate of inflation remaining subdued, real interest rates, particularly loan rates, continued being exceptionally high, in part reflecting the large spreads between deposit and loan rates. The apparent downward rigidity in real interest rates may also be a result of the market's expectation of devaluation, which could raise inflationary expectations even in times of price stability. Because exchange rate expectations do not always respond to exchange rate policy in a predictable manner, containing real interest rates is still one of the most challenging tasks confronting the Indonesian policymakers.

Throughout the 1983-1986 period, rupiah deposit rates moved roughly in line with U.S. dollar rates adjusted for the actual rate of depreciation of the rupiah against the U.S. dollar. However, the downward movement of rupiah deposit rates was rather sluggish, reflecting in part the lag in the adjustment of exchange rate expectations. A similar pattern is evident with regard to movements in SBI and SBPU rates, suggesting that the setting of interest rate targets must have also been constrained by interest rate parity considerations (Table 4).

In an attempt to stabilize both exchange rate expectations and domestic loan rates, Bank Indonesia has been providing forward exchange cover for approved private sector foreign debt obligations through a swap facility at below market rates. In October 1986, access to this facility was liberalized as the previous ceiling on swaps was abolished, and the premium for new swaps of one-, three-, and six-month maturities was raised from 6 percent to 8 percent. The easier access to the swap facility was to be coupled with a more flexible structure of swap premiums that would ultimately align these premiums with interest rate differentials. As of March 1987, however, the Bank Indonesia swap premium remained unchanged at 8 1/8 percent, compared with money market swap premiums of 11-13 percent. The persistence of such wide differentials despite the large devaluation of September 1986 underscores the complexity of coordinating exchange rate and monetary policies in the presence of stubborn exchange rate expectations.

More generally, the question of how to determine the optimal mix of exchange rate and financial policies in open economies is still largely unanswered. The combination of high real interest rates and overvalued exchange rates, in particular, has proven to be destabilizing in several Latin American countries.[22] Further study of the experiences of other countries might cast additional light on the relative advantages and disadvantages of a wider variety of policy mixes.

SOME LESSONS FROM INDONESIA'S EXPERIENCE

Direct Controls Versus Reserve Money Management

The Indonesian experience before the reform underscores the serious shortcomings of monetary policy based on direct controls on the banking system. In the absence of additional checks on the growth of reserve money, binding credit ceilings may force banks to accumulate large amounts of excess liquidity, thereby undermining their incentives to attract deposits. The resulting lack of competition in banking is bound to discourage domestic financial intermediation and is likely to give rise to capital outflows, posing a threat to macroeconomic stability. This was generally the case in Indonesia before the financial reform, when both banks and nonbanks deposited increasing amounts of funds offshore.

These problems can be alleviated by switching to a system of indirect control through reserve money management. In addition to facilitating the attainment of macroeconomic objectives, indirect monetary control would also be conducive to a more integrated, more competitive, and more efficient financial system, as is indicated by Indonesia's recent experience. By controlling reserve money through open market operations, the authorities could liberalize interest rates and encourage competition, while still maintaining a tight rein over the system's overall money-creating and lending potential.

The Rationale for Developing Domestic Currency Open-Market Instruments

While open-market operations can be conducted in foreign or domestic currency assets equally effectively, the Indonesian experience may be quite instructive in underscoring the advantages of developing domestic currency instruments.

From the point of view of monetary control, the availability of a domestic currency instrument allows policymakers one extra degree of freedom, at least in the short run. Open-market operations exclusively in foreign exchange allow the targeting of either the exchange rate or the money supply, but not both. In contrast, the existence of domestic currency instruments could allow the achievement of independent exchange rate and money supply targets through sterilized exchange intervention, at least in the short run. Such intervention may be especially effective in smoothing out the monetary effects of seasonal fluctuations in the central bank's foreign exchange purchases, but it could also help the central bank resist speculative attacks on the currency without giving up monetary autonomy. In the case of Indonesia, one could even argue, with the benefit of hindsight, that the possibility of sterilized intervention could have conceivably sheltered the domestic economy more effectively against the effects of the oil price cycle of the last several years.

Other reasons that favor the introduction of domestic-currency open-market instruments relate to the objectives of financial market development and prudential control. In Indonesia, one can already note the tendencies toward greater integration, wider participation, and more competition in the domestic money market as a result of the introduction of the new monetary instruments. Finally, given the uncertainty with regard to future exchange rate developments, prudential considerations might limit the extent to which excess bank liquidity could be absorbed with sales of foreign assets, and might warrant the introduction of appropriately priced liquid assets in domestic currency.

Financial Reform, External Balance, and Monetary Targeting

So far, the stability of monetary and reserve aggregates in Indonesia does not seem to have been significantly affected by the reform measures, but control over these aggregates could be enhanced in the future. The aggregates have exhibited more or less the same variability before and after the reform, reflecting the authorities' emphasis on interest rate targets since 1983. This emphasis was probably warranted in the wake of the large portfolio shifts following the reform. The decision to target interest rates may have also resulted from the pressure on the exchange rate, and hence on the domestic money market, that followed the extraordinary oil price shock of the last few years. The consequent need to moderate interest rate volatility during this period may have made it impractical to target monetary aggregates. Excessive volatility in interest rates could undermine the soundness and stability of the domestic financial system, and could discourage the further development of the money market. Nevertheless, the recent easing of the pressures on the balance of payments could permit placing more emphasis on monetary and credit aggregates as policy targets. This would allow fuller use of the new monetary instruments and could also encourage money market development. Effective monetary targeting would, however, require greater flexibility in SBI and SBPU rates, and better coordination between open-market and rediscounting operations than has been necessary under interest rate targeting.

CONCLUDING REMARKS

The financial reform initiated by the Indonesian authorities has been highly successful. In addition to assisting the achievement of external balance objectives, the reform measures have promoted the growth and integration of the money market, encouraged competition and efficiency in banking, and enhanced Bank Indonesia's technical ability to control reserve and monetary aggregates. This latter ability might become especially useful in the near future, as the partial reversal of the recent oil price decline helps strengthen Indonesia's balance of payments.

In the period ahead, one of the most challenging tasks will be the gradual move toward a more market-oriented system of determining SBI and SBPU rates.[23] The Indonesian experience indicates that the pace of liberalization of money market rates would depend not only on continued institutional development but also on the choice of policy mix in dealing with domestic and external shocks. In this regard, the interactions between the mix of exchange rate and financial policies on the one hand, and exchange rate expectations and interest rates on the other, play a critical role and require further study.

NOTES

1. The possibility of using sterilized intervention to control both the exchange rate and the money supply may provide asymmetric flexibility. Given any exchange rate level, domestic interest rates can be kept higher than the level necessary to maintain parity with international rates, as long as the resulting inflow of international reserves is sterilized. However, because the central bank's ability to sterilize reserve losses is limited by its stock of international reserves it would be much more difficult to violate the interest rate parity condition in the opposite direction for an extended period of time. The levels of international interest rates and the exchange rate thus only set a floor for domestic interest rates in the longer run. The authorities may have some autonomy in choosing rates above the floor rate, but this rate cannot be lowered without the necessary exchange rate action. For a more detailed discussion on the potentialities and limitations of sterilized intervention see Kenen (1987).

2. This prescription was originally derived in the context of a closed-economy model (Poole, 1970), but it has also been extended -- with appropriate qualifications -- to the case of open economies (Bryant,1980; Benavie, 1983). One interesting result of these open economy models is that, contrary to the common presumption, it is often optimal for the government to lean with the wind in the foreign exchange market, thereby reinforcing any movement in the exchange rate that is produced by market forces (Benavie, 1983; Harkness, 1985). This result, of course, is specific to these models which provide a rather restrictive view of the circumstances under which exchange intervention occurs.

3. For a more detailed discussion of these issues, and for additional references, see Bryant (1980).

4. For a review of the U.S. experience with money supply targeting between 1979 and 1984, also a period of deregulation and financial innovation, see Simpson (1985, pp. 249-72).

5. See, for example, Obstfeld (1986), who shows how balance of payments crises can be precipitated by rational behavior if an exchange rate collapse is expected to set off an inflationary domestic credit policy. By adhering to a domestic credit target even when the exchange rate is under attack, the authorities could help modify such expectations.

6. The reserve requirements are computed on a weekly average basis using contemporaneous reserve accounting. The current ratio of 15 percent -- in effect since January 1978 -- applies to current liabilities, which is a weighted sum, with weights varying according to type of liabilities.

7. There were no issues of 90-day SBIs during April-September 1985.

8. The limit on interbank borrowing was increased to 15 percent of banks' third-party liabilities on August 7, 1985.

9. FICORINVEST established a separate Securities Trading Department to act as marketmaker. This department maintains separate accounts of its marketmaking activities, and does not buy money market paper from its parent company.

10. Interbank transactions through SBPUs, however, also count toward the separate ceiling on each bank's total interbank borrowing, which was originally set at 7.5 percent of third-party liabilities but was subsequently raised to 15 percent.

11. Banks can also borrow from FICORINVEST in excess of their limit by selling their SBPUs under repurchase agreements that expire before the SBPU maturity date; there is no quantitative limit on such repurchase agreements. As of February 1986, the total utilization of this facility by all eligible institutions amounted to 39 percent of their aggregater SBPU line with FICORINVEST.

12. Many smaller banks that do not have access to FICORINVEST can directly discount SBPUs with BI at the discount rate of 17 percent, irrespective of maturity. The use of this direct line of credit from BI seems to have been minimal.

13. The evolution of rates at which bank and nonbank financial institutions can buy or sell SBPUs through FICORINVEST is presented in Table 2. The margin between buying and selling rates for SBPUs at FICORINVEST is subject to a ceiling of three percentage points.

14. Under the new arrangement, BI will buy SBPUs from FICORINVEST at the midpoint between FICORINVEST's buying and selling rate for the remaining maturity, which amounts to a margin of 0.125 percent under FICORINVEST's current rate structure. For FICORINVEST's purchases of SBPUs from BI, FICORINVEST's buying rate for the remaining maturity will apply.

15. The autonomous factors include those that are not deliberately used as tools of monetary policy and whose monetary effects are only incidental, whereas the policy factors include those whose primary purpose is to affect banking system liquidity. This distinction is bound to be somewhat artificial to the extent that one cannot establish unequivocally the intent of each type of central bank operation. In the case of Indonesia, for example, one could readily envisage the use of foreign exchange swaps or liquidity credits for monetary policy purposes. In practice, however, such use has occurred infrequently, if at all, making the above distinction a useful analytical device.

16. Because reserve calculations are actually based on semi-monthly average balances, it would be sensible to recast this discussion in terms of period-average rather than end-period data. Nevertheless, owing to data limitations, the analysis throughout this chapter is based on end-period stocks, under the assumption that this yields a reasonable approximation of underlying trends.

17. The average quarterly rate of change of reserve money declined from 5 percent in the period between the second quarter of 1978 and the first quarter of 1983 to 4.3 percent in the period between the second quarter of 1983 and the second quarter of 1986, but the standard deviation of reserve money growth rose from 4.8 percent to 4.9 percent during the same period. Concurrently, the average quarterly rate of change of rupiah broad money declined from 5.9 to 5.6 percent, while its standard deviation declined from 3.4 to 3.2 percent. These figures suggest that the quarter-to-quarter variability in reserve money and broad money failed to decrease after the reform, despite the replacement of credit ceilings by a system of reserve money management.

18. For an analytical discussion of these issues, see Gordon H. Sellon, Jr., "The Role of the Discount Rate in Monetary Policy: A Theoretical Analysis," reprinted in *Issues in Monetary Policy II*, Federal Reserve Bank of Kansas City (1982), pp. 82-94.

19. For discussion of the difficulties encountered in liberalizing short-term rates in the United Kingdom, see Coleby (1986).

20. With effective reserve ratios on time deposits amounting to 10 percent for state and foreign banks, and 5 percent for other banks, the SBPU rate should exceed the deposit rate by at least three-quarters to one and a half percentage points at current interest rates. This differential should be even wider if banks preferred to be funded through SBPUs to match the maturities of their assets and liabilities or to lower their administrative costs.

21. These considerations also suggest that a wider and more active money market could help increase the responsiveness of loan rates to monetary policy. For a description of the relevant relationships in the U.S. bankers' acceptance market, see Jensen and Parkinson (1986).

22. For a description of the recent experiences of Argentina, Chile, and Uruguay, see Corbo et al. (1986). Sachs (1985) compares the experiences of Latin American and East Asian countries, and argues that trade and exchange rate policies were the most significant cause of the disparity between the performance of these two groups of countries.

23. Recent developments (not covered in this chapter) suggest that the authorities have already moved toward greater flexibility in interest rates, placing more emphasis on quantity targets. This augurs well for the further development of the money market and for a more effective use of open-market operations.

REFERENCES

Aghevli, Bijan B., Mohsin S. Khan, P. R. Narvekar, and Brock K. Short (1979). "Monetary Policy in Selected Asian Countries." *Staff Papers*, International Monetary Fund (Washington), Vol. 26 (December), pp. 775-824.

Benavie, Arthur (1983). "Achieving External and Internal Targets with Exchange-Rate and Interest-Rate Intervention." *Journal of International Money and Finance* 2, pp. 75-85.

Boediono (1985). "Demand for Money in Indonesia, 1975-1984." *Bulletin of Indonesian Economic Studies* 21, No. 2 (August), pp. 74-94.

Bryant, Ralph C. (1980). *Money and Monetary Policy in Interdependent Nations*. Washington, D.C.: Brookings.

Coleby, A.L. (1986). "Changes in Money Market Instruments and Procedures in the United Kingdom." In Bank for International Settlements, *Changes in Money Market Instruments and Procedures: Objectives and Implications*. Basel, Switzerland: BIS, pp. 199-206.

Corbo, Vittorio, Jaime de Melo, and James Tybout (1986). "What Went Wrong with the Recent Reforms in the Southern Cone." *Economic Development and Cultural Change* (April), pp. 607-640.

Harkness, Jon (1985). "Optimal Exchange Intervention for a Small Open Economy." *Journal of International Money and Finance* 1, pp. 101-112.

Jensen, Frederick and Patrick Parkinson (1986). "Recent Developments in the Bankers' Acceptance Market." *Federal Reserve Bulletin* (January), pp. 1-12.

Kenen, Peter (1987). "Exchange Rate Management: What Role for Intervention?" *American Economic Review*, Papers and Proceedings (May), pp.194-199.

Obstfeld, Maurice (1986). "Rational and Self-Fulfilling Balance-of-Payments Crises." *American Economic Review* (March), pp. 72-81.

Poole, William (1970). "Optimal Choice of Monetary Policy Instruments in a Simple Stochastic Macro Model." *Quarterly Journal of Economics*, 84, pp. 197-216.

Sachs, Jeffrey D. (1985). "External Debt and Macroeconomic Performance in Latin America and East Asia." *Brookings Papers on Economic Activity* 2, pp. 523-564.

Simpson, Thomas D. (1984). "Changes in the Financial System: Implications for Monetary Policy." *Brookings Papers on Economic Activity* 1, pp. 240-272.

15

Monetary Policy and Financial Reform in Korea

Thomas A. Layman

The governments of most developing countries intervene extensively in the operations of their financial sectors. In a system where financial markets are fragmented among regions and/or between different classes and groups of borrowers so that funds do not flow efficiently, government intervention is often justified on the assumption that it has a better chance of success in channeling credit to bring about the desired use of physical resources. Intervention can range from total control over all financial institutions and the allocation of capital, to indirect influence over the growth of monetary aggregates and the price of credit through changes in reserve money. In Korea, the experience has been largely one of more control rather than less.

Korea's annual growth rates have averaged over 9 percent in the 25 years since the First Five Year Economic Development Plan was introduced in 1962. Monetary and financial policies have helped ensure the success of the government's economic development plans. During the 1960s and early 1970s, controls over interest rates and credit allocation allowed for continued increases in investment and rapid real growth.

However, as the economy became more complex and dependent on the rest of the world in the mid-1970s, this system of heavy controls began to produce some harmful effects. Fluctuations in oil prices, substantial variations in world interest rates and economic activity, and a huge build-up of external debt necessitated a change to a less regulated financial system. To make monetary policy a more effective tool, the government has embarked on a number of financial reforms which, if continued, will improve efficiency in the financial sector and give more autonomy and control to the central bank.

The development of financial institutions has also played an important role in mobilizing domestic savings to finance productive investments in the economy. However, the financial system that evolved is somewhat unique. Specialized banks were created in the early 1960s in order to direct financial resources to specific areas of the economy. Funds were allocated from the government to these banks and utilized for specific medium- and long-term loans. Often, however, the special banks also accepted deposits and conducted commercial banking business as well. In parallel with these banks was the system of commercial banks, which has also been subject to strong government administrative control, largely the result of direct government ownership of four of the nationwide commercial banks until the early 1980s. These two groups of financial institutions coexisted with an unregulated financial market[1] composed of the curb market (in which borrowers are mostly large corporations, and lenders are a heterogeneous group of businesses and private individuals) and the *kye* market (a form of rotating credit associations where small depositors pool their resources to make installment loans to other members). Given the interactions of the regulated and unregulated markets in providing finance for economic growth, a recurring theme emerges regarding the problems of monetary control and the methods the authorities have used to mitigate those problems.

The purpose of this chapter is to provide an overview of how monetary policy has contributed to the remarkable growth of Korea's economy since the early 1960s. Adjustments in monetary policy must be understood within the context of financial changes that have occurred during this same period. Therefore, the first section of the chapter gives a brief historical overview of financial sector development. The next section describes the instruments of monetary policy and how they have changed within the historical context. The role of monetary policies in contributing to Korea's recent economic performance is analyzed in the third section. The final section discusses some issues which may affect the future conduct of monetary policy in Korea.

FINANCIAL SECTOR DEVELOPMENT

The era of modern banking in Korea dates from the turn of the century, when the government adopted a unified currency law, giving Daiichi Ginko, a Japanese bank first established in 1876, legal status as the sole issuer of currency for the country.[2] During the colonial period, the financial system in Korea developed quite rapidly, but was owned and controlled by the Japanese. Banks were used initially to channel savings into Japanese-owned industrial and commercial enterprises, but later were instrumental in collecting funds to help finance Japan's military advancements. After World War II, the Korean economy and the financial system were shaken by the sudden separation from Japan, resulting in excessive monetary growth and rampant inflation as wartime controls disappeared.

Despite legislation in 1950 to set up a new central bank (the Bank of Korea) and to reorganize the banking sector, it was not until the cease fire with North Korea in 1953 that the government was able to concentrate on industrial and agricultural rehabilitation. To aid in directing financial flows for this reconstruction effort, the government set up several specialized banks under the control of the Ministry of Finance, including the Korea Development Bank (1954) and the Korea Agricultural Bank (1956). Regulation of domestic financial matters was given to a Monetary Board headed by the Minister of Finance and the central bank governor.

Control over the financial system was further concentrated in the hands of the Ministry of Finance in the early 1960s as majority ownership of commercial banks was transferred to the government, and several additional specialized banks were created to support the development of high priority sectors of the economy. For example, the Korea Agriculture Bank was merged with various local agricultural cooperatives into the National Agricultural Cooperatives Federation which, together with the National Federation of Fisheries Cooperatives, allocated rural and agricultural credit. Other directives created the Small and Medium Industry Bank, the Citizens National Bank, the Korea Development Finance Corporation (later renamed the Korea Long Term Credit Bank), the Export-Import Bank of Korea, the Korea Trust Bank, and the Korea Housing Bank. The establishment of local, privately owned banks was encouraged, to support regional development of the economy. To better utilize foreign funds, the government in the late 1960s allowed a limited number of foreign banks to begin branch operations in Korea, and set up the Korea Exchange Bank by breaking off the foreign department of the Bank of Korea.

Table 1 shows that strong investment and export volume growth during the period 1965-1973 allowed real per capita income to rise a remarkable 9 percent per year. Although domestic savings financed the majority of this expansion, capital inflows from abroad were necessary to satisfy the huge financing needs of Korea's rapid industrialization. In response to this demand and the very strict control by the government over both the availability and price of financial capital, a parallel, unregulated money market grew in importance. The majority of short-term credit that flowed to companies through the unregulated market passed through the curb market. Because rates were not controlled (and presumably returns not taxed), savers provided the unregulated market with ample liquidity despite the high risks.

During the early 1970s, concerns over growing balance-of-payments deficits, increased inflationary pressures associated with rising energy prices, and lack of direct control over credit flows through the curb market led the government to allow the formal establishment of investment and short-term finance companies. To attract savings from the unregulated market, the government authorized these nonbank financial institutions to set their deposit interest rates slightly higher than those offered by

Table 1
Macroeconomic Indicators
(percent per year, unless otherwise specified)

	Annual Avg. '65-73	Annual Avg. '73-80	1980	1981	1982	1983	1984	1985	1986
PERFORMANC									
Real GDP growth	11.5	7.5	-3.0	7.4	5.7	10.9	8.6	5.4	11.9
Per capita GDP growth	9.0	5.8	-4.5	5.7	4.0	9.2	7.0	4.2	10.5
Investment growth	23.0	16.0	-10.6	-4.0	12.9	17.1	10.7	4.4	15.0
Investment/GNP	25.1	31.8	32.1	30.3	28.6	29.9	31.9	31.2	30.1
Savings/GNP	21.5	26.4	20.7	20.5	21.6	25.0	27.1	28.1	32.9
Export volume growh	24.3	18.5	11.5	17.5	6.5	16.3	15.6	7.6	13.0
Current account/GNP	-3.6	-5.4	-8.9	-7.2	-3.9	-2.1	-1.7	-1.1	4.7
External debt growth	48.8	30.7	4.3	19.1	14.5	8.9	6.7	8.6	-4.5
External debt ($bil)	0.2[(a)]	4.3[(b)]	27.2	32.4	37.1	40.4	43.1	46.8	44.5
Debt service ratio	11.1	14.5	18.4	20.5	20.9	19.6	20.9	25.2	23.4
Short-term debt/total	10.2	21.1	34.5	31.5	33.5	30.0	26.5	23.0	20.8
Unemployment rate	n.a.	4.0[(c)]	5.2	4.5	4.4	4.1	3.8	4.0	3.8
GNP deflator	14.2	21.5	23.8	15.4	6.6	3.9	3.8	4.1	2.3
POLICY									
Monetary									
Net domestic asset growth	49	33	36	37	35	15	13	19	11
Interest rates:									
Nominal[(d)]	22.7	17.3	20.0	17.0	10.0	10.0	11.5	11.5	11.5
Real[(e)]	8.5	-4.2	-3.8	1.6	3.4	6.1	7.7	7.4	9.2
Fiscal[(f)]									
Deficit/GDP	1.2	1.7	2.2	3.4	3.1	1.1	1.2	1.3	1.8
Expend/GDP	16.0	16.2	20.3	21.7	22.0	20.0	19.5	14.7	19.6
Exchange rate									
REER change[(g)]	n.a.	n.a.	-6.4	1.2	0.2	-5.7	-3.2	-6.4	-12.1

(a) *Outstanding end 1965.*
(b) *Outstanding end 1973.*
(c) *1976-1980.*
(d) *Ceiling lending rate on loans of one year by commercial banks.*
(e) *Nominal rate adjusted by GNP deflator.*
(f) *Central government only.*
(g) *Based on total trade with 10 trading partners, deflated by consumer prices.*

Sources: Institute of International Finance database, Bank of Korea, Economic Planning Board, and Ministry of Finance.

commercial banks. Loan rates were also allowed to be higher, but still far below those offered in the curb market. To ensure that sufficient funds were available for the rapid development of the heavy and chemical industries during the mid-1970s, the government also set up the National Investment Fund, and merchant banking corporations were introduced to raise medium- and long-term funds for business enterprises and to attract additional inflows of foreign capital.

Although helpful in directing funds to high priority sectors, heavy government control of the financial sector in the 1960s and 1970s created some undesirable side effects as the economy became more sophisticated. While growing in number and variety, financial institutions in Korea had little incentive to expand their intermediation capacity or to improve financial technology. Developing credit assessment and portfolio management skills were generally not emphasized, given the government's credit allocation policies and implicit guarantees against ultimate default. The preferential financing techniques also led to a highly leveraged financial structure of industrial enterprises which repressed the development of an active equity market and at the same time limited the effectiveness of traditional tools of monetary policy.

The heavy reliance on foreign funds in the 1960s and 1970s also created problems for the authorities. To encourage the inflow of foreign capital, the government allowed the Korea Development Bank, the Korea Exchange Bank, and later all nationwide commercial banks to issue guarantees for foreign currency loans contracted by domestic business and government enterprises.[3] Although these banks were responsible for the guarantee, the government in effect backed the loans in the event of default. There was less incentive to evaluate projects or to assess risk, because foreign lenders, mainly U.S. and Japanese banks, treated these loans as sovereign risk credits. Not only did this system complicate the control of domestic credit expansion, it also encouraged the rapid build up of external debt, reinforced the use of bank credit versus equity for business expansion, and in recent years contributed to the volume of bad debts on the books of Korean banks.

In recognition of these problems, the government, as a part of the Fifth Five Year Economic Plan (1982-1986), adopted a number of liberalizing measures to enhance the efficiency of financial institutions and to increase the reliance on market mechanisms to allocate capital.[4] As a part of this process, the government decided to privatize the commercial banking sector. Although all five city banks were returned to the private sector by the end of 1983, the government continues to exert considerable influence over the management structure and decision-making process at those banks today.[5]

To foster increased competition between commercial banks, foreign banks were encouraged to open branch operations; two new joint venture commercial banks -- the Sinhan Bank, owned by Korean businessmen in Japan, and the KorAm Bank, owned by Bank of America and several large Korean companies -- were opened in 1982. Between 1981 and 1986, 23 new foreign banks began operations, bringing the total to 54.[6] By adopting the policy of national treatment, certain discriminatory practices which had favored domestic banks over their foreign counterparts were also removed. Among others, restrictions on foreign banks' ability to raise local funds in support of domestic currency loans were amended. By 1986, foreign banks were allowed to access the Bank of Korea's rediscount facilities for export financing and commercial bills, to issue domestic certificates of deposit in limited quantities, and to engage in trust business. In exchange, however, foreign banks have been forced to allocate a portion of their domestic lending activity to priority sectors and to give up some of their preferential foreign exchange swap facilities with the central bank.

In a move to encourage the development of the domestic capital market, the government allowed 15 foreign securities companies to open representative offices. Although prohibited from operating directly in the domestic market, these foreign companies are allowed to own up to 10 percent of those domestic securities companies authorized to conduct international business. Soon foreigners may be allowed to engage directly in capital market activities such as underwriting. In 1987, the government authorized several foreign insurance companies to begin local operations.

Interest rate and financial instrument reforms were also initiated during the Fifth Plan, but progress has been slow. To compete with the rapid growth of nonbank financial institutions, commercial banks were allowed in 1982 to begin selling commercial bills and government bonds with repurchase agreements, and to issue credit cards and money market-type savings deposits. Commercial paper interest rates were also deregulated so that funds from the unregulated market could be attracted. However, loan rates remained strictly controlled, and spreads between deposit and lending rates narrowed. Pressure on bank profits led the government to restore regulation of the commercial paper market by the end of 1982. In a partial move toward liberalization of bank loan rates, interest rate bands were introduced in January 1984 to permit deposit money banks[7] to charge slightly different rates according to credit risk. The ceiling on interest rates for interbank call money was also lifted. Pressures are building for the pace of reform to accelerate, but this will require that the tools of monetary control be strengthened as well.

INSTRUMENTS OF MONETARY CONTROL

At one time or another, the Korean authorities have used all the usual instruments of monetary control -- reserve requirement ratios, open-market operations, and rediscount policy -- but the primary instrument has been direct control over both interest rates and the allocation of credit. Direct control was necessary early on in order to mobilize capital for the country's development programs. In recent years, however, the under-developed nature of Korea's money and capital markets has precluded active use of open-market operations, and the low interest rate policy to stimulate investment has led to a chronic condition of excess credit demand, making discount rate policy largely ineffectual. Given the importance of Bank of Korea credit in financing the government's budgetary deficits, high reserve requirements have also often served as an additional source of tax revenue for the government.

Reserve Requirements

The Bank of Korea fixes the minimum reserve requirements that banking institutions must maintain against their deposit liabilities. The ratios may not exceed 50 percent, but in periods of excessive monetary growth and/or high inflation, the bank is authorized to impose marginal reserve requirements of up to 100 percent of incremental increases in deposits. Prior to 1982, adjusting reserve requirements was the most frequently used instrument of indirect monetary control. For example, in the mid-1960s when a surplus in the balance of payments generated excess liquidity in the financial system, the Bank of Korea raised reserve ratios to 35 percent for demand deposits and to 25 percent for time and savings deposits. In addition, marginal reserve requirements of 50 percent for demand deposits and 45 percent for time and savings accounts were temporarily imposed from October 1966 to March 1967. During the 1970s, reserve ratios were adjusted downward several times, but remained quite high, ranging from 19 to 27 percent for demand deposits and from 12 to 20 percent for time deposits.

The high levels of required reserves and the frequent changes since the mid-1960s have caused the money multipliers to be quite unstable, complicating both the management of bank balance sheets and the growth in the money supply. These difficulties have probably contributed to the low profitability of deposit money banks and are alleged to be one of the causes of the chronic failure by banks to maintain required reserves.[8] In order to shore up their income, the Bank of Korea has often paid interest on these reserves, ranging from 3 to 15 percent per year. In some cases when banks have been unable to meet the required reserves and have had to pay penalties,[9] the Bank of Korea has extended general loans to banks to make up the deficiency, thereby reducing the effectiveness of the reserve instrument. This problem has been largely mitigated since the 1980s, as increased effectiveness of other monetary control instruments has allowed the central bank to reduce reserve ratios several times.[10] Difficulties in controlling the growth of M2 associated with large surpluses in the current account of the balance of payments, however, led the authorities to raise reserve requirements to 7 percent in November 1987.

Open-Market Operations

Prior to the 1960s, there were very few marketable instruments available for monetary control. In part, this resulted from the fact that the government, rather than issuing government securities, relied almost exclusively on direct borrowings from the Bank of Korea to finance its fiscal deficits. New issues of bonds were not attractive for investors either, because of the government's low interest rate policy to stimulate investment activity.

The first serious attempt to develop a means of conducting open-market operations occurred in the early 1960s when the Stabilization Bonds Act was implemented. Under this act, the Bank of Korea can issue special short-term obligations (usually 90 days) in its own name under terms specified by the Monetary Board, with the right of repurchase before maturity as warranted by credit conditions. Although the rate of interest on these issues is supposed to be close to deposit rates of similar maturity, in fact until 1973 the rates were generally below comparable deposit rates. As a result, sales of these bonds were usually allocated among deposit money banks by the Bank of Korea, thereby reducing the effectiveness of this instrument for influencing domestic credit conditions.

Beginning in 1973, the Bank of Korea made these bonds subscribable through public auctions, allowing the rates to be more market determined. Also, the Treasury Bills Act was amended in 1977 allowing the government to issue treasury bills to reduce its reliance on borrowings from the central bank to finance budgetary deficits.

Since 1981, the central bank has actively used monetary stabilization bonds to influence credit conditions. In recent years with the balance of payments turning to strong surplus, the Bank of Korea has issued large amounts of these bonds, mainly to nonbank financial institutions.[11] However, these operations have been expensive for the central bank, with interest payments in 1987 estimated at over 700 billion won, and only partially effective in controlling the growth of domestic liquidity.

Monetary Stabilization Account

To reinforce the reserve requirement policy and also to develop an instrument similar to the open-market stabilization bonds, the Stabilization Account System was introduced in 1967.[12] Under this system, the Bank of Korea can require banks to deposit additional reserves with the central bank. These accounts now earn a competitive rate of interest; only 5 percent when first introduced, the interest rate was raised to 15-17 percent per annum during the 1970s.

The stabilization account has been used quite often since its introduction, especially in recent years, because it can be selective and flexible with attention to each bank's reserve position. As shown in Table 2, the Bank of Korea allowed banks to withdraw 2.2 trillion won from these interest-bearing accounts during 1987, partially offsetting the contractionary effects of the net 4.7 trillion won in monetary stabilization bonds floated during that period. In 1975, the system was divided into A and B accounts. The A account is the same as the original account, but the B account was established to absorb excess liquidity arising from the sale of foreign exchange to the Bank of Korea by the banking system.

Discount and Loan Policy

Since 1968, the rediscount window has been a major source of credit to the banking system. Like all central banks, the Bank of Korea can supply credit directly to the banking system either by rediscounting commercial bills or by extending general loans based on the collateral of certain assets of the banks. Since interest rates are controlled and generally maintained at rates lower than if they were market determined, variations in the discount rate and the rate of interest on general loans have had little influence on the volume of bank credit. Until recently, what counted was not the cost, but the availability of credit.

Typically, the Monetary Board has established two funds each year. The "A-limit fund" provides banks with direct liquidity for loans to special sectors, such as small and medium industry, general investment, and local industry. The "B-limit fund" offsets deficiencies in banks' reserve positions.[13] The Bank of Korea sets the ceiling each year on the availability of general loans and within the limits of these two funds allocates an amount to each bank depending on the reserve and loanable funds position of the bank.[14]

Bills eligible for rediscount consist of commercial bills -- categorized by prime borrowers, ordinary enterprises, and those guaranteed by the Korea Credit Guarantee Fund -- and bills for trade promotion and other sectors designated for preferential treatment. Until the mid-1980s, the latter were automatically rediscounted at full value and thus outside of the control of the Bank of Korea. As of 1987, the central bank provided rediscounts up to 70 percent of the value of commercial bills for small and medium firms, and 30 percent for others. Owing to the balance-of-payments surpluses in 1986 and 1987, the rediscount facility for export bills was progressively reduced, while new facilities to encourage imports, especially capital goods from the United States, were introduced. As of December 1987, general loans accounted for 66.3 percent of the Bank of Korea's total loans and rediscounts, while trade financing and rediscounts on commercial bills comprised 10.5 percent and 15.0 percent, respectively (Table 2).

Direct Controls

The Monetary Board is authorized under the Bank of Korea Act to set maximum interest rates as well as to establish ceilings on the size of each type of loan and deposit for banks. The Board has allocated credit by measures ranging from setting general guidelines to earmarking funds for specific sectors, industries, and even individual firms and projects. As recently as the late 1970s, the government allocated, directly or indirectly, anywhere from 50 to 70 percent of domestic credit, depending upon the classification of "directed" or "policy" loans.[15] The remainder, in theory at least, was allocated at the discretion of the deposit money banks. In reality, these banks exercised very little control over even the residual banking funds.

Heavy and chemical industries as well as the large business firms, called "chaebol," were the major recipients of government-induced capital allocations in the 1970s. However, such an emphasis resulted in a shortage of credit for small and medium businesses. Beginning in 1980, the Monetary Board mandated that 55 percent of incremental increases in local bank loans and 35 percent of nationwide city bank credit be allocated to small and medium-sized firms.[16] Although credit controls for banks were removed in 1982, the credit requirement for small and medium business continues, and the Monetary Board retains the right to impose such controls and ceilings as appropriate.

Over time, the government also adopted an increasingly complex structure of interest rates to give varying amounts of favored treatment to different categories of borrowers. For some borrowers, such as (until recently) exporters, preferential interest rates and large credit allocations worked together. For others, such as much of agriculture, interest rates were kept low but loan amounts were limited as well.

Because of chronic excess demand for funds in the financial market, the maximum interest rate ceilings adopted by the authorities have tended to be considerably lower than the rates prevailing in the unregulated

Table 2
Bank of Korea Balance Sheet
(billion won)

Liabilities

	Total Liabilities (1=2+6+7)	Domestic Liabilities (2=3+4+6)	Deposits of Banks, Govt. & Other (3)	Monetary Stabilization Bonds Outstd. (4)	Monetary Stabilization Accounts (5)	Foreign Liabilities (6)	Reserve/ Undivided Surplus (7)
1978	4859	4372	3946	426	--	297	190
1979	5778	5238	4706	532	--	192	348
1980	7085	5575	4995	530	50	672	838
1981	8570	6400	4466	1660	274	1166	1004
1982	9766	7680	5142	927	1611	1233	853
1983	11342	9113	5376	3360	377	1514	715
1984	13713	11402	5752	4458	1192	1826	485
1985	16260	14324	5906	1900	6518	1694	242
1986	18562	16490	6813	4285	5392	1940	132
1987	25750	24636	12483	9007	3146	1068	46

Assets

	Total Assets (1=2+7)	Domestic Assets (2=3+4+6)	Cash (3)	Loans & Discounts (4)	Foreign Currency Loans to Banks (5)	Loans to Govt. &Other (6)	Foreign Assets (7)
1978	4859	3707	62	1419	632	1594	1152
1979	5778	4507	53	2126	773	1555	1271
1980	7085	5296	99	2715	906	1576	1789
1981	8570	6714	139	3741	604	2230	1856
1982	9766	7401	238	4609	139	2415	2365
1983	11342	9126	395	5766	134	2831	2216
1984	13713	11025	487	7623	130	2785	2689
1985	16260	13278	462	9641	138	3037	2983
1986	18562	15157	276	10157	1340	3384	3404
1987	25750	22309	282	10783	7403	3841	3440

Sources: Bank of Korea, Economic Statistics Yearbook *and* Monthly Bulletin.

money market (for recent years see Table 3). This in turn has caused banks generally to set rates at their maximum level. The adjustment of ceilings has also reflected changes in government priorities regarding overall growth and development of the economy.

MONETARY POLICIES AND ECONOMIC DEVELOPMENT

Since 1961, monetary policy has been particularly influenced by the Ministry of Finance. The Finance Minister as the Chairman of the Monetary Board can exert considerable control, having the power to request reconsideration of the Board's resolutions (a de facto veto power), audit the Bank of Korea's books, and approve its budget. Both the Economic Planning Board and the Ministry of Commerce and Industry have also been involved in constructing and implementing monetary policy, since they are directly in charge of budgetary and planning operations, and trade promotion and industrial development, respectively. Therefore, monetary policy has been and continues to be very closely planned and controlled by the government, with the central bank having very little autonomous power.

Beginning in the 1950s, the annual Financial Stabilization Program set growth targets for nominal M1 and M2 consistent with desired rates of economic growth and inflation. The basis for this exercise, historically at least, has been a simple quantity-theory of money equation.[17] In the ten years or so prior to 1965, monetary policy of Korea was focused on containing the growth of the money supply (M1) in order to reduce inflation. However, the government was not very successful. Excessive money growth and fixed nominal interest rates to stimulate investment resulted in negative real interest rates. During the 1970s the government's primary goal was maintaining domestic growth, and the authorities devoted more attention to broad money (M2) as the main target. With foreign loans rising in the late 1970s, moreover, the Monetary Board reasoned that M2 was more insulated than, for example, targets for domestic credit expansion from external events. Furthermore, a willingness to maintain a competitive exchange rate (i.e., periodic won devaluations in line with inflation differentials) allowed the authorities to conduct an independent monetary policy.

Once an acceptable level of M2 growth was determined, then an associated level of domestic credit was calculated, using the consolidated balance sheet of the banking system and making assumptions concerning projected changes in the net foreign assets and other asset positions of the banking system. Having determined what financial resources were

Table 3
Selected Interest Rates on Deposits and Loans[a]
(percent per annum)

End of Period	1980	1981	1982	1983	1984	1985	1986
DEPOSITS							
Deposit Money Banks							
Household checking	n.a.	14.4	8.0	8.0	6.0	6.0	6.0
Time deposits over 1 year	19.5	16.2	8.0	8.0	10.0	10.0	10.0
Savings deposits	12.3	14.4	8.0	8.0	6.0	6.0	6.0
(over 6 months)[b]						(12.0)	(12.0)
Certificates of deposits (CDs)[c]	--	--	--	--	11.0	12.0	11.5
Nonbank Financial Institutions							
Money in trust (2 years)	22.5	20.6	9.7	10.7	10.7	11.9	11.5
Investment & finance companies							
Bills resold: 8-29 days	13.3	12.2	8.0	7.5	7.5	7.5	7.5
60-90 days	20.4	18.3	9.0	8.5	8.5	8.5	8.5
Mutual credit cooperatives							
Time deposits (1 year)	20.7	18.3	9.0	9.0	10.5	11.0	11.0
Yield on corporate bonds[d]	30.1	24.4	17.3	14.2	14.1	14.2	12.8
Yield on Government Bonds[d]	28.8	23.6	17.3	13.8	14.3	13.9	11.6
LOANS							
Commercial Banks							
Discounts on bills	19.5	16.5	10.0	10.0	11.5	11.5	11.5
Loans for exports	12.0	12.0	10.0	10.0	10.0	10.0	10.0
Overdrafts	21.5	16.5	10.0	10.0	11.5	11.5	11.5
Term loans: Up to 1 year	20.0	17.0	10.0	10.0	11.5	11.5	11.5
3-8 years	20.5	17.5	10.0	10.0	11.5	13.0	12.0
8-10 years	21.5	18.5	10.0	10.0	11.5	13.0	12.0
Other Financial Institutions							
Korean Development Bank							
Equipment for key industries	18.5	18.5	10.0	10.0	11.5	13.0	13.0
Using government funds	13.0	13.0	10.0	10.0	10.0	10.0	10.0
Korea Housing Bank (private)	10.8	18.5	10.0	10.0	10.0	10.0	10.0
Mutual savings & finance companies	--	29.4	20.0	20.0	18.5	18.0	18.0
Agricultural cooperatives	15.0	15.0	10.0	10.0	10.0	10.0	8.0
National Investment Fund (NIF)	10.5	17.5	10.0	10.0	11.5	11.5	11.0
National Housing Fund (NHD)	8.0	18.0	10.0	10.0	10.0	10.0	10.0
Curb market rate[d]	45.0	35.3	30.6	25.8	24.7	24.0	23.2

(a) *All rates are maximum rates.*
(b) *Introduced in April 1985.*
(c) *CD-generated loans are 1 percentage point above CD deposit rates.*
(d) *Annual averages, not maximum rates.*
Source: Bank of Korea, Economic Statistics Yearbook.

available, the planners then decided how they would be allocated, first among preferential areas, then for rediscounts and general loans, and then for bank allocations. Thus, the planning process was very rigid, leaving little room for subsequent changes in monetary policy, even if the original assumptions underlying the program did not hold.

When the government's development strategy shifted in the early 1960s from an import-substitution orientation to export-led growth, financial and credit policies were adjusted accordingly. The heart of the system was automatic approval of low-interest loans by commercial banks to any producer with an export letter of credit or other valid evidence of an export order. During the mid-1960s, subsidized loans were also given to producers of exports. The amount of the loan usually accounted for 80 percent of the domestic production costs, and it ran for 90 to 120 days at an annual interest rate of 6.5 percent. In 1967 interest rates on these types of trade loans and discounts were lowered to 6 percent and remained there through 1973. With inflation averaging over 14 percent per year, real rates for export credits were substantially negative throughout the period. Export producers were given preferential consideration for guaranteed foreign loans used to finance imported machinery for expansion of productive capacity.

Special measures were taken to ensure that suppliers of exporters also benefited from favorable bank loan schemes. In the 1970s, the special program of low interest loans was extended to include the intermediate goods industries, such as steel and petrochemicals, and also to the machinery and construction industries, including shipbuilding. All of these industries were seen as potential export industries or as important intermediate suppliers to export industries. Given these incentives, it is easy to see how resources were shifted to the export sector. The volume of exports grew in excess of 24 percent per year during the period 1965-1973 and by 18.5 percent annually during 1973-1980 (Table 1).

Domestic demand was also stimulated by the surge in investment spending. To mobilize domestic savings, a monetary reform package was implemented in September 1965. Interest rates on bank time deposits were raised dramatically, from 15 percent to 30 percent on 18-month deposits. Loan rates were also increased but by a much smaller amount, and reforms did not affect rates for high priority sector loans, such as export producers, farmers, and many categories of investment loans by special banks. Rediscount facilities were set up at the central bank to provide the subsidy. Quantitative ceilings on nonpriority bank loans were eliminated, however, allowing commercial banks to use their reserves in excess of forced purchases of Bank of Korea stabilization bonds to expand loans.

Within only three months of implementation, time deposits increased 40 percent and then doubled in each of the succeeding three years. Between the end of 1965 and the end of 1969, time and savings deposits rose from 3.9 to 21.0 percent of GNP, and M2 rose from 12.0 to 32.7 percent of GNP (Table 4). Although inflation continued to average 14-18 percent per year, nominal deposit rates were kept sufficiently high to stimulate increases in real savings. The exchange rate, moreover, was adjusted often enough to maintain export competitiveness.

Reductions in the ceilings on loan and deposit interest rates acted in combination with increased inflationary pressures from a 20 percent devaluation of the won during 1970-1971 to cause real rates to turn negative by 1972. The OPEC embargo the following year and the subsequent decline in world economic growth adversely affected Korea's balance of payments. To offset the impact of this deterioration on the domestic economy, the government adopted a stimulative monetary policy stance, which was maintained throughout most of the decade. Real interest rates remained negative until further reforms were introduced in 1981 (Table 4).[18] Not surprisingly, real economic growth continued to be high, although the 7.5 percent annual average during 1973-1980 was lower than the 11.5 percent average rate during the 1965-1973 period (Table 1). External debt also accumulated rapidly as the current account deficits rose as a percent of GNP.

The unfavorable economic developments of 1980 (further increases in oil prices, a devaluation of 21 percent on January 12, a poor agricultural performance, and political unrest) caused the authorities to seek changes that emphasized increased international competitiveness, and price stability through higher domestic savings and monetary discipline. Although interest rates were actually lowered in 1981 in order to stimulate growth in the domestic economy, real interest rates again turned positive as inflationary pressures from the previous year subsided (Table 4). By 1982 domestic growth had improved, fueled largely by further growth in exports, and the government was able to adopt a more conservative policy stance.

Between 1981 and 1985 monetary policy was generally tight, while fiscal policy also turned contractionary. As shown in Table 1, the rate of growth of the net domestic assets of the banking system was reduced progressively from 37 percent in 1981 to 13 percent in 1984. At the same time, nominal bank lending rates fell from 17 percent to 11.5 percent, but with inflation falling real lending rates more than doubled. In 1985 an emerging recession caused largely by a drop in exports prompted some monetary easing and net domestic assets rose 19 percent. The increase in domestic credit was roughly 1.5 times the rise in broad money, as net foreign assets of the banking system fell (Table 5).

Table 4
Financial Structure of Korea, 1962-1986

	M2/ GNP[a] (percent)	M3/ GNP[b] (percent)	Stocks and Bonds/ GNP (percent)	Nominal GNP (% change)	GNP Deflator (% change)	Interest Rate on 1-Year Time Deposits[c] (percent)	Real Return on 1-Year Time Deposits[c] (percent)
1962	14.6	--	15.8	--	18.5	15.0	-3.5
1963	10.9	--	16.8	41.3	29.5	15.0	-14.5
1964	8.9	--	14.9	42.3	29.9	15.0	-14.9
1965	12.0	--	14.4	12.6	6.4	18.8	12.4
1966	15.1	--	12.2	28.7	14.2	30.0	15.8
1967	19.8	--	12.2	23.5	18.9	30.0	14.1
1968	26.4	--	15.0	29.0	18.9	27.6	11.7
1969	32.7	--	18.2	30.4	14.6	24.0	9.4
1970	32.8	--	19.6	27.0	18.0	22.8	4.8
1971	32.1	37.9	18.9	23.4	13.4	21.3	7.9
1972	35.0	40.5	23.9	23.1	16.4	15.4	-1.0
1973	36.8	44.5	24.2	29.5	13.5	12.6	-0.9
1974	32.7	40.5	21.9	39.5	29.5	15.0	-14.5
1975	31.2	38.7	21.3	34.5	25.8	15.0	-10.8
1976	30.3	38.1	22.9	37.5	20.5	15.5	-5.0
1977	32.4	41.5	24.9	30.5	15.8	15.8	0.0
1978	32.7	42.2	27.6	33.7	21.9	16.7	-5.2
1979	31.6	42.8	30.7	29.0	21.1	18.6	-2.5
1980	34.2	48.6	35.7	17.4	23.8	22.9	-0.9
1981	34.7	51.5	42.2	23.1	15.4	18.5	3.1
1982	39.2	61.0	47.5	12.4	6.6	11.0	4.4
1983	38.9	63.8	55.2	16.3	3.9	8.0	4.1
1984	37.2	68.1	57.3	12.6	3.8	10.0	6.2
1985	39.2	75.2	53.8	9.7	4.1	10.0	5.9
1986	40.4	82.5	60.8	15.1	2.3	10.0	7.7

(a) *M2 = M1 + time and savings deposits and resident foreign currency deposits at banks.*

(b) *M3 = M2 + other financial institution deposits, debentures issued, commercial bills sold and CDs.*

(c) *Average for year.*

Sources: Bank of Korea, Economic Statistics Yearbook *and* Flow of Funds Accounts.

Table 5
Monetary Developments and Factors Affecting Liquidity
(changes, trillion won)

	1980	1981	1982	1983	1984	1985	1986	1987
Net foreign assets	-0.8	-1.7	-2.1	-0.7	-1.1	-1.6	1.6	4.5
Net domestic assets	3.5	4.8	6.3	3.7	3.5	5.9	4.0	2.3
Domestic credit	5.0	5.2	5.5	4.3	4.2	6.5	6.1	7.4
Public sector	0.4	1.0	0.4	-0.1	-	-	-	-1.6
Private sector	4.6	4.2	5.1	4.5	4.3	6.5	6.1	9.0
Other items, net	-1.5	-0.4	0.8	-0.6	-0.7	-0.6	-2.2	-5.1
M2 and CDs	2.7	3.1	4.2	3.0	2.4	4.3	5.5	6.8

(percent change, annual rate)

Memorandum:[b]	1980	1981	1982	1983	1984	1985	1986	1987
Domestic credit 1	42	31	25	16	13	18	14	15
Domestic credit 2	48	34	30	19	21	23	18	16
Domestic credit 3	59	41	39	26	33	29	23	18

(a) *Domestic credit 1 is from the monetary survey and includes net credit supplied by monetary institutions, while Domestic credit 2 includes credit extended by nonbank financial institutions, as shown in the financial survey. Domestic credit 3 measures credit supplied only by nonbank financial institutions and development finance institutions, such as the Korea Development Bank.*

Sources: Bank of Korea, Economic Statistics Yearbook *and* Monthly Bulletin.

With export growth rebounding strongly in 1986 and the current account moving into surplus, the monetary authorities were faced with a new problem of rapid accumulation of net foreign assets. An initial target for M2 growth was set at 12-14 percent for the year, based on an expected real economic growth rate of 7 percent. By mid-year when it became apparent that the economy was expanding much more rapidly, the growth target for broad money was revised upward to 16-18 percent. Efforts to adhere to this ceiling led the authorities to mandate foreign debt prepayments by the nonbank sector and a reduction in external borrowings. The central bank also issued massive amounts of monetary stabilization bonds, equivalent to more than one-fourth the increase in M2 during the year. These bonds were priced competitively, with interest rates in excess of 12 percent. Access to foreign exchange swap facilities was also curtailed, which increased the funding costs for foreign branch banks engaging in local currency lending.[19] Moreover, firms whose debt-to-equity ratios exceeded 500 percent (effectively, all of the large firms) were not allowed further access to bank credit. Overall, domestic credit grew by 14 percent, down from 18 percent in 1985, as lending to the private sector eased (Table 5). The growth of M2 was just above target at 18.6 percent. Despite the rise in real interest rates resulting from the deceleration in prices, investment spending continued to grow, reaching a rate of 15 percent.

Concerns over excessive monetary growth were exacerbated during 1987 as the current account surplus continued to grow. In order to contain M2 growth to the 18 percent target, the Bank of Korea again drained liquidity by issuing large amounts of monetary and foreign exchange stabilization bonds. By the end of September, the outstanding level of these bonds reached 4.3 trillion won. However, much of the contractionary effect of these bond issues was offset by increased credit to banks through rediscounts. As previously noted, the Bank of Korea also allowed banks to withdraw a portion of their deposits under the monetary stabilization account.

Continued pressure on the monetary aggregates forced the authorities to raise the reserve requirement ratio to 7 percent and reduce the export loan rediscount ratio in November 1987. The effectiveness of this measure in reducing credit growth was again partly offset by increasing the B-policy loan limit to help banks cover their reserve shortfalls. The monetary growth target was also raised to 20 percent for the year.

In addition, external debt management remained an integral part of domestic monetary policy. The Korean government forced most government entities to prepay a portion of their external debts, and to take advantage of improved credit conditions to refinance more expensive obligations with cheaper funds. In order to encourage the private sector to do the same, the central bank set up special credit facilities through local banks to lend domestic companies foreign exchange. As of the end of December 1987, these foreign currency loans to banks had risen to 7.4 trillion won, while Korea's total external debt had dropped to $35.6 billion from $44.5 billion at the beginning of the year (Tables 1 and 2). Of this decline, over $7 billion was public sector prepayments; the remainder was from the private sector. The authorities also encouraged the 82 largest corporations to substitute debt financings with equity and bond issues.[20]

MONETARY POLICY OUTLOOK

In assessing the performance of monetary policy in Korea during the past 20 years or so, it is difficult to be overly critical given the extraordinary economic success that has been achieved. Although the authorities might have been more cautious after the first OPEC price shock in the early 1970s and thereby kept inflation lower and contained the build-up of external debt, the 1980s have seen thus far a reduction in inflation, a turnaround in the current account balance, and significant declines in external debt outstanding. To be sure, external conditions have been favorable to these recent achievements and have supported even further increases in real per capita income.

The country remains very vulnerable to external shocks, however, such as a decline in growth in industrial countries, a sharp rise in international interest rates, or a sudden reduction of foreign oil supplies. Though unlikely, domestic political upheavals could undermine the country's economic stability. The question of whether monetary policy can continue to be as effective in a less regulated environment in the future therefore arises.[21]

In order to answer this question, a number of issues will have to be resolved. The first concerns the constraints on further deregulation caused by past policies which have resulted in an overreliance by industrial enterprises on bank credit. As shown in Table 6, bank financing was the largest single source of funds raised by the business sector during the decade of the 1970s, and it is only recently that nonbank credit and funds raised in the domestic capital market have become more important. The liberalization of interest rates since 1981 has been characterized by allowing rates on selected instruments to be freed, while others remain controlled. There have also been instances of backtracking.

It is generally assumed that if bank interest rates were fully deregulated, loan rates would rise significantly, at least in the short run. Given the highly leveraged nature of Korean companies, this would put pressure on company balance sheets and could result in a large number of bankruptcies, thereby threatening the soundness of the financial system. Thus far, the government has approached the industrial restructuring of declining industries by shifting the burden of adjustment to commercial banks, thus avoiding adding the problems of business failures to the real economy. Commercial banks, however, are already burdened by significant nonperforming assets, which limit their autonomy and the efficiency of the banking industry in general. To offset the potential losses and the burden of nonperforming loans, the government has increased tax provisions for the sale of collateral against such loans and provided low-cost rediscount loans by the Bank of Korea. The latter has complicated the central bank's ability to drain excess liquidity from the banking system.

Another recurring theme of monetary policy in Korea is the problem of control over monetary aggregates arising from financial flows between the regulated banking institutions and the unregulated curb money markets. The size of the unregulated market was estimated in June 1980 at 1.5 trillion won,[22] equivalent to 12 percent of the average level of banking claims on the private sector during the January to June 1980 period. A 1985 survey conducted by the Citizen's National Bank estimated that the market had grown to 5.1 trillion won,[23] or roughly one-quarter of banking claims on the private sector at the end of the year. Given the importance of this market and the recent growth in the nonbanking financial sector, it is easy to see how data on the banking system's loans and loan rates may not accurately reflect the overall liquidity and credit conditions faced by the private sector. Moreover, the effectiveness of any policy action by the monetary authorities has been greatly reduced by such "leakages out of the system," especially when slower credit growth was desired.

That does not mean, however, that the unregulated market has necessarily been bad for the Korean economy. Until the financial reforms of the early 1980s removed individual bank credit ceilings and allowed more interest rate variation by commercial banks, the unregulated markets served the function of allocating scarce capital to businesses which did not qualify for priority or special discounted credits. As a result, more investment spending took place than would otherwise have been the case, boosting the economy's potential for growth. To deal with the difficulties of monetary control posed by its existence, however, the government elected to support the development of nonbank financial institutions.

In order to compete with the unregulated markets, the government allowed nonbank financial institutions to be less regulated with respect to their asset management and lending rates than banks. Both deposit and lending rates at nonbank financial institutions are therefore higher than corresponding rates at deposit money banks, but are still below those charged in the curb market (Table 3). In terms of monetary sources of borrowing by the corporate sector, the expanded role of nonbank financial institutions has been quite impressive. Nonbanks' share increased from only 15 percent in 1970-1974 to 26.4 percent in 1980-1984, while that of banks decreased from 40.4 percent to 23.8 percent in the same period (Table 6). The difficulty this rapid growth has created for the monetary authorities is evident in the much higher rates of credit expansion by the nonbank financial institutions (23 percent in 1986) than by the banks (14 percent), which are more directly under the control of the central bank (Table 5).

Future changes in capital flows between these financial markets could also have important implications regarding the responsiveness of investment spending to interest rate changes.[24] Increases in interest rates

Table 6
Funds Raised by the Business Sector 1980-1986
(percent of total, except as otherwise noted)

	1965-69	1970-74	1975-79	1980-84	1985	1986
Indirect finance	47.4	55.9	56.5	53.0	73.2	62.0
Banks	37.5	40.4	35.9	23.8	30.6	29.9
Nonbanks	9.9	15.0	20.6	26.4	17.9	10.0
Government loans[a]	-	0.5	0.1	2.8	24.7	22.1
Direct finance	14.6	20.8	23.0	41.0	26.2	32.8
Stocks	14.3	17.8	13.7	20.7	6.7	10.6
Bonds	0.4	1.7	6.5	14.5	13.9	8.8
Commercial paper	-	1.2	2.8	5.8	5.5	13.4
From abroad	37.9	23.3	20.4	6.0	0.6	5.2
Total	100.0	100.0	100.0	100.0	100.0	100.0
(trillion won)	(0.2)	(0.7)	(3.3)	(10.0)	(14.7)	(15.4)

(a) *Government loans, trade credit, and miscellaneous.*
Sources: Bank of Korea, "Flow of Funds," Economic Statistics Yearbook.

in the regulated market have not necessarily led to declines in investment in part because of the availability of credit (at a cost) from the unregulated market and nonbank financial institutions, and in part as a result of rapidly rising exports. Investment demand may become more sensitive to interest rate changes, however, as the government reduces its direct control over interest rates and credit in the regulated market, and the allocation of credit becomes more dependent on individual firm performance and financial soundness. Moreover, if inflationary pressures remain moderate, interest rate differentials between the curb market and other money markets should also decline. During 1987, for example, curb market rates for short-term credits declined to around 18 percent from an average of 23 percent the year before. Combined, these effects should make conventional monetary policy transmission mechanisms more effective.

These factors suggest the importance of continuing the process of financial liberalization, especially of deposit and lending rates for banks, to insure that they are able to compete for deposits and can lend them profitably. Deregulation of interest rates, however, must also be accompanied by improved credit assessment skills and systems of control within the banks. With less direct control, the government must insure that proper auditing and accounting practices are followed. Furthermore, equity capital of commercial banks should be strengthened. Further development of Korea's capital market is essential not only for equity enhancement of banks and business enterprises but also in order to give the monetary authorities more leeway in absorbing excess liquidity caused by the turnaround in the current account balance. By reducing the dependence of companies on bank financing, the banking system will be less vulnerable to internal and external shocks.

It is encouraging that companies have begun the process of issuing convertible bonds and relying more on equity issues to raise new capital (Tables 4 and 6). Forcing companies to reduce their external and domestic liabilities also serves to sterilize the inflow of foreign capital associated with the current account surplus, reduce companies' overleveraged positions, and make the country's external debt more manageable. Further moves in this direction will allow financial liberalization to proceed more rapidly and will increase the ability of the central bank to conduct monetary policy in an effective manner.

Exchange rate and trade policy have always been highly integrated with monetary policy in Korea. With the rapid turnaround recently in the current account and the growing bilateral trade imbalances between Korea on the one hand, and the United States and Japan on the other, the coordination of policy has become even more important. During 1986 and 1987, the authorities were under significant pressure to revalue the won/dollar exchange rate in order to reduce the rising trade surplus with the United States. During this two-year period, the nominal won/dollar exchange rate moved up only 5.5 percent, while on a trade-weighted basis and deflated for relative price changes, the won has depreciated 12.4 percent (Table 1). Not surprisingly, the imbalances have continued to grow. The government, fearing a substantial loss of export competitiveness with a more rapid currency appreciation, elected to adopt trade liberalizing measures to open the economy to greater import growth. While this policy is likely to boost imports somewhat, in the short run it will have little impact on reducing the continued inflow of foreign exchange associated with the rapid growth of exports. Cost push pressures from increased wages in the manufacturing sector could be exacerbated by continued pressure on the monetary aggregates, necessitating further efforts to sterilize the inflow of foreign capital and put increased pressure on domestic interest rates. The maintenance of strong capital controls, moreover, complicates the task, leaving the prepayment of debt as the only means of limiting the rise in foreign assets. In any event, a rise in domestic inflation could result in some loss of export competitiveness. Therefore, a reluctance to adjust the exchange rate upward against the dollar has reduced the ability of the authorities to conduct an independent monetary policy.

Finally, if the process of financial liberalization continues and the central bank is able to rely increasingly on open-market operations and discount rate changes to affect the monetary aggregates, increased autonomy should be given to the Bank of Korea. In the past, close interaction between the various government agencies allowed for better coordination of all policies in order to achieve the government's economic growth objectives. Such coordination, however, also led to relatively inflexible constraints on monetary policy. With greater reliance on market forces in the future, the central bank must have the ability to react quickly to changing domestic and external market conditions. Increased autonomy would also naturally accompany the reduced dependence of the government on direct loans from the central bank to help finance government deficits. Increased use of government bonds will also add marketable instruments for the conduct of monetary policy.

The challenges, therefore, are significant, but favorable external events during 1986 and 1987 have provided the Korean authorities a unique opportunity to accelerate the process of financial liberalization in conjunction with the opening of the rest of the economy to market forces. Assuming that the external environment does not deteriorate markedly over the next few years, the authorities should have ample time to complete the structural transformation now underway.

NOTES

The author wishes to express thanks to Kim Si-Dam, Margaret Shilliday, Jeff Anderson, Paul Rawkins, William Alexander, John Bennett, and Sung Y. Kwack for helpful comments on earlier drafts of this chapter. The conclusions and opinions expressed in this chapter are those of the author and do not necessarily represent those of the Institute of International Finance or any of its membership.

1. Various authors in referring to Korea's financial system have used the terms "official versus unofficial," "organized versus unorganized," and "regulated versus unregulated" markets to describe these two sectors. The latter, adopted by Cole and Park (1983), is used in this study because it best describes the curb and *kye* markets, which are quite organized, recognized by the government as an important part of the country's financial system, and have been very efficient through the years in allocating credit.

2. For an excellent description of Korea's financial history during the colonial period (1910-1945), see Cole and Park (1983, pp. 42-48) and Suh (1978) generally.

3. Cole and Park (1983, pp. 60-61).

4. See Lee (1986) and World Bank (1987, vol 1, pp. 78-99).

5. In 1982-1982 a series of financial scandals rocked the country, and the government had to prevent the Choheung Bank and The Commercial Bank of Korea from collapsing

through direct management intervention and low interest loans. The government also fears that lending practices of the privatized banks could be severely influenced by their majority owners, which tend to be the largest conglomerate business firms. As a result, the authorities continue to approve most top management of the city banks and keep a watchful eye on their general operations. See World Bank (1987, vol. 1, pp. 92-97), Manguno and Kim (1986, pp. 1, 19), and Nakarmi (1987).

6. Two foreign banks, Morgan Guaranty Trust and Wells Fargo Bank, however, downgraded their operations from branches to representative offices. Mellon Bank of Pittsburgh also closed its representative office in early 1987.

7. Deposit money banks include the seven nationwide, so-called city banks, local banks, and specialized banks except for the Korea Development Bank, the Korea Export Import Bank, and the Korea Long Term Credit Bank.

8. As Park (1982, pp. 22-24) points out, the money multipliers in Korea have not only been unstable but are very low by comparison with most other countries at similar stages of development, largely due to the public's preference to hold currency. The low level of profitability by banks is, therefore, compounded by this tendency. See also Cole and Park (1983, p. 241), Bank of Korea (1985, p. 12), and Kwack and Chung (1986, pp. 129-131). As discussed below, there was a significant shift by savers to deposits in investment vehicles which carry market-related interest rates when they were created in 1985 and 1986. Unable to raise loan rates at the same time, this rise in the cost of funds put an additional squeeze on local bank profits, prompting the Bank of Korea to offer additional discount facilities to the banks. See Manguno and Kim (1986).

9. Reserve requirements, of which 25 percent may be held in vault cash, are computed semi-monthly by the Bank of Korea. A penalty of 1 percent of the amount of the average deficiency during that half-month period is imposed by the Bank of Korea. However, this penalty has often been offset by loans from the Bank of Korea (see below). Such loans and interest payments on reserves have not been available to foreign branch banks. See Ito (1984, pp. 456-457) and Bank of Korea (1985, p. 12).

10. The reduction in reserve ratios has also complemented the partial deregulation of deposit and loan interest rates. Although the ceilings on loan rates have been raised somewhat, the banks are still not free to set their rates at a market-determined level. The theoretical justification for allowing both of these measures to occur simultaneously is based on McKinnon's (1980) argument that the reduction in reserve requirements will allow banks to resist increasing loan rates by a greater amount to maintain profit margins.

11. The nonbank financial institutions consist essentially of short-term finance and investment companies, and insurance and securities companies. These are permitted to raise cash and to lend at rates higher than those permitted to banks. They are also allowed to issue and to guarantee bonds.

12. This account was originally suggested by Gurley, Patrick, and Shaw (1965) as a means to offset the fact that banks were simply failing to hold required reserves or invented accounting procedures to conceal their reserve deficiency. See Cole and Park (1983, p. 242).

13. The A-limit loans are broken down into two categories: A1 funds, which as of mid-October 1987 carried an annual interest rate of 6 percent, can be used by commercial banks to support loans to priority sectors such as trading companies and small- and medium-sized firms; A2 funds, which carried a lower interest cost of only 3 percent, can be utilized by banks to offset losses associated with bad loans to such sectors as overseas construction and shipping firms. The B limit loans carried a much higher interest rate, as of mid-October 1987, of 15 percent. By comparison, the general commercial loan rate ceiling set by the Bank of Korea at the time was 11.5 percent.

14. General loans for local business were abolished in 1981. See Ito (1984, p. 456). Often the general loan account has been utilized to provide low interest loans to help individual companies and banks overcome temporary financial difficulties. This was probably the case in December 1984 when one of the large business groups, Kukje, experienced financial problems. The Ministry of Finance instructed the group's four major creditor banks to lend an additional 138 billion won to keep the company afloat. This loan, however, did not resolve the company's problems, and it was later reorganized and merged into other business groups. See Ensor (1985). This practice has continued, although recent problems with a shipbuilding company, Korea Shipbuilding and Engineering Co., have not resulted in the government offering subsidized loans. See Ensor (1987).

15. See Cole and Park (1983, pp. 171-173). Within these policy loans, direct funding from the central bank, either through rediscounts or direct loans to deposit money banks rose from 4.8 percent of total policy loans extended in 1962 to an average of 18 percent during the last half of the 1970s. The proportion funded by foreign loans also rose from virtually none in 1962 to over 16 percent by 1980. See Park (1982, pp. 61-63). Since then these proportions have declined. As of September 30, 1987, the Bank of Korea had extended on an outstanding basis 1.49 trillion won in concessional policy loans. See *Korea Herald* (October 22, 1987, p. 6).

16. Small and medium firms are defined as those whose total assets are less than 1 billion won, the total number of employees is less than 300 in the case of a manufacturing firm and 200 in the case of a service industry. In July 1986, the ratios were lowered to 35 percent for domestic banks, while in the interest of national treatment, foreign banks were required to allocate one quarter of their domestic won lending to such industries as well. See Bank of Korea Annual Report (1986, p. 20). Given the reductions in foreign exchange swap facilities for foreign banks in 1987, however, the Ministry of Finance agreed to enforce less strictly the lending requirements for foreign banks. During the first seven months of 1987, the 46 foreign banks had extended only 13.1 percent of their total won portfolio to small and medium-sized businesses. See *Korea Herald* (October 25, 1987, p. 6).

17. This description, posited by Cole and Park (1983, pp. 256-258), has some empirical support in Park (1982, pp. 67-69).

18. For more detailed description of events during the period 1973-1980, see Kwack and Chung (1986, pp. 126-127), Cole and Park (1983, pp. 270-280), and Park (1982, pp. 73-109).

19. Although more discount facilities at the central bank were opened to foreign banks during the course of 1986, the majority of won funding for these banks has traditionally come through foreign exchange swap arrangements with the Bank of Korea. However,

because of the buildup of foreign assets since 1986, the central bank froze dollar loans of all banks and curtailed the swap facilities offered to foreign banks. See Manguno (1986, p. 18). These facilities were further reduced in 1987.

20. Ensor (1987, p. 6).

21. Some of the pitfalls associated with financial deregulation in developing countries are identified in Dooley and Mathieson (1987).

22. See Cole and Park (1983, pp. 110-170) and Park (1982, pp. 9-10).

23. Kim (1987, pp. 72-73).

24. This point is made most effectively in World Bank (1987, vol. 2, pp. 57-58).

REFERENCES

Bank of Korea, *Annual Report*, various years.

Bank of Korea, *Economic Statistics Yearbook*, various years.

Bank of Korea, *Monthly Bulletin of Statistics*, various years.

Bank of Korea, *Quarterly Economic Review*, various issues.

Cole, David C. and Yung Chul Park (1983). *Financial Development in Korea 1945-1978.* Cambridge: Harvard University Press.

Dee, Philippa S. (1986). *Financial Markets and Economic Development. The Economics and Politics of Korean Financial Reform*, Kieler Studien 198, J. C. B. Mohn (Paul Siesbeck) Tubingen.

Dooley, Michael P. and Donald J. Mathieson (1987). "Financial Liberalization and Stability in Developing Countries." IMF Working Paper 87/19 (March).

Ensor, Paul (1985). "No Aid for Lame Ducks." *Far Eastern Economic Review* 28 (February), pp. 84-85.

Ensor, Paul (1987). "Redefining Korea Inc." *Far Eastern Economic Review* 4 (June), pp. 57-58.

Ensor, Paul (1987). "South Korea Government Orders Loan Repayments." *Far Eastern Economic Review* 4 (June), p.6.

Gurley, John G., Hugh T. Patrick, and Edward S. Shaw (1965). "The Financial Structure of Korea," United States Operations Mission to Korea (July).

IMF. *Financial Statistic Yearbook*, various issues.

Isenstein, Howard (1987). "Foreign Banks Tread Water in Korea," *Euromoney* (July), pp. 114, 118.

Ito, Kazuhis A. (1983). "Development Finance, Growth, and Economic Stability -- TheCases of Korea and Taiwan." In *Two Decades of Asian Development and Outlooks for the 1980s*, edited by T. Haseyama, A. Hirata, and T. Yangihara. Tokyo: Institute of Developing Economics, pp. 270-294.

Ito, Kazuhis A. (1984). "Development Finance and Commercial Banks in Korea." *The Developing Economies* 22, (4), pp. 453-475.

Kim, B.K. (1965). *Central Banking Experiment in a Developing Economy: Case Study of Korea*, The Korea Studies Series, 12. Seoul, Korea: The Korean Research Center.

Kim, Jin-Moon (1987). "A Burgeoning Necessary Evil." *Business Korea* (June).

Korea Herald (1987). "BOK Issues Bonds Worth 6.7 trillion won to Mop Up Liquidity." August 15, p. 6.

Korea Herald (1987). "BOK Extends W1,490 bil. in Policy Loans for Banks." (October 22), p. 6.

Korea Herald (1987). "Alien Banks Deviate from Government Guidelines on Lending." (October 25), p. 6.

Lee, Chong-Hwan (1987). "Korea's Experience with External Debt Management." *Monthly Review*, Korea Exchange Bank (March), pp. 3-29.

Lee, Duk-hoon (1984). "Recent Developments in Korea's Financial Sector." Economic Planning Agency, Tokyo, Discussion Papers #30 (March).

Manguno, Joseph P. and Hyung-Doo Kim (1986). "Seoul Backpedling on Promise to Ease Control Over Banks." *Asian Wall Street Journal* (December 22), pp. 1 and 19.

Manguno, Joseph P. and Hyung-Doo Kim (1986). "Korea Modifies its Banking Regulations." *Wall Street Journal* (December 30), p. 18.

McKinnon, Ronald I. (1973). *Money and Capital in Economic Development*. Washington, D.C.: Brookings Institute.

McKinnon, Ronald I. (1980). "Financial Policies." In *Policies for Industrial Progress in Developing Countries*, edited by J. Cody, H. Hughes, and D. Wall. London: Oxford Press, pp. 93-120.

Nakarmi, Laxmi (1987). "Revitalizing Korean Banks." *Euromoney* (July), pp. 111-114.

Park, Jae-Yoon (1982). *Monetary Policy and Economic Development in Korea*. Joint Research Program Study, No. 29. Institute of Developing Economies, Tokyo (March).

San Tong (1986). *Banking in Korea*. Seoul: San Tong & Co.

Suh, Sang-chul (1978). *Growth and Structural Change in the Korean Economy, 1910-1940*. Cambridge: Council on East Asian Studies, Harvard University.

Viksnins, George J. and Michael T. Skully (1987). "Asian Financial Development: A Comparative Perspective of Eight Countries." *Asian Survey* (May), pp. 535-551.

World Bank (1987). *Korea Managing the Industrial Transition*. Two volumes, Washington, D.C.

16

Monetary Policy in Taiwan, China

Robert F. Emery

The main purpose of this chapter is to examine how Taiwan, China, has used monetary policy to deal with the inflationary impact of the two oil shocks since 1973, and with the more recent problem of a very large rise in foreign exchange holdings. In the open economy of Taiwan, with its heavy reliance on export-led growth, this rise in foreign exchange holdings has sharply expanded the money supply and has created a major challenge to monetary policy's basic goal of maintaining price stability. This chapter describes the basic structure of the financial and foreign exchange systems, discusses recent regulatory changes, and encapsulates the major economic developments since the first oil shock. The central bank's arsenal of monetary instruments and their past uses are then examined, particularly with regard to the large foreign exchange inflow in recent years. Lastly, the central bank's monetary policy performance is assessed, with some suggestions made for additional research on certain topics.

THE STRUCTURE OF THE FINANCIAL SYSTEM

The financial system consists mainly of the central bank (which holds about 29 percent of the assets of all financial institutions), the commercial banks, the postal savings system, and the credit cooperatives. Together, these four groups hold about 88 percent of the assets of all financial institutions. Unlike other developing economies, the postal savings system is relatively important; its share of the assets of all financial institutions rose from less than 1 percent in 1961 to about 11 percent in April 1987.

The other types of financial institutions -- medium-term business banks, insurance, trust, and finance companies -- are very large, yet in early 1987 accounted for only 12 percent of the total assets of all financial institutions. The data in Table 1 provide a more precise indication of the relative importance, as measured by total assets, of the different types of financial institutions.

Of the four main groups, the commercial banks have the greatest amount of assets, accounting for 43 percent -- 40 percent for domestic banks

Table 1
Taiwan, China: Assets of Financial Institutions
(in billions of New Taiwan dollars; as of April 30, 1987)

	Assets	As a Percent of Total	Number of Units
Domestic commercial banks	2,840	40.1	16
Central bank	2,025	28.6	1
Postal savings system	795	11.2	1,157
Credit cooperative associations	362	5.2	74
Credit departments of farmers' associations	341	4.8	285
Medium-business banks	265	3.7	8
Local branches of foreign banks	174	2.5	32
Investment and trust companies	121	1.7	8
Life insurance companies	115	1.6	8
Property and casualty insurance companies	17	0.2	14
Bill finance companies	13	0.2	3
Offshore banking units	7	0.1	15
The Fuh-Wha Securities Finance Company	5	0.1	1
Total	7,080	100.0	1,622

Note: *The above data are not presented on a consolidated basis. To convert to US dollars, the exchange rate at the end of April 1987 was NT$33.02 per US dollar.*

Source: Financial Statistics Monthly. *Central Bank of China, Taipei, May 1987.*

and about 3 percent for foreign banks -- of total assets. The foreign banks have actually lost ground since the mid-1970s when their share was several percentage points higher.

Except for two small private banks (Overseas Chinese Commercial Banking Corporation and Shanghai Commercial and Saving Bank) and one small joint-venture bank, all of the domestic commercial banks are still owned and controlled by the government, which reflects the fact that the government took them over from Japanese ownership after the end of World War II. Unlike the Republic of Korea, Taiwan has made no effort to privatize these banks. All of the directors and the senior management of these banks are appointed by the government. This institutional arrangement undoubtedly enhances the authorities' ability to implement and achieve their monetary policy objectives. In September 1985, a system of deposit insurance was inaugurated, and by mid-1986, about 20 percent of New Taiwan (NT) dollar deposits were covered by the insurance.

Included in the 16 domestic banks are four specialized banks: a development bank, two agricultural banks, and an export-import bank. Despite their charters, most, if not all, of these operate like regular commercial banks. There are also eight medium-business banks, separate from the 16 domestic banks, that provide credits to small- and medium-sized enterprises, but they hold only about 4 percent of the assets of all financial institutions. Of these eight, all but the Medium Business Bank of Taiwan are private.

It is these medium-business banks and three of the specialized banks cited above (a development bank and two agricultural banks) that receive a relatively large portion of the funds deposited in the postal savings system, with the allocation decisions being made by the central bank. The allocation to these particular banks, where most of the funds are used to finance medium-term rather than short-term loans, has implications for the central bank's monetary policy.

Two major factors have contributed to the rapid 31 percent average annual rate of growth in the postal savings system's assets since the mid-1970s. One is the fact that with 1,157 post offices and 422 postal agencies as of April 1987, it is convenient for most residents to deposit in the system. The other factor is that the interest received by the depositors on their accounts is tax free.

The Ministry of Finance is responsible for the formulation of financial regulatory policies and for the licensing of financial institutions, while the central bank is responsible for the conduct of monetary and financial regulatory policies. Although the credit cooperatives are supervised by the Provincial Cooperative Bank, the central bank oversees most financial institutions.

While the open-money market has grown substantially since its establishment in 1976, the long-term capital market has not yet evolved into an important source of capital. Since firms prefer bank financing, and corporate bond issues typically require a bank guarantee, the corporate bond market is very small. At the end of April 1987, the total market value of stocks listed on the stock exchange was NT$975 billion, equivalent to 13.8 percent of the total asset value of financial institutions. Growth of the stock market has been hindered by public distrust of the accounting standards of most corporations and by the fact that most enterprises are family owned. For these and other reasons, government efforts to promote the development of the capital market have not been very successful.

The government has been more successful in its efforts to develop an open-money market, as opposed to the large, quasi-legal curb money market that has existed for decades, particularly the market in postdated checks.[1] In December 1975 the government issued a regulation authorizing the establishment of bills finance companies. Several companies were established in the following years and the market has grown rapidly, increasing from NT$977 million at the end of 1977 to NT$13.4 billion in April 1987. Commercial paper and bankers' acceptances are two of the main money market instruments of the bills finance companies. The development of the money market has increased the options for business finance and has also provided a market-determined money market rate. This has been helpful to the central bank in conducting its interest rate policy, since for many years the authorities have controlled bank deposit and loan rates with few guides to assist them in assessing the market forces affecting interest rates.

Beginning in July 1984, an offshore banking center started to operate in Taipei and by the end of 1986, the number of offshore banking units had increased to 15. The growth in their total assets was rapid in 1984-1985, and a peak of $7.1 billion was reached in February 1986. By April 1987 the total had declined to $6.7 billion. This leveling-off probably reflects in part the weakening position of the US dollar and the general decline in international loan syndications.

Thus, it is evident that the commercial banks play the major role in providing credit to Taiwan's economy, and, together with the postal savings system, enable the central bank to conduct its monetary policy actions.

FINANCIAL REGULATORY CHANGES

Beginning in February 1979, the foreign exchange system for the NT dollar was changed nominally from a fixed rate system to a more flexible, floating rate system. In actual practice, the authorities controlled the rate and did not introduce a true freely floating rate. The rate for the NT dollar has largely been tied to the US dollar with certain exceptions.

According to the government, the rate for the NT dollar is determined daily at the Foreign Exchange Center by a panel of general managers of the five authorized foreign exchange banks in accordance with the amount of US dollars bought and sold on the market during the previous day. But, in fact the central bank has intervened heavily in the foreign exchange market, buying large amounts of US dollars in an attempt to thwart appreciation of the NT dollar against the US dollar. Since September 1985, the NT dollar has been appreciating against the US dollar, its rate of appreciation being particularly rapid since the end of July 1986.

The two main areas of partial deregulation in the economy since the mid-1970s have been interest rates and the foreign exchange system. After a series of unsuccessful, if not regressive, steps begun in 1975 to liberalize interest rates,[2] the government in 1980 implemented four important actions aimed at a significant liberalization of the system. Briefly, these were: (1) authorization for a committee of the Bankers' Association to set, on a monthly basis, actual loan and deposit rates, although the central bank retained the power to set ceilings for both rates; (2) removal of restrictions on interest rates on banks' negotiable certificates of deposit (CDs) and debentures; (3) permission for credit cooperatives and banks to set freely their own bill discount rates; and, (4) exemption from restrictions on interest rates charged on foreign currency loans by foreign bank branches and on long-term letters of credit issued by domestic banks on the basis of foreign borrowing. In 1986, banks were allowed to enlarge the spread between maximum and minimum lending rates to four percentage points, and the central bank reduced the number of deposit ceiling rates from 13 to 4, giving banks a freer hand to set their own deposit rates and term structures.

However, since the major banks continued to be owned and controlled by the government, both the foreign exchange and interest rate liberalization measures during the 1980s simply involved the substitution of a banking cartel for the management of the central bank. Neither the foreign exchange nor the interest rate liberalization measures taken can be regarded as a fundamental shift in policy.

MAJOR ECONOMIC DEVELOPMENTS

During the postwar period, the economy has generally registered high rates of economic growth. From 1975 through 1986, the average annual increase in real gross national product (GNP) was 8.3 percent; in 1986 real GNP rose 11.6 percent (Table 2). During 1976-1978, after adjustment to the first oil shock of 1973-1974, the growth rate was particularly high, averaging 12-1/2 percent, but decreased to an annual rate of about 6 percent in 1979-1982 after the second oil shock of 1979-1980 and during the worldwide recession in the early 1980s.

Current account surpluses and other influences from abroad generated inflationary pressures in the early 1970s. The money stock increased annually at the relatively high rate of 29 percent during 1975-1978, but subsequently dropped to half that level (14 percent) during 1979-1985 in response to various monetary policy measures.[3] However, there was a very large jump of 51 percent in the money stock (M1B) in 1986,

Table 2
Domestic Economic Indicators

	Real GNP Growth (%)	Consumer Price Inflation (% Change)[a]	Domestic Credit Growth (%)	Money Velocity[b]	Budget Balance[c] (%)	Interest Rates: Rediscount Rate	Interest Rates: 1-year Saving[d]	Interest Rates: Loan Rate[e]
1970	11.3	3.6	18.2	6.4	0.9	9.25	9.72	12.60
1971	12.9	2.8	26.4	5.7	0.6	9.25	9.25	12.00
1972	13.3	3.0	19.2	5.1	0.8	8.50	8.75	11.25
1973	12.8	8.2	35.6	4.4	2.4	10.75	11.00	13.25
1974	1.1	47.5	51.2	5.3	3.3	12.00	13.50	14.75
1975	4.3	5.2	32.8	4.4	1.5	10.75	12.00	13.25
1976	13.5	2.5	17.1	4.2	1.3	9.50	10.75	12.00
1977	10.1	7.0	26.6	3.7	0.8	8.25	9.50	10.75
1978	13.9	5.8	26.1	3.2	1.0	8.25	9.50	10.75
1979	8.5	9.8	17.0	3.6	1.7	11.00	12.50	14.50
1980	7.1	19.0	29.1	3.6	-0.6	11.00	12.50	16.20
1981	5.7	16.3	20.4	3.8	-0.3	11.75	13.00	15.25
1982	3.3	3.0	20.0	3.6	-1.0	7.75	9.00	10.75
1983	7.9	1.4	14.9	3.3	-1.1	7.25	8.50	10.25
1984	10.5	-0.0	11.9	3.4	0.1	6.75	8.00	10.00
1985	5.1	-0.2	7.9	3.5	0.2	5.25	6.25	9.50
1986	11.6	0.7	3.3	3.0	0.5	4.50	6.25	9.00

(a) *Yearly average.*

(b) *From 1982, ratio of nominal GNP to monthly average for year of M_{1B}. For earlier years, ratio of nominal GNP to M_1.*

(c) *Ratio to GNP. Fiscal year ends June 30.*

(d) *End of year.*

(e) *Maximum rate on short-term loans. Secured loans for 1970-1979.*

Sources: Annual Report, Central Bank of China, Taipei, Taiwan; Financial Statistics Monthly, Central Bank of China; Financial Statistics, Central Bank of China; Taiwan Statistical Data Book, Council for Economic Planning and Development, Taipei; and Statistical Yearbook, Directorate-General of Budget, Accounting and Statistics, Taipei.

primarily because of large gains in foreign exchange and the shifts in portfolios toward liquid assets to take advantage of the fact that interest rates on transactions accounts did not decline as much as those on longer-term deposit accounts.

Although the annual rate of domestic credit expansion was also high in the late 1970s (21 percent), it has decelerated significantly since 1980 and in 1986 increased only 3 percent. This sharp contrast with the 51 percent increase in the money stock in 1986 reflects the crucial role played by the large increase in foreign exchange holdings stemming from the large current account surplus. Government budget operations have generally not been an expansionary factor in the economy for several decades. There were slight deficits in fiscal 1979-1980 and fiscal 1980-1981 (the fiscal year ends June 30), but even the larger deficits in fiscal 1981-1982 and fiscal 1982-1983 were only equivalent to about 1 percent of GNP. Since fiscal 1982-1983, the budget balance has generally registered a small surplus.

Except for the sharp jump in consumer prices in 1974, Taiwan's inflation rate was relatively low in the 1970s. With the second oil shock, prices again rose rapidly (10 to 19 percent annually in 1979-1981), but since then have been very stable and low (1.1 percent annual average increase in 1982-1985 and a 0.7 percent increase in 1986). July 1987 consumer prices were 1 percent higher than a year earlier. However, this price stability has been strongly threatened by the huge increase in the money supply since late 1985. It remains to be seen whether the authorities can continue to avoid serious inflation, particularly if some of the forces restraining inflation should reverse or become neutral.

Real earnings of employees in manufacturing have increased substantially since the early 1970s, partly reflecting the substantial gains in labor productivity and the success of monetary policy in generally keeping the inflation rate low. Deflating the average annual nominal earnings of manufacturing employees by the consumer price index, real earnings increased at an average annual rate of 7-1/2 percent during 1976-1986. In 1986 real earnings increased 9 percent.

Interest rates during the postwar period have generally reflected changes in prices and other basic developments, but usually with a lag and only on a partial basis (Table 2). The central bank discount rate, for example, which was 11-3/4 percent in 1981 during a period of high inflation (16 percent), declined to 4-1/2 percent by May 1987. Bank loan and deposit rates are still controlled and do not yet fully reflect basic free market conditions.

In the external sector, trade surplus and capital inflows have been important influences over the years on domestic financial markets, particularly the money supply. In 1972-1973 and again in 1977-1978, large trade surpluses expanded the money supply sharply, one important result being a 50 percent increase in the money supply in 1973 and a 47 percent rise in consumer prices in 1974. In 1978, the main factors expanding bank credit and the money supply were the large trade surplus and the inflow of capital. Since 1982 the rapid growth in exports has led to increasingly large current account surpluses (Table 3). By 1986, exports -- at a level of about US$40 billion -- were approximately double their 1980 level. This represented a compound average annual rate of growth in nominal terms of 12 percent. Most of the export gains in the 1980s have reflected an increase in the export of relatively sophisticated manufactured goods such as apparel, machine tools, chemicals, and electronics. Approximately half of the exports have gone to the United States; other major purchasers have been Japan, Hong Kong, and the European Community.

Table 3
International Economic Indicators
(in billions of U.S. dollars, unless indicated otherwise)

	Balance of Payments							
	Exports	Imports	Trade Balance	Current Account	Overall Balance	Exchange Rate:[a] NT$/US$	Reserves[b]	Public External Debt[a]
1977	9.5	-8.4	1.1	0.9	-1.1	38.00	1.3	2.6
1978	12.6	-10.4	2.2	1.6	-2.0	36.00	1.4	2.9
1979	15.8	-14.5	1.3	0.2	0.0	36.10	1.5	3.1
1980	19.6	-19.5	0.1	-0.9	0.1	36.01	2.2	4.1
1981	22.4	-20.6	1.8	0.5	-1.3	37.84	7.2	4.8
1982	21.8	-18.1	3.6	2.2	-2.6	39.91	8.5	5.7
1983	25.0	-18.8	6.3	4.4	-4.9	40.27	11.9	6.3
1984	30.2	-21.0	9.2	7.0	-5.9	39.47	15.7	5.5
1985	30.5	-19.3	11.2	9.2	-9.4	39.85	22.6	4.8
1986	39.5	-22.6	16.9	16.2	-16.6	35.50	46.3	3.4

(a) *End of year.*

(b) *Excluding gold; end of year.*

Note: *Data may not total due to rounding.*

Sources: *Financial Statistics Monthly, Central Bank of China; Financial Statistics, Central Bank of China; Taiwan Statistical Data Book, Council for Economic Planning and Development, Taipei; and Statistical Yearbook, Directorate-General of Budget, Accounting and Statistics, Executive Yuan, Taipei.*

Imports remained remarkably stable from 1980 through 1985, fluctuating within $1-1/2 billion of the $19-1/2 billion level each year. Part of this stability reflected a decline in oil prices after the second oil shock; nevertheless, it is somewhat surprising that imports did not increase more during this period, given the relatively good rate of economic growth. Undoubtedly, high tariffs and various nontariff barriers played a role in restraining imports. In 1986, however, imports rose 17 percent to $22.6 billion and are likely to continue rising in view of the rapid appreciation of the New Taiwan dollar since August 1986. Most imports come from Japan (28 percent), the United States (25 percent), and the oil-exporting countries.

Rapid growth in exports in the 1980s, coupled with stable imports, resulted in a steady and large increase in the trade surplus. From a trade balance averaging only $1.4 billion annually in 1978-1981, the balance grew steadily in 1982-1986, reaching $16.9 billion in 1986; a further increase is likely. The deficit on services has fluctuated between roughly $0.5 and $2 billion annually since the late 1970s, but is likely to decline in the future as a result of substantial earnings from large official holdings of foreign exchange.

As a result of these developments, large and rising current account surpluses began to appear starting in 1982. Between 1982 and 1986, the annual current account surplus increased from $2.2 billion to $16.2 billion, or by approximately $3 billion per year. Reflecting these surpluses, net inflows in the long-term capital account, which were as large as $0.9 billion in 1981, changed to net outflows, reaching $0.8 billion in 1985 and $1.4 billion in 1986. The bulk of these net outflows mainly reflected an excess of official loan repayments over official loans received.

Official holdings of foreign exchange, excluding gold, were only $2.2 billion at the end of 1980, but since then have increased greatly, more than doubling from $22.6 billion at the beginning of 1986 to $46.3 billion by the end of the year. These holdings were second in size in the world after the Republic of Germany at the end of 1986. By July 1987, reserves excluding gold had increased further to $61.0 billion. Gold holdings at the end of 1986 were $1.3 billion (on the basis of official valuation), but $2.2 billion when valued at the London free market price of gold.

Total gross external debt is low relative to international trade. At the end of 1986, the government reported a public external debt of $3.2 billion, with debt service payments equivalent to 4.6 percent of exports of goods and services. Adding private external debt, total gross external debt was roughly $8 billion at the end of 1986. On a net basis, Taiwan, China is a large net foreign creditor, the estimated amount at the end of 1986 being roughly $37 billion.

From 1973 through November 1986, the exchange rate for the NT dollar against the US dollar fluctuated between about 36 and 40 NT dollars per US dollar. But this has changed. As recently as the third quarter of

1985 the average rate was NT$40.3 per US dollar, close to the lowest value of the New Taiwan dollar in decades. The NT dollar has generally appreciated against the US dollar since then, with a particularly rapid appreciation occurring from August 1986 after the United States government began to exert some pressure on the authorities to let the rate appreciate, in view of the large current account surpluses, the rapid rise in the level of foreign exchange reserves, and, especially, the large bilateral trade surpluses with the United States.

To understand better what lies behind Taiwan's large trade surpluses, it is helpful to examine changes in the terms and volume of trade. Rising import prices resulting from the second oil shock in the late 1970s tended to worsen the terms of trade through 1981. But since then, terms of trade have improved as import prices decreased while export prices stabilized or decreased more slowly than import prices. The large increases in the value of exports in recent years have mainly stemmed from gains in export volume, not from a rise in export prices. Import volume, on the other hand, generally declined in 1981-1985, but then increased sharply by 31-1/2 percent in 1986. The problems that these balance-of-payments developments have created for monetary policy are explored next.

MONETARY POLICY INSTRUMENTS

Because of a government policy to avoid large budget deficits or surpluses (Table 2), fiscal policy has not been used to any significant extent as a dynamic instrument for economic stabilization in Taiwan. As a result, most of the burden for economic stabilization has fallen on monetary policy. The power to formulate monetary policy rests with the governor of the central bank. Although the governor is able to take monetary policy actions without consulting the Ministry of Finance, major policy changes are subject to approval by the cabinet.

During the past two decades, the central bank's main instruments for pursuing its monetary policy objectives have been interest rates, open-market operations, and, occasionally, reserve requirements. Of these, changes in reserve requirements have been the least important. Over the 14-year period preceding 1974, commercial bank reserve requirements were changed only four times for demand deposits and five times for time deposits. In addition, the permissible range for reserve requirements (10 to 15 percent) was too narrow through mid-1975 to be an effective tool.

The reserve requirement system was revised substantially in 1975, following a revision of the general banking law. Basically, the system was simplified by unifying the required reserve ratios for all financial institutions and by differentiating the requirement only according to the type and maturity of deposit. The minimum and maximum range was also changed from 10-15 percent to 15-40 percent, thereby giving the central bank more flexibility in setting reserve requirements.

Nevertheless, even after the reform, reserve requirements have not been used by the central bank as a major monetary policy instrument. Reserve requirements have been changed only by moderate amounts four times since mid-1975 (excluding the imposition of a 7 percent requirement against CDs and foreign currency deposits on July 11, 1986). Since May 1979, reserve requirements have generally been reduced, with the reserve requirement for checking accounts, for example, being cut from 30 percent to 23 percent by June 1982. The central bank has apparently been reluctant to raise the reserve requirements to a level near the maximum allowed by law, for fear that it might act as a drag on economic growth. In addition, although the central bank has the power to impose marginal reserve requirements, it has so far not utilized this power. In short, while manipulation of the reserve requirement has been useful at times, it has not been in the forefront of the central bank's efforts to restrain inflation.

On the other hand, open-market operations, which were little used through 1983, have since become quite important and currently appear to constitute the central bank's main monetary weapon. Prior to 1979, the central bank made some limited use of open-market operations.[4] Its regular use of open-market operations began in January 1979. However, during 1979-1983 the amount of central bank credit accommodation far over-shadowed the total amount of commercial paper, Treasury bills, and bankers' acceptances purchased by the central bank. In 1983, for example, central bank credits were NT$122 billion, and open-market purchases were only NT$18 billion. Even as recently as 1984 central bank credit accommodation totaled NT$185 billion, significantly more than the central bank's open-market purchases which totaled NT$129 billion.

But in 1985, with a large inflow of foreign exchange swelling bank reserves, the central bank "... actively undertook open-market operations by auctioning certificates of deposit to banks, accepting deposits from the postal savings system, and issuing savings bonds to the public."[5] It issued NT$9 billion of its own Class B Treasury bills in 1984. The amount of issue increased by NT$51 billion in 1985, but by only NT$3 billion in 1986. The post-1985 deceleration reflects the fact that the central bank's annual issue is subject to a ceiling equal to 20 percent of the central government's total fiscal year expenditures. Beginning in October 1985, central bank issues were supplemented by sales of the central bank's own CDs. These increased by NT$27 billion in 1985 and by NT$372 billion in 1986. Sales were further supplemented by the central bank's sale of its own savings bonds beginning in December 1985; the outstanding amount rose from NT$4 billion at the end of 1985 to NT$67 billion at the end of 1986.

Thus, these three central bank obligations increased from NT$108 billion at the end of 1985 to NT$543 billion at the end of 1986. Including the deposits transferred from the postal savings system and banks, the central bank's total liabilities to the public rose from NT$389 billion at the end of 1985 to NT$1,091 billion a year later. In contrast, its lending to domestic banks declined by NT$65 billion in 1985 and by NT$35 billion in 1986, with the total amount outstanding at the end of 1986 only $54 billion.

The CDs have been offered at relatively attractive interest rates and in several maturities. On March 24, 1987, for example, yields ranged from 4.07 to 5.12 percent, and maturities included six months, one year, and two years. By comparison, the yield on one-year and two-year time savings deposits at commercial banks was 4.75 percent.

Although it is not clear how long the central bank can continue to absorb large amounts of liquidity by issuing bills and accepting postal savings deposits, so far it has been successful in restraining inflation. Since foreign exchange inflow has been the main expansionary factor, the measures taken by the central bank appear to have been appropriate, since curtailment of central bank credits to banks would have had little impact.

Until approximately 1985, interest rate regulation was the main monetary policy instrument used by the central bank. Since the central bank's reactivation in 1961, it has fixed not only the various discount rates that it charges on credits to banks, but has also prescribed the upper limit for bank deposit rates. In addition, it approves the range of interest rates on bank loans proposed by the Bankers' Association.

During the 1970s and early 1980s, the central bank made fairly frequent changes in the discount rate (Table 2). The principal instrument for discounting was eligible bills at the central bank, rather than temporary advances and secured loan refinancing. At the end of April 1987, the central bank had six different accommodation rates: 4.5 percent for bill rediscounts, 5.5 percent for secured loans, 9 percent for temporary accommodations, 6.75 percent for important financing in foreign exchange, 7.5 percent for accommodations in foreign currencies, and 4.5 for export financing. Since the mid-1970s this last rate has generally been the lowest discount rate; being lower than many bank deposit rates, it constitutes a subsidy to exporters. However, since November 1984 the export financing rate has been the same as the basic rediscount rate. Hence, in effect, there have been five -- not six -- discount rates. Unless there are convincing arguments for continuing such a system, it would appear appropriate to reduce the number to two: a basic rate and a penalty rate.

The central bank's basic philosophy since 1961 has been to reduce gradually the interest rate in order to bring it closer to the interest rate levels in industrial countries and to narrow the spread between loan and deposit rates. However, there have been three times since 1961 when the central bank has had to reverse direction and move rates up in order to restrain inflation. This occurred in a mild way in 1968, and more vigorously in 1973 and 1979 in response to the first and second oil shocks, respectively. In January 1974, the central bank rediscount rate was raised to 14 percent from a low of 8-1/2 percent in July 1972, but by that time much of the severe inflation had already occurred. Similarly, the rate also was raised to a high of 13.25 percent in June 1981 from a low of 8-1/4 percent in May 1979 following the 1979-1980 oil shock. But, again this was too late to prevent a substantial increase in prices in 1980 and 1981. In retrospect, it took too long to get the rate up to a truly restrictive level. Clearly, the rediscount rate should have been adjusted more quickly and with greater flexibility. In the future, it would appear advisable for the central bank not to resist moving the rate to a punitive level when the circumstances warrant such action.

Since October 1981, the central bank has steadily lowered all of its accommodation rates. By October 1986, the main rediscount rate had fallen from a peak of 13.25 percent in October 1981 to 4.5 percent in mid-October 1986. Being an open economy, much of this reflected general worldwide deflation and a decline in interest rates after the second oil shock. But the central bank also cut the rate three times in 1985 in an effort to foster economic growth.[6] As things now stand, interest rate policy is not being used actively to deal with the large increase in liquidity that has occurred since 1985, nor would it really be an appropriate instrument. Rather, the main focus now is on open-market operations, particularly the sale of central bank CDs.

CENTRAL BANK'S RESPONSE TO THE LARGE FOREIGN EXCHANGE INFLOW

An important aspect of the central bank's financial structure is that foreign assets constitute a very high proportion of its total assets. In April 1987, net foreign assets accounted for 96 percent of all central bank assets. The proportion was lower in earlier years, not exceeding 42 percent in 1976 and 83 percent in 1984, for example. This trend largely reflects three factors: the absence of much government debt; the relatively small amount of credit accommodation extended to financial institutions; and the rising yearly surpluses on current account in the balance of payments.

To assist it in determining monetary policy, the central bank utilizes three measures of the money supply: M1A, M1B, and M2. Of these, M1B -- which includes currency outside monetary institutions, checking accounts, passbook deposits, and passbook savings deposits -- appears to be the one most frequently used by the central bank in assessing the impact of monetary expansion. M1A is M1B minus passbook savings deposits, and M2 is M1B plus quasi-money. Central bank experience with all three indicators has shown that MlB is the most helpful indicator for purposes of monetary analysis. However, the central bank utilizes all three measures in determining monetary policy.

From 1979 through 1985, M1B did not expand at a particularly rapid rate, given the nature of the economy and its development. During this period the average annual increase in M1B was 14 percent; the income velocity of money has generally slowed since 1981 (Table 2). Various factors have contributed to this decline; especially important has been the low rate of inflation since 1982 which has contributed to the rise of money holdings by firms and individuals.

However, the large foreign trade surpluses of recent years have led to spurts of monetary expansion, resulting in a 51 percent M1B growth in 1986, far above the average annual increase of earlier years. As shown in Table 4, the two main expansionary factors have been the increase in the economy's net foreign assets and in claims on private enterprises, only partly offset by the rise in quasi-money (a contractionary factor). The other contractionary factors have been quantitatively unimportant in recent years. The increase in net foreign assets accounted for 72 percent of the expansion of M1B in 1985 and for 84 percent in 1986. It is also interesting to note that whereas foreign assets held by the central bank accounted for 42 percent of its total assets in 1976, by April 1987 the proportion had increased to 96 percent. This reflects not only the large foreign exchange gains but also an 80 percent decline since 1980 in the bank's other main asset item: claims on domestic banks.

As noted earlier, the authorities in 1986 were able to avoid a substantial increase in the rate of inflation, despite the 51 percent increase in the money supply in 1986. The very large increase in central bank CDs, plus the sale of central bank savings bonds, and the acceptance of deposits from the postal savings system accomplished much of the job of neutralizing the potentially inflationary impact of the large rise in the foreign exchange reserves. However, two other factors have also helped to offset somewhat the expansionary forces in the economy. These are the rise in the national savings rate and the continuing decline in the income velocity of money. The upward shift in the savings function, reflecting a downward shift in the consumption function , represents a basically contractionary

Table 4
Analysis of Changes in Money Supply (M1B)
(In billions of NT dollars)

		Expansionary Factors				Contractionary Factors		
	Increase in M1B	Net Foreign Assets	Claims on Private Enter-prises	Claims on Govt. Enter-prises	Claims on Govt.	Quasi-money	Govt. Deposits	Other Items (net)
1970	5	5	12	3	1	-13	-3	2
1971	11	10	18	4	-2	-16	1	-4
1972	15	25	12	2	0	-23	6	-7
1973	31	21	57	4	3	-16	-21	-17
1974	10	-22	62	19	5	-41	-4	-9
1975	29	-7	70	19	1	-42	-9	-3
1976	33	36	44	11	7	-52	-9	-3
1977	55	41	82	14	0	-77	0	-6
1978	81	84	123	15	7	-88	-32	-29
1979	23	-6	101	34	3	-45	-34	-29
1980	73	-18	151	68	1	-98	5	-35
1981	55	44	116	44	13	-123	19	-57
1982	66	100	154	44	28	-209	-0	-44
1983	95	198	224	-4	6	-276	-24	-29
1984	57	236	211	0	-12	-300	-21	-57
1985	82	375	118	-8	9	-417	-14	18
1986	386	626	107	-2	8	-278	-40	-35

Note: *Due to change in series, pre-1976 data are not strictly comparable with 1976-1986 data.*
Source: *Financial Statistics Monthly, Central Bank of China, Taipei.*

development. From the late 1970s through 1985, gross national savings as a proportion of GNP did not change very much. In 1986, however, it rose by four percentage points to 37-1/2 percent. This substantial increase has helped to offset some of the expansionary forces in the economy.

In addition, there has been a general downtrend in the income velocity of money (GNP/M1B) since 1974, with M1B rising at a faster rate than nominal GNP. From a level of 5.3 in 1974, the ratio declined fairly steadily to 3.4 in 1984. By 1986, it had declined further to 3.0. Part of the explanation for the recent decline has been the drop in interest rates and the generally stable level of consumer prices through the spring of 1987. With lower interest rates and stable prices, firms and individuals have been willing to hold larger money balances since there is less of a loss of purchasing power. The decline in velocity means a smaller expansionary impact from money growth.

Finally, since the autumn of 1985 the New Taiwan dollar has appreciated against the US dollar. This has helped to hold down the rise in prices, particularly since almost half of the economy's imports come from the United States. In addition, the economy has experienced a decline in unit labor costs, as well as a post-1981 drop in the prices of oil and other commodity imports, along with some reductions in import duties.

The government has also taken a number of measures recently to restrain the steady rise in international reserves, by greatly liberalizing foreign exchange transactions. On July 15, 1987, the central bank lifted controls on trade-related transactions on current account and, for the first time in the postwar period, allowed residents to freely hold and use foreign currencies. For capital account transactions, no permission is required for individuals and companies to export capital of $1 million or less per transaction, with an annual limit of $5 million. Capital inflows are limited to $50,000 per year per account, with inward direct foreign investments still subject to approval. The new regulations mark a radical departure from the earlier regime under which people could only legally remit $5,000 per year abroad, and all foreign exchange receipts had to be sold to the central bank for local currency, with the exception of authorized foreign currency deposits. The government hopes that the new regulations will lead to a rise in capital outflows, which will ease pressure on the money supply.

ASSESSMENT OF THE MONETARY POLICY PERFORMANCE

The key monetary issue has been how to deal with the rapid buildup of foreign exchange, which has caused a sharp rise in the money supply, thus posing a serious inflationary threat. In the two earlier inflationary episodes stemming from oil shocks (1973-1974 and 1979-1980), monetary policy relied heavily on interest rate policy. However, in both cases the central bank's actions were too late and too tentative to prevent serious inflation.[7]

It seems clear that these two earlier episodes involved primarily *cost-push inflation*. The large rise in oil prices during the two oil shocks lay behind much of the increase in costs and prices in 1974 and 1980. On the other hand, the current problem is primarily one of excess liquidity, creating the strong possibility of a serious *demand-pull inflation.* Oil and other commodity prices have either declined or stayed weak since 1982. Interest rate policy would be a much less appropriate instrument for dealing with the problem of excess liquidity. Open-market operations are better suited for neutralizing the large gains in liquidity stemming from the rise in net foreign assets. In this regard, the authorities are to be commended for developing vehicles -- such as the central bank's certificates of deposit -- to mop up the large rise in liquidity.

Government authorities have been aided in their fight against inflation by the recent rise in the savings rate and the decline in the income velocity of money. However, the key factor currently is the large issue of central bank CDs. Excess reserves of the deposit money banks have not been large since the spring of 1986, being equal to only about 2 percent of total reserves. In addition, the deposit money banks expanded their loans and discounts by only 5-1/2 percent in 1986. But their holdings of "securities issued by financial institutions," including those of the central bank, did rise greatly: from NT$122 billion at the end of 1985 to NT$498 billion at the end of 1986 and to NT$737 billion in April 1987, reflecting the large issue of central bank CDs.

In summary, the central bank has been successful in restraining inflation through a massive sterilization operation. Consumer prices in July 1987 were only 1 percent higher than in the same period a year earlier. While the avoidance of inflation is commendable, the question remains as to what is the best way to use the existing resources. Is a large buildup of foreign exchange in the economy's best interests? Certainly more of the foreign exchange could be used to improve living standards in various ways, such as improved housing, transportation, communication, and environment. With the depreciation of the US dollar in world financial markets since February 1985, the central bank and other local financial institutions have experienced sizeable losses. Clearly, it would be inappropriate for the current rate of increase in foreign exchange reserves to continue indefinitely, even if this were possible. There is an urgent need for the authorities to take strong basic measures to restore a sustainable equilibrium between the external and domestic sectors. In this regard, the exchange-liberalization measures announced on July 15, 1987, are an important step forward in achieving a better balance between the current and capital accounts, as well as a better allocation of domestic savings. However, there is still room for a further reduction of import tariffs and various nontariff barriers. In addition, it is also very important that the exchange rate for the new Taiwan dollar be allowed to move to a free market level that does not undervalue or overvalue the currency vis-à-vis the currencies of *all* trading partners.

Possible topics for future research include a more intensive examination of the circumstances that determine whether open-market operations or interest rate policies are more appropriate in dealing with inflationary pressures. It would also be helpful to explore, on the basis of hindsight, which of the three monetary aggregates, M1A, M1B, and M2, is the most useful to the authorities in their pursuit of an appropriate monetary policy.

NOTES

1. For details on the curb market, see Cheng (1986, p. 149).
2. For details on the measures taken in the 1970s, see Cheng (1986, pp. 153-54).
3. These data are based on M1B money stock which is the sum of currency issued, checking accounts, passbook deposits, and passbook savings deposits.
4. In August 1972, the central bank sold central bank time certificates of deposit to reduce commercial bank reserves, following a rapid rise in net foreign assets. In April 1973, the central bank for the first time issued its own Class B, 91-day Treasury bills to banks and the general public. During 1977-1978, the central bank again sold its own CDs in order to reduce excess reserves. In a move to broaden the money market, the central bank in November 1983 began to issue Treasury bills on a noncompetitive basis for small investors.
5. See the Foreward, Central Bank of China's *Annual Report* for 1985.
6. Central Bank of China, *Annual Report*: 1985, p. 35.
7. For a more detailed discussion of this subject, see Emery (1984).

REFERENCES

The Central Bank of China. *Annual Report: 1986* (1987a).

The Central Bank of China (Taiwan, China) (1987b). *Financial Statistics Monthly* (May).

The Central Bank of China (Taiwan, China) (1987c). *Balance of Payments* (June).

The Central Bank of China (Taiwan, China) (1987d). *Financial Statistics* (June).

Cheng, Hang-Sheng (1978). "Alternative Balance-of-Payments Adjustment Experiences: Korea and Taiwan, 1973-77." *Economic Review*, Federal Reserve Bank of San Francisco (Summer).

Cheng, Hang-Sheng (1986). "Financial Policy and Reform in Taiwan, China." In *Financial Policy and Reform in Pacific Basin Counties*, edited by H.S. Cheng. Lexington, Mass.: Lexington Books.

Directorate-General of Budget, Accounting and Statistics, Executive Yuan (1987). Taipei: *Monthly Statistics* (March).

Emery, Robert F. (1984). "Postwar Financial Policies in Taiwan, China." *International Finance Discussion Papers*, No. 252. Board of Governors of the Federal Reserve System (December).

International Commercial Bank of China (1980). "Open Market Operations in the Republic of China." *Monthly Economic Survey* (December).

Khatkhate, Deena R. (1977). "Evolving Open Market Operations in a Developing Economy: The Taiwan Experience." In *Finance in Developing Counties*, edited by P.C.I. Ayre. London: Frank Cass and Company, Ltd.

Kuo, Shirley W. Y. (1983). *The Taiwan Economy in Transition.* Boulder, Colo.: Westview Press.

Liang, Fa-Chin (1982). *Monetary Policy in a Small Open Economy: An Econometric Study of Taiwan.* Ph.D. dissertation, Washington University.

Liang, Kuo-Shu (1986). "Financial Reforms Recommended by the Economic Reform Committee, Republic of China." *Industry of Free China* (March).

Liu, Fu-Chi (1970). "Taiwan's Experience of Transition from Inflation to Stability." In *Studies in Monetary Development of Taiwan.* Taipei: Institute of Economics, Academia Sinica.

Lundberg, Erik (1979). "Fiscal and Monetary Policies." In *Economic Growth and Structural Change in Taiwan*, edited by W. Galenson. Ithaca, N.Y.: Cornell University Press.

Perng, Fai-Nan and Yung-San Lee (1986). "Financial Liberalization in Taiwan, ROC." Taipei: Presented by the ROC Delegation at the Tenth Joint Conference of the USA-ROC and ROC-USA Economic Councils, Changhwa Commercial Bank (December).

Tsiang, S.C. (1981) "Monetary Policy of Taiwan." In *Conference on Experience and Lessons of Economic Development in Taiwan.* Taipei: Institute of Economics, Academia Sinica.

Wu, Yuan-Li (1985). *Becoming an Industrialized Nation: ROC's Development on Taiwan.* New York: Praeger.

17

Monetary Policy and Inflation in China

Hang-Sheng Cheng

Future historians are likely to view China's economic reform since 1978 as one of the most notable world economic developments in the last quarter of the twentieth century. In an attempt to modernize the economy, the nation of more than one billion population has tried to extricate itself from an excessively rigid planning system that had suffocated productive incentives and retarded technological progress over the previous 25 years. To date, sufficient progress has been made to suggest that, if the momentum of reform is sustained, China may well become before the end of this century another newly industrial country -- except that, given the size of the economy, the significance of its rise would undoubtedly overshadow that of all the existing newly industrial countries put together.

In the last three years, however, serious difficulties have been encountered to cast doubt on the future of China's economic reform. Since midyear 1984, as enterprises were freed from tight controls to make their own management decisions, a nationwide spending spree has fed to inflationary pressures that threaten the nation's economic and social stability. Since, in China as elsewhere, inflation is essentially a monetary phenomenon, the development of an effective market-oriented monetary policy for assuring noninflationary stable economic growth has become a topmost policy concern.

Monetary policy cannot be separated from the institutional framework in which it is conducted. In China's case, since the role of money and of monetary policy has differed significantly from that in market economies, discussion of the economic setting, both prior to and after the reform, needs to be more extensive than in other cases.

This chapter is structured as follows. It begins with an analysis of the role of money and monetary policy in the economic-planning framework prior to 1979, followed by a sketch of the economic and financial reform that has taken place since the launching of the reform in December 1978. After an overview of the relationship between money and prices from 1952 to 1987 and a survey of recent econometric studies on the subject, monetary developments from 1980 to 1987 are highlighted, for which fairly detailed data are now available, in order to explore the sources of monetary growth during the period -- with special emphasis on the unusually rapid and volatile monetary growth during the last three years. Monetary policy measures that have been taken in the last three years for economic stabilization under economic reform are then reviewed. Finally, the chapter concludes with a brief assessment of these policy measures and suggests the conditions for successful development of a market-oriented monetary policy.

MONEY AND ECONOMIC PLANNING PRIOR TO 1979

Prior to the founding of the People's Republic of China in 1949, China was essentially a private enterprise economy. Aside from infrastructure facilities -- such as railroads, harbors, schools, hospitals, and public utilities -- nearly all means of production were privately owned.

The socialist revolution changed all this. In seven years, all the farms, factories, shops, and banks became either state-owned (i.e., belonging to "all people") or collectives (i.e., owned collectively by members). In either form, all enterprises turned in their profits to the state treasury and were fully compensated by the state for their losses.[1] All economic activities were, at least in theory, conducted in accordance with state plans and under state supervision.

Economic planning in China followed closely the Soviet model. Parallel to an economic plan, which was stated in terms of physical inputs and outputs, was a financial plan stated in money flows. The financial plan consisted of the government budget, the credit plan, and the cash plan. The budget specified the government's receipts and expenditures, the credit plan, the expected sources and uses of banking funds, and the cash plan, the planned changes in currency in circulation.

Within this planning framework, a clear distinction was drawn between cities and rural areas. Urban enterprises were tightly controlled by their respective overseeing bureaus and ministries at the county, municipal, provincial, or national level, on such management decisions as personnel appointment, wages, production, purchasing, and marketing. In contrast, rural communes were largely left to themselves in managing their economic activities, so long as their production quotas were met.

Another distinction between urban enterprises and rural communes has to do with the nation's payments system. Urban enterprises were joined with government agencies to constitute one group within which all payments were effected through their "transfer-balance" accounts in the banks. Rural communes, in contrast, were placed together with households such that payments within this second group as well as between the two groups were all conducted in currency.

The significance of this distinction is that currency was the only means of payment that was freely transferable in pre-reform China. Individual households could hold savings and time deposits in banks, but not checkable deposits. The "transfer balances" of government agencies and enterprises were transferable only with explicit approval of the banks. Before giving approval, the banks in each case had to ensure that the transaction had received prior authorization by proper authorities in accordance with the economic plan. Hence, prior to 1979, only currency in circulation was considered by the authorities as money, and monetary policy consisted primarily of regulating the amount of currency in circulation.

Nominally, regulating currency in circulation was the responsibility of the People's Bank of China, which during most of the period was the nation's banking system itself. An exact copy of the Soviet "mono-bank" model, the system called for a single bank to carry out all the nation's banking functions. At times, for operational efficiency, the mono-bank was supplemented by a few "specialized banks," closely directed and supervised by the mono-bank, in effect no more than operating extensions of the People's Bank. At various times prior to 1979, such specialized banks included the Bank of China for international banking transactions and the Agriculture Bank for banking needs of the rural area. A third bank, the Construction Bank, under the Ministry of Finance, was not a bank at all, its sole function being that of disbursing agent of the Ministry of Finance for capital construction projects.

It might appear that, since the People's Bank of China was in effect the nation's banking system, regulating the nation's currency supply would be simply a matter of managing the People's Bank's own balance sheet. It can be shown that during any period, the increase in the nation's currency in circulation must always be equal to the banking system's net lendings (i.e., gross lendings minus increases in deposits) to the government and enterprises, plus the net increase in the banking system's foreign asset holdings, and minus the increase in household bank deposits:

$$\Delta CU = \Delta(L_G - D_G) + \Delta(L_E - D_E) + \Delta FA - \Delta D_H \tag{1}$$

where CU, L_G, D_G, L_E, D_E, FA, and D_H are currency circulation, bank lending to the government, the government's bank deposits, bank lending to enterprises, enterprise bank deposits, foreign assets, and household bank deposits, respectively; Δ denotes increases.

In fact, however, the People's Bank's ability to manage its own balance sheet was limited. Note that $\Delta(L_G - D_G)$ on the right-hand side of equation (1) represents banks' net lending to the government, which in China's setting was equal to the budget deficit; the second term, $\Delta(L_E - D_E)$, represents banks' net lending to enterprises, which was determined through the credit plan set by the planning authorities; ΔFA, change in foreign assets, was the net outcome of the nation's foreign trade and net foreign borrowing activities, which were also largely out of the People's Bank's control.

Thus, the sum of the changes in currency circulation and household bank deposits, $(\Delta CU + \Delta D_H)$, was endogenously determined by decisions made by authorities elsewhere in the planning system. Within that sum, the People's Bank could in principle attempt to affect the level of household deposits by adjusting deposit interest rates. However, even that was out of its control, as interest rates were set not by the People's Bank but by the State Council, the nation's highest executive organ. Moreover, interest rates were in fact held fixed, seldom used as a policy instrument for adjusting currency circulation, during the 25 years prior to 1979.

That the People's Bank had little control over the nation's currency circulation can be seen from yet another perspective. Parallel to equation (1) is another relation that shows changes in currency circulation to be determined by factors largely outside the People's Bank's control:

$$\Delta CU = (W + A) - C - \Delta(D_H + B_H), \tag{2}$$

which states that during any period the increase in currency circulation (ΔCU) must always be equal to the sum of total wage payment (W) and government purchase of farm products (A), minus household consumption (C), and increases in household holdings of bank deposits (ΔD_H) and government bonds (ΔB_H)[2].

Equation (2) is, of course, the aggregate household budget constraint. By ignoring for the time being the term ΔB_H (from 1959 to 1979 there was little government bond issue), the equation states that the sum of increases in currency circulation and household bank deposits must always be equal to household savings, i.e., aggregate household income minus consumption. In the scheme of economic planning in China prior to 1979, total wage payment, government procurement of farm products, and the supply of consumer products were all subject to decisions made by authorities other than the People's Bank of China. Thus, equation (2) also demonstrates the endogeneity of currency growth in pre-1979 China. In conducting the nation's monetary policy, the People's Bank reacted passively to decisions made elsewhere in the economy.[3]

This is not to say that the People's Bank had no role to play in the formulation of China's monetary policy prior to 1979. On the contrary, its role was considerable. The Bank was responsible for drafting and carrying out both the credit plan and the cash plan. Because it regularly monitored payment flows, it was in a position to report current economic and financial conditions to the economic planning authorities in a timely manner. It also had a voice in proposing adjustments in the physical as well as financial plans for achieving macroeconomic balance. Nevertheless, in spite of all this, it was a subordinate agency. It could propose, but not decide; it might dissent, but must carry out decisions made by higher authorities. It is in this sense that its role was essentially a passive, accommodating one, similar to that of a central bank which is obligated to finance all the government debt at fixed interest rates. In the latter case, too, money is endogenously determined, and monetary policy is essentially passive.

The endogeneity of currency circulation casts attention on the manner in which currency growth was determined. Of particular interest is bank lending to enterprises, because it is in this area that major reform has taken place in China since 1978, with significant impact on the conduct of monetary policy.

Following the Soviet model, banking lending to enterprises was based on the "real bills" doctrine, which holds that overissue of currency cannot arise so long as bank credit is restricted to the financing of current production and sale of real goods.[4] Bank lending was limited to finance only the "circulating capital" needs of enterprises, such as for unexpected fluctuations in inventories, goods in transit, agricultural credit between planting and harvest, etc. Needs for "fixed capital" investment were met through government budget allocation, with no interest and repayment obligations, and through own funds, mainly depreciation allowances. According to an official estimate, fiscal funds financed 73 percent, enterprises' own funds 14 percent, and bank credit only the remaining 13 percent, of the nation's total capital formation in the late 1970s.[5]

This mode of enterprise financing led to many problems. First, zero-cost fiscal financing created perpetual capital shortage. In the absence of any objective criteria, political bargaining was the only mechanism for fund allocation. Second, the artificial capital shortage combined with unrealistically low loan rates[6] meant that banks were constantly under political pressures to extend credits. Third, banks' credit policy was also hampered by a lack of financial accountability. Since enterprise profit and loss were all absorbed by the state treasury, bank lending to enterprises was riskless, being in effect guaranteed by the state treasury. In addition, in the absence of social insurance, the authorities could not let enterprises fall. This led to a particularly pernicious type of lending, with the banks being pressured to extend credit indefinitely to money-losing enterprises in order to keep them afloat, with no hope of ever recovering the funds.[7]

In those circumstances, the only means available to the authorities to restrain unlimited bank lending was the credit plan, which established annual quotas of credit extension for individual enterprises. Each year, from the plan's initial drafting to its final execution, brought an unceasing process of bargaining for priority treatment and extra-quota credit extension. Not infrequently, the People's Bank found itself at the losing end of these wranglings and matching of political clout and will, as it did, for instance, during the Great Leap Forward period (1958-1960).[8]

ECONOMIC AND FINANCIAL REFORM SINCE 1978

Under the leadership of Deng Xiaoping, the authorities made a fundamental decision in December 1978 to begin a comprehensive reform of the nation's economic system. The reform was motivated by widespread dissatisfaction with the nation's economic performance over the preceding 25 years.

From official economic data, however, it might appear odd that there was so much dissatisfaction. From 1952 to 1978, real national income increased at an average annual rate of 6.0 percent, annual per capita real income growth was an average 3.9 percent, and real per capita consumption grew at an average 2.9 percent annual rate.[9] Granted, these were not extraordinarily high rates compared with those of the fastest-growing countries or territories in the world -- such as Japan, Korea, and Taiwan, China -- during the same period, but would likely arouse envy from most of the developing nations.

Perhaps, official statistics do not tell the whole story. Western scholars citing Chinese sources have found a somewhat different picture. For instance, between 1957 and 1978, per capita supply of grain was reported to have fallen by 3.2 percent, that of three main vegetable oils (peanuts, sesame, and rapeseed) by 33.3 percent, and that of cotton cloth by 2 percent.[10] Industry did not do much better. Despite a 75 percent rise in labor productivity from 1957 to 1978, the real wages of industrial workers declined by 17 percent. The culprit appears to have been capital productivity. Between the same two years, although the investment/income ratio increased from 25 percent to an average 36 percent, and the share of "productive" investment (i.e., all capital formation except commercial and residential construction, and business inventory accumulation) in total investment increased from 59 percent to 72 percent, the incremental capital-output ratio more than doubled.[11] That is to say, the nation had been investing more, but getting less in return.

China's new leaders have been refreshingly open and candid in admitting to past errors in economic policy, attributing them to misinterpretation of Marxism, indiscriminate copying of the Soviet model, and overzealous "leftist radicalism." Under the banner of Modernization, a new pragmatism has prevailed in bringing more material incentives and market mechanisms into an otherwise rigidly controlled socialist command economy. Conscious of the enormity and the complexity of the task, the leaders adopted a cautious approach, introducing reform in stages and spreading reform nationwide only after having tested the measures in selected cities and provinces.

Not surprisingly, the reform started first in the rural areas. This was not only because that was where 80 percent of the population resided and the need for improvement in living conditions was the greatest, but also because administratively it was much easier than starting with the urban enterprises. As stated, urban enterprises were tightly controlled in the nation's economic planning framework by layers of interweaving and at times overlapping government agencies in all aspects of the enterprises' operations. From all that, the rural communes were largely exempt. In addition, rural areas were also outside the essentially *demonetized* "transfer balance" payment system in which urban enterprises and government agencies were included.

The rural reform in 1979 consisted of the replacement of rural communes by a production responsibility system, whereby the state signed contracts with individual households to lease land for five years (later extended to 15) in return for a commitment to pay taxes, contribute to rural social-welfare funds, and fulfill plan production quotas. Beyond these, the rural households were free to produce what they chose and to sell on the "free market" at prices which, though still regulated, could be considerably higher than the official prices.

This sweeping reform plus significant increases in the official purchase prices of farm products apparently released a large reservoir of productive initiative and energy formerly dammed up in the communes. Farm output increased rapidly. Moreover, rural industries soon became the fastest growing sector of the Chinese economy.[12]

The success of rural reform as well as the outcome of limited experiments with industrial reform encouraged the leaders in May 1984 to begin spreading the production responsibility system to urban enterprises, and in October 1984 to launch a comprehensive program of urban industrial reform.

The program had several aspects.[13] First, the government was to keep out of direct management of enterprises. Giant government corporations were established to take away from various ministries and bureaus the day-to-day management of enterprises in sectors such as steel, coal, petroleum, petrochemicals, and import-export. Second, the scope of economic planning was greatly curtailed. The number of industrial products under mandatory planning would over time be reduced from 120 to 60 and agricultural products from 29 to only 10 -- compared to a total number of commodities included in mandatory planning of zero in Hungary[14] and 20,000 in the Soviet Union.[15] Enterprises that fell under mandatory planning would continue to be required to produce and deliver to the state output in quantities and at prices as specified in the plan. Their above-quota output could be sold at prices to be negotiated between buyers and sellers, within ranges set by the authorities. Enterprises producing outside the scope of mandatory planning would in principle be free to make their own product decisions, subject to continued state control over prices, access to energy, key raw materials, as well as finance.

Third, enterprises were to be granted substantial autonomy in managing their businesses and eventually to be responsible for their own profits and losses. After paying an income tax and a complex and somewhat bewildering assortment of taxes,[16] the retained profit would be placed in various funds -- such as for additions to the circulating capital, accumulation for fixed-capital investments, and a consumption fund for bonuses and enhancement of worker benefits (such as housing, medical care), in proportions set by the enterprises' supervising ministries or bureaus.

Parallel to economic reform was financial reform, of which three features may be noted. First, enterprise financing was shifted from government budget allocation to retained funds plus bank loans. Only partial data are available to illustrate the shift. In 1965, budgetary allocation accounted for 86 percent of the financing of fixed investment of state-owned enterprises, retained funds 13 percent, and bank loans only 1 percent; ten years later, the ratios shifted to 64 percent, 34 percent, and 2 percent, respectively.[17] The shift reflected a marked trend of decentralization of economic control that began in the early years of the Cultural Revolution (1966-1976).[18]

In 1979, the People's Bank of China was instructed to begin experimenting with medium-term loans for financing fixed-capital formation involving interest and repayment obligations, with a view to enhancing the financial accountability of enterprises in their investment decisions. As bank loans grew rapidly, retained funds also continued to expand, such that by 1985 budget allocation was down to only 26 percent of state enterprises' fixed-capital investment, the share of retained funds rose to 48 percent, and that of bank loans to 23 percent.[19] While the shift was intended primarily for improving the efficiency of capital investment, it also enhanced the importance of the banking system in national finance.

Second, the nation's payment system underwent a major change with respect to enterprises. As stated, prior to 1979, enterprises were grouped together with government agencies in the so-called "transfer balance" circuit, within which all payments were effected through the entities' bank accounts and subject to case-by-case approval of their respective supervising authorities. Since approval was not assured, the funds were not an unconditional means of payment, as currency was. Inflationary pressures arising from this source could be controlled at will by the authorities, regardless of the amount of such balances outstanding.

It is not clear when restrictions on the transferability of enterprises' bank deposits were eased. It appears that by 1983 or 1984 the "ordinary" enterprise deposits in banks became fully transferable without prior approval. These deposits were earmarked for meeting most of enterprises' current outlays -- such as for the purchase of raw materials and energy -- with the major exception of wage payments, which had to be made from enterprises' "special funds" in the banks. Besides wage funds, the special funds also included different categories of fixed-asset investment funds (such as for major repairs, renovations, and new equipment). The use of special funds still required case-by-case prior approval of the supervising ministries or bureaus. However, even with the special funds, administrative controls over their use were considerably eased as a result of the reform in 1984.

Third, major reform has taken place in the structure of the nation's financial institutions.[20] In 1984, an Industrial and Commercial Bank was established to take over all the remaining commercial banking operations of the People's Bank, leaving the latter to concentrate solely on its central banking functions. Earlier, the Construction Bank, which had been no more than a fiscal agent of the Ministry of Finance, began to disburse funds for capital construction projects in the form of interest-bearing loans. The four specialized banks -- the Bank of China, the Agriculture Bank, the Construction Bank, and the Industrial and Commercial Bank -- were to operate as separate identities, with no more unlimited free access to each other's and the People's Bank's funds. Instead, an experimental interbank market was started to allow the banks to borrow from each other, in addition to borrowing from the central bank. In early 1987 a Communications Bank was established de novo in Shanghai by the State Council to build a nationwide branch network and compete with the other banks in their respective domains of operation. Several cities were allowed to open banks for operation in their respective districts.

In the area of nonbank financial activities, a People's Insurance Company of China has been established to handle insurance business, a China International Trust and Investment Corporation to attract foreign private capital and technology, and a China Investment Bank to channel World Bank loans to development projects in China. A fascinating development has been the rapid growth of investment trust companies, operating under the supervision of local banks, that attracted deposits from enterprises, public organizations, and even individuals, for lending to enterprises.[21] Also, informal credit institutions have sprung up in cities and townships to collect funds for financing production and commerce outside normal banking channels -- similar to the curb markets in other developing countries.[22] Finally, industrial bonds have grown so rapidly as to become a concern to central government bond issues.[23] Experiments have also started in a number of cities to permit a few enterprises to issue a limited amount of stocks to the public, and a small stock exchange has been opened in Shenyang and Shanghai.

Thus, since 1979, sweeping economic and financial reform has taken place in China. From the viewpoint of this chapter, the most significant changes are twofold: First, since about the middle of 1984, a large measure of autonomy in spending decisions has been given to enterprises; and second, the major source of enterprise finance has shifted from the central government budget to enterprises' own retained profits plus bank loans. The implication of these two developments is that money has assumed a much larger role in affecting economic activities than previously, and monetary policy must now become a more important tool for macroeconomic stabilization than before the reform.

MONEY AND PRICES, 1952-1987

Although prior to 1979 production and prices in China were controlled by economic planning, the authorities were still concerned about inflationary pressures on the prices of consumer goods. At the retail level, prices were fixed in official stores. However, during most of the period under study, rural households were permitted to sell on the free market their above-quota output at prices higher than the official prices by margins set by the authorities. In recent years, urban enterprises have also been allowed to sell their above-quota output at negotiated prices -- that is, prices individually agreed upon between buyers and sellers -- which, however, must be no higher than comparable free-market prices.[24]

Thus, during the past 35 years, there have been three sets of prices in China: official prices, negotiated prices, and free-market prices. The retail price index compiled and published by the State Statistical Bureau is a weighted average index of the three, with weights (not published) based on their shares in the consumer basket.[25]

Chart 1 compares the amount of currency in circulation with the retail price index for the years 1952 to 1986. The data indicate that, aside from the early 1960s, steady price increases occurred in China only in the 1980s; similarly, currency growth accelerated significantly after 1979.

Chart 1
Currency and Retail Prices, 1952-1986

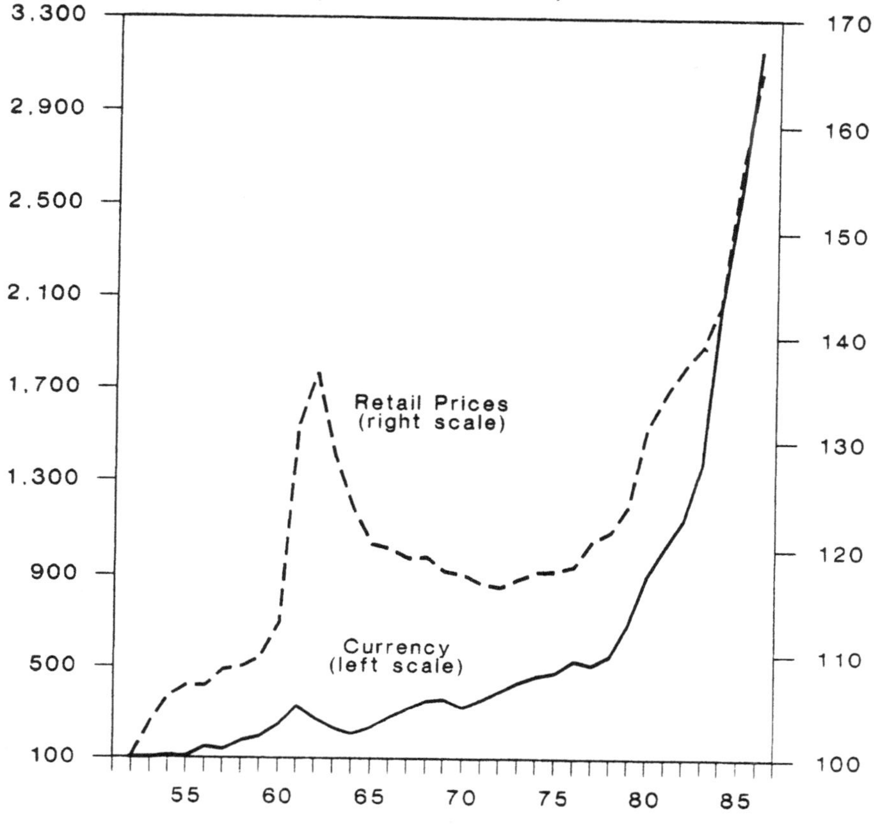

Sources: Statistical Yearbook of China (1986); JETRO China Newsletter (July-August 1987); International financial Statistics (August 1987).

Chart 2 compares the annual currency growth rate with the annual retail price inflation rate. It shows that the annual currency growth rate was singularly unstable throughout the period. Either the People's Bank was uninterested in stabilizing the annual rate of currency growth or, if interested, was unable to attain it. Judging from the bank's own account of how carefully it prepared annual projections of the public's demand for

Chart 2
Annual Changes in Currency and Retail Prices, 1953-1986
(Percent)

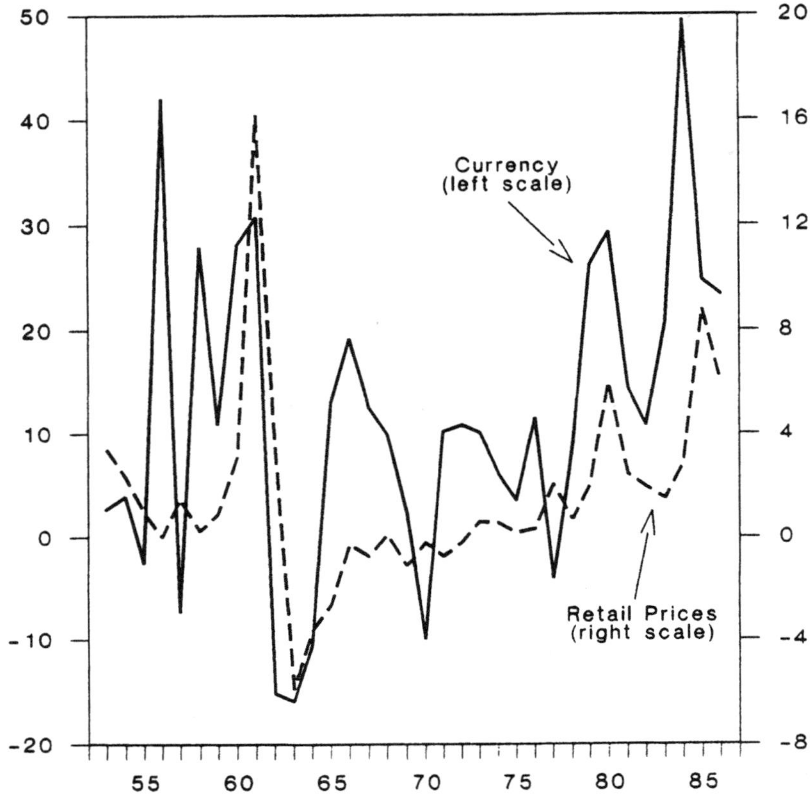

Sources: Statistical Yearbook of China (1986); JETRO China Newsletter (July-August 1987); International financial Statistics (August 1987).

currency and monitored the actual fluctuations in currency circulation,[26] it appears unlikely that the high volatility of currency growth was planned. Thus, it seems that even before 1979, the planning authorities were unable to achieve effective control of currency growth in accordance with their own cash plan.

Examined more closely, the period under survey may be divided into three episodes: 1952-1961, when the currency growth rate averaged 14 percent per year; 1961-1978, when the rate dropped to 3 percent a year; and 1978-1985, when it averaged 21 percent a year. It appears significant that the sharp rise in the retail price index in 1961 (16 percent) was preceded by several years of relatively high currency growth rates, that the stable price period in 1961-1978 coincided with one of exceedingly low money growth rates, and that the period of accelerating inflation since 1979 has been characterized by unusually high currency growth rates.

This cursory comparison of currency growth and inflation rates by itself is insufficient to establish any causal link between the two. The relationship between money and prices in socialist economies is currently a subject of debate among scholars. One controversy centers around the question of whether money is exogenous or endogenous in a socialist economy; another is whether a disequilibrium or an equilibrium approach is more fruitful for studying the demand for money.

Gavin Peebles contends that money (including currency and household bank deposits) in China is *endogenous*, since it is determined by the state's wage payments and purchase of farm products minus the sale of consumer goods; changes in the price level, however, are *exogenous*, since they reflect policy decisions in order to release inflationary pressures arising from excessive money growth.[27] This contrast is exactly the inverse of a basic tenet of most macroeconomic models of market economies, which regards monetary growth as reflecting policy decisions (exogenous) and changes in the price level as resulting from market reactions to the policy actions (endogenous).

Starting from what he calls "purchasing power imbalance" (i.e., inflationary pressure), as measured by the change in the sum of state wage bill and state farm procurement minus the change in real output, Peebles argues that when the authorities in socialist-planned economies face inflationary pressure, they have the option of either keeping prices fixed and letting the inflationary pressure stand, or letting prices rise to the full extent so as to eliminate the inflationary pressure, or a linear combination of the two. He finds a significant positive correlation between the inflationary pressure and the reported retail-price inflation rate in China for each year in the 1953-1982 period.[28] Moreover, for the 15 years (out of 30) in which the annual change in the price level was more than 1 percent, nine years of large price increases were associated with a positive inflationary pressure and four of large price declines were with a negative inflationary pressure.[29] In contrast, he could find no such pattern in the data for the Soviet Union for the years 1953-1978.

These results do not in themselves imply whether money holdings in China were voluntary or involuntary. To the extent that prices were fully flexible, money holdings in China should have been all voluntary; empirically derived equations relating money holdings to income, prices, and other variables could well represent demand for money in China. To the extent that prices were not adjusted flexibly to clear the market, and that besides for purchasing consumer goods there were few alternatives (such as purchase of financial assets), at least part of the money holdings should be involuntary, and empirically derived money demand functions that do not take this into account would necessarily be misspecified.

Gregory Chow, however, dismisses this a priori reasoning and takes the view that the test of pudding is in the eating.[30] He explicitly assumes that according to the quantity theory of money, the demand for money (currency) in China is a function of real income, and tests empirically to see if the assumption can be verified by the data. Using annual data from 1952 to 1983 and assuming lagged adjustments, he finds that the model fits China's data very well. In addition, an empirical equation relating the retail-price inflation rate to the percentage change in the ratio of money to real income explains price fluctuations in China even better than it does for the United States. By implication, Chow finds no evidence of monetary disequilibrium in China during the data period.

Other researchers take the observed official price fixing for granted and presume the prevalence of market disequilibria in the Chinese economy. They have constructed explicit disequilibrium models and tested the models against China's data.[31] Andrew Feltenstein and Ziba Farhadian, for instance, estimate a money-demand function for China on the assumption that at the existing official prices there was an excess demand in the goods market, but households held money with an inflation expectation that was a multiple of the official inflation rate.[32] The model is found to fit well China's data for the period 1954-1983. They find that, on average, households perceived the "true" inflation rate in China to be 2.5 times the official rate.

This brief survey of recent empirical studies on money and prices in China is not intended to be comprehensive nor to take sides in the ongoing debate. Whether a disequilibrium approach or a market-clearing approach fits the Chinese data better, and whether it is better to assume money to be endogenous and prices exogenous rather than the inverse, are questions for econometricians to settle. Whatever the outcome, perhaps few would dispute that an excessive increase in money supply would exert inflationary pressure in the Chinese economy as in other national economies, and that the recent economic reform has enhanced the role of money and monetary policy in China.

MONETARY SURVEY, 1980-1987

Monetary analysis on China has been in the past seriously hampered by lack of data. In recent years, China has released sufficient data to make possible a closer examination of monetary developments in that nation. The data series, published in the "Monetary Survey" section of the International Monetary Fund's *International Financial Statistics*, start from the last quarter of 1979.

Given the data, the first question is: what is money in China? The People's Bank has regarded only currency in circulation as money, because that is what households use to purchase consumer goods; the stability of retail prices is what has primarily interested the authorities. However, there has been recognition that households' savings and time deposits in banks are close money substitutes.[33] Savings deposits can be withdrawn anytime without penalty. Although early withdrawal of time deposits is subject to a penalty equivalent to the interest rate differential between the contractual rate and the actual holding period rate, until recently interest rates have not been high enough to make the penalty a serious deterrent to early withdrawals, when and if consumer goods became available. Moreover, as stated, the "ordinary" portion -- i.e., other than "special funds" -- of the bank deposits of enterprises and government organizations (excluding the central government) can now be used without prior official approval. Conceivably, these balances, too, should be considered as a part of the nation's money supply.

Thus, cumulatively, there are three concepts of money to consider. Currency in circulation (CU) is the narrowest concept. Adding on household savings and time deposits, one obtains money held by households (M_H). Adding further the ordinary deposits of enterprises and government organizations, one arrives at what may be called money held by the public (M_P), i.e., held by all the sectors outside the banking system and the central government.

The choice among the three alternative measures of money must depend on which can best explain and predict the nation's economic activities and changes in the price level. That is an empirical question, which at this stage is not likely to be answerable, given the shortness of the data series. Fortunately, as will be shown, the answer to the question is not critical for the purpose of the present analysis.

Chart 3 shows the growth of the three monetary aggregates from 1979Q4 to 1987Q1.[34] Over the period, all three rose rapidly; both CU and M_P increased more than threefold, at an average annual rate of 25 percent, while M_H rose fourfold at an average annual rate of 27 percent.

Chart 3
Three Monetary Aggregates, 1979Q4 - 1987 Q1
(Billions of Rmb, Log Scale)

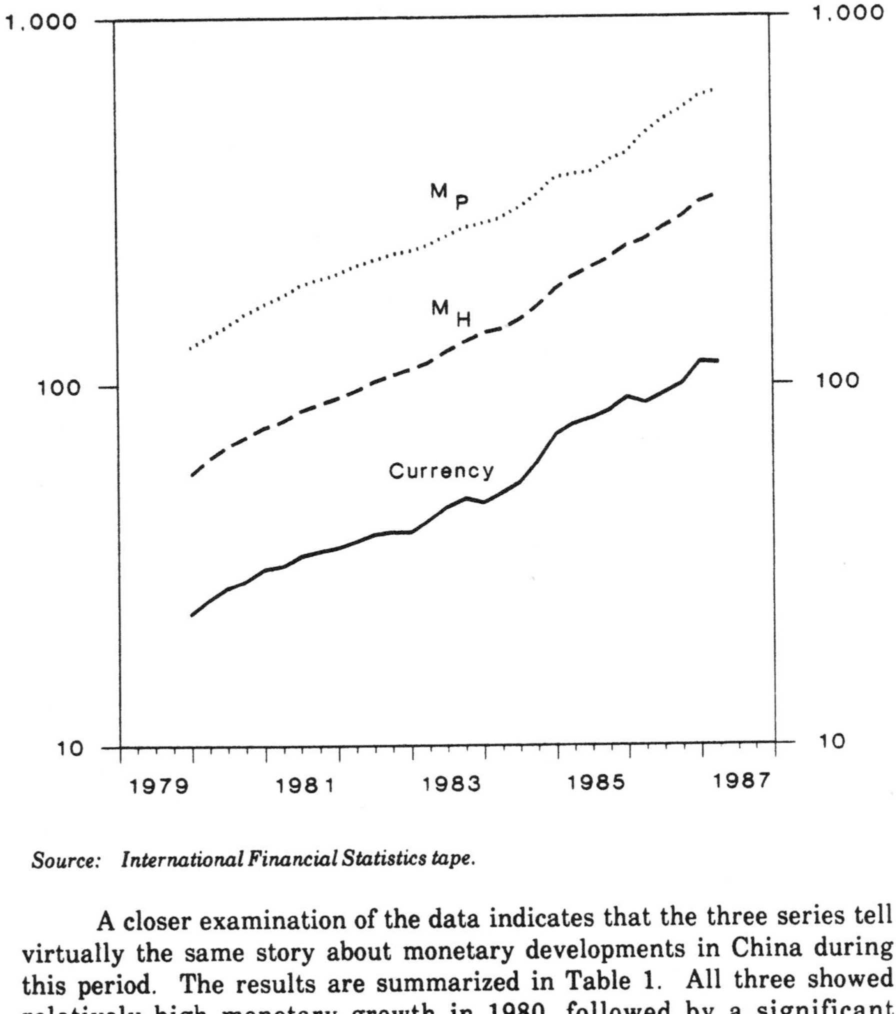

Source: International Financial Statistics tape.

A closer examination of the data indicates that the three series tell virtually the same story about monetary developments in China during this period. The results are summarized in Table 1. All three showed relatively high monetary growth in 1980, followed by a significant slowdown in 1981-1983. The following three years were marked by unusually rapid and highly volatile growth in all three monetary aggregates. During the 13 quarters from 1983Q4 to 1987Q1, all three aggregates doubled, growing at an average annual rate of about 30 percent, compared to their average growth rates of between 15 and 20 percent a year during the preceding three years. Moreover, all three monetary aggregates also became significantly more volatile. The range of variation of currency growth was 4.3 times its average growth rate during the 1984-1987 period, compared to a ratio of 2.3 during the preceding three years; that of M_H growth was 1.6 times, compared to 0.6 times during the earlier period; and that of M_P, 1.7 times compared to 0.9 times for 1981-1983.

Table 1
Quarterly Changes in Monetary Aggregates, Seasonally Adjusted, 1980Q1 - 1987Q1
(Percent)

Quarters or Quarterly Averages	Currency	Household Money Holdings[(a)]	Publicly Held Money[(b)]
1980	7.5	7.6	6.7
1981 - 83	3.6	5.0	4.4
1984Q1	5.8	3.1	2.7
Q2	7.1	5.2	7.2
Q3	13.2	8.9	7.7
Q4	19.9	12.0	11.9
1985Q1	6.6	8.0	1.9
Q2	3.9	5.7	1.9
Q3	5.3	6.3	7.6
Q4	8.0	7.4	4.9
1986Q1	-3.3	3.9	12.8[(c)]
Q2	5.9	8.0	9.1
Q3	6.6	6.8	6.2
Q4	14.2	10.0	8.5
1987Q1	-1.1	4.9	3.7

(a) *Currency plus household savings and time deposits.*

(b) *Household money holdings plus bank deposits of enterprises and government organizations.*

(c) *In a private communication, one communicator suggested that part of the abrupt rise in M_p growth in 1986Q1 was due to inclusion of public deposits at the Construction Bank previously not inlcuded in the series.*

Source: Based on data in International Monetary Fund, International Financial Statistics, various issues.

Rapid monetary growth coupled with high volatility gave rise to serious concerns over the authorities' capability of managing the nation's money supply in the changing economic environment. Nineteen eighty-four was a year of momentous transition. Barely did urban economic reform get started when monetary instability began to rock the national economy. Not surprisingly, questions were raised on the consistency of economic reform with monetary stability, and on what might be done to help achieve stability.

The components of the three monetary aggregates -- currency (CU), household savings and time deposits (D_H), and bank deposits of enterprises and government organizations (D_{EO}) -- are all liabilities of the banking system. In the banking system's consolidated balance sheet, the sum of all the liabilities must be equal to the sum of all the assets, as shown in the following accounting identity:

$$CU + D_H + D_{EO} + D_G + OTHERS = L_E + L_G + FA \tag{3}$$

which is essentially a restatement of equation (1) in a level form, except for the substitution of D_{E0} for D_E to emphasize the inclusion of enterprise and government-organization deposits, and the addition of OTHERS, which is a residual consisting of bank capital and surplus, bank liabilities to international organizations, etc. In China, banks do not lend to households[35] nor to government organizations other than the central government.

The data on the quarterly changes in the components and sources of monetary growth from 1984Q1 to 1987Q1 are presented in Table 2, on the basis of which a number of observations can be made. First, nearly all the rapid and volatile monetary growth during the period can be traced to one single source: bank lending to enterprises. In particular, such lending surged to an extraordinary peak in 1984Q4, receded in the following three quarters, and then rose to successively higher peaks (in absolute amount, not in rate of growth) in 1986Q1 and 1987Q1. The three components CU, D_H, and D_{EO} broadly followed the same path, with the notable exceptions of the currency growth in 1986Q1 and 1987Q1, which fell in both quarters.

Second, the central government contributed minimally to monetary expansion during the period as a whole. During 1985, there appears to have been a deliberate attempt to use fiscal policy to restrain monetary growth. Table 2 shows that the central government reduced its net indebtedness to the banking system by a total of RMB 18 billion, which, though not large compared to the RMB 94 billion bank lending to enterprises, was the single largest restraint to monetary growth that year. The policy was reversed in 1986, when the government increased its net indebtedness to the banking system by RMB 21 billion during the year, more than offsetting the contractionary fiscal effect in 1985.

Third, for the period as a whole, not counting the "black hole" category OTHERS, the foreign sector provided the only significant offset to the strong impetus for monetary expansion arising from lending to enterprises.

Table 2
Monetary Growth, Seasonally Adjusted, 1984Q1 - 1987Q1
(Quarterly changes, billions of RMB)

(A) Components

Quarter		CU	D_H	D_{EO}
1984:	1	2.8	1.5	3.2
	2	3.6	3.8	12.8
	3	7.1	6.1	10.2
	4	12.1	7.3	19.3
1985:	1	4.8	9.7	-7.7
	2	3.0	8.1	-4.2
	3	4.3	8.7	15.6
	4	6.8	9.5	3.7
1986:	1	-3.0	12.3	45.5
	2	5.2	14.4	24.0
	3	6.2	11.7	14.8
	4	14.2	14.0	19.0
1987:	1	-1.3	16.5	7.5

(B) Sources

Quarter		L_E	NL_G	FA	OTHERS
1984:	1	5.3	0.2	3.9	-1.9
	2	14.3	1.1	1.5	3.3
	3	26.1	1.6	0.0	-4.4
	4	52.0	4.9	-2.5	-15.7
1985:	1	19.1	-11.2	-7.4	6.3
	2	18.5	-1.0	-2.9	-7.6
	3	25.1	-0.4	7.8	-3.8
	4	31.0	-5.4	-4.4	-1.1
1986:	1	68.1	10.8	-4.7	-19.4
	2	46.5	4.7	-4.1	-3.4
	3	37.2	2.5	-4.7	-2.3
	4	70.2	2.7	0.7	-26.5
1987:	1	4.9	-1.3	7.1	12.0

CU = *currency in circulation;* D_H = *household savings and time deposits;* D_{EO} = *bank deposits of enterprises and government organizations;* L_E = *bank loans to enterprises;* NL_G = *net bank loans (loans minus deposits*) to the central government;* **FA** = *foreign assets;* **OTHERS** = *bank capital and surplus, liabilities to international organizations, and statistical discrepancy.*

* *Bank deposits of the central government ("budgetary deposits") are included in the quarterly data on "government deposits" but are reported separately only on end-of-year basis in the Statistical Yearbook of China. Quarterly data are estimated by multiplying the ratio of "budget deposits" to "government deposits" at the end of year to "government deposits" for the quarter of that year.*

Sources: Based on International Monetary Fund, International Financial Statistics, various issues, and Statistical Yearbook of China, 1986.

The banking system drew down a total of RMB 10 billion equivalent of foreign assets to pay for the nation's balance-of-payments deficit.[36]

In short, the extraordinarily high and volatile growth rates of the three monetary aggregates in 1984-1987 can all be traced to one single source: bank lending to enterprises. It appears that at various times the authorities have tried to use fiscal and foreign exchange policy measures to offset the monetary impact of bank lending -- with only partial and dubious success. Bank lending to domestic enterprises, therefore, seems to have been the crux of China's monetary control problem in recent years.

ENTERPRISE SPENDING AND MONETARY CONTROL

In view of this finding, one seeks answers to three questions: (1) What factors lie behind the strong enterprise credit demand? (2) What have been the consequences of high monetary growth? (3) What monetary policy and other macroeconomic policy measures have been taken to restrain the strong enterprise credit demand?

As stated, economic reform in China has shifted the principal source of enterprise financing from the central-government budget to the enterprises' own retained profits and bank lending, i.e., "extra-budgetary" financing. In 1984, as reform spread, urban enterprises were told by the authorities that they were to be responsible for their own profits and losses and were to make their own spending decisions.

The managements of the enterprises apparently took the latter instruction, but not the former, seriously. Having long operated in a wage-starved and capital-starved environment, the managements went on a huge spending spree. The national total wage bill spurted 21 percent in 1984, compared to 6 percent the year before, and the national total investment in fixed assets grew 34 percent, compared to 14 percent in 1983.[37]

At first, the spending spree was officially attributed to a combination of two accidental, untoward events.[38] First, in discussing wage reform during the second half of 1984, the authorities decided that in 1985 the payroll of an enterprise would be allowed to rise "in accordance with its economic performance" on the basis of its enterprise's 1984 payroll. Second, at the same time, banks were also advised that their quotas of credit extension in 1985 would be based on the total amount of their loans in 1984. The two announcements called forth a nationwide rush of enterprises to raise wages and banks to extend credits before the end of the year. In the fourth quarter alone, the national total wage bill rose 38 percent; the increase in bank loans in December alone accounted for nearly one-half of the 29 percent increase for the year.[39]

Subsequent developments soon showed that the spurt of wage increases and bank lending in late 1984 was not merely a result of a tactical error in policy-making, but was endemic to the system. Despite stern official warnings and policy measures for restraining spending, fixed investment grew 39 percent and the wage bill 22 percent, in 1985.[40] The increase in total bank lending did decelerate to 21 percent in 1985, compared to 29 percent in 1984, but was still much faster than the average annual rate of 14 percent from 1979 to 1983.[41]

The rapid growth of these aggregates substantially exceeded official plan targets. During the first half of 1985, for instance, capital construction rose 43.5 percent above the level a year earlier, compared to a targeted increase of only 8.8 percent.[42] Fixed investment in state enterprises grew 15.3 percent in 1986, instead of the planned 6.5 percent reduction.[43]

One reason that the planning authorities could not keep investment growth in check was the continued availability of financing. In 1985, the central government did reduce its financing of fixed investment by 4 percent from the 1984 level; however, bank financing increased by 90 percent and financing by enterprises' own funds by 42 percent.[44]

Despite continued price control, retail price inflation rose from 3 percent in 1984 to 9 percent in 1985 and 6 percent in 1986 (Chart 2). Preliminary data indicate that in the first half of 1987 retail prices rose another 6 percent relative to the level a year earlier.[45]

Inflationary pressures were also manifested in the nation's foreign trade. Its trade balance fell from US$2.9 billion surplus in 1982 to a US$1.1 billion deficit in 1984, a whopping US$15.2 billion deficit in 1985, and a US$12.1 billion deficit in 1986.[46] Despite large foreign borrowings, its foreign exchange reserves fell from US$16.7 billion at the end of 1984 to US$10.5 billion at the end of 1986.[47]

The authorities recognized the need for strengthening monetary control in order to restrain national spending without abandoning the goals of economic reform. To underscore the importance of this policy, in March 1985 a powerful member of the Party's Central Committee was appointed to be the new Governor of the People's Bank of China.

Monetary control was tightened.[48] First, supervision over disbursements from enterprises' "wage funds" accounts in banks was enforced more strictly so as to forestall "unauthorized" wage and bonus increases. Second, funds for extra-budgetary investment had to be deposited in banks at least six months (later extended to a year) prior to disbursement. Third, a strict total lending ceiling was imposed on each bank in 1985.[49]

In addition, interest rates were raised in 1986 in order to increase savings and reduce credit demand. However, even after the increases, the one-year deposit rate of 6.1 percent and one-year loan rate of 7.9 percent in August 1985[50] were below the 9 percent inflation rate that year.

Lastly, in 1984, the People's Bank established a reserve requirement for banks as well as a discount facility for adjusting bank reserves.[51] Initially, the reserve requirement varied from 40 percent for urban household deposits to 25 percent for rural deposits and 20 percent for enterprise deposits. In 1985, the rates were reduced and unified to 10 percent for all types of deposits.[52]

Besides monetary policy, a host of other policy measures have been employed for restraining enterprise spending. First, a 10 percent (later increased to 15 percent) tax was levied in October 1983 on all extra-budgetary capital construction spending, with the proceeds earmarked for financing the central government's investments in the energy and transportation sectors.[53] Second, as stated, central government budgetary financing of fixed investment was reduced by 4 percent in 1985. For 1986 and 1987, planned total investment in fixed assets in state enterprises was to remain at about the same level as in 1985, despite price increases.[54] Third, the State Council promulgated in early 1987 a "three guarantees and three restrictions" principle in investment planning to guarantee investments in projects included in the economic plan, in "productive" projects, and in "essential" projects, and to restrict investments in all others.[55] Moreover, massive budget cuts were announced by provincial governments for capital construction spending.[56]

Yet, in spite of all these policy measures -- monetary and otherwise -- investment spending by enterprises kept on rising rapidly. In the first half of 1987, total national expenditures on fixed-asset investment were 21 percent higher than a year earlier, within which "planned" capital construction remained unchanged, but "nonplanned" investment rose 19 percent.[57] Clearly, the policy measures thus far have not been entirely successful in achieving their intended results.

ASSESSMENT

The persistent, strong inflationary pressure in China has presented the policymakers a serious dilemma. On the one hand, economic reform giving farmers and enterprise managers more autonomy in making production decisions has brought on a prosperity and improvement in the standard of living the populace has not seen in recent decades. On the other hand, a nationwide spending spree has been unleashed that has thus far resisted restraining and has threatened to result in accelerating inflation and a destabilization of the economy. On the successful resolution of this dilemma hangs the future of China's economic reform.

In essence, there are two ways to bring down inflationary pressure in any economy: one is by direct control on spending and the other, through regulation of financial flows. Which of the two is better suited to an economy depends on the organizational structure of that economy.

In China's economy before 1979, national spending was controlled directly by economic planning. Finance played a passive role to accommodate and facilitate national spending in accordance with planning. When planning went awry and there was excessive national spending, as during the Great Leap Forward in the late 1950s, the economy was awash with money; inflationary pressures were rampant. All the authorities had to do was to balance the government budget and order the enterprises to reduce investment spending. Excess liquidity soon dried up, and there was no more inflation.

In contrast, in a market economy, the government cannot order businesses to spend or not to spend. When excessive national spending arises, the government has to adjust its budget through fiscal policy and to influence business spending through monetary policy, i.e., by adjusting the cost and availability of finance.

Since 1978, China has moved a considerable way from the command-economy model and has given more autonomy in production decisions to enterprises, without altering the basic structure of the economy. Although the scope of mandatory planning has been substantially reduced, the same economic planning power structure continues to regulate prices, restrict labor mobility, approve bank credits, and decide who gets what essential, scarce inputs and in what quantities. Since the management is still subject to virtually the same set of *external* constraints as before, it can no more be held responsible for the enterprise's profit or loss than before the reform.[58]

This ambiguity of financial responsibility is compounded by a lack of bankruptcy law and social safety net for unemployed workers. Local authorities, including bank branches, have been obliged to sustain money-losing enterprises under their jurisdictions through budget subsidies or through uncollectible bank loans. Under this "soft budget" condition, which prevails in all planned socialist economies,[59] a shift from fiscal financing to bank financing can hardly be expected to enhance the sense of financial responsibility and restrain excessive spending.

Unlike heads of farm households, the managers of urban enterprises are essentially government employees who have been appointed to carry out the government's orders and to look after the welfare of the workers and their families. There is not a clear identification of the enterprises' interest with either the managers' or the workers', as the case has been with farm households. Once given autonomy over the enterprises' operations, the managers have been tempted to raise wages and bonuses to keep workers happy and to replace all dilapidated structures and antiquated equipment with new ones, so long as financing is available.

The reform shifted enterprise financing from government budget to a combination of enterprises' own funds and bank lending -- a situation nearly akin to that which prevails in market economies. Fiscal discipline is no longer a sufficient condition for macroeconomic stability; in addition, there must be effective monetary control.

Yet, the monetary system is not adequately equipped to do the job. Central banking began its separation from commercial banking only about the same time as urban reform began. During 1984, the separation was more in name than in substance. Since banks operated for decades only to accommodate decisions made by economic planning authorities, the nominal separation of the central bank and the specialized banks made little difference in the system's mode of operation. Given the strong enterprise demand for credit, the shift from fiscal financing to bank financing made a rapid growth in enterprise lending almost inevitable.

The situation was further aggravated by a process of decentralization[60] that began in the early 1970s during the Cultural Revolution (1966-1976), when the central government structure was reduced to shambles. Although political stability was re-established in the late 1970s, the center of political power became much more diffused than before. In the national economic planning structure, the provincial and municipal economic authorities possess powers over the economic and financial affairs of their regions far beyond what is conceivable in market economies. Since regional economic interests are not always consistent with the national interest, the provincial or municipal branches of the People's Bank or of the specialized banks were often put in an untenable position with regard to lines of authority.

Under these conditions, it is doubtful that traditional market-oriented, monetary policy instruments -- such as reserve requirement, and discount policy -- would be useful additions to the arsenal for monetary control. In market economies, central bank's actions to reduce bank reserves would tend to raise interest rates and contract national spending through reduced investment demand. In China today, interest rates do not respond to reserve changes; even if they did, investment demand would not likely decline, given the soft budget conditions. A reduction in bank reserves would then be equivalent to a lowering of bank credit ceiling in its effect on aggregate spending.

Moreover, having both reserve requirement and direct credit control in a central bank's arsenal involves a redundancy. The two operate on the two sides (assets and liabilities) of the banking system's consolidated balance sheet, and by construction, the two sides must always be equal. At one time, only one of the two instruments is likely to be binding: if direct credit restraint is binding, reserve requirement must be redundant; if reserve requirement is binding, there must be no need for direct credit restraint. Only by sheer accident would the two restraints be exactly equal.

Which of the two restraints has in fact been binding is hard to say. But, it appears as though that from 1985 to 1987 the authorities relied primarily on direct controls to restrict bank lending. In early 1988, however, in the interest of inducing the banks to be run as autonomous businesses, banks were allowed to increase lending to the extent that they could attract additional deposits.[61] Since competition for deposit was still quite limited, and banks could create deposits at will with no fear of deposit leakage, the policy change amounted to a significant weakening of credit control. It appears, then, that monetary control would have to depend on the central bank's ability to limit total reserve growth.

Ultimately, what is binding on the effectiveness of monetary policy is not the lack of policy instruments, but the institutional framework in which monetary policy is conducted. Economic reform has given the monetary authorities in China greater responsibility than before for restraining national excessive spending. However, in order for any monetary policy instrument, whether credit control or reserve requirement, to be effective, it is critical that the monetary authorities be sufficiently free from political pressures at the national or local levels to accommodate all the spending decisions approved by the political authorities. Unfortunately, it does not appear that this condition is likely to be fulfilled in the near future. However, the other side of the same coin is that progress in industrial reform to strengthen enterprises' financial accountability will enhance the likelihood that monetary policy can one day be used as an effective tool for restraining excessive national spending.

NOTES

The author wishes to thank Laura Shoe for research assistance; and Sven Arndt, Baoshen Chen, Gregory Chow, Luc De Wulf, Martin Fetherston, Milton Friedman, Huayong Ge, John Judd, Thomas von Lupke, Frederic Maerkle, Barry Naughton, P. R. Narvekar, and Gavin Peebles for helpful comments on an early draft of this chapter. Their good deed does not implicate them in any blemishes that remain.

1. Farms, which through the setting of agricultural input and output prices were left with little profits to return to the state treasury, were the exception.

2. See Cheng (1981, pp. 32-33) for a full specification of the budget constraints of the various sectors of the economy; and Naughton (1987, pp. 3-8) for a behavior model that explicitly uses these budget constraints.

3. Scholars on socialist monetary economics have claimed that money plays a relatively minor role in socialist planned economies; see, for instance, Grossman (1966).

4. Cheng (1981, pp. 28-30).

5. Cheng (1981, p. 23). Naughton (1986, Table 1, pp. 628-629) provides a breakdown of the sources of financing of fixed investment in state enterprises for each year 1956-1984.

6. Byrd (1983, Table 11, p. 155) has data on loan rates, 1953-1982.

7. In the literature, this is referred to as the "soft budget" problem. See Kornai (1980).

8. Liu (1980, pp. 100-105).

9. International Monetary Fund (1987b).

10. Johnson (1982, p. 6).

11. State Statistical Bureau (1986). Labor productivity, from p. 273, refers to that of state-owned industrial enterprises; real wage, from p. 573, is the average wage of workers in corresponding enterprises; the investment/income ratio, from p. 49, is the ratio of accumulation to national income available; the ratio of nonproductive to total investment is from p. 54; and the incremental capital-output ratio, from p. 56, refers to increase in national income per RMB 100 capital accumulation.

12. Cheng (1985).

13. Joint Economic Committee (1986); Balassa (1986); De Wulf (1985a); Watanabe (1985); and *The Economist* (1987).

14. Balassa (1986, p. 12).

15. *The Economist* (1987, p. 15).

16. Carver (1986, pp. 121-124); Naughton (1986, pp. 611-613).

17. Naughton (1986, Table 1, p. 629).

18. Naughton (1986, pp. 606-609).

19. State Statistical Bureau (1986, p. 371). Foreign sources accounted for the remaining 3 percent of the total.

20. De Wulf (1985b); Tam (1986); Byrd (1983).

21. Naughton (1986, pp. 616-617).

22. *Ibid.*; Tam (1986, p. 431).

23. Hama (1987, p.4).

24. Watanabe (1985, pp. 49-52).

25. State Statistical Bureau (1986, p. 754).

26. Cheng (1981, p. 26).

27. Peebles (1983, 1984, 1986).

28. Peebles (1986, p. 491).

29. *Ibid.*, p. 492.

30. Chow (1986).

31. Portes and Santorum (1987) presents a useful survey of such models.

32. Feltenstein and Farhadian (1987).

33. Cheng (1981 pp. 27-28).

34. For Mp, *total* enterprise and government-organization deposits are used, rather than "ordinary" deposits, because the latter measure is not separately available.

35. Negligible amounts on an experimental basis, as a part of the recent banking reform, are excepted.

36. Note that in 1985Q3 there was a RMB 8 billion net increase in banks' foreign assets. It did not represent a reversal of this policy, but rather was a result of the large bank borrowing from abroad during that quarter. International Monetary Fund (1987b).

37. Rock Creek Research (1986, pp. 5 and 14).

38. Zhao (1985, p. vii).

39. *Ibid.*

40. State Statistical Bureau (1986, pp. 365 and 559).

41. *Ibid.*, p. 530.

42. Imai (1986, p. 2).

43. Hama (1987, p. 2).

44. State Statistical Bureau (1986, p. 365).

45. *People's Daily* (1987b, p. 1).

46. International Monetary Fund (1987a).

47. International Monetary Fund (1987b).

48. Imai (1986, p. 7); *Far Eastern Economic Review* (1986, pp. 71-72); Central Intelligence Agency (1986, pp. 7-8).

49. This replaced an earlier system in which each bank's total lending was restricted to a certain amount over and above the amount of deposits it could attract.

50. Tam (1986, p. 434).

51. De Wulf and Goldsbrough (1986, p. 228).

52. In a private correspondence, one commentator disagreed with De Wulf and Goldsbrough on this point.

53. Carver (1986, pp. 123-124); Naughton (1986, pp. 609-610).

54. Song (1986, p. II).

55. Zhao (1987, p. 9); Song (1987, p. 16).

56. Apparently, reductions in investment expenditures were ordered not only for provincial government budgets but for enterprises as well. The Jiangsu provincial government, for instance, announced termination or suspension of 919 capital construction projects totaling RMB 830 million, far exceeding the RMB 80 million reduction in its own budgeted investment expenditures. Hama (1987, pp. 3-4).

57. *People's Daily* (1987a, p. 1). Changes in the other components of the total were not reported.

58. Walder (1986) provides a useful analysis of this point through a factual description of the operating conditions of enterprises in China after reform.

59. Kornai (1980).

60. Naughton (1986, pp. 620-622); Walder (1986, pp. 632-634 and 643-644); *The Economist* (1987, pp. 15-17).

61. Private correspondence from a commentator.

REFERENCES

Balassa, Bela (1986). "China's Economic Reforms in a Comparative Perspective." Unpublished (April).

Byrd, William (1983). *China's Financial System: The Changing Role of Banks*. Boulder, Colo.: Westview Press.

Carver, Dean (1986). "China's Experiment with a Fiscal and Monetary Policy." In Joint Economic Committee 1, pp. 110-131.

Central Intelligence Agency (1986). "China: Economic Performance in 1985." A Report Presented to the Subcommittee on Economic Resources, Competitiveness and Security Economics, the Joint Economic Committee, U.S. Congress (March 17).

Cheng, Hang-Sheng (1981). "Money and Credit in China." Federal Reserve Bank of San Francisco *Economic Review* (Fall).

Cheng, Hang-Sheng (1985). "In a Chinese Village." Federal Reserve Bank of San Francisco, *Weekly Letter* (November 1).

Chow, Gregory C. (1986). "Money and Price Level Determination in China." Princeton University Econometric Research Program, *Research Memorandum* 327 (August).

De Wulf, Luc (1985a). "Economic Reform in China: The Recent Policy Changes in Perspective." *Finance and Development* (March).

De Wulf, Luc (1985b). "Financial Reform in China." *Finance and Development* (December).

De Wulf, Luc and Goldsbrough, David (1986). "The Evolving Role of Monetary Policy in China." International Monetary Fund, *Staff Papers* 33, No. 2 (June).

The Economist (1987). "China's Economy: A Special Survey." (August 1).

Far Eastern Economic Review (1986). "China '86." (May).

Fellenstein, Andrew and Farhadian, Zibn (1987). "Fiscal Policy, Monetary Targets, and the Price Level in a Centrally Planned Economy: An Application to the Case of China." *Journal of Money, Credit, and Banking* 19, No. 2 (May).

Grossman, Gregory (1966). "Gold and the Sword: Money in the Soviet Command Economy." In *Industrialization in Two Systems*, edited by Henry Rosovsky. New York: Wiley.

Hama, Katsuhiko (1987). "Further Tightening of the Chinese Economy – The Campaign to Increase Production and Practice Economy." Japan External Trade Organization, *China Newsletter* 69 (July-August).

Imai, Satoshi (1986). "Cooling China's Overheated Economy." Japan External Trade Organization, *China Newsletter* 61 (March-April).

International Monetary Fund (1987a). *Direction of Trade Statistics* Yearbook.

International Monetary Fund (1987b). *International Financial Statistics*, computer tape (July).

Johnson, D. Gale (1982). *Progress of Economic Reform in the People's Republic of China.* Washington, D.C.: American Enterprise Institute for Public Policy Research.

Joint Economic Committee (1986). *China's Economy Looks Toward The Year 2000.* Selected papers submitted to the Joint Economic Committee, Congress of the United States. Volume 1: The Four Modernizations; Volume 2: "Economic Openness in Modernizing China." Washington, D.C.: U.S. Government Printing Office (May 21).

Kornai, Jaros (1980). *The Economics of Shortage.* 2 volumes, New York: North-Holland.

Liu, Hongru (1980). *Money and Banking Problems Under Socialism* (in Chinese). Beijing: China Financial and Economic Publishing Co.

Naughton, Barry (1986). "Finance and Planning Reforms in Industry." In Joint Economic Committee 1, pp. 604-629.

Naughton, Barry (1987). "Macroeconomic Policy and Response in the Chinese Economy: The Impact of the Reform Process." *Journal of Comparative Economics* (forthcoming).

Peebles, Gavin (1983). "Inflation, Money and Banking in China: In Support of the Purchasing Power Approach." Association for Comparative Economic Studies, *ACES Journal* 25, No. 2 (Summer).

Peebles, Gavin (1984). "Inflation in the People's Republic of China, 1950-82." The Royal Bank of Scotland Group, *Three Banks Review* 142 (June).

Peebles, Gavin (1986). "Aggregate Retail Price Changes in Socialist Economies; Identification, Theory; and Evidence for China and the Soviet Union." *Soviet Studies* (October 1986).

People's Daily (1987a). Overseas Edition, in Chinese (August 9).

People's Daily (1987b). Overseas Edition, in Chinese (August 24).

Portes, Richard and Anita Santorum (1987). "Money and the Consumption Goods Market in China." National Bureau of Economic Research Working Paper No. 2143 (February).

Rock Creek Research (1986). *1986 China Statistical Handbook.* Washington, D.C.: Rock Creek Research.

Song, Ping (1986). "Report on the Draft 1987 Plan for National Economic and Social Development." (Delivered at the Fifth Session of the Sixth National People's Congress on March 26, 1987.) Xinhua News Agency *News Bulletin* (April 14).

State Statistical Bureau (1986). *Statistical Yearbook of China.* Oxford: Oxford University Press.

Tam, On-Kit (1986). "Reform of China's Banking System." Trade Policy Research Center, *The World Economy* 9, No. 4 (December).

Watanabe, Kiichi, ed. (1985). *Report on China Dual Economy System and Open-Door Policy.* Japan Center for International Finance Policy Study Series 4 (August).

Zhao, Zhiyang (1985). "The Current Economic Situation and the Reform of the Economic Structure." Report on the Work of the Government Delivered on March 27, 1985 at the Third Session of the Sixth National People's Congress, *Beijing Review* (April 22).

Zhao, Zhiyang (1987). "Report on the Work of the Government." Delivered at the Fifth Session of the Sixth National People's Congress on March 25, 1987. Xinhua News Agency, *News Bulletin* (April 13).

About the Authors

Thomas F. Cargill is professor of economics at the University of Nevada, Reno. He was a visiting scholar at the Bank of Japan, Federal Reserve Bank of San Francisco, Japanese Ministry of Finance and FDIC. He is co-author with Shoichi Royama of "Transition of Finance in Japan and U.S.: A Comparative Perspective," Hoover Institution, Stanford University, 1988. He holds a Ph.D. in economics from the University of California at Davis.

Hang-Sheng Cheng is vice president at the Federal Reserve Bank of San Francisco, in charge of international studies. He was research economist at the U.S. Treasury and the International Monetary Fund and taught at Iowa State University and University of California at Berkeley. He holds a B.A. degree from the National Tsing Hua University, M.A. from the George Washington University, and Ph.D. from Princeton University.

Warren L. Coats is chief of the Operations Division for SDRs and Administered Accounts in the Treasurer's Department of the International Monetary Fund. He was a visiting economist at the Board of Governors of the Federal Reserve System (1979), and Assistant Professor and Assistant Chairman in the Department of Economics at the University of Virginia (1970-1975). He holds degrees from the University of California at Berkeley (B.A.) and the University of Chicago (M.A. and Ph.D.).

Kevin T. Davis is professor of finance at the University of Melbourne. He was senior lecturer at Adelaide University, consultant to the Campbell Inquiry into Australian Financial System, and member of the Review of State Government Financial Management, South Australia. He holds a bachelor's degree in economics from Flinders University of South Australia and a master's degree in economics from Australian National University.

Robert F. Emery is economist, Division of International Finance, at the Board of Governors of the Federal Reserve System. He is also adjunct professor of finance at Southeastern University. He holds degrees in economics from Oberlin College (A.B.) and University of Michigan (M.A. and Ph.D.).

Maxwell J. Fry is professor of economics at the University of California at Irvine. Recently he was visiting fellow at Brasenose College, Oxford University, and advisor to the Governor of the Central Bank of Bangladesh. He holds degrees from the London School of Economics (B.Sc. and Ph.D.), and University of California at Los Angeles (M.A.).

Reuven Glick is senior economist at the Federal Reserve Bank of San Francisco in the international studies section. In recent years he has been assistant professor at the Graduate School of Business, New York University, economist in the International Research Department of the Federal Reserve Bank of New York, and consultant for the Country Policy Department of the World Bank. He holds a bachelor's degree from the University of Chicago and an M.A. and Ph.D. from Princeton University.

John G. Greenwood is chairman of G.T. Management (Asia) Ltd. He also is editor of the *Asian Monetary Monitor*, Hong Kong. He holds an M.A. (honors) degree from Edinburgh University.

Michael M. Hutchison is assistant professor of economics at the University of California at Santa Cruz and a visiting scholar at the Federal Reserve Bank of San Francisco. He holds a bachelor's degree from the University of California at Santa Cruz and a Ph.D. from the University of Oregon.

Homi J. Kharas is senior country economist for Malaysia in the Country Department of the World Bank. He has also worked as an economist in the research department of the World Bank. He holds degrees from Cambridge University (B.A. and M.A.) and Harvard University (Ph.D.).

Miguel A. Kiguel is economist in the Country Economics Department of the World Bank. He has also been assistant professor at the University of Maryland. He holds a Licenciado en Economia from the University of Buenos Aires and a Ph.D. from Columbia University.

Thomas A. Layman is director of the Asia/Pacific section of the Institute of International Finance. He has been a research economist with Mellon Bank and Crocker Bank, and has taught at Arizona State University and North Carolina State University. He holds a bachelor's degree from Vanderbilt University and a Ph.D. from the University of North Carolina - Chapel Hill.

Mervyn K. Lewis is Midland Bank Professor of Money and Banking at the University of Nottingham, England, and visiting professor in economics at Flinders University of South Australia. Recently he has been visiting scholar at the Bank of England, consultant to Australian Financial System Inquiry, and visiting professor at the University of Cambridge and the Business University of Vienna. He holds a bachelor's degree and a Ph.D. from the University of Adelaide and is a fellow of the Academy of Social Sciences in Australia.

David M. Lilien is associate professor of economics at the University of California at Irvine. He is author of *Micro TSP* econometric modeling software for personal computers. He holds a bachelor's degree from the University of California and a Ph.D. from the Massachusetts Institute of Technology.

Donato Masciandaro is junior economist at the Center for Monetary and Financial Economics, Bocconi University in Milan, Italy. Previously he was a teaching and research assistant at the Institute of Political Economics, Bocconi University. He holds a bachelor's degree in economics from that university.

Donald Mathieson is chief of the Financial Studies Division of the International Monetary Fund. Previously he was on the faculty of Columbia University. He holds a bachelor's degree from the University of Illinois and a Ph.D. in economics from Stanford University.

Thomas Mayer is professor of economics at the University of California at Davis. He has taught at West Virginia University, Notre Dame University, Michigan State University, and the University of California at Berkeley. He holds degrees from Queens College (B.A.) and Columbia University (M.A. and Ph.D.).

Lazaros E. Molho is economist at the International Monetary Fund in the European department. He was an assistant professor of economics at Fordham University before joining the IMF. He holds degrees from Yale College (B.A.) and Yale University (Ph.D.).

Ramon Moreno is economist at the Federal Reserve Bank of San Francisco in the international studies section. He was in the United Nations Development Programme from 1973 to 1985, with assignments in

New York, Central America, and the Caribbean. He holds an M.A. from the University of Sussex and an M. Phil. from Columbia University.

V. Sundararajan is chief of the Economics Division, Central Banking Department, of the International Monetary Fund. Before joining the IMF he was assistant professor of economics at New York University. He holds degrees from the Indian Statistical Institute (M.S. in statistics) and Harvard University (Ph.D. in economics).

Guido Tabellini is assistant professor of economics at the University of California at Los Angeles. He has been assistant professor at Stanford University, post-doctoral fellow at Carnegie-Mellon University, visiting scholar at both the Board of Governors of the Federal Reserve System and the Institute of International Economic Studies in Stockholm, and visiting professor at Bocconi University. He holds a Laurea in Economia from the University of Torino, Italy, and a Ph.D. in economics from the University of California at Los Angeles.

Wilima Wadhwa is a graduate student in economics at the University of California at Irvine. She holds degrees in economics from Delhi University (B.A. honors, M.A., and M. Phil.).

Carl E. Walsh is associate professor at the University of California at Santa Cruz and a visiting scholar at the Federal Reserve Bank of San Francisco. In recent years he has been lecturer at the University of Auckland, New Zealand; assistant professor at Princeton University; senior economist at the Federal Reserve Bank of San Francisco; and visiting scholar at the Federal Reserve Bank of Kansas City, Federal Reserve Bank of Philadelphia, and the International Finance Division of the Board of Governors of the Federal Reserve System. He holds an A.B. and Ph.D. from the University of California at Berkeley.

Conference Agenda

Challenges to Monetary Policy in Pacific Basin Countries
September 23-25, 1987

Sponsored by the Federal Reserve Bank of San Francisco

Wednesday, September 23

Welcoming Remarks	Robert T. Parry, President Federal Reserve Bank of San Francisco
Keynote Speech	"The U.S. as an External Debtor" E. Gerald Corrigan, President Federal Reserve Bank of New York

Thursday, September 24

Panel 1	Monetary and Exchange Rate Policy
Chairman	Thomas D. Thomson, Executive Vice President Federal Reserve Bank of San Francisco
Panelists	Donald J. Mathieson, Chief, Financial Studies Division, Research Department International Monetary Fund
	Joseph Bisignano, Assistant Manager Monetary and Economics Department Bank for International Settlements
	Jeffrey Frankel, Professor of Economics University of California, Berkeley
Panel 2	Monetary Policy and Financial Market Developments
Chairman	John P. Judd, Vice President and Associate Director of Research Federal Reserve Bank of San Francisco
Panelists	Reuven Glick, Senior Economist Federal Reserve Bank of San Francisco

Panelists	M. Akbar Akhtar, Vice President and Assistant Director of Research Federal Reserve Bank of New York
	H. S. Kartadjoemena, Deputy General Manager Economics Department Bank of Indonesia

Friday, September 25

Panel 3	Monetary Policy and Fiscal Policy
Chairman	Adrian W. Throop, Research Officer Federal Reserve Bank of San Francisco
Panelists	Guido Tabellini Assistant Professor of Economics University of California, Los Angeles
	Jeffrey Carmichael Representative, New York Reserve Bank of Australia
	Chaiyawat Wibulswasdi, Director Department of Economic Research Bank of Thailand
Panel 4	Monetary Policy and International Capital Flows
Chairman	Hang-Sheng Cheng, Vice President International Studies Federal Reserve Bank of San Francisco
Panelists	Warren L. Coats, Chief, SDR Division Treasurer's Department International Monetary Fund
	Homi J. Kharas, Senior Economist Country Department II, Asia Region The World Bank
	Miguel A. Kiguel, Consultant Country Economics Department The World Bank and Assistant Professor of Economics University of Maryland

Panelists	Michael R. Darby Assistant Secretary for Economic Policy U.S. Treasury Department
	Nicholas P. Sargen, Vice President Bond Market Research Salomon Brothers
Concluding Session	
Chairman	Jack H. Beebe, Senior Vice President and Director of Research Federal Reserve Bank of San Francisco
Panelists	Milton Friedman Senior Research Fellow Hoover Institution
	Michael Keran, Vice President and Chief Economist The Prudential Insurance Company
	Jürg Niehans Professor of Economics University of Bern, Switzerland
	Koichi Takata, Deputy Director Research and Statistics Department Bank of Japan
Adjournment	Robert T. Parry, President Federal Reserve Bank of San Francisco

Conference Participants

Foreign Central Banks

Reserve Bank of Australia

Robert A. Johnston
Governor

Jeffrey Carmichael
Representative, New York

Bank of Canada

Gordon Thiessen
Deputy Governor

Bank Indonesia

H.S. Kartadjoemena, Deputy General Manager
Economics Department

Bank of Japan

Koichi Takata, Deputy Director
Research and Statistics Department

Bank of Korea

Han Do Huh
Assistant Governor

Bank Negara Malaysia

Dato' Jaffar bin Hussein
Governor

Jaafar Ahmad, Advisor/Manager
Economics Department

Bank of Mexico

Jesus Marcos
Director, Financial Programming Department

Reserve Bank of New Zealand

Spencer T. Russell
Governor

David E. Wilton, Manager, Liquidity Management and
Policy Section, Financial Markets Department

Central Bank of the Philippines

Edgardo P. Zialcita
Deputy Governor

Bank of Thailand

Chaiyawat Wibulswasdi, Director
Department of Economic Research

International Organizations

International Monetary Fund

Warren L. Coats, Jr., Chief
SDR Division, Treasurer's Department

Donald J. Mathieson, Chief
Financial Studies Division, Research Department

Jorge Marquez, Assistant Division Chief
Asian Department

V. Sundararajan, Chief
Economics Division, Central Banking Department

World Bank

Homi J. Kharas, Senior Economist
Country Department II, Asia Region

Farrukh Iqbal, Economist
Country Department II, Asia Region

Miguel A. Kiguel, Consultant
Country Economics Department and
Assistant Professor of Economics
University of Maryland

Bank for International Settlements

Joseph Bisignano, Assistant Manager
Monetary and Economics Department

Federal Reserve System

Board of Governors

Michael J. Prell, Deputy Director
Division of Research and Statistics

Robert F. Emery, Economist
Division of International Finance

Federal Reserve Bank of Cleveland

Owen Humpage
Economic Advisor

Federal Reserve Bank of Kansas City

Roger Guffey
President

Federal Reserve Bank of New York

E. Gerald Corrigan
President

M. Akbar Akhtar, Vice President and
Assistant Director of Research

Federal Reserve Bank of Philadephia

Edward G. Boehne
President

Federal Reserve Bank of Richmond

J. Alfred Broaddus, Jr., Senior Vice President
and Director of Research

Federal Reserve Bank of San Francisco

Robert T. Parry
President

John J. Balles
Former President

Thomas D. Thomson
Executive Vice President

Jack H. Beebe, Senior Vice President
and Director of Research

John P. Judd, Vice President and
Associate Director of Research

Hang-Sheng Cheng, Vice President
International Studies

Adrian W. Throop
Research Officer

Reuven Glick
Senior Economist

Carl E. Walsh
Senior Economist

Ramon Y. Moreno
Economist

Other Government Agencies

United States

Michael R. Darby, Assistant Secretary for
Economic Policy, U.S. Treasury Department

France

René Servoise, Consultant, Center for Analysis and
Prevision, Ministry of Foreign Affairs

Academics

Universities

Sven W. Arndt, Professor of Economics
University of California, Santa Cruz

Thomas F. Cargill, Professor of Economics
University of Nevada, Reno

Roger Craine, Professor of Economics
University of California, Berkeley

Kevin T. Davis, Professor of Finance
University of Melbourne

Jeffrey A. Frankel, Professor of Economics
University of California, Berkeley

Maxwell J. Fry, Professor of Economics
University of California, Irvine

Yasushi Hamao, Assistant Professor of Finance
Graduate School of International Relations
and Pacific Studies, University of California, San Diego

Michael M. Hutchison, Assistant Professor of Economics
University of California, Santa Cruz

Herbert M. Kaufman, Director, Center for Financial System
Research and Professor of Economics
Arizona State University

Mervyn K. Lewis, Midland Bank Professor of Money
and Banking, The University of Nottingham, England

David M. Lilien, Associate Professor of Economics
University of California, Irvine

Thomas Mayer, Professor of Economics
University of California, Davis

Jürg Niehans, Professor of Economics
University of Bern, Switzerland

James L. Pierce, Professor of Economics
University of California, Berkeley

Barry N. Siegel, Professor of Economics
University of Oregon

Guido Tabellini, Assistant Professor of Economics
University of California, Los Angeles

On Kit Tam, Senior Lecturer, Department of Economics
and Management, University College
The University of New South Wales

John B. Taylor, Professor of Economics
Stanford University

George J. Viksnins, Professor of Economics
Georgetown University

Wing T. Woo, Assistant Professor of Economics
University of California, Davis

Betty Slade Yaser, Assistant Professor of Economics
School of Business Administration and Public Affairs
University of Houston-Clear Lake

Research Institutes

David C. Cole, Coordinator of Financial and Banking Studies
Harvard Institute for International Development

Milton Friedman, Senior Research Fellow
Hoover Institution

Thomas A. Layman, Director, Asia/Pacific
The Institute of International Finance

Robert Pringle, Senior Fellow, World Institute for
Development Economic Research, Helsinki, Finland

Commercial and Investment Banks

Commercial Banks

J. Alexander Caldwell, Vice President and Manager
Credit and Risk, Corporate and International Banking Groups
The Hibernia Bank

Kathleen B. Cooper, Senior Vice President and
Chief Economist, Security Pacific National Bank

Christopher Kwiecinski, Vice President
Continental Bank

Ronald L. Solberg, Vice President and Senior International
Economist, Security Pacific National Bank

Rod Swanson, Vice President and Senior Economist
First Interstate Bancorp

John O. Wilson, Senior Vice President and Chief Economist
Bank of America

Investment Banks

John G. Greenwood, Chairman
G.T. Management (Asia) Limited, Hong Kong

Nicholas P. Sargen, Vice President
Bond Market Research, Salomon Bros.

Corporations and Economic Consultants

Michael Bazdarich, Proprietor
MB Economics

Robert T. Crow, Chief Energy Economist
Bechtel Financing Services

Robert Einzig, Senior Advisor
Transamerica Corporation

William D. Hermann, Chief Economist
Chevron Corporation

Michael W. Keran, Vice President and Chief Economist
The Prudential Insurance Company

Paul Meek, Principal
PM Consulting

Index

Aggregate demand, Pacific Basin countries, 20-21, 51, 87-88, 92n
Australia, 140t
"Accord," 257, 259, 269
balance of payments, 257, 261
bank bills, 251, 273n
banks, 22, 28, 247-251, 249t, 258-260, 262, 266; commercial, 272n; laws, 149, 262; lending guidance terminated, 25; M3 target, 270
base money, 47, 49, 256t, 258, 263, 265-266, 268
bonds, government, 247, 258, 260t, 265, 269, 272n, 273n; typical of Pacific Basin countries, 5, 33
budget domestic deficit (BDD), 265, 269
Campbell Inquiry into the Financial System, 257, 274n
central bank structure, 10, 135-138, 144-145, 147, 149, 269; Reserve Bank, 249t, 250-251, 256t, 259-271, 260t
certificates of deposit, 259
consumer price index, 253t
credit aggregates, 18, 29-30, 53-58, 95, 270-271
credit controls, 262, 268
current account / GDP, 254t
current account deficits, 252, 254-255, 261
exchange controls, 248, 250
exchange rates, 10, 31, 70, 247-252, 253t, 257-265; affecting money conditions, 210; controls abolished, 17-18, 22-24, 35, 48, 270; floating, 13, 26-27, 88-89
exchange settlement accounts, 250-251, 263-264
exports, 254t
financial deregulation, major events, 278
financial system, 249t
foreign debt, 254-255, 254t
foreign exchange markets, 26-27, 83, 247-251, 259-262, 268-269
Foreign Investment Review Board, 250
Fraser government, 255, 257
government debt, 250-252, 254t, 258, 260-261, 265, 272n
government deficits, 125, 138-139, 250, 260-261, 272n
government expenditure, 102-103, 113, 115, 121n, 124, 257
Australia (continued)
government securities, 28, 70, 149, 247, 250-251, 262-267; LGS ratio, 258-259, 273n; typical of Pacific Basin countries, 5, 23, 33-34, 37
GDP, 88-89, 139, 252, 253t, 254t
imports, 89, 254t
inflation, 88-89, 253t, 255, 257-259, 261
interest rates, 31, 35, 89, 247-248, 251, 253t, 258-259; controls abolished, 10, 17-18, 22-24, 26-27, 31, 35, 48; deposit rates, 24, 70, 270-271; regulations, 10, 22, 149, 262-263; varied, 264-268, 271
international capital controls, 70, 81-89, 250
liabilities of private non-finance sector, 256t
liquidity, 70, 251, 268, 273n; LGS ratio, 258-259, 262, 265-267, 273n
monetary aggregates, 18, 37, 255, 259, 264-266, 270-271
money demand, 268, 271
money growth, 249t, 253t, 255, 256t, 258-259, 271
money markets, 249t, 250-251, 262-263, 266, 269
money supply, 255, 259, 267-268
nonbank financial institutions, 8, 18, 22, 70, 248, 263-268, 270
open-market operations, 10, 70, 250-251, 258, 262-263, 270
overnight settlements float, 267, 273n
portfolio holdings restrictions, 70, 258 259, 267-268
private sector foreign exchange transactions (PSFET), 265-266
rediscount rate, 5, 263-264, 267
re-intermediation, 259, 268
Reserve Bank Act of 1959, 251, 262, 273n
reserve requirements, 264, 271, 274n
statutory reserve deposits (SRDs), 258-259, 262-263, 266-267, 271
stock exchanges, 260, 274n
tender system, 250, 260, 269
Trade Weighted Index, 272n
transmission mechanisms, 247, 262, 270, 272
Treasury bonds (bills), 147, 149, 250-251
treasury financing, 137t

n = note, t = table

Australia (continued)
Treasury notes, 250-251, 262-264, 273n
unemployment, 252, 253t, 255, 257, 262
wages, 252, 255-257, 269

Balance of payments, 17, 20-21, 34, 37, 50, 95-96, 158 (*see also* Australia; China; Indonesia; Korea; Singapore; Taiwan; Thailand);
analytical framework (model), 105-106, 107f., 115-117, 119-120, 124
monetary aggregate control, 136
monetary approach, 153-154
Bank Economic and Social Database, World Bank, 161
Banks, 7-10, 23, 33, 37, 39n (see also Australia; Burma; China; Hong Kong; Indonesia; Japan; Korea; New Zealand; Singapore; Taiwan; Thailand; United States; Western Samoa)
credit, 47, 52-53, 55-57, 79
"Base drift" argument, 39n
Bonds, 116-118, 140t, 154-158, 156t, 160 (see also Australia; Canada; China; Japan; Korea; New Zealand; Philippines; Taiwan; Thailand; United States)
Bretton Woods system, 309
Burma, banks and international capital controls, 371

Callable loan markets, 33
Cambridge-type-demand-for-money function, 121n
Canada, 134, 137t, 138-139, 140t, 145, 150, 197n
bonds, 148
central bank structure, 135-138, 145-146, 148-150
government deficits, 125
government securities, 5, 23, 33-34, 37, 149
Treasury bills, 140t, 149
Capital flow equations, 154, 159, 162, 163t, 164, 167-168
Capital repatriation, 191
CAR (ratio of current account balance to GNP), 159, 163t
Central bank structures, 5, 12, 18, 21-23, 29-30, 33, 132-137 (*see also* Australia; Canada; China; Germany; Hong Kong; Indonesia; Japan; Korea; New Zealand; Singapore; Sri Lanka; Taiwan; Thailand; United Kingdom; United States)
analytical framework (model), 102-103, 106

Central bank structures (continued)
certificates, 10
domestic credit, 54-56, 64n, 100t
domestic credit reaction function, 156t, 158, 160, 167
exchange rates, 82, 121n
exchange rate reaction function, 156t, 158, 167
fiscal and monetary indicators, 140t
government deficits, 95, 97, 154
and gross domestic product, 124
independence, degree of, 125-126, 130
money stock, 84, 128, 153, 158, 174
solvency, 36
treasury financing measures, 137t
China
aggregate household budget constraint, 404
balance of payments, 420
banks, 11, 403-405, 408-410, 418, 420-425
bonds, government, 5, 33, 404
capital construction, 421-422, 427n
capital-output ratio, 406
cash plan, 401-402, 404, 412
central bank structure, 11, 424; People's Bank, 403-406, 409, 411, 415, 421-422
credit controls, 424-425
credit plan, 401-402, 404-405, 421
Cultural Revolution, 403, 424
currency in circulation, 402-405, 410-413, 415-419; monetary growth, 419t
enterprises' bank deposits, transferability restrictions, 409
exchange rates, pegged, 13
exports, 9
extra-quota credit extension, 406
financial reforms, 401-402, 408
foreign borrowings, 421
foreign exchange market, 420-421
"free-market," 407, 410
government agencies, 407
government debt, 405
government deficits, 403-404, 421
government expenditure, 421, 423, 425
Great Leap Forward period, 406, 423
imports, 9
inflation, 401-429
interbank money markets, 11
interest rates, 404-405, 415, 421-422, 424
investment/income ratio, 406, 422, 426n
liquidity, excess, 423
loans, medium-term, 408
modernization, 407
monetary aggregates, 416-420, 419t
monetary policy from 1980, 11
monetary policy prior to 1980, 9

China (continued)
  Monetary Survey, 1980-1987, 415-420
  money demand, 413-414
  money growth, 401-402, 411-413, 416-420, 419t
  money supply, 403, 414-415, 417
  net foreign assets, 403-404, 427n
  nonbank financial institutions, 409-410
  payments system, 402, 408
  pricing, 410-412, 414
  production quotas, 402, 407
  "real bills" doctrine, 405
  reserve requirements, 422, 424-425
  retail price index, 410, 412-414
  "soft budget" condition, 423-424
  State Statistical Bureau, 410
  stock exchange, 410
  taxation, 408
  "three guarantees and three restrictions principles," 422
  "transfer-balance" accounts, 402-403, 407-409
  unemployment, 423
  urban economic reform, 417, 420, 422, 424-425
  urban industrial reform, 407
  wage bill, 420-421
Closed-form solutions, monetary and exchange rate policies, 58-59
Cointegration, 295, 299n
Commodities, 7, 20, 34-36, 51, 309-311, 397, 408
Consumer's intertemporal budget restraint, 127-128
Consumer's lifetime real wealth equation, 127-128, 130-131
Consumption utility function (V), 127-128, 394-395
Crawling peg policies, 60, 248
Credit, domestic, 95, 97, 101, 121n, 124, 165
  expansion, 153, 160-161, 164
  models, 102-106, 107f., 108-109, 114-116, 119, 154-157, 156t
Credit controls, 4-6, 12-13, 17, 19-22, 25, 29, 37 (*see also* Australia; Canada; Hong Kong; Indonesia; Japan; Korea; Malaysia; New Zealand; Philippines; Singapore; Sri Lanka; Taiwan; Thailand; United States; Western Samoa)
  modifications, 47, 60-61, 138
Current account balance (CA), 50, 86-88, 99t, 112-113, 118-121, 155-160, 168 (*see also* Australia; Indonesia; Japan; Korea; New Zealand; Singapore; Taiwan; Thailand; United States)
Current account ratios, 164-165

DDCGR (change in net domestic credit to government sector by GNP), 161-162, 165, 166t
DDCR (change in domestic credit divided by GNP), 159, 162, 163t, 165
DDETY (change in the ratio of foreign debt to GNP), 159, 163t
DDEYS (change in the squared debt ratio), 159, 162, 163t
Deficit financing, 126, 134, 137-138
Disintermediation from the banking system, 33, 293
DNFAR (change in net foreign assets divided by GNP), 161, 165, 166t
DOILP (rate of change in world market dollar price of oil), 161, 165, 166t

EDEXG (expected change in rate of depreciation in foreign exchange rate), 159, 163t, 165
Envelope theorem, 132
Euromarket, 90, 190, 261, 388
European Economic Community (EEC), 280
Exchange rates, 4, 7, 13, 17, 19-23, 29, 34 (*see also* Australia; Burma; China; Fiji; Hong Kong; Indonesia; Japan; Korea; Malaysia; New Zealand; Philippines; Singapore; Sri Lanka; Taiwan; Thailand; United States)
  appreciation, 118-119
  and balance of payments financing, 86
  by the central bank, 121n
  and capital controls, 45t, 46t, 83, 87
  depreciation, 95, 97, 153, 155, 157, 159-162
  fixed, 51-52, 82
  flexibility, 51, 56-61, 62n, 63n, 81-84, 127
  models, 154
  monetary aggregates, 136
  and monetary policy, 37, 43-80
  nominal, 121, 127, 161
  overshooting, 85, 87, 92n, 108-109
  pegging, 37, 47, 51-52, 58, 60
  reaction functions, 162
  spot, 83-84
EXG (exchange rate adjustment reaction functions), 165
Exports, 52, 87, 96, 98t, 111, 155, 168 (*see also* Australia; China; Hong Kong; Indonesia; Japan; Korea; New Zealand; Philippines; Singapore; Taiwan; Thailand; United States)

Feedback-Nash equilibrium, 131-132
Fiji, exchange rates and international capital controls, 72
France, 197n, 247

F tests of the pooling assumption, 162, 166t, 167-168
Funds rate, 209-212, 216, 220n

Germany, 63 n, 126-127, 191, 197n, 389
GG (rate of growth in real GNP), 159, 163t
Gold standard, 32
Government debt, 5, 23, 34, 126, 129, 157 (*see also* Australia; Canada; China; Indonesia; Japan; New Zealand; Singapore; Taiwan; Thailand; United States)
  analytical framework (model), 103-104, 115
  cost of issuing, 127, 131-133, 136-137
  reaction functions, 153-169
Government deficits, 5-6, 55-56, 95, 97-101, 129-134, 138, 154 (*see also* Australia; Canada; China; Hong Kong; Indonesia; Japan; Korea; Malaysia; New Zealand; Philippines; Taiwan; Thailand; United States)
  analytical framework (model), 103-105, 108-109, 111-112, 114-115, 119-120
  and monetary regimes, 125-152
Government intertemporal budget constraint equation, 129, 141
Government policy equations, 165
Granger tests, 220n
Gross domestic product (GDP), 29, 100t, 101-105, 114, 119, 124-126, 132 (*see also* Australia; Canada; Hong Kong; Indonesia; Japan; Korea; Malaysia; New Zealand; Philippines; Singapore; Thailand; United States)
Gross national product (GNP), 30, 98t, 111, 113, 153, 155 (*see also* Indonesia; Japan; Korea; Malaysia; Philippines; Taiwan; Thailand; United States)
  debt/GNP ratio, 160, 162
  nominal, 159, 165

Heteroscedasticity, 298n
Hong Kong
  banks, 179-181
  central bank lacking, 8-9, 28, 32, 173, 179
  certificates of deposit, 196n
  certificates of indebtedness (CIs), 8, 40n, 179, 181, 183
  credit controls, 25, 28
  Exchange Banks' Association, 24, 179
  Exchange Fund, 32, 40n, 179-184, 196n
  exchange rate index, 197n
  exchange rates, 9-10, 32-34, 173, 180-184, 187, 189-199
  exports, 197n
Hong Kong (continued)
  foreign currency assets, 182-184, 187
  government deficits, 184
  government securities, 196n
  gross domestic product, 182-184, 185t, 187, 189, 192, 198n
  Hong Kong Association of Banks, 24-25, 179, 181-182
  Hong Kong dollar, 9, 26-28, 32, 34, 179-185, 188, 191; depreciation, 196n
  imports, 197n, 388
  inflation, 173, 181, 185t, 189-199
  interbank liabilities, 179
  interest rates, 9, 13, 179-183, 188-189, 191; regulations, 17, 24-25
  international capital controls, 26
  liquidity ratios, 32
  Monetary Affairs Branch, 196n
  money creation, 8, 28, 173-174, 179-184, 187, 193-194, 197n
  money demand, 183, 189-191, 193-194
  money growth, 181, 185-187, 186t, 189, 197n
  money market instruments, 196n
  money supply, 173-174, 180
  money velocity, 189, 190t, 191, 198n
  nonbank financial institutions, 182
  offshore markets, 198n-199n
  open-market operations, 180
  "real bills" doctrine, 196
  recessions, 185
  reserve requirements, 40n, 180-181, 183
  treasury bills, 196n
  unemployment, 184, 197n
  wages and labor costs, 192, 194, 198n

IMF Balance of Payments Statistical Yearbook, 198n
Implicit function theorem, 133
Imports, 20, 86-87, 96, 99t, 122n, 124 (*see also* Australia; China; Hong Kong; Indonesia; Japan; Korea; New Zealand; Singapore; Taiwan; Thailand; United States)
Indonesia, 99t, 100t
  auction system, 329-330, 331t, 338-339
  balance of payments, 323, 327-328, 343t, 344, 347, 348n
  banks, 322-325, 327-330, 333-334, 337, 340-342, 341t, 349n; state, 9, 350n
  central bank certificates, 10, 329-330, 331t
  central bank structure, 9-10, 27, 339, 346, 348n, 349n; Bank Indonesia, 321-324, 327-335, 331t, 337-340, 344-345, 347
  commercial paper, 23, 339
  consumer price index, 99t, 198n, 343t

Indonesia (continued)
- credit, domestic, 324, 326, 348n
- credit aggregates, 324-327, 335
- credit controls, 25, 27, 327-328, 342, 345, 349n
- current account, 323, 343t
- discount windows, 332-333, 339
- exchange rates, 10, 99t, 321-327, 338t, 339-347, 343t, 348n; speculation, 330
- exports, 321, 343t
- FICORINVEST (First Indonesian Finance and Investment Corporation), 330-334, 331t, 337, 339-340, 348n, 349n
- financial reforms, 17, 24, 27, 321-322
- foreign debt, 27, 95, 97, 98t, 112, 344-345
- foreign exchange market, 10, 324, 346, 348n
- government debt, 329
- government deficits, 23, 101, 113, 342, 344
- government expenditure, 102-103, 113, 115, 121n, 124
- government securities, 5, 10, 23, 34, 37, 195n
- gross domestic product, 109, 113, 321, 325, 326t, 341-344, 343t
- gross national product, 153, 321
- imports, 109, 343t
- inflation, 321, 326, 341t, 342, 344
- interbank market, 323, 331t, 333-334, 337-338, 342, 348n, 349n
- interest rates, 24, 322-325, 327-329, 331t, 332-333, 335-339, 338t; bank, 341t; deposit, 344; domestic, 342, 344-345, 348n; loan rates, 344, 350n; and money growth compared, 110t; targeting, 346-347
- intermediation, financial, 321, 323, 328, 334, 345
- international capital controls, 27, 124
- liquidity, 327-333, 331t, 336t, 337; banks, 339-340, 345-346, 349n
- monetary aggregates, 18-37, 322, 324-325, 326t, 335, 340, 346-347
- money creation, 345-346
- money demand, 325, 327
- money growth, 110t
- money market, 10, 24, 321-325, 329-333, 331t, 337-340, 345-347; and loan rate responsiveness, 350n
- money supply, 324-325, 346, 348n
- net foreign assets, 327-329, 336t, 346
- nonbank financial institutions, 18, 322, 328-334, 331t, 337-339, 342, 349n
- offset coefficients, 164
- offshore financial markets, 328-329

Indonesia (continued)
- open-market operations, 27, 328-332, 345-347, 350n
- overborrowing, 109
- policy mixes, 344-345, 347
- portfolio shifts, 322, 325, 329, 341-342, 347
- price stability, 323, 344
- promissory notes, 322, 332, 334, 339
- rediscounting, 5, 327-328, 330, 332, 334-337, 336t, 340, 347
- repatriated assets, 328
- reserve requirements, 32, 337
- SBPUs (Surat Berharha Pasar Uang), 331t, 333-335, 336t, 338t, 340-344, 347, 349n
- Sertificat Bank Indonesia (SBI), 329-332, 331t, 334-340, 336t, 338t, 344, 347
- sterilization, 324, 346, 348n
- time deposits, 328, 332, 340, 344, 350n
- trade bills, 333-334
- unemployment, 323

INF (inflation rate), 159, 162, 163t

INFGAP (difference between domestic and U.S. inflation), 161, 165, 166t

Inflation, 6-7, 19-21, 30, 43, 58-59, 85, 115 (*see also* Australia; China; Germany; Hong Kong; Indonesia; Japan; Korea; Malaysia; New Zealand; Philippines; Sinagapore; Taiwan; Thailand; United States)
- analytical framework (model), 103-105, 109-111
- consumer price, 140t
- debt/equity swaps, 120
- divergent rates, 84
- domestic acceleration, 167
- equilibrium rate, 130-131
- exchange rate flexibility, 52, 54, 56-58
- and foreign debt, 95, 97, 101, 103
- gross expected rate, 127, 160-162
- hedges, 154-155, 157-158
- inverse of rate, 130
- issuance of domestic bonds, 116-117
- pressures, 3, 33, 55, 118, 120, 165
- rate desired by central bank, 133, 168
- tax, 112, 122n

Interest rates, 4-8, 12-13, 17-24, 35, 47-51, 81-88, 117-120 (*see also* Australia; Canada; China; Fiji; Hong Kong; Indonesia; Japan; Korea; Malaysia; New Zealand; Philippines; Singapore; Sri Lanka; Taiwan; Thailand; United States)
- ceilings, 29, 59-60, 137t, 138
- domestic real, 60, 62n

Interest rates (continued)
foreign indebtedness, 103, 157
international, 108-109, 110t, 111-113
market-determined, 97
monetary aggregate control, 136
nominal, 92n, 157
world real, 160, 162, 165
Intermediation, financial, 20, 32-33, 85, 271, 287, 292 (*see also* Indonesia)
International capital controls, 4-6, 12-13, 17-23, 45t, 46t, 51, 154 (*see also* Australia; Burma; Fiji; Hong Kong; Indonesia; Japan; Korea; Malaysia; New Zealand; Philippines; Singapore; Sri Lanka; Taiwan; Thailand; United States; Western Samoa)
costs, 86
foreign debt, 95-124, 99t, 100t,
removal or relaxation of, 60, 85
International Financial Statistics, 161
IS curves, 206

Japan, 73, 140t
bankers' acceptances, 238
banks, 9, 25, 73, 90, 230-234; city, 237, 242
bills of exchange, 231-232, 232f.
bonds, 23, 73, 89-90, 148, 231
capital markets, 231, 237-238
central bank structure, 73, 135-138, 146, 148, 150; Bank of Japan, 9-10, 28, 31, 34, 90, 227-243
certificates (gensaki), 24, 26, 89
certificates of deposit, 23-24, 28, 31, 40n, 150, 230, 238
corporate deficits, 230-231, 237
corporate investment spending, 232f.
credit controls, 90, 230-231, 234, 241
current account balance, 89, 228, 230
discount window, 27, 33, 73, 230-233, 232f., 237
disintermediation, 150
exchange rates, 10, 31, 73, 227, 232f., 239, 243; fixed, 228, 238; floating, 13, 26, 88, 234, 237
exports, 228, 389
flow-of-fund patterns, 227, 229-230, 236-237
Foreign Exchange and Foreign Trade Control Law, 73
foreign exchange market, 83
government debt, 23, 140t, 141, 150
government deficits, 125, 140t, 141, 237
government expenditure, 102-103, 113, 115, 121n, 124
government securities, 5, 23, 33-34, 37, 230-231, 238, 242

Japan (continued)
gross domestic product, 139
gross national product, 229t, 232f., 234, 240
gross national product deflator, 229t, 235
"high growth" period, 11, 227-228
imports, 234, 388
inflation, 141, 191, 228, 234-236, 239-241, 243
interbank market, 24, 27, 230-233, 232f., 233f., 237-241, 239f.; rates, 31
interest rates, 10, 17, 48, 89-90, 141, 150, 228; constraints, 31, 231, 235; decontrol, 242; discount, 34, 146, 230-231, 232f., 234, 243; expenditure effect, 234; increase, 237-238; interbank, 232-233, 241-243; regulated, 10, 24, 73, 238, 239f., 241, 243
intermediate credit, 231-232, 233f., 235, 237-238, 239f.
international capital controls, 10, 73, 81-90, 138-139, 230
labor market adjustment, 240-241
loans, 90, 231, 232f., 233f.
markets exempt from interest rate controls, 24
monetarist policy, 239-241
monetary aggregates, 18-37, 73, 228-229, 240
monetary policy transmissions, 239f.
money demand, 227
money growth, 229t, 234-236, 238-239, 241, 243
money markets, 24, 237-238
money supply, 235, 236f., 243
nonbank financial institutions, 18
open-money markets, 231
open-market operations, 146, 238-239, 241-242
policy instruments, 233f., 239f.
portfolio holdings restrictions, 231, 232f., 233f., 237-238, 239f.
pre-reform period, 234
price stability, 235, 238-241, 243
recession, 236, 239
reserve requirements, 146, 150
"stable period," 227-228, 235
Tanaka Plan, 229
Temporary Interest Rates Adjustment Law, 150
time-deposit certificates, 238
trade policy, 374
"transition period," 227-228, 234-235
transmission mechanisms, 238, 241, 243
treasury bills, 89, 148, 242
treasury financing, 137t, 148

Japan (continued)
window guidance, 25, 27-28, 90, 231-234, 232f., 233f., 241; role unresolved, 238-239, 242

Korea, 74
"A-limit fund," 361, 377n
auction system, 360
balance of payments, 355, 359-360, 362, 366
Bank of Korea Act, 362
Banks, 353-359, 356t, 362, 365t, 366, 369-374, 373t; commercial, 377n, 378n; foreign, 376n, 377n; privatized, 376n; state-owned, 9, 11
bonds, 358, 360-361, 365t, 368-370, 373t, 374-375, 376n
central bank structure, 9, 18, 353-355, 358-362, 366, 369-372, 374-375; Bank of Korea, 363t, 364, 375, 376n, 377n
certificates of deposit, 358, 369t
"chaebol," 362
commercial bills, 358, 361-362, 368t
commercial paper, 23, 358, 373t
consumer price index, 99t, 198n
credit, domestic, 357, 362, 364, 367, 370
credit controls, 25-26, 353, 357, 359, 362
curb market, 22, 25, 31-32, 354-357, 365t, 372-373, 375n
current account, 118, 360, 367, 370-371, 374
domestic capital market, 358, 371
Economic Planning Board, 364
exchange rates, 10-13, 34, 99t, 356t, 364, 367, 374
exports, 355, 358, 362, 366-367, 369-374
Fifth Five Year Economic Plan (1982-1986), 357-358
Financial Stabilization Program, 364
First Five Year Economic Development Plan, 353
foreign debt, 95, 97, 98t, 118, 356t, 374; buildup, 353, 357, 367; prepayment, 369-370
foreign exchange market, 361, 369, 374
foreign exchange reserves, 112, 115, 118, 370, 377n, 378n
foreign funds, 373t
government deficits, 355, 359-360, 375
government expenditure, 102-103, 113, 115, 121n, 124
government loans, 373t
gross domestic product, 356t
gross national product, 153, 367, 368t
gross national product deflator, 356t, 368t
imports, 114, 362, 366, 374

Korea (continued)
inflation, 354-355, 359, 364, 366-367, 371, 373-374
interbank market, 358
interest rates, 31, 110t, 353, 355-359, 356t, 359-362, 365t; regulations and types, 25, 73, 364, 366, 368-374, 368t, 376n
intermediation, 357
international capital controls, 27, 74, 124, 374
Korea Credit Guarantee Fund, 361
kye market, 354, 375n
liquidity, 355, 359-361, 369t, 370-371, 374
monetary aggregates, 31-32, 353, 370-372, 374-375
monetary creation, 354, 361-362, 364
money growth, 27, 30-32, 110t, 353, 364, 368-370, 369t
money markets, 18, 355, 358, 362-364, 373
money supply, 359, 364
net foreign assets, 364-365, 369t, 374
nonbank financial institutions, 18, 25, 31, 355, 358-360, 371-373, 376n; funds, 354t, 373t
offset coefficients, 164
open-market operations, 359-361, 375
policy of national treatment, 358
recessions, 367
rediscounting, 5, 358-359, 361-362, 366, 370-371, 377n
reserve requirements, 359-361, 370, 376n
Stabilization Account System, 361
Stabilization Bonds Act, 360
stocks, 368t, 373t
time deposits, 359, 366-367, 368t
trade policy, 374
transmission mechanisms, 373
Treasury Bills Act, 360
unemployment, 356t
unified currency law, 354

Latin American countries, 35, 153, 197n, 345, 350n
LDETY (lagged ratio of foreign debt to GNP), 161, 165, 166t
LDEYS (square of lagged debt/GNP ratio), 161-162, 165, 166t
LIBOR (London interbank offer rate), 110t, 188-189, 196n, 328, 338t
Liquidity, 5-6, 12, 27, 32-33, 47-48 (*see also* Australia; Korea; Malaysia; New Zealand; Singapore; Taiwan; Thailand)
Liquidity Assets and Government Securities Convention (LGS), 149
LM curves, 87, 206

Malaysia, 17, 75, 99t, 100t
bankers' acceptance, 23-24
certificates of deposit, 24
consumer price index, 198n
credit controls, 25, 27
Employee Provident Fund, 117
exchange rates, 26, 75, 99t
foreign debt, 95, 98t, 112, 118, 124
government deficits, 23, 97-101, 113
government expenditure, 102-103, 113, 115, 121n, 124
gross domestic product, 117
gross national product, 117, 153
inflation, 113
interest rates, 24, 110t, 118
international capital controls, 113
money growth, 110t, 118
nonbank financial institutions, 18
offset coefficients, 164
open-market operations, 27
overborrowing, 109
reserve requirements, 32
Monetary policy reaction functions, 158-168
Money-demand functions, 155, 206, 213-214, 335, 414
Money growth (M1, M2, M3), 39n, 40n, 154, 160, 162, 165, 168 (*see also* Australia; China; Hong Kong; Indonesia; Japan; Korea; Malaysia; New Zealand; Philippines; Singapore; Taiwan; Thailand; United Kingdom; United States)
Mutual indemnity principle, 248

New Zealand, 76, 140t
auction system, government securities, 289, 298n
banks, 150-151, 282-284, 286-287, 293, 298n
bank settlement balances, 287, 288t
bonds, government, 148
cash settlement balances, 292, 297
central bank structure, 10, 30, 135-138, 146-148; Reserve Bank of New Zealand, 279, 282-283, 285-287, 289-293, 295
consumer price index, 281t, 291, 298n
credit aggregates, 282, 292
credit controls, 25, 28, 76, 151, 195n, 279, 286; eliminated, 289
current account, 91-92, 281t
discount window, 76, 285, 288t, 289, 291
exchange rates, 10, 76, 91-92, 281t, 290, 292-293, 295-297; control abolished, 17-18, 24, 27, 35, 48; flexible, 285; floating, 13, 27, 88, 287, 288t; partial dollar devaluation, 91; pegged, 279, 285
exports, 280, 281t
New Zealand (continued)
foreign exchange market, 83, 282-283, 285, 296
government debt, 139, 283-285, 287, 288t, 296
government deficits, 76, 125, 134, 138-139, 279-280, 281t, 286; financing of, 289, 295-296
government securities, 30, 76, 150-151, 283-284, 285t, 287-290, 288t; for Pacific Basin countries, 5, 23, 33-34, 37, 139; long-term, 295; short-term, 295
gross domestic product, 280, 281t
imports, 281t, 290
inflation, 91-92, 139, 279-280, 284, 285t, 286, 290-292; decrease, 295, 297
interest rates, 282-287, 285t, 289-290, 292, 295-296, 298n, 299n; controls abolished, 17-18, 27, 35, 48, 279, 288t, 293; regulations, 10, 24, 76, 91-92, 151
international capital controls, 26, 76, 81-88, 90-92, 141, 288t
liquidity, 28, 30; primary, 290-293, 295-297
monetary aggregates, 282, 286, 289-296, 299n
monetary policy measures, 288t
money demand, 292-293
money growth, 280, 281t, 284, 286, 290-291, 294-295
money markets, 283, 298n
money supply, 262
money velocities, 290-291, 294
nonbank financial institutions, 18, 282-284, 292-293, 298n
open-market operations, 10, 76, 151, 279, 288-289, 293
price controls and stability, 280-282, 284, 290-292, 294, 297
reserve requirements, 28, 76, 279, 283-287, 288t, 289, 292-294; removal of, 296-297; tightened, 298n
taxation, 30, 283, 287, 291-292, 297
tender system, 288t
time deposits, 283
treasury bills, 289
treasury financing, 137t
unemployment, 280, 281t
wages, 280-282, 284
Nontradable goods market, 83-84, 118, 198n

OECD (Organization for Economic Cooperation and Development, 97, 273n, 280
Oil Prices, 7, 34, 51, 117, 326, 343t, 346-347
increase and its effect, 160-161, 165, 353, 367, 371, 388-389, 397

Oil Prices (continued)
rate of change in world dollar prices, 155
short-run inelastic demand, 86
weakening of, 113, 322, 342
Ordinary least squares (OLS) estimation procedure, 160, 164

Philippines, 99t, 100t
banks, 34
bonds, government, 116
consumer price index, 198n
credit controls, 24-25
exports, 111
financial reforms undertaken, 17, 24
foreign debt, 39n 95, 97-101, 98t, 115-116, 124
foreign exchange market, 111
government deficits, 101
government expenditure, 102-103, 111, 113, 115, 121n, 124
government securities, 5, 23, 33-34, 37
gross domestic product, 101
gross national product, 153
inflation, 111
interest rates, 24, 110t, 111-114, 116
international capital controls, 112, 116
money growth, 110t, 111-114
nonbank financial institutions, 18
offset coefficients, 164
open-market operations, 27
Prime assets ratios, 262, 267
Private Sector Credit, 294t, 295

Quantity theory of money equation, 364
Quasi reduced-form behavioral equation, 154, 167

Reserve requirements, 5-6, 10-12, 19-20, 27, 32-33, 37, 47-48 (*see also* Australia; Canada; China; Fiji; Hong Kong; Indonesia; Japan; Korea; Malaysia; New Zealand; Singapore; Taiwan; Thailand; United States; Western Samoa)
on foreign borrowing, 45t, 46t
Resource allocations, 83, 85
Risk premia, country-specific, 154-155, 157
Round tripping, 193-194, 198n-199n

Savings function, 394-395
Seigniorage extraction, 4-7, 12, 105, 114-115, 125-127, 136-138, 194
in New Zealand, 284
Shocks, external and real, 4, 50-52, 58, 61, 63n, 168, 295
monetary, 84, 86-87, 158, 168, 285-286

Shocks (continued)
oil, 81, 97, 101, 217-219, 222, 227, 280; effect of first on Taiwan, 381, 385, 393, 396; effect of second on Japan, 236-237, 239, 243; effect of second on Taiwan, 385, 387-390, 393, 396; first, 95, 109, 184-185, 201-202, 309, 312; second, 89, 184-185, 201-202, 312, 317-318, 347
Simonsen rule, 105, 121n
Simultaneous equation bias, 164
Singapore
and Asian dollar market, 26, 174-178, 193-194, 196n, 199n
balance of payments, 32, 77
banks, 175-176, 196n
bonds, government, 39n
Central Provident Fund, 178
commercial paper, 23, 178
credit, domestic, 178
credit controls, 25, 176
current account deficit, 191, 193
exchange rates, 10, 28, 34, 77, 173, 175-179, 189-199; floated, 176; pegged to basket of currencies, 8, 26, 34, 178, 185; pegged to U.S. dollar, 176, 188, 192
exports, 176
foreign exchange market, 8, 176, 247
government debt, 174
government securities, 5, 23, 28, 33-34, 37, 177, 195n
gross domestic product, 184, 185t, 192, 198n
imports, 191-192, 198n
inflation, 8, 173, 175-176, 178-179, 185t, 187-194, 198n
interest rates, 8, 13, 17, 24, 32, 188, 190; deposit, 175
interest tax on investment transactions, 26
international capital controls, 77
liquidity, 77, 174, 178-179
monetary aggregates, 194
Monetary Authority of Singapore, 8, 174-177, 195n, 198n
money creation, 8, 174-176, 194
money demand, 189-190, 198n
money growth, 184-187, 186t, 189-190, 193
money supply, 177, 179
money velocity, 190t, 191
National Wages Council, 198n
1967 Banking Act, 175
nonbank financial institutions, 175, 196n
offshore markets, 193
open-market operations, 177-178
price stability, 195n
recessions, 173, 178-179, 185
rediscounting, 5, 176

Singapore (continued)
reserve requirements, 77, 175, 193, 195n
treasury bills, 174, 195n
unemployment, 184, 197n
wages and labor costs, 192, 194, 198n
Sri Lanka, banks and international capital controls, 78
Stackelberg leader, 129-130
Statutory reserve-deposit system (SRD), 70, 149
Sterilization, 54-55, 63n, 64n, 96, 165, 309, 374 (*see also* Indonesia)
complete, 161, 167
of rising foreign exchange reserves, 115, 118, 120
Sterling standard for currency, 9, 180-181, 183, 307, 316
Switzerland, 167, 197n

Taiwan
balance of payments, 388t, 390, 393
bankers' acceptances, 23, 25, 391
banks, 27, 381-385, 382t, 390, 392, 394, 397, 398n; state, 9, 11
bonds, 383, 391-392, 394
central bank certificates, 10
central bank structure, 9-10, 18, 27, 381-385, 382t, 390-397, 398n
certificates of deposit, 25, 385, 391-394, 397, 398n
commercial bills, 392
commercial paper, 23, 391
consumer price index, 386t, 387-388, 396-397
credit, domestic, 386t
credit controls, 25
curb markets, 22, 25, 131-132, 383-384
current account surpluses, 118-119, 387-390, 388t
debentures, 385
exchange controls, 11
exchange rates, 11, 13, 27, 388t, 389-390, 397-398; pegged, 34, 384, 396
exports, 381, 388-390, 388t, 392
foreign currency deposits, 391
foreign debt, 388t, 389
foreign exchange market, 27, 381, 384-387, 389-392, 394, 396-397
government debt, 393
government deficits, 390
gross national product, 385, 386t, 387, 395
inflation, 386t, 387, 391-394, 396-398
interest rates, 25, 383-387, 386t, 390, 392-393, 396-398
international capital controls, 27, 385
liquidity, 393, 396-397

Taiwan (continued)
money aggregates, 31, 398
money growth, 30-31, 394-395
money markets, 18, 25, 383-384, 398n
money supply, 387-388, 394-396, 395t
money velocity, 386t, 394, 396
net foreign assets, 392-394, 395t, 397, 398n
nonbank financial institutions, 18, 381, 382t, 384
offshore banking units, 39n, 382t
open-market operations, 390-391, 393, 397-398
postal savings system, 381-384, 382t, 391-392, 394
price stability, 381, 387
quasi-money, 394, 395t
recessions, 385
rediscounting, 5, 386t, 393-393
reserve requirements, 390-391
stocks, 383
tariffs, 389, 397
trade balance, 388t
trade surpluses, 389-390, 394
treasury bills, 391, 398n
Thailand, 77, 99t, 100t
balance of payments, 118, 306-307, 309, 310t, 312-314, 319n
banks, 303-306, 304t, 308-309, 311t, 313-314, 317
bills, government, 312
blue chip companies, 318
bonds, domestic, 97, 112, 117
bonds, government, 79, 117-118, 305, 314-315, 318
capital movements, 310t
central bank structure, 11, 307-309; Bank of Thailand, 303-305, 311t, 312-313, 315-318, 319n
commodity price boom, 309-311
consumer price index, 198n, 308t, 309, 312
credit, domestic, 314
credit controls, 23, 25, 79, 315
current account, 309, 310t, 312-313, 316-317
exchange rate, 8, 11, 23, 79, 99t, 306-307, 316-318; fixed, 303, 309, 313
exports, 313, 317
foreign debt, 95, 97, 98t, 124, 314, 316
foreign exchange market, 309
government debt, 118
government deficit, 101, 117-118, 306, 312
government expenditure, 102-103, 113, 115, 121n, 124
government securities, 5, 23, 27, 33-34, 37, 79, 318

Thailand (continued)
gross domestic product, 112, 308t, 309, 312-313
gross national product, 153
imports, 313, 315, 317
inflation, 309, 311-312
interbank rates, 317-318
interest rates, 11, 23, 35, 79, 118, 308t, 312-318; high level, 307; and money growth, compared, 110t; regulation, 25
international capital controls, 23, 34-35, 79, 112
liquidity, 79, 314, 318
monetary base, component sources of, 311t
money aggregates, 18-37
money creation, 309
money growth, 110t, 307, 309, 311-313, 316
money market, 318
net foreign assets, 307, 309, 311t, 312, 319
nonbank financial institutions, 25, 303-306, 304t
offset coefficients, 164
overborrowing, 109
overseas borrowings, 312-313
policy changes, 11, 17, 313
premium savings certificates, 305
private capital outflows restricted, 26
promissory notes, 304
recessions, 311, 313
reserve requirements, 79
restrictions on domestic financial markets, 40n
time deposits, 317
Treasury bills, 309
treasury borrowing, 314
Tradable goods, 35, 57-58, 83-84, 90-91, 255
Trade weights, 197n
Turkey, credit expansion, 165
Two-country framework, 50-51
Two-stage least squares estimates, 162, 168

United Kingdom, 39n, 197n, 251, 271, 280, 305, 350n
United States
Accord of 1951, 205
bankers' acceptances, 350n
banks, 204, 213-214
bonds, treasury, 224t
central bank structure, 3, 10, 40; Federal Reserve, 136-137, 147, 201-209, 216, 220n, 221n, 312-313; independent of Treasury, 126-127, 151, 202, 204-205, 210, 215, 219n; Volcker's disinflationary policy, 202, 205, 209, 218-219
Congress, 147, 205, 209, 220n, 224-225
consumer price inflation, 203

United States (continued)
credit controls, 8, 151
current account balance, 218
depression, 209, 222
discount window, 151, 207-208, 211, 220n
exchange rates, 8, 13, 192, 201, 218, 224t, 384
executive branch influence, 204-205, 209, 212, 224-225
exports, 218, 389
Federal Open Market Committee (FOMC), 147, 203, 207, 210, 214-216, 219-220, 225
government debt, 148
government deficits, 125, 134, 141, 148, 223t, 225
government securities, 5, 23, 33-34, 37, 148, 220n
gross domestic product, 139
gross national product, 40n, 207, 209, 213, 215-216, 223t
GNP deflator, 201, 203, 223t
imports, 218
inflation, 40n, 151, 155, 160-161, 167, 191; and monetary policy, 201-210, 215, 218-219, 221n, 223t
interest rates, 206-207, 209-210, 212-213, 217-219, 220n, 221n, 224t; discount, 225; flexibility, 312-313; regulations, 8
macroeconomic variables, 223t
monetary aggregates, 264-265
monetary target ranges, 211
money demand, 206
money growth, 201, 204, 206-207, 209-219, 221n, 224t; charts, 208, 211, 213
money supply, 207, 211, 221n
money velocity, 212, 214, 219n
nonbank financial institutions, 220n
open-market operations, 207-208, 210, 216, 225
open-market rates, 213
quasi-monetarist experiment, 201, 208-212, 214, 216, 219, 220n
recession, 209, 212, 216-217, 221n, 222
reserve requirements, 8, 151, 208-210, 225
trade policy, 374
treasury bills, 151, 216, 224t
treasury financing, 137t
unemployment, 203-204, 217, 223t, 224
wage and price controls, voluntary, 218

VAR (vector autoregression), 285-286, 298n

Walras' Law, 155
Western Samoa, banks and international capital controls, 80

SPRINGER NATURE

GPSR Compliance

The European Union's (EU) General Product Safety Regulation (GPSR) is a set of rules that requires consumer products to be safe and our obligations to ensure this.

If you have any concerns about our products, you can contact us on ProductSafety@springernature.com

In case Publisher is established outside the EU, the EU authorized representative is:

Springer Nature Customer Service Center GmbH
Europaplatz 3
69115 Heidelberg, Germany

FSC
www.fsc.org
MIX
Papier | Fördert
gute Waldnutzung
FSC® C083411

Kolibri 360 GmbH
Ferdinand-Jühlke-Straße 7
99095 Erfurt, Deutschland
produktsicherheit@kolibri360.de